Prima's Official Strategy Guide

EverQuest

THE RUINS OF KUNARK

An Incan Monkey God Studios Production

Credits

Writing	Melissa Tyler
Statistics	David Ladyman
Additional Writing	Anyka (Glossary Jargon Story), Tuesday Frase, Gary A. Grobson (Group Etiquette, Class-Specific Solo Tactics, Beginner Tactics), Raini Madden, Chris McCubbin, Lawrence Poe (Fiction, Class Advantages, Group Tactics)
Interior Graphic Design	Jennifer Spohrer
Interior Layout	Tuesday Frase, Sharon Frielich, Raini Madden, Jennifer Spohrer, Melissa Tyler
Cover Design and Layout	Raini Madden
Maps	Portions © 1999, 2000 Mike Swiernik and EQAtlas Used here by permission, all rights reserved.
Many Thanks	Team: Gary A. Grobson, Don Vercelli, Lawrence Poe, Thom Terrazas, Andrew Sites, Brad McQuaid, Ryan Palacio, Geoffrey Zatkin, Bill Trost, Kelsey McNair, Daniel Enright
	Players: Craig Smith, Jon Fournie, Kyle Gupton, Anyka, Mike Swiernik
	also Duncan Hudson, Andrew Morris

Important: Prima Publishing has made every effort to determine that the information contained in this book is accurate. However, the publisher makes no warranty, either expressed or implied, as to the accuracy, effectiveness or completeness of the material in this book; nor does the publisher assume liability for damages, either incidental or consequential, that may result from using the information in this book. The publisher cannot provide information regarding game play, hints and strategies, or problems with hardware or software. Questions should be directed to the support numbers provided by the game and device manufacturers in their documentation. Some game tricks require precise timing and may require repeated attempts before the desired result is achieved.

ISBN: 7615-2284-0
Library of Congress Card Catalogue Number: 9964225
Printed in the United States of America

00 01 02 03 BB 10 9 8 7 6 5 4 3 2 1

EverQuest: The Ruins of Kunark

How to Use this Book

Experienced *EverQuest* players may recognize two things about this book right off the bat. The first is that there is more info here than has ever previously been organized about *EverQuest*. Much of this is available on the web, and some of it is available from various screens in the game, but some of it could only come from the *EQ* designers at Verant. In this book, everything is in one place and at your fingertips while playing.

The second thing is that not *quite* everything is included. This is a no-spoiler strategy guide, which avoids revealing things that might give a few players an unfair advantage over the rest. Verant has gone to a great deal of trouble to create a world where people must work together, and it doesn't seem quite fair for every last secret to be revealed in such an impersonal format as a book. So, for instance, there are no descriptions of the deepest, darkest dungeons, or explanations of quests that many have died trying to unravel their secrets.

The sections, and how they are intended to be used, are outlined on this page:

Glossary (p. 8). Players new to *EverQuest* should read this section first! To anyone who isn't familiar with *EQ* jargon, this book will be hard to decipher. We decided to use jargon and slang in this book because experienced players will already be comfortable with it, and new players would do well to learn it before they encounter it in the fast-paced setting of real-time *EverQuest*.

DISCLAIMER

The information in this book was correct at the time of printing. However, *EverQuest* is an ever-changing world and all of this information is subject to change at any time.

Character Creation (p. 22). Creating a character that you can really "get into" is the first and best task in starting off a long, healthy and enjoyable career in Norrath. This is a must-read for people who are thinking of trying out a new race, class or personality in the game.

Community (p. 118). Norrath is kept alive by real people, most nice, some with issues or personal agendas — all of whom expect certain things from the people around them. This section discusses *EverQuest* culture and how it impacts the players.

Words to the Wise (p. 136). Strategies, tips, advice ... all arranged for easy access. Think of it as a FAQ — not a substitute for getting out there, talking to other players and joining a guild — but advice to point you in the right directions.

Cities of Norrath (p. 215). For the urban EQuester, here are maps of the starting cities, plus a list of all the creatures and items that can be found in the nearby "newbie zones," where new players can gain their first few levels of experience.

Items (p. 296) Statistics for weapons, armor, containers, jewelry and objects that can be used as shields.

Creatures (p. 326). Statistics for monsters and critters, from Alligators to Zombies.

Spells (p. 352). Complete info on all spells up to level 24, lists of spells up to level 60.

Note: a very few "spoiler" spells have been omitted from the Spells list.

Table of Contents

Table of Contents

Glossary of Jargon

Jargon Glossary

Because *EverQuest* is such a social experience, it should be no surprise to anyone that it has evolved its own culture ... including words and phrases specific to the *EverQuest* experience. Unfortunately it can be terribly confusing to someone new to the game. On the facing page is an example of what a dyed-in-the-wool *EverQuester* can sound like, taken from a public bulletin board.

Below is a list — not a complete list, but a good start — that may help you understand the jargon of the seasoned *EverQuester*.

Note: *Whenever jargon, defined elsewhere in this glossary, is used in a definition, that word will be in italics.*

**Level number.** Players sometimes refer to other characters by their level. In other words, a 28 Mage is a 28th level magic user.

AoE   **Area of Effect.** Many spells and items do not just affect the target, but anything around the target, as well. This is vitally important to remember in battle, where a spell's "backwash" might also affect the caster, or a weapon's area of effect might awaken creatures that were mesmerized ... and intended to stay that way.

Aggro   **Be aggressive**. When a creature attacks a person, it's "going aggro." Monsters are famous for going aggro on magic users, and the strong fighter-types keep busy taunting them off.

Bait   **Monster Bait.** More commonly referred to as *pulling*. When a character is bait, he (usually a physically strong race/class, although fast helps, too) goes out to get the attention of a local creature and lure it back to where the party's magic users are waiting to destroy it.

Bind   **Reset resurrection point**. Magic users, once they acquire this spell, can reset people's Bind point to their current location. This means that when they're killed, they'll resurrect at their new Bind point, rather than all the way back in their original city. Many mages will bind you to your location if you ask. The nicer you ask, the more likely they'll grant your request. "Oh Great and Noble Mage ..." is a good way to start!

Blue   **A likely win**. A "blue" creature is one that is easy for your character to kill. This is because when you *con* a creature, if the message appears in blue text, it means that the skill level of the creature is much lower than yours. Of course, a critter that's "blue" to a 50th level Necromancer, can often bite the head off your average 10th level bard.

EverQuest: The Ruins of Kunark

OK, I try to play by the rules and also be nice to other players. Here's what happened.

I wanted the tarnished brass key dropped by the Priest of Najena in Unrest. This is the first object in a caster quest for a very nice, no drop caster cloak (Mystic Cloak). I figured I'd get a nice group in the early 30's and try to hold a room on the top floor of the house while camping the Priest.

I got two clerics 32–34 (I'm a 32 Mage) and was waiting to get three more for the group. I went to investigate and the Priest was being camped by a 35 Mage. I told him to give me a tell when he got his key so that I could grab the camp. It was very cordial and he seemed like a nice guy, although kind of stupid to be solo in the house in Unrest.

We decided to pull from the house to the front of the fountains while we were waiting to get a full group, and the larger cleric went in to pull. We got a couple of nice mobs, killed a couple of small trains, etc. At this point, the mage camping the Priest pulled a horrific train, ran by us, and zoned.

I was medding (I think it was still from killing this guy's train actually) when the cleric yelled that he was pulling the Priest. I asked him if there was a Mage around and he said no. I popped up and there was the Priest. We killed him, and waited for about two minutes while the cleric teased me about the key. Finally I looted it.

Then five minutes later the mage shows up and starts yelling about me stealing his camp. Well, I tell you, I felt bad for the guy and tried to give him the key which was (of course) no drop, (else there wouldn't be a problem). I gave him 100pp, which he took and then kept yelling at me.

I asked the cleric, and he said he'd pulled the priest wandering around the house.

Then, two hours later, the mage started accusing me of ks'ing the Priest. This I'm pretty sure is not true, since 1) There was no pet there hitting the Priest, 2) I'm pretty sure the guy wasn't even in the zone, 3) It seems unlikely that a 34 Cleric is going to pull a mob away from an actively engaged 35 mage, who's going to pack a lot of punch with level 34 DD, 4) the mob seemed to be in almost full health when it arrived, and 5) the guy who pulled it said it was loose (I haven't played with him before). If someone tried to take a mob I was fighting and wanted badly, I'd be right on the mob's tail until one of us was dead. Furthermore, we didn't even loot the mob for a couple of minutes and this guy didn't say a word. I probably would have given him the loot if he'd shown up, just out of sympathy.

So, did I do something wrong? I feel bad about getting the loot so easily, when some poor slob had been camping him. I do think he's mistaken about the "ks" thing; all the indications are that the mob was loose. But he certainly has a point about the result — he'd been camping a mob that we got.

(Reprinted with permission by Anyka.)

BRB

Be Right Back. This is more "party talk" — i.e., what you might say to people in your group — than it is a general-use abbreviation. Saying you'll be right back is of shorter duration than being *afk*.

BRT

Be Right There. "Party talk" for letting people know you're on your way. When someone in your party shouts, for instance, that a Hill Giant has suddenly appeared and is trying to beat her to a pulp, it's reassuring to let her know you're heading over to help ... without spending too much time typing out comforting phrases.

BTM

Blue To Me. Refers to a creature/*npc* who is not that difficult to kill. It's much more impressive coming from a high-level character: "Yeah, he may be a city guard to you, but he's btm."

BTW

By The Way. An acronym that has crossed over from Email Quickspeak.

Bubble

Status bar section. Things such as experience, mana and stamina have status bars that have a twisted, segmented look. Each segment looks a bit like a bubble. When you are low on mana, you could say that you have one "bubble" left. Likewise, you could have "one bubble to go before *leveling up*."

Buff/Buffing

Strong. "Buff" is slang for strong. If your character is buff, he or she is probably very good at melee fighting, and can take a lot of damage. "Buffing" someone means making a character temporarily stronger by use of magic.

Camp

Wait. This is different from the hot key command "Camp" that you use right before you exit the game. To "camp" means to hang around an area where you know a monster (or npc) is going to *spawn*, with the intention of killing it and getting its loot. Some monsters spawn regularly, others have to be killed before they will spawn again. Common courtesy is "first come, first fight": if a party is camping a monster, newcomers to the area will let the first ones kill the monster when it appears.

Con

Judge how dangerous. When players target a creature or *npc* and types "/con," they will receive a statement as to have dangerous it would be to pick a fight. Green or blue responses mean the fight should be fairly straightforward. Red text means it would be suicide to begin battle.

Corpse

Dead body. For a period of time (depending on how high your level is) after you're killed, there are two of you. A new "you" is resurrected at your bind point, and the old body is left where it fell. If you can make it back before time runs out and your corpse disappears, you can retrieve your items from your old inventory. If you can't ... well, let's just say the phrase "you can't take it with you" doesn't refer to *EverQuest* corpses. When the corpse goes, so do all the goodies.

EverQuest: The Ruins of Kunark

EverQuest Culture: Jargon Glossary

CU/Cya   ***See you (see ya)***. The "speed typing" version of goodbye. It works perfectly well, but many people don't think it's good role playing.

DD   **Direct Damage**. A type of spell that does direct physical damage to the target, usually all at once. These are usually pretty expensive in terms of mana, but when you need your opponent taken down *right now*, dd is the way to go.

Debuff   **Reduce Strength.** When a strong (sometimes called *buff"* character is rendered weak by a spell, then he or she has been "debuffed."

DOT   **Damage Over Time**. A type of spell that does a certain amount of damage, delivered in increments over a period of time. When a mage is fighting in a party against multiple opponents, it's often more efficient for her to cast several dot spells on the various enemies, wearing them all down and making it easier for others to do clean-up duty, than to concentrate on taking out one particular foe.

EP (Also XP)   **Experience Points**. For every enemy vanquished, a player gets a number of experience points. As experience points accumulate, players move on to the next experience level. Current experience points are measured in the golden bar to the left in the "Personal" screen.

EVAC   **EVACuate.** A spell that Wizards ... and only Wizards ... can cast to teleport their party to another location. There's not a lot of fine control over where the party lands (other than, for instance, "north"), so it's best to use it only when facing annihilation. When someone thinks that the situation warrants a full-scale blind retreat, he'll yell "evac" and hope the wizard doesn't *fizzle* the spell.

Fetch/ Fetcher   **Lure creature**. More commonly referred to as "pulling." When a character "fetches," she (usually a physically strong race/class) goes out to get the attention of a powerful monster and lure it back to where the party's magic users are waiting to destroy it. **Finger-** **Magic user.** More common in speech than in keyboard chatting, "fingerwigglers"

wiggler   are just a casual way of referring to anyone who can use spells.

Fizzle   **Spell failure**. When a magic user attempts to cast a spell and fails, it "fizzles." The mana is consumed, but the spell does not happen. Failure can be caused by several things: moving during time required to cast the spell, being attacked, or just not having enough experience with the spell to cast it consistently.

FM   **Full Mana**. When a mage's mana bar is entirely blue, she has Full Mana and is ready to tackle the world (up to her level, of course).

FYI   **For Your Information**. An acronym that has crossed over from Email Quickspeak. It indicates that the following information may be of use, but is neither a request or a demand.

Green   **A certain win.** When you target a person or creature and type "/con" to determine the likelihood of winning, a response in green text means that unless you stop fighting altogether and simply stand there and take damage, you'll be able to win against the target. (Of course, if the target has friends that get involved, you could be in trouble.)

Grif   **Griffin**. Tough critter, and worth warning others about.

GTG   **Got To Go**. Not a universally common phrase, gtg is a method of warning your party members that you're going to haul tail out of the *zone* rather being killed and resurrecting somewhere inconvenient. Confusingly, it can also mean that you're about to mix it up with the enemy and that folks should get ready for the battle to start.

GTM   **Green To Me**. Refers to a creature/npc who is easy to kill. As in *btm*, it's much more impressive coming from a high-level character: "Yeah, it may be a Hill Giant to you, but it's gtm."

Hate   **Monster Motive**. Creatures prioritize their attacks on who they hate most in a party. For instance, some monsters hate magic users, so they'll attack the mages first. However, they also (logically) hate anyone who's done them the most damage, or anyone who helps out the person they're currently trying to kill. Depending on how it all adds up, a creature will choose whether to stay with its current target or switch its attention to someone else.

"There's the entrance. Are we ready?" Nesmar whispered as he looked at the other members of the Decamen, a party of ten Paladins of Rodcet Nife.

At first, none of the other nine answered. Then, the largest, oldest, and most experienced of the group said, "If our duty is to root out the evil in this lair of Gnolls, then so be it." The burly man pulled his sword and held it high. "I stand ready!"

Nesmar smiled as the others then pulled their swords, raised their shields and made ready to do battle against the evil that threatened Qeynos herself.

HG
    Hill Giant. A not-uncommon creature, the Hill Giant is a serious threat to most characters. Remember, Hill Giants are one of those aggressive, "social" monsters that will come and help out any of their kin in combat. Running away from a hg battle is a common cause of *trains*.

IMHO
    In My Humble Opinion. Another email Quickspeak acronym. Used to soften a statement that everyone may not agree with.

IMO
    In My Opinion. Essentially the same thing as *imho*, above.

Inc
    Incoming. A shorthand way to warn your party that you are *pulling* — either intentionally or unintentionally — a creature back to camp. This gives everyone enough time to stop meditating, stand up and get ready to cast the appropriate spell.

J/K
    Just Kidding. Letting people know when you're kidding is a good idea. Chatting does not convey emotion as much as could be hoped … and it's surprisingly easy to offend someone who misunderstands the spirit in which the statement was given.

K
    'Kay. Short for OK or okay.

Kill stealing
    Unwelcome "help." In *EverQuest*, the person (or party) who does the most damage to a creature is the one who gets the experience points (and *loot*). Common courtesy is to let the person who instigated the combat get the experience points, unless they asked for help. Kill Stealing is especially easy for mages, who can usually do in one spell what it would take several attacks with a conventional weapon to do. Even if you see that someone is about to die, ask before stepping in! It's not unheard of for someone to be publicly accused of Kill Stealing, and thus become an unpopular character on the server.

Kite
    Delay, attack, delay. When someone kites a creature, he casts a spell that temporarily immobilizes it, then casts a dot or dd spell … and then meditates or runs like mad until his mana is back up. At that point, he repeats the process until the creature is dead.

KOS
    Killed On Sight. Due to political reasons, some races or classes will automatically evoke a killing reaction in local creatures and/or npc's. Necromancers, for instance, can expect a kos reception in most cities, as can Dark Elves.

KS
    Kill Stealing. See *Kill Stealing*, above.

LD　**Link Dead**. A sad, sad situation where a player's connection is not good enough — for whatever reason — to adequately control his character. One of the main symptoms is reacting to a situation long after the reaction is appropriate (i.e., swinging at where a creature *used* to be). Being ld in a hostile situation will quickly devolve into real death unless you have party members to defend you.

Level up　**Increase Character Level**. It's the moment everyone waits for: your character has finally earned enough experience points to go up a level. Primarily you get skill points that you can apply toward training, but at certain levels (depending on your character's class) you get access to new skills, spells or both.

loc　**Locate command**. An extremely useful command: typing /loc will give you your current X/Y coordinates. All players should develop the habit of checking their location any time they feel they're about to be killed. It makes finding your corpse much easier.

LOL　**Laughing Out Loud**. A crossover from email, certain phrases attempt to convey the emotion in which a message was either sent or received. Lol means that you thought the previous statement (or event) was funny, and that you or your character is currently laughing.

LOS　**Line of Sight.** Everything that can be seen from a character's first-person perspective is in "line of sight." Things that cannot be seen are very hard to hit. An example of this would be archery.

loot　**Creature inventory**. Any items in a creature's or NPC's inventory, which will become available to the victor upon the death of the owner. (You can take loot from a player character's corpse only if you've both previously agreed to it.)

Also can be a verb, meaning to take the inventory from a creature. "I looted the key" means that you took the key from a fallen enemy's inventory.

Lore Item　**Quest item.** An item that is somehow involved in a quest. Lore Items usually cannot be dropped or given away (although they can be destroyed), which always needs to be considered before picking up the item. They can, of course, be given to the appropriate person, as part of fulfilling the quest.

Lowlies　**Low level character.** This isn't a particularly common term. It's usually referring to characters between Levels 5 and 10.

Mage　**Magic User**. There are many different kinds of magic user in the game, but they're all called mages. Mage is simply the generic phrase.

Med   **Meditate.** Meditating (medding) is a way for magic users (after a certain level) to regenerate mana. The pro is that mana regenerates much more quickly during meditation. The con is that the mage is temporarily "out of the loop" since all she can see is the spell book. That's why it's important for a puller to warn his party that there's a monster incoming — a mage is a sitting duck during meditation.

Mez   **Mesmerize.** Enchanters are the masters of mesmerizing one or more monsters, in order that the fighters can pick them off one by one. A mezzed monster is only quiet and still until it is attack (or the spell wears off), so Enchanters are famous for jumping around, yelling "Don't attack the mezzed mobs!"

MOB   **Mobile OBject.** This is a very common phrase throughout *EverQuest*. Any creatures that is computer-controlled is called a mob. This is often used to refer to hostiles, differentiating them from other computer-controlled characters (*npc's*) such as merchants.

Nerf   **Programmed to be less effective.** When a skill, item or power has its effect decreased by the programmers at Verant, for balance issues, people say it was "nerfed." Verant usually warns people of the impending change, but some people only find out about the change when they try to do something and it doesn't work the way they expect.

Newbie   **Newly created character.** Newbies are 1st through 5th level characters. They tend to stay just outside the city gates, killing small vermin and hoping nothing serious targets them. Remember, every powerful high-level character was once a weak newbie — it's the only way to get started.

Newbie Garden/ Newbie Zone   **Low-level creature area**. Just outside the gates of most cities is an area that is plentifully stocked with low-level creatures. This is to provide the newly created characters with a hunting ground where they can safely ... or fairly safely ... achieve 4th or 5th level.

No drop   **Non-droppable item**. Some items cannot be dropped out of inventory, sold or put in the bank. They are labeled "No Drop" in the description (right click on the item). Usually these are quest items that have a certain action associated with them, such as giving them to a specific person or combining them with other items to create some sort of special weapon, item, etc. These items can only be used in the manner intended, or destroyed.

NP   **No Problem**. Shorthand method of responding to someone's thanks.

NPC   **Non-Player Character**. Any character that is not run by a player is a non-player character. This term is usually used to describe only computer-driven characters, such as merchants or guards.

Nuke	**Powerful Destructive Spell**. "Nuke" is short for "Nuclear Attack" and refers to any spell that will destroy an opponent, or so seriously damage it that it is no longer a serious threat.
OMW	**On My Way**. Omw is shorthand to let another player that you intend to help, and that you'll be there shortly.
OOM	**Out Of Mana**. When a mage is oom, she cannot cast any more spells until she's rested or meditated long enough to regain the mana. It's polite to warn anyone who may be depending on your magical assistance that you aren't going to be much help for a while.
OOS	**Out Of Spells**. The same as *Out Of Mana*, see above.
PC	**Player-Character**. A character played by an actual person, rather than a computer-driven character, such as a guard or merchant.
Pet	**Monster Servant.** These are far from the cute-n-fluffy variety of pets. Certain mages, such as Necromancers and Wizards, can summon monsters that will obey their commands to physically attack targeted opponents. While the pet is attacking, the mage can be casting other spells. The higher the mage's level, the higher the pet's level. Eventually even a pet will be a match for most anyone it meets.
PK	**Player Killer**. A player who kills other players. In *EverQuest*, only players who have mutually agreed to be Player Killers can kill or be killed by other players. This is done by giving the book in your character's starting inventory to a Priest of Discord.

Note: sometimes a player can be "cursed" or "possessed." These unfortunate characters are, for the duration of the possession, monsters. The player cannot control his character at all, and the character will run amok, killing other characters. The tricky thing is that it looks like a player-character, but is temporarily classified as a monster. Like a monster, these out-of-control characters can be killed.

Port	**telePORT**. Teleportation is instantaneous travel between one location and the next. Wizards are the primary class for teleportation, but Druids also achieve some location-specific teleportation spells. It is not uncommon for people to (loudly) request ports to whatever destination they desire.
Power-leveling	**Rapid level acquisition.** When a player does whatever is necessary to rise through the ranks as quickly as possible, she is Powerleveling. This is something learned with experience, and includes ignoring *green* creatures, joining parties, taking on multiple quests, and generally losing a lot of sleep.

EverQuest Culture: Jargon Glossary

Proc
Process an action. Certain items act as though they have magical abilites, and sometimes there is a delay. What the item's "proc" is, is usually something best found out on the battlefield. Alos, how long it takes to "proc" (process) the item's skill is of extreme interest to the owners.

Pull
Lure creature. When a character "pulls," he (usually a physically strong race/class) goes out to get the attention of a powerful monster and lure it back to where the party's magic users are waiting to destroy it.

PVP
Player Versus Player. Actually, you don't *have* to be a player killer to kill another player. There are pvp zones in various cities where players can attack other players. They're usually distinguishable by the copious amounts of blood splashed on the walls and floor.

R
Ready. Pretty much an all-purpose word, it means that the player is ready for whatever is about to happen, whether it's a duel, a teleport or full-fledged battle.

The carriage bounced across the rough road from Crushbone Castle. Suddenly, Sraleth began to chuckle. Soon, the chuckle turned into a hearty laugh. Tradon, Sraleth's aide, had never heard such a sound from his master and looked at her askance.

"My lady," Tradon said, "is there something wrong?"

The Dark Elf swept moisture off her face and examined it as if it were a bug she'd never seen before. She took a deep breath and smiled. "No, my friend, I've just convinced those disgusting Orcs that we are going to help them take Greater Faydark, and that all we want is the satisfaction and future trade agreements."

Tradon furrowed his brow. "And, we really want ...?"

Sraleth sat back on her carriage seat. "You are such an innocent delight, Tradon. Once the Orcs have taken Greater Faydark," Sraleth paused a moment and added, "we take it from the Orcs, a much easier adversary."

Red	**An impossible win**. When you target a person or creature and type "/con" to determine the likelihood of winning, a response in red text means that unless an extremely powerful person is standing nearby, ready to help you out, your opponent will swat you like a bug. The phrase "What would you like your tombstone to say" should be a clue.
Res	**Resurrect.** Some casters have resurrection spells, and can res their friends. Very useful.
RL	**Real Life.** Refers to your life outside of *EverQuest*. As in "I know you're a Qeynos homey, but what's your rl town?"
ROFL	**Rolling On Floor Laughing**. "I think that was funny." Rofl is an acronym that has crossed over from Email Quickspeak.
ROFLMAO	**Rolling On Floor Laughing My Ass Off.** "I think that was extremely funny." An acronym that has crossed over from Email Quickspeak.
Root	**Immobilization spell**. A Root spell is one that keeps the target from moving its feet or legs. This obviously makes it a much more appealing target, and is an integral part of kiting a creature. However, don't be surprised when other creatures do it to you! Times like that is when it's *really* handy to have friends around.
RTM	**Red To Me**. Refers to a creature/npc who is more than your match. Unless you have serious backup, you'd better leave a Red alone. Saying something is rtm is admitting that it's safe from any solo attack from you.
SG	**Sand Giant**. Giants are just dangerous no matter where you meet them. It's very important to recognize a Giant warning when you hear one!
SOW	**Spirit Of Wolf**. A Druid/Shaman spell that makes the target much faster, and therefore safer. It's common to ask for a Druid or Shaman to cast SOW on you before traveling long distances.

Note: Druids and Shamans will usually cast the spell, rarely asking for anything in return. However, you increase your chances and make folks happier with you if you word your request "Noble Shaman, would you bestow" or "Great and Mighty Druid ...." Just saying "sow me" is a little abrupt.

Spam	**Message to everyone**. To "spam" a message is to send it to everyone, regardless of interest. In *EverQuest*, shouting things that are not pertinent to everyone can be annoying. On the other hand, shouting "Train North" is acceptable, since it is *very* important to some people but there's no way to know exactly who.

EverQuest: The Ruins of Kunark

EverQuest Culture: Jargon Glossary

Spawn **Creature Creation**. When an *npc* or creature is killed, after a while it will be recreated at a certain location. This is called "spawning." If it is a creature with particularly interesting loot, frequently players will go to the location and wait for it to spawn, so they can kill it immediately.

Stun **Paralysis spell**. When you stun a target, it loses all ability to move, leaving it entirely at the mercy of its enemy ... in this case, you. On the other hand, the reverse is true: if you get stunned, you're in serious hot water.

Tank/Tanking **Overpowering Strength**. A "Tank" is a player with great physical strength and stamina. A well-balanced party will have a few tanks and several mages. To "tank" something is to overwhelm it with physical force.

Taunt **Enrage**. Several different classes, such as Bards and Warriors, have the ability to *Taunt* an enemy. Essentially this is provoking the enemy to give up its current target and attack the taunter. This is used primarily when the opponent is focusing its attack on a weaker party member, who will be killed unless the enemy breaks off its attack. This is a little like throwing yourself on a grenade, only you have a much better chance of surviving.

Tombstone **Certain death**. When a target is conned and the result is the red text of "What would you like your tombstone to say," then it is certain that you'll lose the battle if you don't have heavy backup. "It looks like a tombstone to me" therefore means that you think failure is inevitable.

TPW **Total Party Wipeout**. When is a party not a party? When it's been tpw'd. Nothing left to do but try to make it back. Times like this is when having everyone in the group bound to the same area is invaluable. There's nothing worse than trying to cross hostile territory alone ....

Train **Creatures following a target.** Two points: some creatures have "buddies" that will join their friend in battle, and creatures you're fighting will follow you until you exit their zone. This means that it's common to see a player running for the zone boundary, while being chased by two or more creatures. This is called "pulling a train." The problem is that once the player exits the zone, the hostile creatures are now free to attack any innocent bystanders who happen to be in the vicinity. Therefore it's common courtesy, under the circumstances, to shout "Train!" so that people can get clear of the zone areas. If you know what direction you're heading, it's good to add that to the warning, so that people at other zone exits don't have to worry.

Twinking	**Giving Equipment.** Occasionally you'll see low-level characters with "too much money, or with better armor than they can afford. They may have been "twinked." This means that the player has taken a high-level character's equipment or money, hidden it in a safe place, and then switched to the low-level character and retrieved it. Many players don't approve of this practice.
Twist	**Successive bard songs**. With enough mana, a Bard can sing two or three songs back to back. This not only varies the effect of his attack (this is, of course, usually used in battle), but there is a period of time when the last song is still in effect while the new song's effects start to kick in ... and that kind of double whammy is a glorious thing.
WTB	**Want To Buy**. Offers up goods for sale. *EverQuest* is as capitalistic as you can get, and if you can find a market for your goods or skills, more power to you.
WTF	**What The F*****. Usually an expression of surprise or incredulity.
WTS	**Want To Sell**. Hope springs eternal ... asking if anyone has a specific item to sell is more likely to get a response if that item is fairly common in a nearby, but dangerous, zone.
WTT	**Want To Trade.** Offers up goods for trade. People tend to hang on to their cash, usually because everyone is saving for some specific goodie, or because they stash it in the bank.
Yellow	**Risky to fight**. A Yellow is not quite a serious as a Red, but it is a serious leap of faith to take one on alone. With a buddy for backup, it's more feasible.
YTM	**Yellow To Me**. Announces to anyone who cares to listen that the creature in question is probably too tough for you in a one-on-one fight, but might be handled with a little help.
XP (also EP)	**Experience Points.** For certain victories, a player gets a number of experience points. As XP accumulates, players move on to the next experience level. Current experience points are measured in the golden bar to the left in the "Personal" screen.
Zone	**Regional Area**. Norrath is divided into zones. When crossing between zones, the message "Loading" appears, along with the zone that the player is about to enter. Certain things are restricted to zones. Creatures, for instance, cannot cross zones. Shouts can only be heard within the speaker's zone. Weather is also a zone-by-zone phenomenon.
	"Zone" can be an action verb, meaning to exit the zone. "He ran by me and zoned" means that he ran past and exited the zone.

EverQuest: The Ruins of Kunark

Character Creation

Characters

The heart and soul of *EverQuest* is roleplaying. When you create your character, you design from the ground up who you will be for hours and hours (and days and days, or if you're like most of us, weeks or months). Creating a persona is essentially kicking off a long-term relationship ... a relationship with yourself.

It's more work than saying "I want to play *EverQuest*" and having someone give you a character, all ready to go. A ready-made character would be defeating the purpose of the game. A really good personality will reflect aspects of your inner self that have been lying abandoned in your subconscious, getting dusty and tattered. That's what makes role-playing fun — being able to exercise all those deep-down inclinations that regular etiquette says isn't acceptable. The challenge is to create a role that you'll be able to play with real flair and panache.

Think about it. Deep down inside, are you dying to call all those rude and ignorant people you meet worm-eating miscreants, and challenge them to a duel? With the right character, it's the natural thing to do. Would you like to face danger? Find it. Do you like to make wisecracks in the face of danger? Do it. Have you always wanted to be the soft-spoken healer that people turn to for help and advice? Now's your chance. In fact, with the right character, you can chuckle at others' pain and mock them when they lose. (Of course, don't be surprised if your dark and nasty character doesn't make a lot of friends and has to lone wolf it most of the time!)

Creating a Character

Obviously it's one thing to say, "You should create a really good persona," and another thing completely to go about making one. Here are some tips that might help you cook up a really interesting on-line character.

Personality. Sit back for a few moments and think about what kind of person you are going to create. What would be fun to play? What sort of personality will this character have? Snippy and brusque, calm and serene, wise-cracking, down-to-earth ... these character traits are like a skeleton for your character. Once you have the basic form, you can go back and flesh out the details.

Note: If you're stumped, you can always "borrow" a personality from a TV show (or movie, book, etc.) that you enjoy. Just be absolutely certain it is a personality you'll feel comfortable playing. Some people feel more confident in maintaining a consistent personality if they can think, "what would so-and-so do in this situation?"

EverQuest: The Ruins of Kunark

Powers and abilities. Once you have an idea about the personality you'd like to work with, the next most important aspect is the character's *modus operandi*. How are you going to function in society? Start with the simple things: will you be a magic user or will you rely on your strength and speed? Once you know that, you're halfway there.

Now, look at your personality and decide how the skills you want are going to mesh with the kind of personality you've picked. Don't get caught in the trap of thinking in stereotypes. Just because you're snippy and brusque doesn't mean you can't be a healer. Healers can be surly and snappish — as long as they keep patching up the wounded, they're still good healers.

Class. (See **Classes**, page. 26.) Now, you may have been told that the very first thing you should do is decide what race you want your new character to be. That works, and you can certainly do it that way if you want. However, there's a good reason to consider class before you consider race. That reason is teamwork.

EverQuest is a very social game. People dealing with people ... that's the way the world works. Unless you decide to create a character that just won't get along with other people (like the lone wolf mentioned earlier who laughs at injuries), you'll probably want to join a party sooner or later. It's the best way to get experience and loot, and generally considered an all around good idea. What does that have to do with class? Well, you're going to have to be able to do something that's of value to your adventuring party.

Classes are essentially occupations. Mind you, they're not jobs (a thing wonderfully unnecessary on the bonny shores of Norrath). They do, however, let people know what they can expect from you, in terms of overall group support. So decide what you want to do, and then choose a race that will allow you to do that.

Note: Healers are usually very popular. There aren't a lot of them, since fighters are easier to play and other forms of magic are flashier. They're useful in a party, though, and can be a very interesting role to play.

Race. (See **Races**, page 74.) After you've decided what class you're interested in, you can then choose from the races are available to you. (Yes, you can choose the race and then choose the class. That's a perfectly valid way to design up a character ... in fact, that's the way the game is set up.)

Choosing a race has certain ramifications. Depending on which race you pick, certain classes, starting cities and physical characteristics become available, and others become off-limits.

Attributes. Depending on your chosen race and class, you will have a different base set of attributes (Strength, Stamina, Agility, Dexterity, Intelligence, Wisdom, Charisma) as well as a certain number of "bonus" points that you can distribute among them. The typical "important" attributes for the class are in bold (and green on the character screen), and it's generally recommended that you add — and add generously — to those particular attributes.

Race and Class Combinations

Below is a chart illustrating which classes characters of different races can belong to.

	Bard	Cler	Druid	Ench	Mag	Monk	Necr	Pala	Rang	Rog	Sham	ShKn	Warr	Wiz
Barbarian										√	√		√	
Dark Elf		√		√	√		√			√		√	√	√
Dwarf		√						√		√			√	
Erudite		√		√	√		√	√						√
Gnome		√		√	√		√	√		√			√	√
Half Elf	√		√					√	√	√			√	
Halfling		√	√							√			√	
High Elf		√		√	√			√						√
Human	√	√	√	√	√	√	√	√	√	√		√	√	√
Iksar						√	√				√	√	√	
Ogre											√	√	√	
Troll											√	√	√	
Wood Elf	√		√						√	√			√	

Basic Race Abilities

Below is a list of basic stats for each race. Note that 20 to 30 points of the bonus are permanently assigned when you select a class.

	STR	STA	AGI	DEX	WIS	INT	CHA	Bonus	Total
Barbarian	103	95	82	70	70	60	55	50	585
Dark Elf	60	65	90	75	83	99	60	50	582
Dwarf	90	90	70	90	83	60	45	50	578
Erudite	60	70	70	70	83	107	70	50	580
Gnome	60	70	85	85	67	98	60	50	575
Half Elf	70	70	90	85	60	75	75	50	575
Halfling	70	75	95	90	80	67	50	50	577
High Elf	55	65	85	70	95	92	80	50	592
Human	75	75	75	75	75	75	75	50	575
Iksar	90	70	90	85	80	75	55	50	595
Ogre	130	122	70	70	67	60	37	50	606
Troll	108	109	83	75	60	52	40	50	577
Wood Elf	65	65	95	80	80	75	75	50	585

Class Ability Modifiers

When you select a class for your character, the basic stats for that character's race are modified according to the table below.

Bonus Points: *You can't spend more than 25 bonus points on any single ability, even if you have 30 bonus points. You also may not take any ability higher than 150, although this only limits the Ogre's Strength and Stamina.*

	STR	STA	AGI	DEX	WIS	INT	CHA	Bonus Ability Points
Bard	+5	–	–	+10	–	–	+10	25
Cleric	+5	+5	–	–	+10	–	–	30
Druid	–	+10	–	–	+10	–	–	30
Enchanter	–	–	–	–	–	+10	+10	30
Magician	–	+10	–	–	–	+10	–	30
Monk	+5	+5	+10	+10	–	–	–	20
Necromancer	–	–	–	+10	–	+10	–	30
Paladin	+10	+5	–	–	+5	–	+10	20
Ranger	+5	+10	+10	–	+5	–	–	20
Rogue	–	–	+10	+10	–	–	–	30
Shadow Knight	+10	+5	–	–	–	+10	+5	20
Shaman	–	+5	–	–	+10	–	+5	30
Warrior	+10	+10	+5	–	–	–	–	25
Wizard	–	+10	–	–	–	+10	–	30

Classes

Bard

Okay, first you need to check your basic assumptions about Bards. If what you picture is a skinny little git with a lute who probably still lives in his parents' house, then you're dead wrong.

A Bard is someone who's got an intense case of wanderlust. He's a guy driven to find out what's on the other side of the mountain, the far shore of the river, or just "thataway." She's a gal who figures there's too much living going on all around to cool her heels in the same place for too long. These are people on the go.

Bards are full of surprises, though. For one thing, those nimble fingers are useful for more than just playing music ... let's just say your average Bard doesn't necessarily feel too hemmed in by local ordinances. They're observant, they're quick, and no one is particularly surprised if some pastries, or ale, or loose change suddenly turns up missing after a Bard passes through. Even from behind closed doors, if you know what I mean.

On the other hand, their songs can stir up some serious mojo. Bards are great in a party, since their spells either directly affect the party's abilities (like increasing Strength or Dexterity), or are very useful on a quest (such as healing or invisibility). Since the life Bards lead involves traveling through dangerous lands and frequently sticking their noses where they don't belong, they are competent at defending themselves when necessary. For a Bard, perfect pitch could mean either a good, clear note ... or a dagger in an enemy's eye. It depends on the situation.

A Bard is an excellent all-around class to choose, although it takes a while to work one up to a truly powerful persona. And don't worry, you don't have to be able to sing or have any songs or stories memorized to be a Bard. It all happens with a touch of a button.

Bard Skills

1	1H Blunt
1	1H Slashing
1	2H Blunt
1	2H Blunt
1	2H Slashing
1	Alcohol Tolerance
1	Baking
1	Begging
1	Bind Wound
1	Blacksmithing
1	Brewing
1	Defense
1	Fishing
1	Fletching
1	Hand to Hand
1	Jewelry Making
1	Offense
1	Piercing
1	Pottery
1	Sense Direction
1	Singing
1	Swimming
1	Tailoring
1	Throwing
1	Tinkering
5	Percussion Instruments
8	Stringed Instruments
10	Dodge
10	Meditate
11	Brass Instruments
12	Forage
14	Wind Instruments
17	Dual Wield
17	Sneak
24	Safe Fall
25	Hide
35	Track
40	Pick Lock
53	Parry
58	Riposte
30	Specialization

More about Bards

Dexterity. How often your attack connects. Since a Bard's main attack consists of playing a musical instrument *really well*, the higher the dex, the higher the likelihood of a spell-song making good. Since the Bard can also wade into melee fighting, which a high dex also improves. This is an important attribute for Bards.

Wisdom. The higher the wisdom, the more mana you get per level jump. Bards get wisdom not so much from their gods, necessarily, but from traveling through different cultures.

Charisma. Mostly, charisma affects how merchants treat you. Frankly, Bards are incredibly likeable. Merchants appreciate the heads-up on current events, people like them because they're fun and full of stories and (more importantly) songs, and kids like them because they're the kind of person their parents don't want them to grow up to be.

Human

Advantages: Sell liked throughout Norrath, highest Strength

Disadvantages: Poor night vision, lower agility

Half Elf

Advantages: Infravision

Disadvantages: None

Wood Elf

Advantages: Infravision, fragging

Disadvantages: None

Bard Spells

Level	Spell	Page	Level	Spell	Page
1	Chant of Battle	364	35	Denon's Dissension	373
2	Chords of Dissonance	366	36	Vilia's Verses of Celerity	450
3	Jaxan's Jig o' Vigor	401	37	Psalm of Purity	416
4	Lyssa's Locating Lyric	408	38	Tuyen's Chant of Flame	449
5	Selo's Accelerando	426	39	Solon's Bewitching Bravura	434
6	Hymn of Restoration	394	40	Syvelian's Anti-Magic Aria	444
7	Jonthan's Whistling Warsong	402	41	Psalm of Mystic Shielding	416
8	Kelin's Lugubrious Lament	402	42	McVaxius' Berserker Crescendo	409
9	Elemental Rhythms	377	43	Denon's Desperate Dirge	373
10	Anthem de Arms	355	44	Cassindra's Elegy	363
11	Cinda's Charismatic Carillon	367	45	Jonthan's Provocation	401
12	Brusco's Boastful Bellow	360	46	Tuyen's Chant of Frost	449
13	Purifying Rhythms	417	47	Niv's Melody of Preservation	413
14	Lyssa's Cataloging Libretto	407	48	Selo's Chords of Cessation	426
15	Kelin's Lucid Lullaby	402	50	Verses of Victory	450
16	Tarew's Aquatic Ayre	445	51	Largo`s Absonant Binding	403
17	Guardian Rhythms	392	51	Selo`s Song of Travel	426
18	Denon's Disruptive Discord	373	52	Nillipus` March of the Wee	413
19	Shauri's Sonorous Clouding	428	53	Song of Dawn	434
20	Largo's Melodic Binding	403	53	Song of Twilight	434
21	Melanie's Mellifluous Motion	410	54	Selo`s Assonait Strane	426
22	Alenia's Disenchanting Melody	354	54	Vilia`s Chorus of Celerity	450
23	Selo's Consonant Chain	426	55	Cantana of Replenishment	363
24	Lyssa's Veracious Concord	408	56	Song of Highsun	434
25	Psalm of Warmth	417	56	Song of Midnight	434
26	Angstlich's Appalling Screech	355	57	Cassindra's Insipid Ditty	363
27	Solon's Song of the Sirens	434	57	McVaxius` Rousing Rondo	409
28	Crission's Pixie Strike	370	58	Jonthan's Inspiration	401
29	Psalm of Vitality	417	58	Niv`s Harmonic	413
30	Fufil's Curtailing Chant	389	59	Denon`s Bereavement	373
31	Agilmente's Aria of Eagles	354	59	Solon's Charismatic Concord	434
32	Cassindra's Chorus of Clarity	363	60	Angstlich's Assonance	355
33	Psalm of Cooling	416	60	Kazumi's Note of Preservation	402
34	Lyssa's Solidarity of Vision	408			

 # Cleric

If you have trouble wrapping your mind around the concept of a man or woman of the cloth wading through battle, hammering enemy heads like a dodging, smashing version of whack-a-mole, then you haven't quite grasped the concept of a Norrathian Cleric. Not all Clerics follow happy, "group-hug" kinds of gods. The appellations "Prince of Hate" and "The Warlord" ought to give you a clue that head-bashing is to some religions what lighting candles is to others. Of course, even Clerics of fairly benevolent gods have subjects upon which they have violent opinions. For instance, most gods have an "if you're dead you should act dead" policy. Therefore — since Cleric spells are gifts from their god — Clerics have at least one "anti-undead" spell per level.

If you can imagine Robin Hood's buddy, Friar Tuck, fighting not only the evil Sheriff of Nottingham but also any local Vampires and Skeletons, you've got the picture.

Clerics aren't very "in your face" about their religion. They don't necessarily grab a person's ear and talk about the benefits of their religion, but instead they act on faith, and hope people pay attention. Since an important part of a Cleric's abilities are god-granted spells, people tend to be respectful, even if they aren't inclined to convert.

Clerics are good in groups, and groups love to have them. Their ability to heal is invaluable to any party of adventurers. They also tend to have effective offensive spells, which work better at a distance (usually) than up-close and personal. Clerics tend to join parties, both because it's safer for them to have one or two bruisers to keep the bad guys at a distance, and because their whole purpose is to get out into the world and show people the way to truth.

Clerics can be a little difficult for an inexperienced player, simply because the character's success depends so much on working well with other player-characters. Of course, if you have no trouble making friends, joining groups, and heading out for adventures — well, hey, healers are always welcome!

Cleric Skills

1	1H Blunt
1	2H Blunt
1	Abjuration
1	Alcohol Tolerance
1	Alteration
1	Baking
1	Begging
1	Bind Wound
1	Blacksmithing
1	Brewing
1	Conjuration
1	Defense
1	Divination
1	Evocation
1	Fishing
1	Fletching
1	Hand to Hand
1	Jewelry Making
1	Offense
1	Pottery
1	Sense Direction
1	Swimming
1	Tailoring
1	Tinkering
4	Channeling
8	Meditate
15	Dodge
30	Specialize Abjure
30	Specialize Alteration
30	Specialize Conjuration
30	Specialize Divination
30	Specialize Evocation

More about Clerics

Wisdom. Clerics are deity-based magic users, of course. (The title kind of gives that away.) Therefore, the higher their wisdom, the more mana they get per level. Let's just say that the gods are not very generous to dumb-head followers.

Strength. Mmm-mmm. No doubt about it, real strength can only help when you battle against the foes of your god ... but wait, there's more! The higher the strength, the more you can carry. That makes everything *much* nicer.

Stamina. Without high stamina, a Cleric can look forward to a short battle and a long search for his poor, abandoned corpse.

Dark Elf

Advantages: Ultravision
Disadvantages: Race is hated

Dwarf

Advantages: Infravision, high Strength, high Stamina
Disadvantages: None

Gnome

Advantages: Infravision, high dexterity, high agility
Disadvantages: Lowest Wisdom

Halfling

Advantages: Infravision
Disadvantages: None

High Elf

Advantages: Infravision, highest Wisdom
Disadvantages: None

Human

Advantages: None
Disadvantages: Poor night vision

Cleric Spells

Level	Spell	Page	Level	Spell	Page
1	Courage	370	14	Halo of Light	392
1	Cure Poison	371	14	Healing	393
1	Divine Aura	374	14	Invisibility versus Undead	401
1	Flash of Light	387	14	Sense Summoned	426
1	Lull	407	14	Smite	434
1	Minor Healing	411	14	Symbol of Transal	444
1	Spook the Dead	437	19	Calm	362
1	Strike	439	19	Daring	371
1	True North	449	19	Endure Magic	379
1	Yaulp	454	19	Extinguish Fatigue	382
5	Cure Blindness	371	19	Holy Might	394
5	Cure Disease	371	19	Spirit Armor	435
5	Furor	389	19	Ward Summoned	451
5	Gate ✓	389	19	Word of Shadow	454
5	Holy Armor ✓	394	19	Yaulp II	455
5	Light Healing ✓	406	24	Bravery	359
5	Reckless Strength ✓	419	24	Counteract Poison	370
5	Stun ✓	439	24	Dismiss Undead	374
5	Summon Drink	441	24	Greater Healing	391
5	Ward Undead	451	24	Hammer of Striking	392
9	Center	364	24	Inspire Fear	400
9	Endure Fire	379	24	Radius of Fear 2	417
9	Endure Poison	380	24	Symbol of Ryltan	443
9	Fear	383	24	Wave of Fear	452
9	Hammer of Wrath	392	29	Abundant Drink	353
9	Invigor	400	29	Counteract Disease	370
9	Root	423	29	Divine Barrier	374
9	Sense the Dead	426	29	Enstill	381
9	Soothe	434	29	Expulse Summoned	382
9	Summon Food	441	29	Guard	391
9	Word of Pain	454	29	Panic the Dead	414
14	Bind Affinity	358	29	Revive	421
14	Cancel Magic	362	29	Word of Spirit	454
14	Endure Cold	379	29	Wrath	454
14	Endure Disease	379	34	Abundant Food	353
14	Expulse Undead	382	34	Atone	356
			34	Blinding Luminance	358

Cleric Spells, cont.

Druid

There's a subtle difference between the mindset of a Bard and a Druid. A Bard likes to go to interesting places, and will travel through the wilderness to get there. A Druid likes to travel through the wilderness, and if there's someplace interesting at the end, so much the better. Got it? Essentially, Druids might be happier if there weren't any cities on Norrath at all ... and quite possibly, if there weren't near as many people, either.

The Druid is the original earth-child. You just haven't seen a tree hugged until you discuss deforestation with a Druid. They get their power from directly tapping into the forces of nature, so they have views on its sanctity. In fact, they are so in tune with the outdoors that most animals won't attack a Druid unless the Druid strikes first. That definitely makes traveling easier. Druids know wood lore, they know herbs and they know how to heal.

By now you're probably thinking they sound all granola and aromatherapy, and wouldn't last a minute in a fight. Not true. Remember, in nature, blood and violence is as much a part of everyday life as sniffing a flower or twitching a whisker. Druids have no qualms about skewering an enemy. To them, arterial spray is nature's liquid fertilizer.

There is a lot of hostile terrain in Norrath, and Druids have magic that makes passage easier and safer. Take a look at their spells (see **Druid**, page 33) and you'll see how magic and nature can combine in a vicious one-two punch that's ruthlessly efficient.

Druids are the catchall class. They do a bit of magic, a bit of fighting, a bit of wood lore, etc. However, when it gets down to the nuts and bolts of skills and abilities, it's important to note that they don't perform any one skill better than everyone else. This is not a "sky rocket to the top" class. This is an "I want to travel places and see things" class. If you want to travel, it's good to either be a Druid, or invite one along.

Druid Skills

1	1H Blunt
1	1H Slashing
1	2H Blunt
1	Abjuration
1	Alcohol Tolerance
1	Alteration
1	Baking
1	Begging
1	Bind Wound
1	Blacksmithing
1	Brewing
1	Conjuration
1	Defense
1	Divination
1	Evocation
1	Fishing
1	Fletching
1	Hand to Hand
1	Jewelry Making
1	Offense
1	Pottery
1	Sense Direction
1	Swimming
1	Tailoring
1	Tinkering
4	Channeling
5	Forage
8	Meditate
15	Dodge
20	Track
30	Specialize Abjure
30	Specialize Alteration
30	Specialize Conjuration
30	Specialize Divination
30	Specialize Evocation

More about Druids

Stamina. Stamina is for the fighter aspect of this class. A good, high-Stamina Druid will be able to stand as solid as an oak tree in battle.

Wisdom. The higher the Wisdom, the more mana they can soak up from the ground. More mana, more spells. In Norrath, wisdom carries a lot more clout than it does in the real world.

Half Elf

Advantages: Infravision

Disadvantages: None

Human

Advantages: Good faction in pro-Druid areas

Disadvantages: Poor night vision

Halfling

Advantages: Infravision

Disadvantages: None

Wood Elf

Advantages: Infravision, foraging

Disadvantages: None

Druid Spells

Level	Spell	Page	Level	Spell	Page
1	Burst of Flame	361	5	Ward Summoned	451
1	Dance of the Fireflies	371	5	Whirling Wind	453
1	Endure Fire	379	9	Endure Cold	379
1	Flame Lick	386	9	Enduring Breath	380
1	Lull Animal	407	9	Firefist	385
1	Minor Healing	411	9	Ignite	395
1	Panic Animal	417	9	Invisibility versus Animals	400
1	Sense Animals	426	9	Light Healing	406
1	Skin like Wood	433	9	Shield of Thistles	429
1	Snare	434	9	Starshine	438
5	Burst of Fire	361	9	Strength of Earth	439
5	Camouflage	362	9	Thistlecoat	447
5	Cure Disease	371	9	Treeform	448
5	Cure Poison	371	14	Befriend Animal	357
5	Gate	389	14	Bind Affinity	358
5	Grasping Roots	390	14	Cascade of Hail	363
5	Harmony	393	14	Expulse Summoned	382
5	Invoke Lightning	401	14	Halo of Light	392

Druid Spells, cont.

Level	Spell	Page	Level	Spell	Page
14	Invigor	400	24	Tremor	448
14	Levitate	405	24	Wolf Form	453
14	See Invisible	425	29	Beguile Plants	357
14	Skin like Rock	433	29	Bramblecoat	360
14	Spirit of Wolf	436	29	Circle of Butcher	366
14	Stinging Swarm	438	29	Circle of Commons	366
14	Summon Drink	441	29	Circle of Karana	366
14	Summon Food	441	29	Circle of Toxxulia	366
19	Barbcoat	357	29	Combust	369
19	Calm Animal	362	29	Counteract Disease	370
19	Cancel Magic	362	29	Counteract Poison	370
19	Careless Lightning	363	29	Ensnare	380
19	Dizzying Wind	375	29	Extinguish Fatigue	382
19	Endure Disease	379	29	Greater Healing	391
19	Endure Poison	380	29	Immolate	398
19	Feral Spirit	384	29	Ring of Misty	422
19	Healing	393	29	Scale of Wolf	424
19	Ring of Butcher	421	29	Shield of Brambles	429
19	Ring of Commons	421	29	Succor: East	439
19	Ring of Karana	422	34	Beguile Animals	357
19	Ring of Toxxulia	422	34	Circle of Feerrott	366
19	Shield of Barbs	428	34	Circle of Lavastorm	366
19	Superior Camouflage	443	34	Circle of Ro	366
19	Terrorize Animal		34	Circle of Steamfont	366
24	Charm Animals	365	34	Circle of the Combines	366
24	Creeping Crud	370	34	Drones of Doom	375
24	Dismiss Summoned	374	34	Earthquake	376
24	Ensnaring Roots	381	34	Endure Magic	379
24	Pogonip	415	34	Expel Summoned	382
24	Resist Fire	420	34	Greater Wolf Form	391
24	Ring of Feerrott	421	34	Lightning Strike	406
24	Ring of Lavastorm	422	34	Regeneration	419
24	Ring of Ro	422	34	Resist Cold	420
24	Ring of Steamfont	422	34	Strength of Stone	439
24	Skin like Steel	433	34	Succor: Butcher	439
24	Spirit of Cheetah	435	39	Avalanche	356
24	Sunbeam	442	39	Circle of Misty	366

Druid Spells, cont.

Enchanter

The first few times players set out to be magic users, they probably won't choose Enchanter. It's not a "stand on your own" class, and it's certainly not flashy. Until someone's been playing in *EverQuest* for a while — and has gone on some serious party-style adventures — it's hard to see the point in a specializing in enchantments. After all, enchantments don't blast your enemy into little smoldering cinders, they don't render you invulnerable or invincible, and you don't get to go around with a frothing, fanged pet at your beck and call. Well, then, what's the point?

The point is, an Enchanter is an absolutely top-notch party member. No doubt about it. If you're designing a character with the goal of getting together with a bunch of friends (or friends-to-be), and seeing what Norrath is all about, choosing an Enchanter will greatly increase the overall success of your group. Success for the group, never forget, means success for all the members.

That's what an Enchanter does: he makes it much easier for his party to be successful. It's not an exotic job description, granted, but being practical and efficient has its own charms. If you can picture yourself standing on the sidelines of a battle, buffing up your own side's abilities and casting spells of confusion on the enemy, you've got the right idea. Just look at the kinds of spells the Enchanter gets right off the bat: *Strengthen*, *Weaken*, *Lull*, plus others.

And don't forget that at Level 12, an Enchanter can cast *Bind Affinity*. (Okay, so all magic users can cast *Bind Affinity*. It's still incredibly useful for a group that travels!) For those who might not understand the glory that is the *Bind Affinity* spell, it means that an Enchanter can reset the location where a person goes when he or she dies. Something that makes an Enchanter really stand out is the ability to do crowd-control. When there's just one monster on the offense, pretty much any party can handle the situation. When there's a horde, keeping on top of the matter becomes trickier. Organization and strategy is an ability that requires experience and level heads. Having an Enchanter on hand who can slow things down with a radius stun helps keep things from spinning out of control.

More about Enchanters

Intelligence. Intelligence is brain-power for book-learners … the more brainpower you got, the more mana you get, the more spells you can cast.

Charisma. Here's a hint. Another word for charismatic is "charming." Enchanters are nothing if not charmers. The more charisma they have, the easier it is for their charm spells to work. It's all a matter of convincing other people to see the world the way you want them to.

Dark Elf

Advantages: Ultravision

Disadvantages: Race is hated

Erudite

Advantages: Highest intelligence

Disadvantages: Poor night vision, low agility

Gnome

Advantages: Infravision

Disadvantages: None

High Elf

Advantages: Infravision

Disadvantages: None

Human

Advantages: None

Disadvantages: Poor night vision

Enchanter Skills

1	1H Blunt
1	2H Blunt
1	Abjuration
1	Alcohol Tolerance
1	Alteration
1	Baking
1	Begging
1	Bind Wound
1	Blacksmithing
1	Brewing
1	Channeling
1	Conjuration
1	Defense
1	Divination
1	Evocation
1	Fishing
1	Fletching
1	Hand to Hand
1	Jewelry Making
1	Offense
1	Piercing
1	Pottery
1	Sense Direction
1	Swimming
1	Tailoring
1	Throwing
1	Tinkering
4	Meditate
16	Research
20	Specialize Abjure
20	Specialize Alteration
20	Specialize Conjuration
20	Specialize Divination
20	Specialize Evocation
22	Dodge

Enchanter Spells

Level	Spell	Page	Level	Spell	Page
1	Lull	407	12	Charm	365
1	Minor Illusion	411	12	Choke	366
1	Minor Shielding	411	12	Ebbing Strength	376
1	Pendril's Animation	414	12	Enduring Breath	380
1	Reclaim Energy	419	12	Illusion: Dark Elf	396
1	Shallow Breath	428	12	Illusion: Erudite	396
1	Strengthen	439	12	Illusion: Halfling	397
1	Taper Enchantment	445	12	Illusion: High Elf	397
1	True North	449	12	Kilan's Animation	403
1	Weaken	452	12	Languid Pace	403
4	Color Flux	368	12	Memory Blur	410
4	Enfeeblement	380	12	Mist	412
4	Fear	383	12	Serpent Sight	423
4	Gate	389	12	Thicken Mana	446
4	Haze	393	12	Whirl till you Hurl	452
4	Illusion: Half-Elf	397	16	Breeze	360
4	Illusion: Human	397	16	Chase the Moon	365
4	Invisibility	400	16	Disempower	374
4	Juli's Animation	402	16	Enchant Electrum	378
4	Mesmerize	410	16	Enthrall	381
4	Suffocating Sphere	440	16	Identify	395
4	Tashan	445	16	Illusion: Barbarian	396
8	Alliance	354	16	Illusion: Dwarf	396
8	Bind Sight	358	16	Illusion: Tree	398
8	Cancel Magic	362	16	Invisibility versus Undead	400
8	Chaotic Feedback	365	16	Levitate	405
8	Enchant Silver	379	16	Mesmerization	410
8	Eye of Confusion	383	16	Quickness	417
8	Illusion: Gnome	396	16	Rune I	423
8	Illusion: Wood Elf	398	16	Sanity Warp	424
8	Lesser Shielding	404	16	Shalee's Animation	428
8	Mircyl's Animation	412	16	Shielding	429
8	Root	423	20	Benevolence	358
8	See Invisible	425	20	Berserker Strength	358
8	Sentinel	457	20	Calm	362
8	Soothe	434	20	Cloud	367
12	Bind Affinity	358	20	Color Shift	368

Enchanter Spells, cont.

Level	Spell	Page	Level	Spell	Page
20	Crystallize Mana	371	34	Anarchy	355
20	Endure Magic	379	34	Boltran's Animation	359
20	Feckless Might	384	34	Cast Sight	363
20	Illusion: Iksar	397	34	Enchant Platinum	378
20	Illusion: Ogre	397	34	Entrance	381
20	Illusion: Troll	398	34	Greater Shielding	391
20	Shifting Sight	430	34	Illusion: Fire Elemental	396
20	Sisna's Animation	433	34	Insipid Weakness	399
20	Sympathetic Aura	444	34	Mana Sieve	409
20	Tashani	446	34	Radiant Visage	417
24	Alacrity	354	34	Rune III	423
24	Beguile	357	39	Aanya's Animation	353
24	Chaos Flux	365	39	Cajoling Whispers	361
24	Enchant Gold	379	39	Celerity	364
24	Illusion: Earth Elemental	396	39	Distill Mana	374
24	Illusion: Skeleton	398	39	Gravity Flux	390
24	Invigor	400	39	Illusion: Drybone	396
24	Major Shielding	408	39	Illusion: Spirit Wolf	397
24	Rune II	423	39	Immobilize	398
24	Sagar's Animation	424	39	Insight	399
24	Strip Enchantment	439	39	Invoke Fear	401
24	Tepid Deeds	446	39	Mind Wipe	410
29	Augmentation	356	39	Pacify	414
29	Clarify Mana	367	39	Rampage	418
29	Clarity	367	39	Resist Magic	420
29	Curse of the Simple Mind	371	39	Shade	427
29	Dyn's Dizzying Draught	376	44	Arch Shielding	356
29	Enstill	381	44	Brilliance	360
29	Feedback	384	44	Color Skew	368
29	Illusion: Air Elemental	395	44	Discordant Mind	374
29	Illusion: Water Elemental	398	44	Extinguish Fatigue	382
29	Listless Power	406	44	Illusion: Werewolf	398
29	Nullify Magic	413	44	Incapacitate	399
29	Obscure	413	44	Pillage Enchantment	415
29	Suffocate	440	44	Rune IV	423
29	Uleen's Animation	449	44	Shiftless Deeds	430
29	Ultravision	449	44	Tashania	446

Enchanter Spells, cont.

Level	Spell	Page	Level	Spell	Page
44	Weakness	452	54	Dementia	372
44	Yegoreff's Animation	455	54	Glamour of Kintaz	390
49	Adorning Grace	354	54	Shield of the Magi	429
49	Allure	355	55	Largarn's Lamentation	403
49	Berserker Spirit	358	55	Memory Flux	410
49	Blanket of Forgetfulness	358	55	Wind of Tishani	453
49	Dazzle	372	55	Zumaik's Animation	455
49	Gasping Embrace	389	56	Augment	356
49	Group Resist Magic	391	56	Overwhelming Splendor	413
49	Kintaz's Animation	403	56	Torment of Argli	447
49	Paralyzing Earth	414	56	Trepidation	448
49	Purify Mana	417	57	Enlightenment	380
49	Reoccurring Amnesia	420	57	Forlorn Deeds	387
49	Shadow	427	57	Tashanian	446
49	Swift like the Wind	443	57	Umbra	449
51	Collaboration	367	58	Bedlam	357
51	Theft of Thought	446	58	Fetter	384
51	Wake of Tranquility	451	58	Wonderous Rapidity	453
52	Boon of the Clear Mind	359	59	Asphyxiate	356
52	Color Slant	368	59	Gift of Pure Thought	390
52	Fascination	383	59	Rapture	418
52	Rune V	423	60	Dictate	373
53	Aanya's Quickening	353	60	Visions of Grandeur	450
53	Boltran's Agacerie	359	60	Wind of Tishanian	453
53	Cripple	370			
53	Recant Magic	418			
54	Clarity II	367			

Magician

If you picture a Magician as someone who can pull a rabbit out of a hat, then you pretty much know the fundamental nature of this class — and no, they don't have the rabbit hidden behind a secret screen. These are magic users who summon something out of nothing. You've got to see how that can be useful.

Since some of the first things that a Magician can summon are food and drink, he immediately starts off with an advantage. While other classes have to spend their first few levels looking around for places that sell muffins and milk (or whatever) or trying to scrounge up enough rat whiskers to be able to afford a meal, the Magician just wiggles her fingers and presto! Dinner is served. What's more, food and drink can be sold for cold cash. Mana for money isn't a bad exchange on a slow day, although it's a recommended primary occupation.

The Magician is a good choice for the new or shy player. They are decent stand-alone characters, and don't have to depend on tagging after tanks for their continued well being. At Level 4 they have access to the *Gate* spell, which affords them a quick route back home should the situation on the road get too dire. (It's important to save enough mana to use the spell, of course.)

Just as important as the useful items they create are the pets they summon. Elemental forces are molded into creatures and set to (usually martial) tasks. The higher the Magician's level is, the stronger the elemental pet. Eventually Magicians can walk across the land with very little fear of the locals — even though they never become very durable as far as hit points or armor class goes.

Magicians also make decent party-members. They can hold their own in a battle (magically, since they tend not to be good in hand-to-hand combat). A steady source of food and drink, of course, is always welcome and by Level 12 they have the much-sought-after *Bind Affinity* that resets a killed player's resurrection point. *Summoning Bandages* is also good if the group is short a real healer.

Magician Skills

1	1H Blunt
1	2H Blunt
1	Abjuration
1	Alcohol Tolerance
1	Alteration
1	Baking
1	Begging
1	Bind Wound
1	Blacksmithing
1	Brewing
1	Channeling
1	Conjuration
1	Defense
1	Divination
1	Evocation
1	Fishing
1	Fletching
1	Hand to Hand
1	Jewelry Making
1	Offense
1	Piercing
1	Pottery
1	Sense Direction
1	Swimming
1	Tailoring
1	Throwing
1	Tinkering
4	Meditate
16	Research
20	Specialize Abjure
20	Specialize Alteration
20	Specialize Conjuration
20	Specialize Divination
20	Specialize Evocation
22	Dodge

More About Magicians

Intelligence. Spells, spells, spells. When you're a magic-user, you're always going to have bookwork to brush up on. More intelligence equals more spell-power per level.

Stamina. Magicians are one of the better solo-player attributes ... and anyone who is going out on their own is well served to be able to shrug off a few direct hits, just in case their faithful pet takes a dirt nap.

Dark Elf

Advantages: Ultravision

Disadvantages: Race is hated

High Elf

Advantages: Infravision

Disadvantages: None

Erudite

Advantages: Highest intelligence

Disadvantages: Poor night vision, Low agility

Human

Advantages: None

Disadvantages: Poor night vision

Gnome

Advantages: Infravision

Disadvantages: None

Magician Spells

Level	Spell	Page	Level	Spell	Page
1	Burst of Flame	361	4	Elementalkin: Air	378
1	Flare	386	4	Elementalkin: Earth	378
1	Minor Shielding	411	4	Elementalkin: Fire	378
1	Reclaim Energy	419	4	Elementalkin: Water	378
1	Summon Dagger	440	4	Fire Flux	385
1	Summon Drink	441	4	Gate	389
1	Summon Food	441	4	Sense Summoned	426
1	True North	449	4	Summon Bandages	440
4	Burn	360	4	Summon Wisp	442

Magician Spells, cont.

Level	Spell	Page	Level	Spell	Page
8	Dimensional Pocket	373	20	Bolt of Flame	359
8	Elementaling: Air	377	20	Elemental Shield	377
8	Elementaling: Earth	377	20	Expulse Summoned	382
8	Elementaling: Fire	377	20	Lesser Summoning: Air	404
8	Elementaling: Water	378	20	Lesser Summoning: Earth	405
8	Eye of Zomm	383	20	Lesser Summoning: Fire	405
8	Flame Bolt	386	20	Lesser Summoning: Water	405
8	Invisibility	400	20	Rain of Fire	418
8	Lesser Shielding	404	20	Renew Summoning	419
8	Renew Elements	419	20	Shield of Flame	429
8	Shield of Fire	429	20	Spear of Warding	435
8	Shock of Blades	430	20	Summon Arrows	440
8	Staff of Tracing	438	20	Summon Waterstone	441
12	Bind Affinity	358	24	Cornucopia	369
12	Burnout	361	24	Everfount	382
12	Cancel Magic	362	24	Flame Flux	386
12	Column of Fire	368	24	Major Shielding	408
12	Elemental: Air	376	24	Malise	408
12	Elemental: Earth	376	24	Shock of Spikes	431
12	Elemental: Fire	376	24	Staff of Runes	437
12	Elemental: Water	377	24	Summoning: Air	442
12	Rain of Blades	418	24	Summoning: Earth	442
12	Summon Fang	441	24	Summoning: Fire	442
12	Ward Summoned	451	24	Summoning: Water	442
16	Acumen	353	29	Burnout II	361
16	Identify	395	29	Dismiss Summoned	374
16	Minor Summoning: Air	411	29	Greater Summoning: Air	391
16	Minor Summoning: Earth	411	29	Greater Summoning: Earth	391
16	Minor Summoning: Fire	412	29	Greater Summoning: Fire	391
16	Minor Summoning: Water	412	29	Greater Summoning: Water	391
16	Phantom Leather	415	29	Inferno Shield	399
16	See Invisible	425	29	Phantom Chain	415
16	Shielding	429	29	Rain of Spikes	418
16	Shock of Flame	430	29	Summon Coldstone	440
16	Staff of Warding	438	29	Sword of Runes	443
16	Summon Heatstone	441	34	Blaze	358
16	Summon Throwing Dagger	441	34	Cinder Bolt	367

Magician Spells, cont.

Monk

Depending on your background, you might not have the right mental image when you think of a Monk. If you picture a pale-faced fellow with a funny haircut and a rope for a belt, you're not quite right. Try this one: you walk into an oriental shrine's consecrated garden and pick the sacred flower ... next thing you know a quiet, mild-mannered groundskeeper kneeling nearby leaps six feet into the air and kicks your head right off your shoulders and into the immaculately tended fish pond. *That's* the kind of monk we're talking about.

The Way of the Warrior is a religious calling to these holy people. The way they figure, the best method for teaching about the afterlife is to personally introduce opponents to their maker. They tend to be quiet, introspective and more than a little scary. Because they rely on speed and skill to succeed, they don't wear anything heavier than leather. With their martial abilities, they rarely tend to need equipment at all. That rhymes with "low-cost maintenance," which is a happy, happy thing. Plus, anything over 14 pounds and they lose their Monk armor class. Have you looked at the prices of good quality armor these days? It's much better to have the ability of not being hit. Of course, they usually believe in leading a simple lifestyle and eschew monetary gain, so they're not famous for walking around in silks and gems, but that's the way the world works.

The Monk is the quintessential warrior. That's all they do, and they do it well. Magic? That's for wusses too afraid to get in close and personal. Weapons? Only for neatniks who don't want to get their hands dirty. Monks wade in and mix it up, using their incredible Agility and Dexterity to keep from being sliced to shreds.

This character actually does pretty well in a group, fulfilling the role of fighter. A Monk who has been augmented by magic spells — especially Enchanter's spells — can be utterly awesome in battle. She makes a good "drawer," because by Level 8 she can sneak out, find the appropriate critter, and then draw it back to the others for a short and sweet slaughter. Her dexterity and agility means she can reliably stay ahead of most monsters.

It's worth noting that Monks start with the skill *Mend*, with which they keep themselves in tip-top shape. However ... *Mend* takes practice, and you may harm yourself while you learn the ins and outs of cellular reconstruction.

Monks are different from the standard role-playing characters, and may be tricky for someone new to *EverQuest* to truly appreciate.

More about Monks

Strength. Strength affects how much damage you do. If you think you don't need strength unless you're going to swing a big weapon, *you* try knocking someone across the room with one kick. Furthermore, it affects how much you can carry, which is a major concern for a Monk. A strong Monk is a happy Monk.

Stamina. Monks have a naturally high Stamina from a life of crafting their bodies into the ultimate war machine. However, more is better. High Stamina is a good thing in a warrior who doesn't wear armor.

Agility. Fast, fast, fast. The faster you are, the more often your enemy misses you. Even better, a high Agility improves your starting armor class. This is commonly considered *the* most important attribute, and is commonly maxed out during character creation.

Dexterity. Akin to Agility, a high Dexterity increases your success in landing an attack. When a Monk tries one of the patented "Monk Moves," it's the Dexterity that counts.

Human

Advantages: Well- liked

Disadvantages: Poor night vision

Iksar

Advantages: Infravision, higher swimming, regeneration

Disadvantages: Race is hated

Monk Skills

1	1H Blunt
1	2H Blunt
1	Alcohol Tolerance
1	Baking
1	Begging
1	Bind Wound
1	Blacksmithing
1	Brewing
1	Defense
1	Dodge
1	Dual Wield
1	Fishing
1	Fletching
1	Hand to Hand
1	Jewelry Making
1	Kick
1	Mend
1	Offense
1	Pottery
1	Sense Direction
1	Swimming
1	Tailoring
1	Throwing
1	Tinkering
3	Safe Fall
5	Round Kick
8	Sneak
10	Tiger Claw
12	Block
15	Double Attack
17	Feign Death
18	Intimidation
20	Eagle Strike
25	Dragon Punch
27	Disarm
30	Flying Kick
35	Riposte

Necromancer

The art of reaching beyond the grave and commanding the dead is the primary skill of Necromancers. They don't tra-la through the woods with the bunnies like Druids, or dabble in "let's all feel good about ourselves" magic like Enchanters. Nope, Necromancers go straight for the throat with spells of destruction and the dark, evil acts of raising the dead. That's actually not a bad career in Norrath, where there are always plenty of dead around, and plenty of creatures that need killing.

A powerful Necromancer is powerful indeed, and fears very little. At a high enough level, one could stand before the gates of a hostile city, idly chatting with anyone inclined to a little light conversation, while his pet single-handedly destroys the guards who have come to take him down. Which is a good thing for him, because most cities will indeed be hostile to his presence, and most guards will treat him as an enemy of the state. The lesson here is two-fold: a Necromancer shouldn't go visiting until he's good and ready, and shouldn't get his feelings hurt when no one likes him.

Well, there's usually *someone* around who will be nice to a Necromancer, and that's anyone who's looking for a lost corpse. It's actually very easy to lose your corpse when you're killed while walking around in unfamiliar territory (let alone doing something guaranteed to make recovery difficult, like traveling beneath the surface of a river). When that happens, people will be more than happy to make friends with a Necromancer, who is adept at finding corpses from the very beginning of his career.

Necromancers don't put a lot of weight into this whole business of "good" magic and "evil" magic. Essentially they consider research to be a noble goal,

Necromancer Skills

1	1H Blunt
1	2H Blunt
1	Abjuration
1	Alcohol Tolerance
1	Alteration
1	Baking
1	Begging
1	Bind Wound
1	Blacksmithing
1	Brewing
1	Channeling
1	Conjuration
1	Defense
1	Divination
1	Evocation
1	Fishing
1	Fletching
1	Hand to Hand
1	Jewelry Making
1	Offense
1	Piercing
1	Pottery
1	Sense Direction
1	Swimming
1	Tailoring
1	Throwing
1	Tinkering
4	Meditate
16	Research
20	Specialize Abjure
20	Specialize Alteration
20	Specialize Conjuration
20	Specialize Divination
20	Specialize Evocation
22	Dodge

Level	Spell	Page	Level	Spell	Page
	Sense the Dead	426	16	Feign Death	384
	Siphon Strength	433	16	Heart Flutter	393
	Clinging Darkness	367	16	Hungry Earth	394
	Endure Cold	379	16	Infectious Cloud	399
	Fear	383	16	Restless Bones	421
	Gate	389	16	Shielding	429
	Grim Aura	391	16	Shieldskin	430
	Leering Corpse	404	16	Spirit Armor	435
	Lifespike	406	16	Voice Graft	451
	Numb the Dead	413	20	Allure of Death	355
	Poison Bolt	416	20	Animate Dead	355
	True North	449	20	Dominate Undead	375
	Bone Walk	359	20	Expulse Undead	382
	Dark Empathy	372	20	Harmshield	392
	Dark Pact	372	20	Identify	395
	Deadeye	372	20	Shadow Compact	427
	Gather Shadows	389	20	Shadow Vortex	428
	Impart Strength	398	20	Siphon Life	432
	Lesser Shielding	404	20	Word of Shadow	454
	Mend Bones	410	24	Breath of the Dead	360
	Shadow Step	427	24	Haunting Corpse	393
	Vampiric Embrace	450	24	Intensify Death	400
	Ward Undead	451	24	Leatherskin	404
	Bind Affinity	358	24	Major Shielding	408
	Convoke Shadow	369	24	Rapacious Subversion	418
	Endure Disease	379	24	Resist Cold	420
	Engulfing Darkness	380	24	Rest the Dead	420
	Heat Blood	394	24	Scent of Shadow	425
	Leach	404	24	Screaming Terror	425
	Lifedraw	405	24	Shadow Sight	427
	Scent of Dusk	424	24	Shock of Poison	431
	Sight Graft	432	29	Boil Blood	359
	Spook the Dead	437	29	Defoliate	372
	Wave of Enfeeblement	452	29	Dismiss Undead	374
	Banshee Aura	357	29	Dooming Darkness	375
	Cancel Magic	362	29	Panic the Dead	414
	Cure Disease	371	29	Renew Bones	419

and have no problem with the ends justifying the means ... espec
are the Necromancers. Still, the rest of the world is kind of hung
business of magic, and that's that.

Because of the blatant hostility of the rest of the world toward
merchants who sell food and drink and who pay cash for items
challenge for even an experienced player, let alone someone just
EverQuest works. If you don't have some friends to adventure w
supplies as necessary, expect to have to use a lot of people skills
bring a Necromancer up through the levels until he's strong enc

More about Necromancers

Intelligence. Intelligence equals book learning equals more spell
pretty much what a Necromancer is all about, it's a good qualit

Dexterity. No armor and everyone in the world out to get you? Dex
attack. Just think of it as buffing up the fingers in preparation for m

Dark Elf

Advantages: Ultravision
Disadvantages: Race is hated

Erudite

Advantages: Highest intelligence
Disadvantages: Poor night vision

Iksar

Advantages: Infravision, regeneration
Disadvantages: Race is hated

Gnome

Advantages: Infi
dexterity
Disadvantages:

Human

Advantages: Bett
Disadvantages: F

Necromancer Spells

Level	Spell	Page	Level	Spell
1	Cavorting Bones	364	1	Lifetap
1	Coldlight	367	1	Locate Corps
1	Disease Cloud	374	1	Minor Shield
1	Invisibility versus Undead	401	1	Reclaim Ener

Necromancer Spells, cont.

Level	Spell	Page	Level	Spell	Page
29	Spirit Tap	437	49	Lich	405
29	Summon Dead	440	49	Paralyzing Earth	414
29	Vampiric Curse	450	51	Dread of Night	375
29	Word of Spirit	454	51	Envenomed Bolt	381
34	Beguile Undead	357	51	Sacrifice	423
34	Call of Bones	361	51	Splurt	437
34	Greater Shielding	391	52	Defoliation	372
34	Invoke Fear	401	52	Manaskin	409
34	Invoke Shadow	401	52	Plague	415
34	Resist Disease	420	52	Scent of Terris	425
34	Root	423	53	Annul Magic	355
34	Steelskin	438	53	Convergence	369
34	Surge of Enfeeblement	443	53	Enstill	381
34	Venom of the Snake	450	53	Minion of Shadows	410
39	Augment Death	356	54	Deflux	372
39	Counteract Disease	370	54	Shadowbond	428
39	Drain Spirit	375	54	Shield of the Magi	129
39	Expel Undead	382	54	Thrall of Bones	447
39	Malignant Dead	408	55	Chill Bones	365
39	Nullify Magic	413	55	Infusion	399
39	Scent of Darkness	424	55	Levant	405
39	Scourge	425	55	Skin of the Shadow	433
39	Summon Corpse	440	56	Cessation of Cor	364
39	Word of Souls	454	56	Sedulous Subversion	425
44	Arch Shielding	356	56	Servent of Bones	427
44	Asystole	356	56	Trepidation	448
44	Cackling Bones	361	57	Conjure Corpse	369
44	Covetous Subversion	370	57	Exile Undead	382
44	Dead Man Floating	372	57	Vexing Mordinia	450
44	Diamondskin	373	58	Immobilize	398
44	Ignite Bones	395	58	Pyrocruor	417
44	Pact of Shadow	414	58	Quivering Veil of Xarn	417
49	Banish Undead	356	59	Devouring Darkness	373
49	Bond of Death	359	59	Emissary of Thule	378
49	Cajole Undead	361	59	Touch of Night	448
49	Cascading Darkness	363	60	Banishment of Shadows	356
49	Drain Soul	375	60	Demi Lich	373
49	Ignite Blood	395	60	Enslave Death	380
49	Invoke Death	401	60	Trucidation	448

Paladin

You can usually recognize a Paladin by that "I'm on a mission from God" look in her eye. That is, in fact, the job description in a nutshell ... to go out and destroy the evil that besmirches the otherwise noble land of Norrath. In general, most people find them a little fanatical and preachy — when they're in a good mood. When they're in a bad mood, people often find them at the far end of a very sharp sword.

If you've taken a look at Norrath recently, you'll understand that the goal of cleansing the world of all those nasty monsters is more than a full time job. Because it's such a handful, Paladins' gods actually pitch in a little, and give them a boost in the form of certain helpful spells. Like *Laying of Hands*, which entirely cures one person (but not more than once a day). Essentially, the more experience they get, the more clerical skills they get. Real Clerics get these skills much faster, but then real Clerics don't spend as much time developing their weapons skills as Paladins do. It's only fair.

Paladins are usually strong, burly types, with enough hit points that they can wade into the middle of a fray without worrying too much about being dismembered in the first few minutes. Frankly, it takes some dedicated whaling to get a Paladin to fall down, and stay there.

The good part about being a Paladin is that you're an obvious benefit to any group, being not only strong, but being (at higher levels) pretty sensitive to where the evil creatures are, and having some very practical spells. A Paladin can also be fairly self-sufficient, and doesn't necessarily have to rely on a group to get the job done.

So ... if there is a nook or cranny in the dark and dusty parts of your soul that yearns to ham up a role to an almost ridiculous extreme ... this is your chance. If being so single-minded about a quest that your friends have to practically drag you away from certain destruction is attractive to you, well, that's what a Paladin does. With a character of this class, let's just say you don't have to be subtle. All you have to do is shout your defiance at the powers of darkness, and swing that sword.

More about Paladins

Strength. Paladins have truth and righteousness and an incredibly strong sword arm. They are major tanks on the battlefield.

Stamina. Unswerving conviction gives Paladins serious stamina. Okay, that and muscles like woven cables. That's why they can take it on the chin and keep on swinging.

Wisdom. This is one of those deity-based issues. It only makes sense that someone who communes directly with a god has a substantial amount of wisdom. At the appropriate time the gods look down and say "art thou a wise Warrior or a pitiable nincompoop?" and dole out the extra mana points accordingly.

Charisma. Merchants like charismatic people ... and well, anyone who will stand between the helpless and the forces of darkness will always be popular with the locals. As for how the forces of darkness feel about Paladins ... you can just say that they always notice when one walks into the room.

Dwarf

Advantages: Infravision, Strength

Disadvantages: None

Erudite

Advantages:

Disadvantages: Poor night Vision

Half Elf

Advantages: Infravision

Disadvantages: None

High Elf

Advantages: Infravision, highest wisdom

Disadvantages: None

Paladin Skills	
1	1H Blunt
1	1H Slash
1	2H Blunt
1	2H Slash
1	Archery
1	Taunt
6	Bash
9	Abjuration
9	Alteration
9	Channeling
9	Conjuration
9	Divination
9	Evocation
10	Bind Wound
10	Dodge
12	Meditate
17	Parry
20	Double Attack
30	Riposte
40	Disarm

Paladin Spells

Level	Spell	Page	Level	Spell	Page
1	Lay on Hands	403	39	Daring	371
9	Courage	370	39	Endure Disease	379
9	Cure Poison	371	39	Greater Healing	391
9	Flash of Light	387	39	Symbol of Ryltan	443
9	Minor Healing	411	39	Yaulp II	455
9	Spook the Dead	437	49	Calm	362
9	True North	449	49	Dismiss Undead	374
9	Yaulp	454	49	Divine Light	375
15	Cure Disease	371	49	Guard	391
15	Hammer of Wrath	392	49	Holy Might	394
15	Holy Armor	394	49	Revive	421
15	Light Healing	406	49	Symbol of Pinzarn	443
15	Lull	407	49	Valor	449
15	Sense the Dead	426	51	Pacify	414
15	Ward Undead	451	52	Force	387
22	Center	364	52	Frenzied Strength	387
22	Endure Poison	380	53	Armor of Faith	356
22	Halo of Light	392	54	Enstill	381
22	Invigor	400	54	Expel Undead	382
22	Invisibility versus Undead	401	54	Hammer of Requital	392
22	Reckless Strength	419	56	Counteract Disease	370
22	Root	423	56	Yaulp III	455
30	Expulse Undead	382	57	Superior Healing	443
30	Hammer of Striking	392	58	Divine Aura	374
30	Healing	393	58	Nullify Magic	413
30	Soothe	434	58	Symbol of Naltron	443
30	Spirit Armor	435	59	Resuscitate	421
30	Stun	439	59	Resurrection	421
30	Symbol of Transal	444	60	Resolution	420
39	Cancel Magic	362	60	Shield of Words	429
39	Counteract Poison	370			

Human

Advantages: None

Disadvantages: Poor night vision

Ranger

For those folks who grew up with a Robin Hood fixation, this is the one, true class. Anyone who wears green, is a top-notch archer and wants to live in the woods is a natural-born Ranger. The same goes for the kids who always wanted to shoot the arrows and track the bad guys by the depth of their of the footprints when they played Cowboys and Indians ... definitely Ranger material. Rangers are the ones who can smell the rain coming, can follow tracks over solid rock, and generally prefer the great outdoors to the safety of a walled-in city. They don't care much for creatures of darkness, mostly because such monsters defy the basic tenets of Mother Nature, and radically mess up the circle of life. Rangers do not have a sense of humor about either Mother Nature or the circle of life. Not even a little bit.

Rangers are another one of the crossover classes, able to do magic after they've been around a while, but always more comfortable with direct confrontation. Actually, one of their best traits is that they're excellent archers ... and a long-range weapon can be a glorious thing. Of course, first you've actually got to *get* the bow, but that's just an inconvenience.

Don't let the Robin Hood comment above convince you that Rangers are primarily woodsmen. They aren't. Concentrate on the "range" in Ranger ... they like to travel (especially over land), and function well in almost every part of Norrath. Snow doesn't faze them, and neither do the wide, open plains.

Rangers are a little bit tricky for a first-time player, but only because they don't have the hit points that other, more beefy classes have. It doesn't take as much to kill a Ranger as it would a Warrior, for instance, but on the other hand, there is a certain comfort in good, old-fashioned speed. Plus, you trade in a little raw power up front for the promise of spells later on — that's not a shabby trade-off.

Rangers do well in groups or on their own. They are not highly sought after, like a healer or some of the flashier magic users, but they do play well with others. Certainly, joining a group makes it easier for them to fight the higher-level monsters, not to mention simply gaining experience points. Of course, once they gain enough experience points to develop spell-casting abilities, they're even more useful to have in a group.

More about Rangers

Strength. Strength is how hard you can hit 'em. There are no fat Rangers. There are no weak Rangers. These guys only eat what they can kill ... the oldest exercise/dieting regimen known to man.

Stamina. Can they take the slings and arrows of outrageous fortune? Well, when you figure these guys would rather be rained on than build a roof, you've got to figure they've got more stamina than they know what to do with. But still, more is always better.

Agility. The higher this ability, the less you get hit. Rangers don't study the ways of the wild for nothing. There's the quick and the dead. You choose.

Wisdom. Hmmm ... lots of time to yourself, studying nature, staying alive, and (eventually) memorizing spells. Wisdom is inevitable. Mana follows.

Half Elf

Advantages: Infravision

Disadvantages: None

Human

Advantages: None

Disadvantages: Poor night vision

Wood Elf

Advantages: Infravision, foraging

Disadvantages: None

Rangers Skills

Level	Skill
1	1H Blunt
1	1H Slashing
1	2H Blunt
1	2H Slashing
1	Alcohol Tolerance
1	Archery
1	Baking
1	Begging
1	Bind Wound
1	Blacksmithing
1	Brewing
1	Defense
1	Fishing
1	Fletching
1	Hand to Hand
1	Jewelry Making
1	Offense
1	Piercing
1	Pottery
1	Sense Direction
1	Swimming
1	Tailoring
1	Taunt
1	Throwing
1	Tinkering
1	Track
3	Forage
5	Kick
8	Dodge
9	Abjuration
9	Alteration
9	Channeling
9	Conjuration
9	Divination
9	Evocation
10	Sneak
12	Meditate
17	Dual Wield
18	Parry
20	Double Attack
22	Intimidation
25	Hide
35	Disarm
35	Riposte

Ranger Spells

Level	Spell	Page	Level	Spell	Page
9	Endure Fire	379	39	Careless Lightning	363
9	Flame Lick	386	39	Dismiss Summoned	374
9	Glimpse	390	39	Healing	393
9	Lull Animal	407	39	Levitate	405
9	Minor Healing	411	39	Skin like Steel	433
9	Skin like Wood	433	39	Spirit of Wolf	436
9	Snare	434	49	Bramblecoat	360
15	Burst of Fire	361	49	Ensnaring Roots	381
15	Camouflage	362	49	Immolate	398
15	Cure Poison	371	49	Resist Fire	420
15	Dance of the Fireflies	371	49	Shield of Brambles	429
15	Feet like Cat	384	49	Superior Camouflage	443
15	Grasping Roots	390	49	Wolf Form	453
15	Invoke Lightning	401	51	Ensnare	380
15	Thistlecoat	447	52	Combust	369
22	Bind Sight	358	52	Extinguish Fatigue	382
22	Enduring Breath	380	53	Strength of Stone	439
22	Harmony	393	53	Storm Strength	438
22	Ignite	395	54	Drones of Doom	375
22	Light Healing	406	54	Skin like Diamond	433
22	Skin like Rock	433	55	Regeneration	419
22	Ward Summoned	451	56	Chill Sight	365
30	Barbcoat	357	56	Greater Wolf Form	391
30	Cancel Magic	362	57	Greater Healing	391
30	Eyes of the Cat	383	58	Nullify Magic	413
30	Invigor	400	58	Shield of Spikes	429
30	Shield of Thistles	429	59	Firestrike	386
30	Stinging Swarm	438	60	Enveloping Roots	381
30	Strength of Earth	439	60	Thorncoat	447
39	Calm Animal	362			

Rogue

You can look at the name "Rogue" one of two ways: rogue means "scoundrel" — someone who cannot be trusted — but it also means someone (or something) different, unhindered by the rules that govern others. They're not quite the same thing, but they're close. Exactly how a Rogue is played is up to you.

Rogues would be the underdogs in the world of Norrath ... except that they're too sharp to fall into that category. They aren't strong, but they're quick and quiet and have a talent for being unexpected. Where a Warrior breaks down a door, a Rogue scales the wall or pries open a window. When a Paladin flourishes a sword and cries defiance at his enemies, a Rogue silently creeps up behind and slips a thin blade past the ribs and into the heart. Both are effective, but one is much more appropriate to the smaller character who can't bench press a packhorse.

Now, while you can play the Rogue as any type of personality you choose, be aware that the skills a Rogue accumulates as he or she lives and learns tend to be of a certain ... to put it politely ... practicality. A Rogue is part acrobat, part assassin, part thief and a whole lot of swashbuckler. A Rogue can swagger and strut, and then disappear into the shadows. The sheer flexibility of the class makes it a lot of fun for the moderately experienced player. First-time players may be frustrated by the lack of muscle or fireworks, since the Rogue is not ideal for a straightforward lifestyle.

In a party, a Rogue's role (usually) becomes a little bit more mellow, at least as far as his comrades are concerned. Rogues are pretty useless in a battle ... unless the bad guys are so distracted by the others that they can slip in from behind and backstab ...but they make pretty good scouts, being inconspicuous enough to see without being seen, and fast enough to be seen without being cut into ribbons. (Now, being seen by someone with a ranged weapon gets a little trickier.) However, when the party goes into the deep, dark and dangerous places, a Rogue can usually spot the traps without setting them off. That's useful!

Be careful, however, about being light-fingered with your party's goods. A Rogue can do more things and see more places when allied with a group, and if you make your party members angry at you, as often as not they'll drop your character, and go out of their way to make sure no one else picks you up.

Rogue Skills

1	1H Blunt
1	1H Slashing
1	2H Blunt
1	Alcohol Tolerance
1	Archery
1	Baking
1	Begging
1	Bind Wound
1	Blacksmithing
1	Brewing
1	Defense
1	Fishing
1	Fletching
1	Hand to Hand
1	Jewelry Making
1	Offense
1	Piercing
1	Pottery
1	Sense Direction
1	Sneak
1	Swimming
1	Tailoring
1	Throwing
1	Tinkering
3	Hide
4	Dodge
6	Pick Lock
7	Pick Pockets
8	Sense Traps
10	Backstab
12	Parry
12	Safe Fall
13	Dual Wield
16	Double Attack
18	Apply Poison
20	Make Poison
21	Disarm Traps
27	Disarm
30	Riposte

More about Rogues

Agility. This practically goes without saying. Ballerinas move with a flowing grace, but they're like lumbering Trolls when compared with a Rogue dodging an attack. Faster is safer.

Dexterity. Dexterity is directly related to how fast a Rogue picks up the special related to the class. The fastest road to a mixed out Backstab is the way to go!

Barbarian

Advantages: Highest strength, slam

Disadvantages: Poor night vision

Dark Elf

Advantages: Ultravision

Disadvantages: Race is hated

Dwarf

Advantages: Infravision

Disadvantages: None

Gnome

Advantages: Infravision

Disadvantages: None

Half Elf

Advantages: Infravision

Disadvantages: None

Halfling

Advantages: Good faction

Disadvantages: None

Human

Advantages: Level faster

Disadvantages: Poor night vision

Wood Elf

Advantages: Infravision, foraging

Disadvantages: None

Shadow Knight

For those people who have a low goody-goody tolerance, the Shadow Knight stands out as an unabashed, really rotten individual ... gloriously so. She has style, presence, and a reputation that's known throughout the world.

This reputation is more often than not inconvenient.

You see, most people in Norrath consider themselves decent, hard-working individuals. This goes for NPCs as well as most of the player-characters. Consequently, a Shadow Knight just isn't welcome most places. City Guards, for instance, will do their level best to keep a Shadow Knight at a safe distance, and most merchants will get annoyingly tight with their goods. If you're lucky, they'll merely up the price ... if you're not, they won't sell you the time of day ... and killing them is more trouble than its worth.

This means that unless you come up with some workarounds, your Shadow Knight isn't going to see as much of Norrath as you might like. Unfortunate and inconvenient, but that's the way of the world.

Workarounds include things such as ... forming parties with other people as nasty as yourself and taking the world by storm. Wizards, Rogues and Necromancers are usually open to the idea. Conversely, you could convince people who are in better graces with the local law setup that you'd make a marvelous tank for their team, and use your new friends as go-betweens on market day. (This means that you'd have to cool your heels outside most city walls while they pocket your cash and walk away, promising to buy you some nice stuff. Hmm.)

Frankly, Shadow Knights are a tough class for the less-experienced player. Not only is it difficult to survive and grow in a hostile environment, and frustrating to deal with people who'd much rather see you dead on the ground, but frankly, it's difficult to play such an implacable persona of evil without regularly dropping out of character ... and dropping out of character dilutes the façade of implacable evil. However, once you get this class up to the higher levels, you've got the world at the tip of your sword point, and there's a lot to be said for that. There is very little in life more satisfying than practicing your evil laugh after you've sucked the life out of your enemy with *Harm Touch* or a good, out-of-the-blue spell. Plus, the freedom of not caring about the feeling of others is, well, disturbingly addictive.

More about Shad. Knights

Strength. You have the strength of your convictions ... or what would have been your convictions if you had ever been captured and put on trial. Strength is how much damage you can do, and Shadow Knights are very interested in doing damage.

Stamina. You are, essentially, one of the roughest, toughest people in Norrath, and can take about as much as you can dish out ... which is much more than most others can handle.

Wisdom. This is one of the prerequisites of being an anti-Paladin. If it sounds too studious, think again ... it's directly related to how much mana you get at subsequent levels, which equals arcane ways of killing people.

Charisma. Well, this isn't going to make merchants eager to sell you things, unless they're from your hometown. It does mean that when you try to convince the dead to do your bidding, they can't think of a reason why not.

Dark Elf

Advantages: Ultravision

Disadvantages: Race is hated

Erudite

Advantages: Highest intelligence

Disadvantages: Poor night vision

Human

Advantages: Better faction than other SK races

Disadvantages: Poor night vision

Iksar

Advantages: Infravision, regeneration, high swimming

Disadvantages: Race is hated

Ogre

Advantages: Infravision, slam

Disadvantages: Race is hated

Troll

Advantages: Infravision, regeneration, slam

Disadvantages: Race is hated

Skills

1	1H Blunt
1	1H Slashing
1	2H Blunt
1	2H Slashing
1	Alcohol Tolerance
1	Archery
1	Baking
1	Begging
1	Bind Wound
1	Blacksmithing
1	Brewing
1	Defense
1	Fishing
1	Fletching
1	Hand to Hand
1	Jewelry Making
1	Offense
1	Piercing
1	Pottery
1	Sense Direction
1	Swimming
1	Tailoring
1	Taunt
1	Tinkering
6	Bash
9	Abjuration
9	Alteration
9	Channeling
9	Conjuration
9	Divination
9	Evocation
10	Dodge
12	Meditate
17	Parry
20	Double Attack
30	Riposte
35	Hide
40	Disarm

Shadow Knight Spells

Level	Spell	Page	Level	Spell	Page
1	Harm Touch	392	39	Expulse Undead	382
9	Disease Cloud	374	39	Heart Flutter	393
9	Invisibility versus Undead	401	39	Resist Cold	420
9	Leering Corpse	404	39	Shadow Vortex	428
9	Lifetap	406	39	Shieldskin	430
9	Locate Corpse	407	49	Breath of the Dead	360
9	Sense the Dead	426	49	Dismiss Undead	374
9	Siphon Strength	433	49	Dooming Darkness	375
15	Bone Walk	359	49	Invoke Fear	401
15	Clinging Darkness	367	49	Shadow Sight	427
15	Endure Cold	379	49	Summon Dead	440
15	Fear	383	49	Word of Spirit	454
15	Lifespike	406	51	Siphon Life	432
15	Numb the Dead	413	52	Malignant Dead	408
15	Shadow Step	427	52	Rest the Dead	420
22	Convoke Shadow	369	53	Boil Blood	359
22	Dark Empathy	372	54	Banshee Aura	357
22	Deadeye	372	54	Panic the Dead	414
22	Engulfing Darkness	380	55	Expel Undead	382
22	Spook the Dead	437	56	Spirit Tap	437
22	Vampiric Embrace	450	56	Steelskin	437
22	Ward Undead	451	57	Vampiric Curse	450
30	Endure Disease	379	58	Cackling Bones	361
30	Feign Death	384	58	Nullify Magic	413
30	Gather Shadows	389	59	Cascading Darkness	363
30	Heat Blood	394	60	Asystole	356
30	Lifedraw	405	60	Drain Spirit	375
30	Restless Bones	421			
30	Wave of Enfeeblement	452			
39	Animate Dead	355			
39	Cancel Magic	362			

Shaman

The Shaman class is like one of those all-purpose camping knives: the kind that has the can opener *and* both types of screwdriver *and* the three-inch saw that can cut down small trees. Shamans have a wide array of skills and abilities. There are very few situations where being a Shaman doesn't come in handy.

You need a healer? A Shaman can do the trick. You need someone to go toe-to-toe with the big uglies? A Shaman has enough hit points to take the punches. How about fingerwaggling some damage in pitched battle? That is also on the résumé. Frankly, they're more at home covering the defensive, clerical side of things, but that's a general inclination, not a genuine restriction.

In fact, the only real restriction is that the Shaman is available for only a very few races: Barbarian, Iksar, Ogre and Troll. As these aren't the most popular races, not many people explore Shamanhood, but it's well worth a try. Keep in mind that a Shaman is a religious character — no such thing as an agnostic Shaman — but that doesn't have to be a main feature of his interaction with others. "My god is not for the likes of you" is a perfectly viable attitude, depending on the deity that you follow.

One of the best things about being a Shaman is that you are very useful in a party, and quite functional as a solo character. In a group, no matter what is needed, a Shaman can be part (if not all) of the solution. Individually, a Shaman can hold his own: fight his own fights, heal his own wounds, make his own way in the world.

Normally the Shaman's flexibility (as well as the fact that Healers are almost universally popular) would make it an excellent class for a new player to choose, but this is not necessarily the case. The problem is that Barbarians can be tricky to get started, and Ogres and Trolls are unwieldy to role play for people not used to it. Also, Ogres and Trolls are generally not well received in most cities, which can be a little disheartening if you're not well versed in the politics of Norrath.

Still, Shamans have a rich variety of choices and abilities at their disposal, and it's definitely worth the time it takes to bring one up to his full potential.

More about Shamans

Stamina. Shamans aren't tough because they're Shamans. They're tough because they are Barbarians, Iksars, Ogres or Trolls. Of course, that's reason enough. You gotta like a spell caster who isn't afraid of a blow to the head … so the more stamina, the merrier.

Wisdom. A spell-caster and a cleric means that wisdom brings more mana at the higher levels.

Charisma. Hmm … well, charismatic as far as Ogres and Trolls can be. Actually, since the Shaman's spells are a very charm-like magic, charisma is an important element of their makeup.

Barbarian
Advantages: Slam, highest wisdom
Disadvantages: Poor night vision, large race

Iksar
Advantages: Infravision, regeneration
Disadvantages: Race is hated

Ogre
Advantages: Infravision, slam
Disadvantages: Race is hated, large race

Troll
Advantages: Infravision, regeneration, slam
Disadvantages: Lowest wisdom, race is hated, large race

Shaman Skills

1	1H Blunt
1	2H Blunt
1	Abjuration
1	Alteration
1	Bind Wound
1	Conjuration
1	Divination
1	Evocation
1	Piercing
4	Channeling
8	Meditate
15	Dodge
30	Specialization

Shaman Spells

Level	Spell	Page	Level	Spell	Page
1	Burst of Flame	361	14	Turtle Skin	449
1	Cure Disease	371	14	Walking Sleep	451
1	Dexterous Aura	373	19	Affliction	354
1	Endure Cold	379	19	Cancel Magic	362
1	Flash of Light	387	19	Endure Magic	379
1	Inner Fire	399	19	Frenzy	388
1	Minor Healing	411	19	Healing	393
1	Strengthen	439	19	Infectious Cloud	399
1	True North	449	19	Insidious Fever	399
5	Cure Poison	371	19	Malise	408
5	Drowsy	376	19	Shrink	432
5	Endure Fire	379	19	Spirit of Cat	435
5	Feet like Cat	384	19	Spirit Strength	437
5	Fleeting Fury	387	19	Vision	450
5	Frost Rift	388	24	Cannibalize	362
5	Gate	389	24	Counteract Disease	370
5	Scale Skin	424	24	Creeping Vision	370
5	Sicken	432	24	Envenomed Breath	381
5	Spirit Pouch	436	24	Frost Strike	389
5	Summon Drink	441	24	Invigor	400
9	Cure Blindness	371	24	Poison Storm	416
9	Endure Disease	379	24	Protect	416
9	Light Healing	406	24	Regeneration	419
9	Sense Animals	426	24	Resist Cold	420
9	Serpent Sight	427	24	Scale of Wolf	424
9	Spirit of Bear	435	24	Spirit of Cheetah	435
9	Spirit of Wolf	436	24	Spirit of Monkey	436
9	Spirit Sight	437	24	Spirit of Ox	436
9	Summon Food	441	29	Alluring Aura	355
9	Tainted Breath	444	29	Befriend Animal	357
14	Bind Affinity	358	29	Counteract Poison	370
14	Burst of Strength	361	29	Greater Healing	391
14	Disempower	374	29	Invisibility	400
14	Endure Poison	380	29	Listless Power	406
14	Enduring Breath	380	29	Quickness	417
14	Invisibility versus Animals	400	29	Raging Strength	418
14	Levitate	405	29	Resist Fire	420
14	Root	423	29	Rising Dexterity	422
14	Spirit of Snake	436	29	Tagar's Insects	444
14	Spirit Strike	437	29	Ultravision	449

Shaman Spells, cont.

Level	Spell	Page	Level	Spell	Page
34	Companion Spirit	369	49	Plague	415
34	Enstill	381	49	Rage	418
34	Fury	389	49	Strength	438
34	Health	393	51	Immobilize	398
34	Malisement	409	51	Talisman of Jasinth	444
34	Nimble	413	51	Turgur's Insects	449
34	Resist Disease	420	52	Insidious Decay	399
34	Scourge	425	52	Regrowth	419
34	Shifting Shield	430	52	Spirit of Scale	436
34	Talisman of Tnarg	445	53	Cripple	370
34	Winter's Roar	453	53	Deliriously Nimble	372
39	Assiduous Vision	356	53	Superior Healing	443
39	Blinding Luminance	358	53	Talisman of Shadoo	444
39	Cannibalize II	363	54	Cannibalize III	363
39	Chloroplast	365	54	Ice Strike	395
39	Deftness	372	54	Riotous Health	422
39	Extinguish Fatigue	382	54	Shroud of the Spirits	432
39	Furious Strength	389	55	Annul Magic	355
39	Gale of Poison	389	55	Spirit of the Howler	436
39	Glamour	390	55	Talisman of Kragg	444
39	Insidious Malady	399	55	Torrent of Poison	447
39	Resist Poison	420	56	Acumen	353
39	Togor's Insects	444	56	Bane of Nife	356
39	Venom of the Snake	450	56	Celerity	364
39	Vigilant Spirit	450	56	Paralyzing Earth	414
44	Agility	354	57	Malosini	409
44	Alacrity	354	57	Manicial Strength	409
44	Blizzard Blast	359	57	Talisman of the Brute	444
44	Guardian	391	57	Talisman of the Cat	444
44	Guardian Spirit	391	58	Mortal Deftness	412
44	Incapacitate	399	58	Talisman of the Rhino	445
44	Nullify Magic	413	58	Talisman of the Serpent	445
44	Resist Magic	420	58	Tigir's Insects	447
44	Stamina	438	59	Pox of Bertoxxulous	416
44	Talisman of Altuna	444	59	Talisman of the Raptor	445
49	Abolish Disease	353	59	Unfailing Reverence	449
49	Charisma	365	59	Voice of the Berserker	451
49	Dexterity	373	60	Avatar	356
49	Envenomed Bolt	381	60	Malo	409
49	Frenzied Spirit	387	60	Torpor	447
49	Malosi	409			

Warrior

The Warrior is a marvelously uncomplicated character. Simple in concept, this class can be like a clean sheet of paper or an empty canvas: more than almost any other class, the job description of Warrior can be adapted to fit almost any personality or history you care to create. It also is very forgiving to players who are unfamiliar with *EverQuest*. Warriors are straightforward and direct: they hit creatures. If they can't kill their opponents, they have more time — because they have more hit points — to recognize that they're in trouble and head for help.

Warriors are not necessarily good and noble, or evil either, as far as that goes. There are intellectual Warriors, and also big brutes that just whack whatever comes within swinging distance. Polite or brusque, gregarious or loners, devout or devil-may-care ... Warriors do what they want to do.

Warriors do well in parties, but they can also hold their own alone. In a group, they tend to fulfill two roles. First, they protect the fingerwagglers from any non-magical damage. If a magic user (a healer, especially) seems to be losing control of the situation, a Warrior should be on hand for rescue work. The second role is that of "pulling." While the high-powered magic users sit around and recharge mana, Warriors go and flush out some monsters, then lure them back to the mages. Once there, the mages perform whatever quick-fry spells they prefer, the experience and loot is shared, and then they go back to meditating while the Warriors go out to pull more critters.

Be aware that Warrior is a very popular class, and while a Warrior (or more) is very useful to a group, there are always plenty around. Don't expect strangers to just walk up and offer you a place in their party ... you'll need to hunt around for one and (usually) ask to join. On occasion, you might need to form your own group. If you decide to go this route, *definitely* make friends with a healer. Warriors and healers need each other.

One of the benefits of the Warrior class is that nearly every race has a version of Warrior. The Erudites are too snooty and over-educated for sword work, and High Elves are too refined for such barbarity, but other than that, all Norrathians seem open to the idea of physical confrontation.

More about Warriors

Strength. The stronger the Warrior, the more damage is done per hit. Strength wins a fight.

Stamina. Stamina, which translates to hit points, makes the Warrior more durable.

Agility. Big people have a reputation for being clumsy, but clumsy Warriors have a reputation for being corpses. Agility here means quick and effective weapon work and more hits per stab.

Barbarian

Advantages: Slam, high strength and stamina
Disadvantages: Poor night vision

Dark Elf

Advantages: Ultravision
Disadvantages: None

Dwarf

Advantages: Infravision
Disadvantages: None

Gnome

Advantages: Infravision
Disadvantages: None

Half Elf

Advantages: Infravision
Disadvantages: None

Halfling

Advantages: Infravision
Disadvantages: None

Human

Advantages: None
Disadvantages: Poor night vision

Iksar

Advantages: Infravision, regeneration
Disadvantages: None

Ogre

Advantages: Infravision, slam, high strength, high stamina
Disadvantages: Race is hated, large race

Troll

Advantages: Infravision, regeneration, slam, high strength, high stamina
Disadvantages: Race is hated, large race

Wood Elf

Advantages: Infravision, foraging
Disadvantages: None

Warrior Skills

1	1H Blunt	1	Brewing	1	Taunt
1	1H Slashing	1	Defense	1	Throwing
1	2H Blunt	1	Fishing	1	Tinkering
1	2H Slashing	1	Fletching	6	Bash
1	Alcohol Tolerance	1	Hand to Hand	6	Dodge
1	Archery	1	Jewelry Making	10	Parry
1	Baking	1	Kick	13	Dual Wield
1	Begging	1	Offense	15	Double Attack
1	Berserking	1	Piercing	25	Riposte
1	Bind Wound	1	Pottery	35	Disarm
1	Blacksmithing	1	Sense Direction		
		1	Swimming		
		1	Tailoring		

# Wizard

The Wizard is the class for people who have no problem with delayed gratification. As with all classes, you essentially have to work your way up from next to nothing. With other classes, however, you usually have something more to start with ... more stamina, more speed, more something. The Wizard is the proverbial ninety-pound weakling until she works her way up to real power. Even then, she's still a ninety-pound weakling, she just happens to be able to keep enemies at a safe distance by killing them with high-octane magic. A Wizard who tries to use physical power in a fight is either confused or suicidal. End of story.

A Wizard who's been around is a Wizard with power: Power to travel, power to destroy. In fact, at the tender age of 4th Level, a Wizard can return home on command ... as long as there is enough mana. Which means that survival is simply a matter of mana management. That helps. By 20th Level, a Wizard can actually teleport to just outside certain cities, which is also useful. That means that travel is faster, easier, less expensive, and much, much safer.

However, it takes a while to get to 20th Level. By 5th Level, then, it's time to go out and see the world ... but frankly it's a dangerous place out there. Medium-level Wizards can really benefit from joining parties and using their formidable direct-damage spells against hostile creatures. It won't be too long before the rest of the party relies on the Wizard as a major monster-masher.

As far as personality goes, it really depends on which race you choose, as to whether you're going to need an "attitude" or not. Not all races can be Wizards ... in fact, only a handful are eligible. Dark Elves and Erudites — if you're going to play in character — are not the most casual races in Norrath. They strut, they sneer, and they make it clear that they consider even their friends to be barely worth considering. High Elves can be aloof, but can unbend enough to make real friendships with others. Gnomes and Humans don't have as many issues, on a racial level, as the other wizarding races do. With them, relationships are more on a person-by-person basis. However, pretty much across the board, Wizards are a proud class and can't abide a lack of respect. After all, for Wizards it's especially easy to take their toys and, in a shower of sparkles, go home.

More about Wizards

Intelligence. A Wizard has a higher than average intelligence, and they're not afraid to let you know, either. High intelligence equals more mana per level, which is definitely something to brag about in their circles.

Stamina. Wizards are a class that often solo, and stamina is always important for anyone who might face the world without a friend to protect her back. Especially since pets unfortunately have a way of occasionally dying at inopportune times. It helps if a wizard doesn't crumble like spun-sugar at the first blow.

Dark Elf

Advantages: Ultravision

Disadvantages: None

Erudite

Advantages: Highest intelligence

Disadvantages: Poor night vision, low agility

Gnome

Advantages: Infravision

Disadvantages: None

High Elf

Advantages: Infravision

Disadvantages: None

Human

Advantages: Good faction

Disadvantages: Poor night vision

Wizard Skills	
1	1H Blunt
1	2H Blunt
1	Abjuration
1	Alcohol Tolerance
1	Alteration
1	Baking
1	Begging
1	Bind Wound
1	Blacksmithing
1	Brewing
1	Channeling
1	Conjuration
1	Defense
1	Divination
1	Evocation
1	Fishing
1	Fletching
1	Hand to Hand
1	Jewelry Making
1	Offense
1	Piercing
1	Pottery
1	Sense Direction
1	Swimming
1	Tailoring
1	Throwing
1	Tinkering
4	Meditate
16	Research
20	Specialize Abjure
20	Specialize Alteration
20	Specialize Conjuration
20	Specialize Divination
20	Specialize Evocation
22	Dodge

EverQuest: The Ruins of Kunark

Wizard Spells

Level	Spell	Page	Level	Spell	Page
1	Frost Bolt	388	16	Project Lightning	416
1	Minor Shielding	411	16	Shielding	429
1	Numbing Cold	413	16	Shieldskin	430
1	Shock of Frost	431	20	Elemental Shield	377
1	Sphere of Light	435	20	Enstill	381
1	True North	449	20	Fay Gate	383
4	Fade	383	20	Fire Spiral of Al'Kabor	385
4	Gate	389	20	Force Shock	387
4	Glimpse	390	20	North Gate	413
4	Icestrike	395	20	Sight	432
4	O'Keils Radiation	414	20	Tishan's Clash	447
4	Root	423	20	Tox Gate	448
4	See Invisible	425	20	Track Corpse	448
4	Shock of Fire	430	24	Cast Force	363
8	Column of Frost	368	24	Cazic Gate	364
8	Eye of Zomm	383	24	Column of Lightning	368
8	Fingers of Fire	384	24	Common Gate	369
8	Fire Bolt	385	24	Frost Shock	388
8	Lesser Shielding	404	24	Leatherskin	404
8	Sense Summoned	426	24	Levitate	405
8	Shadow Step	427	24	Lightning Storm	406
8	Shock of Ice	431	24	Major Shielding	408
12	Bind Affinity	358	24	Nek Gate	412
12	Cancel Magic	362	24	Ro Gate	422
12	Firestorm	385	24	West Gate	452
12	Frost Spiral of Al'Kabor	388	29	Bonds of Force	359
12	Gaze	390	29	Energy Storm	380
12	Halo of Light	392	29	Evacuate: North	382
12	Resistant Skin	420	29	Fay Portal	383
12	Shock of Lightning	431	29	Inferno Shock	399
16	Bind Sight	358	29	Magnify	408
16	Flame Shock	386	29	North Portal	413
16	Heat Sight	394	29	Shock Spiral of Al'Kabor	431
16	Identify	395	29	Thunder Strike	447
16	Invisibility	400	29	Tox Portal	448
16	Lightning Bolt	406	29	Yonder	455
16	Pillar of Fire	415	34	Cazic Portal	364

Wizard Spells, cont.

Level	Spell	Page	Level	Spell	Page
34	Circle of Force	366	51	Draught of Fire	375
34	Combine Portal	369	51	Pillar of Frost	415
34	Evacuate: Fay	381	51	Tishan's Discord	447
34	Greater Shielding	391	52	Abscond	353
34	Ice Shock	395	52	Lure of Frost	407
34	Lava Storm	403	52	Manaskin	409
34	Nek Portal	412	52	Tears of Druzzil	446
34	Nullify Magic	413	53	Annul Magic	355
34	Steelskin	438	53	Inferno of Al'Kabor	399
34	Thunderclap	447	53	Jyll's Static Pulse	402
39	Chill Sight	365	54	Pillar of Lightning	415
39	Common Portal	369	54	Shield of the Magi	429
39	Concussion	369	54	Thunderbold	447
39	Evacuate: Ro	382	54	Voltaic Draugh	451
39	Force Spiral of Al'Kabor	387	55	Draught of Jiva	375
39	Immobilize	398	55	Lure of Flame	407
39	Lightning Shock	406	55	Plainsight	415
39	Ro Portal	423	55	Tears of Solusek	446
39	Shifting Sight	430	56	Jyll's Zephyr of Ice	402
39	West Portal	452	56	Markar's Discord	409
44	Arch Shielding	356	56	Retribution of Al'Kabor	421
44	Conflagration	369	57	Draught of Ice	375
44	Diamondskin	373	57	Evacuate	381
44	Elemental Armor	376	57	Eye of Tallon	383
44	Evacuate: Nek	382	57	Pillar of Flame	415
44	Force Strike	387	58	Fetter	384
44	Frost Storm	388	58	Lure of Lightning	407
44	Gravity Flux	390	58	Manasink	409
46	Alter Plane: Hate	354	58	Tears of Prexus	446
46	Alter Plane: Sky	355	59	Flaming Sword of Xuzl	386
49	Evacuate: West	382	59	Invert Gravity	400
49	Ice Comet	395	59	Jyll's Wave of Heat	402
49	Markar's Clash	409	59	Vengeance of Al'Kabor	450
49	Paralyzing Earth	414	60	Disintegrate	374
49	Rend	419	60	Lure of Ice	407
49	Supernova	443	60	Sunstrike	443
49	Wrath of Al'Kabor	454	60	Winds of Gelid	453
51	Atol's Spectral Shackles	356			

"**F**rogloks," Rhasees said as he stood in front of an army of his beleaguered people, "we prepare for battle. It has been bad enough to defend ourselves against the trolls from without. Indeed, we thought we had found blessed refuge in these sunken ruins. Now, we must find somewhere in these ruins the evil that consumes even our own dead … and destroy it!"

Several in the front ranks whispered, "Hoptor," while others murmured "Thaggelum."

"Yes! You name our enemy!" Rhasees cried as we walked to the front of the ranks.

The whispering increased in volume until everyone was croaking, "Snag the Thaggelum! Chop the Hoptor!"

Races

Barbarian

Barbarians ... you've got to admire them. No other race can get away with wearing a kilt while strolling through the woods, humming a tune and knocking off defenseless creatures. "Whack, smack, add loot to the pack" is their motto. Barbarians are one of the largest races in Norrath, and both the female and male versions of Barbarians are built like tanks. In fact, they're essentially organic war machines. Weighing in at 500+ pounds each, they tend to steamroll just about anything they run across.

Even though they're direct descendants of the God of Valor and Goddess of Love, Barbarians didn't really inherit any traits other than tolerance and a slight tendency toward Good over Evil. Barbarians eat, drink and pursue violence every day of their lives. They prefer a good, solid fistfight to that flashy magic stuff, and tend to use the intelligence they have to plan their next raid or hunt. The typical Barbarian loathes regular bathing, intimate conversation and any sort of social gathering. Fear is looked upon as a despicable trait, and those who possess it are quickly stomped on and cast aside. Slamming comes naturally — almost unconsciously — and they're phenomenally talented at smashing things and creatures in order to acquire bones, pelts, coins and other loot.

Frankly, Barbarians don't have too many career choices. Most prefer to channel their great strength, stamina and agility into developing Warrior skills. There's also a strain of less physical (but just as ruthless) Barbarians that choose to become Shamans instead and slowly grow into their potential. The *really* shy and shady loner types assume the career of a Rogue and don't peak until they've gained a lot of experience. Barbarians are quite egotistical about their career, and are constantly boasting and arguing among themselves as to who's better at what. Once Warriors and Shamans slurp down enough ale to drown their differences, though, they're the best of friends and make an incredible team out in the wild.

At an early age, Barbarian youth become accustomed to swimming in the frigid waters of Everfrost. Many choose to team up and venture out for riches and fame elsewhere in Norrath. No one really has a problem with Barbarians that visit their cities — after all, wouldn't you want one on *your* side? Evil Elves, Iksar, Ogres and Trolls, however, often silently spit behind their backs as they walk past. Few would dare to take on a wandering Barbarian in face-to-face combat. Of course, those who have highly developed magical skills and ranged weapons have less to fear from these mundane fighters.

Starting City	Halas		
Occupations	Rogue, Shaman, Warrior		
Racial Tensions	Dark Elves, Iksar, Ogres, Trolls		
Special Abilities	Slam		

	STR	STA	AGI	DEX	WIS	INT	CHA	Bonus AP
Rogue	103	95	92	80	70	60	55	30
Shaman	103	100	82	70	80	60	60	30
Warrior	113	105	87	70	70	60	55	25

Dark Elf

Ah, the lure of evil! Here's the background: all races in Norrath were hand-created by one god or another in their quest for power and balance. However, the "good" and "evil" gods weren't very good at communicating. This made Innoruuk, the Prince of Hate, very angry. As revenge, he slowly crafted his own brood (the Teir-Dal), which turned out to be just as evil as himself. Like their creator, Dark Elves are deceitful creatures who love to inflict pain and suffering on anyone around them — especially if they benefit by it. Loyalty isn't really in the Elven vocabulary, and many a Dark Elf has backstabbed her own brethren in order to achieve some goal.

While other races screaming a war cry and wading into battle, Dark Elves prefer to Hide and cast magic. (It's *much* more fun to watch your opponents panic and run around in circles while you cast a painful spell on them.) Dark Elves feel it's perfectly within their right to create chaos and spread evil. They often take great pleasure in misleading others, perhaps by sending newbies into the nearest Piranha-infested pond to retrieve a few platinum. Dark Elves have no real use for timetables, do-gooders or promises. Instead, life is guided by their immediate wants and pleasures.

Much to their disgust, Dark Elves share the pointed ears of other elves — but have white hair and bluish-black skin. They're quick to dismiss all other races with disdain, especially if someone dares to compare them to a lowly Wood Elf. Unlike their arboreal cousins, Dark Elves prefer roots to branches. They live underground and can see perfectly well in the dark.

The enjoyment of inflicting suffering is the hallmark trait of a Dark Elf. Likewise, hiding is both the preferred defense and attack for Dark Elves, no matter what they do for a living. Some choose magic, while others prefer to sneak behind-the-scenes as a Rogue, Warrior, Shadow Knight or Cleric.

Except for similarly twisted individuals, most Dark Elves won't tolerate other races in Neriak. That feeling's quite mutual throughout Norrath. Because of this bad rap, Dark Elves have a hard time getting from Point A (Neriak) to Point B, C, D, E ... you get the idea. The only way to travel is to kill someone that's hated in your destination city — Orcs, Gnolls, Rogues, Elven slaves. That's always a risky, double-edged sword, though, since raising your faction standing outside Neriak usually alienates Dark Elves in your hometown.

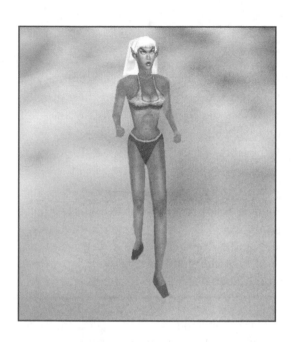

Starting City	Neriak
Occupations	Cleric, Enchanter, Magician, Necromancer, Rogue, Shadow Knight, Warrior, Wizard
Racial Tensions	Barbarians, Erudites, Half Elves, High Elves, Humans, Iksar, Wood Elves
Special Abilities	Ultravision

	STR	STA	AGI	DEX	WIS	INT	CHA	Bonus AP
Cleric	65	70	90	75	93	99	60	30
Enchanter	60	65	90	75	83	109	70	30
Magician	60	75	90	75	83	109	60	30
Necromancer	60	65	90	85	83	109	60	30
Rogue	60	65	100	85	83	99	60	30
Shadow Knight	70	70	90	75	83	109	65	20
Warrior	70	75	90	75	83	99	60	25
Wizard	60	75	90	75	93	109	60	30

Dwarf

Behind the backs of the other Norrathian gods, Brell Serilis established a secret, magical portal into the bowels of Norrath and planted the Dwarven race. He planned his new people to be just as deceitful and sneaky as himself, while also making them impeccably loyal so they'd become devout followers. He crafted them to be short, strong, mobile and ambidextrous — after all, mining cavern space is a difficult task, and he believed in efficiency.

In the eyes of most Dwarves, being short isn't bad. They don't seem to mind their lack of height — pound for pound and inch for inch, they handily outperform most races in tests of strength and agility. Their second most obvious feature is ... well, let's just say that Dwarves never worry about going bald. (A running joke among other races is that Dwarven men keep the toupee makers in business, while Dwarven women keep the smithies busy making razors. Males often duel over this comment, since female facial hair is considered quite attractive in their culture.)

Dwarves have about the same level of Charisma as Ogres and Trolls — which is close to none at all. But, all of them believe in one thing strongly, whether that something is their task at hand, life's work, or deity. (Very few Dwarves are agnostic.) No matter what their role, they'll gladly give it their all. Most Dwarves pursue the life of a Paladin or Warrior, Cleric or Rogue. All are good and proper ways to make a living (excepting thievery, of course).

Time after time, opponents underestimate the power of a Dwarf in combat. More than one has let loose a hearty chuckle after knocking off a bigger target, or after giving a helping hand to a huge Ogre friend who's fallen in battle. Dwarves normally have lots of friends and stick together at any cost. In general, the Dwarven race is tolerant of everyone else, and vice-versa. Even Dark Elves will allow them into Neriak (this is not to say, however, that they won't take advantage of their presence). This sort of neutrality leads Dwarves to join with characters of all sorts and wander about the continents. Be wary of Dwarven Rogues, however — not all of them are honest enough to split loot evenly with the rest of the party.)

Starting City	Kaladim
Occupations	Cleric, Paladin, Rogue, Warrior
Racial Tensions	Iksur
Special Abilities	Infravision

	STR	STA	AGI	DEX	WIS	INT	CHA	Bonus AP
Cleric	95	95	70	90	93	60	45	30
Paladin	100	95	70	90	88	60	55	20
Rogue	90	90	800	100	83	60	45	30
Warrior	100	100	75	90	83	60	45	25

Erudite

If you ever notice an Erudite hacking away with a pick or associating with a lowly Barbarian, find the nearest Paladin or Wizard and beg for a healing spell — you must be suffering from delusions. Because Erudites are highly evolved Humans ... who are, in turn, highly evolved Barbarians ... they pride themselves as being superior to all other races. Erudites ignore their apparent Barbaric heritage, claiming instead to be descendants of Erud, one of the original Human leaders who left the relative safety of Qeynos and Freeport to seek out sorcery and magical power.

All Erudites are dark and frail, and muscles are an undesirable trait in either gender. Physical labor leaves a bad taste in the mouths of all Erudites, who prefer to concentrate instead on their intellect and magical skills. At a tender age, all young Erudites are persuaded to follow the path of the arcane arts. This little exercise in brainwashing has shaped the hometown of Erudin as a whole. Now, an Erudite's worth to society is measured entirely by his or her spellcasting ability. (And fashion statement — they're famous for their elaborate clothing and armor, especially Paladins.)

As vain as they are, most Erudites pursue a neutral or slightly compassionate career as Magician, Enchanter or Wizard. Some less ethical members of this race turn to the life of a darkly aligned Necromancer. Though much more rare, Erudites do occasionally become Paladins or Clerics with good intentions. A lot of what an Erudite says and does is determined by his or her deity — followers of Solusek Ro, for instance, could really care less about what happens to other people.

While others portray them as arrogant, self-righteous and weak, Erudites can't possibly fathom why anyone would ever question their superiority over the other races. It's not even an option to consider, in their opinion. For this reason, guards and townsfolk in other cities rarely welcome Erudites with open arms. Those that do recognize their potential, however (and are willing to shrug off a constant stream of insults), will find one a welcome force in their group. Whatever an Erudite lacks in physical development, he or she makes up twicefold with a superior intellect and a spell or two. Taking the power of magic into account, the advantage of having even a low-level Erudite in your party becomes quite clear.

Starting Cities	Erudin, Paineel	
Occupations	Cleric, Enchanter, Magician, Necromancer, Paladin, Wizard	
Racial Tensions	Dark Elves, Iksar	

	STR	STA	AGI	DEX	WIS	INT	CHA	Bonus AP
Cleric	65	75	70	70	93	107	70	30
Shadow Knight	70	75	70	70	83	117	75	20
Enchanter	60	70	70	70	83	117	80	30
Magician	60	80	70	70	83	117	70	30
Necromancer	60	70	70	80	83	117	70	30
Paladin	70	75	70	70	88	107	80	20
Wizard	60	80	70	70	83	117	70	30

Gnome

Shorter and slimmer than Dwarves, Gnomes are another brainchild of Brell Serilis. Gnomes are famous throughout the land for their childlike curiosity and a love for tinkering and magic. What with their high intelligence, this makes them a fantastically interesting race to associate with. So what if they're not quite as strong or hirsute ... who needs such frippery when you've got brains to spare and a good personality?

Gnomes have fewer hair follicles than Dwarves, and are smarter and generally friendlier. They've got a decent sense of humor (despite all the height-deficiency jokes they hear) and are easygoing. Appearance-wise, they sport Elf-like ears and pale coloring from years of dwelling underground. Their intense love for all things technical amuses the other races, but even the Dwarves who supply them with ore recognize that Gnomes have a unique gift for tinkering.

Even though they get along famously with everyone else, Gnomes aren't travelers at heart. They're perfectly content to remain in the dark and tinker the days away. Most prefer to hang around their hometown of Ak'Anon and wait for everyone else to come visit them. Ak'Anon is always alive with the ever-present clicking and clacking sounds of "Clockwork" robots, which perform all required physical labor without complaint. They repeatedly refuse to export these magical, robotic creations to other cities, but gladly welcome all visiting races except for the Iksar. The only friction surfaces when travelers slay their guards for money — though Gnomes aren't particularly concerned with being loyal, they like their guards. Of course, this doesn't stop travelers from trying.

High intelligence prequalifies a Gnome for a career in the magical arts, though a persevering individual can make a living as a Warrior. Many choose to follow good causes (or at least neutral ones). Equally as often, strong agility and dexterity ratings lead the less scrupulous to become Rogues. Down any road they follow, Gnomes are hard to hit due to their small stature and quickness.

As part of a party, Gnomes have fewer magical skills to offer than other races, but they're far more humble than Erudites and way more trustworthy than Dark Elves. Besides, you can pick on them without too much fear of retribution.

Starting City	Ak'Anon
Occupations	Cleric, Enchanter, Magician, Necromancer, Rogue, Warrior, Wizard
Racial Tensions	Iksar

	STR	STA	AGI	DEX	WIS	INT	CHA	Bonus AP
Cleric	65	75	85	85	77	98	60	30
Enchanter	60	70	85	85	67	108	70	30
Magician	60	80	85	85	67	108	60	30
Necromancer	60	70	85	95	67	108	60	30
Rogue	60	70	95	95	67	98	60	30
Warrior	70	80	90	85	67	98	60	25
Wizard	60	80	85	85	67	108	60	30

Half Elf

Because Norrath has so many Wood Elves and so many Humans, it only makes sense that there's a large Half Elf population. (We'll spare you the details here on how that happened … it's not too hard to figure out.) They've got the same adorable pointy ears and sharp features of their good-looking cousins, but otherwise look more Human than Elf … and can actually get a tan.

Half Elves get less respect than they deserve in Norrath, considering their ancestry. Humans slightly distrust them, and even the other Elven races don't entirely accept Half Elves as one of their own — mostly out of pure vanity. (What? Mate with a filthy Human?) Iksar, Ogres and Trolls don't like Half Elves and can be quite mean, but at least the other races treat them pretty decently. Most often, Half Elves roam around with Humans and Elves.

Despite their dual upbringing, Half Elves inherited the best of both worlds as far as their ancestry's concerned. Probably the biggest advantages that Half Elves have are their ability to see at night (Infravision). Their Agility and Dexterity ratings are nothing to sneeze at, either. With these abilities, Half Elves can master anything from the art of magic to battle to thievery … it's all a matter of personal preference. Bards, Druids, Rangers, Rogues, Paladins and Warriors are all commonplace, and Half Elves are no less competent in one than another.

Half Elves occupy Felwithe, Freeport, Kelethin and Qeynos, a cross-continental luxury that few races enjoy. With such wide choices in starting cities, traveling isn't normally a problem. Many a happy Half Elf has found a group to adventure with — especially with Bards, who are well-liked by nearly everyone. Because they travel so often, Half Elves can be a good source of information to visitors in the region.

Starting Cities	Qeynos, Freeport, Kelethin, Felwithe
Occupations	Bard, Druid, Paladin, Ranger, Rogue, Warrior
Racial Tensions	Dark Elf, Iksar, Ogres, Trolls
Special Abilities	Infravision

	STR	STA	AGI	DEX	WIS	INT	CHA	Bonus AP
Bard	75	70	90	95	60	75	85	25
Druid	70	80	90	85	70	75	75	30
Paladin	80	75	90	85	65	75	85	20
Ranger	75	80	100	85	65	75	75	20
Rogue	70	70	100	95	60	75	75	30
Warrior	80	80	95	85	60	75	75	25

Halfling

Some people claim that a Dwarf or Gnome must have been introduced into the Human bloodline at some point to create the short, hairy breed of Halflings, though the Halflings argue differently. Sure, it's true enough that they resemble Humans, and that they're also one of the more nimble and agile races in the world, but that's it. The rumor stops there. Instead, they chalk up their abilities to years of successful breeding.

Even without a great Charisma, Halflings get along just fine with all other races (except the Iksar, who'd rather not associate with anyone at all). Outstanding Dexterity and Agility come naturally, and they're natural travelers. Because of this, Halflings have developed peaceful relations with all other races.

Physically, Halflings sort of look like Humans. Short and stocky, but light on their feet, they're the prank masters of Norrath. Turn your head, and you're likely to see them zip off and Hide as you merrily head down the path toward danger. They'll eventually Sneak up behind you and give you a good scare ... and have a good laugh. But after all, someone's got to keep the adventure interesting. Curiosity is their mainstay trait. So, watch out when grouping with them; Halflings like to meander out to inspect something that looks interesting, but that something just might turn out to be big and dangerous. Or something in your pack might just turn up missing.

Because they're so open-minded and curious about the world, few Halflings actually hang around Rivervale for long. Their calling as a Cleric, Druid, Rogue or Warrior often leads them far from home.

"Hail, there, boatman," the Halfling said. "Where, along this canal, may a wanderer, such as myself, find a peaceful night's rest?"

The Iksar pushed his pole so that his flatbottom ferry would nestle closer to the small, pale customer. His reptilian eyes warily studied the little creature. After a beat, he replied, "No man such as you can rest peacefully within these walls, traveler."

The Halfling put his hand on his sword hilt and tried to stand taller. "Can you take me to an inn or not?"

"That, I can do," the boatman said with a sneer, "as long as you make no conditions on your safety ..."

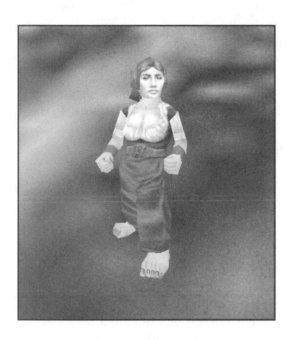

Starting City	Rivervale						
Occupations	Cleric, Druid, Rogue, Warrior						
Racial Tensions	Iksar						
Special Abilities	Infravision						

	STR	STA	AGI	DEX	WIS	INT	CHA	Bonus AP
Cleric	75	80	95	90	90	67	50	30
Druid	70	85	95	90	90	67	50	30
Rogue	70	75	105	100	80	67	50	30
Warrior	80	85	100	90	80	47	50	25

High Elf

Okay, take a typical Erudite. Strip away the elaborate clothing, alter the appearance drastically, add night vision and pointy ears, and you've got a High Elf. They're just about as arrogant, and they have the same natural talent for casting magic. High Elves are to the elven race what Erudites are to the Human race. Add to that a long history of degradation (their words, not ours), and you've got the makings for one snobby race.

Truly reclusive, High Elves consider themselves the royal supremists of all things Elven. They guard their secrets carefully, most of the time by speaking in their native tongue. High Elves reproach the behavior of commoners — Half Elves, Wood Elves and the like — and greatly despise Ogres, Trolls and Iksar. Rarely will they lower themselves to associate even with Humans, lest their base behaviors permeate the sacred High Elf culture.

High Elves may be full of themselves, but to a point, they have a point. (There's that point pun again ....) They're much more intellectual than Wood Elves or Half Elves, and they know it. If cornered, High Elves will admit that they don't own the strength of a Human (but they'll keep their fingers crossed). They're beautiful, light-skinned and thin, and their Infravision ability and Agility rating definitely give them bragging rights over some of the other races. For this reason, they usually associate only with their own kind; others aren't advanced enough to realize that they should be bowing in submission.

High Elves hate groveling around in the dirt in hand-to-hand combat, which is probably why they prefer magic. They'd much rather toss aside their sword and let loose a sound round of spell attacks. Clerics, Enchanters, Magicians and Wizards are popular, while some of the less vain High Elves devote themselves to good and join the Paladin class.

High Elves can travel freely throughout the land, except for the darker cities. If you can keep a High Elf happy and don't mind a light banter concerning who's better than who, invite one to join your group on an adventure. On the spellcasting side, you can't go wrong ... just make sure you've got a tank (buffed up fighter) as well.

Starting City	Felwithe							
Occupations	Cleric, Enchanter, Magician, Paladin, Wizard							
Racial Tensions	Iksar, Ogres, Trolls							
Special Abilities	Infravision							

	STR	STA	AGI	DEX	WIS	INT	CHA	Bonus AP
Cleric	60	70	85	70	105	92	80	30
Enchanter	55	65	85	70	95	102	90	30
Magician	55	75	85	70	95	102	80	30
Paladin	65	70	85	70	100	92	90	20
Wizard	55	75	85	70	95	102	80	30

Human

Even though over a dozen races exist in Norrath, a disproportionate number of players still choose to be their Human selves in the game. Perhaps it's out of vanity ... or maybe just because people have heard that Humans can pursue nearly any occupation. Either way, Humans are the standard yardstick in Norrath to which all other races are compared.

Humans have taken over a good portion of Norrath. While they're not welcome in the dark cities of Elves, Iksar, Ogres or Trolls, Humans can travel virtually anywhere else they please.

The best thing about being Human is that there are few preconceptions as to what being Human entails. You've got all kinds — your do-gooders, lone serial player killers, lost newbies, common townsfolk, and seekers of power and fame. Perhaps this is why Humans can pursue any occupation except for that of a Shaman — theoretically, they're way too civilized for that. Until the recent arrival of the Iksar, Humans were the only race that could produce Monks.

Freeport and Qeynos are both bustling metropoli fueled by mostly Human townsfolk and merchants. Whatever you want to find will be there, and if it's not, it's easy to leave. (Both of these Human starting cities have ports of call that lead to other locations.) Because Humans welcome most other races into their cities, they're quite open-minded and have few prejudices against non-evil characters. (Not quite as often, dark Humans will group up with dark characters ... outside the city gates, of course.)

The giant sat and fondled the blonde hair of his new human chamber attendant. "Have you ever witnessed a meeting of the Ring of Scale, human woman?"

Kelisa stepped back from the giant and the lock of her hair fell from his massive fingers. "No, I was taken against my will only recently. If Erollisi blesses my escape, I won't be here to see the next one either."

The giant laughed and the gold door decorations rattled. "Do you know how to escape magic bonds, human woman?"

The angry flush on Kelisa's face told the giant that she didn't, but she answered, "I'll find a way."

Starting Cities	Qeynos, Freeport
Occupations	All but Shaman
Racial Tensions	Dark Elves, Iksar, Ogres, Trolls

	STR	STA	AGI	DEX	WIS	INT	CHA	Bonus AP
Bard	80	75	75	85	75	75	85	25
Cleric	80	80	75	75	85	75	75	30
Druid	75	85	75	75	85	75	75	30
Enchanter	75	75	75	75	75	85	85	30
Magician	75	85	75	75	75	85	75	30
Monk	80	80	85	85	75	75	75	20
Necromancer	75	75	75	85	75	85	75	30
Paladin	85	80	75	75	80	75	85	20
Ranger	80	85	85	75	80	75	75	20
Rogue	75	75	85	85	75	75	75	30
Shadow Knight	85	80	75	75	75	85	80	20
Warrior	85	85	80	75	75	75	75	25
Wizard	75	85	75	75	75	85	75	30

Iksar

Norrathians have Cazic-Thule, Lord of Fear, to thank for the presence of the Iksar. Fed by centuries of enslavement to the Shissir snake men, the Iksar have ingested a deep hatred toward all other races. (That explains why everyone hates Iksar, and why they hate everyone else.) Though their period of enslavement bred resentment, it also gave the Iksar the chance to amass knowledge of many evil rituals. To this day, the secretive guilds and factions in Cabilis carry out many of these dark traditions. Most involve practices that spread destruction and hate. This isn't the Iksar's fault, really — they act out of fear of their diety, not allegiance.

Intimidating and hard as nails, Iksar are basically the meanest race on the planet. Even Dark Elves don't hold quite this deep a grudge. They keep to themselves, but remain capable of striking down a weaker opponent with one swift kick or punch. Iksar only allow a select few to enter their precious city of Cabilis — you've got to be extremely evil, and you've got to be high level enough to take care of yourself. So, don't go in and make fun of a lizzie's sssevere lisssp problem and essspect to live long.

Despite their little speech impediment, Iksar are completely intelligent and wise to the ways of the world. Having grown up with a large appendage dragging behind them, they also possess great agility and balance. This combination comes in handy in a variety of classes, including Necromancer, Shadow Knight, Shaman and Warrior. Even though Iksar and Humans have nothing else in common, they can both be Monks … a great combat occupation, since it immediately awards Kick plus two other combat attacks. Being slightly amphibious, Iksar can also hold their breath for an extended period of time and see fairly well underwater.

Young Iksar spend their formative years swimming through the Swamp of No Hope hunting leeches and other game, something they always return to for pleasure's sake. There's nothing quite as refreshing as a dip in the swamp and the feel of rotting moss oozing between your scaly toes ….

Starting City	Cabilis (New Sebilis)
Occupations	Monk, Necromancer, Shadow Knight, Shaman, Warrior
Racial Tensions	All
Special Abilities	Regeneration, Infravision, Foraging, Vulnerability to Cold (Major), Resistance to Fire (Minor), Armor Class bonus

	STR	STA	AGI	DEX	WIS	INT	CHA	Bonus AP
Monk	75	75	100	95	80	75	55	20
Necromancer	70	70	90	95	80	85	55	30
Shadow Knight	80	75	90	85	80	85	60	20
Shaman	70	75	90	85	90	75	60	30
Warrior	80	80	95	85	80	75	55	25

Ogre

"Me go bash. Ya, I like bash and smash lots an lissen to meez frienz de tiny peeple. Me steppen on dem lots and makken dem not so happee, doh." Typical Ogre-speak isn't always easy to understand, but you've got to admit it's got a certain charm coming from the mouth of a 10-foot, several-hundred-pound character. How other races describe an Ogre, however, depends on who's doing the talking. According to the Dark Elves, they're sort of clumsy and dumb as a rock, but sometimes useful. To Humans and other Elves, they're scary and dumber than a giant rat. Barbarians simply find them annoying. To Gnomes and Dwarves, Ogres are gargantuan creatures that can make great allies ... as long as they watch their step.

Ogres spend more time on the battlefield than anywhere else. Not that they're really trying to perfect their natural Bash skill — it's just what comes naturally to them. It doesn't take much to make an Ogre happy — a few good meals every hour and occasional good loot should do the trick. Because of this, most of them end up becoming Warriors. A few ambitious Ogres try their hand at being a Shadow Knight or Shaman (some even succeed) but magical abilities aren't something that comes easily to them.

Though quite unattractive to other races, with their misshapen bodies and tusks, the Ogres' most desirable traits are their visible ones — height, weight and sheer force. Whatever qualities you can't see are pretty much absent, except for an excellent Stamina rating. That's only fair, since a mentally buffed up Ogre would make for a nearly unconquerable combination. (You can almost achieve the same thing by pairing up a dumb Ogre with a smart Dark Elf, though.)

Ogres are evil by nature, but are by no means tricky. They're not often violent without provocation, unless you happen to be of a race they don't get along with. They like Trolls. They like other Ogres. They don't really like Humans, but they're striving to form a Human-like society inside their home city of Oggok — albeit uncouth and unorganized. When Ogres get together for a meaningful social experience, it usually involves gulping down a few gallons of ale, burping a lot, scratching in inappropriate places, then mightily lumbering out into the wilderness for a good duel or to see what's on the dinner menu. If it gets dark in the meantime, no problem — Ogres are blessed with Infravision.

Starting City	Oggok	
Occupations	Shadow Knight, Shaman, Warrior	
Racial Tensions	Barbarians, Erudites, Half Elves, High Elves, Humans, Iksar, Wood Elves	
Special Abilities	Slam, Infravision	

	STR	STA	AGI	DEX	WIS	INT	CHA	Bonus AP
Shadow Knight	140	127	70	70	67	70	42	20
Shaman	130	127	70	70	77	60	42	30
Warrior	140	132	75	70	67	60	37	25

Troll

The basest of all Norrathian civilizations, Trolls are just downright ugly. They fell into the ugly green gene pool, and traded brains for bad looks before they emerged from the swamps. Their genders are nearly indistinguishable, except for the fashionable, two-piece bikini that all females wear. But whatever they lack in appearance, they make up for in strength, fighting ability, fast hit point regeneration, and a natural ability to see in the dark.

Like Ogres, Trolls are a bit evil and majorly dumb. It's not surprising, then, that these two races get along just dandily. The main difference between the two is that Ogres are actually trying to improve themselves, while Trolls are happy rolling around in dust and grunting after a good romp in the woods. They enjoy Slamming any opponent, defenseless or not, and enjoy it even more when there's notable pain and suffering involved. Eavesdrop in on a good post-hunt bragging session, and you'll see what we mean.

Because the Trolls' home city of Grobb is little more than an undeveloped, cesspool, many of its citizens wander over to Oggok at a young age to pursue a trade skill or buy various supplies. Shadow Knights and Shamans nearly always defect as well. Some Warriors leave, but most apparently enjoy wading around the swamps in South Antonica and can often eke out a meager living killing and scavenging game there.

Thaxes, the Troll leader, moved on his belly like a snake to the top of the hill. He knew he had to take care because it was more difficult to keep the top of a Troll's head from being spotted from the other side. However, he need not have worried. When his eyes crested the top, he discovered that he and his two companions were quite alone in the area. He waved them up.

Dis and Cronah crawled on their hands and knees anyway.

"Looks empty," Thaxes said before anyone could beat him to the assessment.

Dis started to stand. "We go in then."

Cronah stopped him and pulled him back down. "It's full of Humans that be fallen. You — you sure you want do this?"

Thaxes cuffed Cronah. "Then stay here if want, but no sharing with Trolls scared of puny humans, live or dead!"

Starting City	Grobb							
Occupations	Shadow Knight, Shaman, Warrior							
Racial Tensions	Barbarians, Erudites, Half Elves, High Elves, Humans, Iksar, Wood Elves							
Special Abilities	Slam, Infravision							

	STR	STA	AGI	DEX	WIS	INT	CHA	Bonus AP
Shadow Knight	118	114	83	75	60	62	45	20
Shaman	108	114	83	75	70	52	45	30
Warrior	118	119	88	75	60	52	40	25

Wood Elf

Anyone who grew up longing to live in a treetop fort will appreciate Kelethin, home of the Wood Elves. It's no ordinary place, and they're no ordinary tree dwellers. Naturally graceful from years of traipsing across branches and swinging bridges, Wood Elves possess extraordinary Agility and Dexterity. They lack the intelligence of High Elves, but are still smarter than Humans and don't act nearly as high and mighty about it. Considered to be one of the best-looking races in Norrath (well, okay, *they* consider themselves to be one of the best-looking races of Norrath), Wood Elves are quiet, introspective and somewhat shy among strangers.

Their primary element is Nature, and Wood Elves prefer to be surrounded by it at all times. This usually steers them toward a career as a Bard, Druid or Ranger, though Rogues and Warriors have their place as well. Their keen Infravision removes the barrier of darkness — even in the dead of night, Wood Elves can find their way around the countryside and Hide from foes if need be. They're also very nimble and fast, and can outrun just about any enemy that's chasing them. Food and drink are never a problem either, since Foraging is an innate skill. If you still don't want to add a Wood Elf to your group, then maybe you should put aside your prejudice against Elves and give one chance.

Wood Elves sense balance in nature, and likewise try to be fair and just in everything that they do. Rogues may maintain that they're an exception to that rule, but even the best of thieves will usually limit her pilfering and backstabbing to those who deserve it. Wood Elves do most things in moderation, including drinking. (A fall or two from the treetops is enough to cure the urge for that extra ale.)

It's a rare sight to see a Wood Elf make his or her home anywhere other than Kelethin or out on the open range. Those that seek a new life in one of the four nearby cities fold effortlessly into other cultures and make great company. Wood Elves possess great Charisma and are well-liked by their non-evil peers, race notwithstanding.

Starting City	Kelethin
Occupations	Bard, Druid, Ranger, Rogue, Warrior
Racial Tensions	Dark Elves, Iksar, Ogres, Trolls
Special Abilities	Hide, Foraging, Infravision

	STR	STA	AGI	DEX	WIS	INT	CHA	Bonus AP
Bard	70	65	95	90	80	75	85	25
Druid	65	75	95	80	90	75	75	30
Ranger	70	75	105	80	85	75	75	20
Rogue	65	65	105	90	80	75	75	30
Warrior	75	75	100	80	80	75	75	25

Abilities

Strength (STR)

This is your physical power.

STR determines how much you can carry without being encumbered.

STR increases the maximum and average damage you inflict in combat.

STR influences how quickly you learn many offensive skills.

Stamina (STA)

This is your health and constitution.

STA reflects your ability to perform strenuous tasks without becoming exhausted.

STA is used to calculate your hit points (HP).

STA determines how long you can hold your breath.

Agility (AGI)

This is your physical dexterity.

AGI helps determine your defensive abilities: it affects how often you are hit, and to a lesser degree how much damage you take. The higher your Agility, the less likely you are to be hit by melee combat.

AGI affects how quickly you learn some defensive skills.

Dexterity (DEX)

This is your hand-to-eye coordination.

DEX helps determine your accuracy and spellcasting capability in combat.

DEX helps calculate your missile combat skills.

DEX helps determine if you're interrupted when you're hit while casting a spell.

DEX affects how quickly you learn weapon skills.

DEX affects how quickly you learn Rogue skills.

DEX affects how hard you hit with a bow.

DEX affects how often your weapon procs — applies any special abilities it has.

Wisdom (WIS)

This is willpower and faith.

WIS determines how much mana a Cleric, Druid, Shaman, Paladin or Ranger has (per experience level).

WIS (if higher than INT) affects how quickly you learn many skills.

WIS helps determine the casting abilities of Shaman, Druids, Rangers, Clerics and Paladins.

WIS helps resist spells that affect your mind.

Intelligence (INT)

This is your intellect.

INT helps determine the casting abilities of Wizards, Enchanters, Magicians, Necromancers, Shadow knights and Bards.

INT affects how quickly you learn most skills (especially if it's higher than WIS).

INT, WIS & Mana

INT or WIS determines how easily you can learn most skills in the game. Usually the higher stat is used for this calculation, but only INT (not WIS) is used for some skills.

INT or WIS also determines how much mana you have to work with. You get a set amount of mana with every new experience level you achieve; that amount is determined by your INT (for Magicians, Enchanters, Necromancers, Enchanters and Shadow Knights) or WIS (for Clerics, Druids, Shamans, Rangers and Paladins). How much mana you get per experience level can range from under 10 to over 20, so your INT/WIS is crucial to your ability to function as a caster.

Of course, if you can't cast spells, mana doesn't do you any good. Paladins, Rangers and Shadow Knights don't start accruing mana until you can actually start casting spells.

Charisma (CHA)

This is a combination of your physical beauty and charm.

CHA is used primarily to calculate how various NPC factions react to you. The higher your charisma, the less likely they will be adversely affected by actions that would lower your standing with a group. This modification is very limited (that is, a pretty and charming murderer is still a murderer).

CHA affects how much merchants will charge you for items, and how much they will pay you for items. (This also depends upon your standing with the merchant's faction.)

Higher CHA increases your chance to *Charm*.

Higher CHA increases the chance you receive divine intervention in some very high level spells.

Combat

In combat, your Agility, Class and Defense skill affect how often you're hit.

Your Armor (AC) and Defense skill affect how much damage you take.

Being the chamberlain to a dragon was difficult on the best days. Besthal, an ice giant who had served the Lady Vox for decades was praying that this latest scheme would work out.

"Have you heard anything?" Besthal asked one of the entrance guards.

"No, Lord Besthal," the guard replied. "But they have not been gone that long. That barbarian, Hanaar, is smart, and his fellow warriors are strong. They will get word to us."

A long, low moan echoed throughout the caverns. Several stalactites fell near from the reverberations.

Besthal sighed. "I hope they bring word from Lord Nagafen soon."

Skills

Level Limits. For most skills, the highest a skill can go is no higher than 5 times your current level, plus 5. For example, if you're currently at level 20, your highest skill could be no higher than 105 [(20 x 5) + 5 = 105].

Skill Caps. There are absolute caps on most skills (but the cap will often depend on your class). You can't exceed this cap no matter how much experience your character has. For about half the skills, the maximum you can achieve in a skill — its skill cap — is level 200.

Trade Skills. There are no level limits or skill caps on trade skills — there is no limit at all to your progress in a trade skill (except having the cash to continue practicing the skill ...).

Skills	Bd	Mk	Ro	Wr	Pl	Rn	Dr	Cl	Sm	SK	En	Mg	Wz	Nc
Trade[1]	1	1	1	1	1	1	1	1	1	1	1	1	1	1
General[2]	1	1	1	1	1	1	1	1	1	1	1	1	1	1
Basic Combat[3]	1	1	1	1	1	1	1	1	1	1	1	1	1	1

Additional Combat Skills

Class	Bd	Mk	Ro	Wr	Pl	Rn	Dr	Cl	Sm	SK	En	Mg	Wz	Nc
Piercing	1		1	1		1			1	1	1	1	1	1
Throwing	1	1	1	1		1					1	1	1	1
1H Slashing	1		1	1	1	1	1			1				
2H Slashing	1			1	1	1				1				
Archery			1	1	1	1				1				
Taunt				1	1	1				1				
Berserking				1										
Dodge	10	1	4	6	10	8	15	15	15	10	22	22	22	22
Parry	53		12	10	17	18				17				
Riposte	58	35	30	25	30	35				30				
Disarm		27	27	35	40	35				40				
Double Attack		15	16	15	20	20				20				
Dual Wield	17	1	13	13		17								
Bash				6	6					6				
Kick		1		1		5								
Intimidation		18				22								

[1] Baking, Blacksmithing, Brewing, Fletching, Jewelry Making, Pottery, Tailoring, Tinkering
[2] Alcohol Tolerance, Begging, Fishing, Sense Direction, Swimming
[3] Offense, Defense, Hand to Hand, Bind Wound, 1H Blunt, 2H Blunt

Monk Skills

Skill	Bd	Mk	Ro	Wr	Pl	Rn	Dr	Cl	Sm	SK	En	Mg	Wz	Nc
Mend		1												
Safe Fall	24	3	12											
Round Kick		5												
Tiger Claw		10												
Block		12												
Feign Death		17												
Eagle Strike		20												
Dragon Punch		25												
Flying Kick		30												

Rogue Skills

Skill	Bd	Mk	Ro	Wr	Pl	Rn	Dr	Cl	Sm	SK	En	Mg	Wz	Nc
Sneak	17	8	1			10								
Hide	25		3			25				35				
Pick Lock	40		6											
Pick Pockets			7											
Sense Traps			8											
Backstab			10											
Apply Poison			18											
Make Poison			20											
Disarm Traps	30		21											

Ranger Skills

Skill	Bd	Mk	Ro	Wr	Pl	Rn	Dr	Cl	Sm	SK	En	Mg	Wz	Nc
Track	35					1	20							
Forage	12					3	5							

Bard Skills

Skill	Bd	Mk	Ro	Wr	Pl	Rn	Dr	Cl	Sm	SK	En	Mg	Wz	Nc
Singing	1													
Percussion Inst.	5													
Stringed Inst.	8													
Brass Inst.	11													
Wind Inst.	14													

Casting Skills

Skill	Bd	Mk	Ro	Wr	Pl	Rn	Dr	Cl	Sm	SK	En	Mg	Wz	Nc
Channeling					9	9	4	4	4	9	1	1	1	1
Meditate	10				12	12	8	8	8	12	4	4	4	4
Research											16	16	16	16
Alchemy									25					
Casting Skills					9	9	1	1	1	9	1	1	1	1
(Abjuration, Alteration, Conjuration, Divination, Evocation)														
Specialize Skills							30	30	30		20	20	20	20
(Specialize: Abjure, Alteration, Conjuration, Divination, Evocation)														

Trade (Craft) Skills

Trade skills in *EverQuest* allow you to construct useful items from component pieces. You construct these things to help you in your profession, as well as providing a secondary source of income. To get started with a trade skill, visit a merchant of the skill you wish to learn. He will have the books and kits which you will need to begin your career.

Once you've carefully read a book appropriate to your trade skill and acquired the component pieces necessary to build the item, you may attempt to construct it. Start by right-clicking on the container used for the trade skill. This will open a window to which you drag the component parts from your inventory to the available slots in the container. Double-check that all of the correct parts have been placed in the container, then click on the "Combine" button.

If you skillfully worked your trade skill you will get a new item(s). If you blundered, all of the disposable components usually disappear anyway, along with all of component pieces placed into the container.

There is no maximum to your advancement in a trade skill — no level limits or skill caps — but advancing gets much harder after you reach skill level 200.

Baking

Allows anyone to produce a wide variety of baked goods. Examples include Bixie Crunchies, Lizard-On-A-Stick, and Dwarf Chops.

You must have access to an Oven for this skill.

Blacksmithing

Allows anyone to manufacture valuable metal items, including lockpicks, muffin tins, and iron boots.

You must have access to a Forge for this skill.

Brewing

Allows any inhabitant of Norrath to produce potent alcoholic beverages, including Mead, Short Beer, Kalish and Halas Heaters.

You must have a Still for this skill.

Fletching

Allows anyone to construct a wide variety of bows and arrows. Examples of Fletching products include the Elm Linen Bow and a Class 1 Point Porcelain Arrow.

You must have a Fletching Kit for this skill.

Jewelry Making

Allows anyone to fashion jewelry gems and precious metals. Examples of Jewelry include the golden hematite choker, engagement rings and wedding rings.

You must have a Jewelry Kit for this skill.

Pottery

Allows people to craft clay into pottery. Examples of hand-made pottery include the small bowl, small clay container and clay deity.

You must have a Pottery Wheel and Kiln for this skill.

Tailoring

Allows anyone to sew fine leather items from hides and pelts. Examples include a raw hide tunic, a tattered backpack and a tattered belt.

You must have a Tailoring Kit for this skill.

Tinkering

Allows Gnomes to fabricate mechanical items, including a collapsible fishing pole, Gnomish fireworks and a spyglass.

You must have a full toolbox for this skill.

"What the devil is that sound?" Meson asked his Iksar guide.

"It is only the wind, great warrior," Slith replied. "Do you fear the wind?"

Meson had traveled with Slith long enough to recognize the sarcastic tone in his voice. However, even Slith's petulance wasn't going to curb Meson's enthusiasm. "Those are the Howling Stones, aren't they? We're near the entrance that we seek."

Slith shook his head. "Excitement to enter this dread realm is misplaced, barbarian."

Meson started toward the howling sound, but the reptilian turned and walked back the way they had come.

"Aren't you coming?" Meson asked.

Loudly enough for Meson to hear, Slith shouted over his shoulder, "I am no fool. Rumors say to beware the Portals of Mist and to use the howling markers to teleport back here." Slith turns and grins. "But they are only rumors."

General Skills

All classes can begin practicing the General skills immediately. Their skill cap is 200.

Alcohol Tolerance

Begging

Fishing

Fishing allows people to pull fresh fish from larger bodies of water. It requires a Fishing Pole and Fishing Bait.

Sense Direction

Swimming

Combat Skills

All classes can begin learning the most basic Combat skills immediately, but the more combat-oriented your class, the further and more rapidly you can advance in the skill.

INT-based casters (Magicians, Wizards, Necromancers and Enchanters) earn less experience in normal combat than do other classes, can only advance to about 3 x their experience level, and have lower caps on overall advancement.

Non-casters (Warriors, Monks and Rogues) advance the fastest, with higher experience limits (about 5 x their experience level) and higher skill caps (if they're capped at all).

Mixed casters (Rangers, Paladins, Bards and Shadow Knights) and WIS-based casters (Clerics, Druids and Shamans) fall between these two extremes.

Basic Combat Skills

All classes can begin practicing the following six skills immediately.

- Offense
- Defense
- Hand to Hand
- Bind Wound
- 1H Blunt
- 2H Blunt

Led by Srathar, the Toriz Keale Ze tribe of Iksar sent a party of its best warriors to recover the sacred stone stolen from them by two rival Iksar tribes. They stumbled upon these their quarry at a temple dedicated to Cazic-Thule.

Many of the band lost their lives in the battles that took them further and further into the temple. Deeper and deeper they went until only five remained. Beaten and bleeding, they finally entered a large chamber. There it was. Their sacred stone. Exhausted, they stumbled toward the altar.

As Srathar reached for the gem on the altar, a veneer of stone fell from the surface of one of the giant statues by the door. The largest Iksar any of the warriors had ever seen stepped out with his sword raised.

Srathar snatched the gem and pressed it into the palm of the youngest warrior. "Carry this home," were the final words spoken by any of that noble band of Iksar but the one who remained to tell the tale.

Additional Combat Skills

The more specialized combat skills must be acquired gradually. You might expect that the Warrior always learns each of these skills earlier than the other classes, and can progress farther with them, but that's not the case. The Monk starts using a couple of these skills first (Dodge, Dual Wield), while the Rogue can advance farther in Piercing and Throwing than the Warrior.

Despite all that, this is the Warrior's category. She's not far off the lead with any of these skills (except Dual Wield and Intimidation), and is usually the first to acquire any of them. One skill — Berserking — can only be learned by a Warrior.

Archery

Warrior	1	(max 240)
Ranger	1	(max 240)
Rogue	1	(max 240)
Paladin	1	(max 75)
Sh. Kn.	1	(max 75)

Piercing

Rogue	1	(max 250)
Warrior	1	(max 240)
Ranger	1	(max 240)
Sh. Kn.	1	(max 210)
Bard	1	(max 210)
Shaman	1	(max 200)
Necro	1	(max 110)
Wizard	1	(max 110)
Magician	1	(max 110)
Enchanter	1	(max 110)

Throwing

Rogue	1	(max 250)
Warrior	1	(max 200)
Monk	1	(max 200)
Ranger	1	(max 113)
Bard	1	(max 113)
Necro	1	(max 75)
Wizard	1	(max 75)
Magician	1	(max 75)
Enchanter	1	(max 75)

1H Slashing

Warrior	1	(max 250)
Rogue	1	(max 250)
Ranger	1	(max 240)
Paladin	1	(max 225)
Sh. Kn.	1	(max 225)
Bard	1	(max 225)
Druid	1	(max 175)

2H Slashing

Warrior	1	(max 250)
Ranger	1	(max 240)
Paladin	1	(max 225)
Sh. Kn.	1	(max 225)
Bard	1	(max 200)

Taunt

Warrior	1	(max 200)
Paladin	1	(max 180)
Sh. Kn.	1	(max 180)
Ranger	1	(max 150)

Berserking

Warrior   1   (max 200)

Dodge

Monk   1   (max 230)

Rogue   4   (max 210)

Warrior   6   (max 175)

Ranger   8   (max 137)

Paladin   10   (max 155)

Sh. Kn.   10   (max 155)

Bard   10   (max 155)

Cleric   15   (max 75)

Druid   15   (max 75)

Shaman   15   (max 75)

Necro   22   (max 75)

Wizard   22   (max 75)

Magician   22   (max 75)

Enchanter 22   (max 75)

Parry

Warrior   10   (max 230)

Rogue   12   (max 230)

Paladin   17   (max 205)

Sh. Kn.   17   (max 205)

Ranger   18   (max 185)

Bard   53   (max 75)

Riposte

Warrior   25   (max 225)

Rogue   30   (max 225)

Paladin   30   (max 200)

Sh Kn.   30   (max 200)

Monk   35   (max 225)

Ranger   35   (max 150)

Bard   58   (max 75)

Disarm

Monk   27   (max 200)

Rogue   27   (max 200)

Warrior   35   (max 200)

Ranger   35   (max 55)

Paladin   40   (max 70)

Sh. Kn.   40   (max 70)

Double Attack

Warrior   15   (max 245)

Monk   15   (max 250)

Rogue   16   (max 245)

Paladin   20   (max 235)

Sh. Kn.   20   (max 235)

Ranger   20   (max 235)

Dual Wield

Monk   1

Rogue   13   (max 245)

Warrior   13   (max 240)

Ranger   17   (max 240)

Bard   17   (max 200)

Bash

Warrior   6   (max 240)

Paladin   6   (max 200)

Sh. Kn.   6   (max 200)

Kick

Monk   1   (max 250)

Warrior   1   (max 210)

Ranger   5   (max 205)

Intimidation

Monk   18   (max 200)

Rogue   22   (max 200)

Monk Skills

The Monk doesn't need weapons for his style of play — he has access to a wide variety of special unarmed combat attacks, starting at experience level 5. In addition, he can Mend what needs fixing, and can Feign Death when all else fails, starting at level 17.

Mend

Monk   1   (max 200)

Safe Fall

Monk   3   (max 200)

Rogue   12   (max 94)

Bard   24   (max 40)

Round Kick

Monk   5   (max 225)

Tiger Claw

Monk   10   (max 225)

Block

Monk   12   (max 225)

Feign Death

Monk   17   (max 200)

Eagle Strike

Monk   20   (max 225)

Dragon Punch

Monk   25   (max 225)

Flying Kick

Monk   30   (max 225)

Bard Skills

Only the Bard can learn these skills. They are necessary to cast any of the related spells. For example, if the Bard doesn't know Percussion Instruments, she can't cast any percussion-based spells. They all have a cap.

Singing

Bard   1   (max 200)

Percussion Instruments

Bard   5   (max 200)

Stringed Instruments

Bard   8   (max 200)

Brass Instruments

Bard   11   (max 200)

Wind Instruments

Bard   14   (max 200)

Rogue Skills

If you need it sneaky, the Rogue's got what you need. While other classes can learn a few of these skills, the Rogue starts far earlier than other classes in every one of them, usually by at least 20 levels.

Sneak

Rogue	1	(max 200)
Monk	8	(max 113)
Ranger	10	(max 75)
Bard	17	(max 75)

Hide

Rogue	3	(max 200)
Ranger	25	(max 75)
Bard	25	(max 40)
Sh. Kn.	35	(max 75)

Pick Lock

Rogue	6	(max 200)
Bard	40	(max 100)

Pick Pockets

Rogue	7	(max 200)

Sense Traps

The Sense Traps skill only works on traps with moving parts (that is, not on invisible walls, floors and so forth).

Rogue	8	(max 200)

Backstab

Rogue	10	(max 225)

Make Poison

Rogue	20	(max 200)

Apply Poison

A Rogue can apply a poison in his inventory temporarily to his primary weapon. The effect of successfully applying poison and hitting an opponent will vary, depending on the type of poison used.

Rogue	18	(max 200)

Disarm Traps

Like Sense Traps, this skill only works on traps with moving parts. Activate Disarm Traps by clicking on an appropriate trap. Success is based both on your skill level and the type of trap.

Rogue	21	(max 200)
Bard	30	(max 100)

Ranger Skills

The Ranger is master of these two outdoor skills, but the Druid and Bard can acquire expertise in them, as well.

Track

Ranger	1	(max 200)
Druid	20	(max 50)
Bard	35	(max 100)

Forage

Allows nature-oriented classes to find food and water. Examples are grubs, berries and rabbits.)

Requires no components or other tools.

Ranger	3	(max 200)
Druid	5	(max 200)
Bard	12	(max 55)

Caster Skills

Channeling

Necro	1	(max 200)
Wizard	1	(max 200)
Magician	1	(max 200)
Enchanter	1	(max 200)
Cleric	4	(max 200)
Druid	4	(max 200)
Shaman	4	(max 200)
Paladin	9	(max 215)
Sh.Kn.	9	(max 215)
Ranger	9	(max 215)

Meditate

Necro	4	
Wizard	4	
Magician	4	
Enchanter	4	
Cleric	8	
Druid	8	
Shaman	8	
Bard	10	(max 1)
Paladin	12	(max 226)
Sh. Kn.	12	(max 226)
Ranger	12	(max 226)

Research

Only the pure INT-based casters can research spells. They can all begin researching at level 16. The WIS-based casters don't need to research spells, and the Shadow Knight finds it easier to acquire spells other ways.

Spell research is similar in theory to the trade skills. Specific items are place into a container, combining to produce a new item.

Tomes. To research a spell, you must have a tome specific to your class. These can be purchased in your guild hall.

Wizards use a Lexicon

Magicians use an *Elemental Grimoire.*

Enchanters use a *Tome of Endless Enchantments.*

Necromancers use a *Book of Dark Bindings.*

Instruction Books and Languages. Research instruction books can also be purchased in your guild hall. All instruction books are written in languages other than Common. To learn the fundamentals of a language, you must train one point in the language with your guild master. Once you've learned the fundamentals, you can advance your linguistic skills through use — usually by listening to someone speak in that language.

Spell Components. Your research instruction book lists the components needed to produce a scroll. Spell components can be found scattered throughout the world — they appear randomly on different creatures, so you don't have to 'camp' a spot to get a certain component. Components are each specific to a single caster class, and they can be stored and traded — ask around. 13 of the 14 classes out there can't use the research component that you need.

Research components are usually found on intelligent creatures, or on creatures that are innately magical.

Necro	16	(max 200)
Wizard	16	(max 200)
Magician	16	(max 200)
Enchanter	16	(max 200)

Caster Skills (cont.)

Casting Skills

All five of the basic casting skills have the same minimum experience level for a given class — level 1 for pure casters, and level 9 for mixed casters.

Abjuration

Alteration

Conjuration

Divination

Evocation

Cleric	1
Druid	1
Shaman	1
Necro	1
Wizard	1
Magician	1
Enchanter	1
Paladin	9
Sh. Kn.	9
Ranger	9

Specialize Skills

Only the pure casters can specialize in the casting skills. Specializing in a particular casting skill improves your performance in that type of spell — increasing the chance it will succeed — but prevents you from specializing(to any great extent) in any other type of spell. You can only take one of the Specialize skills past level 50.

Specialize Abjure

Specialize Alteration

Specialize Conjuration

Specialize Divination

Specialize Evocation

All five of the specialized casting skills have the same minimum experience level for a given class. INT-based casters (Magicians, Wizards, Necromancers and Enchanters) can start specializing at experience level 20, while WIS-based casters (Clerics, Druids and Shamans) must wait until level 30 to specialize.

Necro	20	(max 200)
Wizard	20	(max 200)
Magician	20	(max 200)
Enchanter	20	(max 200)
Cleric	30	(max 200)
Druid	30	(max 200)
Shaman	30	(max 200)

Alchemy

Only the Shaman can learn Alchemy. It works in many ways like a trade skill, but the Shaman can't start practicing it until reaching experience level 25, and it has a cap on it. A Shaman uses Alchemy to concoct potions.

The Shaman must have a Medicine Bag in which to mix the potions. Examples of potions that can be concocted are Charming Deceit and Troll's Essence.

Shaman	25	(max 200)

Character Creation: Caster Skills

The wild-eyed woman in tattered and torn clothing had been babbling since she entered the smoky tavern. "The eyes glowed," she said while widening her own eyes. "Glowed red. And it laughed. A crazy laugh. It wouldn't stop. Stood over the drawbridge and laughed." She held her hands over her ears and opened her mouth wide, but only a pathetic mewling came out.

A group of friends sat in at a corner table by the fireplace. They thought they would be undisturbed there as they made their plans.

"You!" she shouted as she pointed a trembling finger at them. "You, strangers! I know why you're here." The warrior sitting in the outside chair almost evaded the mad Iksar's grasp. She clutched at his shoulder and caught the edge of his armor. "Melt to bone, you will," she whispered.

The tavern keeper pulled the woman away from the group of adventurers. When he returned, they asked him where she had been to have such a fright?

"She and her husband thought to serve the master of Karnor's Castle, but it is difficult to serve that master." The keeper leaned on the table. "First, you have to die."

Deities of Norrath

(Ag) Agnostic

(PB) Bertoxxulous, the Plaguebringer

(KT) Bristlebane Fizzlethorpe, the King of Thieves

(FL) Cazic-Thule, the Faceless

(PHt) Innoruuk, the Prince of Hate

(RK) Karana, the Rainkeeper

(QL) Erollisi Marr, the Queen of Love

(LB) Mithaniel Marr, the Lightbringer

(PHl) Rodcet Nife, the Prime Healer

(OL) Prexus, the Oceanlord

(TQ) Quellious, the Tranquil

(BP) Solusek Ro, the Burning Prince

(DB) Brell Serilis, the Duke of Below

(SH) The Tribunal, the Six Hammers

(MA) Tunare, the Mother of All

(WQ) Veeshan, the Wurmqueen

(WL) Rallos Zek, the Warlord

Barbarian All start in Halas.

	Ag	PB	KT	FL	PHt	RK	QL	LB	PHl	OL	TQ	BP	DB	SH	MA	WQ	WL
All start in Halas																	
Rogue	Ag		KT											SH			
Shaman														SH			
Warrior	Ag													SH			WL
Dark Elf All start in Neriak.																	
Cleric					PHt												
Enchanter	Ag				PHt												
Magician	Ag				PHt												
Necromancer					PHt												
Rogue	Ag		KT		PHt												
Shadow Knight					PHt												
Warrior	Ag				PHt												WL
Wizard	Ag				PHt							BP					
Dwarf, All start in Kaladim.																	
Cleric													DB				
Paladin													DB				
Rogue	Ag		KT										DB				
Warrior	Ag												DB				

Erudite All start in Erudin, except Necromancers, who start in Paineel

	Ag	PB	KT	FL	PHt	RK	QL	LB	PHl	OL	TQ	BP	DB	SH	MA	WQ	WL
Cleric										OL	TQ						
Enchanter	Ag									OL	TQ						
Magician	Ag									OL	TQ						
Necromancer				FL													
Paladin										OL	TQ						
Wizard	Ag									OL	TQ	BP					

Gnome All start in Ak'Anon

	Ag	PB	KT	FL	PHt	RK	QL	LB	PHl	OL	TQ	BP	DB	SH	MA	WQ	WL
Cleric		PB	KT										DB				
Enchanter	Ag	PB											DB				
Magician	Ag	PB											DB				
Necromancer		PB															
Rogue	Ag	PB	KT										DB				
Warrior	Ag	PB											DB				WL
Wizard	Ag	PB										BP	DB				

Human O = Oeynos, F = Freeport

	Ag	PB	KT	FL	PHt	RK	QL	LB	PHl	OL	TQ	BP	DB	SH	MA	WQ	WL
Bard	Ag		KT			RK	QL	LB	PHl	OL	TQ	BP	DB	SH	MA	WQ	WL
	(FQ)		(FQ)			(Q)	(F)	(F)	(Q)	(FQ)	(FQ)	(FQ)	(FQ)	(FQ)	(FQ)	(FQ)	(FQ)
Cleric		PB			PHt	RK	QL	LB	PHl								
		(Q)			(F)	(Q)	(F)	(F)	(Q)								
Druid						RK									MA		
						(Q)									(Q)		
Enchanter	Ag	PB			PHt	RK	QL	LB	PHl								
	(FQ)	(Q)			(F)	(Q)	(F)	(F)	(Q)								
Magician	Ag	PB			PHt	RK	QL	LB	PHl								
	(ΓQ)	(Q)			(F)	(Q)	(F)	(F)	(Q)								
Monk	Ag										TQ						
	(Q)										(F)						
Necromancer		PB			PHt												
		(Q)			(F)												
Paladin						RK	QL	LB	PHl								
						(Q)	(F)	(F)	(Q)								
Ranger						RK									MA		
						(Q)									(Q)		
Rogue	Ag	PB	KT		PHt	RK	QL		PHl								
	(FQ)	(Q)	(FQ)		(F)	(Q)	(F)		(Q)								
Shadow knight		PB			PHt												
		(Q)			(F)												
Warrior	Ag	PB			PHt	RK	QL	LB	PHl								WL
	(FQ)	(Q)			(F)	(Q)	(F)	(F)	(Q)								(FQ)
Wizard	Ag	PB			PHt	RK	QL	LB	PHl			BP					
	(FQ)	(Q)			(F)	(Q)	(F)	(F)	(Q)			(FQ)					

Half-Elves
Q = Qeynos, F = Freeport, K = Kelethin, 3 = Qeynos, Freeport & Kelethin, Fw = Felwithe

	Ag	PB	KT	FL	PHt	RK	QL	LB	PHl	OL	TQ	BP	DB	SH	MA	WQ	WL
Bard	Ag (3)		KT (3)			RK (Q)	QL (F)	LB (F)	PHl (Q)	OL (3)	TQ (3)	BP (3)	DB (3)	SH (3)	MA (3)	WQ (3)	WL (3)
Druid						RK (Q)									MA (QK)		
Paladin						RK (Q)	QL (F)	LB (F)	PHl (Q)						MA (Fw)		
Ranger						RK (Q)									MA (QK)		
Rogue	Ag (3)	PB (Q)	KT (3)			RK (Q)	QL (F)		PHl (Q)						MA (K)		
Warrior	Ag (3)	PB (Q)			PHt (F)	RK (Q)	QL (F)	LB (F)	PHl (Q)	OL (3)				SH (3)	MA (K)		WL (3)

Halfling   All start in Rivervale

	Ag	PB	KT	FL	PHt	RK	QL	LB	PHl	OL	TQ	BP	DB	SH	MA	WQ	WL
Cleric			KT														
Druid						RK											
Rogue	Ag		KT										DB				
Warrior	Ag												DB				WL

High Elf   All start in Felwithe

	Ag	PB	KT	FL	PHt	RK	QL	LB	PHl	OL	TQ	BP	DB	SH	MA	WQ	WL
Cleric															MA		
Enchanter	Ag					RK	QL	LB							MA		
Magician	Ag					RK	QL	LB							MA		
Paladin															MA		
Wizard	Ag					RK	QL	LB				BP			MA		

Iksar   All start in Cabilis

	Ag	PB	KT	FL	PHt	RK	QL	LB	PHl	OL	TQ	BP	DB	SH	MA	WQ	WL
Monk				FL													
Necromancer				FL													
Shadow Knight				FL													
Shaman				FL													
Warrior				FL													

Ogre   All start in Oggok

	Ag	PB	KT	FL	PHt	RK	QL	LB	PHl	OL	TQ	BP	DB	SH	MA	WQ	WL
Shadow Knight				FL													WL
Shaman																	WL
Warrior	Ag			FL													WL

Troll   All start in Grobb

	Ag	PB	KT	FL	PHt	RK	QL	LB	PHl	OL	TQ	BP	DB	SH	MA	WQ	WL
Shadow Knight				FL	PHt												
Shaman				FL	PHt												
Warrior	Ag			FL	PHt												WL

Wood Elf   All start in Kelethin

	Ag	PB	KT	FL	PHt	RK	QL	LB	PHl	OL	TQ	BP	DB	SH	MA	WQ	WL
Bard	Ag		KT			RK	QL	LB	PHl	OL	TQ	BP	DB	SH	MA	WQ	WL
Druid															MA		
Ranger															MA		
Rogue	Ag		KT			RK									MA		
Warrior	Ag					RK									MA		WL

EverQuest: The Ruins of Kunark

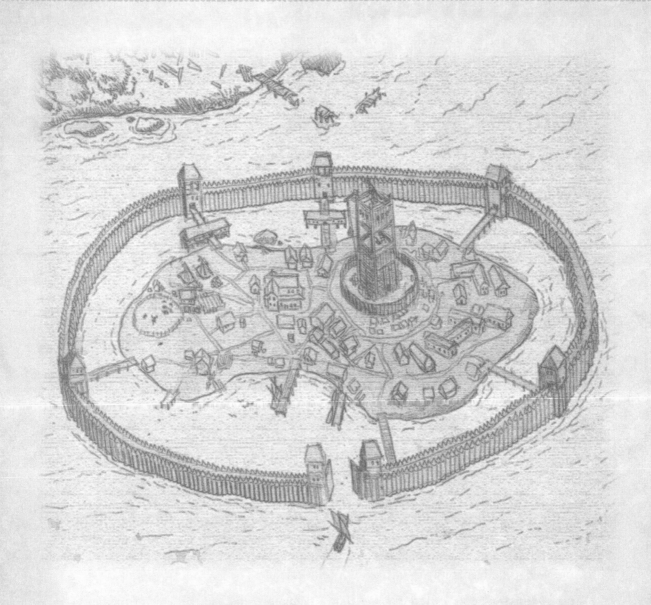

Community

Etiquette

EverQuest has been around for a long while now, and people have developed ways of doing things that makes everything go a little smoother. Some are common sense, and some are game-specific. Of course, these aren't rules, so you don't *have* to pay attention to them, but ....

Skills

Begging. Using the begging skill is fine, if it's in character. Asking higher players to give you things "just 'cause" tends to annoy people.

Rogue Safe Fall. Remember that falls that are no longer dangerous to you (because you have *Safe Fall*) can seriously hurt other people. Be cautious where you lead friends or party-members.

Camping

Ownership. If a party is at a spawn site, respect their camp and don't pull from that area. Especially if they are in a room, everything in that room is "theirs."

If you want to camp a site, but someone else is already there, you can ask if you can take the next turn. Usually people who are "power-leveling" will let you take a turn. If they don't, wish them luck and find another camp site, or if necessary, dungeon.

Combat

Tactics. Discuss your battle tactics with your group mates, and try to take people's needs into account. For instance, if a Rogue asks you to keep on the other side of the mob from him, try to do it. If a mage asks you not to hit the mezzed monsters, try to steer clear of them.

Medding Mages. Don't get angry if a magic user doesn't do much during a fight, until you're *sure* he didn't do much. Sometimes someone who meds most of the time will provide just the right DD blast or healing spell when you need it. First find out what their technique is, then make comments as to what you were expecting.

Mezzed Monsters. Don't hit a monster that a magic user has mezzed. One of the most useful things that a magic user can do is to "mez," or mesmerize, several creatures in a crowd, thus allowing the fighters to concentrate their efforts on fewer active enemies. However, once a mezzed creature is attacked, it wakes up.

EverQuest: The Ruins of Kunark

Tank Duty. Fighters with lots of hit points should keep themselves between the bad guys and the magic users. Sure, the finger-wagglers can usually take care of themselves, but they can be doing much more useful things if they can concentrate on strategy.

/Assist. If someone asks you to /assist him in a battle, /assist him (by targeting him and typing /assist). Don't insist on fighting your own mob ... that might be what you want to do, but in a group, fight like part of the team, not a solo fighter.

Constructive Criticism. If people are doing things in a fight that you think is detrimental, /tell them *individually* what problem you think each one is creating. Keep it private and they're less likely to get defensive about it.

Emotes

Descriptions. Describe your character's emotions or actions, rather than just spelling it out. It's fine to say "Permia is happy," but it's better to say "Permia smiles at all around her." Making people *see* the experience is better (more enjoyable) than just telling them what the experience is. (For a list of pre-programmed emotes, see **Emote Commands**, page 122.)

Using emotes improves the game for you and everyone around you. Come up with some catchy lines, assign them to hot keys, and use them. "Trioss howls with victory." "Permia checks for a broken nail." "Haloxx wipes his bloody blade on his fallen enemy's hair." (Don't spell out your name, just type either /em or a colon.)

GMs

Petition Politely. If something happens and you need to ask the GM for some sort of fix, ask promptly, ask clearly and ask politely. If the GM isn't on, you can ask a guide to pass your requests along, or you can ask for the GM's email address and forward the requests that way. Don't repeat your requests more than once a day, and *always* be polite. The GMs have a list of rules that outline what they can and can't do, so if you get a negative answer, don't take it out on the GM!

Kiting

Controlled Kiting. If you're going to kite a creature (hurt it, stun it, run away and repeat), don't stun it and then run toward other people. It's dangerous for all involved. Hit it, hold it, and then run into unpopulated areas.

Loot

Announce Loot. If you're in a dungeon and find loot that you don't need, drop it on the ground and yell out what you found and where it is. For instance: "Rune of Froon at pos35 neg58." (If it's no-drop, of course, don't pick it up!) You'll make friends wherever you go.

Safe Times. If you're playing solo and want to "poke around" in places that are famous for being death-traps, you might want to give those areas a try on busy weekends. There will be so many weekend-warriors camping the critters that it'll be fairly safe (well, not necessarily suicide ...). Just be very careful not to interfere with anyone else's plans.

Ask Nicely. People are often willing to let you loot — in a controlled fashion — after their battles ... especially if you offer services like healing. If you're in an area that has a common (or rare) drop that you're looking for, just ask if you could trade services for it, if they find it. If they don't want it themselves, they're usually more than happy to be helpful.

Names

Short and Sweet. Pick a name that's easy for people to type, since if they are going to talk to you with a /tell command, they have to type in your name. Especially pay attention to capital I's and lower case L's. They look similar.

Newbies

Be Helpful. If you want to up your skill levels, make a newbie's day by casting an unexpected buff or heal on them. Or, give them a "hand-me-down" item you no longer need.

Out Of Character

OOC Mode. This mode allows players who want to immerse themselves in the fantasy of Norrath to filter out the text. Anything that your character wouldn't say — from comments about the server to asking what the current Superbowl score is — are considered OOC. Remember, OOC comments are heard throughout the zone.

No OOC Mode. It really depends on the etiquette of the individual server, but many people consider it polite to type "ooc" before any out of character comments, rather than use the /ooc command. This keeps your comments local, instead of zone-wide.

Pulling

Double-check. Be very careful not to pull more than your party can handle. That may sound obvious, but be sure and check that what you're pulling is *all* you meant to pull.

EverQuest: The Ruins of Kunark

Watch Your Pulls. If you're pulling a mob from a distance, try not to pull it through anyone's camp. It only confuses things, and it's potentially dangerous, as well.

Keep Control. If you're pulling or kiting a creature and it goes agro on an innocent passer-by, that's your fault and you should apologize.

Roleplaying

Spin Control. It's accepted that roleplaying a certain race may make your character hostile to certain other races. That's a good thing, and makes the Norrath experience more immediate and compelling. However, if your language is going to be very "sharp," or your targets seem to be taking offense for real, you might want to drop out of character momentarily and /tell them that you are teasing or insulting them "in character" only.

Stay Local. Try to keep idioms local to Norrath language. Same goes for insults, etc.

Make a Description. You can create your own description of your character (physical, social or whatever). Right-click on your character's picture (upper-right hand corner in gameplay) and type in the description. Your name will change to from dark blue to purple, and anyone who right-clicks on you will see the description. Also, your character will no longer show class or level to a /who command.

Rudeness

/Ignore. For every rude person there are a hundred nice people. If you encounter someone who's a real pill, just /ignore him or her, and forget it.

Walk Away. Don't like the way someone is playing? Go somewhere else. Norrath is way too big a place to let jerks ruin your good time.

Travel

All for One. If one or more of your group can't see in the dark, don't travel in the dark unless you can find something that helps them out. It's just no fun walking around blind.

Typing

Spell It Out. Sometimes punctuation can get lost. If it's important, spell it out. The big issue is coordinates. For example, if you want to write the coordinates "+35 -38," it's better to type either "pos35 neg58" or "(plus) 35 (minus) 58."

Emote Commands

Emotes are a way of describing what your character is doing. Usually, emotes are something typed in by the player (example: Narra kicks her fallen enemy.), however some emotes have shortcut commands. In those cases, all you have to do is type the command and the full sentence appears in your chat box. In most cases, there's an animation to go with the emote command.

Below is a list of emotes and what they do. For these examples, Narra is the player's character. Mac is the name of her target, when she has one.

Emote	Animated?	If you have a target	If you have no target
/agree	Yes	Narra agrees with Mac.	You agree with everyone around you.
/amaze	Yes	You gasp at Mac in amazement.	You are amazed!
/apologize	Yes	You apologize to Mac whole-heartedly.	You apologize to everyone.
/applaud	Yes	You applaud Mac's performance.	You give a round of applause.
/bird	Yes	Narra makes a rude gesture at Mac.	You make a rude gesture.
/bite	No	You bite Mac on the leg.	You look around for someone to bite.
/bleed	Yes	Narra bleeds all over Mac.	You bleed quietly.
/blink	Yes	You blink at Mac in disbelief.	You blink in disbelief.
/blush	Yes	Narra blushes at Mac.	You blush profusely.
/boggle	Yes	You boggle at Mac, shaking your head and looking confused.	You boggle, shaking your head and looking confused.
/bonk	No	You bonk Mac on the head.	You look around for someone to bonk.
/bored	Yes	You inform Mac that you are bored.	You inform everyone that you are bored.
/bounce	No	Narra bounces around Mac.	You bounce with excitement.
/bow	Yes	Narra bows before Mac.	You bow.

/brb	Yes	You let Mac know that you will be right back.	You announce that you will be right back.
/burp	Yes	Narra burps loudly at Mac.	You burp loudly.
/bye	Yes	Narra waves goodbye to Mac.	You wave goodbye to everyone.
/cackle	Yes	Narra cackles gleefully at Mac.	You cackle gleefully.
/calm	No	Narra tries to calm down Mac.	You look peaceful and calm.
/cheer	Yes	Narra cheers at Mac.	You cheer.
/chuckle	Yes	Narra chuckles at Mac.	You chuckle.
/clap	Yes	You clap happily for Mac — hurray!	You clap your hands together — hurray!
/comfort	No	Narra comforts Mac.	You need to be comforted.
/congra -tulate	Yes	You congratulate Mac on a job well done.	You congratulate those around you on a job well done.
/cough	Yes	Narra coughs at Mac.	You cough.
/cringe	Yes	Narra cringes away from Mac.	You cringe.
/curious	Yes	You look at Mac curiously.	You look around you curiously.
/cry	Yes	Narra cries over Mac.	You cry.
/dance	Yes	You grab hold of Mac and begin to dance with him.	You stand on your tip-toes and do a dance of joy!
/drool	Yes	Narra drools all over Mac.	You drool — something must have you excited!
/duck	Yes	Narra ducks behind Mac.	You duck.
/eye	Yes	Narra raises an eyebrow at Mac.	You raise an eyebrow inquiringly.
/finger	Yes	Narra makes a rude gesture at Mac.	You make a rude gesture.
/flipoff	Yes	Narra makes a rude gesture at Mac.	You make a rude gesture.
/frown	Yes	Narra frowns at Mac.	You frown.
/gasp	Yes	You gasp at Mac in astonishment.	You gasp in astonishment.
/gesture	Yes	Narra makes a rude gesture at Mac.	You make a rude gesture.
/giggle	Yes	Narra giggles at Mac.	You giggle.
/glare	Yes	Narra turns an icy glare on Mac.	You glare at nothing in particular.

/grin	No	Narra grins evilly at Mac.	You grin evilly.
/groan	Yes	Narra groans at the sight of Mac.	You groan.
/grovel	Yes	Narra grovels before Mac.	You grovel pitifully.
/hail	No	You say "Hail Mac."	You say "Hail."
/happy	Yes	Narra is very happy with Mac.	You are so happy.
/hug	No	Narra hugs Mac.	You hug yourself.
/hungry	Yes	You let Mac know that you need food, badly.	You need food, badly.
/introduce	Yes	You introduce Mac.	You introduce yourself. Hi there!
/jk	No	You let Mac know that you were JUST KIDDING!	You were JUST KIDDING!
/kneel	Yes	You kneel before Mac in humility and reverence.	You kneel down.
/laugh	Yes	Narra laughs at Mac.	You laugh.
/lost	No	You inform Mac that you are completely lost.	You look completely lost.
/massage	No	You massage Mac's shoulders.	You look around for someone to massage.
/moan	Yes	Narra moans at Mac.	You begin to moan.
/mourn	Yes	You lower your head and mourn the loss of Mac.	You lower your head and mourn the loss of the dead.
/nod	Yes	Narra nods at Mac.	You nod.
/panic	No	Narra panics at the sight of Mac.	You panic and scream.
/peer	Yes	You peer at Mac, looking him up and down.	You peer around intently.
/plead	Yes	You plead with Mac desperately.	You plead with everyone around you.
/poke	No	Narra pokes Mac.	You poke yourself.
/point	Yes	You point at Mac. Yeah you!	You point straight ahead.
/ponder	Yes	You ponder Mac. What is going on with him?	You ponder the matters at hand.
/puzzle	Yes	You look at Mac, completely puzzled.	You look completely puzzled.
/raise	Yes	You look at Mac and raise your hand.	You raise your hand.

/ready	Yes	You ask Mac if he is ready.	You let everyone know that you are ready!
/roar	Yes	Narra emits a low rumble and then roars at Mac.	You emit a low rumble and then roar like a lion.
/rofl	No	Narra rolls on the floor laughing at Mac.	You roll on the floor laughing.
/rude	Yes	Narra makes a rude gesture at Mac.	You make a rude gesture.
/salute	Yes	You snap to attention and salute Mac crisply.	You salute the gods in pure admiration.
/shiver	Yes	You shiver at the thought of messing with Mac.	You shiver. Brrrrrr.
/shrug	Yes	You shrug at Mac.	You shrug unknowingly.
/sigh	Yes	You sigh at Mac.	You sigh, clearly disappointed.
/smirk	No	You smirk mischievously at Mac.	You smirk mischievously.
/smile	No	Narra beams a smile at Mac.	Narra smiles.
/snarl	Yes	You snarl meanly at Mac.	You bare your teeth in a terrible snarl.
/snicker	Yes	You snicker softly at Mac.	You snicker softly.
/stare	Yes	You stare dreamily at Mac, completely lost in his eyes.	You stare at the ground.
/tap	Yes	You tap your foot as you look at Mac impatiently.	You tap your foot impatiently.
/tease	No	You tease Mac mercilessly.	You look about for someone to tease.
/thank	Yes	You thank Mac heartily.	You thank everyone.
/thirsty	No	You let Mac know that you need drink, badly.	You need drink, badly!
/veto	Yes	You veto Mac's idea!	You veto the idea.
/wave	Yes	Narra waves at Mac.	You wave.
/welcome	Yes	You welcome Mac warmly.	You welcome everyone.
/whine	No	You whine pitifully at Mac.	You whine pitifully.
/whistle	Yes	You whistle at Mac appreciatively.	You whistle a little tune.
/yawn	No	You yawn rudely in Mac's face.	You open your mouth wide and yawn.

Rules and Policies

Okay, now *these* are the rules ....

Why "Play Nice" Policies?

March 14, 2000

Hello Everyone,

Back in October, Jeff Butler, *EverQuest*'s Customer Service Manager, outlined some new Customer Service Guidelines in the Producer's Letter. Shortly after these policies were publicized, we announced that their implementation would be postponed pending some revisions necessary to insure enforceability and consistency across the servers and different levels of our Customer Service organization. Last week, our policy team completed their public revision of those policies, and we are ready to implement them at this time. Before we get in to the wording of the "Play Nice Policies", I'd like to take a moment to discuss their spirit, and why we feel that they are necessary.

EverQuest almost daily continues to astound everyone involved with it. Nearly one year since we opened our doors, *EverQuest* boasts a community of current players numbering nearly 200,000, most of whom still play on a daily basis. In all actuality, *EverQuest* has gone beyond what could be described with a term such as "community". We are all, in fact, part of the *EverQuest* Society.

Like any society, each person has the ability to place his or her mark upon it. The vast majority of people in our society do their best to insure that their mark is positive, by abiding to the laws that we, much like the government, bring forward. Some of you choose to become pinnacles of honor, dignity, and respect in your individual communities by forming guilds, promoting honorable actions by your members, and by supporting *EverQuest* on your web-sites.

Also like any society, we have our underbelly, a relatively small number of people who live to prey upon the honorable. It is frequently the goal of these people to see to their desires, no matter the effect of their actions upon others around them. They are the ones who claim ownership of servers, zones, or spawns, and cause or threaten harm to anyone who does not share their disregard and contempt. They are the ones who live, not to enjoy the game with everyone else, but to enjoy at everyone else's expense.

For the first few months after *EverQuest*'s release, we felt that a policy of non-interference in many of these matters was warranted. However, we continued to lose good players. This was

EverQuest: The Ruins of Kunark

not due to any deficiency or dissatisfaction in the game, but due to dissatisfaction with the treatment that they received from their fellow players, and the perceived inability of our Customer Service department to intervene. Late last year, we made a commitment to our players to begin playing an active role in many of these situations.

The intent of these policies is to provide the players with general guidelines for what is or is not acceptable behavior in *EverQuest*, and give them with the opportunity to work out differences prior to involving the *EverQuest* Customer Service Staff. Naturally, in a game as multifaceted as *EverQuest*, we are not able to cover every possible issue that could arise as part of these policies. In these cases, it is the spirit of a rule that will prevail over any discrepancies in the letter.

Play Nice Policies

A revision to the GM/Guide FAQ and the Rules of Conduct. The policies below are now in effect and will be reflected in the GM Guide/Conduct FAQ in the near future.

Kill Stealing

Kill Stealing will now be regarded as disruption and will result in disciplinary action when witnessed by any *EverQuest* Customer Service Representative (EQCSR). The EQCSR will review these situations on an individual basis and issue a decision which is considered binding upon all parties involved. Kill Stealing is defined as the killing of a mob for any reason that is already fighting or pursuing another player or group.

The intent of this rule is to discourage and make note of habitual Kill Stealers, not to punish those who honestly try to work together or those who make an honest mistake. Its enforcement by the *EverQuest* Customer Service Staff will reflect this philosophy.

Contested Spawns

There are cases where two or more groups wish to kill the same thing. In these cases, the groups are required to compromise. If an equitable compromise cannot be reached between the players prior to *EverQuest* Customer Service Staff involvement, the EQCSR will mandate a binding compromise. Refusing to abide by a compromise mandated by an EQCSR will be considered disruption. It is therefore strongly suggested that the groups make every attempt to reach a compromise that they can live with prior to involving an EQCSR, who may mandate a compromise that does not suit you to the extent that a player-devised compromise would.

Note: A "group" in this case is defined as a party of one or more characters that are united in a common belief or goal and are capable of completing that goal.

Foul Language

Excessive use of foul language in an inappropriate context, including swear words, real-world racial slurs, and other language that is not consistent with the fantasy environment and designed to hurt, will be considered a disruption. The existence of the filter (`/filter`) is not a license to be profane.

Harassment

Harassment is defined as specifically targeting another player or group of players to harm or inconvenience them. Harassment can take many forms, as it goes to the state-of-mind of the person or party on the receiving end of the action. However, in order to account for those who are excessively thin-skinned, the EQCSR involved will make a determination as to whether or not the average person would feel "harassed" and act accordingly.

Zone/Area Disruption

Zone/Area Disruption is defined as any activity designed to harm or inconvenience a number of groups rather than a specific player or group of players. This includes things such as:

❖ Monopolizing most or all of the kills in an area.

❖ Deliberately blocking a doorway or narrow area so other players cannot get past.

❖ Refusing to cooperate with the other parties at a contested spawn site after having been instructed to do so by an EQCSR.

❖ Making excessive and inappropriate use of zone-wide communications (`/shout`, `/ooc`, `/auction`).

Reports of Fraud

Fraud in all transactions between players will result in disciplinary action when confirmed by an internal EQCSR. Fraud is defined as falsely representing one's intentions to make a gain at another's expense. Examples of this activity include but are not limited to offering to recover possessions from the corpse of another player and refusing to return that property to its owner as well as using flaws in a secure trade window to deprive someone of one of their items.

Guilds

Disciplinary issues involving guilds will also be addressed on a broader basis. Guilds whose members habitually violate any of the Rules of Conduct or Play Nice Policies may be disbanded. In addition, monopolizing numerous spawn areas with the intent to exclude other players will not be permitted. If investigated and verified by an internal EQCSR, monopolizing will result in the disbanding of the guild.

Training NPCs

The intentional training of NPCs will result in immediate disciplinary action when witnessed by an EQCSR. We are aware that accidents often happen causing unintentional trains, and will scrutinize each report of this activity closely.

Abuse

Though the following have always been in the GM/Guide FAQ, this letter is probably a good place to reiterate some of the items that we consider abuse:

❖ **Hate Mongering** — participation in or propagation of Hate literature, behavior, or propaganda related to real-world characteristics.

❖ **Sexual Abuse or Harassment** — untoward and unwelcome advances of a graphic and sexual nature. This includes virtual rape, overt sexual overtures, and stalking of a sexual nature.

❖ **Attempting to Defraud a CS Representative** — petitioning with untrue information with the intention of receiving benefits as a result. This includes reporting bug deaths, experience or item loss, or accusing other players of wrongdoing without basis for it.

❖ **Impersonating a Customer Service Representative** — falsely representing yourself to another player as a Guide or a Verant Interactive employee.

❖ **CS Personnel Abuse** — sending excessive /tells to a CS Representative, excessively using say or other channels to communicate to a CS Representative, making physical threats, or using abusive language against a CS Representative.

❖ **Using Threats of Retribution by GM Friends** — attempting to convince another player that they have no recourse in a disagreement because favoritism is shown to one of the parties by the Verant Interactive or Guide staff.

It is recommended that players make judicious use of the /report command when reporting abuse. The proper course of action is to file a report, then file a petition informing the *EverQuest* Customer Service Staff that a report has been filed.

PvP Servers

The PvP Servers are a special case for many of the policies listed here. When one makes the decision to play on a PvP Server, they are in essence agreeing to play on a server where compromise is decided on the basis of who has the power to kill whom.

By the same token, we expect that the people on those servers will apply PvP combat in all situations where it is called for, as a resolution to the problem. As such, the *EverQuest* Customer Service Staff will decline to intervene in cases where a PvP alternative exists, such as at disputed spawns where the parties involved have the ability to attack each other.

Though the PvP environment does eliminate a few of the problems experienced on the normal servers, there are a few more PvP-specific problems that are created.

Causing Experience Loss

Intentionally causing experience-loss to other players in the PvP environment is illegal in all cases and will result in a warning when witnessed by an EQCSR. This includes things such as intentionally training NPCs, and purposefully allowing an NPC to get the final blow in combat. We do understand that there are cases where the experience-loss is unintentional, and will take no action unless a person earns a reputation of causing unintentional experience-loss.

Much like how the Kill Stealing rule applies to those on the blue servers, this rule is designed to discourage and make note of those who do it habitually, thus betraying the spirit of PvP. As a note, the EQCSR will not in any case provide a resurrection for someone who was caused experience loss in PvP, intentionally or otherwise. This is one of the dangers of playing on a PvP server.

Bind-point/Corpse Camping

Killing someone over and over again while at his or her bind-point or while they are in the process of retrieving their corpse is illegal and will result in a warning when witnessed by an EQCSR. You are expected in all cases to give someone a reasonable amount of time to recover their corpse and leave the area prior to attacking again.

Conversely, the person recovering their corpse is expected to do so and retreat to safety promptly. In other words, sitting next to your corpse and taunting someone while daring them to attack you so that you can **/petition** them is bad form, and would result in a warning if witnessed by an EQCSR.

The EQCSR in attendance will decide what is reasonable in these cases. It is highly recommended that the people involved make equitable arrangements prior to involving the *EverQuest* Customer Service Staff.

Roleplay

Though *EverQuest* is a role-playing game, the claim of "role-play" will not be accepted in defense of any of the antisocial behaviors mentioned above. As an example, you are in no case (PvP or otherwise) allowed to "Train" a guard onto an enemy in protection of your homeland. In another example, a Rogue is not allowed to steal someone's corpse under the guise of role-playing a thief.

By all means we want to encourage you to play your role, we just cannot allow that role-play to be done at another's out-of-game expense.

To quote the Producer's Letter from October 20, 1999, Verant GM-Administrators review records of disciplinary incidents on a daily basis. Action is taken based on the severity and nature of the offense, and/or the number of warnings issued to the customer. These actions may include but are not limited to, temporary suspension or permanent banning from the game. Be advised that you may not receive any notification or warnings, in-game or otherwise, prior to disciplinary action being taken against your account.

We ask that everyone give these new policies some time before judging their effectiveness. Our intent is to further our philosophy that no one player should ever be allowed to intentionally ruin the gameplay experience of another, a philosophy to which we are firmly committed. These policies will continue to adapt as we learn new ways to deal with particular issues, and discover new issues that need to be specifically addressed.

Thank you,

Gordon Wrinn

Internet Relations Manager

Verant Interactive, Inc.

EQ On-Line Sites

These sites were current and long-running at the time of publication, but we can't guarantee they will always be there when you need them.

General

Allakhazam
http://everquest.allakhazam.com/
A no-holds-barred source of facts, including an index of quests and how to complete them.

Crossroads of Norrath
http://con.xrgaming.net/
A goldmine of facts.

EQ Atlas http://www.eqatlas.com/
An excellent source of consistently high quality maps for a large number of areas.

EQ Links http://www.eqlinks.com/
A mind-boggling array of *EverQuest* links.

EQ Stratics http://eq.stratics.com/
An all-purpose site that includes comments on current events, a variety of forums, etc.

EQ's Best Link Site
http://members.home.net/federici2753/
MainPage.html
Another mind-boggling array of *EQ* sites.

EQGuide http://www.eqguide.com/
A good, no-spoiler site with a comfortable feel.

EQlizer
http://www.gameznet.com/eq/cgi-bin/viewnews.cgi?profileClassic
A lot of information, without being too much of a spoiler-fest.

EverHybrid http://www.everhybrid.com/
Ranger, Paladin, Shadow Knight, Bard ...

EverLore http://www.everlore.com/
Updated daily by *EverQuest* players. Good spells lists and news section.

EverQuest Corner http://www.eqcorner.com/
Good info, good forums, and good site list.

EverQuest Express
http://www.eqx.simplenet.com/
A genuine on-line newspaper that comes out weekly. There are stories, editorials and an excellent Q&A section. The archives are easily accessible.

EverQuest Glossary
http://amtgard.pinkpig.com/everquest/eqglossary.htm
A comprehensive *EverQuest* jargon glossary.

EverQuest Vault http://eqvault.ign.com/
A vault of information, and a wealth of bulletin boards on nearly all conceivable subjects.

Maximum EverQuest
http://www.maximumeq.com/
A ton of information, well laid out.

The EverQuest Tavern
http://clubs.yahoo.com/clubs/theeverquesttavern
Sit back and chat awhile.

The Official EverQuest Site
http://www.station.sony.com/everquest/
The one and only official home page.

EQ Headquarters http://www.eqhq.com/
It discusses everything from character creation to current events.

EverQuest: The Ruins of Kunark

Magic Users

Casters Realm http://eq.castersrealm.com/
Maintains a recommended Database of Official Posts ... plus news, spells, creation guides, and info, info, info.

Class-Specific

Bard

Concert Hall
http://www.attcanada.net/~reaper/
Outstanding Bard site.

Soerbaird
http://www.sok.org/soerbaird/
An organization for *EQ* bards.

Cleric

EQ Cleric
http://eqcleric.gameglow.com/
Outstanding Cleric site.

Druid

EQ Druids   http://www.eqdruids.com/
Outstanding Druid site.

The Druids Grove
http://server3.ezboard.com/bthedruidsgrove
Another outstanding site for Druids.

Enchanter

The Enchanted Circle
http://www.terrapinsolutions.com/enchant/
index.cgi
A helpful guild for all enchanters, regardless of race, server or other affiliations.

Magician

The Mage Compendium
http://www.homenetwork.fsnet.co.uk/
Mage_Compendium/The Magician Site
An outstanding site.

The Magician's Library
http://cor.simplenet.com/Mage/
Research, skills, hints, commands and more.

Monk

EverQuest Monks
http://kadanit.com/eqmonks/
Outstanding Monk site.

Necromancer

EQNecro.com http://www.eqnecro.com/
An outstanding site.

Paladin

Paladins of Norrath
http://www2.hpcdsb.edu.on.ca/~jeff_cameron/
Outstanding Paladin site.

Ranger

EverQuest Rangers
http://www.geocities.com/eqrangers/
Outstanding Ranger site.

Rogue

The Safehouse
http://www.guildboss.com/safehouse/
Outstanding Rogue site (and a lot of fun!).

Shadow Knight

EQ Shadow Knights   http://sk.eqhq.com/
Definitive, yes. Info dump, definitely.

Shaman

Ultimate Shaman Guide
http://gladstone.uoregon.edu/~jwindshe/usg/
A little confusing, but very informative.

Warrior

Swordstrike
http://www.eqportal.com/Warrior/swordstrike/
Lots of info, plus inspiring Warrior Music.

Wizard

Graffe's Wizard Compilation
http://www.graffe.com/
Wizard info and a great "hot" map.

The Wizard's Tower
http://www.soerbaird.com/wizard/
A good site for Wizards.

The small gnome paced in his office. "I'm hiring you to protect my mine from the kobolds. Here's the map of the mines and the maze to … well, nevermind where that maze goes. Now, get out and protect!"

Hanaar, a tall barbarian, and his two clansmen glanced at each other. The unspoken words between them were: not only can we kill kobolds, we can also kill little gnomes if they annoy us too much.

The warrior guards stepped out of the office and walked toward their posts. However, after they were out of sight of the gnome's office, Hanaar whispered, "I can't believe our good fortune. A map directly to the old wurm Nagafen. Lady Vox will be sure to reward us when we return to Permafrost with this news."

Words to the Wise

Exploring Antonica

by Gary Grobson

Tunaria, now called Antonica, is the most populated area in the world. The cities of Qeynos, Freeport, Surefall Glade, Rivervale, Neriak, Oggok, Grobb, High Keep, and Halas serve to show how great a land Antonica truly is.

Qeynos is officially the home of the Half Elves, but is actually more populated with Humans. Many guild masters call Qeynos home, and for those that are not of the light path, below Qeynos lies the Catacombs where those humans who follow darker ways lurk. Some of the greatest evil lies under the city, while some of the greatest heroes walk the lands above.

Freeport is the City of Humans, and a city at war. North Freeport has become the last stronghold for the honorable Paladins, as the Freeport Militia have seized control of East and West Freeport. Tensions are high, and the battle continues. There are many secrets in Freeport waiting to be discovered. Be careful of your actions unless you want to enter the war on one side or another.

Surefall Glade is the home of the Rangers and Druids of Antonica. While other guild masters can be found in this realm, none are finer then the true followers of the Glade. Even Tunare herself would be proud to witness the Glade. Sacred animals are protected in the Glade, so poachers beware of upsetting the Druids and Rangers who call Surefall Glade home.

Rivervale is the home of the Halflings, a city bursting with energy. One cannot help but get involved with the never-ending festivities in this unusual city where the mayor is only a few feet tall. In this great metropolis, while many may think that no evil could ever hide, there are dark secrets to be discovered. Mind the dogs and watch your step if you are of the races "over-blessed in height," for Rivervale is a city of both mystery and adventurous quests.

Neriak is the home of the followers of Innoruuk and his creation, the Dark Elves. While some disbelievers in the "Father's Faith" may be welcome in the Foreign Quarter to buy goods and supplies, past this area lies only the purest hatred. Beware any "Lightwalker" who enters this city, for the Prince of Hate knows no limits. For those who follow the dark path, this city's rough streets have the beauty of great illusions and wicked glory. Some of the greatest magic in the lands can be found here ... for those who dare call Neriak home.

Oggok is the home of the Ogres, an outpost suited only to those large of foot. Supplies and rations can be found here, as well as a few quests, but this is not for the small or kind-hearted. Those who wander past the bouncers into this city have found a quick and unexpected death from bouncers' weapons. Even though this city is one of the smallest in the realm, there is adequate protection from most would-be thieves and trespassers.

The Trolls call **Grobb** home, or "Hoom" as many may say. Troll "Bashers" like to defend the outer parts of the city, as if the inside of the city was worth anything except for cold, hard food, and perhaps a large club to hit things with. Most of the area is in disarray, with not even water control; streams flow

EverQuest: The Ruins of Kunark

freely, and seemingly unnoticed, through the city. Caves, for the most part, are the buildings, and evil eyes are ready to spring from the lairs of the least civilized of the races.

High Keep is a human outpost between the cities of Qeynos and Freeport. Not much is known about this place: it is easily missed when traveling the High Pass between the greater cities. The young adventurer should only seek what is needed before continuing quickly onward to areas that suit their adventuring needs; however, most humans and allies of the race are allowed to rest here for the night.

The great city of **Halas** is home to the proud "Wolves of the North," the Barbarians. While still having one of the lowest standards of living compared to some of the races, the Barbarians have evolved further then the Trolls and Ogres in both the art of Shamanism and living conditions. Without a question the coldest city in Norrath, there are great trades, quests, and deeds to be shared with the peoples of this land. While many are tolerated in this city due to the "Rogues of the White Rose," the Barbarian Guards are the strongest in the Lands of Antonica, and there is but one punishment for crossing the Wolves: Death.

Not only has this land some of the greatest cities, but also perhaps the greatest adventure zones as well. Blackburrow, Paw, Cazic-Thule, Solusek's Eye and others are all located on this continent. To miss adventuring any of them (at the correct time in your career) is a great loss, and many have created secondary characters to simply hunt a zone they missed at the appropriate time in their character's life.

Blackburrow is the home of the Sabretooth Gnolls, whose influence is seen both in Everfrost and Qeynos Hills. This burrow is their final stronghold upon the lands, as the Barbarians and Humans wage a winning war against them. While this zone is designed for the very young to the young, it can be hard to survive a full alarm of Gnolls coming to save their commander. So popular a place is this to adventure that great heroes from across the lands — as far as Ak'Anon and Felwithe — come to prove their honor against these beasts.

Paw was once a great colony of the Splitpaw Gnolls, and was within this lifetime taken over by an opposing clan. Clan Torn Ear has complete control over the dungeon, and only the shattered souls of the Splitpaw Clan remain, enslaved or imprisoned. Although it was once an area safe for the young to travel, now only the experienced may enter the lair with a hope of survival, and only the toughest can go to the deepest depths to challenge the leaders of the Clan Torn Ear.

The Temple of Cazic-Thule is the home to the lizard men who worship Cazic-Thule. There is rumor that Cazic's presence is so great, he sent his own Avatar of Fear to oversee the training of Cazic's greatest creation for world domination. Only experienced characters should enter this realm — and take good time to learn its mysteries — for many before have been sacrificed to the faceless god. The temple constructed by the lizard men is confusing, by design, intending to entrap those who walk on the land without the blessing of their god. It's definitely a zone that should not be missed by those passing from Young to Mastery level.

Between the dungeons lie many lands to be traveled and explored. **Everfrost** is the frozen tundra of the North. Here Snow Orcs challenge the Barbarians in the land of ice and snow, where the "Wolves of the North" earn their manhood. Every character can find adventure in this area, from the very young to the masters of the lands. If the greatest icy tundra is not hard enough, there are stories of the great Necromancer Miragul who founded the black arts of magic somewhere beneath the snow. Truly, it's a land that all should see.

The Karanas are the lands named after Lord Karana, the god of the rains. The largest outdoor regions of Antonica are patrolled on the western edge by the Guards of Qeynos, but their protection only goes so far. In the Southern Karana areas lie the civilizations of the Centaurs and Aviaks, areas that advanced players come to experience. Eastern Karana is home to many hazards, but still many brave souls attempt to tame this great land. The Karanas are home to many great races that have flourished upon Lord Karana's blessed lands. Rangers and Druids skilled in tracking are necessary to find many of the spots missed by those who simply walk through this area.

Lake Rathetear is another land with scattered tribes of many races. This is a young- to experienced-area where many can find quests, adventures and unique encounters. The lake itself is rumored to be haunted, as undead have been seen at night in those places where the living walk during the day. Many are the reports of mysterious deaths which leave no corpses, and it's not known if something lives in the lakes, or if the undead resurrect the bodies to join their army of evil.

The Desert of Ro is geographically divided into Northern Ro, Southern Ro, and the Oasis of Marr. Creatures that can survive the dry climate do well here: snakes, spiders, mummies, and the undead. Younger to experienced players do the best in this realm, but beware the Sand Giants who roam these sands. This desert once boasted a great city, but long ago it was erased from view in a great sand storm.

The Commonlands have scattered human settlements of many vendors and citizens. The Freeport Militia has many outposts here, spreading its influence in the world. Many creatures live in this area ... it is rich in adventures and opportunities. Hill Giants, once living within the Commonlands, have mostly moved to the Karanas, as well as the great Griffons, but there are still some who prey on the weak who walk these paths.

Qeynos Hills is the land between the great city of Qeynos and Surefall Glade. This area has both patrolling Guards from Qeynos and Druids from Surefall to keep the area safe for those pushing farther from the city gates. There are stories of uprisings of undead in this area, but none have been seen in many moons.

EverQuest: The Ruins of Kunark

Innothule Swamp is the least tamed in all the lands of Antonica, if not all of Norrath. Swamp Spiders and Snakes are common, as well as both wandering and posted Troll Bashers from the nearby city of Grobb. The Frogloks' young are born and take their first steps onto the land here. While it's a very confusing area to be explore, it is still safe for the younger dark races to hunt. Of course, those young from non-evil races may find themselves smashed instead of saved by the protectors of the lands, if they should flee from creatures of the swamp.

Kithicor Forest was once a very peaceful land, but that was before the time of war ... before Innoruuk. In the greatest conflict in modern history, the Daughter of Innoruuk, Avatar of Tunare, did battle upon these lands that lie between Lanys and Fironia. In an action condemned by the gods, Father Innoruuk protected his only daughter from defeat, not for love (because that god has not the knowledge of such an emotion), but for pride. Unwilling to have his daughter conquered by a follower of Tunare, he opened forever a rift in space between Norrath and the Plane of Hate. This severing of the dimensions killed everything in the forest, and hundreds of Warriors' blood soaked the lands of Kithicor. While Tunare's blessing keeps the forest safe during the day, Innoruuk's hatred haunts the night. Therefore, younger parties are safe enough during the day, but only the experienced and masters dare set foot into the forest at night. Many younger characters have learned the meaning of the word fear while watching the sun set upon the forest with the protection of Rivervale still a ways off.

The Feerrott is a thick rainforest, known to be the stomping grounds to many young Ogres and the bouncers that protect them. Many undead and lizard men also call this home, making it a great area for the young and old alike. Secrets lie behind trees and rocks, and many have found themselves lost in the rainforest, shouting for anyone to assist them.

Rathe Mountains is a dangerous crossing between Lake Rathe and The Feerrott. Giants, Cyclopes, undead, lizard men, and many others make this a hunting ground for experienced parties. While there are many settlements of merchants and gypsies along the way, not many will lend a hand to help a stranger in need. There are stories of great mystical flying cat-like creatures, but recent travelers from the lands have not confirmed these.

Beholders Maze, also known as King Xorbb's Maze, is the territory of several Evil Eyes, Minotaurs, and a race consisting of living rock. There are also patrols from the nearby goblins of Runnyeye, making this a hostile area — at best — to cross, and rewarding for experienced players to hunt in. Groups of younger players who work well together can survive, but even the more experienced players cannot hope to simply cross the maze and continue on their journeys.

Misty Thicket lies between the town of Rivervale and the Runnyeye Citadel. This is a land protected well by the Guardians of the Vale, filled with creatures that wander this area. Younger characters do well here, well protected by several outposts of Guards from Rivervale. Beware the goblin guards near Runnyeye, and be certain you are ready to engage them, for it is a long way to the outposts from there.

Nektulos Forest is the land outside of Neriak, and is controlled by the children of Innoruuk. This forest is not as thick as many of the other forests of Norrath, but there are still many dangers. Well-guarded by the Dark Elf guards of Neriak, as well as towering, walking golems that have been enchanted to protect the fledgling villains, the lands are almost under constant attack from those who are scared of what these grim-eyed children may grow up to be. Halflings especially are trying to reclaim these once-safe lands from the dark forces, but to this date have only won a tenuous foothold.

Lavastorm is a disaster waiting to happen. Active volcanoes spew forth streams of lava; these are the youngest mountains in Norrath. The temperatures are extreme, and many creatures who thrive in the heat call this land home. Reports of Fire Drakes have been confirmed, as well as walking cousins of these creatures, while Fire Elementals leap from the lava at prey. This zone, while good for many of the younger parties, still holds great dangers since rocks have been known to work loose ... forming puddles of molten rock.

Near Lavastorm is the **Temple of Solusek Ro**, where some of the greatest quests in the lands can be found. Beware those who wish to challenge the power of the Prince of Fire, for whosoever crosses this dread god will find fiery hatred behind his mask. The quests are considered the supreme adventures to be had by the experienced player, although betraying the god of Ro will find those handing out the quests to be suddenly savage opponents. All are equal in the Prince's eyes, as it is only deeds that measure the man, not his race.

Exploring Faydwer

Faydwer is the second-most populated land, and has many places for learning, growing, and adventuring. The great cities of Kelethin, Felwithe, Ak'Anon, and Kaladim are here, as well as Castle Mistmoore. This is the home of the Elves, Dwarves and Gnomes ... and many political factions.

Kelethin is the tree city of the Wood Elves, located in the center of Greater Faydark. Wood Elves feel at home in a city far above the ground, and have little fear of falling. They are safe in the trees, while the Orcs that pillage the land cannot reach them. What events occur dirtside is seldom noticed above, as the bards play their music, and some of the finest bows and armor are made.

Felwithe, a city bordering Greater Faydark, is the home of the High Elves, and is home not only to great magic, but to a race steeped in tradition. From the Paladins and Clerics, to some of the most capable casters in the realm, Felwithe has several notable quests, and is a great resource for magic users.

Kaladim, is the city of the Dwarves, and industry is the trademark of those within. Great mines lie deep within the city, and gems and ore are well used by these great of artisans. Taller races beware, for this town was built for the race of Dwarves. Barbarians maybe welcome, but the folk of the town are not about to start making taller buildings to convenience the likes of them.

Ak'Anon is the home of the Gnomes, where some of the greatest inventors of the lands come to discuss ideas and concepts. Great mechanical creatures have been built to make the Gnome's lives easier. Everything is of interest in the city, for the knowledge of all to learn. The Ak'Anon zoo is famous in

Norrath, as only the Gnomes could devise with such a concept for their people to enjoy. Knowledge is everything, never evil nor good, but simply information to be processed, refined and consumed.

The Butcherblock Mountains lie outside of Kaladim, and are protected by the "Storm Guard" of the Dwarves. These scattered mountains and great hills have paths that have been traveled long before any humans set foot on the lands of Faydwer. Many wandering creatures are here, and younger characters can grow strong hunting them, taking time to wonder at a very strange monument. It is, in fact, a large chess set, with pieces that look as though the gods themselves once played with them, but now lie in ruins within a mountainous alcove. Some lesser undead are all that remain from what must have been the god's pastime.

Dagnor's Cauldron enters off of the Butcherblock Mountains, and some consider it the most dangerous traveling terrain in Norrath. Take time as you tour this land, for it is easy to misjudge the steep slopes and rapid descents ... and be injured in a fall. Aqua Goblins have set up many camps in this area, and stage frequent ambushes on those that cross the Cauldron. There are rumors of a legendary underwater city to be found here, but no recent travelers' reports can confirm this.

The Estate of Unrest was once a place of great joy, before an extreme dishonor was done upon the land. The estate is now haunted, and all within are now undead or a minion of the undead. This is an area where many experienced undead hunters come to test their faith, as the estate seems to be moan with despair over past crimes. The undead never cease defending the estate, and the source of unrest has never been found.

Clan Crushbone is the final stronghold of the Orcs on Faydwer. An entire legion of Orcs still remains active here, in Emperor Crush's service. They train each other for battle against the Elves, a constant threat as it appears that the Orcs are gaining ground in Greater Faydark. This is the proving ground for many Elves, and those who have established themselves as great Orc slayers often go on to become legends in the Elven community. Those who fail often end up as slaves to the Orcs, unable to free themselves from the never ending lash of the whip. Rumors have it that the Dark Elves are supplying the Orcs with weapons and counsel on how to make a final assault on Kelethin and Felwithe. How deep the involvement of the Dark Elves goes is not yet known.

Lesser Faydark is a peaceful forest where many mysterious creatures live, hidden to those who cannot look with trusting eyes. Brownies, Fairies and other small creatures of magic hide in this zone which knows nothing of modern ways, but only the ways of nature and of ages past. Stories were told long ago that the most magical of creatures, the unicorns, used to be seen on moonlit nights, but these mythical creatures have not been seen in a long time. Perhaps a faithful Elf in the moonlight can still see these creatures if he lies still enough in the woods.

Steamfont Mountains is the area where Gnomes have settled down. Many watchmen of the King of Ak'Anon stand guard near the city and its environs. Drakes, Minotaurs, and many smaller creatures make this a great zone for the younger to even some experienced players. Several Gnomes have won fame and favor with the King for duties against the Minotaurs. Many Gnomes put new inventions on display; the most noted was a great clockwork spider that malfunctioned immediately after being unveiled. The Gnome creator of this failed project still answers to this date for the chaos it caused.

The Ocean of Tears separates the world in a land of many islands and adventures. Ranging from the Young to Mastery level, each of these islands has a story and history behind it. From Pirates to Spectres to Aviaks, there are as many different forms of life on the islands as there are fish in the sea.

Exploring Odus

Odus is the home of the Erudites, who broke off from Qeynos to form their own society. Erudin is the center of life for Odus, but no longer the only city on the continent. Paineel, the city of outcast heretics, now stands in defiance of the High Council of Erudin. Toxxullia Forest is the only common ground between these areas, and is in contention by both factions of the Erudite race.

Erudin is a city of great knowledge and refinement. It is by far the most civilized city (by at least Erudite reckoning), is protected by many Sentinels, and the noble council overviews all. The knowledge of many generations is stored within the largest library in the lands, even fading by comparison the heretics' version in Paineel. Deeper inside the city is the great Palace of Erudin. The ruling council and leaders decide on the truest forms of magic of the greatest casters in the realm.

Paineel is the city of outcast heretics — those who study the arts of Necromancy — located on the opposite side of Toxxulia Forest. Inside, followers of Cazic-Thule bring forth a new school of Clerics, the Fell Blade Shadow Knights, and the ruling class of the Necromancers. Do not be fooled by the appearance of this city. Even though it is nearly as refined as Erudin, it is a dark and evil site. Isolationist at heart, this city is well defended by the Shadow Knights and Necromancers who study; they have the secrets of the original first Necromancer, Miragul.

Kerra's Ridge is the land ruled by the Kerrans, a cat-like people fighting for existence against extinction at the hands of the Erudites. This is a younger dungeon, and groups of newer Erudites can find fame and glory worthwhile to anyone starting a career in the arts of magic or faith. There are reports that the Heretics have set up an outer school on a nearby island, but those who have set out to verify this information failed to report back. For those opposed to the Heretics, and are of the suitable age, this could be a quest to fulfill.

Erud's Crossing has but a single island between Odus and Antonica, which appears to be a volcano that made an island within recent years. This island has been taken by a group of Kerrans who appear to have revolted against those at Kerras Ridge, and have a good colony to start a new life. A ship traveling between Qeynos and Erudin has been lost in the area, and hopes are high that survivors may be found, but as time goes by, this hope diminishes. This island is good for younger to slightly more experienced parties, and is a great break from other areas to get away from the worries of everyday life on a more tropical vacation.

Exploring Kunark

Unfortunately, the land of the Iksar has yet to be explored … and this is a no-spoiler book. However, rumors abound. Throughout this book are fictional "hints" as to what might be found within the mysterious land.

Classes

Bard

Be a Bard's Bard. A Bard who can help a group with his magical songs (and what bard can't?) will always be welcome in a group ... but a Bard who is a storyteller or poet will be welcomed no matter where he goes. Someone who gets into the role enough to actually recount the glories of past battles or wax poetical on whatever topic he feels might appeal to a Norrathian will often get tips, free drinks and lots and lots of friends.

Allocating Ability Points. (Recommended) Add points until Dexterity and Charisma are at least 100 apiece. Strength is useful, but at later levels it is very easy to get items that improve your Strength, so don't spend too much on that ability. Any leftover points can be spent at will ... remember, a higher Agility never hurts.

Travel. It's usually wise to travel with a weapon in hand, instead of an instrument. Sometimes combat happens when you least expect it. Although it may seem like a good idea to travel while playing a song or two, always consider your reaction time if you're attacked unawares. You can always sing in places that are potentially dangerous, and get at least partial effect.

Travel Song. The Bard travel song cancels the *Spirit of Wolf* speed spell and doesn't do anything if you're wearing Journeyman boots.

Haste. The haste buffs works with any item of increased speed, although haste items are rare until you're of quite a high level.

EverQuest: The Ruins of Kunark

Encumbrance

Bundle up. To keep things as light as possible, use a large sewing or fletching kit.

Don't be a packrat. One kit (or bag even) full of stuff is plenty.

Change out your cash. Don't carry copper and silver if you can switch it for gold. Keep your extra cash in a bank, preferably close to a good source of instruments you intend to buy.

Shop wisely. If you know you're going to want an instrument, buy it. Odds are it weighs less than the money did.

Be a philanthropist. If you've got more money than you can spend, donate some to someone who does you a good turn.

Get some Strength items. The more powerful the Strength items, the more armor you can wear.

Armor

If you're going to go the melee route in battle, or if you're going to solo it, definitely budget for bronze armor. This includes finding the right Strength items so you don't cripple yourself by wearing it.

Songs

Remember to have the right person targeted when you start each song!

A song works much better if you use the appropriate instrument. For example, while you can sing *Jaxan's Jig o' Vigor* — and it will have an effect — it will be more effective if you use a drum or other percussion instrument.

Remember that you have to train at least one point in any skill (for instance, Stringed Instruments skill) before you can start to increase your experience. (This does not include skills that you had at level one.)

Twisting. Start a song. When you see the text saying the song is in effect, turn it off and start the next one. Twisting usually means three songs, and then you start off with the first one again. You can use three different spells, or two of the same spell and one other one. It's entirely up to what you need at the moment.

Some spells don't last long enough to twist. Bard clarity and mana songs are good examples. You can usually get around this by devoting two "slots" to the short songs, and using only one other song.

Tactics

Strengths and weaknesses. Before you go into battle, talk about what people feel their roles are and what you feel your best abilities are, and then work out a plan for how your Bard skills will help the outcome.

Healing. Because singing mana songs is not the best use of your skills during combat, ask (politely) that Clerics only heal people who are running low. If a Cleric spends all his time healing, the Bard will be spending all his time trying to get his mana back up ... or more likely, you'll just ignore him, and your group will be short one useful Cleric.

Taunters. Make sure the group is clear that a Bard needs two or three taunters to keep you from being killed in no time flat.

Pulling

Think twice about using Chords of Dissonance. It riles up the mobs for quite a distance. Remember, be careful what you pull, and don't risk pulling more than your group can handle.

Combat

Adjust. Pay attention to how much damage you do in combat. If you're not pulling your weight, for whatever reason, rethink your strategy and concentrate on supporting the other folks.

Mana. Play melee songs during combat, mana songs during downtime.

It's usually more effective to buff up your tanks and debuff the enemy than it is to play mana songs for your magic users. Usually, casters have a good idea about mana conservation ... and if or when they need help restoring their mana, they can always ask you nicely.

(Recommended) Some spells work really well together, if you have the experience to play them together. For instance: *Anthem de Arms*, *Largo's* (or *Melodic Binding Melanie's Mellifluous Binding*) and the *Hymn of Restoration*. That way you've increased your own side's strength and speed, you've lowered your enemy's armor class and speed and have spread some healing around.

(Recommended) *Hymn of Restoration* is a great combat spell, since it usually keeps your mages from having to cast heal. That frees them up to concentrate on doing the most damage at the most opportune time.

(**Recommended**) *Anthem de Arms* and *Brusco's Boastful Bellow* are great songs during battle.

Downtime

If a Cleric is low on mana, and no one is in danger of dying from their wounds (i.e., there won't be another fight before you're ready for it), it makes more sense for the Bard to do the healing (clarity, clarity and *Hymn of Restoration*). This way the Cleric can med up, and everyone gets a mana-free healing.

Twisting songs during downtime can make you crazy. If your group is into power-leveling, or you've just spent a lot of time in combat, you're going to be working constantly for *hours*. Everybody ought to get a break between battles. Ask around to find out what song your group would like you to keep going during downtime, and don't do more than that unless you've got a good reason.

Cleric

The good news is that a Cleric can cast spells *and* wear armor *and* wave around a weapon, and is a generally useful person to have around ... and everybody is aware of that, and welcomes your company.

The bad news is that buying armor, weapons and spell will leave you strapped for cash for most of your life. Also, you're not particularly cut out for solo work.

Starting off

Your first goal is to accumulate money for your first spells. Go out and fight the vermin near your city until you reach 5th level.

At lower levels you can do fine as a solo player, but you really should get in the habit of either forming groups or asking if you can join groups.

Once you've got all your spells, start saving for some armor. Yes, that will take a while.

Spells

(**Recommended**) If you don't have naturally good night vision, get really familiar with *Halo of Light*. Until you've got that one, half the day is closed to you.

(**Recommended**) When you reach level 5, you get the opportunity to learn more spells. Some of the most useful are *Furor* (more damage than *Strike*), *Gate* (emergency exit to bind site), *Holy Armor* (higher AC), *Cure Disease* (you can get sick from sick vermin and Mummies), *Light Healing* (hooray! It's a start on your soon-to-be greatest talent), and *Ward Undead* (extra damage to undead). *Summon Drink* also comes in handy.

Words to the Wise: Classes

(Recommended) When you reach level 9 (finally) you get even more spells, particularly *Root*, *Summon Food*, *Center* and *Hammer of Wrath*. *Root* keeps the enemy in place, which is a tactic you will use for the rest of your career. *Summon Food* is good (plus it's nice to complete the set, since you should already have *Summon Drink*). *Center* really helps your hit points, and also helps your AC. *Hammer of Wrath* is a weapon that you can use until you log out. Free weapon ... gotta love it!

Races

Dwarf. Dwarves get an amazing amount of Strength and a high Dexterity, both of which are useful in combat. High Dexterity means magical attacks connect more often, and high Strength means more damage. Strength also increases the ability to carry things, always a good thing for anyone who plans to carry weapons, armor, etc. They also have a higher Stamina, which no one ever complains about.

High Elf. Cleric spells are fueled by mana ... mana is dependent on Wisdom ... Wisdom is what High Elves have in boatloads. In other words, High Elves are spell-casting machines when it comes to Cleric-type spells. When it comes to mana, these folks are better and faster, without having to scrounge all over Norrath for jewelry and other enchanted items to buff up their magical abilities.

Human. Regular Humans have a good "medium" ground for Clerics. They are stronger than Elves, so can immediately wear more armor, and they have a higher natural Agility than dwarves. Agility is, essentially, what allows you to dodge. You can cast while you dodge, no problem, but if someone actually *hits* you, your spell will automatically fizzle. A major downside to Humans is, as always, that old can't-see-in-the-dark issue. However, by level 9 you can summon your own light, which pretty much solves that problem.

Halfling. An unusual choice for Cleric, but it works. Your Wisdom is good enough for you to survive as a spellcaster, and your super-high Agility and Dexterity means you're not only efficient in a fight, but you're less likely to be interrupted when casting.

Armor

A word to the wise: save up and buy armor, because creatures are going to go out of their way to rip your liver out.

Commands

Put a heal spell in your #1 skill slot. That keeps it close to hand for when you need it.

F8 selects the nearest NPC, usually your nearest enemy in a fight, and F1 selects yourself. Get in the habit of healing yourself by typing F1 then 1, then retarget for the next attack by hitting F8.

Combat

Max out stats, especially Strength and AC, before battle.

Use *Yaulp.* Use it a lot.

Begin casting immediately after the mob swings and hits/misses. That way you get the longest amount of uninterrupted time. (It's not long, but it's the best possible.)

Specialization

Note: See also **Specialization**, page 209.

Specialization means casting a type of spell with less mana. Figure out which ones you use the most. After a battle, including bringing everyone back up to health afterwards, scroll back and count how many healing spells, buff spells, anti-dead spells, etc., you used.

If you find that you're primarily healing and resurrecting, then you want to specialize in Alteration.

If the number of times you prep your team for battle with buff spells tops the list, then you want to specialize in Abjuration.

If you hang out with Paladins who can't sleep at night if they haven't cleaned the zone of undead, then you're probably looking at Evocation for your specialty.

If, of course, your Cleric has strong personal opinions — a role-playing indication of what his specialization would be — then that's the way you should go. In all things, have fun.

Druid

Starting Off

Spells. Druids are a great, all-around class. However, your first priority is getting spells. Make money, buy spells.

Arms. The second thing you should acquire is probably a good weapon. Ask around. Not all weapons are worthwhile for Druids.

Armor. Next, armor. Sure, if the Druid has a habit of getting chewed up by bad guys, get the armor first, and *then* the weapon.

One school of thought is that it is a waste of money for a Druid to buy lesser, more affordable items, but instead should save up and buy the best available. One really high-AC item, with the rest of the armor being everyday leather, saves you money in the long run, until you can afford to buy whatever you want (if and when that day ever comes).

Friends. Talk to people and make friends. The best way to get into groups is to know a lot of people, and ask the ones you're friendly with if you can join. If there are a lot of Druids in the area, it can sometimes take a while to find a party. Friends will almost always let you join!

It doesn't matter. When it gets right down to it, race isn't really that important to a Druid. Why? Because the Druid is such an all-around character that any ability set is pretty useful. Decide race on how you want to role-play the character, and then hunt up items to improve your weak stats.

Groups

Druids are great with groups. They don't really specialize in any one area (like spells or combat), but they get pretty good in all of them. This means that there is rarely an emergency where a Druid won't be able to help.

Experience

Guilds. Check around the cities for quests that you can do. They make gaining experience a lot more fun than just slaughtering critters in the newbie gardens. Check out your guild hall, and talk to other folks in your city.

Groups. Don't be afraid to join parties and go hunt up mobs. At lower levels you won't lose any experience, and at higher levels you'll have spells, etc., to make the fighting easier.

Converse. Talk, talk, talk. Talk to any friendly high-level Druids (and there are almost always more friendly people than otherwise) for advice. Talk to folks your own level to find what they thought was interesting, lucrative or just plain fun. Talk to the people in your group about what they'd find most useful from a Druid.

Death stories are the most useful pieces of information you can get from someone your own level. What couldn't they handle? What were their mistakes? What will/won't they do next time?

Enchanter

Eyes Open. Enchanters must have good situational awareness. They are always running around looking at a fight from different angles, watching the members' health bars (especially the healers — Enchanters should always have a rune ready to go if the healer is getting clobbered), and reading the scrolling messages to watch for other monsters that enter the fray.

Hang in there. Levels 20-24 are awful for Enchanters. The Enchanter is weak then, so he will want to get into a group; however, a lot of groups don't really want an Enchanter until they are a bit higher. The smart Enchanter will educate a potential group on his capabilities and spells. For instance, Mesmerization will appeal to a lot of groups.

Be creative. Jewelry Making is a favorite trade for Enchanters. The really successful ones are quite wealthy ... and can always find friends.

Quests

Metal. If an Enchanter worships Erollis Marr, she could get her metal enchantment spells in Neriak (along with money). One place to find the Stein is Oggok (be sure to avoid the Shadow Knight guild).

Coins. In their travels, if Enchanters find coins like the old silver ones, they should keep them. They are for the final Tashan series quest.

Sand Giants and such like can chew through melee classes, yet most Enchanters (indeed, most casters) can kill them fairly easily. This comes in handy!

Attributes

For an Enchanter, both Intelligence and Charisma are important. Which attribute is the most important depends on the situation. An Enchanter can divide her items into two groups: Intelligence or Charisma. If she's doing a lot of mesmerizing or charming, Charisma items are called for; for casting fear or DD spells, Intelligence is the way.

Spell Strategies

Creative combinations of spells. If an Enchanter finds that he has to put on the visage of an unwelcome race or class, he can cast *Illusion: Dark Elf* first (for example), then cast *Invisibility* over it. He would need to stay away from classes that could see through the illusions, of course. (This is done by conning at a distance. If it cons more hostile than "indifferent," then it can see through *Invisibility*. It may not have noticed the interloper yet, but it will.) If the Enchanter then needs to enlist aid from someone of the "illusioned" race, he could drop the *Invisibility* and cast *Alliance*. When the item or assistance was acquired, he could then *Gate* out.

Consider religion at creation. If the Enchanter wishes to use her spells for secretive reasons, she should consider being agnostic. For example, even with the use of faction-improving spells, she could get into trouble with good city guards if she were the follower of an evil god, or vice versa.

Dealing with Magic Resistance. One of the Enchanters' main spells is *Tashan*, which lowers Magic Resistance by 10+. Any enemy casters will have less resistance once the Enchanter casts this spell.

EverQuest: The Ruins of Kunark

Area of Effect spells. AoE Mesmerize needs room. Enchanters should make sure to tell their groups to back up a monster, if necessary, so they don't mesmerize themselves.

Specialization

Enchanters have many schools to choose from for specialization. The first one a young Enchanter might look at would be Abjuration. This skill is all about buffing shield spells. Another would be Conjuration. This is used to summon the Enchanter's animations as well as some of his combat spells. Evocation is the heart of the Enchanter's direct damage spells. Divination is the key for all of the shape shifting spells. The final school an Enchanter might want to concentrate in would be Alteration since most of the combat-related spells fall into this category.

Combat

Gate is always a good spell to have loaded, in case something goes wrong.

Charm. Enchanters can charm one monster to attack another monster and then decrease the attributes on the monster that their pets are attacking. Of course, all of this takes monitoring, but it can be quite effective.

Resistance. Monsters with poison and high magic resistance are difficult for Enchanters — not many of their spells will work well.

Solo. An Enchanter can cast a damage spell, then *Whirl* on her target and sit down to meditate. Then, stand up and cast a damage spell, and *Whirl* again. Repeat until the monster is killed.

Group tactics

Communicate. In addition to working out strategies and tactics before battle, Enchanters need to be very clear with their parties about when they want help and when they don't. Sometimes, a well-meaning Warrior can mess up a perfectly good spell — especially when the Warrior is wielding an area-effect weapon too close!

Debuff. First off, Enchanters should *Mesmerize* and then debuff the monster that the party is about to beat on, and then move on to the next one. The goal is to give the party a target, and then mez the rest of the opposition.

Wait for it. The Enchanter should kill monster/NPC casters last. She has a line of stun spells that can be alternated to keep the monster from casting ever (unless one is resisted). If she kills the monster casters last, she can focus 100% of her attention on the monster caster and not have to step out of battle and *Mesmerize* other monsters. Even with simple stuns, most of the time the NPC caster won't get a spell off.

Buff. Enchanters should buff everyone in the group with *Strengthen* and *Haze*. The *Strengthen* spell gives about 5-10 extra Strength; the *Haze* spell gives about that amount in Armor Class. It make a big difference; plus, as they are buffs, they can be cast before battle, and the mana can be regained before the battle.

Pet Tactics

Pet weapons. An Enchanter should buy a short-delay, high-damage weapon for her pet — or get summoned daggers from players, or the best — a shadowman weapon — if she can get her hands on one. Also, to help out her pet, she should debuff the monster, cast *Whirl* along with her color series to keep the monster from attacking.

If the pet is about to die ... The Enchanter should cast *Fear*. This will stop the monster from beating on the pet and give him some free damage on the monster. Thus the Enchanter gains some time to aid his pet and get ready to cast a few stun spells, then *Fear* again, *Whirl* and run a short distance away. By then, his pet will get the monster's attention back and finish it off.

Important information. An Enchanter pet cannot be controlled in any way. It attacks when its master is attacked — that's about it. So when the Enchanter uses a pet, she should cast a spell or attack with melee, to taunt the monster for a moment. Then the pet will join in and the Enchanter can step back and play from there.

Pet healing. Pets regenerate their hit points at ten times the rate that players do.

Get the best. Enchanters should cast and recast for pets until they get the most dangerous pet around. Enchanters need to remember that their pets are there to take the beating so they don't.

Spells on the pet and the Enchanter. The Enchanter should buy cat's eyes agates and cast *Rune I* (at least) on herself and her pet before battle. Cast *Quickness* on her pet during combat and *Languid Pace* on her target. Also, a shield spell and some sort of cloud, like *Haze* or *Mist* should be on her and her pet.

Pet-kiting. Enchanters can get a monster on their pets, hit the monster with a debuff or so, get away from the thick of things and — keeping an eye on the pet's hit points — meditate. As soon as the pet goes down, cast another pet. When the monster runs at the Enchanter again, the pet will take it. Of course, if the Enchanter has enough mana, he should run through the buffs for his pet (speed and strength, usually).

Tanking for the pet. Enchanters have to meditate after a fight, so there's also going to be time to recover some hit points. Therefore, getting hurt a bit, if it gives the pet more time to finish off the monster, is definitely an option. Dodge if possible (after level 22) and keep that skill maxed! If the mob is attacking but missing the Enchanter, while the pet is attacking and connecting, that's definitely a short-lived enemy.

Races

Dark Elf Enchanter. Dark Elves aren't popular, and their Charisma is practically non-existent, but they make up for it with Intelligence and Wisdom, Dexterity, and Agility. Besides, there is no vision like ultravision — it's much clearer than infravision. Counteract the low Charisma by stocking up on Charisma-boosting charms.

Gnome Enchanter. Along with all the attributes needed for an effective Enchanter, Gnomes have a great newbie zone (Misty Thicket) to increase in levels.

EverQuest: The Ruins of Kunark

Magician

Lingo. When a non-Magician says "mage," it means either magic user or Magician. When a Magician says "mage," it means Magician.

Experience

Work up a character profile that's more than summoning things ... maybe the mage likes to go fishing, make pots, etc. Magic is good, but a real personality makes it worthwhile.

Spells

Night vision. Use *Summon Heatstone*.

Sit and summon. It takes a long, long time to get adept at summoning. Simply sit and summon items for as long as you can take it. Once you have the items, give a gift (or three) to anyone who's pleasant.

Practice summoning food and water, and sell it to passers-by who are KOS in nearby cities. After all, not everyone can summon food and drink from thin air when they need it.

Specialization. Evocation is mostly direct damage. Conjuration is summoning, from pets to food to weapons, although there are some DD conjurations. When given the options to specialize, nearly every Magician goes for conjuration.

Pets

Sometimes it can save your life to kill your pet. This may seem like a bad thing, but they're actually very useful if your pet is getting into something that you *really* don't want to deal with. There are some items that will "instant kill" your pets.

Monk

Kick it. Monks have the uncanny advantage of being able to kick, throw melee punches and issue ranged attacks — all at the same time. It doesn't take long to improve kicking skills, so throwing a few practices into kicking isn't a bad idea. After a Monk character gains a few levels, accurately-landed round kicks look really cool ....

Mend. Sort of like the Paladin's *Lay on Hands* spell, Mending is a good skill to improve on during or after battle. It can't be used more than once a day or so at lower levels, but that gets better with practice. The only real drawback to Mend is that using it unsuccessfully causes damage instead of healing it. Ouch.

Combat

Don't even try to learn a weapon. Weapons are not only superfluous — a Monk's moves are just as deadly as a blade — but they are too heavy. A Monk will not be able to perform up to expectations if she's weighted down with unnecessary items.

Take it slow. Fight cautiously until you get Dual Attack and Feign Death. Monks are amazing fighters ... but they are a little underpowered at the outset. It can be a bit frustrating for a newbie.

Strategic withdrawal. If you're out-matched ... run! A Monk can easily outpace his enemies (although creatures in Norrath never give up the chase until you're out of zone). Since Monks are often loners, learning to perform tactical withdrawals is a survival trait.

Magic w/o spells. Regular attacks (hand attacks) don't become magical in and of themselves no matter how high the Monk's level — the Monk will need to get magical items, such as gloves, to have a magical hand-to-hand hit. However, the skills acquired at later levels, such as Flying Dragon Kick, are magical in nature.

Iksar. Iksar Monks immediately start off with Dual Wield ability, so once you can come up with a second weapon you're ready to rock. Of course, Iksar don't start off with two weapons, but you can't have everything. And never forget the ever-present tail attack.

Pulling

Feign Death. Monks are great pullers, but ... pulling a manageable number of mobs (one or two) is the goal. In case of a train, Feign Death to keep from overwhelming your camp. Pulling a train to camp can mean instant wipeout, and it will be all your fault.

Feign Death will sometimes not work on the highest-level mobs. Know your enemies.

Switch off. Monks are great tanks *and* great pullers, so if there's another puller in the party, switch off to keep things interesting.

Skills

Practice. Always be practicing skills that you think are necessary. Sense Heading (particularly useful during solo work), Kick and always and especially Mend.

Practice Feign Death in your downtime. It may feel silly to be playing possum without a hint of danger nearby, but it's better than spending skill points.

Mend. Mend is going to be one of your most often used skills, so it might be worth spending a few spell points on it when you're in those troubled-teen levels. It's better than practicing, because a flubbed Mend hurts.

Mend works as often as your skill is high. In other words, if your skill is 75, your attempts to Mend will work 75% of the time. It takes a long time to get consistently good.

Feign Death. Any extended capabilities for solo playing will rely on your knowing when to Feign Death and when to run for the border.

Flying Dragon Kick. After you get your basics down, save up your skill points for Flying Dragon Kick. Flying Dragon Kick is definitely one of the coolest skills available to anyone.

Dragon Punch and Intimidation are also good, no doubt about it, and also worth the skill points.

Clothing

Silk. You want to wear silk, specifically Cured Silk. You should be well on your way to a complete Cured Silk fashion statement by level 15.

A Monk with time on his hands and no luck getting Cured Silk can always develop the skill of Tailoring. It's the hard way, but it's a good feeling to wear only your own, hand-crafted clothes. If a Monk isn't into self-sufficiency, who is?

Magic. Magical gloves may sometimes impart the "special kick" ability, similar to magical boots. Who knows why, but there it is.

Equipment

Ask your own, ask nicely. Gaining levels can be a little intimidating, but a trip down to your guild and a whole lot of polite discussions with the older Monks can be invaluable. Monks can't carry very much, so they are apt to be generous.

Cash it in. Also, being helpful to people tends to be a lucrative pastime for Monks. Since you can't really carry much in the way of items, anything a Monk gets should be immediately sold for cold, hard cash. Other classes have to spend time thinking "will this be useful later?" Monks always travel light — and don't count on weapons and shields for their success.

Allocating Ability Points

Don't spend hours stressing over how to allocate points: they won't make *that* big a difference. That said, there are different reasons to put points different places.

Agility. Allocate enough skill points to get Agility up past 75. Agility acts as armor class — it essentially represents your ability to dodge a blow. However, remember that once you get Feign Death, you're only going to be killed if you're careless.

Strength. Strength is a good place to put ability points. Let's face it, the Monk is a damage dealer, and the higher the Strength, the more damage is dealt.

On the other hand, there are an awful lot of Strength-buffing items out there. If you have reason to think you'll survive to get them, you can pull back on the Strength allocation and put it elsewhere.

Necromancer

Races

Dark Elves are by far the most popular Necromancer race. They have night vision and free entrance to any "evil" areas.

Erudite Necros have such a high Intelligence that they get more mana than Humans, but no one much likes them, and they don't get the night vision that Dark Elves do.

Human Necromancers will level faster than Dark Elf or Erudite Necromancers.

Gnomes have a higher Dexterity than any other Necromancer race, which improves their chance of getting through a spell uninterrupted. They also have night vision — and it's always handy to see in the dark.

Skills

If you're an Erudite, just go ahead and make the most of your best skill — max out your Intelligence. That plus any Intelligence-raising items that you get will make you a phenomenal spellcaster.

Combat

A good weapon makes a big difference until the Necro goes pure spellcaster.

Know who your NPC friends are, and don't kill anything that will ruin your faction with them. For instance, if you've got a good thing going with the Ogres at Oggok, don't kick up dirt in their neck of the woods.

See **Solo Tactics: Root and Direct Damage** (page 174) and **Kiting** (page 175).

Kiting. Necromancers are the kings of kiting, especially reverse kiting.

DoT. Damage over Time spells are always useful, if you've got the time and mana to spend on it during battle. Your pet will almost always be your main damage-dealer.

Courtesy. Don't cast *Fear* on a creature when it would endanger nearby people. If it needs to be lured to a safe place before kiting, then lure it. (Even if the Necro is a hard-as-nails baddie who doesn't care about anyone's safety, the player should be careful. Be creative, and you can come up with a reason why the Necro would kill in privacy.)

Also, don't cast *Fear* on your mob when you're fighting with a group. It makes thing too unpredictable for party tactics.

Traveling

Unloved. Necromancers are not welcome in most cities. Accept that fact, because it's going to be true for your entire career.

Paineel. Erudite Necromancers start off in Paineel. That's good news and bad news. The good news is that it's easy for newbies to level up in Paineel. There are plenty of creatures in the newbie garden and lots of quests in the city, and tons of time to build up skills and cash. The bad news is that any quests will really lower faction with the rest of the Erudites ... eventually it will be hard to sneak (with dignity) off the island.

Older Erudite Necromancers will often give you a teleport of off Odus, if you can find any.

Loot

Words, not cash. Necromancer's Words are not really in high demand to anyone but Necromancers. In a group you can ask that you get first dibs on any Words that are dropped, and people will normally be more than pleased to do so ... of course, you'll be last on the list for cash, but it's worth it.

Pets

Leering Corpse. Use a pet as soon as you can (level 4). Lower-level pets aren't much use, really, but you get more experience, so it's worth it.

Best is best. Especially at lower levels, if you have enough bone chips, keep summoning pets until you get the best one in the area.

Or don't. Many Necromancers rely entirely on spells, and never use a pet. It can be done — and you get more experience points per battle — it's just much, much harder.

Soloing

Necromancers are excellent soloists — though there are many places where they aren't welcome. Wizards will often sell food and drink. Also, newbies are useful for buying things in the city — for the right price.

Groups

Be a joiner. Necromancers are better soloists than almost any other class ... but soloing up to 60 can be mind-numbingly boring and repetitive. Keep the enjoyment factor in mind, and join a group and do a dungeon or two.

EverQuest: The Ruins of Kunark

Thank a tank. Lower-level critter-crunching goes faster and easier if you can find a tank to join you. Necros are much more vulnerable at lower levels than most others, and it's nice to have someone there when the mana runs out. Once you get high enough to summon a pet that's actually useful, you won't need the tank backup anymore.

Necro-buddies. Fighting with another Necromancer means less experience per creature, but also means twice the *Fear* and darkness spells. Two Necros almost never have to zone to escape a rogue creature.

When grouping with another Necromancer, it's especially vital to communicate what you're about to do.

Spells

DOT or not. All Necromancer Damage over Time spells will stack. However, if the effect of the spell is not improved by accumulation — such as a paralyzing spell, where the mob is either paralyzed or it's not — it's a waste of time to cast it again.

No *Fear*. Don't use fear spells in small places like dungeons. Spells like *Shock of Poison* or *Venom of the Snake* are safer for all concerned ... that and sending in your pet, of course.

Specialization

There are three kinds of spells that a Necromancer tends to use the most. Conjuration (spells like *Clinging Darkness* and *Shock of Poison*), Alteration (such as *Heat Blood* and *Siphon Life*), and Evocation (most things having to do with the dead). By the time you get to the point where you can Specialize, you'll know which spells you favor.

Paladin

Allocating Skill Points

It's good to have an Agility of at least 75.

Strength should be around 85.

Any points left over should go into Wisdom for mana accumulation. Yes, Paladins are at heart just "wade-in-and-kill-it" fighters, but once you get high enough to get the good spells, you're going to want to use them.

Races

Dwarves are always good for any melee-based class, because they have such a high Strength. Moreover, they have a good base Wisdom, which means more mana in the long run.

Half Elves are good - average stats, plus you get night vision.

High Elves have great Wisdom, but because their Strength is low you're going to be shopping for Strength items pretty early on.

Erudites have good stats, but nothing is significantly outstanding. They don't have night vision *at all*, and it's a long time to Level 22 and *Halo of Light*.

Humans are good all-around, but not special in anything. No night vision, unfortunately, and no light spell until Level 22.

Weapons

At lower levels, use Bash and One-Handed Slash. The short delay is valuable in a fight until you get to higher levels.

Slice or smush. Most Paladins will have a preference for either slashing or blunt weapons. (Most by far prefer the edged weapons.) It's best to decide early on, and allocate skill points to one or the other, instead of dividing them between the two.

Hammer of Wrath. Some Paladins prefer the One-Handed Blunt skill because even death won't disarm them. Paladins get *Hammer of Wrath* early on (relatively), but that doesn't mean it's particularly useful ... unless you've practiced One-Handed Blunt. Of course, by the time you get to Level 15 and the *HoW*, you've probably already got a weapon you like, and may be saving for one that's better than a hammer, even one that's a gift from your god. Still, it's nice to always have a weapon you can use in event of an emergency.

Use both hands. At higher levels, your delay is shortened, and you can benefit from the higher damage of a two-handed slashing weapon. However, as long as you use a one-handed weapon, you can use a shield (useful) and Bash with it (even more useful). So keep in mind when deciding whether to give up your one-handed weapon: are you more comfortable with a shield or with a more powerful weapon?

No delay. At the highest levels, you're doing so much more damage that once again it's the delay that's the hindrance, so one-handed weapons become the weapon of choice again.

Group

Join. Paladins usually do better in groups than as a soloist. They *can* solo, and solo well, but the higher they get, the harder it gets. By around Level 40, most either give up soloing or they give up their character.

Adapt. Paladins do a lot of things well, without really specializing in any one thing. They can tank, they can cast. What they *should* do in a group is fit their actions to the needs of the particular band of people they're with.

Paladins do two things particularly well: tanking and healing. With a few buffs, they can wade in wreak havoc with the best of them. Or, they can hold back, protect the magic-users and heal up anyone teetering on death's doorstep.

Generally, whether a Paladin plays a tank or a healer depends on how many Warriors are in the group. More than two fighters, the Paladin should be a healer. Less than two, the way to go is tanking.

Combat

No undead. Combat against undead? Paladin is the fighter-cleric for you!

Caster companion. Very popular partners with casters, especially casters who can deal out direct damage. They are wonderful tanks, and make excellent taunters to keep the enemy off the casters — with their AC they don't have to worry about taking a couple of shots to the chin. They also have heal spells to keep anyone from dying should anyone's health get too low.

Ranger

Bag it. Rangers by definition travel pretty light, so you've got a low encumbrance. Get backpacks, sewing kits, fletching kits, or whatever to help you organize your loot. Quite often you can get items like these on quests you can find around cities.

Dress nicely. Rangers can use *most* of the better weapons and armor. Banded remains a respectable choice into the upper 20s.

Skill Point Allocation

Allocation can go two ways.

Go Wide. There are so many useful skills available to a Ranger (depending on what you plan to do with the character) that many people simply allocate one skill point to each skill as it becomes available.

Go Deep. Since a Ranger is primarily a melee class, another good idea is to concentrate on 2-Handed Slash. Investing all (or nearly all) of the skill points in 2-Handed Slash, and it will work well until Dual Wield. Of course, yes, coins will have to be spent on a good 2-handed weapon.

Combat

Equip yourself. Your initial weapon isn't very good (no one's ever is), so keep an eye on any auctions going on. Moreso than many other groups, a Ranger is as good as his weapons.

Go for double damage. When Dual Wield is available, practice it by having a dirk or dagger in one hand, and a sword (or a Barbed Leather Whip) in the other.

Go for max damage. Given the choice between 2-Handed Slash and 1-Handed Slash, remember that 2-Handed does more damage. 1-Handed is great with a shield, but then, shields are heavy, and there's the encumbrance issue ... and Rangers don't get Bash, anyway. So, unless there's a good reason not to, go for the 1-Handed Slash.

Beware of planes. Rangers are great tanks in any non-planar situation. However, tanking on the planes will take some planning. Basically, a Ranger will have to go all out on AC. Buffing the AC up as high as possible makes it survivable.

Groups

Cash. Money and experience are easier to come by groups — especially at lower levels.

Ask a caster. Rangers are a melee class, so they partner well with casters. Particularly Shamans, since both are nature-based classes. The Shaman's buffs and the Ranger's *Snare* and attacks are quite a combination.

A Necromancer/Ranger alliance works well, with the Ranger essentially performing the role of "pet." The Necromancer casts a darkness spell, followed by *Fear*, and the Ranger does the damage. This works out better for the Necromancer, because the Ranger can recognize an emergency situation where the mob needs to be taunted away from the caster. The Ranger also does well by it, because not only does the Necromancer keep the target occupied, one way or another, but in a tough area can summon a pet for backup.

For Rangers who want to play the traditional bow-slinging fantasy Ranger, partnering up with a Magician to do *Summon Arrows* is a good thing. (Of course, there are those who point out that a well-trained Ranger can do more damage in melee than with even an infinite supply of arrows.)

Track. Perhaps the most useful skill to have in most groups is the ability to locate (track) whichever kind of animal they're interested in. That way, everyone gets what they want: more experience points.

Pulling

Slowly. Rangers are good pullers. *Flame Lick* followed (quickly) by *Snare* will have a creature following you back to camp ... angry but slow, just the way you like 'em.

Ye olde bow and arrow. At lower levels, before you get spells, the best way to pull creatures is to use archery. It works like a charm, and if you learn fletching it's not that expensive. You can usually find someone to sell you a bow at "discount" prices near the fletching supply places. Look for a higher-level Ranger — they're most likely to know how — and ask very nicely.

Spells

Snare. It's godlike. Use it.

Although a Ranger's spells are not as varied as the Bard's, being able to buff (*Skin like Diamond*, *Feet like Cat*), do direct damage (*Burst of Fire* and the lightning spells), cast *Camouflage*, as well as things like *Enduring Breath* (that's waterbreathing, and very handy) and *Cure Poison* are all amazingly useful things.

Rogue

Character Creation

Abilities. In developing a Rogue, think Dexterity (for better use of higher level weapons), a little extra Strength (for higher max damage, and loot-carrying ability), Agility (for not being hit) and Charisma (for better prices when fencing goods). Frail races should put few extra points in Stamina. Count up the STR/DEX/AGI/STA and go for 75 points or more ... any less, and survivability takes a nose-dive. Always remember, there are magical items for further stat improvements.

Attitude. First of all, it takes the right mindset. Rogues believe, deep down in their heart, that everything "acquired" from others is somehow owed to them. "That'll teach them to goof off and not pay attention." It's a conservation issue, really ... it's not healthy for people to have too much stuff.

Rogues aren't one of the "usual" classes ... they have extremely useful skills that most classes don't have. More than that, they've got *attitude*. It takes a flat-out stubborn person to play a Rogue. It's a matter of personal style ... and backstabbing like mad.

Leveling. Soloing a Rogue is very, *very* difficult and it takes forever to level.

Races. Gnomish Rogues are pretty much on their own ... their guild generally tries to disassociate itself from the young.

Half-Elven Rogues lose a ton of XP whenever they die (after level 5, of course).

Combat

Go for the back. Get behind them whenever possible. No one can Backstab from the front.

Dual Wield. Use the fastest weapons available. When facing a caster, the goal is to interrupt the spell.

Stick with it. Eventually a Rogue gets to use "special" weapons that proc, plus a little poison on the ol' blade never hurts ....

Pick the place. Duel or fight, whenever possible, in a place near a steep incline. Safe Fall down the slope and hope they follow. Falling can really leave folks vulnerable.

Tank 'em. Barbarians should Backstab ... and Slam!

Player vs. Player. Be sneaky and underhanded in duels. Success depends on getting behind the opponent. People who whine about a Rogue's "moving too much" should be Backstabbed. People who don't turn fast enough should be Backstabbed. Anyone who challenges a Rogue to a duel should *definitely* be Backstabbed.

Groups

Don't be a target. Rogues are secondary melee fighters. They can't take a full assault ... but if a tank distracts the mob, the Backstab damage is phenomenal!

Think. In a fight, Rogues have to think more about tactics ... Sneak? Arrows? Evade and run? Backstab?

Coordinate. It's *very* important that a Rogue's group understands about staying on the far side of the enemy from a Rogue. If they don't, don't join that group again!

It's not easy at all to backstab creatures because they're so fast at turning around. That's why it's so hard to solo, and why in a group it's helpful if someone distracts the enemy while the Rogue slides the knife in between the fourth and fifth ribs.

Evade. Evade is also handy in groups, because it works like a "reverse taunt." While the fighters are usually good at taunting the opponent, sometimes it just isn't enough. Their taunts plus Evade usually gets the mob back on to the tank, where it belongs.

Rogue Invisibility

How to Sneak and Hide. The secret, when a Rogue is young and naïve — and prone to skill failure — is to Hide first. When it finally succeeds, there's all the time in the world to try Sneak until that succeeds as well. Sneaking first means the Rogue's only got once chance to Hide ... after that, Sneak has to be reapplied. Guess it's not so very sneaky to keep trying — and failing — to Hide!

Why to Sneak and Hide. Most things that see through Sneak still won't see an "invisible" Rogue.

Sneak and Hide equals "invisible to the undead."

A Rogue who is Sneaking and Hiding can't run, so it's pretty slow going, but it's worth it.

Once a Rogue makes level 20, invisibility is pretty consistently successful.

Rogues' "invisibility" never breaks unless they attack or are hit by a trap (or someone particularly clever spies you).

When to Sneak and Hide. In case of low hit points, Evade and run! Only at a safe distance should a Rogue try Sneak and Hide.

Sneak and Hide is incredibly useful for exploring (i.e., scouting spawns) if it's used to check for "surprise" mobs that might train with the pull.

It's also great for pulling friends' corpses out of dangerous areas, as well as just for showing off a little. Rogues are the best for retrieving corpses, hands down.

A talented and prudent Rogue can sneak into towns that don't normally welcome them and do a little quiet business. Just be careful of anything that can see Invisible! Best bet in all cases is to assume that *everyone* might see through it.

Remember. A lazy Rogue is a dead Rogue. A distracted Rogue is a dead Rogue. A hasty Rogue is a dead Rogue ....

Backstab

Practice makes perfect. Backstab will improve much faster in a group ... and the goal is to get that skill as high as possible. Why? Because the more creatures pulled, the more backstabbing opportunities there are.

Safe Fall

An expert Safe Faller can jump off of a wizard teleport partway up and feel no pain. It's not suggested to jump off the very top ... even if it's survivable, it's usually not worth it.

Safe Fall in the desert is a happy thing ... just be careful when leading, since other people can get hurt by the steep dunes.

Slow down. As long as they don't run, Rogues can go down most inclines. Take it one step at a time.

Practice. Improve Safe Fall by finding a steep wall at the edge of a zone, and run up and down it. Angle the approach and "bounce" or trip a few times on the way down. Each bump has a chance of improving Safe Fall, but done right, it doesn't hurt too much.

Other Skills

Pottery. With serious coin outlay, Pottery can be maxed (168) at level 1.

Poison. Poison is incredibly hard for a Rogue to make profitable. The necessary things are expensive and scattered all over Norrath. It's great if friends help out, but otherwise, it's just a very difficult hobby.

Evade. Evade is a combat skill, so use it in battle.

Pickpocket. Failing Pickpocket means consequences will follow. Always have a Plan B ready.

Something useful —preferably against a blue mob — is to Sneak and Hide to get behind the monster, Backstab, Pickpocket ... and *immediately* Autoattack. Then when Pickpocket is available again, click off Autoattack, hit Pickpocket, and then Autoattack again as fast as possible. Use hotkeys!

Shadow Knight

Leveling Up

Move through the newbie levels quickly. Shadow Knights don't level up as quickly as some of the other classes. Rapidly gaining experience in a newbie garden (for example, Paineel's newbie garden is a good place to gather bone chips) — as well as earning money to purchase necessities such as armor — can help the Shadow Knight sooner attain the levels where the more powerful spells are available.

Attributes. As for any magic user, increased Intelligence gets even more useful at high levels of the Shadow Knight class.

(Not recommended) Since Shadow Knights have limited carrying space and are somewhat weak at lower levels, they are more prone to "twinking" — a practice where players take a high-level character's equipment and money, and stash it in a safe place where a low-level character can retrieve it. Most players don't approve of this method.

Spells

Pet Spell. Shadow Knights enjoy the double benefit of a fighter's high strength and stamina, plus the ability to cast spells. Once the pet spell becomes available, the Shadow Knight becomes a fierce adversary.

Invisibility. The invisibility spell is the Shadow Knight's best defense. Use it well. Use it often. It will allow the Shadow Knight to move around in cities and areas where they are marked to be killed on sight.

Little-known spells. Many players don't know the spells that Shadow Knights have available, such as *Deadeye*, *Gather Shadows*, *Feign Death*, or any of the darkness spells. This can work to the Shadow Knight's advantage in a confrontation.

Traveling

Surly guards. Hey, Shadow Knights aren't out to win any popularity contests. Pay attention to the cities you visit. Shadow Knights are not welcome everywhere and, in fact, some city guards (such as in Qeynos) have standing orders to kill Shadow Knights on sight. Freeport and Neriak streets are open to Shadow Knights.

Combat

Vs. red NPCs. Best to party with strong characters and Clerics.

Mesmerizing spells during combat. Damage over time (DoT) spells (such as the darkness spells) will wake up a mesmerized enemy. Don't do it unless you *want* it to wake up. However, if you do want to break the mez, it's a great way to get it to come after you, instead of going after the caster who spelled it.

Tank your pet. Give your pet high-damage weapons whenever you can afford to. If you've got a magician who can summon weapons ... you're good to go!

Shaman

The "usual" job description. Selfishness is very rare in Shamans. Often, it is the Shaman who work to keep everyone else alive. Remember, the Shaman can also use some powerful weapons; however, those weapons are mostly used to fend away an enemy so a friend can be healed.

Combat

1H Blunt. A one-handed blunt weapon should be in every Shaman's inventory.

2H Blunt. Higher-level Shamans are more capable with two-handed blunt weapons.

New weapons. Check for new weapons — such as new Shaman spears — that may be added from time to time!

Unique role in a party. Shamans can play a vital role in a well-balanced party (the Shaman, a Warrior or two, Bard, magic user, Druid and/or Cleric, for example) and never take the offense. Keep the Warriors going with *Burst of Strength* spells and everyone moving quickly with *Spirit of Wolf* (haste) spells.

DOT the targets. The Shaman will get the longest benefit (more damage for less mana) from a DoT spell (such as *Infectious Cloud*) by casting it on a monster and running toward waiting offensive party members. Of course, it's always advisable to keep those party members healed as the combat progresses.

Stack spells. This is especially valuable in a long combat situation. The Shaman can stack several DoT spells and then get out of the way to heal the other party members.

For example, you can stack *Affliction*, *Insidious Fever* and *Malise* because they don't have overlapping effects. In other words, all damage over time (DoT) spells of the same type do stack. Moving spells, such as *Drowsy* and *Walking Sleep,* don't stack. Area of effect (AoE) spells (such as *Infectious Cloud*) stack with DoT spells.

Keep it going. Continually keep a strength Spell, a Stamina spell and a haste spell (such as *Strength*, *Inner Fire*, and *Spirit of Wolf*) on all the members of your party.

Spell smarter, not harder. If the party has another magic user with attribute-enhancement spells, don't overlap and waste mana. For example, you might let the Enchanter buff Strength while the Shaman buffs everything else.

Cleric on hand. At level 24, the Shaman can get the *Regeneration* spell which can really lighten the Cleric's load by regenerating hit points on the tanks.

Pets. At level 34, the Shaman gets a wolf pet that can melee for the Shaman. Oh yeah, the wolf is definitely something to look forward to!

Training

Weapon training. There are some great two-handed weapons available to a Shaman. Keep this skill, as well as one-handed weapons, as high as you can. However, don't disregard Piercing. Some of the new Shaman spears look pretty good.

Warrior

AoE. Wide-area effect weapons aren't always welcome in a crowd. They may be great for Warriors, but the damage might unmez the nearby creatures. Groups should always perform an equipment check prior to setting out for a long adventure.

Walk with a wolf. Adventurous Druids and Warriors form a lot of lasting friendships in *EverQuest*. The Druid has the power to instill the *Spirit of Wolf*, buff, and teleport ... and the Warrior's skills speak for themselves.

Specialize. Those well-versed in the ways of the Warrior recommend specializing in a particular weapon skill at higher levels.

Combat

Combat with Clerics. Clerics and Warriors work well in a real battle with numerous enemies. The "why" of that statement can be summed up in one word — healing.

If a speedy, constant battle is the preferred mode of attack, Clerics work best with Warriors. For attacks in a relatively safe area where a target can be leisurely tracked and attacked with downtime in between hunts, Druids and Warriors work best.

Have a party. Many Warriors claim that the best hunting groups of all consist of a Warrior (for bashing), a Druid (for tracking) and a Cleric (for healing). Add in an Enchanter and a couple more Warriors, and the party is complete.

Wizard

Races

Humans are pretty well-rounded in their statistics, but they lack racial infravision, something that can be a boon to a low-level Wizard. (Wizards get the *Heat Sight* spell later on).

Erudites have high INT and, usually, the most mana, however, because of their attitudes, they have pretty bad relations with some of the other races (like Humans) and won't be able to sell their goods at the local market. They also have the worst vision of all the races.

High Elves seem to make better Paladins or Clerics than Wizards.

Gnomes have good Intelligence (on par with dark Elves), they are pretty neutral with all races, they have infravision, and they have a great starting area.

Abilities

INT suggestion. Wizards should put all but 5 of their starting points into Intelligence. This attribute determines how fast the Wizard can learn anything and how much mana the character will have, which is vital to the longevity of this class. The other five points? The Wizard should keep putting as much as she can into Intelligence, even raising it to 200, before worrying about just increasing mana. Increasing the attribute increases more than just mana.

Combat

Offense. Wizards are very good at offense, with many powerful spells. They have the most damage potential in the shortest amount of time; however, it is difficult (if not impossible) to hit anything 6 levels or more above the caster. Unfortunately, Wizards are the only pure casting class without pets.

Defense. A Wizard is very bad at defense, very vulnerable to attack (low armor class), and has few hit points. This is a good reason for the Wizard to belong to a party, rather than solo, and to belong to a guild. If the player prefers to solo, he should consider the Magician or the Necromancer classes, as those classes are much better for soloing.

Embrace limitations. Stop carrying a weapon around Level 18. The Wizard might try relying on her spells alone once her level is high enough and she has a good, well-rounded spell book.

Armor. The first wearable armor for Wizards comes off of Orc Pawns. Cloth armor is also sold in shops. There are armorsmiths who can make armor for Wizards, but they are a specialized group of armorsmiths.

Traveling

Wizards can teleport, (which is a good defense, in a way) and this is an excellent commodity to sell ... as long as the Wizard doesn't mind the constant requests for teleports from everyone.

Only the Wizard can take people to the Planes of Sky and Hate, but she shouldn't. The components are expensive and the Planes are deadly to any but the toughest groups.

Spells

Early in their careers, Wizards get immobilization spells, which help in defense, as long as the player watches his mana supply.

Mana conservation. Wizards need to know how much their spells hit for and how much they cost to cast. It may be drudgery at first, but becomes second nature, and will save your life at times. When the Wizard drops to low mana, she becomes a juicy target for any monster. Consider keeping mana levels between 60-80% during a battle because the Wizard may be asked to evacuate the group with a teleport spell.

Fizzles. Wizards need to keep practicing their spells and keep the skills they use maxed out for their level. Once the skill gets high enough, fizzles occur rarely.

Research. Wizards should wait until level 20 and throw everything into practicing research. They need to remember to put a practice point in the Research skill and obtain a lexicon (usually from their guild vendor). There are 2 runes that have to be put into the lexicon before you can make any spells.

Meditating. This is simply recharging for the Wizard. For a Level 10+ Wizard who is part of a group, one strategy is to cast a strong (and costly) damage spell at the beginning, go meditate during the middle of the battle, and be ready to cast another strong damage spell or the *Root* spell at the end.

Level 1 Spells. Many Wizards find these spells worthless. They should save their money. After Level 4, the Wizard should go to their guild and put a point into meditation, a must skill for casters.

Area of Effect Spells. These spells (in a train situation) need special circumstances— a nice tight area, plenty of crowd control for the monsters about to key in on the caster and no new spawns in the nearby area waiting to start their own train. *Icestrike* and *Firestorm* spells are great for low-level wizards. Immobilize the target with a *Root* spell, cast *Icestrike* or *Firestorm*, let the beast take all the hits and then repeat.

Stun Spells. Wizards will eventually obtain a couple of stun spells, which can be their best spells. They give the Wizard instant control of a situation, if the spell sticks. Higher-level monsters have higher magic resistance, which makes it harder to make these spells stick. However, players need to bear in mind that stun spells only last so long — have an immobilization spell ready, just in case.

Interruptions. If a monster is going to hit the Wizard while she is casting another spell (for example, when *Root* times out), she should go ahead and take the hit or miss, and then cast the spell before the monster has the chance to hit her again. That way, the Wizard gets the spell off without being interrupted.

Dodge. At level 22, the Wizard can practice Dodge. Level 20-24 are hell levels, so Wizards get plenty opportunities to practice Dodge right off the bat.

Races

Barbarian

Classes and groups. There is an ongoing argument among players as to which is better, the Warrior or Shaman. It's really a symbiotic relationship — they make a great "tank" combination — one smashes, the other one heals. Barbarians and Clerics from other races can work well together, too.

Pull up roots. As a Barbarian, it's relatively easy to live in other cities as long as you can make it through the wilderness. The only places you want to avoid are the "dark" cities that are home to Ogres, Trolls and Dark Elves — Barbarians are KOS to them.

Raise faction. If you want to raise your faction standing with just about everyone in Norrath, kill any of the races mentioned above.

Pound 'em. Barbarians have the innate ability to Slam your opponents. Rogues especially benefit from this at higher levels.

Wear steel. Barbarians can wear medium or large armor, which not many can say.

Leap. If you're being attacked, try jumping as your opponent strikes. This can often put you out of his reach and make him miss, or help put distance between you and the monster if you're running away. (Even Barbarians should know when to quit a fight!)

Start at Home. The starting city of Halas has plenty of lucrative quests, and the game animals in the nearby wilderness have the reputation of carrying lots of coins.

Dark Elf

Disappear. Dark Elves can Hide and have Night Vision. Use both to best advantage.

Take quiet time. Hiding can come in handy if you get the urge to sit down and meditate for a while. Target the most dangerous opponent around, then Hide from it over and over and over. Eventually, that creature will leave you alone.

Hunt a chest. Dark Elves acquire a lot of things, but can't get containers very easily at low levels. So, the Necromancer guild quest is a good way to pick up a storage container early on. (It doesn't pay you much, but you receive a chest for your efforts.)

Find the back door. As a Dark Elf, traveling to other cities is difficult. You'll have to resort to being sneaky and covert. All port cities have underground caves or sewers you can use to bypass the guards at the gate. Look (or ask around) for a secret entrance hidden in the exterior walls.

Sneaking into a port city and grabbing a boat to somewhere else, you means jumping ship before you reach the next city. It's usually better than facing the KOS guards.

Faction

Make nice. Another way to get into non-evil cities is to kill other races that are hated there. This raises your faction standing with guards and commoners alike, depending on the race. (Let it be noted that Dark Elves don't do anything out of compassion ... they merely use everyone else in the world to get what they want.)

To get into Freeport, kill Orcs (this doesn't go over well with the Indigo Brotherhood)

To get into Blackburrow or SplitPaw, kill Gnolls.

To get into Kaladin, kill Rogues.

To get back in good standing with the Indigo Brotherhood in Neriak, kill Elven slaves.

Who do you hate? Others can raise their faction with Dark Elves by killing Halflings.

Freeport Faction. Try the "Note" quests in the tunnels of Freeport — this will raise your faction standing with the guards in Freeport (as well as some in Qeynos).

Trouble with Freeport shops? Seek out Pardor the Blessed and the Shady Swashbuckler.

DE Faction is initially dubious with most other races, but eventually (specifically, by killing lots of Crushbone Orcs), even the other Elves can become amiable. The Orcs are a double-edged sword, however, so only do that if you've left Neriak for good.

Completing evil-oriented quests in Neriak will raise faction with the guards there.

Choose not to choose. Agnostics get poorer service in Neriak than followers of Innoruuk. However, Agnostics do better with most other races than followers of the Prince of Hate.

Agnostics can sometimes get guards in Neriak friendly by getting them drunk. Give them bottle after bottle of red wine (especially the one guarding the letter of Innoruuk), and they'll eventually be friendlier.

Pet death. If you hide while you have a pet, it commits suicide. But, if you move so that your pet can't "see" you, it won't kill itself.

EverQuest: The Ruins of Kunark

Dwarf

Life after death. If you die as a Dwarf, you don't resurrect in your home city; instead, end up in your home playing zone (the Butcherblock).

Sense heading. Dwarves have a great sense of direction, so use Sense Heading as much as you can early on. Learn your starting area before you wander out into the wild, and always know which direction is "safe."

Warrior. Because of their size, Dwarves are harder to hit in combat. Combine this with nearly unmatched Strength (Ogres have more), and you've got a great Warrior.

As a Dwarven Warrior, you can wear a full suit of bronze armor — no other race can do so.

Paladin. Dwarves are an overlooked class for the most part — examine the stats, and you'll see why they make great Paladins.

Faction. Take on the Bone Chip quest early (talk to NPCs near the Paladin guild in Kaladim) — it'll boost your level and give you some notable items.

Rogue/Cleric. Dwarven Rogues and Clerics benefit most from practicing on a single weapon. Good trade skills are Tailoring and later, Blacksmithing.

Short legs. For obvious reasons, Dwarves have a hard time running away from their opponents.

Erudite

Max it out. You're better off allocating lots of points to Intelligence at the outset, since this determines your maximum mana at higher levels.

Blind, blind, blind. Erudites lack the ability to see in the dark, greatly limiting their powers at night. This makes the Tox forest area quite an obstacle for low-level characters.

Ripped. Due to their rude manners, Erudites often get bum deals from merchants in other towns. This is a good argument to keep your bind point set to Erudin. Hometown shops do have their advantages.

Get the goodies. If you chose Quellios as your deity, Erudites can find a lot of quests at the Temple of Quellios. Some of them can even be completed more than once.

Pick it up. Because they're so intelligent, Erudites have no problem with the learning curve, and can pick up something in no time flat. Languages? No problem. Skills? Even less of a problem.

Hunting. Some Erudites prefer to do their low-level killing in Qeynos or Halas — they claim that the loot's better there.

However, if you're an Erudite Necromancer, don't go to Qeynos directly. The guards will kill you on sight. You can, however, take a boat and dive off before it docks. Under the dock, there's an entrance to the Qeynos aqueduct system.

Gnome

Steamfont, again? If you die as a Gnome, you don't go back to your home city; instead, you resurrect in your home playing zone (the Steamfont Mountains).

Just that kind of face. Gnomes are an extremely neutral race, so merchants everywhere will deal with you.

Like a viper. Gnomes can strike fast in combat and move out of the way even faster.

Infravision. Gnomes can see other creatures in the dark, but have a hard time making out the terrain.

Sitting ducks. As cruel as it seems, you can hunt at the Ak'Anon zoo. This doesn't fall favorably upon your standing with the "good" citizens, but the Dark Reflection faction sure likes you afterward.

Five-finger discount. Gnomes make good Rogues, especially if you allocate a lot of ability points to intelligence. (That helps you learn skills more quickly at higher levels.)

Auto-evade. Gnomes hardly ever have to duck while running — quite useful in some cases.

Half Elf

Take a measurement. Half Elves can only wear only medium-sized armor.

Lazy levelers. Half Elves earn experience more slowly than non-hybrid races. They just do.

Career counseling. This isn't the smartest race — so choose an occupation that gives more wisdom, or allocate more points to it.

Track for cash. Half Elves can Track. Other characters will often pay handsomely for you to locate a specific creature.

Moonlight serenade. Half Elves make good Bards due to their high Charisma. The only other race that can yield Bards is Human, and Half Elves are have infravision ....

Halfling

Now you see them ... Halflings are the best at Sneaking and Hiding — a great asset for those that exhibit Roguish behavior or who just like to have fun with their group.

Lazy Levelers, also. One drawback Halflings have is that they earn experience more slowly than most other races, except Half Elves. It's that confused blood-line.

Shrub-huggers. According to many players, Halfling Druids are a great race/class combination.

Easy to miss. Halflings have good Dexterity and Agility, so they're able to evade shots and don't get hit as often in combat.

Home sweet home. Halflings are very fond of their home continent. Even those that wander about Norrath eventually return home.

EverQuest: The Ruins of Kunark

High Elf

Sharp as daggers. High Elves are true masters of magic because they possess both high Wisdom and Intelligence, something no other race can claim.

Frail as toothpicks. As a High Elf, you have to learn to travel light. Your frail back just can't take any excess weight. So, try to find a weightless container as soon as you can.

Talk in tongues. Remember, you can speak Elven. Take advantage of this when you need to be discreet.

Faction. Faction standing can sometimes be a problem for High Elves who wish to visit darker cities associated with Ogres, Trolls and Dark Elves.

On the flip side, High Elves don't have the faction problems that Dark Elves do. Humans find you dubious, Dwarven merchants don't really like you, and Gnomes don't especially like conversing with you, but they won't kill you on sight.

Most High Elves are killed on sight at Oggok and Neriak, but if your nature is rather dark, you might get in by killing the right enemies.

Human

Allocating points. Humans are about as center-of-the-road as you can get. That's not a bad thing, it's just a starting place. There are lots of items that will help buff up whatever abilities are best for the chosen class.

Melee types should make fast friends with casters for buffs, and casters should make friends with Enchanters, for charmed jewelry.

Monks. Humans are one of only two races whose members can become Monks. They're the only monks who don't have major faction issues.

Human Monks can hit more often and avoid hits more often than most other race/class combinations.

Level up. Yes, it's true — Humans earn experience more quickly than other races.

Humans are quite popular in a group setting because they tend to increase level (level up) quickly. This means you have more friends ... but also more competition.

Night-blind. One major disadvantage to being Human is the lack of Night Vision. If you want light as a low-level character, you have to carry a lantern, fire beetle eye or some other light source. At higher levels, you can gain items or spells that help you see.

Remember that no-drop candle, and don't worry about using it up. It lasts forever.

Iksar

Master taunters. There is no better race than the Iksar for sheer taunting ability — they have Dual Wield from the outset. To add extra oomph to the skill, try an Iksar Monk. Yowza!

Grow another one. Iksar have regenerative powers. Like Ogres, they're hard to keep down. As soon as they get up, Tanks should be ready to do quick damage, and Casters should have the next spell locked and loaded.

Aqua lizard. Iksar are excellent swimmers, right off the bat. That's helpful more often than should be expected. Keep in mind that even though Norrath port cities always have water-entrances through sewers or whatnot, even the dark races residing within aren't friendly.

Know the score. Iksar are a remarkably rounded-out race ... not short, not weak, not night-blind. They've got an extra attack (the tail), can Dual Wield, and are excellent tanks and casters. The drawback, and it's a big drawback, is that they're universally despised and feared. Of course, that has it's own charm, in a way.

Forage. Lizards aren't particular about what they eat ... or rather, what they like isn't too hard to find. Extra legs don't bother them, shall we say. Practice up, and pretty soon living off the land will be much better than trying to buy provisions from foreign merchants who — let's say it one more time — all hate Iksar.

Train the tail. Iksar are the only one who can flail a tail ... work it for all it's worth.

Stay at home. There are many quests, and *lots* of hunting in Kunark. Curious Iksars should be dead certain they're ready to face a hostile world — in a large group — before starting off to explore the rest of Norrath.

Don't trust anyone. Just because an Iksar is a "dark" race, it doesn't mean that other dark races are friendly. Nobody likes you, and you don't like anyone else. Gregarious Iksars should stay outside the city limits and see if any passing groups are looking for a scaly tank or caster.

Put it off. Avoid the Dreadlands and the Frontier Mountains — neither place is safe for an Iksar.

Ogre

Slice 'em. Concentrate on two-handed slash weapons. They'll give better results than others. Carry a lot of bandages for battlefield healing, and set off for a good solo session.

Strong but slow. Ogres have the highest base hit point value, which means they can absorb a lot of blows. However, Ogres aren't so hot at evading strikes.

Play porter. Ogres can carry an amazing amount of loot. Make friends with powerful casters by offering to carry their extra stuff.

Bash 'em. Ogres can naturally Slam their opponents, and can greatly improve Slam by practicing Bash. (Of course, that's only after a few levels. Shamans don't get Bash at all.)

Don't eat your friends. Ogres aren't liked much by others — perhaps because they enjoy munching on their opponents. But people who can forge a friendship with an Ogre, actually find them extremely helpful.

Got problem wit dat? Ogres have a small vocabulary, which is a lot of fun to work with.

Train at home. Don't travel beyond Oggok, Grobb and Neriak until you've leveled up a bit — merchants elsewhere don't like to sell to you. Some NPCs will even kill you on sight.

Don't eat the merchants, either. Ogres usually get bad prices in other towns due to low Charisma ... or just because merchants elsewhere figure they're too dumb to notice.

Gotta hate stumpies. Other races can improve their standing with Ogres by smashing up Dwarven slaves in Crushbone.

Troll

Keep coming back. Trolls can regenerate health amazingly fast — and that's even without regen items, that is.

Surprise slam. Trolls have the natural ability to see in the dark and Slam their opponents.

Ultra tank. In the Strength and Stamina department, Trolls are surpassed only by Ogres.

Ultra dumb. Trolls learn skills more slowly than other races — this should come as no surprise, given their lack of intelligence.

Slaughter and scavenge. The Innothule swamp near Grobb is a good source of loot, especially if there are high-level characters around. Many of those who stick around would rather give away useless goods than go visit a merchant to sell them.

Go shopping. Grobb doesn't have many of the items you need to develop specific trade skills (like an oven or forge). Check out the neighboring city of Oggok … and make sure you're nice to the bouncer guards there so that you don't get forcefully evicted.

Wood Elf

Don't look down. Wood Elves live in a treetop city. Yes, trees. High up, off the ground. Take care not to fall off any ledges — it'll kill you until you've gained a few levels and upped your maximum health points.

One way to keep an eye on the ever-present ledge is to pan your view down slightly.

Stat build. If you're one of the weaker Wood Elf classes (like a Druid), boost up your Strength at the start. It'll really help later and keep you from having to tote around tons of Strength-boosting equipment.

Hand-me-downs. Wood Elves can wear small or medium armor. This can be an advantage, since other races often accidentally buy armor sizes they can't wear. What better way to get it off their hands than to hand it over to a friendly Wood Elf?

Nice froggie. Don't kill Frogloks unless you want trouble later.

Skill Balance. Practice your 1H and 2H skills in equal increments so that you'll keep both of them approximately the same level. If the disparity is too great, you might find yourself in trouble during battle.

Weight balance. Because of your weight limitations, you often have to choose between carrying equipment to protect yourself or staying light enough on your feet to run.

Slow Rangers. Wood Elf Rangers gain experience more slowly than other Ranger races.

EverQuest Tactics

By Gary Grobson

Solo Tactics

There are several tactics available to those wishing to engage monsters without the assistance of another character. The use of these is highly dependent upon what class you are playing. While *EverQuest* is designed as a massive multi-player online game, there are times when strong characters can take matters into their own hands with a favorable outcome. See **Solo Tactics**, page 174.

Overpowering Your Enemy — Beginner Difficulty

This is designed for the melee classes in the game. While it's extremely difficult in the higher levels to gain experience by simple brute force, at lower levels it can be done quiet easily. It's a simple enough tactic: hit target with weapon, repeat.

If you are stronger then your foe, you will be victorious. This is the simplest of all soloing tactics, but don't expect it to remain this simple at higher levels for those in melee classes. Eventually all melee classes will need the assistance of at least another player to gain experience in *EverQuest*.

Root and Direct Damage — Moderate Difficulty

This is designed for the primary casters with capability of completely stopping the movement of an enemy.

Root and Nuke works best when you surprise your target by rooting it, then hitting it with the best direct damage spells available. For this to work correctly, you must have enough mana to convert into direct damage to dismiss your target. Be ready to cast root again, because assault of a target with Direct Damage has been known to break the root spell, and you will need to reapply it to do this tactic correctly.

If you run out of mana, you have basically two choices: Fight or Flight. Most casters are not the masters of melee combat, and can be crushed easily in a hand-to-hand situation. If the mob is low enough on health, and you believe that if you can take him down by hitting him with your staff or dagger, feel free to engage the enemy and hope for the best. If you do not believe that you can handle the wounded target in melee combat, then flee. It is better to run and get more mana, or to let a guard finish you target, then it is to lose experience to an untimely death.

Kiting —
Moderate Difficulty

This is the term that was given to the tactic of constructive fleeing. There are many spells that will affect the movement rate of the target. *Snare*, *Darkness*, and *Bonds of Force* are all examples of spells that will make your target move a lot slower then normal. This tends to upset the target, and it will give chase. The concept behind the tactic is to stay far enough away from the target that you can cast a spell on the target before the distance between the two are closed.

The best class suited to this tactic is the druid. Normally Druids have speed-enhancing spells on them, such as *Spirit of Wolf*, which allows them to move faster then normal. Combined with the fact that the target mob will have a speed-reducing spell placed upon them, this gives the Druid the advantage of speed.

Running from the target, and releasing a spell against the creature that does either direct damage, or damage over time, then fleeing again before being able to be hit is the secrets to kiting.

Reverse-Kiting —
Advanced Tactic

This came into existence when Necromancers found a way to take the tactic of kiting, and refine it to a safer and more efficient way of killing. The secret to this tactic is to start kiting a mob, but cast *Fear* on it instead of *Root*. This way, instead of the mob chasing you and able to do damage (if it catches you), you are chasing the mob and able to do damage to it. A "feared" mob won't fight if it can run — so don't root it. What's even better, a feared mob that is running while simultaneously being attacked by a pet has damage being done to it constantly.

There is a standard way to reverse-kite:

1. Get a high-speed spell placed upon you.

2. Cast a speed-reducing spell on the target.

3. Cast *Fear* on the mob.

4. Sic the pet on the target.

5. Stack DOTS on the creature to seal its fate while staying far enough back to cast *Fear* if the spell wears

This will normally finish the Reverse-Kiting.

Reverse Kiting by far is the most advanced and efficient way to solo a monster. The only drawback is the fact that doing this in any zone except an outdoor area can lead to the mob finding help. Having three more monsters jump into the equation drastically reduces the survivability quota of any reverse-kiting character.

Class-Specific Solo Tactics

By Gary Grobson

Bard

Don't do it. Yes, it's possible, but Bards need friends (read: an audience) to be at their best. The best advice for soloing would be, play a haste song, don't stop for long enough to get into trouble, and just explore.

Cleric

Clerics are limited to soloing undead most of the time, an area in which they shine.

By using root followed by undead direct damage, a Cleric can usually overcome most undead at similar levels. Out of all the other classes, only the Necromancer has similar firepower against undead.

Since undead are abundant all over the realm of Norrath, this class can do well in many areas. Considering the high demand for Clerics, there is little need for this class to solo, but it is possible when conditions are right.

Druid

Druids are the masters of kiting. By using combinations of snare, DOTS and DDs, they can solo from early levels all the way up.

If soloing, keep the Druid outdoors, where there powers really shine, because kiting in dungeons is hazardous to any Druid.

EverQuest: The Ruins of Kunark

Enchanter

Enchanters have the ability to completely cripple a target by decreasing their abilities to the point of feebleness. Keep in mind, of course, that even though the creature may be feeble, it's still not dead yet.

While Enchanters get pets, these don't respond to commands, so the Enchanter must be attacked before the pet acts.

Enchanters are adequate at doing "Root Bombing," but have a special way of soloing some creatures. This is to charm a creature and having it attack another one. The trick is to keep at least one charmed at all times, because if the charmed creature breaks free of the spell, they will both come to attack the Enchanter. Note that a clever Enchanter will assist the charmed NPC, because if it loses, the Enchanter gets no experience.

If the charmed NPC (pet) wins, it may be heavily wounded, so when it breaks free of the spell it can be killed for experience.

Magician

Magicians can summon the best pets in Norrath, despite what Necromancers say.

Having the strongest pets means good soloing. The idea is a modified root and DD (by having the pet do the rooting), or keeping the monster taunted to the point the NPC is as good as rooted. At that point, the trick is to kill the NPC before it kills your pet. By accomplishing this, you stay alive.

If multiple NPC creatures become aggro on your pet, you can have the pet take the heat while you make a run for safety.

Monk

Monks also are most suited to using the overpowering tactic for soloing. They are pure fighters, strong and fast.

The advantages to the Monk over the Warrior are the skills of Mend and Feign Death. If a Monk gets into trouble, the first skill in a Monk's arsenal of abilities is Mend. While this skill is much more effective at higher levels, it will immediately heal a lot of hit points, possibly turning the tide of the battle.

The advantage of the Monk at higher levels is that an escape route may not be necessary. Feign Death is the ability to play dead and have the assaulting mob believe you have ceased to exist. Many times this will save the Monk's life. Constantly practice Feign Death, because many a Monk has died when his display of death was a little less then convincing then it should have been. Practice makes perfect.

Necromancer

Necromancers are the most lethal of all solo characters. Regardless of zone, dungeon, town, outdoor, indoor, or no door, this class can handle the heat.

With both *Feign Death* (level 16) and *Harmshield* (level 20), they are the only class with 2 get-out-of-death-free cards. This is not to belittle the power of *Gate*, *Shadowstep*, speed reducing spells, *Fear*, and *Screaming Terror*.

Very experienced Necromancers, even with solo, should not die very often, and if they do many times will be the result of a failed skill, a fizzled spell, or a misjudged distance or creature.

Necromancers can do every form of soloing except brute force, which they have no reason to do except at the earliest of levels, before their pets become skeletal powerhouses.

It is not uncommon to find Necromancers who haven't touched a creature with melee past level 12. Use any of the basic (spell and *Feign Death*) or advanced soloing techniques (see **Solo Tactics**, page 174), including the rare charm spells ala the Enchanters — all will work well with Necromancers.

Paladin

Paladins are the opposite of Shadow Knights in many ways, and are designed to survive attacks better then the other Melee Classes and Hybrids. They not only have the high hit points, they can heal themselves when necessary. Thus the Paladin defies death over and over to continue his crusade against his target.

Often going up against undead is a much better choice for soloing with a Paladin, because of the Direct Damage (some specifically anti-undead) spells blessed upon a Paladin by his or her god.

Use stuns and *Yaulp* at moderate to higher levels.

Ranger

Rangers are suited not only to overpowering tactics, but can also use some of the Root and Direct Damage tactics at higher levels.

They are the masters of the use of the Bow, and can hit for damage at a distance from a rooted mob, or use many arrows in kiting them without use of much mana.

Rangers should familiarize themselves with their surroundings and use outdoor areas to their advantage.

Rogue

Rogues are a non-caster melee class. The Rogue does the less damage compared than other pure melee classes at lower levels, but have increased abilities and skills in other areas that make them a joy to play.

By using Hide, a Rogue steps into shadows. By using Sneak, he stays hidden and creeps on his opponent. The idea is to cause an extreme amount of damage at the start and hope to survive the rest of the fight. While this is still overpowering the target, there is a lot more skill involved in playing a Rogue.

If you have the ability to apply poison, do so for the initial attack. This way, you are backstabbing, inflicting a poison, and catching your target off guard. Rogues are very good at disarming an opponent, so if your enemy has a weapon, take it.

Keep your eye on an escape route just in case the fight goes sour, and remember that Rogue's primary role is in a group, not as a solo artist.

Shadow Knight

Shadow Knights are designed as the most offensive class in the game. Everything about a Shadow Knight is based around overpowering your target with a great combination of strength, spells, pets, lifetaps, and brute force tactics.

The Shadow Knights are great at terrorist tactics, and have a modified reverse-kiting that is both dangerous and efficient at higher levels.

1. Start off with a *Darkness-series* spell, to slow your opponent.

2. Follow it quickly by a *Fear* spell, and command your pet to attack the target.

3. Chase the creature and engage it in melee by hitting it in the back.

4. Make sure you recast *Darkness* and *Fear* before they wear out if possible

Simply bully your target to death.

If the situation turns sour, remind the target that you are a Shadow Knight, and don't take kindly to a counterattack by Harm Touching the creature, which will normally turn the tide of battle in a solo fight back to the side of the Shadow Knight.

Shaman

Shamans are the "jack of all trades," and until higher levels, the master of none. This makes their soloing presence limited to "blue" mobs most of the time.

They can kite, but will normally run out of mana and end up having to engage the NPC near the end of the fight in melee.

Another class that is usually in high demand for groups, Shamans should limit soloing at least until their first pet spell.

Warrior

There is but one efficient Solo Tactic for a Warrior, and that is to overpower the foe within a melee battle.

When dealing with dangerous targets, have an escape route in mind. This escape route should take you to the nearest creatures that are hostile to the target you are fighting, such as Guards, or to the nearest Zone border.

Soloing is a great way to make experience, but remember that deaths reduce the amount of experience gained quickly.

Wizard

Wizards are the masters of Direct Damage. By using their *Root* spell in combination with direct damage, they are a force to be reckoned with.

While casters at higher levels can kite using *Bonds of Force* instead of *Root*, the most effective way still is Root-Direct damage.

At higher levels, they take Root-Direct Damage tactics to new extremes. "Room-Bombing" as it is affectionately known to some of the Wizards is a very viable way to level.

However, be careful. "Root Bombing" a creature that another player is already engaging is called "Kill Stealing" and seriously looked down upon by other players. Solo Wizards are the most notorious for "Kill Stealing," and those that use this tactic often find themselves at high levels, but with a terrible reputation and no one to group with to take out creatures for high level experience and items.

Group Tips & Tactics

by Lawrence Poe

Bard

When it comes to joining groups, Bards are one of the best classes in the game. They are 100% group oriented. When grouped, Bards need to analyze their list of songs and play the ones that best suit the occasion.

When traversing Norrath, a good way to make quick time is to designate one person in the group as the point man and have the others (Bard included) use the /FOLLOW command. Once you get moving, the Bard can play his level five song *Selo`s Accelerando*, which increases movement rate. This way the Bard never gets ahead of the party and no one gets out of range of his song.

In combat, Bards have many choices to make when it comes to what songs to play. The Chant series, which starts with the level 1 song *Chant of Battle*, will add to your party's combat stats of Strength, Dexterity, Agility and AC. These songs get increasingly more powerful and eventually start adding group haste. There are also songs that add to the party's resistance to Fire, Cold, Magic, Disease, and Poison. Another option that the Bard can choose is the Debuff songs: songs that, while not doing damage to enemies, will make it much harder for the enemy to hurt the party. Some of these songs are the

level 8 song *Kelin's Lugubrious Lament* which lowers the target's attack speed, and the level 23 song *Selo's Consonant Chain* which lowers the target's movement rate and keeps runners at bay.

Bards can also aid in downtime. When not in combat, Bards should play the level 6 *Song Hymn of Restoration* to help the party regain hit points faster. Some higher-level songs will help the casters of the group regain mana faster, and they usually stack with the Enchanter spell *Clarity*. Some other very useful songs for Bards are *Tarew's Aquatic Ayre* (grants party water breathing), *Shauri's Sonorous Clouding* (grants the party invisibility), and later on there's even a song for levitation.

Song "stacking" or "twisting" is another important tactic for Bards. To do this you start a song and wait for the message indicating the song has started, then start the next song. That means both songs will be affecting your party at the same time. At the most you can have four songs stacked — if you are very skilled in the art — and the songs you wish to stack have the right casting times.

The most important thing every Bard needs to understand is that he amplifies the party. The Bard songs can give the party a major advantage over any enemies they face. Because of this the Bard should always try to remain out of danger of death, sometimes this means staying back from combat unless absolutely necessary.

Cleric

Clerics are responsible for the health of the party. Their main job is to keep everyone alive — which is not a job for the faint of heart, or the easily panicked. For a Cleric, the most efficient way to heal your party members is to use the F keys to select your teammates, as sometimes in a high lag or hectic situation it's difficult to target people with the mouse cursor. Another trick is to face away from the action: by not facing the fight you cut down on the video lag and are able to get your spells off faster.

Clerics can do more than just heal, they also have the best hit point and armor class buffs in Norrath. Before and during a battle, they need to make sure the party is always buffed with the hit point, Symbol and armor class lines of buffs. Other spells that the priest needs to be aware of are the Stun line of spells. These spells are very useful as they prevent melee enemies from attacking the party, and when fighting casters, Stun interrupts their spells.

Clerics also get Direct Damage spells — although while these spells do a fair amount of damage they should only be used when absolutely necessary. The problem with DD spells is they attract unwanted attention to the Cleric. Instead, when Clerics are attacked they should try to back away, hoping the NPC will leave them alone. However, if an enemy continues to attack, *do not run*. Instead, stand still (yes, you can yell for help) so the tanks of the group can attack and taunt the enemy away. Running just means the melee types of the group will have to chase the enemy around, and that just makes it harder for them to taunt it/kill it.

Druid

Druids are another group-friendly class: they have hit point buffs, heal spells, damage shield, stat buffs and resistance buffs. When playing a Druid you should always keep a damage shield (such as *Shield of Thistles*) on the melee fighters in the group, as well as something from the regeneration line of spells (like *Invigor*).

Druids also need to make sure to use the spell *Snare* on any NPC the group is fighting. When the NPC is snared, it can't run when it becomes low on health. Snaring creatures will significantly reduce the number of trains the party has to deal with, since it can't get away to group with its friends.

Another very useful group tactic for Druids is kiting. (See **Kiting**, page 175.) When fighting in a group, and the group has more than one opponent, the Druid can snare any Extra NPCs and kite them until the party has finished the one they are currently fighting.

Enchanter

Enchanters are very useful in groups: they have the ability to buff the party, as well as debuff any NPCs the party is fighting. They are also excellent at crowd control.

When grouping, it is important to make sure you use your Haste spells on all melee classes in the group: these spells will increase their attack rate, allowing them to kill NPCs faster. Just as the Enchanters should be "hasting" their party, they should also be slowing their opponents using the *Languid Pace* spells. These spells work the opposite of the haste spells: they lessen the amount of damage the NPC can do to the party. When grouped with other casters, Enchanters should always use the *Tashani* spells to lower the NPCs magic resistance. The *Rune* line of spells adds magical damage-absorbing skin to the target — this spell can be very useful on melee types who need extra "armor" to make a tough pull. Another, and perhaps the most popular Enchanter spell is a higher-level enchantment to increase the rate at which mana is regenerated, an absolute must have for any high level caster.

Buffs aside, the most important tactic for group play of an Enchanter is playing "traffic cop." When the party is facing multiple enemies, the Enchanter can use the level 4 spell *Mesmerize* to render the excess opponents unable to move. This tactic is key for breaking spawns up so that you can pull one or two at a time. It can also be used to give a Wizard or Druid time to get off a Group Gate spell.

Magician

Magicians are the master summoners of Norrath. They pull something out of nothing ... that's their job.

They can summon weapons for Corpse recovery or party members' pets, they can summon food and drink, and they can summon pets of their own. Magicians also pack fairly good damage spells, second only to the Wizard, in fact.

Magicians also have the best damage shields. It's always worth the mana and time it takes to cast damage shields on the melee fighters, especially since the damage shield does damage to the attacker.

When in groups, Magicians should choose what pet to summon based on the opponents they will be facing. When fighting NPCs that are mainly casters, the Air Elemental needs to be used — it casts spells that interrupt the NPC's spellcasting. When in groups where Magician's pet will be doing a lot of heavy fighting, the Earth Elemental is a good choice: it has the most hit points. Fire Elementals cast a damage shield on itself, so it also is useful when your pet will be tanking. Lastly is the Water Elemental, the middleman, which is the all-around pet that can be used in any situation.

Monk

Monks in *EverQuest* are very good at melee combat, great scouts, and excellent pullers. When in a group, the Monk should always be the scout. Once she has the ability to feign death — so the NPCs think the Monk is dead and leave her alone — she is a puller beyond compare. (Feign Death means no accidental trains.)

Feign Death has more than one use, though. It's also good for clearing the path of hostile creatures. When entering a new area, the Monk can run into a hostile area, attract the attention of any NPCs blocking the party's path, lead them away, and then Feign Death so the party has time to get past.

Another trick involving Feign Death is the Feign pull. In this process, the Monk will go to a group of NPCs and attack. She will lead the NPCs away a bit, then Feign Death. The NPCs will wander off, one by one, while the Monk waits patiently. When only one is left, she'll get back up and return to the group This tactic can be very useful for breaking up a spawn in a dungeon.

Necromancer

Necromancers can summon skeletons as their pets — the higher the Necro's level, the stronger the skeleton. When playing in a group, Necromancers should never be without their pets, since it's a tough melee fighter, and a big help in a fight.

Necromancers are the masters of Damage Over Time spells. However, it is important to remember not to stack all of your DOT spells on the NPC at once, since if you do this the NPC will decide it *really* wants to kill you, and be very hard to taunt away.

Necromancer *Lifetap* spells should be used any time the Necromancer has taken damage. You can't ask for better than a spell that does damage to the NPC as well it gives HP back to the Necromancer. The first DOT the Necromancer should cast is the DOT *Lifetap* spell. At higher levels, there are more powerful spells in the *Lifetap* category.

Disease spells can be used to negate an opponent's ability to regain hit points, so these spells should usually be cast early in a fight.

Paladin

Paladins are a hybrid class — a cross between a melee fighter and caster. As a "tank," it is a Paladin's responsibility to make use of the Taunt skill to attract the attention of an opponent onto them.

When fighting one-handed and using a shield, Paladins need to keep an eye open for NPCs casting spells. Whenever the NPC tries to cast, the Paladin needs use his Bash skill to interrupt the NPC's casting.

Paladins are also like Clerics. Paladins can use combat spells, unless there's a "real" Cleric in the group. Paladins can cast spells to renew hit points, and buff the armor class of the party, although the spells they have will always be of lesser effectiveness than the spells of a same-level Cleric.

Paladins also should make use of the Stun line of spells. A stunned opponent is unable to attack, or in the case of a caster, has her casting interrupted.

Paladins also get heal spells, and in times may be called on to heal party members. Frankly, this should always be the last resort since Paladins are not very efficient healers.

Finally, the Paladin has the innate ability to Lay Hands once per day. With Laying of Hands, the Paladin can completely heal himself or a party member. This can be invaluable in matters of life and death.

Ranger

Rangers are also a hybrid class — part melee fighter and part spell caster.

As a "Tank" it is the Ranger's primary responsibility is to use the taunt skill to attract the attention of any opponent away from the frail casters. Rangers can also use the Kick skill to interrupt enemy casting.

Rangers receive Druid spells as well as some spells unique to their class. Druid-type spells can buff the party's Strength and Agility. At later levels, Rangers have access to heal spells, though like Paladins, Rangers should only be called on to heal as a last resort. Rangers eventually get the ability to cast *Spirit of the Wolf*. This spell increases movement rate and is highly sought after by citizens of Norrath. *SOW* can be useful when fighting in outdoor areas, as it will allow the party members to run for the zone should an NPC prove too strong for them.

During fights, Rangers should always make use of the *Snare* spells. By casting *Snare* on an opponent the Ranger can prevent it from running away and getting help from other NPCs, thus drastically cutting down the number of trains the party has to tackle.

Rangers should freely use their direct damage and damage over time spells while in combat, because not only do these damage an opponent, but they also help the Ranger taunt creatures away from casters. The Damage over time spells will also help kill any runners that get away.

Rogue

Rogues are excellent party members. They can do the most single-blow damage of any class in Norrath, and due to their ability to Sneak and Hide they make very good scouts.

When in combat, Rogues should always watch for opportunities to Backstab, since the Backstab attack delivers much more damage than a regular attack. In fact, Rogues should explain to the rest of the group that they should fight *away* from the Rogue, to increase the Backstab opportunities.

When fighting NPC spell casters, Rogues should watch for the casting message, then circle behind the NPC and deliver a Backstab — NPCs cannot turn while casting spells. Rogues get the ability to Disarm at level 27. They should try to make use of this skill when facing armed opponents, since a disarmed NPC does much less damage.

Shadow Knight

Shadow Knights are a melee/caster class.

It is a Shadow Knight's duty to taunt the opponent away from weaker casters and onto himself. They have the hit points to take the blows.

When fighting single-handed, Shadow Knights should use their shield to Bash. Bashing interrupts an enemy's casting, rendering them unable to complete their spells.

Shadow Knight spells are primarily offensive. They should always use *Siphon Strength* to lower the opponent's strength while simultaneously raising their own. They have access to several damage over time spells. These spells will help kill runners that get away. Damage spells, especially the higher-level ones, should always be cast when fighting, not only because they do damage but because they also help to taunt NPCs away from regular magic-users.

All Shadow Knights have the innate ability to Harm Touch once per day. Harm Touch delivers a massive amount of damage to the target. This ability should be reserved for matters of life or death, since you don't get more than one at a time. Shadow Knights also have the spell Feign Death, which allows them to pull NPCs the same ways Monks do.

Shaman

When in groups, a Shaman should always make sure to buff the party with Stat buffs, haste buffs, and the Talisman line of spells (to add hit points). Shamans should always focus on debuffing opponents with their Slow spells (such as *Drowsy*), and *Malise* which lowers the enemy's resistances.

Shamans also have an assortment of direct damage spells and damage over time spells, but these should only be used after they have debuffed the enemy and the tanks have had sufficient time to taunt the NPCs away.

Shamans also have access to the heal spells — though not as good as a Cleric — and they can heal fairly efficiently. In situations where the Shaman is playing the healer role, the Shaman should make use of the F keys to target group mates when casting heals on them. (See **Cleric**, this section, page 181.)

Warrior

Warriors are the true tanks of Norrath. They have the most hit points, their armor yields the best armor class, and the weapons they can use weapons do the most damage. Tanks are best used to protect the magic users, although they are also the front-runners, first to wade into battle.

When in groups, Warriors should always use the Taunt skill to attract the attention of all NPCs that the party is engaging, excepting any that are mesmerized.

Warriors should also make use of the Kick skill to interrupt casting of NPCs.

Warriors make good pullers because they have the most hit points, and unless there is a Monk or a Shadow Knight in the group they should handle all pulling responsibilities.

Wizard

Wizards are the masters of offensive spells, although they're painfully low in hit points.

In groups, Wizards have two roles, Nuker and Group Gate maker.

Wizards should always allow the melee types to dish out around 20 percent damage to an opponent before casting. Once this has happened, the Wizard can begin to throw direct damage spells at the opponent, *cautiously*. Caution must be used since too many direct damage spells cast in succession will anger the NPC onto them.

At higher levels, Wizards also have a stun line of spells, which should be used (and used often) to prevent NPCs from attacking. Stuns also work as an interruption for NPC spell casting.

Should an NPC aggro on the Wizard it is important not to run, since running will make it harder for the tanks to taunt the enemy off of you.

The other function of Wizards in groups is group gating. There are two types of group gate, Portal and Evacuate. Evacuate spells have shorter casting times, but there is a greater chance that someone will be left behind. Portal spells are usually the better choice because the chance of someone being left behind is greatly reduced. Wizards should always have one of these spells memorized and ready to go.

Multi-Group Tactics

by Gary Grobson

There are times and places where a single group is just not strong enough to handle the task at hand. Examples of these are Dragons, Gods and high-level dungeon "Bosses." For these types of usually high-level encounters, multi-group tactics must be used. There are many differences between single group and multi-group tactics. Setup, Deployment, and Communications are the biggest factors to a successful engagement.

Setup

For almost all cases, four groups of six (24 players in all), working together can handle almost any single encounter. At this point, setup of these groups becomes more necessary then total numbers. A group of twenty-four dedicated, and well-communicating players can easily accomplish more then 100 independent players. This has been proven many times in the Lands of Norrath. Keep in mind, the common rules of balanced parties do not always apply to multi-group tactics. There can be specialized groups made up of certain classes or roles that have a specific task assigned to them. How they are established and deployed is up to the dictates of the members of the group.

A pulling group is made up primarily of the melee classes (Monks, Warriors, Rogues) but Shadow Knights have become popular on many servers. The idea of the pull is to bring as few NPC's to the multi-group as possible, so that the victory is easy and without death.

Deployment

Deployment of the groups is depends heavily on situation. There are times that it is beneficial to "pull" an NPC from its current location to the rest of the group by a single player or a team of players, and then ambushing it will a full barrage of melee and DD attacks.

If a full attack is called for, make sure it is clearly communicated, that everyone knows, and that all groups do, in fact, engage the enemy.

Communication

Communication is key to solving the many problems that face a large group of players. The answer is to use different channels for different tasks. /SHOUT may be reserved for the overall organizer and pullers only. Have all other communications be used in either /OOC, or if everyone is in the same guild, then guildchat. This way everyone knows what is important to be heard, and nothing important is missed.

While this has become common on most servers, some of the newer servers still need to learn that this kind of communication is key to surviving and thriving in a high-risk area.

Group Etiquette

by Gary Grobson

The rewards of teamwork is one of the greatest reasons for playing *EverQuest*. However, there is much more to grouping then hitting ACCEPT and following your role.

Splitting Money

One consideration is the fact of loot. There are two types of loot in the game: coin and items. When dealing with coin, there are two acceptable ways of divvying it up. First is to simply turn on AUTOSPLIT, and let the computer do the work for you. There is only one drawback to autosplit, and that is the looter will always receive the coins that are not evenly divisible.

For this example, lets say there is a group of 4. Someone in the group loots an NPC. The NPC has 2 platinum, 3 gold, 4 silver, 5 copper. The split to the looter would be 2 platinum, 3 gold, 1 silver, 2 copper. The rest of the group would receive 1 silver and 1 copper. This is because the loot system does not "make change." You cannot split a single coin between players. This is a big issue, so keep it in mind when choosing this method.

The second method is to have one trusted member of the group loot all NPC's with autosplit off. By using the /SPLIT command, the trusted member then can split all loot at one time, and it is much more accurate to split the coin.

Splitting Items

One of the largest conflicts between groups is the handling of item treasure. When hunting creatures that have specific, named items, know beforehand how the issues of treasure allocation will be handled — just to avoid fights after the treasure has been acquired.

The most common way is to split by greatest need. For example, a Warrior has no need for a robe, or a Wizard a sword. The group should always give preference to those who can use the item before those who cannot.

If there is more then one player who has a need for an item, or an item that no one has a need for (but all would like), the most common way of distribution is the lottery system. Basically, anyone that is involved in the lottery of the item does a /ROLL 1 100. This generates a random number between 1 and 100. Whoever rolls the highest number wins the item in question.

Normally the winner of an item doesn't receive a second item until everyone else in the group has received one. This insures that the entire party profits from the adventure.

Being compassionate to the other members in the group has great benefits. Remember that everyone in the game desires the nicest items and great piles of coin. Your reputation for kindness to others will spread through Norrath, and others may base their decision on accepting you into a group — or leaving you out of a group — depending on that reputation. Dickering for and winning one nice item, at the cost of sitting out of many future groups, is a mistake that many newer adventures make ... once.

Acquiring Items

by Gary Grobson

There are four basic ways of getting items in the world of Norrath (besides being handed one from another player). Each has different difficulty levels and reward values. Knowing how to get these items is one of the enjoyable challenges that *EverQuest* provides.

Shop Goods

The most straightforward method is simply buying the item. There are hundreds of vendors in *EverQuest*, selling not only the store's own inventory, but also many items (including equipment) that other players have sold to the vendors. If you've got the coin, this is a simple way to get the basic items that any player needs to survive.

There is also a very large player driven economy on *EverQuest*, and in many cities you will find items for sale by use of the /AUCTION channel. Learning the "street" value of items before purchasing or selling anything is something that takes a while to get used to, but there are many players who take pride in making money simply through trade.

Treasure

The next easiest means of item acquisition is treasure. You need a sword, an NPC that you can defeat in front of you, and a victory. Defeat the NPC in battle, and whatever prize it's carrying shall be yours.

Knowing where the most desired items in the game are comes from much exploration. These are the items that must be won, that have great stories behind them.

Handmade Items

Making items with "Trade Skills" can be confusing at first, but the items will be imbued with pride and value to the person making them. Armor, jewelry, bows, and many other kinds of items can be made by players who have practiced the right skills.

Be warned that NPC vendors in *EverQuest* aren't going to sell an item for less than they would pay for it. Therefore be advised that you simply cannot make items and sell them to vendors for a profit. You make profit by selling things to other players, not NPCs.

Quest Items

Questing is what makes *EQ* as great as it is. There are quests released with the game that have yet to be figured out. There are many varieties of quest items — from things that a newer player might consider disappointingly average, to the incredible Fiery Avenger sword for Paladins. The learning, adventuring, and completion of the quest are joys of the game that players learn to love.

Note that many of the items and parts to the quest are "No Drop", which means there will be no shortcuts, or the final item will never be able to leave your inventory. New quests continue to go into the game all the time, and those first to figure them out often become part of Norrath history.

Newbie Tips

Tech it up. The Options screen has some options that may make it easier to see at night, depending on what race a player is playing. Some races (Elves, Iksar, Dwarves, Gnomes and Trolls) have special night vision abilities, but others (like Erudites) are blinder than bats at night. The Gamma slider bar can offset that problem by making things a bit brighter.

Hot Buttons

Hot Buttons make life on the run a bit easier. The first step is to open the Abilities window and assign all available skills to the Macro Buttons there.

The second step is to click and hold on frequently used buttons. A copy then "floats" on the cursor and can be dropped onto an empty slot on the left side of the interface screen. Any clickable button on the interface can be copied onto an empty slot. That button can then be pressed whenever a player needs a particular attack, spell, chat message or other function.

Combat. Combat attacks and other offensive skills are used more than just about any other buttons, so it's a good idea to copy all of those onto Hot Buttons right from the start.

Organize. Six Hot Button "banks" exist. Clicking the small number above the slots changes banks. One could be dedicated to non-combat actions (Walk/Run, Camp, Sit, Hail) while another holds spells or combat attack types.

View

Pan around. Those pesky little creatures in the newbie garden are often short and hard to keep track of during an attack. Players learn early on that panning the view around helps tremendously. Numpad ③ and ⑨, as well as the right mouse button, pan the view. Numpad ⑤ re-centers the view.

Panning the view also works particularly well when swimming underwater. The character swims in whatever direction the view is pointing.

The Big View. The large world of *EverQuest* is too big to fit in that tiny playing view, so most players opt to hit ⓪ and cycle through to an enlarged, transparent view.

Combat

Do this first, always! This is the very, very first rule of combat — and one that most players find out the hard way during their first few hours of play. MOVE THE AUTO-ATTACK KEY! There's nothing more frustrating to a new player than trying to strike up a conversation with an NPC and accidentally not bringing up the chat bar first. That means the first time you type in the letter Ⓐ, thinking that you're just talking to a merchant, you attack him. The result is a disastrous bludgeoning that leaves an ugly stain on the sidewalk and leaves the new player dazed, dead and confused.

Con as a way of life. "Conning" is not swindling ... it's just a measure of how a character stacks up against a targeted opponent. Right-clicking on any character (or person, for player-killers) displays a colored text message. For real newbies, red and yellow critters should be avoided at all costs. White and blue ones are okay (they award experience), and so are green ones (they don't give experience, but they still yield loot).

Scram. Generally, it's a smart, smart idea to run when only three or four health point bubbles remain. Unless, of course, dying sound better than running all the way back to the edge of the zone.

Not all created equal. Not all monsters that con the same color are equally easy (or challenging) to kill. Some are bigger and badder than their friends. If something seems to be taking longer to kill, it's probably one of the better specimens of the species.

Run to daddy. In most towns, guards at the gate will kill any monsters that try to run through it. Newbies quickly realize this and use it to their advantage when a train of skeletons or equally dangerous critters are chasing them.

Group Combat

The way it works. During a group fight, all members' damage is added together. After the creature dies, the entire group is awarded party experience.

If two groups are attacking something simultaneously, the group that does the most damage gets to loot the corpse.

Hate list. Monsters like to attack whoever's hitting them the hardest. Their immediate person of choice varies, and they can be "redirected" by either Taunts or blows.

All for one. During a group fight, everyone should try to keep an eye on everyone else's health bar. (The bars for all group members appear on a player's interface when he or she clicks FOLLOW to join the group.) If someone's getting slammed, that person can quit fighting for a moment (or run) and the other players can concentrate on the attack. Hopefully, the monster will focus his attack on another group member.

The greater sum. Grouping up with other players is a highly effective method of banding together to take down a monster that no one newbie can take down individually. Many a group of newbies has successfully killed off a white or yellow monster by combining their attacks.

General

Typing coordinates in the chat bar can be problematic: the positive and minus signs occasionally get dropped out. It's better to spell it out. 305.78, -200.66 would be spelled (pos)305.78 (neg)200.66.

Crying out a plea for help (/SHOUT) is one of those semi-annoying but really useful things new players can do in the game. There are tons of experienced players roaming the zone, and a good portion of them will respond to new players that are having a problem — as long as /SHOUT isn't overused.

/SHOUT is generally reserved for desperate situations. For example:

/SHOUT Where in the heck is the Warrior's Guild?!
(a newbie can't find his guild and shouts out in frustration...)

/OOC Mee notta knowa where ta find da wolfie puppies! Give da poor Ogre a tipsy?
(a new Ogre can't find a recipient for his note and speaks out of character)

/SHOUT Ack!! Incoming Skellies!!
(a new spellcaster's spell fizzled and she's just got two skeletons chasing her to the edge of the zone.)

Quests

Go to the guild. A newbie's first quest is always to find his or her guild and turn over the note in the Inventory window. This is really very easy if the new player's willing to ask around to track down the guild hall. Plus, the recipient is always happy to see new faces and usually hands out a small quest and reward item in return.

Quest again. Training is the next step after meeting the guildmaster. He (or she) will send the new player off to the next stop on the newbie journey — namely, a visit to Master So-and-So for a little training. (New players get a few freebie practices, and gain more with experience.)

The book of discord. That little book in the Inventory window may seem rather vague and useless at first, but it's really not. It's a major component of the game — if a newbie wants to join the ranks of player killers (PKs), the

book must be handed over to a Priest of Discord or similarly evil character. Most new players, though, destroy the book immediately and forget about player-killing altogether.

Dying

Dying is not a bad thing for aspiring players. In fact, until level 5, dying gives you back nearly everything you had at the start. New food, new drink, and a new little book. That's the best time to go exploring ... .

Binding. Binding is a term that often leaves new players going "Huh?" What it refers to is the spot where a character regenerates when he or she dies. Higher-level spellcasters will usually reset someone's bind point for a price upon request, or at in return for a compliment or a nice favor.

Self-looting. Dead characters do have one advantages throughout their gaming life — they can track down their body and loot it, but no one else can. (This isn't true for player-killers, who usually get some money and an item if they succeed in killing another player.)

Bodies aren't always easy to find, however.... especially if the character was lost before he or she died. So, most people choose to leave coins and really valuable stuff in the bank if they're about to venture out into dangerous or uncharted territory.

The /CONSENT command (followed by another character's name) can be given by the dead player upon resurrection. This does allow another player to loot the corpse, which can be handy if the resurrectee is miles away and the group's standing over his or her original, dead body.

Corpse-dragging. If a corpse seems irretrievable because of time or physical location, /CONSENT can be used in conjunction with /CORPSE to move the body to a better place. The resurrected player can then go loot his or her corpse and pick up everything.

Spells

Hard life. Casting spells is no easy matter — first, there's the task of scribing the spell, then there's memorizing it, and then there's practicing it until it can actually be cast without fizzling. Then there's the meditating (later on) and the finding money for spells, and so on ....

Pick and choose. The spell gem inventory slots (little cutouts on the left side of the interface screen) can hold eight memorized spells at a time. That doesn't mean magic users are limited to only eight, but it does mean that only eight can be available for casting at any given time.

Money

Baby bread. The best way to earn money at the start is to go out and kill small game, then sell the loot to merchants in the city. This should yield enough to keep a new character fed, watered and clothed through a level or two.

Items that stick. Some items are "No-Drop," which means they can't be given away, traded, sold or dropped. Usually, no-drop and lore items are part of class-specific quests. They *can* be destroyed, although that's a last-resort, usually.

Food

Despite differences in price, one type of food or drink doesn't last longer than another.

Alcohol does not count as drink. Milk, yes. Water, yes. Ale, no.

Time

Time flies by at a manic pace in *EverQuest*. First it's night, then it's day, and then it's night again. Expect to see many days go by in Norrath per one 24-hour session in front of the keyboard.

The /TIME command lets players know a) what time it is in Norrath and b) what time it is in the real world.

When a character camps and exits the game, time screeches to a halt. It still progresses in the game world, but upon returning, everything else will remain exactly the same (health, fatigue, physical location, etc.).

The only thing exempt from standstill time is a character's corpse. After death, the corpse clock starts ticking. How long the corpse takes to decay depends on the character's level, and whether the player's still logged into the game or not. Higher-level corpses last longer, and young corpses don't last long at all. The morale here is don't log out after dying!

Grouping

Organizing a Party

Looking to group with a specific race or class? Prefer to travel with characters around your level? Players can use the following commands to locate the kind of companions with whom they might like to form a party.

/WHO: This command gives players a list of the characters in their zone, the character's name, race, class, and level (unless the player is in anonymous mode, or role-playing mode, in which case it will just indicate the name). Players can also modify this command to filter out information they don't want; for example, type /WHO NECROMANCER and learn all the necromancers in the zone, or /WHO 5 to find all the level 5 players in the zone.
NOTE: At lower levels, there is no experience gain if members of your group are 3 or 4 levels above you, so knowing who is the right level is very handy.

/FRIEND <name>: This command will put (name) on the character's friend list. To see which of the friends on the list are playing, the player can type /FRIEND ALL. Players find this useful when they already have a bunch of people they like to group with and want to see if they are available.

/TELL: This command will send a private message to another player. This can be useful to ask others if they want to join the player's party without having to shout and bother everyone else in the zone.

/SHOUT: This is the easiest way to find group members, but it can be overused and annoying. Consequently, a lot of players keep /SHOUT turned off. To use, simply shout something like "/SHOUT Lvl 9 Ranger looking for party!" and wait for replies.

/GROUP, /G: This works a little like /tell, only it allows players to talk privately within their group.

/INVITE and **/DISBAND**: These are also selections on the character's interface screen. To invite someone to join the player's group, target the player and click the INVITE button. The invitee will either accept or decline. If he or she accepts, joining the player's group is automatic. To then leave the group or disband it, click the DISBAND button.

Splitting the Loot

Nothing's worse than a bunch of players standing around bickering over who gets what. The AUTOSPLIT button will help somewhat, but the non-money loot will still have to be divided by the players. Many times, the easiest way is to loot by taking turns alphabetically. Elect someone to keep track of whose turn it is to loot so there are no fights. (See also **Group Etiquette**, p. 120.)

Groups

Players should not join a group if they're only going to be able to play for less than an hour. Use those short visits to solo or explore, look for quests or just talk to NPCs.

Group Leader

Choose a group leader and let that group leader decide who will lure the creatures, who will stand back and heal players, or who will be the zone guide. That way, parties won't end up with two or more members luring beasties back to the group and suddenly having more monsters than the group can fight. Every party needs a leader to come up with quick decisions on the details so the players can get back to the fun of the game instead of arguing.

As the group leader

One of the main responsibilities of a good group leader is to make sure the entire party is following before heading off somewhere. Double- and triple-check to make sure everyone is where they're supposed to be. It's easy to get lost in Norrath ... and no one will be happy if hunting has to be suspended to find that lost group member (especially the one who got left behind)!

Group Responsibilities

Be ready. If a player joins a group to go fight at Chessboard in Butcherblock, she should be ready to go there. The prepared party members will be pretty annoyed if the dwarf has to run to Kaladim to get food/water/sell items, etc. Players should do those things before joining the group.

Wait for the casters. If they're not ready to attack a creature, no one is ready.

Let one person choose the target. One specific tank should target the next mob to be attacked, type /ASSIST and let everyone go at it at once.

Casters, don't sweat the small stuff. If the creature is an easy kill for the party, magic users should save those huge spells (and thus conserve mana) for another time.

Track everyone's hit points. If a party member's hit points are getting too low, other members of the group should taunt the creature away, cast a heal spell, or both.

Finally: Keep talking, people! Assign hot keys to common commands, if you have to, but let people know what's happening.

For More information, see **Etiquette**, page 118.

Combat

Trains

Communication. Players in a party should keep saying how many opponents are up, whether they are tough or weak opponents, what target is being attacked, and if any new monsters have popped in.

Be aware. Party members should cycle through camera angles during a fight to check for wandering beasties. Of course, players should alert their party as soon as anything hostile is sited and if it seems like it will interfere.

It's been said before: Relocate that AUTO-ATTACK hot key! The default seems to cause more attacks on friendly NPCs than on monsters!

Try this. If the character pulling the monster goes around a corner, the monster won't always follow.

Newbie alternative. Low-level Enchanters can use *Enthrall* to mesmerize 1 or 2 of the weakest monsters attacking the party. Then, the Warriors can work on the tougher ones.

Know about any magical weapons. Weapons enchanted with area of effect spells can awaken a mesmerized monster. Just when the Enchanter thinks all the monsters are asleep, a weapon in the proximity wakes one or all of them up! With 40+ level melee types, it's always good to check this beforehand.

Mesmerized Targets

If the party has an Enchanter or other class that can use Mesmerize, have her cast it upon a monster. The monster sits there, unable to fight. Mesmerize is broken if any damage is done to the creature. The /ASSIST command targets a monster that player X is fighting. If everyone in the party uses it, they can easily target a single monster and attack it simultaneously.

Tip for /ASSIST. Players should set their text macros to /ASSIST. It allows players to readily assist other party members.

NOTE: If the player is in the role of puller (See Jargon Glossary, p. 8) and runs off to bring back more than one monster to fight, she must keep one monster targeted and keep her AUTO-ATTACK on. /ASSIST does not work unless the player is attacking her target.

Killing mesmerized monsters. Players should not wake a mesmerized monster with melee. Learn what the character's class can do that is considered a taunt. For Warriors, use the TAUNT button. For Rangers, taunt/*Snare*/*Flamelick* is a good combination. When everyone is ready to attack the monster, one of the magic users should cast a damage over time spell that won't awaken it immediately. The party should follow this strategy with another taunt/attack/taunt volley.

Use Area of Effect spells. Players of level 30+ should consider using AoE mesmerization spell at a good distance to stop the monster.

Armor Class

Buff the AC. Generally speaking, items that increase armor class are more valuable than items that merely increase strength. Upping armor class — even by only a few points — makes a big difference, especially when going soloing.

Pare down. Always take the time to really examine accumulated possessions closely. When someone — especially a caster-type — is carrying too much, Agility and AC suffer. However, think carefully before getting rid of strength-enhancing gear — with armor it's often the difference between being find and being encumbered.

Dueling

Claustrophobia/Agoraphobia. When casters take on fighter types in a duel, they'll normally try to fight in a wide-open area. That way, they can kite their opponents (in other words, knock them silly with an immobilizing spell, then cast damage, then run away while they regain mana). One good way for a fighter to counteract this — if the casters can't be forced into a smaller area — is to hit them with very long-range weapons. They hate that.

To the pain. It has been known for two people to fight to the not-quite-death, by agreeing to fight up to a certain point — for instance, one bubble of health. (However, watch out for liars that might take advantage of you and kill you anyway, however ...).

Group

Assign roles. Grouping is without a doubt one of most enjoyable ways to spend *EverQuest* time. Make sure, however, that the potential groups have a strategy... otherwise, everyone might end up attacking one monster while another goes unnoticed. The best way to group is to elect one player (usually a fast-moving Ranger or Warrior) to draw critters toward the group. Before the mob arrives, decide who's going to do what — especially if the approaching monster is bringing friends.

This one's almost too simple, but often neglected — let people do what they do best ... but get everything sorted out *before* you go into your first battle together.

Don't forget to taunt. Monsters tend to stick to one target at a time. If someone in the group is getting wasted by a creature who's focused on him or her, have the nearest Ranger or Paladin taunt the creature and divert its attention away with a good whack or two.

Strafing Workaround

There is no STRAFE LEFT or STRAFE RIGHT key in *EverQuest*. To be honest, players won't find a lot of use for strafing since they select a target and start swinging. However, a player can hold down the STRAFE key and use the TURN LEFT and TURN RIGHT keys to strafe in that direction.

Player-vs-Player

Dress down. With the exception of folks who've got gold and plats just pouring out of their pockets, it's wise to carefully consider what equipment to carry when going solo. In PvP-land, cool stuff is an invitation to be killed and looted. Losing that great piece of equipment that took so long to get can be quite a letdown. For this reason, some players prefer to keep a "nice" set of expensive armor on reserve for group play, and wear a less-expensive second set while going it alone. Don't be an obviously valuable target — it's safer that way.

Fizzle 'em. When battling a finger-wiggler (caster-type), one of the biggest offensive moves is to interrupt the opponent's spellcasting as often as possible. The best way to do this is to use the fastest weapon and the best shield possible.

Blind 'em. Paladins — when in doubt, blind 'em with *Flash of Light*.

Know the rules. Contrary to popular belief, all PvP servers were not created equally. The regular PVP server is Rallos Zek, while Tallon Zek and Vallon Zek are team PvP servers. What this means is that on Rallos Zek, everyone is out to kill everyone else. With the other servers, it's Group A vs. Group B vs. Group C vs. Group D.

Group A:	Humanoid (Barbarian, Erudite, Human)
Group B:	Evil (Dark Elf, Iksar, Ogre, Troll)
Group C:	Elven (Half Elf, High Elf, Wood Elf)
Group D:	Small (Dwarf, Gnome, Halfling)

Start with the basics. All of the PvP servers are well-populated. However, we strongly urge players to spend some time getting to know *EverQuest* on a regular, non-PvP server before you decide to join the PvP ranks. Keep in mind that on any PvP server, corpses can be looted for any inventory items on them.

Taunt

There are two ways to taunt a creature — Taunting, or simply knocking the critter around a little. When facing a group of monsters, it's often possible to stir the pack into a near-riot by taunting the individual members or casting damage-over-time (DoT) spells.

High-quality taunts. Some spells and actions are better taunting tools than other types of spells or actions. Direct damage (DD) Enchanter spells work quite well. So do any area affect spells that work on the monster group as a whole (for instance, a spell that diminishes the strength of all members). DoT spells and snares take longer to work, but can backfire if the mob gets too angry.

All of the healer-types are pretty good at taunting, even if it is rather indirectly. This is why: *Harm Touch* (as well as other healing and curing spells) heals group members, which makes the monster mob very, very angry. After all, the healer is undoing all the monster's hard work. Nine times out of ten, the mob will quickly turn to find the source of the spell. Of course, the healer then needs someone to protect him or her ....

The old-fashioned way to get a monster's attention is to step directly in front of it and attack. Boy, they notice that!

The rapid touch. The faster a group can deliver hits to a mob, that madder it'll get. Monks are particularly good at this (especially Iksar monks, who have dual attacks from the start), as are Backstabbing Rogues.

Tank task. Been elected as the group's tank? A tank's main task is to watch out for his fellow group members and see who the monster is focusing on. This is, of course, while he's simultaneously fighting the good fight.

Take it on the chin. When getting aggro'd on (seem to be bearing the brunt of a critter's attack), the best advice is to stand completely still, quit fighting, and yell for help. Yes, that sounds a bit counterproductive for a battle, but it's not. It's harder to help people who run around like lunatics.

Shields up. Any Warrior in a less-than-powerful group should invest in the best shield possible. Maybe other party members will be willing to chip in a plat or two — after all, who knows when the tank is going to be the group's last, best hope against an unexpected train?

Picking a Server

Go low. The CHOOSE A SERVER screen has more than one function. Yes, it gives you a wide choice of servers from which to choose. It also tells you how many players are online at that particular time. It helps to watch servers for a few days during the times you're most likely to play. Sometimes, it's more fun to play on servers with lower populations.

Find the crowds. On the flip side, older servers with lots of established players can be a source of reward and wealth. What better way for a 30th level Paladin to unload a rusty two-handed blade or old armor than to give it to a newbie player for cheap? What's 5pp to a player brimming with hundreds of plats? Be nice, play nice, and make nice, high-level friends... it's often worth the effort.

Sprechen Sie Orc? Despite the vast array of in-game languages, players sometimes find it difficult to communicate with other players from other countries. Players from outside the United States should do some checking around to find servers containing other players with of the same nationality. For instance, Veeshan has a relatively high number of Asian players, and Solusek Ro is home to many German players.

Find your own. Newer servers mean more newbie players. Ask other players, poke around on the chat boards, and then select a server. When it comes to grouping and leveling up quickly, it pays off to make a lot of friends who are at similar levels.

Guilds

Players can create a newbie character to see how the factions change when the character joins, and what the quests are against.

Joining a guild

Guilds are where people can find training and can be very important to the advancement of the character. For example, players might want to be in a guild for Wizards, to help in researching new spells, armor, weapons, etc. Or, players might want to belong to a guild that is Dwarves, or all Good Guys, or Evil role-players, or whatever.

Research the guild. Players should not be in a hurry to join a guild. Talk to members and see if they are happy with the guild. Party with members of the guild (if they let non-guild members in) and see who they fight against and why. The character might end up in a guild that is always going to war with other guilds for inconsequential reasons. Players definitely need to be wary of guilds that might damage their character's reputation.

Questions to ask. What are people saying about the guild? What is the reputation of the various members? What time of day (real time) do most of the members play? Do you have common interests with the members? Plus consider: do you like the people within the guild whom you've met?

Communication. This is a good indicator of whether a guild is good or not. Do they maintain communication among the members of the guild?

Wait to join. Players should spend the lower levels of their characters really learning *EverQuest* before they join a guild. There's too much basic stuff that needs to be taken in: how the game works, who the races are, what the different classes do, religions, etc. By the time characters reach level 12-17, they have enough experience and knowledge to make an educated decision about joining a guild. Meet people and make friends, and the guild invitations will follow!

Roleplaying

Immersion roleplaying. One of the best ways to have a good time in *EverQuest* is to assume the personality of a certain race and class. Come up with good stories, and stick to them. Don't worry about what other players think, even if they're all ROFL — nearly everyone appreciates a player who takes the time to create an interesting personality.

Spend some time making up the fantasy life you've always wanted to have. Make a new character who's an Erudite orphan, taken in by a great Wizard and carefully taught every spell from the tender age of two? Detail an Ogre past including a family history of thick blood and schizophrenia? Explain why the Human Monk gave up a life of wealth and riches and decide to roam Norrath?

Drop hints. When a character has a quirk, give other players clues as to why that particular trait exists. Does your steaming hatred of Trolls stem from a childhood of being teased? Allude to it. Does she have a traditional "fight song" that she sings before each fight? Put in on a hot key, or just talk about it. Drop hints why the fearless character has an unnatural loathing of bridges? You can use conversations, but emotes in particular are helpful in defining your character (see **Emotes**, p. 122).

Think like an Iksar, or whatever. Being a good role-player means getting into a character. Leave your real personality behind and be consistent in your tone and actions. Before long, you'll be spending time in your real life thinking about your fantasy life!

Pick an easy name. Here's an important one — *keep the name simple!* Remember, other players who want to say anything other than "Hey, you!" must type in by hand. Feel free, of course, to make it match the character's background or personality ... just try to keep in relatively short and easy to spell. Other players will appreciate it.

Give some slack. Get to know other players before judging them too harshly. Just because someone comes across as brash, rude and insensitive doesn't make him or her a mean person. Talk, converse, ask questions ... who know what mysteries will surface after a few deep conversations over a few ale.

Stay off-channel. If you're a true role-player, don't overuse /SHOUT and /OOC. For offline discussions with other players, try /TELL and starting the line OOC without the "/".

Interface

Views

There are 3 different user interface views for characters in *EverQuest*:

1. **Full-Screen.** The player will see all the action with no interface at all except for important messages, such as LOADING ZONE or YOU ARE DEAD. Players need to be very familiar with keyboard commands to use the view effectively.

2. **Half-Screen.** This is the most used set-up for most players. The entire action is still viewable, but the really important interface buttons are available. Text flows across the top of the screen.

3. **Interface-Screens.** Players default to this set of screens after character creation. This is the view where the player can open up character inventory, see character skill levels, etc.

Customization/ Options Menu

EverQuest has taken into account that not every player enjoys the same interface and has built in options to tailor the game to the individual's preferences. For example, the player can re-map keyboard commands. (See the *EverQuest* manual.) Check out the options menu for choices, such as MOUSE LOOK.

Hot Buttons

Highly Recommended. Check the *EverQuest* manual and set up the character "hot buttons." Each character is given 6 groups of 6 buttons — that's 36 hot buttons for each character. To switch between the 6 groups, the player will either click the arrow buttons above the boxes or hold [Shift] and hit [1]-[6]. Each of the 6 buttons in the group is mapped to the [1]-[6] keys on the keyboard.

Mapping the buttons. Players left click and hold on almost anything in the User Interface. When a BUTTON ICON appears, the player can then take that BUTTON ICON and drop it into an empty hot box. This works for everything from memorized spells to the programmable text macros.

Important Note: Hot button groups do not necessarily carry on to other characters. For example, players can set up hot buttons for spell casting characters differently from warrior characters.

Example: Bard

The player should consider a set of hot boxes for quick access to useful Bard songs, another set up for melee weapon and instrument changes, and a third one set up for traveling.

Suggested organization: most frequently used spells on hot box group 1, weapons and other often-used items on hot box group 2, and a set of items used when traveling on hot box group 3. Of course, players should organize their hot boxes in ways that best fits their playing style.

Text Macros

Players have 12 social buttons they can use to set up the most commonly used text commands, such as controlling pets, dialog during battle, emotes, etc. The player right-clicks on a "Social" box to bring up a dialog box. Then, he or she will type in a short description, multiple commands, and/or spoken text. Players can have up to five different messages (one on each line) per macro.

Example: Necromancer

The player would type in:

>   /say I command thee to kill!
>   /pet attack

Characters around the necromancer will "hear" the "/say" and then see the pet respond and attack.

Limitations: Players cannot use two "say" statements in one macro, but they can use one "say" with various commands.

Try lines similar to the following example:

>   /pet guard me
>   /say Deathfang, to my side!
>   :snaps his fingers.

Auctions

The player can hit [Shift][↑] to scroll back through previous messages. Or, fill the custom box with text and switch the chat to auction.

Players can also extend a message for auctions by just repeating the /AUCTION (up to five times per macro) and continuing their text.

Items

Focus Items

Stay-ability. Focus items are kind of like non-perishables — they're needed to cast a spell, but they don't vanish afterward. For instance, some spells require a Fire Beetle eye. Once the spell is cast, the eye remains intact in the caster's inventory.

Elemental focus items. Magicians typically have to complete quests to get four elemental focus items — a shovel, broom, stein and torch: Earth, Air, Fire and Water, respectively. (A stein is a kind of mug.) Once acquired, these items make magicians capable of conjuring up some pretty powerful pets. Common rumor states that focus items aren't usable until a character reaches higher levels. This isn't true, however. At low levels, their advantage may go unnoticed. At higher levels, they're much more powerful.

Going back to the elemental focus items, Water and Earth have their very own Staves of Elemental Mastery. They aren't easy to find by any standard — let's just that they're highly useful when it comes to pets ....

Money

Take the time. The old adage "Good things are worth working for" holds true in *EverQuest*. Many of the trade skills (smithing armor, fletching, jewel-making, etc.) can be particularly profitable if a player is willing to put effort into selling them.

Dungeon loot. For characters at higher levels, good loot can be hard to come by. The less-populated places end up yielding valuable items more often, especially when it comes to dark, dangerous dungeons. Risk-taking is part of the game — players who want better stuff should be willing to take a few more risks to acquire it.

The old-fashioned way. Most of the time, class-based quests yield pricey items more often than the "hunt what's around — kill it — loot it — sell it" method of doing things. Because of this, quests that are specific to an occupation (Monks, Necros, Warriors, etc.) are fairly intricate and send players scurrying around all over the place. The lesson here is that valuable things can be acquired with lots of effort instead of lots of platinum.

Pal around. Group, group, group for profit! The more players that can help out at a camp site or on a quest, the better. It's much more efficient for a group to help its individual members than it is for each player to go at it solo. A group can help a player earn more money and better items in less time.

Being nice for profit. At newbie levels, it's tough enough to support oneself and stay stocked up on food and drink. It does get a bit easier as characters reach higher levels (presumably because harder creatures give out better loot), but good equipment still wears a heavy price tag. A lot of higher-level players have more cash than they could possibly need and go through occasional periods of generosity. It never hurts to look nice, hopeless and poor in front of a rich crowd ....

Experience & Levels

Rapid ascent. It's an indisputable fact of *EverQuest* that some races and classes level up faster than others. Some of this is due to brute strength (Warriors), faster attack speeds (Monks), faster health point regeneration (Iksar and Trolls) or basic racial advantages. Players should spend a considerable amount of time thinking hard about what race/class combination they should choose for their character.

HP disparities. Killing monsters in certain zones can provide more experience than the same monster in another zone. Some zones award more experience than others, or give more experience for mob fights.

Grouping for gain. In nearly all cases, grouping together helps players level up faster.

The bleeding obvious. Dying subtracts some experience from the experience bar in the Persona screen. Logically, dying more often subtracts more experience points. To level up, try not to die. This means develop strategies and play with people you work well with.

Zones

Train etiquette. Angry mobs and trains have been known to chase players for miles, or more accurately, to the edge of the closest zone. Zoning is a great evasion method — players run into an adjacent zone, and the monsters can't follow. While this is very convenient for the chasee, it's very inconvenient for any innocent victims who happen to be hanging around the zone area when the train comes in. /SHOUT a warning and let folks know what's coming in.

The endless question. An ongoing debate among players is whether or not water zoning is possible. In some places it is ... sometimes ... but don't depend on it as your escape method of choice.

Newbie garden

Start slow. In Northern Cabilis (Field of Bone), the green terrain has the "safe" newbie creatures. Decaying skeletons are about the worst thing players will find ... and, in groups, or at least at Level 2 or so, players can easily handle them. The yellow, sandy terrain has harder monsters. There is a definite line between it and the green area. The walled canyon, just north of the gate, has things that will be red for a player (not a good idea to attack) for a long while. However, with a well-balanced group, players should be able to lure even one of those out and successfully defeat it.

Traveling

Cloud direction. Clouds head from east to west, which is an enormous help in figuring out what direction is where.

Big, dangerous & magnetic. Dropped swords will land with point-northward, just like a compass.

/LOC. Learn how to read the /LOC coordinates.

The first number indicates how far north or south you are. If it's a positive number, it's north. If it's a negative number, it's south. The bigger the number (disregarding negativity), the farther north or south you are.

The second number indicates how west or east you are. Positive numbers are west, negative numbers are east.

The third number is altitude. Positive numbers are higher than lower numbers.

Therefore: Halas might be 305.78, -200.66 which means it's in the northwest part of the world.

Also: Cabilis might be -266.44, -221.15, meaning it's in the southeastern part of the world.

Races

Language

Book languages. Not that many players (at least not many new ones) bother to speak in their native tongue, if they have one. No, it's not really necessary for having a good time, but it can have its advantages. Caster-types, for instance, need to use special languages to interpret some scrolls and books.

Speaking in code. Two of the player-vs.-player servers (Tallon Zek and Vallon Zek) service ongoing racial wars. Each set has languages that are intelligible among the races in that group, but less so among other races. For example, the Dark races (Dark Elves, Iksar, Ogres and Trolls) all speak Dark … a potentially useful tool on the battlefield.

Practice (again). The best way to improve a language skill is to listen or speak with other characters in that tongue.

Occasionally, players who want to improve their skill in a particular language set up language-learning parties, complete with ale, food and good stories. Stay alert for them.

Check it out. A character's spoken language can be switched by right-clicking on the Text Display window. One field in the window that appears shows the currently selected language. Clicking the name of the language cycles through all of the character's possible tongues.

Night Vision

There's a difference between ultravision (owned solely by Dark Elves) and infravision (possessed by other night-sighted races). Dark Elves have night vision because they can use different kinds of light (not just spectral light) to see. The others "see" heat as a kind of light, so they're never completely in the dark.

Diplomacy

A friend of my enemy ... Many races (and creatures) won't attack at first, but if players kill a lot of them, certain faction standing will lower and, eventually, previously congenial NPCs will kill the player on sight (KOS). An example is Frogloks: if players are performing a quest that requires going through the swamps, they need to be aware that Frogloks of all levels roam about the marshes. So, it might be a good idea to keep them on your side, at least for a while. Another example would be wolves ... NPC Druids are never happy with people who slaughter wolves.

Loot. If a player decides not to stay in the Frogloks' or Druids' good graces and attack, they do carry loot and are pretty easy to kill. Sometimes it can be a hard decision.

Skills

Begging

Begging is one of those skills that many players toss aside as useless. Yes, it can take a *long* time to improve, but an Excellent rating in Begging can eventually yield platinum coins and a measurable amount of experience. The flip side of the coin, so to speak, is that some NPCs grow highly agitated when begged and have been known to attack players.

Begging from pets is a safe way to improve the Begging skill.

Instill Doubt

Instill Doubt is another one of those seemingly less-useful skills that has its advantages if used at the right time and place. It's also one of those skills that takes a while to raise. Some creatures attempt to run away if successfully intimidated, but end up running smack dab into a wall or other hard structure instead.

Some players maintain that Instill Doubt works best when the user stands directly in front of the target and doesn't move, speak or hit or get hit.

Instill Doubt actually works similarly to a fear-causing spell. (If the monster successfully resists it, you'll see a message.)

One of the best times to use Instill Doubt is when an entire group (or several members) is low on mana and health. Instill Doubt might give everyone just enough time to zone.

Blacksmithing

Blacksmithing is one of the very profitable trades in the game. The ultimate goal for most smiths is to make banded armor, very good armor, and also cheap armor for low-level players.

Beginning. Players should create a character that has really high Intelligence or can do charisma attribute increases (such as Enchanters and Shaman). The high Intelligence will help the player learn skills faster, and high Charisma means cheaper prices when buying and selling to the stores. Enchanters would be the best for both Intelligence and Charisma reasons.

Raising the skill. Player smiths can either make metal bits (quite a few metal bits to raise the skill, so get used to making them) or sharpen rusty weapons. They must be bladed weapons, obviously, because sharpening staves or maces is a fool's task. The easy way is to go to the guild and put 20 points into smithing, however, past that point only old-fashioned, persistent work will pay off.

Recipe for metal bits. Players need to get two pieces of ore (separated) and non-summoned (store-bought) water.

Recipe for scalers. The next project is to make scalers. They require 1 flask of water, 1 metal bit, and 1 scaler mold that costs about 6 silver.

And so on ... If the smith has high Intelligence she should quickly raise her skill. Soon enough she will be at the point where scalers are trivial to make and ready to move on to more costly and difficult skewers.

Safe Fall

In those particularly hilly or elevated points in Norrath, Safe Fall can be a lifesaver. In a group setting, however, those without this skill will have a harder time keeping up with members that do possess Safe Fall. Party members should keep a close eye on the terrain instead of following the leader blindly.

The only way to improve Safe Fall is to fall. Small falls down ramps, steep hills, etc. — it's the frequency, not height, that has the effect.

Boats with ramps are a convenient place to improve Safe Fall. What else is there to do on a long journey?

Jewelry-Making

This is a very interesting trade for a spellcaster. When the player's skill level hits about 20, he can make silver jewelry. With a skill around 25, he can work silver and amber. At level 8 an Enchanter can begin enchanting the silver.

Starting. The best way to learn how to make jewelry is to make it ... all the time . Unenchanted is fine, just keep making it, selling it, making more, and so on, to raise the skill. Progress will be slow and, yes, it'll be expensive. High Wisdom gives the jeweler less failure as she learns, while high Intelligence will help her learn faster. If the jeweler can find charisma buffs, she won't lose as much money over the course of her education. All jewelers should be aware that they need about 50 pp to start and mastering the craft will take every copper you can scrounge. However, jewelry making is a profitable pastime eventually.

Spellcaster Issues

Meditation

Spellcasters should constantly remind themselves of the cardinal rule of spellcasting — cast, rest and meditate. Hour after hour after hour. Meditating is the best way to restore mana, and mana is everything.

Even while meditating, spellcasters can keep an eye on the battle. The hit point bars for the character, group members and monsters give valuable clues as to when it's time to mez or heal again.

Ability Points and Enhancements

Charisma. Charisma is a good thing for a spellcaster — higher charisma gives a slightly better chance of success (or at least fewer resists by mobs that aren't conning red).

Charisma helps spellcasters charm wild beasts. Wood Elves in particular can benefit from a combination of high Charisma (boosted with + CHA items) and the *Befriend Animal* spell. They can then send the charmed animal into combat against an equal or slightly better opponent. So what if it dies? By then, the second creature (the one under attack) should be somewhat close to dying as well. One good direct damage spell will finish the kill for the caster.

Mana max. Once a spellcaster's mana ceiling hits 200 or so, resists are few and far between.

Intelligence. Intelligence-enhancing items have the desirable side effect of increasing a spellcaster's maximum mana storage potential. (This is true for non-deity-based-mages, but not Cleric casters.) The more + INT items a casting character wears, the more mana he or she can acquire.

Offensive vs. Defensive. One important point to note is that casting non-offensive spells will improve magical skills, but won't necessarily award experience. Attacking mobs (either with spells or weapons) is still the most prevalent way to gain experience.

Combat

Crowd control. The best way to control a group of critters is to use Conjure first, then follow up with Divination or Alteration.

Not the face! Spellcasters aren't known to put up a good fistfight ... that's a task best left up to muscle-ridden tanks.

Double-whammy. Fighting and casting classes form a useful symbiotic relation — they can both benefit from one another's talents. One really effective strategy players have developed for partner play is this: a tank and a spellcaster team up, the spellcaster buffs up the tank, the tank goes after something that normally cons yellow or red, and then both characters attack the creature. Simple and sweet.

Pets

To summon up a pet, spellcasters need an appropriate spell and usually gems, bone chips or some other sort of catalyst. The pet's power is limited, of course, by the caster's current level and abilities.

To arm, or not to arm. Generous spellcasters often arm their pets with a weapon. The only problem with doing this, though, is that pets sometimes get greedy and refuse to give it up at the end of a fight.

Elemental pets. Magicians have access to four elemental pets — Fire, Earth, Air and Water. Each has its pluses and minuses, and some players are sure to argue that one is better than the other. Which pet to summon in a specific situation, however, depends on the opponent and the combat environment.

· Fire has less hit points than water, but shields the caster and has better attack potential.

· Earth has lots of hit points, but is pretty low on Dexterity and Agility.

· Water boasts a reasonable number of hit points and delivers a fair amount of damage.

· Air has great Dexterity and Agility, but doesn't have much of a punch.

Elementalings are baby Elementals — not as high-level, and not as powerful.

Specialization

There can only be one. Specializing in certain types of spells (Abjuration, Alteration, Conjuration, Divination or Evocation) pays off once the caster's gained level 51 in any one area. Spells falling into the specialized category take less mana to cast, and fizzle fewer times. The downside is that specializing in one area prevents the caster from attaining anything higher than level 50 in any other area.

Cash up front. Spellcasters who want to specialize should toss a few practice points at their guild. In order to hit the magical number of 50 in any skill, casters have to practice each and every skill at least once.

Keep them straight. Specializing in a magical category isn't the same thing as specializing in one skill. (For example, Conjuration and Specialize Conjuration aren't the same thing.)

Just FYI. Trainers offer up Specialization skills in the following order: Alteration, Conjuration, Abjuration, Evocation, and Divination.

Keep count. Specialization enables you to cast certain types of spells with less mana. If you can't make up your mind what sorts of spells you'd like to specialize in, just figure out which ones you use the most. After a battle, including bringing everyone back up to health afterwards, scroll back and count how many healing spells, buff spells, anti-dead spells, etc., you used.

Abjuration	Buffing up your party-mates.
Alteration	Healing and traveling (including Evacuation).
Evocation	Direct Damage spells.
Conjuration	Damage over Time spells.

Mechanics of specialization

INT-based Casters — Specialization available at Level 20

WIS-based Casters — Specialization available at Level 30

Element of chance. Chance determines the likelihood of whether a casting will receive the specialization bonus: the higher the caster's specialization skill, the higher the likelihood. When the determination is positive, the bonus will reduce the mana used on the spell and the chance of the spell fizzling. When the caster doesn't get the specialization bonus, the spell is still cast with normal mana cost and fizzle chance.

NOTE: Specialization does not increase chance of recovering after interruption. This is based purely on Channeling. Specialization does not make spells cast faster. This is a fixed amount.

Choosing fields of magic. A caster can specialize in all five fields of magic, but only one field can exceed a skill of 50. Whichever skill first exceeds 50 becomes the primary specialization of the caster from that time on.

Changing specialties. Players can alter their specialty by completing a quest in the Temple of Solusek Ro.

Raising skills. When a caster puts one practice point into a skill, it will increase in level by approximately 25. Initially, a caster should spend 1 point in each of the five casting skills. Then, players need to pick the specialization, memorize a Level 1 spell of that type, and cast it on themselves for an hour or so until they reach a skill of 51, thereby setting their specialization.

NOTE: The max skill limit on specialization is 5 + (5 x Level), with a maximum of 200.

EverQuest: The Ruins of Kunark

Specialization considerations

The magic user should first study the **Spells** (p. 352) and learn what spells are in what class. For example, if an Enchanter is thinking of specializing in Evocation, she would notice that only a few spells use this skill. Therefore, it would be a bad idea.

Before making a decision about specialization, the spell caster should:

· Count the number of spells which will benefit from the specialization

· Think about the situations those spells can be used in

· Determine how often those spells are used

· Consider the average mana cost of that class of spells

Enchanter. Enchanters really only have two choices for specialization: Alteration (includes immobilization spells, haste spells, slowing spells, damage over time spells, charms, and most attribute increases and decreases) and Conjuration (includes mesmerizing spells). Most Enchanters choose Alteration as their field of specialization since 80% of their spells are under this skill.

Magician. There are two main choices when selecting a specialization as a Magician: Evocation (AoE and a few DD spells) or Conjuration. The Magician's decision is just a matter of preference, but most choose Evocation because that's used during battle. Conjuration spells are often used (in fact, most of the Magician spells are in Conjuration); but, the casting is during non-critical times ... so they just med back up.

Wizard. There is really no choice for Wizards: Evocation. In battle, Wizards are the big bastions of destruction.

Necromancer. Necromancers have perhaps the hardest choice of all. There are three classes of magic ... all powerful additions for a Necromancer: Alteration (DoT spells, lifetap spells, and undead charms/useful during combat), Evocation (includes damage spells/useful during combat), and Conjuration (includes pet summoning, darkness and disease series of spells).

NOTE: Most Necromancers specialize in Alteration, with Conjuration second and Evocation, third.

Cleric. For Clerics, the choices of specialization are Alteration (includes heals, cures, immobilization and resurrection spells) and Evocation (good for many solo Clerics). However, since a lot of the Cleric's Alteration spells are mana drains and the heal spells are so vital to a party, the Cleric should seriously consider specializing in Alteration.

Druids. Druids have 3 choices of specialization: Conjuration (DoT spells/good for solo Druids), Alteration (buffs, healing and gates) and Evocation (DD spells/big mana burners). Choosing among these three groups of spells for the Druid is difficult. The only inclination would be for party Druids to specialize in Alteration. Other than that, the Druid character needs to consider her gameplay and choose along those lines.

Shaman. Shamans have two real choices: Alteration (includes immobilization spells, haste spells, slowing spells, damage over time spells, and most attribute increases and decreases) and Conjuration. Alteration is a pretty safe bet, but if Shaman players attack more, and enhance less, then Conjuration is still worth considering.

Fun

Before a character reaches level 5, he doesn't lose experience points when he dies. Therefore, the player should put all valuables, such as what his guildmaster gives him and his money, into the bank and go exploring. Norrath is whole world, and it's worth getting out and seeing it.

NOTE: No-Drop items are especially useful on a PvP server, since you can wear them without fear that they'll be taken off your corpse.

Quests

Players might consider creating a "throw away" character to perform a quest before they let their primary character do it. That way players find out what factions get raised without any penalty to the main character.

Twinking

Players should expect to get flak from people who don't agree with twinking (See **Jargon Glossary**, p. 8). Long-time players have a pretty good idea what equipment can be had at different levels.

Spell Tips

Feign Death

Here's a trick — the SIT button springs a character from the *Feign Death* position to a standing one.

Bind Spell

Who can bind where. "Regular" casters — Cleric, Druid, Shaman, Necromancer, Wizard, Magician and Enchanter — can be bound at any location. "Mixed" casters — Paladin, Shadow Knight, Ranger, Bard — only bind in cities, as well as non-casters. In other words, a Cleric could bind himself or a Necromancer in Qeynos Hills, but could only bind a Paladin in Qeynos.

How to know if it has worked. Players will receive a message from the spell saying that they have been bound to the area. If a player doesn't get that message, even if the spell was cast, he is not bound and when he dies, he will return to his old bind point.

The caster will get a message if the spell fails, but may not think, or in the case of certain conniving Dark Elves, may not choose to tell the target.

Binding bugs. It is possible for Bind to get bugged, but it's rare. If a player receives the "You feel yourself bind to the area." message and then dies and returns to her old bind point, she should petition and ask for help. (Or, if anything unusual happens, she should petition a GM for help.)

Camouflage Spell

Outdoor only. This spell can only be used out of doors and can only be cast on others if they are grouped with the caster. Indoors, players need to make sure they are in a group with someone who can cast an Invisibility spell.

Note: The length of Camouflage is extremely random. Players should keep the skill for casting Camouflage maxed: they will find that it lasts longer.

Thicken Mana Spell

This spell creates a vial of viscous mana that can then be used for making enchanted armor. Not *all* kinds of Enchanter armor, but enough.

Cities of Norrath

The Mapmaker

Mylord,

I trust this missive finds you in good health, if indeed it finds you at all. I had only returned to the port to replenish my supply of parchment, when I was informed by the captain that he would soon be departing for home. He kindly offered to carry my humble report to your eyes.

This new land is all I could ever dream it would be, and more! I must confess that my musical endeavors have quite fallen by the wayside. Indeed, the head of my drum is even now playing host to a careful tracing of an inland lake some six days journey from our anchorage (I believe I mentioned that I had run out of parchment). I have become utterly consumed with the task of committing the contours of great Kunark at last to paper. I think I have almost a third of the whole landmass sketched out now, and hope to have the rest in no more than a year, at which time I can start the even more massive task of making my charts fit for your sight. Have I found here my life's calling? Indeed, it may be so.

I wander hither and yon quite overwhelmed by the infinite possibilities of this land. Shall I follow the river that winds to the east, or seek out the peaks that loom to the north? I have learned much about both my craft and myself. It is most difficult, for example, to take an accurate compass reading while one is being pursued by a pride of lions, owing to the frequent necessity of evasive action. Although the actual distance covered between attempts was minuscule, the problem of reestablishing a true baseline under the formidable time pressure of leonine attention proved to be both frustrating and potentially life-threatening. In the end, however, I triumphed, when I discovered simultaneously that the trunk of a long pine can be climbed, with a sufficiently rapid run-up, and that said pines make both a good vantage point for geographical survey and a passably comfortable bower for the night.

I apologize for the brevity of this account, when indeed I have so much to report. However, the captain's departure cannot be delayed. As for myself, I once again hear the call of the expanses. There is a rumor of a most fascinating high meadow to the southwest, which none have been able to cross owing to the unfortunate presence of dragon-like Sarnaks. Therefore, I have every reason to hope that I shall be the first! Excitement quite overwhelms me.

Ever your obedient servant,
Muse, bard and cartographer

Cities of Norrath

EQ Atlas

www.eqatlas.com

To serious EverQuest adventurers, a good map is the magic mirror that lets them see the world as it really is. It saves time, saves resources, and saves lives.

Exploring is half the fun of questing ... but anyone who's spent hours wandering through zones, confused and frustrated, knows that being lost is neither "exploring" or fun.

EQ Atlas has an excellent array of high-quality maps, not just of cities, but also of the myriad areas in between. Muse, the Half Elf Bard/Cartographer, has been wandering Norrath since the early days of the Beta, drawing maps and making them available to his fellow adventurers.

Even more, there is first-hand expert advice on the best ways to survive exploration and find your way back home.

It's definitely worth a bookmark.

All maps are copyright EQ Atlas Web Site, and used here with permission.

Using the Maps in this Book

Places of interest are marked on each map and listed in the key below the map. Items that you can find at these locations are listed in parentheses where applicable. Please note that in addition to things you can buy (like food or cloth armor), these lists include things you might see and possibly use (like an oven or brew barrel) and occasionally people. Also, the lists are very general — a merchant listed as selling plate armor may not have all pieces of armor in every size, for example. And of course, items merchants keep in stock are subject to change as the game changes.

The maps are followed by lists of items and creatures found in the major newbie zones outside these cities. As *EverQuest* is a living, breathing game it is always possible that things we've listed are no longer available, or things we haven't listed are out there. We've provided the lists as a hint to the opportunities and dangers that lie outside city walls.

Antonica

The first stop for any traveler from abroad should surely be the main continent of Antonica. From broad green meadows to lush forests and frosty plains, our favorite island presents a breathtaking image of all four seasons at once. This jewel of Norrath supports the most acceptable of our thirteen known races, each with its own region and rich heritage. We wish you a warm welcome throughout the land, and hope you find your travels relaxing and pleasurable. Let us take a few moments to guide you through our bright and beautiful land...

Halas, nestled comfortably in between several snow-capped mountain ranges on the northernmost tip of Antonica, is home to most of the world's Barbarians. Further south in Rivervale, the land of the Halflings, the temperature rises to a breezy and comfortable 70° year round. Surrounded by lakes and rivers, this area has evolved into the most desirable vacation spot in the land — as evidenced by those visitors who return season after season.

Hardier travelers who want to mingle with several cultures may opt to visit the eastern seaboard. This region harbors the most varied terrain, races and native life in the land. From the Dark Elves' forested city of Neriak to the ever-alive Human and Half-Elf city of Freeport, visitors are always amazed by the unpredictable, exciting events and happenings in this region.

Southern Antonica may lack the wealth and goods present elsewhere on the island, but the true explorer or avid spelunker can't help but appreciate the unexplored lands surrounding Oggok (home of the Ogres) and Grobb (city of the Trolls). Caves, wild marshlands and historical ruins abound, many still untouched by progress or culture.

After an extended tour of the mainland, most travelers take a few days' rest in Qeynos, a tolerant, predominantly human city that rests on the western edge of Antonica. This famous port city bustles with mercantile activity both day and night, lending to its well-earned reputation as the City of Infinite Trade. From here, we hope you'll opt to continue your voyage onward to Norrath's other continents, each with something new to offer.

Freeport

Marsheart's Chords was full tonight—of singers warming up their voices, strummers tuning their lutes, and travelers eager to listen.

Angel leaned close to her lover, Mykel, and said, "That guard said to come here to learn about the city, but this is a group of entertainers. Don't they deal in fantasy?"

Mykel caressed Angel's hair, "Where do you think they get their stories from, love?"

A hush fell on the crowd as the night's entertainment began. There were stories of love and valor. Tales of the gods and their faithful. Songs of magic and wonderment.

When it was all done, Mykel turned to Angel and said, "Well, there you have it. You need to see this Tara Neklene in the Magician's Tower of the Arcane Scientists and help her with her important research. I, a humble cleric of Mithaniel, will be off to visit the Marr Hall of Truth and rid it of the pestilence that has infested the peaceful waters there."

"But those were just stories," Angel argued.

Mykel smiled as he kissed Angel's hand. "Meet me here tomorrow evening. Tell me about your story and I'll let you know about mine."

Located on the eastern coast of Antonica, Freeport is a starting city for Humans and Half-Elves. In this humming port city you will find all manner of goods and refreshment for sale. In particular, travelers in search of spirits to quench their thirst won't be disappointed.

The city is divided into three zones: north, east and south. Boats depart from the docks in East Freeport for the Ocean of Tears and various ports of call.

Newbies who wish to venture outside of town will do well to stick to the East Commonlands, which lie just to the west of West Freeport.

West Freeport

to North Freeport

to North Freeport

to North Freeport

← to East Commonlands

1

2

3

4

5

13

9

10

8

14

6

7

11

12

to East Freeport

to East Freeport

Map by Mike Swiernik

1. Lady Merchant (brewing supplies)
2. Ogre Merchant (pickled items)
3. Freeport Militia
4. Lady Merchant (cloth armor)
5. Magicians, Enchanters and Wizards Guilds (tomes, gems, violet robes)
6. Warriors Guild (weapons, forge)
7. Arena (PvP)
8. Smithy (weapons, pottery wheel/kiln)

9. Tavern (alcohol)
10. The Stage
11. Cooking Shop (food, cooking supplies/recipes, pottery wheel/kiln)
12. Ashen Order (Monks Guild, weapons, musical instruments)
13. Torlig's Herbs and Medicines (potions, crystals, mistletoe)
14. Empty (oven)

EverQuest: The Ruins of Kunark

East Freeport

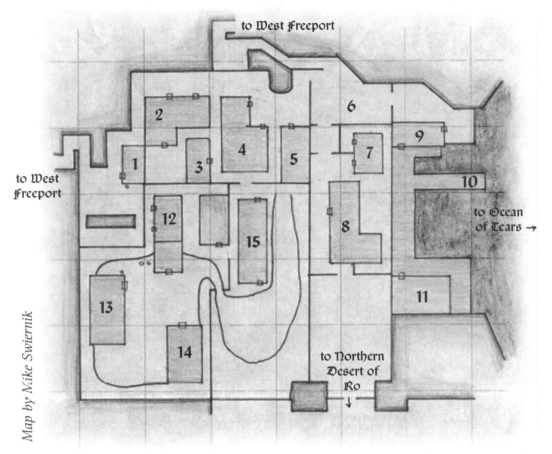

to West Freeport

to West Freeport

to Ocean of Tears →

to Northern Desert of Ro ↓

Map by Mike Swiernik

1. Armor by Ikthar (chain/plate armor, armor molds, clay, forge)
2. Trader's Holiday (blacksmithing molds/books, alcohol, brew barrel, oven)
3. Tavern (alcohol)
4. Felith and Bard Imported Goods (alcohol, blacksmithing books, molds)
5. Leather and Hide (leather armor/ patterns)
6. Priest of Discord
7. Grub and Grog Tavern (alcohol, oven)
8. Freeport Inn (food, lanterns, etc.)

9. Port Authority (fishing supplies)
10. Boats to Butcherblock Mountains, rest of Faydwer
11. Seafarer's Roost (beers, brew barrel)
12. Inn (secret entrance to Necromancers, Shadow Knights and Rogues Guilds, Guildmasters for other evil races)
13. Gord's Smithy (weapons, bags)
14. Chops and Hops (alcohol, oven)
15. Hallard's Resales (weapons, KOS dog named Scraps)

North Freeport

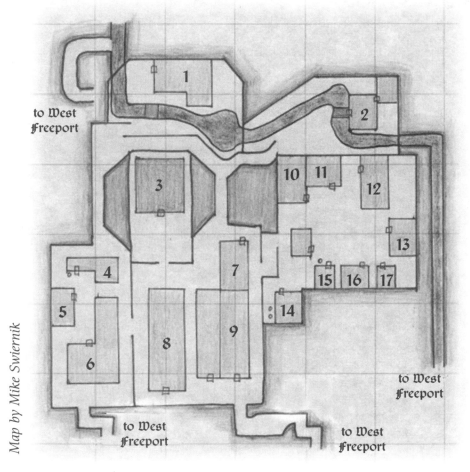

to West Freeport

to West Freeport

to West Freeport

to West Freeport

Map by Mike Swiernik

1. Office of Landholders
2. Hall of Truth (Paladins Guild)
3. Temple of Mithaniel Marr (Clerics and Paladins Guilds)
4. Groflah's Forger (ore, weapons, clay, steel boning, sharpening stones, forge)
5. Marsheart's Chords (Bards Guild, weapons, musical instruments)
6. Freeport City Hall
7. Coalition of Trade Folks (food)
8. Guard House

9. "The Blue Building" (jewelry supplies)
10. Jade Tiger Den (food)
11. Tassle's Tavern (alcohol, brew barrel)
12. Emporium (cloth items, forge)
13. Bank of Freeport
14. Tavern (food, brew barrel, oven, pottery wheel/kiln)
15. Empty (oven)
16. General Goods (food)
17. Clothier Shop (pottery sketches, cloth armor)

EverQuest: The Ruins of Kunark

East Commonlands Newbie Zone

Personalities

Altunic Jartin	High Lord Elisar	Lyth Spellstar	Shadow Warrior
Battle Chanter	High Paladin of Tunare	Master Elementalist	Shady Swashbuckler
Blademaster Arishan	High Priest of Brell	Mstr. Enchantress Kalystari	Silent Fist Master
Bubar	High Priest of Three	Math Wintersong	Silent Fist Warrior
Cavalier of Thunder	High Priest Z'Kuvel	Merra Clayfinger	Squire Narl
Cavalier of Tunare	High Priestess of Brell	Metha Wintersong	Steel Warrior General
Chaplain of Brell	Innkeep Blaise	Mith Wintersong	Steel Warrior Lieutenant
Dena Loommistress	Innkeep Calen	Mytha Wintersong	Steel Warrior Sergeant
Elder Battle Chanter	Innkeep Dolman	Paladin of Tunare	StormGuard Corporal
Elder Enchantress of Three	Innkeep Elora	Pardor the Blessed	StormGuard General
Elder Priest Dunnik	Innkeep Fenia	Parthar	StormGuard Lieutenant
Elder Priest of Brell	Innkeep Harold	Ponila Quickfingers	StormGuard Sergeant
Elder Ritualist Ka'Visan	Innkeep Juna	Priest of Brell	Vali Greenwhisper
Elder Wizard	Innkeep Leo	Priestess of Brell	Veli Greenwhisper
Elder Woodsman	Jagged Pine Tracker	Priestess of Three	Voli Greenwhisper
Enchantress of Three	Jelda Needlefinger	Rinna Lightshadow	Vuli Greenwhisper
Essence Lord Laenari	Joryd Longarms	Romya	Warlord Spruance
Feir'Dal High Wizard	Katha Firespinner	Rugged Woodsman	Wizard Adept
General Melkar	Knight of Tunare	Senior Elementalist	Wizard of Three
General Sa'Ralis	Lady of the Pine	Senior Wizard	
Germe Threadspinner	Lord Shin Ree	Sergeant Slate	
Guards	Loric Weaver	Shadow Master	

Teir'Dal

Teir'Dal Bishop	Teir'Dal Elder Ritualist	Teir'Dal Lieutenant	Teir'Dal Ritualist Adept
Teir'Dal Chaplain	Teir'Dal Elite	Teir'Dal Priest	Teir'Dal Senior Ritualist
Teir'Dal Corporal	Teir'Dal High Priest	Teir'Dal Ritualist	Teir'Dal Sergeant

Others

air elemental	ghoul	moss snake	rattlesnake
asp	giant scarab	orc apprentice	shadow wolf
bixie	giant spider	orc centurion	skeleton
black bear	griffin	orc legionnaire	spiderling
black wolf	large spider	orc oracle	willowisp
darkweed snake	lesser mummy	orc pawn	young kodiak
decaying skeleton	lion	orc weaponsmith	zombie
fire beetle	lioness	puma	

Items

Ale
Alliance Robe Blue, Yellow
Aloe Swatch
Amber
Arrow
Axe
Backpack
Balm Leaves
Bandages
Basic Pottery
Bat Fur, Wing
Battle Worn Great Staff,
    Long Sword,
    Morning Star, Scimitar,
    Short Sword, 2-Handed
    Sword, Warhammer
Bear Meat
Belt Pouch
Binelen's Quick Treats,
    Succulence
Bixie Parts, Stinger
Black Pearl
Black Wolf Skin
Block of Clay
Blood of Velious
Bloodstone
Bloodstone Ring
Bone Chips
Bottle
Bottle of Kalish, of Milk
Box of Lute Strings
Bracelet of Chaotic Intellect
Brandy
Breastplate of Afflation
Breath of Ro, of Solusek
Broken Block of Ore, Axe,
    Bastard Sword, Battle
    Axe, Flail, Halberd,
    Long Sword, Mace,
    Scimitar, Short. Spear,
    Spear, Two Hnd. Batt.
    Axe, 2-Hand. Hammer,
    2-Handed Sword,
    Warhammer
Buckler
Bundled Bone Arrow Shafts,
    Ceramic Arrow,
    Steel Arrow Shafts,
    Wooden Arrow
Burned Out Lightstone

Cactus Pie
Carnelian
Cask
Cat's Eye Agate
Chunk of Meat
Cloth Cap, Cape, Choker,
    Cord, Gloves, Pants,
    Shawl, Shirt, Sleeves,
    Veil, Wristband
Club
Compass
Cracked Giant Scarab
Cracked Staff
Cup of Flour
Dagger
Dark Elf Parts
Deathfist Pawn Scalp,
    Slashed Belt
Dragonwart
Dwarf Meat
Dwrvn. Bar Room Table Leg
Elemental Grimoire
Elf Leaf
Emerald
Enchanted Battleworn
    Bastard Sword,
    Battleworn Great Staff,
    Battleworn Long Sword,
    Battleworn Morning
    Star, Feir'Dal Bastard
    Sword, Feir'Dal Great
    Staff, Feir'Dal Long
    Sword, Fine Steel
    Bastard Sword, Fine
    Steel Great Staff, Fine
    Steel Long Sword, Fine
    Steel Morning Star,
    Fine Steel Rapier,
    Teir'Dal Bastard Sword,
    Teir'Dal Great Staff,
    Teir'Dal Long Sword
Essence of Rathe
Eye of Serilis
Faded Salil's Writ Pages
Faded Velishoul's Tome
Feir'Dal Dagger, Great
    Staff, Long Sword,
    Morning Star, 2-
    Handed Sword,
    Warhammer
Field Point Arrowheads

Fine Steel Dagger, Great
    Staff, Long Sword,
    Morning Star, Rapier,
    Scimitar, Short Sword,
    Spear, 2-Hand. Sword,
    Warhammer
Fire Beetle Eye, Leg
Firing Sheet
Fish Scales
Fish Wine
Flame of Vox
Footpads of the Monkey
Frosting
Garnish
Gator Gulp Ale
Ghumim's Classical Dishes
Ghumim's Delights
Giant Scarab Egg Sack
Giant Snake Fang, Rattle
Glass Shard
Glove of Rallos Zek
Gold Ring
Golden Earring, Pendant
Grapes
Greater Lightstone
Griffon Feathers
Grizzly Bear Skin
Gypsy Wine
Hematite
High Elf Parts
High Quality Bear Skin,
    Cat Pelt
High Quality Firing Sheet
Honey Mead
Hooked Arrowheads
How To Sew: Large Sizes,
    Medium Sizes, Small
    Sizes
Human Head
Ice of Velious
Illegible Cantrip
Iron Ration, Visor
Jade
Jade Earring, Ring, Shard
Jasper
Jug of Sauces
Kite Shield
Lapis Lazuli
Large Bag

Large Block of Clay
Large Buckler
Large Cloth Cap, Cape,
    Choker, Cord, Gloves,
    Pants, Shawl, Shirt,
    Sleeves, Veil,
    Wristband
Large Groove Nocks
Large Kite Shield
Large Lantern
Large Round Shield
Large Snake Rattle
Large Snake Skin
Large Targ Shield
Large Tower Shield
Large Wooden Shield
LarkSpur
Lightstone
Lined Vial Sketch
Lion Meat
Loaf of Bread
Lockpicks
Longbow
Low Quality Bear Skin
Malachite
Malagil's Compend. Vol. 1
Malagil's Compend. Vol. 2
Mead
Meat Pie
Medium Groove Nocks
Medium Quality Bear
    Skin, Cat Pelt
Mithril Dwarven War Pick
Mithril Earring
Mixxy's Delicacies Vol 1
Mixxy's Delicacies Vol 2
Nilitim's Grimoire Pages
Oasis Water
Obtenebrate Claymore
On Languages
Onyx
Opal
Orc Pawn Pick
Packet of Kiola Sap
Parrying Dagger
Tasarin's Grimoire Pages
Pearl
Pearl Earring, Ring,
    Shard

Items, Cont.

Peridot
Petrified Bark Leggings
Piece of Parchment
Pristine Giant Scarab
Puma Skin
Quality Firing Sheet
Quill
Quiver
Rapier
Rat Ears
Ration
Raw-hide Belt, Boots, Cloak, Gloves, Gorget, Leggings, Mask, Shoulderpads, Skullcap, Sleeves, Tunic, Wristbands
Red Wine
Rehim's Robe
Ringmail Boots, Bracelet, Cape, Coat, Coif, Gloves, Mantle, Neckguard, Pants, Skirt, Sleeves
Rohand's Edibles, Sea Treats
Round Shield
Ruined Bear Pelt, Cat Pelt, Lion Skin, Wolf Pelt

Rune of Al'Kabor, Ap'Sagor, Arrest, Attraction, Banding, Conception, Concussion, Consumption, Contortion, Crippling, Disassociation, Dismemberment, Embrace, Expulsion, Falhalem, Frost, Fulguration, Howling, Impetus, Infraction, Karana, Nagafen, Neglect, Opression, Paralysis, Periphery, Petrification, Presence, Proximity, Rallos Zek, Rathe, Regeneration, Solusek Ro, Sorcery, Substance, the Astral, the Catalyst, the Combine, the Cyclone, the Helix, the Inverse, Trauma, Tyranny, Velious, Xegony
Rusty Axe, Bastard Sword, Battle Axe, Broad Sword, Dagger, Halberd, Halberd, Long Sword, Mace, Morning Star, Rapier, Scimitar, Scythe, Short Sword, Shortened Spear, Spear, 2-Handed Sword, Warhammer
Salil's Writ Pages
Sealed Vial Sketch
Set of Bone Arrow Vanes, Ceramic Arrow Vanes, Wooden Arrow Vanes

Several Parabolic Cut, Round Cut Fletchings, Shield Cut Fletchings
Shadow Wolf Pelt
Short Ale
Short Beer
Short Sword
Shotglass
Shuriken
Silver Amulet, Earring, Ring, Tipped Arrowheads
Skull Mask of Innervation
Small Bag
Small Block of Clay
Small Box
Small Buckler
Small Cloth Cap, Cape, Choker, Cord, Gloves, Pants, Shawl, Shirt, Sleeves, Veil, Wristband
Small Groove Nocks
Small Kite Shield
Small Lantern
Small Round Shield
Small Sewing Kit
Small Targ Shield
Small Tower Shield
Small Wooden Kite Shield
Small Wooden Shield
Snake Egg, Fang, Rattle Pieces, Scales, Venom Sac
Sorin's Treats on the Go
sparkling saphire
Spices

Spider Legs, Silk, Venom Sac
Spiderling Eye, Legs, Silk
Splintering Club
Staff
Star Rose Quartz
Talisman of Tranquility
Targ Shield
Tears of Prexuz
Teir'Dal Dagger, Great Staff, Long Sword, Morning Star, Rapier, Scimitar, Short Sword, 2-Hand. Sword, Warhammer, Robe Red
Telryd's Exspansive Writ, Writ
The Scent of Marr
Throwing Axe, Knife
Tiny Dagger
Token of Generousity
Topaz
Torch
Tower Shield
Turquoise
Unfinished Brass Trumpet
Vaashar's Sweet Revege, Sweet Treats

Grobb

Grobb, the starting city for Trolls, lies at the far southeastern tip of Antonica. Compared to a busy metropolis like Qeynos, Grobb is relatively small and somewhat limited in resources, but residents are able to fnd all they need in the way of necessities like food, armor and weapons.

Innothule Swamp separates the Troll city from its neighbors. Newbies who quail not at the thought of slogging through decaying flora and fauna might find this a very rewarding place. Not the spot for a second vacation home, perhaps, but potentially lucrative nonetheless.

"Here deal," Sohog said to Mixac. "I help you get bones for Hukulk and you gets to be Nightkeep." Sohog grabbed Mixac's tunic and drew him close. "You go through swamp to desert with me. Kill fire beetles for eyes for Basher Nanrum."

Mixac shrugged. "Thought fire eyes a lie." When Sohog pulled him closer, Mixac added, "But, it deal."

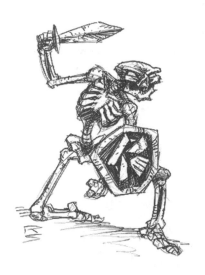

EverQuest: The Ruins of Kunark

Grobb

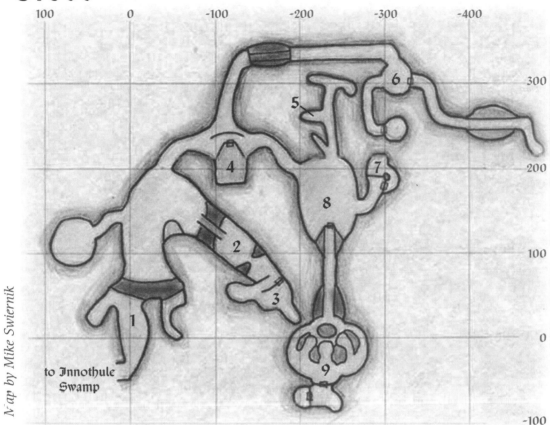

Nap by Mike Swiernik

to Innothule Swamp

1. Priest of Discord
2. Warriors Guild (weapons)
3. Merchant (brewing supplies, alcohol, bags)
4. Merchant (weapons, leather/chain/plate armor) Merchant (food, boots, fletching equipment, bows, arrows) outside

5. Merchant (jewelry)
6. Shadow Knights Guild (ore, sharpening stones, clay, weapons)
7. Bank
8. Shaman Trainers (medicine bags)
9. Shamans Guild

Innothule Swamp Newbie Zone

Personalities

Basher Oggrik	Fandl Arathin	Jyle Windstorm	Stragak
Basher Sklama	Forager Grikk	Lynuga	Sylp Tyanathin
Basher Smag	Gwynn Marthank	Peltin Funter	Tal Godin
Basher Trak	Hogus Durmas	Rell Ostodl	Tann Cellus
Bunk Odon	Jars Legola	Slayer Captain	Zepin Winsle
Dark Deathsinger	Jojongua	Spore Guardian	Zimbittle

Frogloks

froglok	froglok forager	froglok tad
froglok fisherman	froglok guard	

Others

bull alligator	giant rat	shadowed man	young water moccasin
decaying skeleton	giant water moccasin	skeleton	zombie
earth elemental	kobold hunter	snake	
fat alligator	large rat	swamp alligator	
fungus man tracker	lesser kobold	troll slayer	
fungus spore	lesser mummy	water moccasin	

Items

Ale	Essence of Rathe	Huge Mushroom Head	Mithril Earring
Alligator Skin, Tooth	Eye of Shadow	Human Flesh	Netted Cap, Cape, Choker, Girth, Gloves, Mantle, Mask, Pants, Shirt, Sleeves, Wristband
Amber	Faded Salil's Writ Pages	Hunting Bow	
Arrow	Faded Velishoul's Tome	Ice of Velious	
Backpack	Fine Steel Dagger, Great Staff, Long Sword, Morning Star, Rapier, Scimitar, Short Sword, Spear, 2-Hand. Sword, Warhammer	Intestine Necklace	Nilitim's Grimoire Pages
Bandages		Iron Ration, Visor	Noble's Crest
Bead Necklace		Ivandyr's Hoop	Ochre Liquid
Belt Pouch		Jade	Ogre Arm
Bone Chips		Jade Earring, Shard	Parrying Dagger
Bottle of Kalish		Lapis Lazuli	Patch of Shadow
Bronze Mace, Morning Star	Frog Eye Necklace	Large Bag	Pearl
	Froglok Meat	Large Patchwork Boots, Tunic	Pearl Shard
Brutechopper	Froglok Tadpole Eye, Flesh		piece of Rat Fur
Cat's Eye Agate	Gator Meat	Large Ruby	Rat Ears, Foot, Meat, Tooth, Whiskers
Chunk of Meat	Giant Rat Ear, Pelt, Whiskers	Large Snake Skin	
Cloth Cap, Cape, Choker, Cord, Gloves, Pants, Shirt, Sleeves, Veil, Wristband		Long Sword	Ration
	Giant Snake Fang, Rattle	Longbow	Raw-hide Boots, Cloak, Gloves, Gorget, Leggings, Skullcap, Tunic
	Glowing Gloves	Malachite	
	Gold Ring	Mask of Shadow	
Copper Amulet, Band	Hand of Shadow	Mead	
Cracked Staff	Hematite	Midnight Mallet	
Dwarf Meat	High Elf Flesh, Parts		

Items, cont.

Ringmail Boots, Bracelet, Cape, Coat, Coif, Gloves, Mantle, Neckguard, Pants, Skirt, Sleeves

Round Shield

Rune of Arrest, Attraction, Attraction, Banding, Concussion, Consumption, Contortion, Disassociation, Expulsion, Falhalem, Fulguration, Howling, Karana, Nagafen, Periphery, Presence, Proximity, Rathe, Solusek Ro, Sorcery, Substance, the Catalyst, the Cyclone, the Inverse, Trauma, Xegony

Rusty Axe, Bastard Sword, Battle Axe, Broad Sword, Dagger, Halberd, Long Sword, Mace, Morning Star, Rapier, Scimitar, Short Sword, Shortened Spear, Spear, Warhammer

Salil's Writ Pages

Senior Apprentice Robe

Shadowed Ball, Battle Axe, Book, Halberd, Long Sword, Mace, Morning Star, Rapier, Scimitar, Scythe, Spear, 2-Hand. Hammer, 2-Hand. Sword

Shining Stone

Short Beer

Silver Amulet, Stud

Small Bag

Small Box

Snake Egg, Fang, Scales, Venom Sac

Spell: Abolish Disease, Abundant Food, Affliction, Alter Plane: Hate, Anarchy, Atone, Beguile Animals, Beguile Undead, Blaze, Blinding Luminance, Call of Bones, Cast Sight, Cazic Portal, Charm, Cinder Bolt, Circle of Feerrott, Circle of Force, Circle of Lavastorm, Circle of Ro, Circle of Steamfont, Companion Spirit, Counteract Disease, Counteract Poison, Drones of Doom, Earthquake, Enchant: Platinum, Endure Disease, Endure Magic, Endure Poison, Enstill, Entrance, Envenomed Bolt, Envenomed Breath, Evacuate: Fay, Expel Undead, Force, Frenzied Strength, Fury, Gate of Poison, Greater Shielding, Greater Wolf Form, Health, Ice Shock, Illusion: Fire Elemental, Infectious Cloud, Insidious Fever, Insidious Malady, Insipid Weakness, Invoke Fear, Invoke Shadow, Lava Storm, Lightning Strike,

Spell: Malisement, Mana Sieve, Minor Conj.: Air, Minor Conj.: Earth, Minor Conj.: Fire, Minor Conjur.: Water, Nek Portal, Nimble, Nullify Magic, Plague, Poison Storm, Radiant Visage, Regeneration, Resist Cold, Resist Disease, Resist Fire, Resist Poison, Root, Rune III, Scourge, Shifting Shield, Sicken, Steelskin, Steelskin, Strength of Stone, Succor: Butcher, Superior Healing, Surge of Enfeeblement, Symbol of Pinzarn, Tainted Breath, Talisman of Tnarg, Thunderclap, Tremor, Valor, Venom of the Snake, Winter's Roar, Word of Health

Splintering Club

spore mushroom

Tasarin's Grimoire Pages

Tears of Prexuz

The Captain

The Scent of Marr

Thex Dagger

Topaz

Troll Parts

Turquoise

Undead Froglok Tounge

Velishoul's Tome Pages

Very Large Pelt

Water Flask

Wooden Shield

Words of Abatement, Absorption, Allure, Burnishing, Cazic-Thule, Cloudburst, Collection (Caza), Dark Paths, Derivation, Detachment, Detention, Dimension, Discernment, Dissolution, Duration, Duress, Efficacy, Endurance, Eradication, Eventide, Haunting, Imitation, Incarceration, Materials, Mistbreath, Motion, Neglect, Obligation, Possession, Quivering, Recluse, Resolve, Reviviscence, Spirit, the Element, the Psyche, the Sentient (Azia), the Sentient (Beza), the Spoken, the Suffering, Transcendence, Tyranny

Worn Great Staff

Woven Cap, Cape, Collar, Girth, Gloves, Leggings, Mantle, Mask, Sleeves, Tunic, Wristbands

Zimbittle's Pouch

Zombie Skin

Halas

The Barbarians have managed to construct a fairly cozy little town out of the frozen wastelands they call home. Such achievements don't come easily, however, as the rough-and-tumble nature of the residents may attest. The wandering traveler will find Halas rich in food, alcohol, weapons and the tools to make them.

Boats for the Everfrost Peaks leave from the dock at the south of town. Newbies should check out the Everfrost and Blackburrow Newbie Zones, which are just outside the city (take the raft across the pond in front of the main gate).

"Hail, lassies," McQuaid asked Salona and Drasa as they stepped into the Bar and Stout. "What can I get for you?"

"Something strong to drown the bad taste of a disappointing day," Salona replied as they both slipped onto a barstool.

McQuaid turned to pull a draught of his strongest grog as an older man sat next to Salona. "You know, the Warrior's Guild is always on the lookout for people strong like you. Perhaps direction is all you need. Speak with Lysbith McNaff. She'll send you after a worthy goal."

"And, after you've found what McNaff wants," McQuaid laughed, "you can drag your beaten body over Waltor Felligan's for healing. He'll fix you up in return for a favor."

Halas

Map by Mike Swiernik

1. Dog Pens
2. Pit of Doom (Warriors Guild, weapons)
3. Shamans Guild (alchemy supplies)
4. Dok's Cigars (food, pottery supplies)
5. The Golden Torc (steel/iron torques, pottery wheel/kiln)
6. Rogues Guild
7. Bank, Merchants (weapons, food) Rogue Trainers, Priest of Discord (outside)
8. Mac's Kilts (cloth/leather armor, sewing kits/patterns)
9. McDaniel's Smokes and Spirits (alcohol, smithing supplies), Merchant (food, oven) outside

10. Merchant (food, alcohol, pottery/brewing supplies)
11. McPherson's Bloody Blades (chain/plate armor, bows, arrows, fletching supplies, forges)
12. McQuaid's Bar and Stout (alcohol, brew barrel)
13. Yee Magik (weapons, medicine bags)
14. The Bound Mermaid (fishing supplies)
15. Merchants (food, cooking supplies, pottery patterns)

Everfrost Newbie Zone

Personalities

Arnis McLish	Granin O'Gill	Redwind	Tanosh
Bandl McMarrin	Iceberg	Ristia	Tarquin
Bonn McMarrin	Karg IceBear	Seria O'Danos	Tartain
Bryndin McMill	Lich of Miragul	Snowflake	Tasvan
Dansie McVicker	Lish McMarrin	Starn Bearjumper	Tinish
Dark Assassin	Martar IceBear	Sulgar	Trankia
Dom McMarrin	Megan O'Reilly	Sulon McMoor	Tundra Jack
Garn McMarrin	Miragul	Talin O'Donal	

Others

decaying skeleton	ice goblin caster	polar bear cub	vengeful lyricist
giant wooly spider	ice goblin diver	scrawny gnoll guard	vengeful soloist
glacier bear	ice goblin scout	skeleton	white wolf
gnoll guard	ice goblin whelp	snow leopard	wooly mammoth
gnoll pup	icy orc	snow orc shaman	wooly mammoth calf
goblin diver	large wooly spider	snow orc trooper	wooly spiderling
ice boned skeleton	orcish mountaineer	snow wolf	
ice giant	polar bear	vengeful composer	

Blackburrow Newbie Zone

Personalities

Lord Elgnub	Master Brewer	Tranixx Darkpaw

Gnolls

gnoll brewer	gnoll guardsman	patrolling gnoll	scrawny gnoll
burly gnoll	elite gnoll guard	gnoll pup	gnoll shaman
gnoll commander	gnoll high shaman	gnoll scout	

Others

brown bear	giant snake	razorgill
giant plague rat	grizzly bear	

EverQuest: The Ruins of Kunark

Items for Both Newbie Zones

(e) = only found in Everfrost; (b) = only found in Blackburrow

Ale
Amber (e)
Armor and Weapons Guide (e)
Arrow (b)
Baby Joseph Sayer (b)
Backpack
Backpack Pattern (e)
Bandages
Barbarian Head (e), Rib (e)
Basic Blacksmithing (e)
Bead Necklace
Bear Meat
Belt Pattern (e)
Belt Pouch
Black Pearl (e)
Blackburrow Cask (b)
Blackburrow Gnoll Pelt (b), Skin (b)
Bloodstone
Bloodstone Ring
Bloody Dagger (b), Dirk (e), Mantle (e)
Bone Chips (e)
Bottle of Kalish
Breath of Ro (c)
Bronze Battle Axe, Dagger (e), Long Sword, Mace, Main Gauche (e), Morning Star, Rapier (e), Shortened Spear (e), Spear (e), 2-Handed Sword
Buckler (e)
Burned Out Lightstone (e)
Carnelian
Caster Beads (e)
Cat's Eye Agate
Chunk of Meat
Clay Totem (b)
Cloak of the Ice Bear (e)
Cloak Pattern (e)
Cloth Cap, Cape, Choker, Cord, Gloves, Pants, Shawl (e), Shirt, Sleeves, Veil (e), Wristband (e)

Combine Dagger (e)
Copper Amulet, Band, Skull Ring (b)
Cracked Staff
Crystallized Marrow (e)
Delius Thyme's Diary Pages (e)
Elven Charm Necklace (b)
Emerald (e)
Emerald Ring (e)
Empty Bottle of Elixir (e)
Essence of Rathe (e)
Faded Salil's Writ Pages (e)
Faded Velishoul's Tome
Fine Steel Dagger (e), Great Staff (e), Long Sword (e), Morning Star (e), Rapier (e), Scimitar (e), Short Sword (e), Spear (e), 2-Handed Sword (e), Warhammer (e)
Fire Emerald (e)
Fire Opal (e)
Fish Scales (b)
Flame of Vox (e)
Fleeting Quiver Pattern (e)
Fresh Fish (b)
Frost Giant Toes (e)
Giant Snake Fang (b), Rattle (b)
Gigantic Zweihander (e)
Glacier Bear Pelt (e)
Glove of Rallos Zek (e)
Gnoll Fang, Head (b), Paw (b), Pup Scalp
Goblin Ice Necklace (e)
Gold Ring (e)
Golden Earring, Pendant (e)
Gorget Pattern (e)
Greater Lightstone (e)
Grizzly Bear Skin (b)
Hematite
High Quality Bear Skin (b)
How To Sew: Large Sizes (e), Medium Sizes (e), Small Sizes (e)

Hunting Bow (b)
Ice of Velious
Ichor (e)
Ingot of the Devout (e)
Iron Ration
Jade (e), Earring (e), Ring (e), Shard
Jasper
Lantern Casing Mold (e)
Lapis Lazuli
Large Bag
Large Belt Sectional Mold (e)
Large Boot Mold (e)
Large Bracer Sectional Mold (e)
Large Cloak Sectional Mold (e)
Large Cloth Cap, Cape, Choker, Cord, Gloves, Pants (e), Sandals, Shawl, Shirt, Sleeves, Veil, Wristband
Large Gauntlet Mold (e)
Large Gorget Mold (e)
Large Helm Mold (e)
Large Leggings Sectional Mold (e)
Large Mail Sectional Mold (e)
Large Mantle Sectional Mold (e)
Large Mask Mold (e)
Large Raw-hide Belt, Boots, Cloak, Gloves, Gorget, Leggings, Mask, Shoulderpads, Skullcap, Sleeves, Tunic, Wristbands (all e)
Large Sewing Kit (e)
Large Sleeves Sectional Mold (e)
Large Wooden Shield
Leather Boots (e)
Lightstone (e)
Low Quality Bear Skin (b)
Lupine Claw Gauntlets (e)
Malachite

Mammoth Meat (e), Rib Bone (e), Skin (b), Tusks (e)
Mask Pattern (e)
Mead
Medium Quality Bear Skin (b)
Miragul's Head (e), Robe (e)
Mithril Amulet (e), Earring (e)
Needle Mold (e)
Nilitim's Grimoire Pages (e)
Old Stained Robe (e)
One Half of Elixir (e)
One Hand Pick (e)
One Quarter of Elixir (e)
Onyx
Onyx Earring (b)
Opal (e)
Opal Bracelet (e)
Parrying Dagger (e)
Parrying Pick (e)
Patch of Gnoll Fur
Pearl (e), Earring (e), Necklace (e), Ring (e), Shard
Peridot (e)
Polar Bear Cloak (e), Skin (e)
Puma Skin (e)
Quiver Pattern (e)
Rat Bone Necklace (b)
Rat Ears (b), Tooth (b), Whiskers (b)
Ration
Raw-hide Belt, Boots, Cloak, Gloves, Gorget, Leggings, Mask, Shoulderpads, Skullcap, Sleeves, Tunic, Wristbands (all b)
Red Sr Apprentice Robe (e)
Robe of the Evoker (e)
Ruined Bear Pelt
Ruined Blackburrow Gnoll Pelt (b)

Items

Ruined Cat Pelt (e)

Ruined Wolf Pelt (e)

Rune of Al'Kabor, Ap'Sagor (e), Arrest (e), Attraction, Banding (e), Conception (e), Concussion (e), Consumption (e), Contortion (e), Crippling (e), Disassociation, Embrace (e), Expulsion, Falhalem (e), Frost (e), Fulguration (e), Howling (e), Impetus (e), Infraction (e), Ivy (e), Karana, Nagafen (e), Neglect (b), Opression (b), Paralysis (e), Periphery (e), Petrification (e), Presence, Proximity (e), Rathe (e), Solusek Ro (e), Sorcery (e), Substance (e), the Astral (e), the Catalyst (e), the Combine (e), the Cyclone (e), the Helix (e), the Inverse (e), Trauma, Tyranny (e), Velious (b), Xegony

Rusty Axe (e), Bastard Sword (e), Battle Axe, Broad Sword, Dagger, Flail (b), Halberd (e), Long Sword, Mace, Morning Star, Rapier, Scimitar (e), Scythe, Short Sword, Shortened Spear, Spear, Spiked Shoulderpads (b), 2-Handed Hammer (b), 2-Handed Sword, Warhammer

Salil's Writ Pages (e)

Sapphire (e)

Shattered Caster Beads (e)

Short Beer

Shoulderpad Pattern (e)

Silver Amulet (e), Earring, Ring, Stud

Small Bag

Small Box

Small Mammoth Tusks (e)

Snake Egg (b)

Snake Venom Sac (b)

Songs: Agilmente's Aria of Eagles (e), Alenia's Disenchanting Melody (e), Angstlich's Appalling Screech (e), Cassindra's Chorus of Clarity (e), Chant of Battle (e), Denon's Dissension (e), Lyssa's Solidarity of Vision (e), Lyssa's Veracious Concord (e), Melanie's Mellifluous Motion (e), Psalm of Cooling (e), Psalm of Mystic Shielding (e), Psalm of Purity (e), Psalm of Vitality (e), Psalm of Warmth (e), Selo's Consonant Chain (e), Solon's Song of the Sirens (e), Syvelian's Anti-Magic Aria (e)

Spells (all e): Abolish Disease, Abundant Drink, Affliction, Alluring Aura, Augmentation, Befriend Animal, Boil Blood, Bramblecoat, Burnout II, Circle of Butcher, Circle of Commons, Circle of Karana, Circle of Toxxulia, Clarity, Combust, Counteract Disease, Counteract Poison, Curse of the Simple Mind, Dismiss Summoned, Dismiss Undead, Divine Barrier, Dooming Darkness, Endure Disease, Endure Poison, Energy Storm, Ensnare, Enstill, Envenomed Bolt, Envenomed Breath, Evacuate: North, Extinguish Fatigue, Fay Portal, Feedback, Gale of Poison, Greater Healing, Greater Summoning (Air, Earth, Fire, Water), Guard, Immolate, Infectious Cloud, Inferno Shield, Inferno Shock, Insidious Fever, Insidious Malady, Listless Power, Magnify, North Portal, Nullify Magic, Obscure, Panic the Dead, Phantom Chain, Plague, Poison Storm, Quickness, Raging Strength, Rain of Spikes, Renew Bones, Resist Disease, Resist Fire, Resist Poison, Revive, Ring of Misty, Rising Dexterity, Scourge, Shield of Brambles, Shock Spiral of Al'Kabor, Sicken, Spirit Tap, Succor: East, Suffocate, Summon Coldstone, Summon Dead, Tagar's Insects, Tainted Breath, Thunder Strike, Tox Portal, Ultravision, Vampiric Curse, Venom of the Snake, Word of Spirit, Wrath, Yonder

Spider Legs, Silk, Venom Sac (all e)

Spiderling Eye, Legs, Silk (all e)

Spiked Collar (b)

Splintering Club

Star Rose Quartz

Star Ruby (e)

Steel Torque (e)

Studded Leather Collar (b)

Sweaty Shirt (e)

Tailoring (e)

Tasarin's Grimoire Pages

Tattered Leather Boots (b)

tattered note (e)

Tears of Prexuz (e)

The Scent of Marr (e)

Thimble Mold (e)

Tishans Kilt (e)

Topaz (e)

Turquoise

2-Handed Sword (e)

Velishoul's Tome Pages

Warthread Kilt (e)

Water Flask

Werewolf Skin Cloak (e)

Whip Pattern (e)

White Wolf Skin (e)

Wing of Xegony (e)

Wolf Meat (e)

Wooden Shield

Wooden Totem (b)

Wooly Fungus (e)

Words of: Abatement (e), Absorption, Acquisition (Beza) (e), Allure, Anthology (b), Bidding (e), Bondage (e), Burnishing (e), Cazic-Thule, Cloudburst, Collection (Azia) (e), Collection (Beza) (e), Collection (Caza) (e), Convocation (e), Crippling Force (e), Dark Paths (e), Derivation (e), Descrying (e), Detachment, Detention (e), Dimension, Discernment, Dissolution (e), Dominion (b), Duration (e), Duress (e), Efficacy (e), Endurance (e), Enlightenment (b), Eradication (e), Eventide, Grappling (e), Haunting (e), Imitation (e), Incarceration (e), Materials (e), Mistbreath, Motion (e), Neglect (e), Obligation (e), Odus (e), Possession, Projection (e), Quivering (e), Radiance (b), Recluse, Refuge (b), Requisition (e), Resolve (e), Reviviscence (e), Seizure (e), Spirit (e), the Element (e), the Ethereal (e), the Extinct (b), the Psyche (e), the Quickening (b), the Sentient (Azia) (e), the Sentient (Beza), the Spectre (e), the Spoken (e), the Suffering (e), Transcendence, Tyranny (e)

Worn Great Staff

Wrath Orc Wristbands (e)

Wristband Pattern (e)

"Y ou are new here," the wine steward said as he looked down his nose at Krasath, a dark elf necromancer, and her dark elf warrior companion, Kr'santh.

"Perhaps we are," Kr'santh said indignantly.

"Well, I'm sure you won't be able to afford anything here," the steward said and turned to his next customer.

A tall, wiry warrior stepped between Kr'santh and the retreating steward. "I can tell by your pride that you are a warrior. If you seek the gold to pay for The Rack's wines, seek out Trizam N'Tan at the Cauldron of Hate."

"But, I am no warrior," Krasath said. "I study the dark arts."

"Ah," the older warrior said, "then it is to The Dead that you should go. An old friend is seeking assistance. His name is Noxhil V'Sek."

Neriak

The Dark Elves carved out an extensive for themselves, invisible to the prying eyes of outsiders. One enters Neriak from Nektulos Forest, through the first zone of the city, which is known as the Foreign Quarter. Few but the Dark Elves continue through this zone to the next, known as Neriak Commons. The single entrance to the final zone, Third Gate, lies at the far side of the Commons.

Neriak is a sizable city, offering its residents not only the basic necessities of life, but also goods of a higher order, such as wines, fine plate armor, and magicial supplies of all kinds. The mansions of the Third Gate are reputed to be quite fine, indeed.

Such wealth is of course not immediately available to all, and newbies are advised to seek their fame and fortune (or at least earn bed and board) in the Nektulos Forest Newbie Zone near the entrance of the city.

Neriak Foreign Quarter

to Nektulos Forest

to Neriak Commons

Map by Mike Swiernik

1. Guard Hall
2. The Smugglers Inn (alcohol, brewing/pottery supplies, food, etc.)
3. Silk Underground (cloth armor, sewing kits)
4. Dranas Bread and Butcher (food, cooking supplies, oven)
5. Slugs Tavern (alcohol, brew barrel)
6. Market View (alcohol, brewing/pottery supplies, food, etc.)
7. Merchants (shoes, bags), kiln, pottery wheel

8. Merchant (weapons)
9. Ogre Merchants (smithing books, molds)
10. Armor Shop (ring armor, forge)
11. Pig Stickers (weapons)
12. Merchant (Shaman spells) [[??]]
13. Shadow Knights Guild
14. Warriors Guild (alcohol, weapons)
15. Bites 'n' Pieces (oven, food, etc.)
16. Shinie Things (jewelry metal)

EverQuest: The Ruins of Kunark

Neriak Commons

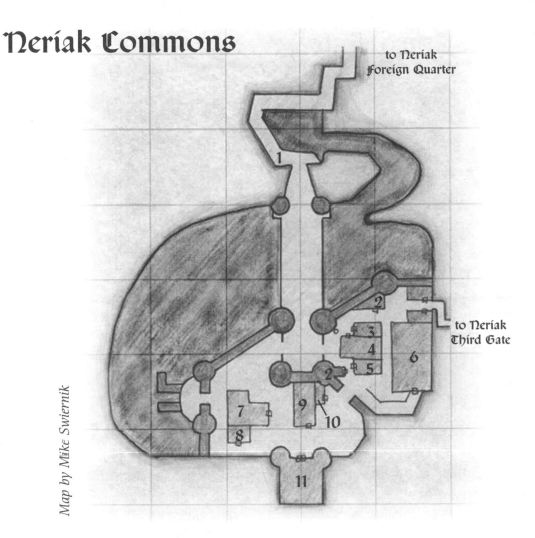

Map by Mike Swiernik

to Neriak
Foreign Quarter

to Neriak
Third Gate

1. Priest of Discord

2. Entrances to underground:
   Neriak Bank, The Burnished Coin, The
   Refined Palate, The Bounty of the Earth
   and The Blind Fish (alcohol, books,
   brew barrel, clay, cooking supplies, food,
   lightstones, ore, oven, potions,
   sharpening stones)

3. Smithy (ring armor, weapons)

4. Adamant Armor (plate armor)

5. Forge House (alcohol)

6. Enchanters, Magicians and Wizards
   Guilds (each sells supplies for that class)

7. Toadstools (alcohol, armor molds),
   Merchant (fishing supplies) outside

8. The Bleek Fletcher (fletching kits/supplies)

9. The House of D'abth (food, etc.)

10. The Dashing Form (cloth armor, sewing
    kits)

11. Warriors Guild

Neriak Third Gate

Map by Mike Swiernik

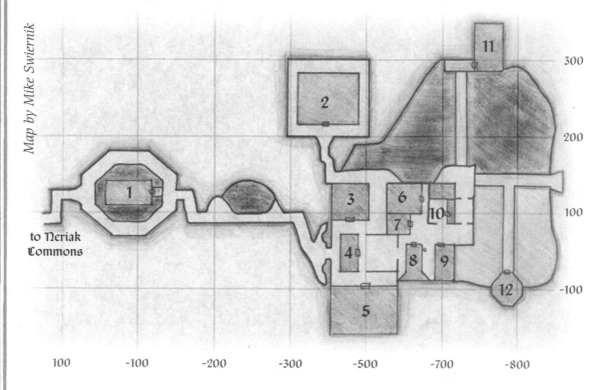

to Neriak
Commons

1. Temple of Innoruuk (Clerics Guild, weapons)

2. Necromancers and Shadow Knights Guilds (equipment for these classes)

3. Library (spells)

4. Furrier Royale (leather armor/patterns/ kits)

5. Rogues Guild

6. The Maidens Fancy (alcohol, brew barrel, Dark Elf ambassador, Ironforge prisoner)

7. The Bauble (jewelry supplies)

8. Cuisine Excelsior (alcohol)

9. The Rack (wines)

11. X'Lottl Mansion

12. J'Narus Mansion

Nektulos Forest Newbie Zone

Personalities

Bink	Gollee	Initiate Pool	Quester Hannin
Cannix	Guard E'Brona	Initiate Rambel	Rauner
Captain N'Farre	Guard E'tru	Initiate Umbra	Rollis
Corporal D'Abth	Guard F'Losta	Jossle	Sergeant C'Orm
Corporal J'Rais	Guard N'Lan	Klimmer	Sergeant J'Narus
Corporal X'Horn	Guard T'Aba	Leatherfoot Deputy	Snitch
Corporal X'Tis	Guard T'Quetal	Leatherfoot Medic	Travis Two Tone
Dragoon J'len	Guard V'Lex	Mardoon	
Dragoon T'Sanne	Guard X'Onnu	Master Whoopal	
Dragoon V'tai	Hamer	Neophyte Edel	
Dragoon X'Lottl	Himmel	Neophyte Halle	
Foley	Initiate Abber	Neophyte Hazel	
Forley	Initiate Guanin	Quester Dunden	
Gammer	Initiate Hart	Quester Hannil	

Others

bixie	iron guardian	shadow wolf	will o' wisp
black bear	large piranha	shadowed man	young kodiak
black wolf	large spider	skeleton	zombie
darkwater piranha	lesser mummy	spiderling	
decaying skeleton	moss snake	stone guardian	
fire beetle	orc runner	tree snake	

Items

Bear Meat
Bixie Parts, Stinger
Black Wolf Skin
Bloodstone
Bloodstone Ring
Bone Chips
Bronze Bastard Sword, Halberd, Long Sword, Mace, Morning Star, Short Sword, 2-Handed Sword
Burned Out Lightstone
Carnelian
Chunk of Meat
Cloth Cap, Cape, Choker, Cord, Gloves, Pants, Shirt, Sleeves, Veil, Wristband
Cracked Staff
Crushbone Belt
Dragoon Dirk
Eye of Serilis
Eye of Shadow
Faded Salil's Writ Pages
Faded Velishoul's Tome
Fine Steel Long Sword, Scimitar, Short Sword, 2-Handed Sword
Fire Beetle Eye, Leg
Fish Scales
Flame of Vox
Fresh Fish
Glove of Rallos Zek
Glowing Gloves
Golden Earring
Greater Lightstone
Grizzly Bear Skin
Hand of Shadow
High Quality Bear Skin
Ice of Velious
Jade Shard
Jasper

Large Snake Skin
Leatherfoot Raider Skullcap
Lightstone
Long Sword
Low Quality Bear Skin
Mask of Shadow
Medium Quality Bear Skin
Onyx
Parrying Dagger
Tasarin's Grimoire Pages
Patch of Shadow
Pearl Shard
Raw Darkwater Piranha
Raw-hide Boots, Cloak, Gloves, Gorget, Leggings, Skullcap, Tunic
Round Shield
Ruined Bear Pelt
Ruined Wolf Pelt
Rune of Al'Kabor, Arrest, Attraction, Banding, Conception, Concussion, Consumption, Contortion, Disassociation, Dismemberment, Embrace, Expulsion, Falhalem, Fulguration, Howling, Infraction, Karana, Nagafen, Neglect, Opression, Paralysis, Periphery, Petrification, Presence, Proximity, Rallos Zek, Regeneration, Solusek Ro, Sorcery, Substance, the Catalyst, the Combine, the Cyclone, the Helix, Trauma, Tyranny, Velious, Xegony
Runner Pouch

Rusty Axe, Bastard Sword, Battle Axe, Broad Sword, Dagger, Flail, Halberd, Long Sword, Mace, Morning Star, Rapier, Scimitar, Scythe, Short Sword, Shortened Spear, Spear, 2-Handed Battle Axe, 2-Handed Hammer, 2-Handed Sword, Warhammer
Salil's Writ Pages
sealed letter
Shadow Wolf Pelt
Shadowed Ball, Battle Axe, Book, Halberd, Long Sword, Mace, Morning Star, Rapier, Scimitar, Scythe, Spear, 2-Handed Hammer, 2-Handed Sword
Shining Stone
Silver Earring
Silver Ring
Small Cloth Cap, Cape, Choker, Cord, Gloves, Pants, Sandals, Shawl, Shirt, Sleeves, Veil, Wristband
Snake Egg, Fang, Scales
Spider Legs, Silk, Venom Sac
Spiderling Eye, Legs, Silk
Splintering Club
Star Rose Quartz
Velishoul's Tome Pages
Wolf Meat
Wooden Shield
Words of Abatement, Absorption, Acquisition (Azia), Allure, Anthology, Bidding, Cazic-Thule,

Cloudburst, Coercion, Collection (Azia), Collection (Beza), Convocation, Dark Paths, Derivation, Descrying, Detachment, Detention, Dimension, Discernment, Dissemination, Dissolution, Dominion, Duration, Duress, Efficacy, Endurance, Enlightenment, Eradication, Eventide, Haunting, Imitation, Materials, Mistbreath, Motion, Neglect, Parasitism, Possession, Projection, Purification, Quivering, Radiance, Recluse, Refuge, Resolve, Reviviscence, Rupturing, Seizure, Sight, Spirit, the Element, the Extinct, the Incorporeal, the Quickening, the Sentient (Azia), the Sentient (Beza), the Spectre, the Spoken, the Suffering, Transcendence, Tyranny
Worn Great Staff
Zombie Skin

Grasog and Oc stood over their mutual lizard man kill in the Feerrott Marsh. Grasog said, "Me gets meat for Soonog in Greenblood Guild Hall."

"Me gets tail for Horgus," Oc the Ogre warrior said.

The Ogres nearby looked confused. Grason and Oc just grinned at each other and walked off to their next kill.

Oggok

Oggok, home city of the Ogre race, is located in central southern Antonica. At first glance, it may not appear much, but a substantial portion of the city is hidden in underground tunnels. City merchants stock almost everything the inhabitants and the occasional traveler might require, including food, various types of armor and weapons, and alchemy supplies.

Newbies can rustle up a living in the Feerrott to the south of town, at relatively little risk to life and limb. As swamps go, this one's not so bad ...

Oggok

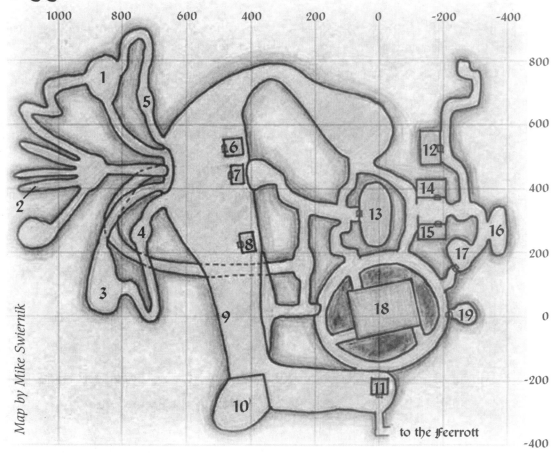

Map by Mike Swiernik

to the Feerrott

1. Shamans Guild
2. Ambassador K'Ryn
3. Merchant (weapons)
4. Merchant (food), pottery wheel, kiln
5. Merchant (boots)
6. Merchant (shield)
7. Merchant (weapons)
8. Merchant (boxes)
9. Priest of Discord
10. Merchant (arrows, fletching supplies)

11. Merchant (food, etc.)
12. Merchant (food, oven)
13. Shadow Knights Guild (weapons)
14. Merchant (leather/cloth armor)
15. Merchant (chain/plate armor, forge)
16. Shaman Trainer (alchemy supplies, weapons)
17. Merchant (food, alcohol, brew barrel)
18. Warriors Guild
19. Bank

The Feerrott Newbie Zone

Personalities

Bouncer Flerb
Bouncer Fug
Bouncer Hurd
Bouncer Prud
Bup
Cyndreela

Dark Assassin
Drizda Tunesinger
Duga
Fugla
Grak
Innkeep Gub

Innkeep Morpa
Mugu
Murg
Murga
Roror

Lizard Men

lizard man broodling
lizard man warrior

lizardman forager
lizardman mystic

lizardman scout
lizardman watcher

Others

bat
black wolf
decaying skeleton
dry bones skeleton
froglok tad
giant bat

green snake
hatchling
infected rat
jungle spider
jungle spiderling
large piranha

lesser scarab
minor scarab
shadow wolf
skeleton
snake
spectre

swamp alligator
tree snake
zombie

Items

Amber
Armor and Weapons
    Guide
Ashwood Bow Staff
Backpack Pattern
Bandages
Basic Blacksmithing
Bat Fur, Wing
Belt Pattern
Binelen's Quick Treats,
    Succulence
Black Pearl
Black Wolf Skin
Bloody Dirk
Bloody Mantle
Bone Chips
Bottle of Milk
Bowyers Guide
Box of Lute Strings
Breath of Ro

Bronze Battle Axe,
    Dagger, Long Sword,
    Mace, Main Gauche,
    Rapier, Scythe,
    Shortened Spear, Spear,
    2-Handed Sword
Chunk of Meat
Chunk of Ogre Flesh
Cloak Pattern
Cloth Cap, Cape, Choker,
    Cord, Gloves, Pants,
    Sandals, Shawl, Shirt,
    Sleeves, Veil,
    Wristband
Combine Dagger
Cracked Staff
Crude Stein
Cup of Flour
Dagger
Darkwood Bow Staff
Elm Bow Staff

Emerald
Emerald Ring
Faded Salil's Writ Pages
Faded Velishoul's Tome
Fine Steel Dagger, Great
    Staff, Long Sword,
    Morning Star, Rapier,
    Scimitar, Short Sword,
    Spear, 2-Handed
    Sword, Warhammer
Fire Beetle Eye, Leg
Fire Emerald
Fire Opal
Flame of Vox
Fleeting Quiver Pattern
Fletching Kit
Fresh Fish
Froglok Tadpole Eye, Flesh
Frosting
Garnish

Gator Meat
Ghumim's Classical Dishes
Ghumim's Delights
Glove of Rallos Zek
Gold Ring
Golden Pendant
Gorget Pattern
Hemp Twine
Hickory Bow Staff
How To Sew: Large Sizes,
    Medium Sizes, Small
    Sizes
Ice of Velious
Iron Ration
Jade
Jade Earring, Ring, Shard
Jug of Sauces
Lantern Casing Mold
Large Belt Sectional Mold
Large Boot Mold

Items, cont.

Large Bracer Sectional Mold
Large Cloak Sectional Mold
Large Cloth Cap, Cape, Choker, Cord, Gloves, Pants, Sandals, Shawl, Shirt, Sleeves, Veil, Wristband
Large Gauntlet Mold
Large Gorget Mold
Large Groove Nocks
Large Helm Mold
Large Leggings Sectional Mold
Large Mail Sectional Mold
Large Mantle Sectional Mold
Large Mask Mold
Large Raw-hide Belt, Boots, Cloak, Gloves, Gorget, Leggings, Mask, Shoulderpads, Skullcap, Sleeves, Tunic, Wristbands
Large Sewing Kit
Large Sleeves Sectional Mold
Large Snake Skin
Linen String
Lizard Meat
Lizard Tail
Lizardman Scout Fife
Loaf of Bread
Mask Pattern
Mead
Medium Groove Nocks
Mithril Amulet, Earring
Mixxy's Delicacies Vols 1, 2
Mystic Doll
Needle Mold
Netted Cap, Cape, Choker, Girth, Gloves, Mantle, Mask, Pants, Shirt, Sleeves, Wristband

Nilitim's Grimoire Pages
Oak Bow Staff
Opal
Opal Bracelet
Parrying Dagger
Tasarin's Grimoire Pages
Pearl
Pearl Earring, Necklace, Ring, Shard
Peridot
Planing Tool
Quiver Pattern
Rat Ears, Tooth, Whiskers
Ration
Raw-hide Belt, Boots, Cloak, Gloves, Gorget, Leggings, Mask, Shoulderpads, Skullcap, Sleeves, Tunic, Wristbands
Rohand's Edibles, Sea Treats
Round Shield
Ruined Wolf Pelt
Rune of Al'Kabor, Ap'Sagor, Arrest, Attraction, Banding, Conception, Concussion, Consumption, Contortion, Crippling, Disassociation, Embrace, Expulsion, Falhalem, Frost, Fulguration, Howling, Impetus, Infraction, Karana, Nagafen, Paralysis, Periphery, Petrification, Presence, Proximity, Rathe, Solusek Ro, Sorcery, Substance, the Astral, the Catalyst, the Combine, the Cyclone, the Helix, Trauma, Tyranny, Xegony

Rusty Axe, Bastard Sword, Battle Axe, Broad Sword, Dagger, Dagger, Flail, Halberd, Long Sword, Mace, Morning Star, Rapier, Scimitar, Scythe, Short Sword, Shortened Spear, Spear, 2-Handed Hammer, 2-Handed Sword, Warhammer
Sack of Cursed Hay
Salil's Writ Pages
Sapphire
Scythe
Shadow Wolf Pelt
Short Beer
Shoulderpad Pattern
Silk String
Silver Amulet
Small Groove Nocks
Small Lantern
Snake Egg, Fang, Scales
Sorin's Treats on the Go
Spices
Spider Legs
Spiderling Eye, Legs, Silk
Splintering Club
Standard Bow Cam
Star Ruby
Tailoring
Tears of Prexuz
Thimble Mold
Topaz
Torch
Unfinished Brass Trumpet
Vaashar's Sweet Revege, Sweet Treats
Velishoul's Tome Pages
Vinegar
Water Flask
Whip Pattern
Whittling Blade

Wing of Xegony
Wolf Meat
Wooden Shield
Words of Abatement, Absorption, Acquisition (Beza), Allure, Bidding, Bondage, Cazic-Thule, Cloudburst, Collection (Azia), Collection (Beza), Convocation, Crippling Force, Dark Paths, Derivation, Descrying, Detachment, Detention, Dimension, Discernment, Dissolution, Duration, Duress, Efficacy, Endurance, Eradication, Eventide, Grappling, Haunting, Imitation, Materials, Mistbreath, Motion, Neglect, Odus, Possession, Projection, Quivering, Recluse, Requisition, Resolve, Reviviscence, Seizure, Spirit, the Element, the Ethereal, the Sentient (Azia), the Sentient (Beza), the Spectre, the Spoken, the Suffering, Transcendence, Tyranny
Worn Great Staff
Wristband Pattern
Xectia's Favored Flavors, Hot Pie
Zombie Skin

Qeynos

Ah, the bustling city of Qeynos — home to Humans and Half-Elves, and waystation for travelers of Norrath. Qeynos is divided into two zones, North and South. Most merchants have set up shop in South Qeynos, and boats leave from the docks to the west of this zone.

A larger than average number of Qeynosians are young and upwardly mobile, and newbies will find abundant resources in the Newbie Zones of Qeynos Hills and the Plains of Karana surrounding the city.

"**R**ats and bats and snakes!" the young warrior said to the evening gate guard. "The merchants hardly pay anything for what I gather."

"Experienced in killing rats, are you?" the guard asked. "Sneed Galliway's having a big rat problem. Help him and he might consent to pay you more."

The swordsman rolled his eyes. "And, after I kill one more rat?"

The guard grinned at the young man's ambition. "After that, go see Brin Stolunger. He hangs around the Arena. He might know of a way to make bat wings and snake scales useful."

South Qeynos

1. Tin Soldier (forge, chain armor)
2. The Wind Spirit's Song (Bards Guild), Merchants (Bard songs, weapons)
3. Fharn's Leather and Thread (leather armor, sewing kit/patterns)
4. Bag 'n' Barrel (bags, pottery wheel/kiln)
5. Nesiff's Wooden Weapons (weapons), Merchant (arrows, fletching supplies) outside
6. Lion's Mane Inn (alcohol, brew barrel)
7. Tax Hall
8. Qeynos Hold (bank)
9. Tunnel to underground
10. The Herb Jar (spells, potions, books, lightstones, Magician supplies)
11. Enchanters, Magicians and Wizards Guilds (trainers, spells Wizard supplies)
12. Merchants (cloth/leather/ring armor)
13. Fireprides (chain/leather/plate armor, shields)
14. Merchant (leather/ring armor, shields, forge)
15. Boats to Erud's Crossing, Erudin
16. Mermaid's Lure (fishing supplies)
17. Merchants (cloth armor, sewing kits, bags, axes, weapons)
18. Grounds of Fate (PvP area), tunnel to underground
19. Warrior Training Hall
20. Tunnel to underground
21. Port Authority
22. Voleen's Fine Baked Goods (food, brewing supplies, cooking supplies, oven)
23. Fish's Ale (alcohol, brew barrel)
24. Temple of Thunder (Paladins/Clerics trainers, spells, weapons, sheilds)

Renara had tried many ways to find her guild in Qeynos, and to find the temple of Bertoxxulous where she could pay tribute to her god. Unfortunately, many of the directions she had been given up until now were wrong. It was always difficult for Renara to trust anyone, but she was desperate. She finally ran into a caster called Grein who was willing to help her.

He cast a spell on her. "That should make it so you can breathe underwater." Then, he jumped from a nearby bridge into the water. "Follow me," he said with a grin.

Renara looked into the water. There were others down there!

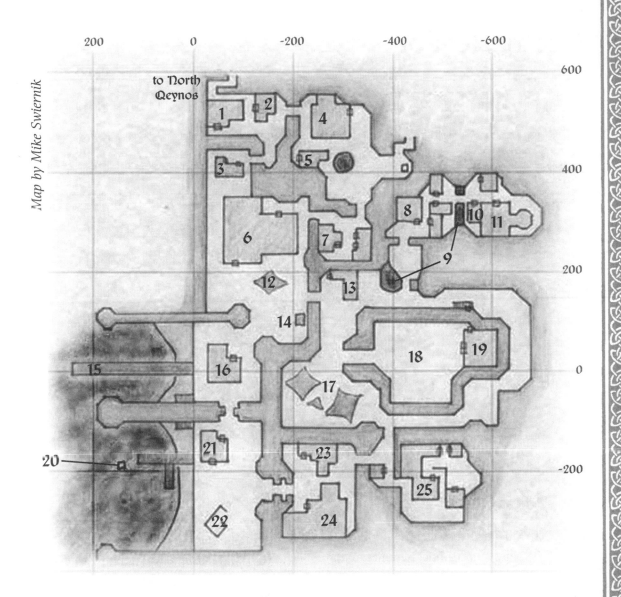

Map by Mike Swiernik

to North Qeynos

North Qeynos

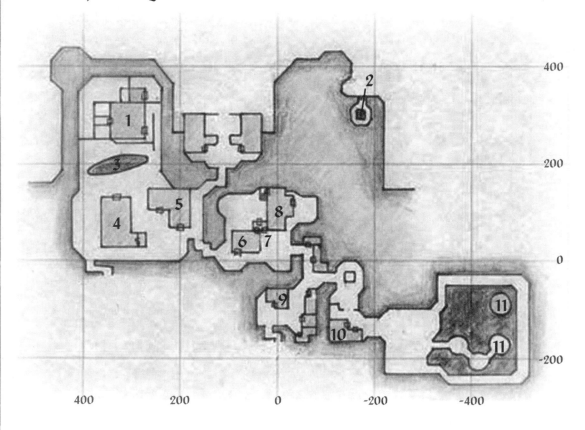

1. Order of the Silent Fist (Monks Guild), Merchant (weapons, bags, bandages)
2. Kliknik Tunnel to underground
3. Reflecting Pond (tunnel to underground)
4. Crow's Pub & Casino (alcohol, brew barrel, tunnel to Thieves Guild)
5. Galliway's Trading Post (food, etc.)
6. Ironforge's (weapons, medicine bags)
7. Jewelbox (jewelry supplies)
8. Ironforge's Estate
9. The Cobbler (boots)
10. Merchants (weapons, Paladin spells)
11. Teleport to Temple of Life, Cleric and Paladin Trainers

Western Plains of Karana Newbie Zone

Personalities

Alysa
Analya
Anderia
Basil
Brenzl McMannus
Brothers Chintle, Estle, Trintle
Caninel
Carlan the Young
Chief Goonda
Choon
Chrislin Baker
Cleet Miller, Cleet Miller Jr
Draze Slashyn
Einhorst McMannus
Froon
Frostbite
Furball Miller
Gindlin Toxfodder
Gomo Limerin
Grebin Sneztop
Guards
Habustush Gikin
Henina Miller
Innkeeps Danin, Rislarn
Junth McMannus
Kobot Dellin
Kyle Rinlin
Lander Billkin
Lars McMannus
Lempeck Hargrin
Linaya Sowlin
Maldin the Old
Minda
Minya Coldtoes
Misla McMannus
Mistrana Two Notes
Misty Storyswapper
Nachh
Ollysa Bladefinder
Paglan
Parcil Vinder
Quegin Hadder
Rongol
Ronly Jogmill
Sera McMannus
Silna Weaver
Spinner
Tarnar
Tiny Miller
Tolony Marle
Tukk
Tyzer
Ulrich McMannus
Vanikk
Yiz Pon

Others

bandit
black wolf
brigand
brown bear
cyclops
farmer
fire beetle
ghoul, ghoul messenger
giant beetle
giant spider
grizzly bear
hill giant
lion, lioness
mist wolf
ogre guard, priestess, shaman, shamaness
scarecrow
shadow wolf
skeleton
Splitpaw assassin
treant
troll basher, runner
werewolf
willowisp
young lion, lioness
zombie

Northern Plains of Kunara Newbie Zone

Personalities

Ashenpaw
Barkeeps Jeny, Milo
Bilbis Briar
Briana Treewhisper
Bristletoe
Brother Nallin
Bunu Stoutheart
Callowwing
Capt Linarius
Cordelia Minster
Cory Bumbleye
Ezmirella
Fixxin Followig
GrimFeather
Grimtooth
Guards
Innkeeps Disda, James
Korvik the cursed
Lieutenant Midraim
Mrysila
Nul Aleswiller
Regis the Reverent
Romella
Romi
Roule
Shiel Glimmerspindle
Swiftclaw
Tak Whistler
Timbur the tiny
Watchman Dexlin
Xanuusus
Zahal the Vile

Others

borer beetle
druid
farmer
ghoul
griffawn, griffenne, griffon
grizzly bear
hill giant
lion, lioness, highland lion
pincer beetle
raider
scythe beetle
silvermist wolf
skeleton, tiny skeleton
treant
willowisp
zombie

Southern Plains of Karana Newbie Zone

Personalities

Brothers Drash, Qwinn
Coloth Meadowgreen
Cracktusk
Ghanex Drah
Gnashmaw
Gnawfang
Grizzleknot
Groi Gutblade
High Shaman Grisok

High Shaman Phido
Jale Phlintoes
Knari Morawk
Krak Windchaser
Kroldir Thunderhoof
Lady Arlena
Lord Grimrot
Marik Clubthorn
Mroon

Narra Tanith
Quillmane
Sentry Alechin
Shakrn Meadowgreen
Shamans Lenrel, Ren'Rex
Synger Foxfyre
Tarn
Tash
Tesch Mas Gnoll

Tigia
Topaz
treant
Trumpy
Turnin
Ulan Meadowgreen
Vhalen Nostrolo

Qeynos Hills Newbie Zone

Personalities

Axe Broadsmith
Baobob Miller
Barn Bloodstone
Buzzlin Bornahm
Chanda Miller
Colyn IronBark
Cros Treewind
Gnasher Furgutt

Gornolin
Guards
Hadden
Hefax Tinmar
Hilda WildRunner
Holly Windstalker
Isabella Cellus
Konem Matse
Lars McMannus

Marton Sayer
Mira Sayer
Misty Storyswapper
Mogan Delfin
Neclo Rheslar
Niclaus Ressinn
Pinata
Pyzjn
Rephas

Scruffy
Sir Edwin Motte
Talym Shoontar
Tol Nicelot
Tovax Vmar
Varsoon
Wyle Bimlin

Gnolls

gnoll hunter

gnoll pup

gnoll scout

gnoll watcher

Others

bat
brown bear
dread corpse
fire beetle
fish

giant rat
gray, grey wolf
grizzly bear
large bat
large rat

large snake
mangy rat
piranha
rabid grizzly, wolf
skeletal messenger, monk,

spearman
skeleton, decaying, putrid,
  strange, warbone
snake
willowisp

Items for All Four Newbie Zones

(h) = in Qeynos Hills; (n) = in Northern Plains of Karana; (s) = in Southern Plains of Karana; (w) = in Western Plains of Karana; no notation (e.g., Ale) = in all four zones

Ale
Amber
Animal Cookie Mold (h)
Armor and Weapons Guide (h,w)
Arrow (h,s,w)
Ashwood Bow Staff (s)
Aviak Charm (s)
Aviak Feathers (s)
Axe (s,w)
Backpack
Backpack Pattern (w)
Bag of Troll Guts (n)
Balm Leaves (n)
Bandages
Bandit Sash (n,s,w)
Barbarian Cookie Mold (h)
Barbarian Head (h,w)
Bark Shield (s)
Barley (w)
Basic Blacksmithing (h,w)
Basic Pottery (w)
Bat Fur (h), Wing (h)
Batfang Headband (w)
Batskull Earring (w)
Bayle List I (h)
Bead Necklace (h,n,w)
Bear Meat (h,n,w)
Bear-hide Belt (h), Boots (h,s), Cape (h), Jerkin (n)
Beartooth Necklace (s)
Belt of Flesh Hooks (n)
Belt Pattern (w)
Belt Pouch
Belt Sectional Mold (h)
Binelen's Quick Treats (w)
Binelen's Succulence (w)
Black Headband (s)
Black Pearl
Black Sapphire (w)
Blackened Iron Bracers (s), Crown (s), Legplates (s), Mail (s)
Blessed Silver Wand (n)

Block of Clay (w)
Bloodstone (n,s,w), Ring (n,s,w)
Blue Training Robe (h)
Bone Armplates (w)
Bone Chips
Bone Legplates (w)
Boot Mold (h)
Bottle (n,w), of Kalish, of Milk (w)
Bottom of Broken Staff (h)
Bowyers Guide (s)
Box of Lute Strings (n,w)
Box of Undead Brownie Bones (n)
Bracer Sectional Mold (h)
Brandy (n,w)
Bread Tin Mold (h)
Breath of Ro (n)
Broad Sword (n,s)
Bronze Axe (n,s,w), Bastard Sword (n,s,w), Battle Axe, Boots (w), Bracers (n,w), Breastplate (w), Claymore (n), Collar (w), Dagger, Flail (n,w), Gauntlets (w), Girdle (w), Greaves (w), Halberd (n,s), Halberd (w), Helm (w), Long Sword, Mace, Main Gauche (n,s,w), Mask (w), Morning Star (n,s,w), Pauldrun (w), Rapier (n,s,w), Scimitar (h,n,w), Scythe (n), Short Sword (h,s,w), Shortened Spear (n,s,w), Spear (n,s,w), 2-Handed Battle (h,n,w), 2-Handed Hammer (n,w), 2-Handed Sword, Vambraces (w), Warhammer (n,w)
Buckler (h,s)
Bull Elephant Tooth (s)

Bundled Bone, Ceramic, Steel Wooden Arrow Shafts (w)
Bunker Battle Blade (n)
Burned Out Lightstone (h,n,w)
Busted Prayer Beads (w)
Cake Round Mold (h)
Carnelian (n,s,w)
Carrot (n)
Case of Blackburrow Stout (h)
Cask (n,w)
Cat's Eye Agate (h,n)
Chainmail Neckguard (n), Skirt (n)
Charger Hoof Chips (s)
Chipped Bone Bracelet (w), Collar (w)
Chunk of Meat
Cloak of Leaves (s)
Cloak Pattern (w)
Cloak Sectional Mold (h)
Cloth Cap, Cape, Choker, Cord, Gloves, Pants, Sandals (s), Shawl (s,w), Shirt, Sleeves, Veil (n,s,w), Wristband
Combine Dagger, Long Sword, Scimitar, Short Sword, 2-Handed Sword (all n)
Compass (n)
Concordance of Research (n)
Container Base Mold (w)
Container Lid Mold (w)
Copper Amulet (h,n,w)
Copper Band (h,n,w)
Cracked Flute (s)
Cracked Staff
Crafted Bracers (s), Breastplate (s), Gauntlets (s), Greaves (s), Helm (s), Pauldrun (s), Plate Boots (s), Vambraces (s)
Crown of Leaves (s)

Crysknife (h,n,s)
Crystal Ring (n)
Crystal Shard (w)
Cup of Flour (w)
Cyclops Skull (s)
Cyclops Toes (s,w)
Dagger (h,s,w)
Dagger of Dropping (s)
Dareb's Skull (s)
Darkwood Bow Staff (s)
Decaying Heart (s)
Diamond (w)
Dirge of the ForgeFire (w)
Diseased Wolf Pelt (h)
Double-bladed Bone Axe (s)
Dragonwart (n)
Drom's Champagne (h)
Dual-Edged Blade Mold (w)
Dufrenite (w)
Dwarf Bones (s), Meat (h)
Dwarven Ale (n)
Earring of Magic Reflection (h)
Elf Leaf (n)
Elm Bow Staff (s)
Elven Wine (n)
Emerald, Ring (n,w)
Empty Chalice (w)
Engagement Ring (s)
Essence of Rathe (n,w)
Eye of Serilis
Eye of Shadow (s)
Faded Salil's Writ Pages
Faded Velishoul's Tome
Feathered Leggings (s)
Field Point Arrowheads (w)
File Mold (w)
Fine Steel Dagger, Great Staff, Long Sword, Morning Star, Rapier, Scimitar, Short Sword, Spear, 2-Handed Sword, Warhammer
Fire Beetle Eye (h,n,w), Leg (h,n,w)

Items for All Four Newbie Zones, cont.

Fire Emerald (n,w), Ring (w)

Fire Opal (n,w)

Firing Sheet (w)

Fish Scales (h)

Fish Wine (h,n,w)

Fishbone Earring (h)

Fishcakes (w)

Fishing Bait (h)

Fishing Pole (h,n,w)

Fishing Spear (w)

Flail (w)

Flame of Vox

Fleeting Quiver Pattern (w)

Fleshy Orb (h,w)

Fletching Kit (s)

Fresh Fish (h,w)

Fresh Piranha (h)

Frosting (w)

Garnish (w)

Gauntlet Mold (h)

Ghumim's Classical Dishes (w)

Ghumim's Delights (w)

Giant Laceless Sandal (n)

Giant Rat Ear (h), Pelt (h), Whiskers (h)

Giant Snakespine Belt (w)

Giant's Reminder String (n)

Gigantic Chipped Tusk (s)

Gigantic Cracked Tusk (s)

Glass Shard (w)

Glove of Rallos Zek

Glowing Black Stone (h)

Glowing Bone Collar (w)

Glowing Gloves (s)

Gnawfangs Pelt (s), Tooth (s)

Gnoll Fang (h,w), Head (h)

Gnoll Hide Lariat (s)

Gnoll Pup Scalp (h)

Gnoll Slayer (h)

Gnome Cookie Mold (h)

Gold Ring

Golden Ear Stud (h,n,s), Earring (n,s,w), Pendant

Gorget Mold (h)

Gorget Pattern (w)

Granite Earring (n)

Grapes (n,w)

Grathin's Invoice (h)

Great Staff (n,s,w)

Greater Lightstone (h,n,w)

Griffenne Charm (n), Downfeather (n)

Griffon Eye (n), Feathers (n), Talon Gloves (n)

Grilled Rat Ears (h)

Grizzleknot Bark (s)

Grizzly Bear Skin (h,n,w)

Guard Bracelet (h,n,w)

Gypsy Medallion (n)

Gypsy Wine (h,n)

Halberd (s)

Hand Drum (s)

Hand of Shadow (s)

Head of Ghanex Drah (s)

Head of Shen (s)

Heavy Steel Blade Mold (w)

Helm Mold (h)

Hematite (h,n,w)

Hemp Twine (s)

Hickory Bow Staff (s)

High Quality Bear Skin (h,w)

High Quality Cat Pelt (n,s,w)

High Quality Firing Sheet (w)

High Quality Lion Skin (n)

High Quality Wolf Skin (h)

Hill Giant Toes (n,w)

Hilt Mold (w)

Hinge Mold (h,w)

Hollow Skull (w)

Honey Mead (h,n,w)

Hooked Arrowheads (w)

Hops (w)

Horn (s)

How To Sew: Large Sizes, Small Sizes (w)

Hulking Spiked Club (s)

Human Heart (w)

Hunting Bow (h,s)

Ice of Velious

Ingot of the Reverent (n)

Intestine Necklace (w)

Iron Ration

Iron Shackles (n)

Iron Visor (h,n,s)

Jacinth (w)

Jade, Earring, Ring, Shard

Jasper (n,s,w)

Jug of Sauces (w)

Karana Clover Shipment (w)

Kite Shield (s)

Koalindl Fish (w)

Lambent Stone (n,w)

Lantern Casing Mold (h,w)

Lapis Lazuli (h,n,w)

Large Bag

Large Belt Sectional Mold (w)

Large Block of Clay (w)

Large Boot Mold (w)

Large Box (n)

Large Bracer Sectional Mold (w)

Large Cloak Sectional Mold (w)

Large Cloth Cap, Cape, Choker, Cord, Gloves, Pants, Shirt, Sleeves

Large Container Base Mold (w)

Large Container Lid Mold (w)

Large Gauntlet Mold (w)

Large Gorget Mold (w)

Large Groove Nocks (s,w)

Large Helm Mold (w)

Large Iron Armplates (n), Visor (s)

Large Lantern (n)

Large Leggings Sectional Mold (w)

Large Mail Sectional Mold (w)

Large Mantle Sectional Mold (w)

Large Mask Mold (w)

Large Raw-hide Belt, Boots, Cloak, Gloves, Gorget, Leggings, Mask, Shoulderpads, Skullcap, Sleeves, Tunic, Wristbands (all n,s,w)

Large Ringmail Belt (s), Boots (s), Bracelet (s), Cape (s), Coat (s), Coif (s), Gloves (s), Mantle (s), Neckguard (s), Pants (s), Sleeves (s)

Large Sewing Kit (w)

Large Sleeves Sectional Mold (w)

Large Snake Skin (h)

Large Wooden Shield

LarkSpur (n)

Leather Belt (s), Boots (s), Gloves (h,s)

Leggings Sectional Mold (h)

Letter of Recommendation (h)

Lianna's Flute (n)

Lightstone

Lined Vial Sketch (w)

Linen String (s)

Lion Meat (n,s,w)

Lion-skin Leggings (n)

Lionhide Backpack (s)

Loaf of Bread

Locket (s)

Lockpicks (n,s)

Long Sword (s)

Longbow (h,s,w)

Low Quality Bear Skin (h,w)

Low Quality Lion Skin (n)

Low Quality Wolf Skin (h)

Lupine Runed Armband (s,w)

Items for All Four Newbie Zones, cont.

Lute (s)
Mail Sectional Mold (h)
Main Gauche (w)
Malachite (h,n,w)
Malt (w)
Mammoth Tusks (s)
Mandolin (h,s,w)
Mantle Sectional Mold (h)
Mask Mold (h)
Mask of Shadow (s)
Mask Pattern (w)
McMannus Clan Dagger (w)
Mead
Meat Pie (n,w)
Medium Groove Nocks (s,w)
Medium Quality Bear Skin (h,w)
Medium Quality Lion Skin (n)
Medium Quality Wolf Skin (h)
Mist Wolf Pelt
Mistletoe (n)
Mithril Amulet (n,w)
Mithril Earring
Mixxy's Delicacies Vol 1 (w), Vol 2 (w)
Mortar and Pestle (w)
Mroons Toy (s)
Muffin Tin Mold (h)
Needle Mold (w)
Needle of the Void (s)
Nilitim's Grimoire Pages (n,w)
Note To Cassius (s)
Oak Bow Staff (s)
Ogre Swill (h)
Old Delivered Book (w)
Onyx (n,s,w)
Opal
Opal Bracelet (n,w)
Order of Thunder (w)
Packet of Kiola Sap (n,w)
Pair of Bent Spectacles (n)
Parrying Dagger (n,s,w)
Patch of Gnoll Fur (h,w)

Patch of Shadow (s)
Patchwork Boots (h,s), Pants (s), Sleeves (s), Tunic (s)
Pearl, Earring, Necklace (n,w), Ring, Shard
Pegasus Feather Cloak (s)
Peridot
Pestilence Scythe (s)
Pie Tin Mold (h)
Piece of Rat Fur (h)
Pine Needles (n)
Piranha Tooth (h)
Planing Tool (s)
Polished Bone Hoop (h,n,s)
Pommel Mold (w)
Pot Mold (h)
Potion of Disease Warding (h)
Potion of Sustenance (h)
Pouch of Evidence (h)
Prayer Beads (w)
Preserved Split Paw Eye (s)
Puma Skin (w)
Purple Headband (s)
Purse (n)
Putrid Bear Hide (h)
Putrid Rib Bone (h)
Qeynos Kite Shield (h,n,w)
Quality Firing Sheet (w)
Quartz Crystal (h,n,s)
Quiver (n,w)
Quiver Pattern (w)
Rat Ear Pie (h)
Rat Ears, Foot, Meat, Tooth, Whiskers (all h)
Rat Shaped Ring (w)
Ration
Raw-hide Belt (h,n,w), Boots, Cloak, Gloves, Gorget, Leggings, Mask (h,n,w), Shoulderpads, Skullcap, Sleeves, Tunic, Wristbands (h,n,w)
Red Wine (h,n,w)
Reinforced Boots (n)

Rice (w)
Ring of Shadows (s)
Ringmail Boots, Bracelet, Cape, Coat, Coif, Gloves, Mantle, Neckguard, Pants, Skirt, Sleeves (all h,n,s)
Robe of the Lost Circle (s)
Rohand's Edibles (w)
Rohand's Sea Treats (w)
Round Shield (n,s,w)
Ruby (w)
Ruby Crown (w)
Ruined Bear Pelt (h,n,w)
Ruined Cat Pelt (n,s,w)
Ruined Lion Skin (n,s,w)
Ruined Wolf Pelt
Rune of: Al'Kabor, Ap'Sagor (n), Arrest, Attraction, Banding, Conception, Concussion, Consumption, Contortion, Crippling (n), Disassociation, Dismemberment, Embrace, Expulsion, Falhalem, Frost (n), Fulguration, Howling, Impetus (n), Infraction, Ivy (n), Karana, Nagafen, Neglect, Opression, Paralysis, Periphery, Petrification, Presence, Proximity, Rallos Zek, Rathe (n,w), Regeneration, Solusek Ro, Sorcery, Substance, the Astral (n), the Catalyst, the Combine, the Cyclone, the Helix, the Inverse (n,w), the One Eye (w), Trauma, Tyranny, Velious, Xegony
Runed Oak Bow (s)
Runed Totem Staff (s)
Runes and Research Vol. I (n), Vol. II (n)

Rusty Axe, Bastard Sword, Battle Axe, Broad Sword, Dagger, Flail (n,s), Halberd, Long Sword, Mace, Morning Star (n,s,w), Rapier, Scimitar, Scythe, Short Sword, Shortened Spear, Spear, 2-Handed Battle Axe (h), 2-Handed Hammer (n,s), 2-Handed Sword (h,s,w), Warhammer
Sack of Hay (w)
Salil's Writ Pages
Sapphire (n,w)
Sapphire Necklace (w)
Scaler Mold (h)
Scimitar (n,s)
Scythe (w)
Sealed Letter (h)
Sealed Missive (h)
Sealed Vial Sketch (w)
Senior Apprentice Robe (n)
Serpent Insignia Collar (s,w)
Serrated Blade (s)
Set of Bone Arrow Vanes (w)
Set of Ceramic Arrow Vanes (w)
Set of Wooden Arrow Vanes (w)
Several Parabolic Cut (w)
Several Round Cut Fletchings (w)
Several Shield Cut Fletchings (w)
Shadow Wolf Pelt (s,w)
Shadowed Ball (s), Battle Axe (s), Book (s), Halberd (s), Long Sword (s), Mace (s), Morning Star (s), Rapier (s), Scimitar (s), Scythe (s), Spear (s), 2-Handed Hammer (s), 2-Handed Sword (s)
Sheer Bone Mask (w)
Sheet Metal (h)

Items for All Four Newbie Zone, cont.

Shining Stone (s)
Shiny Card (n)
Short Ale (n,s,w)
Short Beer
Short Sword (n,s,w)
Shotglass (n,w)
Shoulderpad Pattern (w)
Shovel (w)
Shuriken (w)
Silk String (s)
Silver Amulet, Earring, Ring (n,s,w), Stud (h,n,w)
Silver Tipped Arrowheads (w)
Silverish Scimitar (s)
Skewer Mold (h)
Skull (h)
Sleeves Sectional Mold (h)
Small Bag
Small Block of Clay (w)
Small Box
Small Buckler (h)
Small Cloth Cap (h,s), Cape (h,s), Choker (s), Cord (h,s), Gloves (s), Pants (h,s), Sandals (s), Shawl (s), Shirt (h,s), Sleeves (s), Veil (s), Wristband (h,s)
Small Container Base Mold (w)
Small Container Lid Mold (w)
Small Groove Nocks (s,w)
Small Iron Visor (n)
Small Lantern (n,w)
Small Mammoth Tusks (s)
Small Raw-hide Belt, Boots, Cloak, Gloves, Gorget, Leggings, Mask, Shoulderpads, Skullcap, Sleeves, Tunic, Wristbands (all n)
Small Ringmail Belt, Boots, Bracelet, Cape, Coat, Coif, Gloves, Mantle, Neckguard, Pants, Sleeves (all n)

Small Ringmail Pants (s)
Small Round Shield (n)
Small Sewing Kit (w)
Small Wooden Shield (h)
Smoker Base Mold (h)
Smoker Support Mold (h)
Snake Egg (h), Fang (h), Scales (h)
Snakeskin Gloves (w), Jerkin (w), Mask (w)
Songs (all s): Chant of Battle, Chords of Dissonance, Hymn of Restoration, Jaxan's Jig o' Vigor, Lyssa's Locating Lyric, Selo's Accelerando (all s)
Sorin's Treats on the Go (w)
Spear (s,w)
Spell: Alacrity (s), Barbcoat (n), Befriend Animal (w), Beguile (s), Bravery (s), Breath of the Dead (s), Burst of Fire (s), Camouflage (s), Cancel Magic (n), Cannibalize (s), Careless Lightning (n), Cast Force (s), Cazic Gate (s), Chaos Flux (s), Charm (s), Charm Animals (s), Column of Lightning (s), Common Gate (s), Companion Spirit (w), Cornucopia (s), Counteract Disease (s), Counteract Poison (s), Creeping Crud (n,s), Creeping Vision (s), Cure Poison (s), Dismiss Summoned (n,s), Dismiss Undead (s), Dizzying Wind (n), Enchant: Gold (s), Endure Disease (n), Endure Poison (n), Ensnaring Roots (n,s), Envenomed Breath (s), Everfount (s), Feet like Cat (s), Flame Flux (s), Frenzied Spirit (w),

Spell: Frost Shock (s), Frost Strike (s), Grasping Roots (s), Greater Healing (s), Guardian Spirit (w), Hammer of Striking (s), Haunting Corpse (s), Inspire Fear (s), Intensify Death (s), Invigor (s), Invoke Lightning (s), Leatherskin (s), Levitate (s), Light Healing (s), Lightning Storm (s), Lull (h), Lull Animal (s), Major Shielding (s), Malise (s), Minor Shielding (h), Nek Gate (s), Pogonip (n,s), Poison Storm (s), Protect (s), Regeneration (s), Resist Cold (s), Resist Fire (n,s), Rest the Dead (s), Ring of Feerrott (s), Ring of Lavastorm (s), Ring of Ro (s), Ring of Steamfont (s), Ro Gate (s), Rune II (s), Shadow Sight (s), Shield of Barbs (n), Shock of Poison (s), Shock of Spikes (s), Skin like Steel (n,s), Snare (s), Spirit of Cat (s), Spirit of Cheetah (s), Spirit of Ox (s), Strip Enchantment (s), Summoning (Air, Earth, Fire, Water) (s), Sunbeam (n,s), Superior Camouflage (n), Symbol of Ryltan (s), Tepid Deeds (s), Thistlecoat (s), Tremor (n,s), True North (h), Vigilant Spirit (w), Wave of Fear (s), Weaken (h), West Gate (s), Wolf Form (s)
Spices (w)
Spider Legs, Silk, Venom, Venom Sac (all w)

Spiked Ball Mold (w)
Spit (h)
Splinted Bronze Cloak (w)
Splintering Club
Split Paw (s)
Split Paw Hide Belt, Gloves, Mask, Tunic (all s)
Split Paw Tooth Necklace (s)
Staff (w)
Standard Bow Cam (s)
Standing Legs Mold (h)
Star Rose Quartz (n,s,w)
Star Ruby (n,w)
Star Ruby Earring (w)
Steel Torque (n,s,w)
Strategic Map of Kithicor (w)
Superb Bear Hide (n)
Superb Lion Skin (n)
Superb Wolf Hide (n)
Suspension (w)
Tailoring (w)
Tanned Split Paw Skin (s)
Targ Shield (n)
Tasarin's Grimoire Pages
Tattered Belt (h)
tattered Cloth Note (w)
Tattered Cloth Sandal (h)
Tattered Note (h)
Tattered Skullcap (s)
Tears of Prexuz (n,w)
Tentacle Whip (n)
The Scent of Marr (n,w)
Thimble Mold (w)
Throwing Axe (s)
Throwing Knife (n,s,w)
Throwing Spear (w)
Thunderhoof Quiver (s)
Top of Broken Staff (h)
Topaz
Topknot Headband (s)
Torch (h,n,w)
Torn Cloth Tunic (h,s)
Tower Shield (s)
Treant Staff (s)

Items for All Four Newbie Zone, cont.

Troll Cookie Mold (h)
Troll Parts (s)
Turquoise (h,n,w)
Turtleshell Helm (w)
2-Handed Battle Axe (s)
Unfinished Brass Trumpet (n,w)
Vaashar's Sweet Revege (w)
Vaashar's Sweet Treats (w)
Velishoul's Tome Pages
Velvet Choker (h,n,s)
Very Tiny Crumpled Skeleton (n)
Vial of Rabid Froth (s)
Vial Sketch (w)
Vinegar (w)
Warped Great Staff (h,n,w)
Water Flask
Werewolf Claws (s,w), Pelt (s,w)
Werewolf-hide Jerkin (n)
Whip Pattern (w)

White Wine (n,w)
Whittling Blade (s)
Winds of Karana sheet 1 (s), 2 (n)
Wine Yeast (w)
Wing of Xegony (n)
Winged Headband (h)
Wolf Meat
Wolf-hide Belt (h), Boots (h), Cape (h), Cape (s), Sleeves (n)
Wood Elf Parts (n)
Wooden Flute (s)
Wooden Heart (n,s,w)
Wooden Shards (n,s,w)
Wooden Shield
Words of: Abatement, Absorption, Acquisition (Azia), Acquisition (Beza) (n), Allure, Anthology, Bidding, Bondage (n), Burnishing (n), Burnishing (w), Cazic-Thule, Cloudburst,

Words of: Coercion, Collection (Azia), Collection (Beza), Collection (Caza) (n,w), Convocation, Crippling Force (n), Dark Paths, Derivation, Descrying, Detachment, Detention, Dimension, Discernment, Dissemination, Dissolution, Dominion, Duration, Duress, Efficacy, Endurance, Enlightenment, Eradication, Eventide, Grappling (n), Haunting, Imitation, Incarceration (n,w), Materials, Mistbreath, Motion, Neglect, Obligation (n,w), Odus (n), Parasitism, Possession, Projection, Purification, Quivering, Radiance, Recluse, Refuge, Requisition (n),

Words of: Resolve, Reviviscence, Rupturing, Seizure, Sight, Spirit, the Element, the Ethereal (n), the Extinct, the Incorporeal, the Psyche (n), the Psyche (w), the Quickening, the Sentient (Azia), the Sentient (Beza), the Spectre, the Spoken, the Suffering, Transcendence, Tyranny
Worn Great Staff
Wrist Pouch (n,s,w)
Wristband Pattern (w)
Xectia's Favored Flavors (w)
Xectia's Hot Pie (w)
Yeast (w)
Yellow Headband (h)
Zap Doodle Tonic (h)
Zombie Skin (n,s,w)

Rivervale

The pleasant tunnel town of Rivervale lies almost at the exact heart of Antonica. It isn't a large town, but it has everything its resident Halfings need to live prosperous lives. Most of the merchants and shops are clustered near the more highly traveled entrance from the Misty Thicket, while more specialized establishments are generally located at the end of branching tunnels.

Newbie adventurers might try cutting their teeth exploring the Misty Thicket Newbie Zone just outside of town.

Tall strummed his lute and sang the story of Greenley, the man who could not believe that he could profit so much in one day!

"Greenley's knowledge and wisdom ha' been blessed by Reebo Leafsway, guildmaster of druids; while Greenley's pouch bulged from the reward of hard work, well done!"

Elleanne nudged her friend. "Do you think there really is a Reebo Leafway?"

"Of course not," her friend Dilling replied," 'tis only a bard's tale."

Or, is it? Elleanne thought to herself.

Cities of Antonica: Rivervale

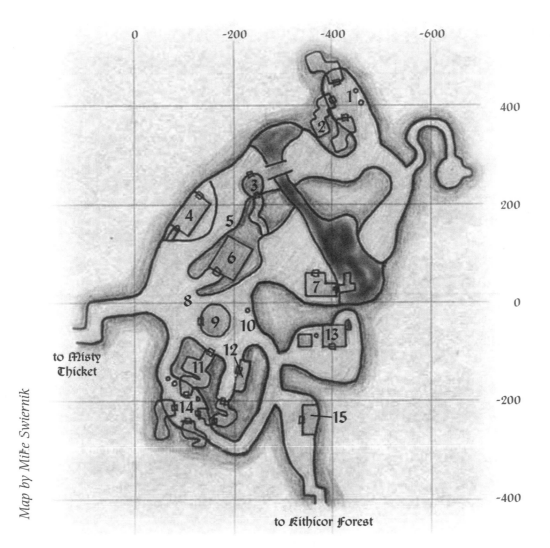

Map by Mike Swiernik

to Misty Thicket

to Kithicor Forest

1. Pottery wheel/kiln
2. Nyla Gubbin's house
3. Merchant (bags, fishing supplies)
4. Weary Foot Rest (inn)
5. Bard
6. Town Hall, Leatherfoot Hall (bank, Warrior Guild, weapons)
7. Merchant (fishing supplies, food, etc.)
8. Priest of Discord

9. Rogues Guild
10. Brew barrel
11. Merchant (potions)
12. Merchant (leather armor/patterns, chain armor)
13. Druids Guild (veggies, forge, oven)
14. Pottery wheel, oven, forge
15. Clerics Guild (weapons)

Misty Thicket Newbie Zone
Personalities

Bim Buskin	Deputy Looh	Eizosze	Joogl Honeybugger
Blixkin Entopop	Deputy Qeynos	Ember	Lil Honeybugger
Brock Brawlbottom	Deputy Tagil	Faano Windmaker	Mooto
Bronin Higginsbot	Deputy Uplin	Guardian Braster	Relia Wastein
Deputy Asler	Deputy Vastin	Guardian Gasten	Slaythe
Deputy Budo	Deputy Vix	Guardian Killen	Sonsa Fromp
Deputy Drebo	Deputy Widd	Guardian Yillirum	Tipa Lighten
Deputy Felp	Deputy Yassin	Gunrich	Topper Drodo
Deputy Keld	Dralfling	Hanga Wiskin	

Goblins

goblin alchemist	goblin warrior	goblin whelp
goblin shaman	goblin warrior	goblin worker

Klaknak

Klaknak drone	Prince Klaknak	Queen Klaknak
Klaknak warrior	Princess Klaknak	

Others

bat	fire beetle	lesser mummy	shadow wolf
bixie	giant bat	mangy rat	skeleton
bixie drone	giant rat	moss snake	spiderling
bixie queen	giant scarab	orc apprentice	tree snake
black bear	giant spider	orc centurion	young kodiak
black wolf	giant wasp	orc legionnaire	zombie
decaying skeleton	large bat	orc oracle	
dread corpse	large rat	orc pawn	

Items

Ale	Brandy	Copper Amulet, Band	Fish Wine
Amber	Broad Sword	Cracked Giant Scarab	Flame of Vox
Backpack	Bronze Bastard Sword,	Cracked Staff	Froglok Leg
Bandages	Battle Axe, Halberd,	Deathfist Pawn Scalp	Giant Fire Beetle Eye, Leg
Bat Fur, Wing	Long Sword, Mace,	Deathfist Slashed Belt	Giant Rat Ear, Pelt,
Bead Necklace	Short Sword, 2-Handed	Deputy Tagil's Payment	Whiskers
Bear Meat	Sword	Eye of Serilis	Giant Scarab Egg Sack
Belt Pouch	Buckler	Faded Salil's Writ Pages	Giant Wasp Eye, Legs,
Bixie Parts, Stinger	Carnelian	Faded Velishoul's Tome	Stinger, Venom Sac,
Black Wolf Skin	Cat's Eye Agate	Fine Steel Dagger, Great	Wing
Bloodstone	Chunk of Meat	Staff, Long Sword,	Glove of Rallos Zek
Bloodstone Ring	Clay Totem	Morning Star, Rapier,	Gold Ring
Bone Chips	Cloth Cap, Cape, Choker,	Scimitar, Short Sword,	Golden Earring
Bottle of Kalish	Cord, Gloves, Pants,	Spear, 2-Hand. Sword,	Grizzly Bear Skin
Bracelet of Beetlekind	Shirt, Sleeves, Veil,	Warhammer	H.K. 106
	Wristband	Fire Beetle Eye, Leg	Halfling Head

Items, cont

Hematite
High Quality Bear Skin
Honey Mead
Honeycomb
Ice of Velious
Illegible Cantrip
Iron Ration
Jade
Jade Earring, Shard
Jasper
Kedgemail Gauntlets
Lapis Lazuli
Large Bag
Large Banded Gauntlets
Large Banded Leggings
Large Cloth Cap, Cape, Choker, Cord, Gloves, Pants, Shirt, Sleeves
Large Leather Cloak, Gloves, Leggings, Shoulderpads, Sleeves, Tunic, Wristbands
Large Snake Skin
Large Wooden Shield
Leather Shoulderpads, Tunic
Legionnaire Shoulderpads
Long Sword
Low Quality Bear Skin
Malachite
Mead
Medium Quality Bear Skin
Mithril Earring
Onyx
Orc Pawn Pick
Parrying Dagger
Tasarin's Grimoire Pages
Pearl
Pearl Shard
piece of Rat Fur
Potion of Poison Warding
Pristine Giant Scarab
Rat Ears, Foot, Meat, Tooth, Whiskers
Ration

Raw-hide Belt, Boots, Cloak, Gloves, Gorget, Leggings, Mask, Shoulderpads, Skullcap, Sleeves, Tunic, Wristbands
Red Wine
Ribcage Chest Armor
Round Shield
Ruined Bear Pelt, Wolf Pelt
Rune of Al'Kabor, Attraction, Conception, Disassociation, Dismemberment, Embrace, Expulsion, Falhalem, Fulguration, Infraction, Karana, Nagafen, Neglect, Opression, Paralysis, Periphery, Petrification, Presence, Proximity, Rallos Zek, Regeneration, Substance, the Combine, the Helix, Trauma, Tyranny, Velious, Xegony
RunnyEye Warbeads
Rusty Axe, Bastard Sword, Battle Axe, Broad Sword, Dagger, Flail, Halberd, Long Sword, Mace, Morning Star, Rapier, Scimitar, Scythe, Short Sword, Shortened Spear, Spear, 2-Hand. Hammer, 2-Handed Sword, Warhammer
Salil's Writ Pages
Shadow Wolf Pelt
Shattered Warbeads
Short Ale
Short Beer
Silver Amulet, Bracelet, Earring, Ring, Stud
Small Bag
Small Box

Small Buckler
Small Cloth Cap, Cape, Choker, Cord, Gloves, Pants, Sandals, Shawl, Shirt, Sleeves, Veil, Wristband
Small Leather Gloves, Leggings, Sleeves
Small Raw-hide Belt, Boots, Cloak, Gloves, Gorget, Leggings, Mask, Shoulderpads, Skullcap, Sleeves, Tunic, Wristbands
Small Round Shield
Small Wooden Shield
Snake Egg, Fang, Scales
Spear
Spider Legs, Silk, Venom, Venom Sac
Spiderling Eye, Legs, Silk
Splintering Club
Squad Ring
Star Rose Quartz
Topaz
Turquoise
Velishoul's Tome Pages
Vermiculated Armplates, Boots, Bracelet, Gloves, Leggings, Tunic
Water Flask
White Wine
Wolf Meat
Wooden Shield

Words of Absorption, Acquisition (Azia), Allure, Anthology, Bidding, Cazic-Thule, Cloudburst, Coercion, Collection (Azia), Collection (Beza), Convocation, Derivation, Descrying, Detachment, Dimension, Discernment, Dissemination, Dissolution, Dominion, Enlightenment, Eradication, Eventide, Haunting, Imitation, Materials, Mistbreath, Parasitism, Possession, Projection, Purification, Radiance, Recluse, Refuge, Reviviscence, Rupturing, Seizure, Sight, Spirit, the Element, the Extinct, the Incorporeal, the Quickening, the Sentient (Azia), the Sentient (Beza), the Spectre, the Spoken, the Suffering, Transcendence, Tyranny
Worn Great Staff
Zombie Skin

Faydwer

The gods have blessed Faydwer with some of the most glorious forests on Norrath. In the northwest, the Greater Faydark forest surrounds Felwithe, home to high elf and half-elf alike. The city of the wood elf, Kelethin—arguably the most unique city in the world—is located among the high branches of the tall trees of the Greater Faydark! .

To the south of Felwithe, over the Elizerain Lake and Steamfont Mountains, is the city of Ak'Anon, populated mostly by those industrious gnomes. An interesting side trip would be to visit Dragonscale Hills outside of Ak'Anon.

Along the southern coast of Faydwer, bordering the Timorous Deep, are the Wayunder Lake, the Loping Plains with Kanthok's Ridge to the north, and Dagnor's Cauldron in the lower, southern tip of the continent.

Just north of the Cauldron lies Kaladim, the grand city of the dwarves, along with the Lesser Faydark forest, the Butcherblock Mountains and the Hills of Shade.

EverQuest: The Ruins of Kunark

Ak'Anon

Kaxan stood at the crossroads and thought, That merchant told me a gnome named Larkon Theardor at the Library of something or other would have a job for me. And, that bard, Danask, said that his fellow singer, Lyra, had an errand of value.

Kaxan shrugged and walked off to find this library. Surely, the work from there would be more noble than that from a bard.

Ak'anon is located on the far end of Faydwer's southeastern peninsula. To reach it, one must pass over the Steamfont Mountains, making this little hamlet all the more remote from its Elven neighbors to the north. Still, the Gnomes who call Ak'anon home like it that way, for although they hold few strong animosities toward others, they are happy keeping to themselves and their tunneled city.

But Ak'anon is by no means a boring place, it has not only the usual attractions of a city its size, but also a fine palace, a zoo and other spots of interest that are worth a look.

Newbies can cast about for things to sell in the Steamfont Mountains — the single entrance and exit to Ak'anon leads directly to and from them, at the southern end of town.

Ak'Anon

1. Necromancer/Evil Cleric trainers, Merchants (dark gold robes, spells)

2. Evil Warrior trainer

3. Evil Rogue trainer

4. Merchant (tinkering supplies)

5. Abbey of Deep Musing (Cleric trainers), Merchants (weapons), secret entrance to Rogues Guild, Merchants (Rogue weapons)

6. The Smithy (weapons)

7. Merchant (weapons, forge)

8. Merchants (bags, boxes, food, other goods), Bard

9. Merchant (shoes)

10. Library Mechanamagica (Enchanter/ Magician/Wizard trainers), Merchants (spells, gold robes, spellcaster supplies)

11. Merchant (cloth armor)

12. Merchants (food, fishing supplies, lightstones, potions)

13. Ak'anon Palace (King Ak'anon, oven, pottery wheel/kiln)

14. Warriors Guild (Warrior trainers), Merchant (weapons)

15. Merchant (fishing supplies), Merchant (cloth armor, sewing kits) outside

16. Priest of Discord, Merchant (food, other goods)

17. Bank of Ak'anon, Merchants (gems)

18. Merchants (jewelry metals)

19. Ak'anon Zoo

20. Merchants (cloth armor, food, weapons, shields, other goods)

21. Merchant (fletching supplies)

22. Bar (brew barrel, alcohol)

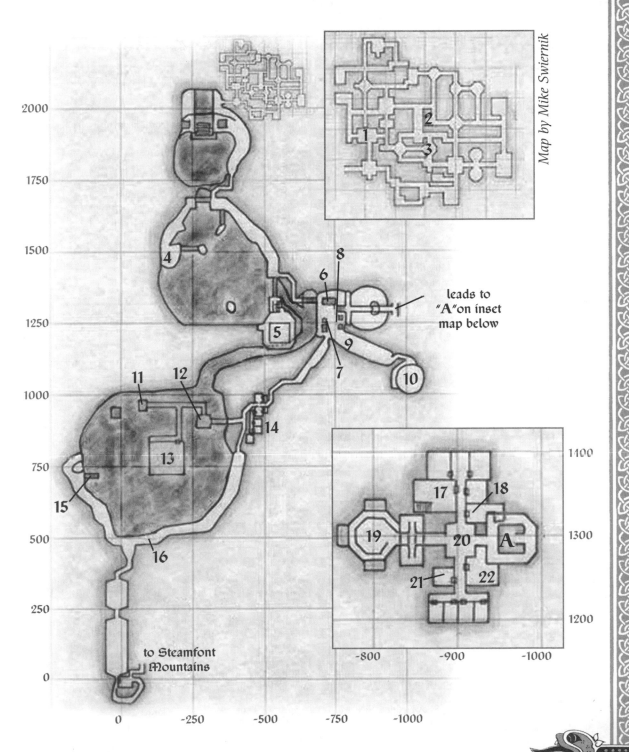

Map by Mike Swiernik

leads to "A" on inset map below

to Steamfont Mountains

Steamfont Mountains Newbie Zone

Personalities

Bom Knotwood
Brona Frugrin
Bugglegupp
Byrola Bendil
Cardizzin
Cargo Clockwork
Charlotte
Crisyn
Crumpy Irontoe
Deputy Fylo

Dimlore Stormhammer
Driver Bryggin
Feddi Dooger
Finkel Rardobaen
Fodin Frugrin
Frebin Tinderhue
Freed Fimplefur
Frugo Prigdish
Genda Minyte
Glaneon Priddlepril

Glen Garginburr
Godbin Strumharp
guards
Jogl Doobraugh
Legyn Sarawyn
Lodrand Dindlenod
Meldrath The Malignant
Nilit Druzlit
Oren Furdenbline
Phiz Frugrin

Thagrim Toridrorn
Thetherthag Wakintrob
Tindo Frugrin
Torodrane Frompwaddle
Watchman Dreeb
Watchman Halv
Watchman Mylz
Watchman Prenn
Watchman Prynn
Zondo Hyzill

Minotaurs

Minotaur Guard
Minotaur Hero

Minotaur Lord
Minotaur Sentry

Minotaur Slaver

Kobolds

kobold

kobold runt

kobold scout

kobold shaman

Others

decaying gnome skeleton
decaying skeleton
earth elemental
giant diseased rat
gnome skeleton

harpy
infected rat
large plague rat
large rat
lesser ebon drake

nilits clockwork
puma
rogue cleaner
rogue clockwork
runaway clockwork

skeleton
spiderling
young ebon drake

Items

Ale
Amber
Animal Cookie Mold
Backpack
Backpack Pattern
Bandages
Barbarian Cookie Mold
Basic Blacksmithing
Bat Fur
Bat Wing
Bead Necklace
Belt Pattern, Pouch
Binelen's Quick Treats,
    Succulence
Black Pearl
Blackbox Fragment
Block of Clay
Bloodstone
Bloodstone Ring

Bone Chips
Bottle
Bottle of Kalish, of Milk
Bread Tin Mold
Broken Mntar. Lord's Horn
Bronze Dagger, Main
    Gauche, Rapier,
    Shortened Spear, Spear
Buckler
Butcher Knife
Cake Round Mold
Carnelian
Cat's Eye Agate
Chunk of Meat
Cloak Pattern
Cloth Cap, Cape, Choker,
    Cord, Gloves, Pants,
    Shawl, Shirt, Sleeves,
    Veil, Wristband

Copper Amulet, Band
Cork
Cracked Staff
Cup of Flour
Dagger
daily log
Dwarf Meat
Emerald
Essence of Rathe
Eye of Serilis
Faded Salil's Writ Pages
Faded Velishoul's Tome
Fine Coral Mesh
Fine Steel Dagger, Great
    Staff, Long Sword,
    Morning Star, Rapier,
    Scimitar, Short Sword,
    Spear, 2-Handed
    Sword, Warhammer

Fish Scales
Fishing Bait, Pole
Flame of Vox
Fleeting Quiver Pattern
Fresh Fish
Frosting
Garnish
Gears
Ghumim's Classical Dishes,
    Delights
Glove of Rallos Zek
Gnome Cookie Mold,
    Decapited Head, Meat,
    Tinkered Toy
Gnomish Bolts
Gold Ring
Golden Earring, Pendant
Gorget Pattern
Grease

EverQuest: The Ruins of Kunark

Items, cont.

Harpy Wing
Hematite
Hinge Mold
How To Sew: Large Sizes, Medium Sizes, Small Sizes
Ice of Velious
Icon of the Devout
Infected Rat Livers
Iron Pellet, Ration
Jade
Jade Earring, Ring, Shard
Jasper
Jeweller's Kit
Jrnl. of Gimblestan XIV, XV
Jug of Sauces
Lantern Casing Mold
Lapis Lazuli
Large Bag
Large Block of Clay
Large Brick of Ore
Large Lantern
Large Sewing Kit
Leather Boots
Legacy of Jewel Craft
Lime Coated Meshing
Malachite
Mask Pattern
Mead
Medium Quality Cat Pelt
Metal Fastening, Rod, Shaft, Twine
Micro Servo
Minotaur Battle Axe, Hero Shackles, Horn
Mithril Earring
Mixxy's Delicacies Vols 1, 2
Muffin Tin Mold
Needle Mold
Nilitim's Grimoire Pages
Onyx
Opal
Parrying Dagger
Tasarin's Grimoire Pages
Pearl
Pearl Earring, Ring, Shard
Peridot
Pie Tin Mold
piece of Rat Fur
Pot Mold
Puma Skin
Quiver Pattern

Rat Ears, Foot, Meat, Tooth, Whiskers
Ration
Raw Bamboo
Reflective Shard
Rohand's Edibles, Sea Treats
Ruby
Ruined Cat Pelt
Rune of Al'Kabor, Arrest, Attraction, Banding, Concussion, Consumption, Contortion, Disassociation, Dismemberment, Expulsion, Fulguration, Howling, Karana, Neglect, Opression, Presence, Rallos Zek, Rathe, Regeneration, Solusek Ro, Sorcery, the Catalyst, the Combine, the Cyclone, the Helix, the Inverse, Trauma, Velious, Xegony
Rusted Blackbox
Rusty Battle Axe, Dagger, Flail, Long Sword, Mace, Morning Star, Rapier, Scythe, Short Sword, Shortened Spear, Spear, 2-Handed Hammer, 2-Handed Sword, Warhammer
Salil's Writ Pages
Scaler Mold
Scrap Metal
Senior Apprentice Robe
Sharkskin Tubing
Sharpening Stone
Shiny Card
Short Beer, Sword
Shoulderpad Pattern
Silk Lined Steel Helm
Silver Amulet, Earring, Ring, Stud
size 4 gizmo, sprocket
size 5 gizmo, sprocket
size 6 gizmo, sprocket
Skewer Mold
Skull of Meldrath
Small Bag
Small Block of Clay
Small Box

Small Brick of Ore
Small Cloth Cap, Cape, Choker, Cord, Gloves, Pants, Sandals, Shawl, Shirt, Sleeves, Veil, Wristband
Small Mold: Boot, Gauntlet, Gorget, Helm, Mask
Small Iron Visor
Small Lantern
Small Sectional Mold: Belt, Bracer, Cloak, Leggings, Mail, Mantle
Small Piece of Ore
Small Raw-hide Belt, Boots, Cloak, Gloves, Gorget, Leggings, Mask, Shoulderpads, Skullcap, Sleeves, Tunic, Wristbands
Small Ringmail Belt, Boots, Bracelet, Cape, Coat, Coif, Gloves, Mantle, Neckguard, Pants, Sleeves
Small Round Shield
Small Sleeves Sect. Mold
Smoker Base Mold
Smoker Support Mold
Snake Scales
Sorin's Treats on the Go
Spell: Bramblecoat, Combust, Counteract Disease, Counteract Poison, Drones of Doom, Earthquake, Endure Magic, Ensnare, Expel Summoned, Extinguish Fatigue, Greater Healing, Immolate, Lightning Strike, Regeneration, Resist Cold, Shield of Brambles, Strength of Stone
Spices
Spider Legs, Silk
Spiderling Eye, Legs, Silk
Spit
Spriket
Sprockets
Staff of the Observers
Standing Legs Mold
Star Rose Quartz
Steel Lined Gloves
Tailoring

Tears of Prexuz
Telescope Lens
The Scent of Marr
Thimble Mold
Toolbox
Topaz
Torch
Troll Cookie Mold
Troll Parts
Turquoise
Vaashar's Sweet Revege, Sweet Treats
Velishoul's Tome Pages
Vinegar
Water Flask
Whip Pattern
Wood Elf Parts
Wooden Shield
Words of Abatement, Absorption, Acquisition (Azia), Allure, Anthology, Burnishing, Cazic-Thule, Cloudburst, Coercion, Collection (Caza), Dark Paths, Detachment, Detention, Dimension, Discernment, Dissemination, Dominion, Duration, Duress, Efficacy, Endurance, Enlightenment, Eventide, Haunting, Incarceration, Mistbreath, Motion, Neglect, Obligation, Parasitism, Possession, Purification, Quivering, Radiance, Recluse, Refuge, Resolve, Rupturing, Sight, the Extinct, the Incorporeal, the Psyche, the Quickening, the Sentient (Beza), the Suffering, Transcendence
Worn Great Staff
Wristband Pattern
Xectia's Favored Flavors
Xectia's Hot Pie
Zombie Skin

Felwithe

Felwithe is perhaps the most beautiful city on Norrath, with its fair walls and elegant buildings. Built by the High Elves in time immemorial it is also home to many Half-Elves, and a temporary waypoint for travelers of all but the Dark Races.

The sole entrance to the town is through the Greater Faydark, over a bridge across an artificial pond. Perhaps because of the protection and seclusion afforded by these ramparts, the city is normally quite peaceful Just inside the ramparts is the zone of South Felwithe, where most shops are located. Continuing through the heart of the city, the traveler will discover a path leading to North Felwithe and the guilds of magic arts.

For the newbie, the forest of Greater Faydark just outside the city entrance contains many useful resources. Although the way is by no means without peril, especially for a lone traveler, Felewithe shares this newbie zone with the Wood Elves of Kelethin, which lies to the west.

The party split at the gate and agreed to meet back up that evening. They had all heard enough rumors and tales to drive the most sane creature totally crazy.

"We were told that the magic part of the city was this way," Llanth said just as they reached a long pier leading to an island in the middle of a lake.

Her friend Stong laughed. "Looks like we're to prove that we are fish before we can prove we can do magic." He pointed to a square building. "That's the Wizards Guild. Go see if there is such a person as Tarker Blazetoss." Then, he pointed to another building directly across from the pier. "I'll try to find the magician looking for spell components."

"Meet back here in about an hour," Llanth said as they headed to the edge of the island and began to swim toward their respective destinations.

EverQuest: The Ruins of Kunark

South Felwithe

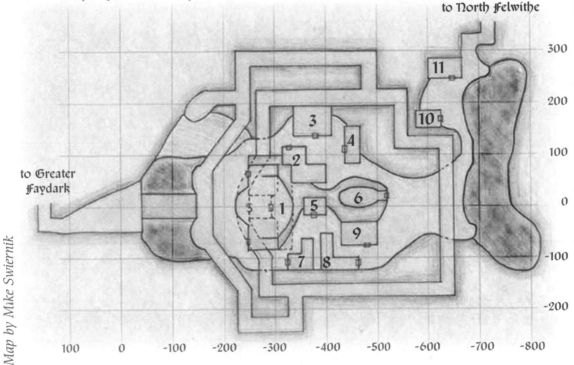

Map by Mike Swiernik

1. Paladins Guild (weapons), Priest of Discord, secret tunnels to ramparts

2. Tovanik's Venom (alcohol, brew barrel)

3. Traveler's Home (inn)

4. Shop of All Holos (cloth armor, boots, gems)

5. Beyond Faydark (food, other goods)

6. Clerics Guild (blunt weapons)

7. Faydark's Bane (fletching supplies/kits, sewing kits, leather armor/patterns, pottery wheel/kiln)

8. Emerald Armor (chain/plate armor, blunt/sharp weapons, shields)

9. Felwithe Keeper (bank)

10. Bait and Tackle (fishing supplies)

11. Felwithe Fish House (fishing supplies, oven, outside — jewelry, metals, gems)

North Felwithe

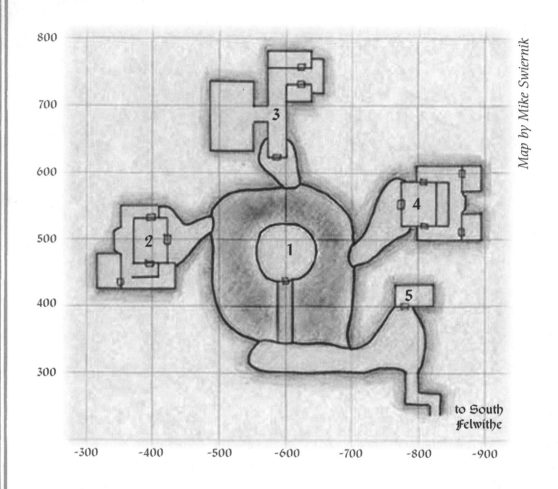

Map by Mike Swiernik

1. Gate Room to Guilds
2. Wizards Guild
3. Magicians Guild
4. Enchanters Guild
5. Merchants (cloth armor, sewing kits, jewelry supplies, common spells)

EverQuest: The Ruins of Kunark

Greater Faydark Newbie Zone

Personalities

Alania Peaceheart
Aleena Lightleaf
Astar Leafsinger
bandit
Banker Willaen
Barkeeps Aanlawen, Lysslan, Manlawen, Myrisa, Sissya, Syntan, Tuviena, Tvanla, Uultanu
Beleth Streamfoot
Bidl Frugrin
Bilrio Surecut
Captain Silverwind
Cerila Windrider
Devin Ashwood

Dill Fireshine
Expin
Gallin Woodwind
Geeda
Grynn
Guards
Heartwood Master
Hendricks
Horth Evergreen
Idia
Innkeeps Anisyla, Larya, Linen, Wuleran
Jakum Webdancer
Kindl Lunsight
Laren
Lieutenant Leafstalker

Lily Ashwood
Linadian
Maesyn Trueshot
Merchants Aianya, Aildien, Ainaiana, Aluuvila, Aluwenae, Gaeadin, Gerienae, Gililya, Iludarae, Kaeluase, Kanoldar, Kweili, Kwein, Laedar, Lanin, Legweien, Linolyen, Minamas, Muvien, Neaien, Nildar, Nluolian, Nyssa, Sylnis, Tananie, Tegdian, Tenra, Tiladinya, Tilluen, Tinolwenya,

Tuluvdar, Uaylain, Ueaas, Weaolanae, Winerasea
Priest of Discord
Ran Sunfire
Regren
Salani Tunfar
Serilia Whistlewind
Sindl Talonstrike
Sylia Windlehands
Tylfon
Uleen Laughingwater
Verth Mistwielder
Zelli Starsfire

Others

bat
black wolf
brownie scout
decaying skeleton

drunkard
fae drake hatchling
faerie courtier, duchess, guard, maiden, noble, royal guard

giant wasp drone
orc centurion, hatchetman, oracle, pawn, shaman
pixie trickster

widow hatchling
will-o-wisp

Items

Ale
Amber
Animal Cookie Mold
Animal Template
Armor and Weapons Guide
Arrow
Ashwood Bow Staff
Axe
Backpack
Backpack Pattern
Bandages
Banded Orc Vest
Barbarian Cookie Mold
Barbarian Template
Bark Potion
Basic Blacksmithing
Basic Pottery
Bastard Sword
Bat Fur
Bat Wing
Battle Axe
Bead Necklace
Bearskin Gloves

Belt Pattern, Pouch
Belt Sectional Mold
Black Wolf Skin
Block of Clay
Bloodstone
Bloodstone Ring
Bone Chips
Boot Mold, Pattern
Bottle
Bottle of Kalish, of Milk
Bowl Sketch
Bowyers Guide
Box of Lute Strings
Bracer Sectional Mold
Brandy
Brazen Brass Kilij
Bread Tin Mold
Breath of Ro, Battle Axe, Dagger, Long Sword, Mace, Main Gauche, Rapier, 2-Handed Sword, Warhammer
Brownie Parts, Bone Arrow Shafts, Ceramic

Arrow, Steel Arrow Shafts, Wooden Arrow
Burned Out Lightstone
Cake Round Mold, Sketch
Cap Pattern
Carnelian
Cask
Cast-Iron Rapier
Cat's Eye Agate
Ceramic Lining Sketch
Chain Coif
Chainmail Bracelet, Cape, Coat, Gloves, Mantle, Neckguard, Skirt
Chipped Bone Rod
Chunk of Meat
Cloak Pattern
Cloak Sectional Mold
Cloth Cap, Cape, Choker, Cord, Gloves, Pants, Shawl, Shirt, Sleeves, Veil, Wristband
Cloudy Potion
Club

Combine Great Staff
Container Base Mold
Container Lid Mold
Copper Amulet, Band
Cracked Staff
Crimson Potion
Crushbone Belt
Dagger
Darkwood Bow Staff
Dirge of the ForgeFire
Dirty Green Tunic
Dual-Edged Blade Mold
Dufrenite
Dwarven Ale
Egg-Shaped Pumice
Electrum Bar
Elm Bow Staff
Elven Bread, Trail Mix, Wine
Emerald, Emerald Ring
Essence of Rathe
Faded Brown Tunic
Faded Salil's Writ Pages

Items, cont.

Faded Velishoul's Tome
Faerie Wing, Dust
Field Point Arrowheads
File Mold
Fine Steel Dagger, Great
    Staff, Long Sword,
    Morning Star, Rapier,
    Scimitar, Short Sword,
    Spear, 2-Handed
    Sword, Warhammer
Fire Emerald
Firing Sheet
Fish Gill Extract
Fish Wine
Fishing Bait, Pole, Spear
Flail
Flame of Vox
Fleeting Quiver Pattern
Fletching Kit
Flight Arrow
Fresh Fish
Fur Lined Boots, Shoes
Gauntlet Mold
Giant Wasp Venom Sac
Glass Shard
Glove of Rallos Zek
Glove Pattern
Gnome Cookie Mold,
    Template
Gnomish Spirits
Gold Bar, Ring
Golden Earring
Gorget Mold, Pattern
Grapes
Great Staff
Greater Lightstone
Green and Tan Tunic
Gypsy Wine
Halberd
Hand Drum
Harvest Crystal
Heart of the Pure Druid
Heavy Steel Blade Mold
Helm Mold
Hematite
Hemp Twine
Hickory Bow Staff
High Quality Firing Sheet
Hilt Mold
Hinge Mold
Honey Mead

Hooked Arrowheads
Horn
How To Sew: Large Sizes,
    Med. Sizes, Small Sizes
Hunting Bow
Ice of Velious
Iron Armplates, Legplates,
    Mask, Ration
Jade
Jade Earring, Ring, Shard
Jasper
Jeweller's Kit
Kite Shield
Lantern Casing Mold
Lapis Lazuli
Large Bag
Large Block of Clay
Large Bowl Sketch
Large Box
Large Container Base Mold
Large Container Lid Mold
Large Groove Nocks
Large Jar Sketch
Large Lantern
Large Sewing Kit
Large Tattered Skullcap
Leather Belt, Boots, Cloak,
    Gloves, Gorget,
    Leggings, Mask,
    Shoulderpads, Skullcap,
    Sleeves, Tunic,
    Wristbands
Legacy of Jewel Craft
Leggings Sectional Mold
Lightstone
Lined Vial Sketch
Linen String
Loaf of Bread
Lockpicks
Long Sword
Longbow
Lute
Mace
Mail Sectional Mold
Malachite
Mandolin
Mantle Sectional Mold
Mask Mold, Pattern
Mead
Medicine Bag
Medium Bowl Sketch

Medium Groove Nocks
Medium Jar Sketch
Mistletoe
Mithril Earring
Morning Star
Muffin Tin Mold, Sketch
Murky Vial
Needle Mold
Nilitim's Grimoire Pages
Oak Bow Staff
Ogre Swill
Old Green Tunic*
Old Worn Gray Tunic*
Onyx
Opal
Orc Hatchet
Packet of Kiola Sap
Pale Green Potion
Pant Pattern
Parrying Dagger
Tasarin's Grimoire Pages
Patchwork Boots, Pants
Pearl, Pearl Earring, Shard
Peridot
Pie Tin Mold, Sketch
Pixie Dust, Wing
Planing Tool
Plate Gauntlets, Girdle
Platemail Helm
Platinum Bar
Pommel Mold
Pot Mold, Sketch
Potion of Light Healing
Purse
Quality Firing Sheet
Quiver, Quiver Pattern
Rapier
Ration
Raw Bamboo
Raw-hide Boots, Cloak,
    Gloves, Gorget,
    Leggings, Mask,
    Shoulderpads, Skullcap,
    Sleeves, Tunic,
    Wristbands,
Red Wine
Ringmail Coif, Skirt
Robe of Discord
Round Shield
Royal Jelly
Ruby

Ruined Wolf Pelt
Rune of Al'Kabor,
    Ap'Sagor, Attraction,
    Attraction, Conception,
    Concussion, Crippling,
    Disassociation,
    Embrace, Expulsion,
    Falhalem, Frost,
    Fulguration, Impetus,
    Infraction, Karana,
    Nagafen, Neglect,
    Opression, Paralysis,
    Periphery, Petrification,
    Presence, Proximity,
    Rathe, Substance, the
    Astral, the Combine,
    the Helix, the Inverse,
    Trauma, Tyranny,
    Velious, Xegony
Rusty Axe, Bastard
    Sword, Battle Axe,
    Broad Sword, Dagger,
    Flail, Halberd, Long
    Sword, Mace, Morning
    Star, Rapier, Scimitar,
    Scythe, Short Sword,
    Shortened Spear, Spear,
    2-Handed Hammer,
    2-Handed Sword,
    Warhammer
Salil's Writ Pages
Sapphire
Scaler Mold
Scimitar
Scouts Blade
Scouts Cape
Sealed Vial Sketch
Set of Bone, Ceramic,
    Wooden Arrow Vanes
Several Parabolic Round,
    Shield Cut Fletchings
Sheaf Arrow
Sheet Metal
Short Ale, Beer, Bow, Sword
Shotglass
Shoulderpad Pattern
Shuriken
Silk String
Silver Amulet, Bar,
    Earring, Ring, Stud,
    Tipped Arrowheads
Silvermesh Leggings
Skewer Mold, Sketch
Sleeve Pattern
Sleeves Sectional Mold

Items, cont.

Small Bag
Small Block of Clay
Small Box
Small Buckler
Small Cloth Cap, Cape, Choker, Cord, Gloves, Pants, Sandals, Shawl, Shirt, Sleeves, Veil, Wristband
Small Container Base Mold
Small Container Lid Mold
Small Deity Sketch
Small Groove Nocks
Small Iron Boots
Small Jar Sketch
Small Lantern
Small Leather Boots
Small Patchwork Boots, Cloak, Pants, Sleeves, Tunic
Small Raw-hide Leggings
Small Sewing Kit
Small Steel Plate Boots
Small Tattered Belt, Gloves, Gorget, Mask, Shoulderpads, Skullcap, Wristbands
Smoker Base Mold
Smoker Sketch
Smoker Support Mold
Song, Alenlus Disenchanting Melody, Angstlichs Appalling Screech, Anthem of Arms, Brusco's Boastful Bellow, Cassindras Chorus of Clarity, Chant of Battle, Chords of Dissonance, Cinda's Charismatic, Crission's Pixie Strike, Denon's Disruptive Discord, Elemental Rhythms, Guardian Rhythms, Hymn of Restoration, Jaxan's Jig o' Vigor, Jonthan's Whistling Warsong, Kelin's Lucid Lullaby, Kelin's Lugubrious Lament, Largo's Melodic Binding, Lyssa's Cataloging Libretto, Lyssa's Locating Lyric, Niv's Melody of

Preservation, Psalm of Cooling, Psalm of Mystic, Psalm of Purity, Psalm of Vitality, Psalm of Warmth, Purifying Rhythms, Selo's Accelerando, Shauri's Sonorous Clouding, Solon's Song of the Sirens, Syvelian's Anti-Magic Aria, Tarew's Aquatic Ayre
Spear
Spell: Allure of the Wild, Barbcoat, Befriend Animal, Beguile Animals, Bind Affinity, Bind Sight, Bramblecoat, Burst of Fire, Burst of Flame, Calm Animal, Camouflage, Cancel Magic, Careless Lightning, Cascade of Hail, Charm Animals, Cure Disease, Cure Poison, Dance of the Fireflies, Dismiss Summoned, Dizzying Wind, Drones of Doom, Endure Cold, Endure Disease, Endure Fire, Endure Poison, Enduring Breath, Ensnaring Roots, Expulse Summoned, Eyes of the Cat, Feet like Cat, Feral Spirit, Firefist, Flame Lick, Form of the Great Wolf, Gate, Glimpse, Grasping Roots, Greater Wolf Form, Growth, Halo of Light, Harmony, Healing, Ignite, Immolate, Invigor, Invisibility vs Animals, Invoke Lightning, Levitate, Light Healing, Lull Animal, Minor Healing, Pack Spirit, Panic Animal, Resist Fire, Ring of Butcher, Ring of Commons, Ring of Karana, Ring of Toxxulia, Savage Spirit, See Invisible, Sense

Animals, Share Wolf Form, Shield of Barbs, Shield of Brambles, Shield of Thistles, Skin like Rock, Skin like Steel, Skin like Wood, Snare, Spirit of Cheetah, Spirit of Wolf, Starshine, Stinging Swarm, Strength of Earth, Summon Drink, Summon Food, Superior Camouflage, Terrorize Animal, Thistlecoat, Treeform, Ward Summoned, Whirling Wind, Wolf Form
Spider Legs
Spiderling Eye, Legs, Silk
Spiked Ball Mold
Spit
Splinted Cloak
Splintering Club
Spring Crystal
Staff
Staff of Discord
Standard Bow Cam
Standing Legs Mold
Star Rose Quartz
Star Ruby
Steel Bracers, Breastplate, Collar, Greaves, Greaves, Mask, Pauldrun, Vambraces
Tailoring
Targ Shield
Tarnished Axe, Bastard Sword, Battle Axe, Dagger, Long Sword, Scimitar, Short Sword, Spear
Tattered Belt, Gloves, Mask, Skullcap
Tears of Prexuz
Telescope Lens
The Scent of Marr
Thimble Mold
Throwing Axe, Knife, Spear
Topaz
Torch
Treant Bow Staff
Troll Cookie Mold
Troll Template

Tunic Pattern
Turquoise
2-Handed Hammer, Sword
Unfinished Brass Trumpet
Velishoul's Tome Pages
Vial of Swirling Smoke
Vial Sketch
Warhammer
Wasp Wing
Water Flask
Whip Pattern
White Wine
Whittling Blade
Wing of Xegony
Wolf Meat
Wood Elf Parts
Wooden Flute
Words of Absorption, Acquisition (Beza), Allure, Anthology, Bidding, Bondage, Burnishing, Cazic-Thule, Cloudburst, Collection (Azia), Collection (Beza), Collection (Caza), Convocation, Crippling Force, Derivation, Descrying, Detachment, Dimension, Discernment, Dissolution, Dominion, Enlightenment, Eradication, Eventide, Grappling, Imitation, Incarceration, Materials, Mistbreath, Obligation, Odus, Possession, Projection, Radiance, Recluse, Refuge, Requisition, Reviviscence, Seizure, Spirit, the Element, the Ethereal, the Extinct, the Psyche, the Quickening, the Sentient (Azia), the Sentient (Beza), the Spectre, the Spoken, the Suffering, Transcendence, Tyranny
Worn Great Staff
Wrist Pouch
Wristband Pattern

Kelethin

A distracted traveler might walk past Kelethin without seeing it. It lies not before, but above one, nestled within the leafy crowns of the ancient trees of Greater Faydark. Here the Wood Elves have built their home atop wooden platforms that ring the treetrunks. The platforms are linked to one another with bridges, and lifts convey creatures from the platforms to the ground.

Alongside the descendants of the Wood Elves who built the arboreal city, one finds Half-Elves who make it their home and visitors from all races friendly to the Wood Elves. Kelethin is deceptively full of resources — one finds numerous merchants of food, alcohol, armor, weapons, gems and other goods.

Kelthin shares the Greater Faydark Newbie Zone with Felwithe, which lies on the eastern edge of that forest. See **Greater Faydark Newbie Zone**, p. 267.

"Ah," Sirenas said, "the Faydark is the only place to live."

His wife, Karadin, smiled. "After visiting Felwithe, I cannot imagine living there." She caressed the tree trunk nearest the platform. "Tunare has blessed us."

Sirenas sighed. "However, I tire of the menial chores we've done so far."

"The talesayer last night spoke of Dill Fireshine's need," Karadin said. "Seek out the ranger guildmaster and I'll visit the Heartwood Master. Perhaps, now that we're more experienced, we can begin to assist our guilds."

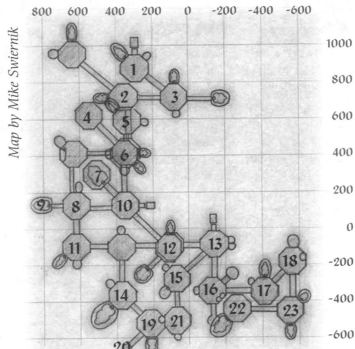

Map by Mike Swiernik

1. Orc Lift to ground, Inn, Merchants (pottery sketches, food, other goods)

2. Merchants (elven food, food, other goods)

3. Tavern (alcohol), Merchant (plate armor)

4. Merchants (racial alcohol, common gems)

5. Tavern (alcohol), Merchant (plate armor)

6. Upper platform: Sparkling Glass (metals, rare gems, elven food, oven)

   Lower platform: Merchants (pottery/fletching supplies), Warriors Guild

7. Heartwood Tavern (alcohol)

8. Merchant (food, other goods)

9. Tavern (alcohol)

10. Priest of Discord Lift to ground Merchants (armor molds, sheet metal, food, other goods)

11. Bank, Merchant (potions)

12. Upper platform: abandoned

    Lower platform: Packwearer's Goods (bags, boxes), Bards Guild

13. Lift, Merchants (sewing supplies, food, other goods)

14. Faydark's Champions (Rangers Guild)

15. Inn (food, other goods), forge, Merchant (potions, weapons)

16. Merchant (leather armor)

17. Inn (food, other goods)

18. Merchants (smithing supplies, weapons, cloth armor, pottery wheel/kiln)

19. Druids Guild (brew barrel)

20. Bilrio's Smithy (weapons, medicine bags)

21. Merchants (chain armor, boots)

22. Rogues Guild (weapons)

23. Trueshot Bows (fletching supplies), Merchants (bow supplies), Tavern (alcohol, Ranger spells)

Kaladim

The Dwarves built the town of Kaladim in the midst of one of their works in progress, the mines beneath Butcherblock Mountains. Like all underground cities, this one is very defensible — a single entrance leads from the mountains into South Kaladim. The city is designed in a loop, and the entrance tunnel soon branches to the east and west, with each branch taking you through the shops and guilds of the town into North Kaladim.

Needless to say, the merchants of Kaladim sell everything one could possibly need to pursue a living in the mines. Those who feel their fortunes lie along a different path might seek to start in the Butcherblock Mountains to the south of the city.

"Of course, I'm dwarf enough!" Fuzzbeard exclaimed. He had finally found out where his hero, Gunlok Jure, was, and this nobeard was doubting his ability. "If I weren't in such a hurry, I'd show you!"

"Old Nultal Malfoot needs skunk glands," Fuzzbeard's tormentor said. "Maybe you should start there, eh?"

Everyone in Irontoe's laughed as Fuzzbeard headed out to locate the Hall of Paladins.

South Kaladim

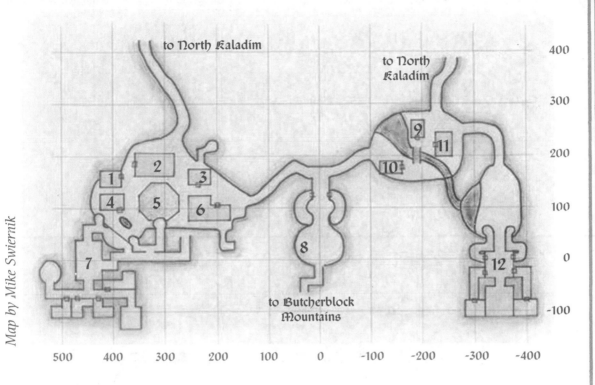

Map by Mike Swiernik

1. Tanned Assets (leather armor)
2. Irontoe's Eats (alcohol)
3. Staff and Spear (swords, fletching supplies)
4. Redfist's Metal (shields, weapons, forge)
5. The Arena (not PvP)
6. Pub Kal (alcohol, brew barrel), Bard outside
7. Warriors Guild

8. Priest of Discord
9. Merchant (potions)
10. Merchant (bags)
11. Gurtha's Ware (shoes, cloth armor, pottery supplies)
12. Castle (king)

North Kaladim

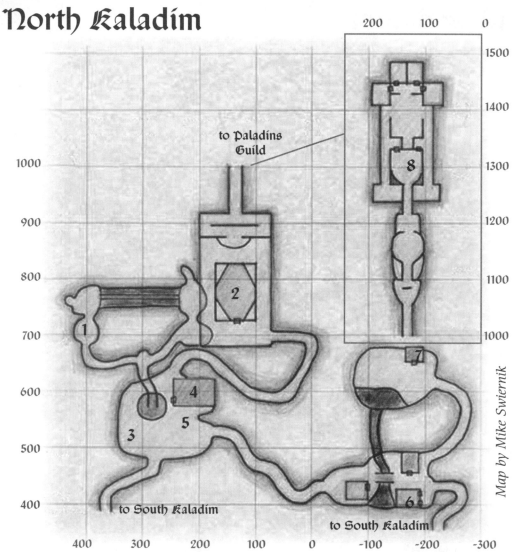

Map by Mike Swiernik

1. Merchant (*gems*)
2. Clerics Guild (*weapons*),
   Merchant (*food*) outside
3. Pottery Wheel/Kiln
4. Watsbone Treasure and Assay Office
   (*bank*)

5. Merchants (*weapons, mining supplies*),
   Rogues Guild members
6. Everhot Forge (*weapons, chain/plate
   armor, jewelry metal, rare gems, forge*)
7. Graybloom Farms (*grapes, brew barrel,
   oven*)
7. Paladins Guild

EverQuest: The Ruins of Kunark

Butcherblock Mountains Newbie Zone

Personalities

Alga Bruntbuckler	Doran Glosglen	Glynn Smeltpot	Nyzil Bloodforge
Alun Bilgum	Dru Razbind	Guards	Parn Gylwyn
Aralin Gwalmyr	Durkis Battlemore	Gundl	Peg Leg
Atwin Keladryn	Ellona	Happ Findlefinn	Qued
Ayen Rundlor	Felen Razdal	Iglan Thranon	Signus Boran
Balen Kalgunn	Fugan Mumfur	Inudul Dumirgun	Siltria Marwind
Barma Dunfire	Gamin Griststone	Izbal Brightblaze	Stump Rundl
Blyle Bundin	Ganhar Dundam	Kaila Rucksack	Tagnis Ginfarr
Corflunk	Gand Truelink	Kalvyn Bynfurr	Thar Kelgand
Crytil Dunfire	Gann Dunbull	Keldyn Dunfire	Trendel Bittlespin
Dalbar Tarbrind	Gibi Bilgum	Lann Dabldrin	Urazun Thranon
Darm Dundam	Glath Galadendal	Magnus Boran	Zarchoomi
Deldryn Splendyr	Glorin Binfurr	Margyl Darklin	
Delin Ironblend	Glubbsink	Naeneth Glynspurr	
Den Ironblend	Glynda Smeltpot	Nalda Griststone	

Goblins

aqua goblin, shaman, wizard	goblin grunt, shaman, warrior, whelp, wizard

Others

aviak chick	giant bat	large spider	SironaBane
bat	giant scarab	lowland basilisk	snake
decaying dwarf skeleton	Krag Chick	orc centurion, oracle, pawn, runner	Stormbreaker
dwarf skeleton	Krag Elder	rock spiderling	undead bishop, king, knight, pawn, rook
dwarven bandit	large skunk	Shuttle	worker scarab
emerald drake	large snake		

Items

Ale
Amber
Animal Cookie Mold
Armor and Weapons Guide
Arrow
Aviak Chick Talon
Aviak Talon
Backpack, Pattern
Bandages
Barbarian Cookie Mold
Barma's Tongue
Basic Blacksmithing
Basic Pottery
Basilisk Tongue
Bat Fur, Wing
Bead Necklace
Belt Pattern, Pouch
Binelen's Quick Treats, Succulence
Block of Clay
Bloodforge Hammer
Bloodstone
Bloodstone Ring
Bone Chips
Boot Pattern
Bottle
Bottle of Kalish, of Milk
Brandy
Bread Tin Mold
Bronze Battle Axe, Dagger, Long Sword, Mace, Main Gauche, Morning Star, Rapier, Shortened Spear, Spear, 2-Handed Battle, 2-Handed Sword
Buckler
Cake Round Mold
Cap Pattern
Carnelian
Cat's Eye Agate
Chalice Case
Chunk of Meat

Clay Totem
Cloak Pattern
Cloth Cap, Cape, Cord, Pants, Shirt, Wristband
Container Base Mold
Container Lid Mold
Copper Amulet, Band
Cracked Giant Scarab
Cracked Staff
Crushbone Belt
Crytil's Tongue
Cup of Flour
Dagger
Dirge of the ForgeFire
Dual-Edged Blade Mold
Dwarf Head, Meat
Dwarven Axe
Essence of Rathe
Faded Salil's Writ Pages
Faded Velishoul's Tome
File Mold
Fine Steel Dagger, Great Staff, Long Sword, Morning Star, Rapier, Scimitar, Short Sword, Spear, 2-Handed Sword, Warhammer
Firing Sheet
Fish Wine
Fishing Bait, Pole
Flame of Vox
Fleeting Quiver Pattern
Frosting
Garnish
Ghumim's Classical Dishes, Delights
Giant Scarab Egg Sack
Glass Shard
Glove of Rallos Zek
Glove Pattern
Glynda's Tongue
Glynn's Tongue
Gnoll Paw

Gnome Cookie Mold
Gnome Meat
Gold Ring
Golden Earring
Gorget Pattern
Gundl's Tongue
Heavy Steel Blade Mold
Hematite
High Quality Firing Sheet
Hilt Mold
Hinge Mold
Holy Partisan of Underfoot
Honey Mead
How To Sew: Large Sizes, Med. Sizes, Small Sizes
Hunting Bow
Hurrieta's Tunic
Ice of Velious
Iron Ration, Visor
Jade, Jade Earring, Shard
Jasper
Jug of Sauces
Keldyn's Tongue
Lantern Casing Mold
Lapis Lazuli
Large Bag
Large Block of Clay
Large Container Base Mold
Large Container Lid Mold
Large Lantern
Large Sewing Kit
Large Snake Skin
Lined Vial Sketch
Loaf of Bread
Malachite
Margyl's Tongue
Mask Pattern
Mead
Mithril Earring
Mixxy's Delicacies Vols 1, 2
Muffin Tin Mold
Needle Mold
Nilitim's Grimoire Pages

Ogre Head
Onyx
Pant Pattern
Pearl, Shard
Pie Tin Mold
Pommel Mold
Pot Mold
Pristine Giant Scarab
Quality Firing Sheet
Qued's Tongue
Quiver Pattern
Ration
Raw Bamboo
Red Wine
Ringmail Boots, Bracelet, Cape, Coat, Coif, Gloves, Mantle, Neckguard, Pants, Skirt, Sleeves
Riptide Spear
Rohand's Edibles
Rohand's Sea Treats
Rune of Al'Kabor, Arrest, Attraction, Attraction, Banding, Conception, Concussion, Consumption, Contortion, Disassociation, Embrace, Expulsion, Falhalem, Fulguration, Howling, Infraction, Karana, Nagafen, Paralysis, Periphery, Petrification, Presence, Proximity, Rathe, Solusek Ro, Sorcery, Substance, the Catalyst, the Combine, the Cyclone, the Helix, the Inverse, Trauma, Tyranny, Xegony
Runner Pouch
RunnyEye Warbeads
Rusty Axe, Bastard Sword, Battle Axe, Broad Sword, Dagger,

Items, cont.

Flail, Halberd, Long Sword, Mace, Morning Star, Morning Star, Rapier, Scimitar, Scythe, Short Sword, Shortened Spear, Spear, 2-Handed Battle Axe, 2-Handed Hammer, 2-Handed Sword, Warhammer

Salil's Writ Pages

Scaler Mold

Scarab Carapace

Scarab Eye

Scarab Legs

sealed letter

Sealed Vial Sketch

Senior Apprentice Robe*

Shattered Warbeads

Short Ale

Short Beer

Shoulderpad Pattern

Silver Amulet, Earring, Ring, Stud

Skewer Mold

Skunk Scent Gland

Sleeve Pattern

Small Bag

Small Belt Sectional Mold

Small Block of Clay

Small Boot Mold

Small Box

Small Bracer Sectional Mold

Small Bronze Boots, Bracers, Breastplate, Collar, Gauntlets, Girdle, Greaves, Helm, Mask, Pauldrun, Vambraces

Small Buckler

Small Chain Coif

Small Chainmail Belt, Bracelet, Cape, Coat, Gloves, Mantle, Neckguard

Small Cloak Sectional Mold

Small Cloth Cap, Cape, Choker, Cord, Gloves, Pants, Sandals, Shawl, Shirt, Sleeves, Veil, Wristband

Small Container Base Mold

Small Container Lid Mold

Small Gauntlet Mold

Small Gorget Mold

Small Helm Mold

Small Iron Armplates

Small Iron Legplates

Small Iron Mask

Small Iron Visor

Small Lantern

Small Leather Belt, Cloak, Gloves, Gorget, Leggings, Mask, Shoulderpads, Skullcap, Sleeves, Tunic, Wristbands

Small Leggings. Mail, Mantle Sectional Molds

Mask Mold

Small Raw-hide Belt, Boots, Cloak, Gloves, Gorget, Leggings, Mask, Shoulderpads, Skullcap, Sleeves, Tunic, Wristbands

Small Ringmail Belt, Boots, Bracelet, Cape, Coat, Coif, Gloves, Mantle, Neckguard, Pants, Sleeves

Small Sewing Kit

Small Sleeves Sectional Mold

Small Splinted Bronze Cloak

Small Wooden Leg

Small Wooden Shield

Smoker Base Mold

Smoker Support Mold

Snake Egg

Snake Fang

Snake Scales

Sorin's Treats on the Go

Spell: Avalanche, Banish Summoned, Chloroplast, Circle of Misty, Drifting Death, Enveloping Roots, Firestrike, Nullify Magic, Pack Regeneration, Resist Disease, Resist Poison, Shield of Spikes, Skin like Diamond, Spikecoat, Storm Strength

Spices

Spider Legs, Silk, Venom Sac

Spiderling Eye, Legs, Silk

Spiked Ball Mold

Spit

Splintering Club

Standing Legs Mold

Star Rose Quartz

Tailoring

Tasarin's Grimoire Pages

Tears of Prexuz

The Scent of Marr

Thimble Mold

Topaz

Torch

Troll Cookie Mold

Tunic Pattern

Turquoise

Vaashar's Sweet Revege

Vaashar's Sweet Treats

Velishoul's Tome Pages

Vial Sketch

Vinegar

Warbone Chips

Water Flask

Whip Pattern

White Wine

Wood Elf Parts

Wooden Shield

Words of Abatement, Absorption, Allure, Bidding, Burnishing, Cazic-Thule, Cloudburst, Collection (Azia), Collection (Beza), Collection (Caza), Convocation, Dark Paths, Derivation, Descrying, Detachment, Detention, Dimension, Discernment, Dissolution, Dissolution, Duration, Duress, Efficacy, Endurance, Eradication, Eventide, Haunting, Imitation, Incarceration, Materials, Mistbreath, Motion, Neglect, Obligation, Possession, Projection, Quivering, Recluse, Resolve, Reviviscence, Seizure, Spirit, the Element, the Psyche, the Sentient (Azia), the Sentient (Beza), the Spectre, the Spoken, the Suffering, Transcendence, Tyranny

Worn Great Staff

Wrist Pouch

Wristband Pattern

Xectia's Favored Flavors

Xectia's Hot Pie

Odus

The reason that Odus was chosen by Erud all those years ago is quite simple. This continent holds all the perfect climates for the up and coming magic users! From the Grand Plateau in the north to The Barren Coast in the southeast, there simply is no better place to practice the arcane arts.

After taking Erud's Crossing from Qeynos, we begin our tour in Erudin, the main city on Odus. Nestled on the Grand Plateau, the city holds all the arcane guilds, except one.

Necromancers are blessed with their own city of Paineel on the western coast, just north of The Hole. Special tours of The Hole can be arranged through your guild assistants.

In the center of the continent are the Stonebrunt Mountains, which separate Toxxulia Forest from the Vasty Deep. This part of the land holds a cornucopia of spell components — from mosses in the forest to the fur of monsters in the Stonebrunts to scales of creatures in the Vasty Deep.

Another location of note is the warm waters of the Gulf of Uzun in the south. Kerra Isle to the west, south of the Abysmal Sea, should be avoided.

EverQuest: The Ruins of Kunark

Erudin

Enoust had just finished singing. The crowd dispersed, but not before they filled his hat with many coins. He smiled at the woman who was trying to dig a coin out of her almost empty pouch. "I can see, m'lady, that you are a bit down on your luck."

She blushed and turned to walk away in embarrassment.

Quickly gathering his hat and coins, the bard caught up with the woman. "Forgive me. I do not mean to distress you. I only wish to tell you that I heard of opportunities galore at the Temple of Divine Light. You are a good soul, are you not? A cleric, yourself, perhaps?"

When she nodded, he continued, "Ah, I can always spot the people to know! Speak with Cleric Guildmaster Leraena Shelyrak or Cleric Lumi Stergnon. When you've filled that pouch with more coins than you know what to do with," Enoust said with a wink, "I will gladly take one or two in payment for any amusement I may afford you."

Home to the Erudites, a race which broke with Humans long ago to follow the higher arts of knowledge, Erudin is a secluded city on the northwest coast of Odus. Qeynos lies just across Erud's crossing, and boats traffic between the two. From the Erudin Docks area, the traveler must teleport into Erudin itself. Merchants of various goods lie within, those catering to practitioners of magic are generally clustered within Erudin Palace, which is linked to Erudin by teleporter.

Citizens of Erudin share the Toxxulia Forest Newbie Zone with the inhabitants of Paineel, which lies within that forest (see **Toxxulia Forest Newbie Zone**, p. 284) However, "sharing" is a word used only loosely here, as in truth the Erudites openly despise the Paineelians as heretics and outcasts, and attempt to destroy any that they find.

Erudín

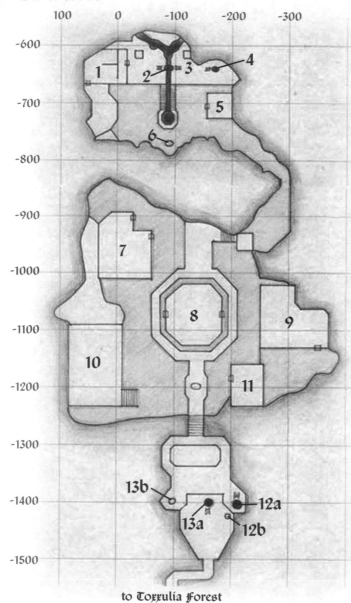

to Toxxulia Forest

Map by Mike Swiernik

1. Temple of Divine Light (Clerics/Paladins Guilds), Merchants (weapons, cloth armor)

2. Teleporter to Erudin Palace

3. Bard

4. Teleporter to Erudin Docks

5. City Armory (chain/plate armor)

6. Arrival platform for teleporters from Erudin Palace and Docks

7. Erudin Surplus (food, boxes, brew barrel, pottery wheel/kiln, other goods) Merchant (cloth armor, oven) outside

8. Erudin City Library (Bard songs, various Cleric/Mage Enchanter/Wizard spells)

9. Deepwater Knights, Followers of Prexus (Clerics/Paladins Guilds), Merchants (weapons, forge) outside

10. Vasty deep Inn

11. Blue Hawk's Food (food, alcohol, cooking books, brew barrel, oven, other goods)

12a. Teleport to platform 12b.

13a. Teleport to platform 13b.

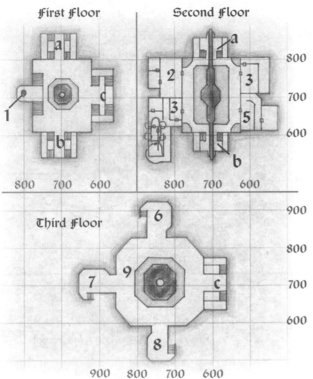

First Floor

Second Floor

Third Floor

Maps by Mike Swiernik

Erudin Palace

Letters indicate connecting staircases.

1. Teleporter to Erudin (bottom), Arrival platform from Erudin (top)
2. Bank of Erudin
3. Erudin City Office (bags, prison)
4. Sothure's Fine Gems (gems, metals, jewelry supplies)
5. Vials of Vitality (jewelry supplies, potions, lightstones)
6. Tower of the Crimson Hands (Wizards Guild), Merchants (spells, crimson robes, books, gems)
7. Tower of the Gate Callers (Magicians Guild), Merchants (spells, blue robes, gems, Magician equipment)
8. Tower of the Craft Keepers (Enchanters Guild), Merchants (spells, gold robes, gems, spell components)
9. Merchant (spells)

Erudin Docks

1. Merchant (bags, boxes)
2. Erudin Port Authority
3. Merchant (cooking supplies, food)
4. Priest of Discord
5. Teleporter to Erudin
6. Arrival platform for teleport from Erudin
7. Boats to Qeynos

Paineel

Paineel is a city in exile. Its inhabitants were once followers of Erudite, like their brothers and sisters the Erudites, to the north. However in times past they turned away from the teachings of Erud, following their own path into the powerful dark arts of Cazic-Thule. The Erudites persecuted them as heretics, leaving the Paineelians to found a new home deep within Toxxulia Forest on the ruins of a much older settlement.

Erudin lies not far to the North through the Toxxulia Forest Newbie Zone. However, considering the animosity between the Erudites and the Paineelians, adventurers best not travel to far from the city unaccompanied and unarmed for combat either physical or magical.

Sathys had been in Paineel for some time and had been enjoying increasing notoriety with his necromancer faction. Last night, he had heard of two new opportunities. A young apprentice stumbled into Sathys' favorite tavern and complained about a very strong skeleton in the initiates yard. Also, a cleric told a tale about undead rats that her guildmaster, Sern Adolia, was looking to eradicate.

After a bit of hit and miss, Sathys got a tip that the person he needed to speak with was Noclin Saah. The opportunity to stop the skeleton had much more appeal to Sathys than going after more rats!

EverQuest: The Ruins of Kunark

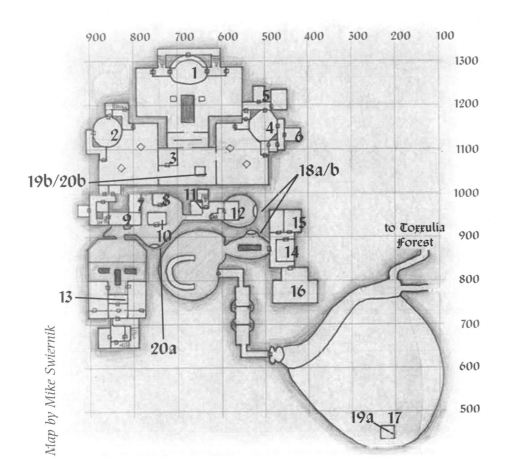

Map by Mike Swiernik

1. Overlord's Hall
2. Library
3. Shop (pottery wheel/kiln)
4. Tabernacle of Terror (Clerics Guild)
5. Merchant (chain mail armor, weapons)
6. Merchants (shields, weapons)
7. False Idols (pottery supplies/wheel/kiln)
8. The Final Reckoning (bank)
9. Shackled Spirits (dancing skeletons, alcohol, brew barrel, inn upstairs)
10. Superior Supplies (food, alchemy supplies, other goods)
11. Good Ivy's Tasty Treats (food, cooking supplies, oven)
12. Sinfully Handsome (cloth/leather armor)
13. The Abbatoir (Necromancers Guild)
14. The Fell Blade (Shadow Knights Guild)
15. Merchant (plate armor, forge)
16. PvP area
17. Observatory
18. Reciprocal teleporters (you can depart/arrive from either a or b)
19. Reciprocal teleporters
20. Reciprocal teleporters

Torxulia Forest Newbie Zone

Personalities

Aglthin Dasmore
Cyria Lorewhisper
E'lial B'rook
Emil Parsini
Erudin Emissary
Islan Hetston

Jalen Goldsinger
Jonly Smithin
Martyn Firechaser
Merchant Bogun
Phaeril Nightshire
Poachers Bogun, Dell, Hill, Shelli, Topi, Unil, Willa

Quana Rainsparkle
Rungupp
Sentinels Bogun, Creot, Drom, Flavius
Shintar Vinlail
Stylla Parsini

Tran Lilspin
Veisha Fathomwalker
Win Karnam
Xylania Rainsparkle

Kobolds

kobold caster
kobold runt

kobold scout
kobold sentry

kobold shaman
kobold watcher

weird kobold

Others

abandoned heretic pet
briar snake
decaying skeleton
fire beetle
fish

giant piranha
heretic prophet, recruiter
Ilanic's skeleton
infected rat
moss snake

palace courier
piranha
pixie
skeleton
skunk, large skunk

spiderling
The Gate Bandit
thistle snake
widow hatchling
willowisp

Items

Aglthin's Fishing Pole
Ale
Amber
Aquamarine
Armor and Weapons Guide
Arrow
Arrow of Contagion, Fire, Frost, Lightning, Poison, Stunning
Backpack
Bandages
Basic Blacksmithing
Battle Staff
Bead Necklace

Belt Pouch
Belt Sectional Mold
Binelen's Quick Treats, Succulence
Bloodstone
Bloodstone Ring
Blue Jr Apprentice Robe
Blue Sr Apprentice Robe
Bone Chips, Shield
Bones
Book of Ancient Restoration
Boot Mold
Bottle

Bottle of Kalish, of Milk
Bracer Sectional Mold
Broken Block of Ore
Bronze Bastard Sword, Halberd, Long Sword, Short Sword, Two Handed Sword
Burned Out Lightstone
Carnelian
Cask
Cat's Eye Agate
Cloak Sectional Mold
Copper Amulet, Band
Cracked Staff

Crate of Potions
Cup of Flour
Dagger
Doctrine of Wizardry
Elemental Grimoire
Emerald
Emissary Head
Empty Crystal Sphere
Essence of Rathe
Eye of Serilis
Faded Velishoul's Tome
Fine Steel Dagger, Rapier, Spear

Others

Fire Beetle Eye, Leg
Fish Scales
Flame of Vox
Fractured Femur
Fresh Fish
Frosting
Garnish
Gauntlet Mold
Ghumim's Classical Dishes, Delights
Glove of Rallos Zek
Gold Jr Apprentice Robe
Gold Ring
Gold Sr Apprentice Robe
Golden Earring
Gorget Mold
Greater Lightstone
Half of a Spell
Helm Mold
Hematite
Ice of Velious
Ipsor's Enlightenment III, IV
Iron Ration, Visor
Jade, Jade Earring, Shard
Jasper
Jug of Sauces
Kobold Hide
Lantern Casing Mold
Lapis Lazuli
Large Bag
Large Box
Large Snake Skin
Leather Gloves
Leggings Sectional Mold
Lexicon
Lightstone
Loaf of Bread
Mail Sectional Mold
Malachite
Malagil's Compendium Vols. 1, 2
Mantle Sectional Mold
Mask Mold

Mead
Mithril Earring
Mixxy's Delicacies Vols. 1, 2
Nilitim's Grimoire Pages
Odd Kobold Paw
On Languages
Onyx
Parrying Dagger
Tasarin's Grimoire Pages
Peacekeeper Staff
Pearl, Pearl Shard
Peridot
Phaeril Nightshire's Head
Piece of Parchment
Poacher's Head
Purse
Quill
Quiver
Rapier
Rat Ears, Tooth, Whiskers
Ration
Rehim's Robe
Ringmail Boots, Bracelet, Cape, Coat, Coif, Gloves, Mantle, Neckguard, Pants, Skirt, Sleeves
Rohand's Edibles, Sea Treats
Rune of Al'Kabor, Attraction, Disassociation, Dismemberment, Expulsion, Falhalem, Fulguration, Karana, Karana, Nagafen, Periphery, Presence, Proximity, Rallos Zek, Rathe, Regeneration, Substance, the Combine, the Helix, the Inverse, Trauma, Xegony
Rusty Axe, Bastard Sword, Battle Axe,

Broad Sword, Dagger, Halberd, Long Sword, Mace, Mining Pick, Scimitar, Short Sword, Two Handed Sword, Warhammer
Senior Apprentice Robe
Sentinal Creots Head
Sheet Metal
Short Ale
Short Beer
Silver Amulet, Earring, Ring, Stud
Skunk Scent Gland
Sleeves Sectional Mold
Small Bag
Small Box
Small Buckler
Small Leather Belt, Cloak, Skullcap, Sleeves, Wristbands
Snake Egg, Fang, Scales
Sorin's Treats on the Go
Spices
Spider Legs
Spiderling Eye, Legs, Silk
Splintering Club
Staff
Star Rose Quartz
Tears of Prexus
Telryd's Exspansive Writ
Telryd's Writ
The End of an Age
The Scent of Marr
The Wizard's Canon
Throwing Knife
Tiny Dagger
Tome of Endless
Topaz
Treant Resin
Troll Head
Troll Parts
Turquoise
Useless Cloth Cap

Vaashar's Sweet Revege, Sweet Treats
Veisha Fathomwalker's Head
Veisha's Engagement Ring
Velishoul's Tome Pages
Vinegar
Water Flask
Water of Povar
Wolf's Eye Agate
Words of Absorption, Acquisition (Azia), Allure, Burnishing, Cazic-Thule, Cloudburst, Coercion, Collection (Caza), Derivation, Detachment, Dimension, Discernment, Dissemination, Dissolution, Eradication, Eventide, Haunting, Imitation, Incarceration, Materials, Mistbreath, Obligation, Parasitism, Possession, Purification, Recluse, Reviviscence, Rupturing, Sight, Spirit, the Element, the Incorporeal, the Psyche, the Sentient (Azia), the Sentient (Beza), the Spoken, Transcendence, Tyranny
Worn Great Staff
Wrist Pouch
Xectia's Favored Flavors
Xectia's Hot Pie
Zombie Skin

Kunark

Kunark is the most mysterious of all the continents and, therefore, of high interest to intrepid travelers. The main city of the Iksar is Cabilis, built near the Lake of Ill Omen, central to the continent. The palace of Emperor Vekin is under construction and is expected to be a glorious structure befitting the ruler of the Iksar race.

Any other information we have on Kunark is rumor. It is shared here with the proviso that the traveler be forewarned.

The history of these lands — indeed, the history of all of Kunark — befits the names of known areas of the island. Across the Frontier Mountains, to the northwest of Cabilis, are the Burning Wood (the remnant of a draconian struggle) and the Overthere. Northeast of Cabilis is the renowned Field of Bone, site of much interest to those who wish to do battle.

Other areas include the Broken Teeth mountains, Trakanon's Teeth, the Emerald Jungle (reported lair of Trakanon himself), the Hills of Disdain, and The Dreadlands.

EverQuest: The Ruins of Kunark

Cabilis

Cerisss had spent enough time exploring Cabilis and he was running out of food. He knew he had to get busy. Merchants were always an annoying lot when it came to gossip, so Cerisss went to the Haggle Barons building and listened. He got two names. Klok, a merchant, needed some help and Warlord Zyzz was paying for killing those irritating scorpions!

Whatever one's opinion of the Iksar, the reports of Cabilis paint a picture of a town as elaborate and extensive as any on Norrath. Divided into an east and west zone, and surrounded by a number of newbie zones, Cabilis is rumored to support a thriving local merchant trade, which offers everything from the basics of food and water to precious gems armors of rare hides.

West Cabilis

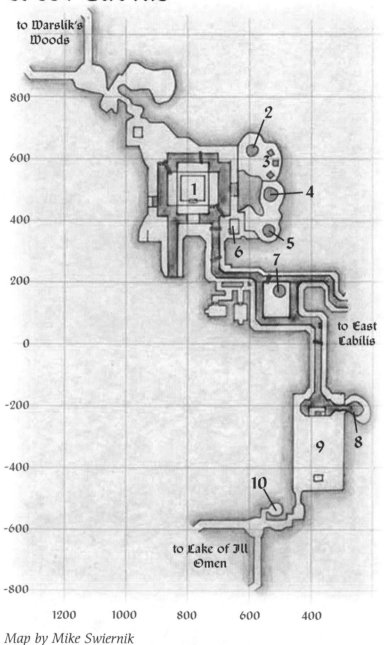

to Warslik's Woods

to East Cabilis

to Lake of Ill Omen

1. Necromancer Guild Hall
2. Merchant (weapons)
3. Merchant (leather armor)
4. Merchant (food)
5. Merchant (cloth armor)
6. Embalmer (embalming supplies)
7. Merchants (alchemy supplies, potions, lightstones, dufrenite)
8. Merchants (necromancer spells)
9. Arena (PvP area)
10. Iksar Hermit

Map by Mike Swiernik

EverQuest: The Ruins of Kunark

East Cabilis

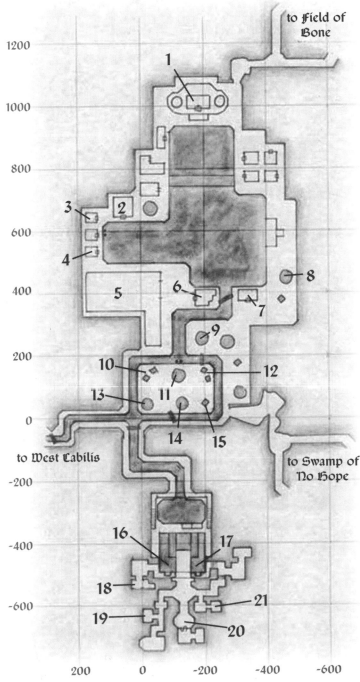

to Field of Bone

to West Cabilis

to Swamp of No Hope

1. Shamans and Shadow Knights Guild Hall
2. The Black (bank)
3. Merchant (gems, jewelry kit)
4. Merchant (pastries, cookbooks)
5. Court of Pain (Monks Guild)
6. The Haggle Baron (bristle silk armor)
7. The Haggle Baron
8. Merchant (food)
9. Merchant (pottery supplies, pottery wheel/kiln outside)
10. Merchant (cloth armor)
11. Merchant (food)
12. Merchants (food, musical instruments)
13. Merchant (bags, boxes)
14. Merchant (rhinoskin armor)
15. Merchant (wilderness survival gear)
16. Merchant (weapons, forge)
17. Merchant (weapons)
18. Merchants (weapons, shields)
19. Merchant (Lupine scale armor)
20. Warrior Guildmaster (trainers)
21. Merchant (cook/lore books)

Map by Mike Swiernik

Feild of Bone Newbie Zone

Personalities

Crusader Bodli	Gharg Oberbord	Klok Acet, Canip, Naman, Tugin	Trooper Chikzik, Grouko, Harpin, Mozo, Taer
Crusader Quarg	Jairnel Marfury		Warlord Zyzz

Iksar

iksar bandit	iksar footpad	iksar marauder
iksar brigand	iksar manslayer	iksar pariah

Others

bonebinder,bonebinder hatchling	carrion beetle hatchling	rogue shaman	skeletal jester
bonecrawler, bonecrawler hatchling	carrion shredder	scalebone skeleton	skeleton, decaying, greater, militiskeleton
burynai burrower, excavator, sapper	emerald fencer, scarab	scaled wolf, wolf cub, hunter, pup, stalker, wolf tracker	Sythrax guardian
burynaibane spider	greater scalebone		tangrin
	heartsting scorpion, large	scorpion, large, giant	targishin
	lesser charbone skeleton	servant of Sythrax	
	lesser icebone skeleton		

Lake of Ill Omen Newbie Zone

Personalities

Bruiser Noz	Klok Foob, Gnask, Sargin, Vydl	Trooper Curlish, Digdul, Eshzik, Frogzin, Hegwez, Kylpog, Larrin,	Selbat
Crusader Deezin, Swype			Warlord Geot

Goblins

goblin brawler	goblin scout	goblin spirit caller	goblin watcher
goblin hunter	goblin skirmisher	goblin warlord	goblin whelp
goblin outrider	goblin soothsayer	goblin warrior	

Iksar

iksar bandit	iksar exile	iksar manslayer	iksar pariah
iksar brigand	iksar footpad	iksar marauder	

Sarnak

sarnak adherant	sarnak crypt raider	sarnak hatchling	sarnak youth
sarnak broodling	sarnak dragoon	sarnak recruit	
sarnak conscript	sarnak flunkie	sarnak revealer	

Others

barracuda, bloodgill, deepwater, large, stuffed	charbone skeleton, lesser	sabertooth cat, cub, grimalkin, kit, kitten, tiger, tigress	skeleton, decaying, greater, war boned
bloodgill goblin	greater icebone		
	greater scalebone	scalebone skeleton	
	icebone skeleton, lesser		

EverQuest: The Ruins of Kunark

Swamp of No Hope Newbie Zone

Personalities

Blackbone, Blackwing
Bleeder
Bloodgorge, Bloodskull, Bloodvein
Bulsgor
Captain Nedar
Crackclaw
Crookspine
Crusader Litia, Savot
Deadeye
Dred

Dreesix Ghoultongue
Ebon Bloodrose
Fakraa the Forsaken
Fangor
Farik the Vile
Fisherman Grik
Footman Moglok
Frayk
Froszik the Impaler
Galeech, Gluttik, Gorge
Grimewurm

Grizshnok
Heartblood Fern
Horkak the Dead
Ichorspike
Klok Bygle, Gokrok, Migo, Roshin
Mystic Dovan
Old Hangman
Scalek
Soblohg
Thirgus, Torgis

Trooper Gubb, Harkee, Inkin, Keat, Lorgen, Nilzik, Nodfod, Nubb
Two Tails
Vissix
Warlord Hikyg
Weeping Mantrap
Woggir
Zagran the Mad

Iksar

iksar bandit
iksar brigand

iksar exile
iksar footpad

iksar manslayer
iksar marauder

iksar pariah

Froglok

escaped froglok slave
froglok berserker
froglok bounder
froglok escort

froglok fisher
froglok gaz knight, shaman, warrior
froglok impaler

froglok raider
froglok shin shaman
froglok skipper
froglok tad

froglok ton shaman, warrior
froglok tuk knight, shaman, warrior
froglok vis shaman

Others

bloodvein mosquito
charbone skeleton
decaying skeleton
giant bloodvein mosquito
giant marsh leech
giant mire leech
giant morass leech
giant mosquito
giant swamp leech

greater scalebone
greater skeleton
icebone skeleton
insatiable devourer
insatiable gnawer
insatiable nibbler
large bloodvein mosquito
large mosquito
lesser charbone skeleton

lesser icebone skeleton
man eating creeper, fern, plant, shrub, vine
marsh leech
mire leech
morass leech
mosquito
scalebone skeleton
scourgewing mosquito

skeleton
swamp leech
venomous lamprey
venomwing
war boned skeleton

Warsliks Woods

Personalities

Captain Gideen	Klok Dogron, Gragin,	Troopers Agash, Elpiz,	Troopers Roklon, Syldon,
Crusader Eaxl, Myxl	Kogrin, Nogolin,	Gepwyz, Kroniz,	Uzin, Walrun
	Rogalin, Ryre	Lunmiz, Melzok, Olon,	Warlord Vyzer

Goblins

goblin agressor	goblin hunter	goblin spirit caller	goblin whelp
goblin bloodtracer	goblin outrider	goblin thief	goblin witchdoctor
goblin bonecaster	goblin scout	goblin warlord	
goblin brawler	goblin skirmisher	goblin warrior	
goblin hextracer	goblin soothsayer	goblin watcher	

Iksar

iksar bandit	iksar exile	iksar knight	iksar marauder
iksar brigand	iksar footpad	iksar manslayer	iksar pariah

Scaled Wolves

scaled wolf	scaled wolf elder	scaled wolf pup	scaled wolf tracker
scaled wolf cub	scaled wolf hunter	scaled wolf stalker	

Others

decaying skeleton	forest giant, evergreen,	rogue shaman	skulking, brute, pygmy
	greenwood, sapling	skeleton	brute, brutling, runtling

Items for All Four Newbie Zones

(f) = found in Field of Bone; (l) = found in Lake of Ill Omen; (s) = found in Swamp of No Hope; (w) = found in Warsliks Wood; no notation (e. g., Amber) = found in all zones

Aloe Swatch (w)	Bloodstone Ring	Cinched Stomach Pouch	Sword (f), Warhammer
Amber	Bone Chips	Copper Amulet, Band	Fire Emerald Ring (f,s)
Axe	Book Binder (w)	Cracked Giant Scarab (f)	First Half of Torn Note (f)
Backpack (w)	Bottle (w)	Diamond (f,s)	Fish Scales (l)
Battle Axe	Breath of Ro (f,s)	Dried Froglok Leg	Fishing Bait
Bead Necklace	Brittle Iksar Skull	Earthworm Munch (f,s,w)	Fishing Pole
Beetle Bake	Busted Froglok Slave	Emerald (l,w)	Flame of Vox (l)
Belt Pouch (w)	Shackles (s)	Essence of Rathe (f)	Flask of Bloodwater
Bixle Berry Pie (s)	Cabilis Pale Ale	Eye of Serilis (l)	Foobscale Coif (l)
Black Pearl (l,w)	Carnelian	Faded Salil's Writ Pages	Fresh Fish (l)
Black Sapphire (f,s)	Cask (w)	(f,l)	Froglok Bounder Javelin
Bladder of Lizard Milk	Cat's Eye Agate	Faded Velishoul's Tome	(s)
Bloodgill Harpoon (f),	Chalp Diagram (w)	Fine Steel Long Sword,	Froglok Escort Fife (s),
Trident (w)	Charred Bone Box (f),	Scimitar (f), Short	Hex Doll (w)
Bloodstone	Shards (f)	Sword, Two Handed	Froglok Tad Eye (s),

EverQuest: The Ruins of Kunark

Items for All Four Newbie Zones, cont.

Tongue (s)
Frogskin Shield
Geozite Tool (f,s,w)
Giant Blood Sac (s)
Giant Scarab Egg Sack (f)
Glove of Rallos Zek (l)
Goblin Hunter Javelin (l,w)
Goblin Scout Beads (l,w)
Gold Ring
Golden Earring
Golden Pendant (l,w)
Halberd
Hematite
Ice of Velious
Iksar Bandit Mask (f)
Iksar Head (s)
Iksar Witch Doll (w)
Iron Cudgel of the Mystic (f), of the Prophet (s)
Jacinth (f,s)
Jade, Earring, Ring (l,w), Shard
Jasper
Jawless Skull (w)
Koada'Dal Blood Doll (l,w)
Lapis Lazuli
Large Bag (w)
Large Box (w)
Large Iron Visor (f)
Large Lantern
Large Ringmail Belt (f), Boots (f), Bracelet (f), Cape (f), Coat (f), Coif (f), Gloves (f), Mantle (f), Neckguard (f), Pants (f), Sleeves (f)
Large Scorpion Pincer (f)
Leech Husk (s)
Legion Order
Lens of Sorts (s)
Loose Scale (f,w)
Mace
Machete
Malachite
Mandible (f)
Maneater Plant Salve
Medicine Bag
Misscribed Gate (w)
Misscribed Lifetap (w)

Mithril Earring
Nilitim's Grimoire Pages (f,s)
Onyx
Opal (l,w)
Ornate Tin Box (s)
Pages of a Poem (w)
Pages of Tome (s)
Patch Hide Ab Guard, Arm Guards, Bracers, Collar, Gloves, Mask, Poncho, Sandal, Skullcap (f,s,w), Shoulder Guard
Pearl, Earring (l,w), Ring (l,w), Shard
Peridot (l,w)
Pristine Giant Scarab (f)
Purification Tablet
Quiver (w)
Ration Bladder
Rhinohide Backpack
Ripped Tapestry (l)
Ruby (f,s)
Ruby Crown (f,s)
Rune of: Al'Kabor, Ap'Sagor (f,s), Arrest (f), Attraction, Banding (f), Conception (l), Concussion (f,s), Consumption (f), Contortion (t), Crippling (f,s), Disassociation, Dismemberment (l), Embrace (l), Expulsion, Falhalem, Frost (f,s), Fulguration, Howling (f), Impetus (f,s), Infraction (l), Karana, Nagafen, Neglect, Opression, Paralysis (l), Periphery, Petrification (l), Presence, Proximity, Rallos Zek (l), Rathe (f,s), Regeneration (l), Solusek Ro (f), Sorcery (f), Substance, the Astral (f,s), the Catalyst (f, the Combine (l), the Cyclone (f), the Helix (l), the Inverse (f), Trauma, Tyranny (l), Velious, Xegony

Rusty Scythe (l)
Sabertooth Cub Canine (l)
Sabertooth Dagger (f,s,w)
Sabertooth Kitten Canine (l)
Salil's Writ Pages (f,l)
Sapphire Necklace (f,s)
Sarnak Hatchling Brain (l), Raider Brain (l), Whelp Head (l)
Scaled Curskin (f,w)
Scaled Wolf Hide (f,w)
Scorpion Pincer (f)
Second Half of Torn Note (f)
Shrub Lettuce (s)
Silver Amulet, Earring, Ring, Stud
Skipping Stone (s)
Skull Chest (f)
Skull with I (l)
Slave Shackle Bag (s)
Small Bag (w)
Small Lantern
Small Mosquito Wing (s)
Soldier's Dull Pike (s)
Spear
Spider Legs (f)
Spider Silk (f)
Spider Venom Sac (f)
Star Rose Quartz
Star Ruby Earring (f,s)
Strange Writing on a Bookmark (s)
Survival Staff
Targ Shield
Tasarin's Grimoire Pages
Tattered Note (w)
Tears of Prexuz (f,s)
Teir'Dal Sooth Doll (w)
The Scent of Marr (f)
Throwing Axe
Ticket Stub (s)
Tiny Glowing Skull (w)
Topaz
Torch (f,s,w)
Torn Tapestry (l)
Tracker's Water Extractor
Turquoise
Velishoul's Tome Pages
Warhammer
Watcher Signal Torch (l,w)

Wing of Xegony (f,s)
Words of: Abatement (f), Absorption, Acquisition (Azia) (l), Acquisition (Beza) (f,s), Allure, Anthology, Bidding (l), Bondage (f,s), Burnishing (f), Cazic-Thule, Cloudburst, Coercion (l), Collection (Azia) (l), Collection (Beza) (l), Collection (Caza) (f), Convocation (l), Crippling Force (f,s), Dark Paths (f), Derivation, Descrying (l), Detachment, Detention (f), Dimension, Discernment, Dissemination (l), Dissolution, Dominion, Duration (f), Duress (f), Efficacy (f), Endurance (f), Enlightenment, Eradication, Eventide, Grappling (f,s), Haunting (f,l), Imitation, Incarceration (f), Materials, Mistbreath, Motion (f), Neglect (f), Obligation (f), Odus (f,s), Parasitism (l), Possession, Projection (l), Purification (l), Quivering (f), Radiance, Recluse, Refuge, Requisition (f,s), Resolve (f), Reviviscence, Rupturing (l), Seizure (l), Sight (l), Spirit, the Element, the Ethereal (f,s), the Extinct, the Incorporeal (l), the Psyche (f), the Quickening, the Sentient (Azia), the Sentient (Beza), the Spectre (l), the Spoken, the Suffering (f,l), Transcendence, Tyranny
Wrist Pouch (w)

"That idiot! We ssshould jusst leave him in there!"

"Now, Palou," Tsear, the other Iksar hatchling, said, "he'sss of our clutch. We left him alone too long and he ran into that tomb. It'sss our resssponsibility. We look out for each other."

Palou paced. His tail thrashed through the underbrush, marking his frustration with his clutchmate. The three of them were hatched at the same time and had always remained together. "Do you realize what that tomb isss?" Palou asked.

Tsear shrugged. "Jussst an old tomb. They're everywhere."

Palou looked around and pointed to the cliff face. "Sssee that? It'sss a landmark that tellsss me thisss isss the Crypt of Dalnir." Palou let that sink in a moment. "No one leavesss that tomb, Tsssear."

Tsear stood and started for the entrance. "We have no choice."

Palou grabbed a rock and knocked Tsear out. As he drug his clutchmate away from the cave, he said to an unconscious Tsear, "Like you sssaid. We look out for each other."

EverQuest: The Ruins of Kunark

Items

Items
Armor & Clothing

Clothing: it's more than just a fashion statement in Norrath. (Well, to most people it's more.) Even the most basic sort of clothing counts as armor, and in the hostile outlands of EverQuest, armor is your friend. There are thousands of pieces of armor and other clothing that you can wear in EverQuest. Each item gives you at least some defensive protection expressed by its Armor Class (AC); the higher the AC, the better the protection. As with all other items, we're listing the more common armor and clothing here, along with a few of the more exotic pieces. As with all values in this book, the values listed here are approximate numbers. Merchants tend to pay you less, and charge more, than the value listed here for any item. Those pieces whose values are out of proportion to their AC obviously have additional qualities that will bear investigating, if you can get your hands on them.

Some armor and clothing is sized, fitting just small, medium or large characters. Sized items have three weights listed (**S**mall, **M**edium and **L**arge); all other items fit everyone and have just one weight. (Actually, a very few items are just available for small or large characters; in those cases, the weight is listed under Small or Large.) The only difference between a small, medium or large piece of armor or clothing — other than who can wear it — is its weight: all items of a type have the same AC, value and take up the same number of slots.

A word to the wise. Now, depending on character preferences and their own personal issues, some people will try to pick out clothing and armor according to how it looks, rather than how effective it is. There's nothing wrong with that. Just be aware that the same article of clothing might not look exactly the same on one person as it does on another. There might even be some subtle differences on a gender basis. Before you drop an ungodly amount of platinum on a pair of boots you expect will complete your Shadow Knight's all-black ensemble, ask around. Sometimes it looks one color under the market awnings but changes to an unacceptable color when you put them on.

Armor & Clothing Locations / Slots

Not all armor and clothing that fit on your head are helmets. Caps, coifs and several other items also protect your head. This first list includes most of the various types of clothing, grouped by the location you can wear them. It should help you figure out where to put that new spaulder or cingulum you acquire. The body location abbreviations in parentheses appear in the tables throughout this section.

Head (Hd). Cap, Coif, Crown, Halo, Headband, Headgear, Helm, Skullcap, Turbin (Turban)

Face (Fc). Facemask, Mask, Snout Guard (?), Snout Mount (?), Veil, Visor

Neck (Nc). Bevor, Choker, Collar, Gorget, Neckguard

Chest (Ch). Breastplate, Coat, Gi, Jerkin, Mail, Rib Pad, Robe, Shirt, Tunic

Shoulders (Sh). Amice, Harness, Mantle, Pauldrun, Shawl, Shoulderpads, Shoulder Guard, Spaulder

Back (Bk). Cape, Cloak, Poncho

Waist (Wst). Ab Guard, Belt, Cingulum, Cord, Girdle, Girth, Rib Pad, Sash, Skirt, Tassets, Waistband

Arms (Arm). Armband(s), Arm Guards, Armplates, Sleeves, Vambraces

Wrists (Wri). Bracelet, Bracer(s), Manacle, Trinket (?), Warband, Wristband(s)

Hands (Hnd). Fists (?), Gauntlets, Gloves, Handwraps

Legs (Lg). Greaves, Leggings, Legplates, Pants, Pantaloons, Shin Guards, Skirt, Trousers, Kilt

Feet (Ft). Boots, Clogs, Lined Shoes, Sandals, Slippers

Comparative List of Chest Armor & Clothing

Our second list is a selection of various chest armor and clothing, ordered from lowest to highest AC. This should give you a rough idea of what is available in Norrath, how much protection it will give you, and how much it will cost.

Item	Size	S	M	L	AC	Value
Sparring Rib Pad	1		0.2		2	90
Netted Shirt	2		0.5		4	500
Bristle Silk Tunic	2		1		4	250
Cloth Shirt	2	0.8	1	1.3	4	500
Curscale Tunic	2		1		5	250
Raw Silk Robe	2		0.4		6	850
Woven Tunic	2		0.5		6	1300
Damask Robe	2		1		6	1300
Patchwork Tunic	2	2.6	3.5	4.4	6	150
Cured Silk Gi	2		0.1		8	1750
Mesh Tunic	2		0.5		8	2600
Gossimer Robe	2		1		8	2600
Leather Tunic	2	2.6	3.5	4.4	8	2600
Rhino Hide Chest Guard	2		3.5		8	4400
Raw-hide Tunic	2	3.9	5.3	6.6	8	1300
Small Scarab Breastplate	2		6		8	4000
Werewolf-hide Jerkin	2		1		9	2800
Studded Tunic	2	2.6	3.5	4.4	9	1900

Item	Size	S	M	L	AC	Value
Bear-hide Jerkin	2		3.5		9	2600
Snakeskin Jerkin	2		3.5		9	2600
Split Paw Hide Tunic	0		4		9	400
Reinforced Tunic	2	2.6	3.5	4.4	11	2600
Dwarven Ringmail Tunic	2		4.5		12	4600
Chainmail Coat	2	5.6	7.5	9.4	12	70000
Lupine Scale War Tunic	2		7.5		12	70000
Bloodforge Mail	2		9		12	400
Blackened Iron Mail	2		9		12	7000
Ringmail Coat	2	7.5	10	12.5	12	4400
Brown Chitin Protector	3		10		12	32000
Bloodstained Tunic	2		6.5		13	4900
Banded Mail	2	5.6	7.5	9.4	15	4400
Chitin Shell Armor	2		6.5		17	3500
Steel Breastplate	3	7.5	10	12.5	17	75000
Bronze Breastplate	3	9.4	12.5	15.6	17	4400

Sets of Armor & Clothing

The third list includes various sets of armor and clothing, sorted by material. Here you can find stats on all the pieces of cloth, leather or banded armor (for example) that can be acquired. We don't note any magical qualities for any of these items, and the rarest armors aren't listed here, either. Some things you just have to find out on your own.

The following sets of armor are loosely grouped into related sets — i.e., cloths, hides, and metals or other hard materials. Within each section (Cloth, for example), items are listed by armor class, from lowest to highest.

Item	Size	S	M	L	AC	Value
Cloth						
Veil (Fc)	1	0.2	0.2	0.3	1	160
Choker (Nk)	1	0.2	0.2	0.3	1	160
Shawl (Sh)	1	0.2	0.3	0.4	1	180
Cord (Wst)	1	0.2	0.2	0.3	1	180
Wristband (Wri)	1	0.2	0.3	0.4	1	180
Cap (Hd)	1	0.2	0.2	0.4	2	200
Cape (Bk)	2	0.4	0.5	0.6	2	260
Sleeves (Arm)	1	0.3	0.4	0.5	2	220
Gloves (Hnd)	1	0.3	0.4	0.5	2	260
Sandals (Ft)	1	0.4	0.5	0.6	2	260
Pants (Leg)	2	0.5	0.7	0.9	3	340
Shirt (Ch)	2	0.8	1	1.3	4	500
Tattered (T) & Patchwork (P)						
T Mask (Fc)	1	0.3	0.4	0.5	2	150
T Gorget (Nk)	1	0.4	0.5	0.6	2	150
T Shoulderpads (Sh)	1	1.1	1.5	1.9	2	150
T Belt (Wst)	1	0.8	1	1.3	2	150
T Wristbands (Wri)	1	0.8	1	1.3	2	150
T SkullCap (Hd)	1	0.5	0.6	0.8	3	150
P Cloak (Bk)	2	1.5	2	2.5	3	150
P Sleeves (Arm)	1	1.1	1.5	1.9	3	150
T Gloves (Hnd)	1	1.1	1.5	1.9	3	150
P Boots (Ft)	1	1.9	2.5	3.1	3	150
P Pants (Leg)	2	3	4	5	4	150
P Tunic (Ch)	2	2.6	3.5	4.4	6	150

Item	Size	S/M/L Wt	AC	Value
Silk, Bristle				
Veil (Fc)	1	0.2	1	130
Neckerchief (Nk)	1	0.2	1	130
Shawl (Sh)	1	0.3	1	90
Sash (Wst)	1	0.2	1	90
Wristband (Wri)	1	0.3	1	90
Cap (Hd)	1	0.2	2	100
Cape (Bk)	2	0.5	2	130
Sleeves (Arm)	1	0.4	2	110
Gloves (Hnd)	1	0.4	2	130
Stockings (Feet)	1	0.5	2	130
Knickerbockers (Leg)	2	0.7	3	170
Tunic (Ch)	2	1	4	250
Silk, Cured				
Mask (Fc)	1	0.1	2	700
Collar (Nk)	1	0.1	3	950
Mantle (Sh)	1	0.1	3	1350
Sash (Wst)	1	0.1	3	950
Wristbands (Wri)	1	0.1	3	950
Headband (Hd)	1	0.1	4	1200
Cloak (Bk)	2	0.1	4	1350
Sleeves (Arm)	1	0.1	4	1350
Handwraps (Hnd)	1	0.1	4	1350
Sandals (Ft)	1	0.1	4	950
Leggings (Leg)	2	0.1	5	1600
Gi (Ch)	2	0.1	8	1750

Item	Size	S	Wt M	L	AC	Value
Silk, Raw						
Mask (Fc)	1		0.4		2	325
Collar (Nk)	1		0.4		2	390
Mantle (Sh)	1		0.4		2	450
Sash (Wst)	1		0.4		2	455
Wristbands (Wri)	1		0.4		2	390
Headband (Hd)	1		0.4		3	450
Cloak (Bk)	2		0.4		3	450
Sleeves (Arm)	1		0.4		3	450
Gloves (Hnd)	1		0.4		3	450
Sandals (Ft)	1		0.4		3	450
Leggings (Leg)	2		0.4		4	450
Robe (Ch)	2		0.4		6	850
Woven						
Collar (Nk)	1		0.1		2	600
Girth (Wst)	1		0.1		2	700
Mask (Fc)	1		0.1		2	500
Mantle (Sh)	1		0.2		2	900
Wristbands (Wri)	1		0.2		2	600
Cap (Hd)	1		0.2		3	800
Cape (Bk)	2		0.4		3	900
Gloves (Hnd)	1		0.3		3	900
Sleeves (Arm)	1		0.3		3	800
Leggings (Leg)	2		0.4		4	1100
Tunic (Ch)	2		0.5		6	1300
Hide, Bear						
Belt (Wst)	1		1		4	700
Boots (Ft)	1		2.5		5	2000
Gloves (Hnd)	1		2.1		5	2000
Cape (Bk)	2		2.5		6	2400
Jerkin (Ch)	2		3.5		9	2600
Hide, Patch						
Sandals (Ft)	1		0.3		1	20
Ab Guard (Wst)	1		1		2	125
Bracers (Wri)	1		1		2	125
Mask (Fc)	1		0.4		2	125
Collar (Nk)	1		0.5		2	125
Shoulder Guard (Sh)	1		1.5		2	125
Arm Guards (Arm)	1		0.4		3	160
Gloves (Hnd)	1		1.5		3	125
SkullCap (Hd)	1		0.6		3	125
Poncho (Bk)	2		0.5		4	150

Item	Size	S	Wt M	L	AC	Value
Hide, Drake						
Sleeves (Arm)	1		0.1		4	4100
Leggings (Leg)	2		0.1		5	4500
Hide, Raw						
Mask (Fc)	1	0.5	0.6	0.8	2	500
Belt (Wst)	1	1.2	1.5	2	3	700
Gorget (Nk)	1	0.6	0.8	0.9	3	600
Shoulderpads (Sh)	1	1.6	2.2	3	3	900
Wristbands (Wri)	1	1.2	1.5	1.9	3	600
Boots (Ft)	1	3	3.8	4.6	4	900
Cloak (Bk)	2	2.2	3	3.7	4	900
Gloves (Hnd)	1	1.6	2.2	3	4	900
SkullCap (Hd)	1	0.7	0.9	1.2	4	800
Sleeves (Arm)	1	1.8	2.2	3	4	800
Leggings (Leg)	2	4	6	7.5	5	1100
Tunic (Ch)	2	3.9	5.3	6.6	8	1300
Hide, Rhino						
Snout Guard (Fc)	0		0.4		2	1000
Collar (Nk)	0		0.5		3	1200
Shoulderpads (Sh)	1		1.5		3	1800
Waistband (Wst)	1		1		3	2800
Wrist Guard (Wri)	1		1		3	1400
SkullCap (Hd)	1		0.6		4	1600
Cape (Bk)	3		2		4	3600
Arm Guards (Arm)	1		1.5		4	2600
Gloves (Hnd)	1		1.5		4	1800
Boots (Ft)	1		2.5		4	1800
Leggings (Leg)	2		4		5	4200
Chest Guard (Ch)	2		3.5		8	4400
Hide, Split Paw						
Mask (Fc)	0		0.5		3	400
Gloves (Hnd)	0		2		4	400
Belt (Wst)	0		1		5	200
Tunic (Ch)	0		4		9	400
Hide, Wolf						
Slippers (Ft)	1		0.5		2	260
Belt (Wst)	1		1		3	700
Gloves (Hnd)	1		1.3		4	1800
Boots (Ft)	1		2.5		4	2000
Cape (Bk)	2		2		5	2400
Sleeves (Arm)	1		1.5		5	1600

Item	Size	S	M	L	AC	Value
Leather						
Mask (Fc)	1	0.3	0.4	0.5	2	1000
Gorget (Nk)	1	0.4	0.5	0.6	3	1200
Shoulderpads (Sh)	1	1.1	1.5	1.9	3	1800
Belt (Wst)	1	0.8	1	1.3	3	1400
Wristbands (Wri)	1	0.8	1	1.3	3	1200
SkullCap (Hd)	1	0.5	0.6	0.8	4	1600
Cloak (Bk)	2	1.5	2	2.5	4	1800
Sleeves (Arm)	1	1.1	1.5	1.9	4	1600
Gloves (Hnd)	1	1.1	1.5	1.9	4	1800
Boots (Ft)	1	1.9	2.5	3.1	4	1800
Leggings (Leg)	2	3	4	5	5	2200
Tunic (Ch)	2	2.6	3.5	4.4	8	2600
Studded						
Mask (Fc)	1	0.3	0.4	0.5	2	750
Gorget (Nk)	1	0.4	0.5	0.6	3	900
Shoulderpads (Sh)	1	1.1	1.5	1.9	3	1300
Belt (Wst)	1	0.8	1	1.3	3	1000
Wristbands (Wri)	1	0.8	1	1.3	3	900
Cloak (Bk)	2	1.5	2	2.5	4	1400
Sleeves (Arm)	1	1.1	1.5	1.9	4	1200
Gloves (Hnd)	1	1.1	1.5	1.9	4	1400
Boots (Ft)	1	1.9	2.5	3.1	4	1400
SkullCap (Hd)	1	0.5	0.6	0.8	5	1200
Leggings (Leg)	2	3	4	5	5	1600
Skirt (Leg)	2	3	4	5	5	1600
Tunic (Ch)	2	2.6	3.5	4.4	9	1900
Reinforced						
Mask (Fc)	1	0.3	0.4	0.5	3	1000
Gorget (Nk)	1	0.4	0.5	0.6	4	1200
Shoulderpads (Sh)	1	1.1	1.5	1.9	4	1800
Belt (Wst)	1	0.8	1	1.3	4	1400
Wristbands (Wri)	1	0.8	1	1.3	4	1200
Cloak (Bk)	2	1.5	2	2.5	5	1800
Sleeves (Arm)	1	1.1	1.5	1.9	5	1600
Gloves (Hnd)	1	1.1	1.5	1.9	5	1800
Boots (Ft)	1	1.9	2.5	3.1	5	1800
SkullCap (Hd)	1	0.5	0.6	0.8	6	1600
Leggings (Leg)	2	3	4	5	6	2200
Skirt (Leg)	2	3	4	5	6	2200
Tunic (Ch)	2	2.6	3.5	4.4	11	2600

Item	Size	S	M	L	AC	Value
Banded						
Mask (Fc)	1	0.8	1	1.3	4	2400
Gorget (Nk)	1	1.5	2	2.5	5	1100
Mantle (Sh)	1	2.6	3.5	4.4	6	3200
Belt (Wst)	1	1.9	2.5	3.1	6	2800
Bracers (Wri)	1	1.5	2	2.5	6	1400
Boots (Ft)	2	3.8	5	6.3	6	2700
Cloak (Bk)	3	3	4	5	7	3600
Sleeves (Arm)	1	2.6	3.5	4.4	7	2600
Gauntlets (Hnd)	1	3	4	3	7	2300
Lg Gloves (Hnd)	1			5	7	2300
Helm (Hd)	1	3.4	4.5	5.6	8	2700
Leggings (Leg)	2	4.1	5.5	6.9	8	4200
Mail (Ch)	2	5.6	7.5	9.4	15	4400
Sparring Equipment						
Facemask (Fc)	1		0.2		2	80
Collar (Nk)	1		0.2		2	80
Shoulder Pads (Sh)	1		0.3		2	90
Rib Pad (Ch)	1		0.2		2	90
Headgear (Hd)	1		0.2		3	100
Arm Guards (Arm)	1		0.4		3	110
Grappler Gloves (Hnd)	1		0.4		3	130
Clogs (Ft)	1		0.5		3	130
Shin Guards (Leg)	2		0.7		4	170
Harness (Sh)	2		1		5	250
Bronze						
Mask (Fc)	1	1.4	1.9	2.4	5	2400
Collar (Nk)	1	3.7	5	6.2	6	1100
Girdle (Wst)	1	3.8	5	6.2	7	2800
Bracers (Wri)	1	3.8	5	6.3	7	1400
Pauldrun (Sh)	1	4.2	5.6	7	8	3200
Splinted Cloak (Bk)	3	5.1	6.7	8.6	8	3600
Vambraces (Arm)	1	6.1	8.1	10.1	8	2600
Boots (Ft)	2	6.1	8.1	10.1	8	2700
Gauntlets (Hnd)	1	4.7	6.2	7.9	9	2300
Helm (Hd)	1	5.6	7.5	9.4	10	2700
Greaves (Leg)	3	7	9.4	11.8	10	4200
Breastplate (Ch)	3	9.4	12.5	15.6	17	4400

EverQuest: The Ruins of Kunark

Item	Size	Wt S	M	L	AC	Value
Ring						
Iron Visor (Fc)	1	1.1	1.3	1.7	3	2400
Neckguard (Nk)	1	2	2.7	3.3	5	1100
Mantle (Sh)	1	3.5	4.7	5.9	5	3200
Belt (Med: Skirt) (Wst)	1	2.5	3.3	4.1	5	2800
Bracelet (Wri)	1	2	2.7	3.3	5	1400
Boots (Ft)	2	5	6.7	8.4	5	2700
Cape (Bk)	3	4	5.3	6.7	6	3600
Sleeves (Arm)	1	3.5	4.7	5.9	6	2600
Gloves (Hnd)	1	4	5.3	6.7	6	2300
Coif (Hd)	1	4.5	6	7.5	7	2700
Pants (Leg)	2	5.5	7.3	9.2	7	4200
Coat (Ch)	2	7.5	10	12.5	12	4400
Blackened Iron						
Grotesque Mask (Fc)	1		1		3	9000
Crown (Hd)	1		6		5	12000
Collar (Nk)	1		3.5		5	1500
Spaulder (Sh)	1		5		5	5000
Waistband (Wst)	1		4		5	2200
Bracers (Wri)	1		3.5		5	1500
Boots (Ft)	2		6.5		5	2600
Sleek Cape (Bk)	3		2		6	6000
Armplates (Arm)	1		5		6	2800
Gloves (Hnd)	1		5.5		6	3000
Legplates (Leg)	2		7		7	3600
Mail (Ch)	2		9		12	7000
Chain (C) & Iron Mail (I)						
I Torque (Nk)	1	0.2	0.2	0.3	1	160
I Mask (Fc)	1	0.8	1	1.3	3	12000
C Neckguard (Nk)	1	1.5	2	2.5	5	16000
C Mantle (Sh)	1	2.6	3.5	4.4	5	56000
C Skirt (Wst)	1		2.5		5	22000
C Belt (Wst)	1	1.9		3.1	5	22000
C Cingulum (Wst)	1	2.5	2.5	2.5	5	22000
C Bracelet (Wri)	1	1.5	2	2.5	5	14000
I Boots (Ft)	2	3.8	5	6.3	5	26000
C Cape (Bk)	3	3	4	5	6	60000
I Armplates (Arm)	1	2.6	3.5	4.4	6	28000
C Gloves (Hnd)	1	3	4	5	6	30000
C Coif (Hd)	1	3.4	4.5	5.6	7	30000
I Legplates (Leg)	2	4.1	5.5	6.9	7	36000
C Coat (Ch)	2	5.6	7.5	9.4	12	70000

Item	Size	Wt S	M	L	AC	Value
Plate (P)/Steel (S)						
S Torque (Nk)	1	0.4	0.5	0.6	3	1200
S Mask (Fc)	1	1.1	1.5	1.9	5	10000
S Collar (Nk)	1	3	4	5	6	14000
S Bevor (Nk)	1	3.4	4.5	5.6	7	14500
P Girdle (Wst)	1	3	4	5	7	28000
S Bracers (Wri)	1	3	4	5	7	24000
S Pauldrun (Sh)	1	3.4	4.5	5.6	8	35000
Splinted Cloak (Bk)	3	4.1	5.5	6.9	8	38000
S Vambraces (Arm)	1	4.9	6.5	8.1	8	32000
S Plate Boots (Ft)	2	4.9	6.5	8.1	8	33000
P Gauntlets (Hnd)	1	3.8	5	6.3	9	46000
P Tassets (Wst)	1	3.4	4.5	5.6	9	35000
P Helm (Hd)	1	4.5	6	7.5	10	35000
S Greaves (Leg)	3	5.6	7.5	9.4	10	40000
S Breastplate (Ch)	3	7.5	10	12.5	17	75000
Damask						
Veil (Fc)	1		0.2		2	500
Collar (Nk)	1		0.2		2	600
Amice (Sh)	1		0.3		2	900
Sash (Wst)	1		0.2		2	700
Wristbands (Wri)	1		0.3		2	600
Cap (Hd)	1		0.3		3	800
Cape (Bk)	2		0.5		3	900
Sleeves (Arm)	1		0.4		3	800
Gloves (Hnd)	1		0.4		3	900
Leggings (Leg)	2		0.7		4	1100
Robe (Ch)	2		1		6	1300
Gossimer						
Veil (Fc)	1		0.2		2	1000
Collar (Nk)	1		0.2		3	1200
Amice (Sh)	1		0.3		3	1800
Sash (Wst)	1		0.2		3	1400
Wristbands (Wri)	1		0.3		3	1200
Cap (Hd)	1		0.3		4	1600
Cape (Bk)	2		0.5		4	1800
Sleeves (Arm)	1		0.4		4	1600
Gloves (Hnd)	1		0.4		4	1800
Leggings (Leg)	2		0.7		5	2200
Robe (Ch)	2		1		8	2600

Item	Size	S	M	L	AC	Value		Item	Size	S	M	L	AC	Value
Mesh								**Scarab, Small**						
Mask (Fc)	1		0.1		2	1000		Helm (Hd)	1	1.5			4	1000
Gorget (Nk)	1		0.1		3	1200		Boots (Ft)	1	4.5			4	3000
Mantle (Sh)	1		0.2		3	1800		Breastplate (Ch)	2	6			8	4000
Girth (Wst)	1		0.1		3	1400		**Curscale**						
Bracers (Wri)	1		0.2		3	1200		Snout Mount (Fc)	1		0.2		2	80
Helm (Hd)	1		0.2		4	1600		Choker (Nk)	1		0.2		2	80
Cape (Bk)	2		0.4		4	1800		Shawl (Sh)	1		0.3		2	90
Armbands (Arm)	1		0.3		4	1600		Belt (Wst)	1		0.2		2	90
Gauntlets (Hnd)	1		0.3		4	1800		Wristband (Wri)	1		0.3		2	90
Leggings (Leg)	2		0.4		5	2200		SkullCap (Hd)	1		0.2		3	100
Tunic (Ch)	2		0.5		8	2600		Cape (Bk)	2		0.5		3	130
Netted								Sleeves (Arm)	1		0.4		3	110
Mask (Fc)	1		0.1		1	160		Gloves (Hnd)	1		0.4		3	130
Choker (Nk)	1		0.1		1	160		Boots (Ft)	1		0.5		3	130
Mantle (Sh)	1		0.2		1	180		Leggings (Leg)	2		0.7		4	170
Girth (Wst)	1		0.1		1	180		Tunic (Ch)	2		1		5	250
Wristband (Wri)	1		0.2		1	180		**Ebon Mail**						
Cap (Hd)	1		0.2		2	200		Boots (Ft)	2		3.8		6	2700
Cape (Bk)	2		0.4		2	260		Sleeves (Arm)	1		2.6		7	2600
Sleeves (Arm)	1		0.3		2	220		Gloves (Hnd)	1		3		7	2300
Gloves (Hnd)	1		0.3		2	260		Coif (Hd)	1		3.4		8	2700
Pants (Leg)	2		0.4		3	340		Leggings (Leg)	2		4.1		8	4200
Shirt (Ch)	2		0.5		4	500		Tunic (Ch)	2		5.6		15	4400
Bloodforge								**Lupine Scale (S) & Claw (C)**						
Helm (Hd)	1		6		5	500		S Snout Guard (Fc)	1		1		3	12000
Bracers (Wri)	1		3.5		5	400		C Gauntlets (Hnd)	3		0.2		4	5500
Boots (Ft)	2		6.5		5	400		S Collar (Nk)	1		2		5	16000
Armplates (Arm)	1		5		6	400		S Mantle (Sh)	1		3.5		5	56000
Gauntlets (Hnd)	1		5.5		6	500		S BloodSash (Wst)	1		2.5		5	22000
Legplates (Leg)	2		7		7	400		Forged Bracers (Wri)	1		2		5	14000
Mail (Ch)	2		9		12	400		Forged Boots (Ft)	2		5		5	26000
Bloodstained								S Cape (Bk)	3		4		6	60000
Mantle (Sh)	1		3.5		6	3200		S Arm Plates (Arm)	1		3.5		6	28000
Bracelets (Wri)	2		3.5		7	4900		Forged Fists (Hnd)	1		4		6	30000
Gloves (Hnd)	2		2.5		8	4900		S Coif (Hd)	1		4.5		7	30000
leeves (Arm)	2		3.5		9	4900		S Leggings (Leg)	2		5.5		7	36000
Leggings (Leg)	2		4.5		9	4900		S War Tunic (Ch)	2		7.5		12	70000
Coif (Hd)	2		2.5		13	4900								
Tunic (Ch)	2		6.5		13	4900								
Boots (Ft)	2		3.5		13	4900								

Miscellaneous Armor & Clothing

This final list includes various bits of armor and clothing that don't fit into a more complete set. They are sorted by location, beginning with your head and running down to your feet. As always, we don't note any magical qualities for any of these items, nor do we list all possible pieces.

Item	Size	Wt S	M	L	AC	Value
Head						
Shazda Turbin	2		0.2		0	500
Crown of Leaves	1		0.4		1	4300
Kerran Tribal Headband	1		0.2		1	200
Rat Fur Cap	1		0.3		1	22
Nightshade Wreath	1		0.1		1	2500
Savant's Cap	1		0.3		2	3500
Topknot Headband	1		0.4		3	4700
Kerran Headband	0		0.1		4	0
Runed Circlet	1		1		4	2300
Shimmering White Shroud	2		2.5		5	5600
Circlet of Mist	1		0.1		5	3000
Helm of Hukulk	1		1		5	2100
Siryn Hair Hood	1		0.2		5	4800
Zaharn's Coronet	1		5		5	3750
Winged Headband	1		1		7	2100
Opoline Helm	1		6		8	20000
Neck						
Rat's Foot Necklace	0		0.1		0	1
Snake Fang Necklace	0		0.1		0	20
Fishbone Necklace	0		0.5		3	0
Spiked Collar	1		0.5		3	1200
Studded Leather Collar	1		0.5		3	1200
Velvet Choker	1		0.5		3	1200
Iron Leash Collar	1		3.5		4	1500
Etched Ivory Charm	1		0.5		5	2600
Steel Gorget	1	3.4	4.5	5.6	8	15000

Item	Size	Wt S	M	L	AC	Value
Face						
Magical Woven Eyepatch	0		0.1		0	0
Mask of Shadow	1		0.2		0	0
Bonechipped Mask	1		0.4		2	100
Froglok Skin Mask	1		0.4		2	1000
Glowing Mask	1		0.4		2	1000
Moss Mask	1		0.1		2	3000
Patch of Shadow	1		0.4		2	100
Snakeskin Mask	1		0.4		2	1000
Turquoise Eyepatch	1		0.1		2	3100
Gorilla Hide Mask	1		0.1		3	3000
Incandescent Mask	1		0.4		3	2000
Leering Mask	1		0.4		3	4500
Lizardskin Tribal Mask	1		0.2		3	4500
Serpentskin Eyepatch	1		0.1		3	2500
Acumen Mask	1		0.5		4	2400
Bloodstone Eyepatch	1		0.1		4	2500
Mask of Empowerment	1		0.4		4	5200
Transparent Mask	1		0.4		4	5200
Ferrous Visor	1		0.8		5	2400
Ivory Mask	2		0.5		6	4000

Item	Size	S	M	L	AC	Value
Chest						
Alliance Robe Blue	2		0.5		4	500
Alliance Robe Yellow	2		0.5		4	500
Robe of Recovery	2		2.5		4	0
Teir`Dal Robe Red	2		0.5		4	500
Robe of the Initiate	2		3.5		5	1000
Thaumaturgist's Robe	2		3.5		5	2500
Robe of the Augmentor	2		1		6	1300
Robe of the Elementalist	2		1		6	1300
Robe of the Evoker	2		1		6	1300
Robe of the Ritualist	2		1		6	1300
Fire Goblin Skin	2		2.5		7	2600
Frost Goblin Skin	2		3.5		7	2600
Green Silken Drape	2		3.5		8	25000
Flowing Black Robe	2		3.5		8	3500
Robe of the Keeper	2		3.5		8	1250
Robe of the Seeker	2		3.5		8	1250
Gnomish Environment Suit	2		3.5		9	2800
Reserve Militia Tunic	2		5		9	100
Robe of Enshroudment	2		3.5		9	3500
Robe of the Elements	2		3.5		9	3500
Snakeskin Jerkin	2		3.5		9	2600
Werewolf-hide Jerkin	2		1		9	2800
Erudehide Tunic	2		3		10	0
Foremans Tunic	2		0		10	2800
Syythrak Hide Vest	1		0		10	2800
Dwarven Ringmail Tunic	2		4.5		12	4600
Lockjaw Hide Vest	2		1.5		12	4500
Basalt Carapace	3		10		14	50000
Charred Guardian Breastplate	3		9		16	7500
Minotaur Ribcage	2		7.5		16	4400

Item	Size	S	M	L	AC	Value
Shoulders						
Shawl of the Wind Spirit	1		0.4		1	80
Gilded Cloth	1		0.3		3	5700
Rusty Spiked Shoulderpads	1		2.5		3	1800
Prayer Cloth of Tunare	1		0.3		3	1800
Bloodsoaked Raiment	1		0.3		4	4000
Nature Walker's Mantle	1		2.5		4	1800
Worn Leather Shoulderpads	2		2		4	0
Lizardscale Mantle	1		2.5		5	3600
Mystical Back Straps	1		0.3		5	18000
Prayer Shawl	1		0.4		5	18000
Sphinx-Hide Mantle	1		2.5		5	1800
Squallsurge Shawl	1		0.3		5	18000
Barnacle-covered Pauldron	1		4.5		6	3500
Earthshaker's Mantle	1		2.5		7	1800
Glowing Pauldrons	1		4.5		9	15000
Griffon Wing Spauldors	1		2.5		9	1800
Songweaver's Mantle	1		2.5		9	1800
Steel Epolets	1	3.4	4.5	5.6	9	36000
Steel Spaulders	1	3.4	4.5	5.6	10	37500

Items: Armor & Clothing

Item	Size	Wt S	Wt M	Wt L	AC	Value
Back						
Black Leather Cloak	2		1		1	1800
Rat Pelt Cape	2		0.5		1	40
Cape of Midnight Mist	1		0.1		2	4500
Thick Black Cape	2		2		3	450
Cloak of the Undead Eye	2		3.5		4	400
Embroidered Black Cape	1		0.3		4	6400
Molten Cloak	2		2.5		4	4400
Twice-Woven Cloak	2		1.5		4	1800
Cloak of Leaves	3		2		5	4800
Faded Cloak	2		0.5		5	40
Festering Cloak	2		0.5		5	500
Mountain Lion Cape	3		3		5	600
Nightmare Hide	2		2		5	1800
Polar Bear Cloak	3		3.5		5	600
Runescale Cloak	2		2		5	2400
Scouts Cape	2		1.5		5	2400
Werewolf Skin Cloak	3		0.3		5	6000
Cloak of Jaggedpine	2		1.5		6	2400
Grizzly Hide Cloak	3		3.5		6	600
Kodiak Hide Cloak	3		3.5		6	600
Thermal Cape	3		4		6	60000
Mammoth Hide Cloak	2		2.5		7	2400
White Wolf-hide Cloak	3		0.3		7	4800
Cloak of the Ice Bear	3		3.5		8	3800
Lizardscale Cloak	2		2.5		8	4800
Mystic Cloak	2		0.5		8	40

Item	Size	Wt S	Wt M	Wt L	AC	Value
Waist						
Fish Scale Belt	1		0.5		1	4000
Braided Cinch Cord	1		0.2		2	2400
Giant's Reminder String	1	0.5			2	1200
Lizardscale Belt	1		1		2	3800
Girdle of Health	1		1		3	3000
Braided Ivy Cords	1		0.3		4	2500
Wooden Belt	1		1		4	2400
Belt of Flesh Hooks	1		0.2		5	2300
Troll-hide Belt	1		1		5	2400
Black Iron Girdle	1		2		6	3500
Dweamorvine Garland	1		0.5		8	4000
Pegasus-Hide Belt	1		1		8	2400
Thick Banded Belt	1		0.5		8	4000
Girdle of Faith	1		1		10	2400
Arms						
Embroidered Black Sleeves	1		0.4		4	8400
Gatorscale Sleeves	1		0.3		6	1600
Barbed Armplates	1		4		7	1500
Wrists						
Bracers of Battle	1		1		3	2200
Legionnaire's Bracer	1		2		3	320
Clay Bracelet	1		1		4	3000
Granite Bracer	1		0.8		5	4300
Sejah Ghulam Bracer	1		0.2		5	0
Hollowed Bone Bracers	1		2.5		6	1600
Iron Shackles	1		2.7		7	2800
Silver-Plated Bracer	1		1		7	1300
Symbol of Loyalty to Vox	1		0.3		7	1400

Item	Size	Wt S	M	L	AC	Value
Hands						
Copper Skull Ring	0		0.1		0	500
Enchanted Gloves	1		1.5		0	0
Gleaming Gloves	1		1.5		0	0
Used Merchants Gloves	1		0.2		0	5
Brown Leather Gloves	1		0.2		1	450
Cutthroat Insignia Ring	0		0.1		1	215
Dusty Bloodstained Gloves	1		0.4		2	1200
Impskin Gloves	1		1.5		2	1800
Tiger Hide Gloves	1		1		2	2400
Bone Fingered Gloves	1		0.4		3	1500
Ratskin Gloves	1		2		3	1000
Black Silk Gloves	1		1.5		4	1800
Elf-hide Gloves	1		1		4	2400
Gloves of Strength	1		1.5		4	1800
Glowing Gloves	1		1.5		4	900
Griffon Talon Gloves	1		0.5		4	3500
Shiny Silk Gloves	1		0.4		4	1200
Snakeskin Gloves	1		1.5		4	1800
Lionskin Gloves	1		1.1		5	2000
Incandescent Gloves	1		1.5		6	1800
Charred Gauntlets	1		4.5		7	5300

Item	Size	Wt S	M	L	AC	Value
Legs						
Large Cloth Kilt	2			0.9	3	340
Feathered Leggings	2		2		4	6800
Silversilk Leggings	2		0.7		4	3400
Large Leather Kilt	2			5	5	2200
Tishans Kilt	1		0.8		5	2200
Warthread Kilt	2		1		5	500
Lion-skin Leggings	2		4		6	2200
Mammoth Hide Leggings	2		4		6	2200
Gatorscale Leggings	2		0.4		7	2200
Silvermesh Leggings	2		3.5		7	2800
Barbed Legplates	2		6.5		8	1700
Gorilla Hide Leggings	2		2		8	6800
Icy Greaves	3		7.5		8	40000
Thick Leather Apron	1		1		8	1400
Silver-plated Leggings	2		5.5		10	3700
Large Steel Kilt	3			9.4	15	40000
Feet						
Tattered Cloth Sandal	1		0.3		1	20
Fur Lined Shoes	1		0.5		2	260
Soft Leather Shoes	1		0.7		3	900
Elven Boots	1		2		4	5000
Firewalker Boots	1		2.5		4	1800
Fur Lined Boots	1		2.5		4	1800
Soft Leather Boots	1		0.7		4	1800
Soiled Boots	1		2.5		4	1800
Tattered Leather Boots	1		0.9		4	1800
Kobold-hide Boots	1		2.5		5	3600
ShadowBound Boots	1		1.2		5	7500
Charred Boots	2		5.5		6	3300
Dwarven Work Boots	2		5		8	2600

EverQuest: The Ruins of Kunark

Weapons

Norrath is a dangerous place, and most people (Monks excluded, of course) feel that having a nice, stout weapon close to hand makes life a little bit more survivable. Here's a list of the weapons you'll encounter ... information for the common ones are included.

Damage (Dmg) lists the maximum base damage with this weapon. An average strike will inflict up to this many points of damage (although the defender's AC and other factors can reduce the damage). Your own abilities and current condition might increase or reduce the damage when you strike. For instance, spells or charms that buff or debuff your character affect the amount of damage you do.

Delay (Del) lists how many seconds it takes between strikes with this weapon (for an average character). Your own abilities and current condition might reduce or increase this time. A slow spell will, obviously, increase the delay spell.

Magic (Mag). Some of these weapons are enchanted. Sometimes that means only that it can hurt creatures immune to normal weapons. You'll have to find one and experiment with it to discover its magical properties.

Values. As with all values in this book, the values listed here are approximate numbers. Merchants tend to pay you less, and charge more, than the value listed here for any item.

One-Handed Slashing Weapons

Weapon	Dmg	Del	Size	Wt	Mag	Value
Axe						
Bronze	5	3.3	2	7.5		1 8 0 0
Dwarven	6	2.6	2	4.0		5 0 0 0
Rusty	5	3.6	2	6.5		5 0
Silvery War	6	2.2	2	2.5	√	1 9 0
Tarnished	5	3.4	2	6.5		5 0
Normal	6	3.1	2	6.5		3 3 0 0
Bastard Sword						
Bronze	7	4.2	2	10.0		3 5 0 0
Forged	7	3.3	2	6.5		3 5 0 0
Rotted	14	3.1	2	0.5	√	6 0 0 0
Rusty	6	4.2	2	9.0		2 4 0
Tarnished	6	4	2	9.0		2 4 0
Normal	8	3.9	2	9.0		1 2 0 0 0

Weapon	Dmg	Del	Size	Wt	Mag	Value
Battle Axe						
Bronze	6	3.7	2	9.5		2 8 0 0
Cast-Iron	6	3.3	2	9.5		2 8 0 0
Ivory Bladed	8	3.5	2	8.5		√125 0 0 0
Minotaur	8	3.7	2	8.5		3 5 0 0
Rusty	6	4.2	2	8.5		1 9 0
Shadowed	7	3.5	2	8.5	√	0
Tarnished	6	4	2	8.5		1 9 0
Normal	7	3.5	2	8.5		1 0 0 0 0

One-Handed Slashing Weapons, cont.

Weapon	Dmg	Del	Size	Wt	Mag	Value	Weapon	Dmg	Del	Size	Wt	Mag	Value
Blade							Scimitar						
Enchanted							Alloy	5	1.9	2	4.5	√	50 000
Steel War	6	3.2	2	5.0	√	3 000	Battle Worn	5	2.4	2	5.0		5 900
Serrated	6	2.8	2	2.5	√	4 600	Bronze	5	3.2	2	8.5		2 300
Steel War	6	3.2	2	5.0		2 500	Cast-Iron	5	2.4	2	7.5		6 000
Brazen Brass Kilij	10	3.5	2	8.5	√	35 000	Combine	5	2.4	2	5.0	√	38 000
Broad Sword							Fine Steel	5	2.4	2	5.0		5 900
Bronze	5	3.2	2	8.5		1 800	Obsidian	7	2.7	2	5.0	√	3 800
Rusty	5	3.6	2	7.5		60	Rusty	5	3.5	2	7.5		190
Tarnished	5	3.4	2	7.5		60	Shadowed	5	2.5	2	7.5	√	0
Normal	6	3.2	2	7.5		3 300	Silverish	6	2.2	2	3.5	√	3 500
Broadsword							Solvedi	6	2.2	2	3.0	√	3 500
of the Void	14	4.6	2	4.5	√	6 000	Tarnished	5	3.3	2	7.5		190
Cat o' Nine Tails	9	3.6	2	8.0	√	500	Teir'Dal	5	2.4	2	4.7		5 900
Claw (Scrounge's)	5	3	2	2.5		3 200	Well-Balanced	5	2.1	2	8.5	√	50 000
Claws (Mystical							Normal	5	2.5	2	7.5		6 000
Claws of Jojo)	4	1.9	2	3.0	√	3 200	Short Sword						
Falchion of the							Battle Worn	4	2.3	2	4.0		5 500
Koada'Vie	6	2.4	2	3.5	√	500	Bronze	4	2.7	2	6.0		280
Gladius	7	2.9	2	2.5	√	4 600	Cast-Iron	4	2.7	2	5.0		50
Langseax	6	2.3	2	4.0	√	500	Combine	4	2.3	2	4.0	√	35 000
Long Sword							Fine Steel	4	2.3	2	4.0		5 500
Alloy	6	2.3	2	5.0	√	50 000	Ivory Handled	5	2.7	2	4.0	√	70 000
Battle Worn	6	2.8	2	5.0		6 000	Rusty	4	2.8	2	5.0		50
Bronze	5	3.2	2	8.5		3 200	Sharp	4	2.3	2	5.0		2 000
Cast-Iron	6	3.2	2	7.5		200	Tarnished	4	2.6	2	5.0		50
Combine	6	2.8	2	5.0	√	50 000	Teir'Dal	4	2.3	2	3.6		5 500
Feir'Dal	6	2.8	2	5.0		6 000	Normal	4	2.4	2	5.0		2 000
Fine Steel	6	2.8	2	5.0		6 000	Short Sword						
Ivory Handled	7	3	2	5.0	√	100 000	of Swiftness	4	2	2	5.0	√	7 500
Rusty	5	3.5	2	7.5		200	Sword						
Shadowed	6	2.9	2	7.5	√	0	(Bone Handled)	6	3	2	7.5		5 000
Tarnished	5	3.3	2	7.5		200	Sword of Runes	7	2.7	2	6.5	√	0
Teir'Dal	6	2.8	2	4.7		6 000	Tomahawk						
Well-Balanced	6	2.5	2	8.5	√	50 000	(Polished Granite)	6	2.6	2	6.5	√	3 300
Normal	6	2.9	2	7.5		12 000	Whip						
Elven	6	2.8	2	2.5	√	2 500	Leather	5	3	2	5.0		200
Machete (Cast-Iron)	3	2.7	2	5.0		50	Tailor-made	7	3.3	2	6.0		3 500
Pick							Tentacle	4	2.5	2	5.0	√	2 000
Rusty Mining	4	3.8	2	6.5		10							
Tarnished Mining	4	3.6	2	6.5		10							
Normal	6	3.6	2	6.5		500							
Rat Tail (Giant)	5	2.7	2	5.0		600							

Two-Handed Slashing Weapons

Weapon	Dmg	Del	Size	Wt	Mag	Value
Axe						
Blood Riven	19	4	3	10.0	√	5 000
Double-bladed						
Bone	18	4.8	2	9.0	√	6 000
Bastard Sword						
Blackened Iron	20	4.7	2	9.0	√	2 400
Enchanted Battleworn	20	4.2	2	8.5	√	5 000
Enchanted Feir`Dal	20	4.2	2	8.5	√	5 000
Enchanted Fine Steel	20	4.2	2	8.5	√	5 000
Enchanted Teir`Dal	20	4.2	2	8.5	√	5 000
Ruined Steel	17	4.4	2	8.5	√	5 000
Tainted Steel	20	4.2	2	8.5	√	5 000
Blade						
(Bunker Battle)	10	4.6	3	13.0	√	800
Claymore						
Bone Bladed	17	4.5	3	10.0	√	4 500
Bronze	8	4.8	3	11.0		3 900
Cast-Iron	7	3.7	3	10.0		3 900
Normal	11	4.3	3	10.0		18 000
Cleaver						
(Ivory Handled)	12	4.3	3	11.0	√	200 000
Flamberge						
(Obsidian)	20	5	2	9.0	√	2 400
Halberd						
Bronze	10	5.2	4	15.0		4 600
Cast-Iron	15	5	4	13.5		8 000
Ivory Bladed	15	4.9	4	14.0	√	250 000
Ruined	14	5	4	14.0	√	0
Rusty	10	5.6	4	14.0		320
Shadowed	14	5	4	14.0	√	0
Shiny Brass	16	4.8	4	15.0	√	4 600
Normal	14	5	4	14.0		28 000
Holy Partisan of Underfoot	14	4.6	4	12.0	√	8 000
Langseax of the Wolves	19	4.4	3	9.5	√	10 000
Reaper of The Dead	12	4	3	13.0	√	13 000
Reed Cutter	8	4.8	3	13.0		3 700
Scythe						
Bronze	8	4.8	3	13.0		3 700
Cast-Iron	9	4.7	3	3.5		3 700
Rusty	8	5.1	3	12.0		200
Shadowed	11	4.5	3	12.0	√	0
Tarnished	8	4.9	3	12.0		200
Threshing	11	3.9	3	12.0	√	13 000
Normal	11	4.5	3	12.0		13 000
Trident (Bloodgill)	10	5.3	4	14.0	√	500
Two Handed Axe						
Silvery	21	4.8	3	13.0	√	3 000
Bronze	9	4.6	3	14.0		4 200
Rusty	9	4.9	3	13.0		300
Tarnished	9	4.7	3	13.0		300
Two Handed Battle Axe	12	4.4	3	13.0		23 000
Two Handed Sword						
Battle Worn	12	4.3	3	10.0		7 000
Bronze	9	4.7	3	13.0		4 200
Cast-Iron	12	4.3	3	10.0		7 000
Combine	12	4.3	3	10.0	√	100 000
Feir'Dal	12	4.3	3	10.0		7 000
Fine Steel	12	4.3	3	10.0		7 000
Forged	12	4.4	3	11.0		5 000
Rusty	9	5	3	12.0		300
Shadowed	12	4.5	3	12.0	√	0
Tarnished	9	4.8	3	12.0		300
Teir'Dal	12	4.3	3	9.5		7 000
Normal	12	4.5	3	12.0		22 000
Two-Handed Axe						
Alloy	16	3.7	3	10.5	√	100 000
Dwarven	14	4.3	2	6.5		6 000
Well-Balanced	16	4.8	3	14.0	√	100 000
Alloy	14	3.2	3	10.0	√	100 000
Well-Balanced	14	4.2	3	13.0	√	100 000
Zweihander (Gigantic)	18	3.9	3	10.0	√	12 000

Piercing Weapons

Weapon	Dmg	Del	Size	Wt	Mag	Value
Blade (Scout's)	5	2.4	2	2.5	√	3200
Crookstinger	4	2.1	2	5.0	√	3200
Crysknife	4	2.1	2	5.0	√	3200
Dagger						
Bronze	3	2.2	1	3.0		280
Cast-Iron)	3	2.2	1	2.5		30
Charred)	3	2.1	1	3.0		300
Combine)	3	1.9	1	2.4	√	30000
Ebon)	3	2	1	3.0		400
Feir'Dal)	3	1.9	1	2.3		4500
Fine Steel)	3	1.9	1	2.4		4500
Ivory Handled)	4	2.3	1	2.4	√	60000
Mithril)	4	2.1	1	2.4		4500
Rusty)	3	2.4	1	2.5		30
Sabertooth)	3	2.2	1	2.5		30
Sacrificial)	5	2.1	2	2.5	√	4500
Tarnished)	3	2.2	1	2.5		30
Normal 1	3	2	1	2.5		2000
Normal 2	3	2.1	1	2.5	√	0
Dagger of Dropping	4	2.2	0	1.5	√	450
Dagger of Symbols	5	2	1	2.5	√	0
Dirk						
Bloody	6	2.2	1	1.0	√	150
Ceramic	4	2	1	3.0		2000
Fork (Runed Bone)	5	2.9	2	4.5		2400
Giant Snake Fang	5	2.7	2	5.0		500
Harpoon (Darksea)	10	2.8	3	7.0	√	4800
Impaler (Orc)	7	2.4	1	3.0	√	7500
Javelin (Temple)	5	3.8	3	7.0		130
Knife (Shadowed)	3	2	1	2.5	√	2000
Main Gauche						
Bronze	3	2.3	1	4.0		1800
Cast-Iron	5	2.5	1	3.5		4500
Normal	3	2.2	1	3.5		4000
Pugius	5	2.1	1	2.5	√	4900
Rapier						
Alloy	6	2.3	2	3.5	√	50000
Bronze	4	2.8	2	6.0		4500
Burning	7	2.3	2	3.5	√	5000
Cast-Iron	4	2.3	2	5.0		150
Combine	5	2.3	2	5.0	√	50000
Enchanted Fine Steel	5	1.9	2	4.5	√	5000

Weapon	Dmg	Del	Size	Wt	Mag	Value
Rapier (cont'd)						
Enchanted Teir`Dal	5	1.9	2	4.5	√	5000
Feir'Dal	5	2.3	2	4.7		5900
Fine Steel	5	2.3	2	5.0		5900
Ruined Teir`Dal	6	2.5	2	4.5	√	5000
Rusty	4	3.1	2	5.0		50
Shadowed	5	2.5	2	5.0	√	0
Tainted Teir`Dal	5	1.9	2	4.5	√	5000
Tarnished	4	2.9	2	5.0		50
Teir'Dal	5	2.3	2	4.7		5900
Well-Balanced	6	2.5	2	6.0	√	50000
Normal	5	2.5	2	5.0		13000
Rapier of Defense	5	2.4	2	5.0	√	5000
Scorpion Telson	4	3	2	6.0		500
Seax	3	2.1	1	3.0		1200
Shank (Cast-Iron)	2	2.4	1	1.0		10
Shard						
Jagged Metal	5	2.7	2	5.0		500
Sharp Metal	5	2.7	2	5.0		500
Short Spear						
Ashenwood	6	2.2	2	5.0	√	4800
Cast-Iron	5	2.6	2	6.0		3800
Slave1	5	4.5	4	12.0	√	15000
Snake Fang	5	2.6	2	5.0	√	0
Spear (Barbarian Hunting)	10	3.3	3	7.0	√	4800
Spear						
Bone	6	2.9	3	6.5	√	2500
Bronze	5	3.2	3	8.0		3100
Cast-Iron	6	2.7	3	7.0		6500
Combine	6	2.7	3	6.8	√	60000
Dull Wooden	7	3.3	3	7.0	√	4800
Feir'Dal	6	2.7	3	6.4		6400
Fine Steel	6	2.7	3	6.8		6400
Fishing	5	3.2	2	5.0		130
Ivory Shafted	7	3	3	6.8	√	120000
Ivory	7	3	3	6.8	√	135000
Kerran Fishing	5	3	2	5.0	√	500
Kerran War	8	3.4	3	5.0	√	60000
Riptide	6	3.3	2	4.5	√	2400
Runed	7	3.3	3	7.0	√	4800
Rusty Shortened	4	3.2	2	5.0		130
Rusty	5	3.8	3	7.0		200

Weapon	Dmg	Del	Size	Wt	Mag	Value
Spear (cont'd)						
Shadowed	6	2.9	3	7.0	√	0
Shortened Bronze	5	3.4	2	6.0		2500
Shortened	5	2.9	2	5.0		9000
Tailor-Made	6	2.8	2	7.0		5500
Tarnished Shortened	4	3	2	5.0		130
Tarnished	5	3.6	3	7.0		200
Teir'Dal	6	2.7	3	6.4		6400
Normal	6	2.9	3	7.0		11000

Weapon	Dmg	Del	Size	Wt	Mag	Value
Spear of Warding	6	2.7	3	7.0	√	0
Sticker (Goblin)	6	3	3	7.0	√	4800
Stiletto of the Bloodclaw	6	2.3	2	3.5	√	4500
Swordfish Bill	4	3	2	6.0		500
Tesch Val Sinisch	9	3.3	3	7.0	√	4800
Trident (Coral)	8	3.8	2	4.5		2400
War Spear (Ebon)	8	3.1	3	7.0	√	4800
Whip (Cinctured)	5	3	2	5.0		100

One-Handed Blunt Weapons

Weapon	Dmg	Del	Size	Wt	Mag	Value
Club						
Hulking Spiked	6	2.6	2	4.5		6000
Ivory Spiked	9	4	2	10.0	√	50000
Splintering	4	2.8	2	6.0		280
Normal	4	2.7	2	5.0		2000
Crook (Glowing Wooden)	11	3.5	3	8.5	√	5000
Femur (Noclin's)	5	3.5	2	4.0	√	0
Flail						
Bronze	6	3.7	2	10.0		3500
Cast-Iron	6	3.7	2	10.0		3800
Harvest	7	3.3	2	9.0	√	5000
Tarnished	5	3.5	2	9.0		190
Normal	7	3.6	2	9.0		12000
Gavel of Justice	5	3.4	2	7.5	√	1000
Hammer of Requital	7	2.9	2	5.0	√	0
Hammer of Striking	6	2.9	2	5.0	√	0
Hammer of Wrath	6	3.2	2	5.0	√	0
Mace						
Bronze	6	3.8	2	9.0		3500
Dwarven	8	3.5	2	4.5		3800
Orcish	7	3.9	2	9.0		5500
Screaming	8	3.5	2	8.0	√	5000
Shadowed	7	3.7	2	8.0	√	0
Normal	7	3.7	2	8.0		12000

Weapon	Dmg	Del	Size	Wt	Mag	Value
Morning Star						
Battle Worn	8	3.8	2	10.0		6200
Bronze	7	4.3	2	11.0		4800
Cast-Iron	8	4	2	10.0		5000
Cold Iron	9	3.5	2	4.5	√	3600
Combine	8	3.8	2	10.0	√	25000
Enchanted Battleworn	7	3	2	9.0	√	5000
Enchanted Fine Steel	7	3	2	9.0	√	5000
Feir'Dal	8	3.8	2	10.0		6200
Fine Steel	8	3.8	2	10.0		6200
Forged	8	3.8	2	9.0		3500
Orcish	8	4.3	2	11.0		6500
Shadowed	8	4	2	10.0	√	0
Tarnished	6	4.2	2	10.0		240
Teir'Dal	8	3.8	2	9.5		6200
Normal	8	4	2	10.0		15000
Rod						
Golden	6	3	2	4.0	√	1000
Modulating	8	2.6	2	1.0	√	0
Scepter of Flame	7	2.9	2	4.5	√	10000
Scepter of Rahotep	9	3.8	2	4.5	√	5000
Sceptre (Bronze)	8	4	2	8.0	√	10000

One-Handed Blunt Weapons, cont.

Weapon	Dmg	Del	Size	Wt	Mag	Value
Staff						
Cracked	5	3.2	3	8.5		1 2 0 0
Darkwood	5	2.8	3	6.5	√	5 0 0
Fire Crystal	5	2.8	3	6.5	√	4 3 0 0
Gnomish	5	2.8	3	6.5		2 0 0 0 0
Ice Crystal	5	2.8	3	6.5	√	4 3 0 0
Ivory Inlaid	5	2.5	3	6.5	√	4 5 0 0 0
Listlyn	5	2.9	3	8.5	√	0
Slime Crystal	5	2.8	3	6.5	√	4 3 0 0
Survival	4	2.8	2	6.0		2 8 0
Tinlyn	5	2.6	3	8.5	√	0
Water Crystal	5	2.8	3	6.5	√	4 3 0 0
Whispering	5	3.1	3	8.5	√	0
Normal	5	2.8	3	6.5		4 3 0 0
Staff of Fire	5	2.5	3	6.5	√	5 0 0 0
Staff of Temperate						
Flux	6	3	3	4.0	√	1 0 0 0
Stein of Moggok	6	2.8	1	2.5	√	5 0 0 0
Stein of Ulissa	6	2.5	3	3.5	√	5 0 0 0

Weapon	Dmg	Del	Size	Wt	Mag	Value
Wand						
Blessed Silver	5	2.5	2	1.0	√	1 0 0 0
Glowing Silver	5	2.5	2	1.0	√	1 0 0 0
Incandescent	5	2.5	2	1.0	√	6 0 0 0
Silver	5	2.5	2	1.0	√	1 0 0 0
Weeping	5	2.5	2	1.0	√	1 0 0 0
Warclub						
Cast-Iron	4	2.8	2	6.0		2 5
Normal	6	3.2	2	5.0		6 0 0 0
Warhammer						
Battle Worn	6	3	2	7.3		5 6 0 0
Bronze	5	3.3	2	8.5		1 7 0 0
Combine	6	3	2	7.3	√	4 3 0 0 0
Dwarven	7	3.3	2	7.5		4 5 0 0
Feir'Dal	6	3	2	7.3		5 6 0 0
Fine Steel	6	3	2	7.3		5 6 0 0
Tarnished	4	2.8	2	7.5		1 8 0
Teir'Dal	6	3	2	6.7		5 6 0 0
Normal	6	3.2	2	7.5		6 0 0 0

Two-Handed Blunt Weapons

Weapon	Dmg	Del	Size	Wt	Mag	Value
Great Staff						
Battle Worn	9	3.6	3	10.0		6 5 0 0
Cast-Iron	7	4	3	11.0		4 3 0 0
Combine	9	3.6	3	10.0	√	4 2 5 0 0
Feir'Dal	9	3.6	3	10.0		6 5 0 0
Fine Steel	9	3.6	3	10.0		6 5 0 0
Ivory Inlaid	10	3.5	3	10.0	√	8 5 0 0 0
Ivory	10	3.5	3	10.0	√	1 0 0 0 0 0
Teir'Dal	9	3.6	3	9.5		6 5 0 0
Warped	7	4	3	11.0		4 9 0 0
Worn	6	4	3	10.0		0
Worn	6	4	3	10.0		2 0 0
Normal	9	3.8	3	10.0		1 8 0 0 0
Mroons Toy	20	7	3	12.0		4 5 0 0
Shovel	4	2.7	2	6.0		3 5 0
Staff of Runes	9	3.6	3	2.5	√	0
Staff of Symbols	10	3.4	3	2.5	√	0
Staff of the Khanza	9	3	3	8.0		0

Weapon	Dmg	Del	Size	Wt	Mag	Value
Staff of Tracing	7	4	3	2.5	√	0
Staff of Warding	8	3.8	3	2.5	√	0
Staff						
Bonethunder	9	3.6	3	10.0	√	7 5 0 0
Runed Totem	9	3.7	3	11.0	√	3 5 0 0
Sap Sheen	10	3.4	3	7.5	√	5 0 0 0
Thunder	5	3.1	3	8.5	√	1 2 0 0
Treant	10	3.5	3	9.5	√	5 0 0 0
Stave (Burnished						
Wooden)	15	4.5	3	11.0	√	4 9 0 0
Two Handed Hammer						
Bronze	8	4.5	3	14.0		7 0 0 0
Cast-Iron	13	5.1	3	13.0		6 5 0 0
Rusty	7	4.5	3	13.0		3 0 0
Shadowed	13	5.1	3	13.0	√	0
Normal	13	5.1	3	13.0		2 5 0 0 0
War Maul (Ogre)	17	5	3	13.0		5 0 0 0

Standard Bows

You can make a standard bow out of five different types of wood: hickory, elm, ashwood, oak and darkwood (from weakest to strongest). You can carve it with a whittling blade, shape it with a planing tool, or leave it rough. You can string it with hemp, linen or silk, and you can add a cam or two cams (two cams make it a compound bow), or leave it a recurve bow. There are 63 different bows you can make, in all. Each weighs 4 pounds and is size 3.

The stronger the wood, the greater the damage (**Dmg**) and **Range**, but the greater the refire **Delay** between shots, as well. Adding any features to your bow reduces the refire delay, but also reduces the damage it inflicts. Adding features also costs more and increases its **Value**.

Part	Dmg	Range	Delay	Value
Wood				
Hickory	10	50	5.0	2 0 0
Elm	13	75	5.1	2 0 0 0
Ashwood	16	100	5.8	15 0 0 0
Oak	21	125	6.5	65 0 0 0
Darkwood	25	150	6.8	215 0 0 0
Drawstring				
Hemp Twine	-	-	-	+1 0
Linen String	-1	-	-0.4	+2 0
Silk String	-2	-	-0.8	+5 0

Part	Dmg	Range	Delay	Value
Tooled				
None (Rough)	-	-	-	-
With Whittling Blade (Carved)	-1	-	-0.4	+2 0 0
With Planing Tool (Shaped)	-2	-	-0.9	+10 0 0 0
Cam *				
None (Recurve)	-	-	-	-
1-Cam	-1	-	-0.5	+37 0 0 0
Compound (2-Cam)	-2	-	-1.0	+74 0 0 0

* Yes, cams *increase* damage in the real world, but Norrath isn't exactly the real world, is it?

Some woods can not be crafted into all types of bows. For each type of wood, these are the bows that can be crafted:

Wood	Rough	Carved	Shaped	No Cam	1-Cam	Compound
Hickory	√	no	no	√	no	no
Elm	√	√	no	√	no	no
Ashwood	√	√	√	√	no	no
Oak	√	√	√	√	√	no
Darkwood	√	√	√	√	√	√

To help you understand, let's assemble a few sample bows:

Sample Bow	Wood	Tooling	String	Cam	Damage	Range	Delay	Value
A	Hickory	None	Hemp	None	10	50	5.0	2 1 0
B	Elm	Carved	Hemp	None	12	75	4.7	4 0 1 0
C	Ashwood	Carved	Linen	None	14	100	5.0	17 0 2 0
D	Oak	Shaped	Linen	1-Cam	17	125	4.7	112 0 2 0
E	Darkwood	Shaped	Silk	Compound	19	150	4.1	299 0 5 0

Standard Arrows

There are 216 different arrows that you can make, given all the possible combinations of head, shaft, fletch and nock. Rather than list all 216, we're going to tell you what each part of the arrow costs, and how it affects the arrow's performance, and give a couple of examples so that you can figure out what you need to know when making or buying arrows. First, all standard arrows (the ones you can make) weigh 10 to the pound and are size 1. Up to 20 can be stacked in a slot. Each arrow must have a head, a shaft, a fletch (or vane) and a nock. Some of these don't modify the arrow's performance, but each part is necessary — for example, a wood shaft doesn't add to the arrow's damage, but you'd have a tough time firing an arrow that didn't have a shaft.

Part	Dmg	Range	Value
Head			
Point	+1	–	4
Hooked	+2	–	6 3
Silver Tip	+3	–	* 7 6 3
Shaft			
Wood	–	–	–
Bone	+1	–	+ 1 4
Ceramic	+2	–	+ 2 1 9
Steel	+3	–	+ 5 3 9

Part	Dmg	Range	Value
Fletch			
Round Cut (CLASS 1)	–	+50	–
Parabolic Cut (CLASS 2)	–	+100	+ 6
Shield Cut (CLASS 3)	+1	–	+ 2 9
Wood Vane (CLASS 4)	+1	+25	+ 1 2 9
Bone Vane (CLASS 5)	+1	+75	+ 2 5 9
Ceramic Vane (CLASS 6)	+2	+50	+ 6 6 6
Nock			
Large Groove	–	–	–
Medium Groove	–	+25	+ 2
Small Groove	–	+50	+ 7

Again, to help you understand, let's assemble a few sample arrows:

Sample Arrow	Head	Shaft	Fletch	Nock	Damage	Range	Value
a	Point	Wood	Round Cut	Large Groove	+1	+50	4
b	Point	Bone	Parabolic Cut	Large Groove	+2	+100	2 2
c	Point	Bone	Shield Cut	Medium Groove	+3	–	4 9
d	Hooked	Ceramic	Wood Vane	Medium Groove	+5	+50	4 1 3
e	Hooked	Ceramic	Bone Vane	Small Groove	+5	+125	5 4 8
f	Hooked	Steel	Ceramic Vane	Small Groove	+7	+100	1 2 7 5

*Silver-tip (formerly "bladed") arrows are somewhat different. First, they're magical — they can hurt creatures who can only be hurt with magical weapons. Second, although the base cost for a silver tip is almost 8 gold (7 6 3), the total cost for the arrow is halved, so that the most expensive arrows (particularly those with steel shafts and ceramic vanes) actually cost *less*, and sell for less, with a silver tip added to them. Here are a few silver-tip arrows:

Sample Arrow	Head	Shaft	Fletch	Nock	Damage	Range	Value
g	Silver Tip	Wood	Round Cut	Large Groove	+3	+50	3 8 2
h	Silver Tip	Ceramic	Wood Vane	Medium Groove	+6	+50	5 5 7
i	Silver Tip	Steel	Ceramic Vane	Small Groove	+8	+100	9 8 8

Bow & Arrow Stats

The final stats for any bowshot you fire depend on both the bow and the arrow you use. Combine the stats for both to get the expected results:

Sample Bow	Sample Arrow	Damage	Range	Delay
A	a	11 (10 + 1)	100 (50 + 50)	5.0
B	c	15 (12 + 3)	75 (75 + 0)	4.7
C	e	19 (14 + 5)	225 (100 + 125)	5.0
D	g	20 (17 + 3)	175 (125 + 50)	4.7
E	I	27 (19 + 8)	250 (150 + 100)	4.1

Other Bows

There are other bows to be found in Norrath, besides the ones you can make. Here are a few of them. Note that you can fire any arrow with any bow.

Bow	Damage	Delay	Size	Wt	Range	Magic	Value
Elven Shortbow	7	4	3	4.5	50		4 0 0 0
Gnomish Composite Bow	16	4.3	3	3.5	100		5 0 0 0
Hunting Bow	5	4.3	2	3.5	50		2 4 0
LarkTwitter Bow	14	4.2	3	4.5	100	√	5 0 0 0
Longbow	8	5.1	3	5	100		3 5 0 0
Runed Oak Bow	21	4.3	3	4.5	125	√	4 0 0 0
Short Bow	6	4	2	3.5	50		3 6 0 0

Other Arrows

There are other arrows to be found, as well, include your basic "arrow."

Arrow	Damage	Size	Wt	Range	Magic	Value
Arrow	+1	1	0.1	+25		8
Flight Arrow	+1	1	0.1	+150		2 0 0
Glass Arrow	+1	1	0.1	+100	√	2 0 0
Gloomwater Arrow	+10	1	0.1	+150	√	2 5 0 0
Gnomish Longrange Arrows	+4	1	0.1	+150		1 0 0
LarkTwitter Arrow	+6	1	0.1	+150	√	1 0 0 0
Sheaf Arrow	+3	1	0.1	+50		2 5 0
Shimmering Arrow	+1	1	0.1	+100	√	2 0 0

Thrown Weapons

In addition to bows and arrow, there are other ranged weapons in *EverQuest*, which can be thrown. Here are some of the more basic thrown weapons.

Thrown Weapon	Damage	Delay	Size	Wt	Range	Magic	Value
Halfling Knife	12	4.2	1	0.5	60		1 0 0
Knife of Luclin	10	3.3	1	0.3	75	√	nfs
Shuriken	4	2.6	1	0.5	60		1 0
Shuriken of Quellious	7	2.3	0	0.1	100	√	nfs
Throwing Dagger	6	3.6	1	0.5	55	√	nfs
Throwing Knife	5	3.6	1	0.5	45		1 0
Turmoil Warts	9	2.4	1	0.3	125	√	9 0 0

Ammunition Slots

You have a slot for ammunition. If the slot has just one item left (for example, one arrow or one shuriken), *EverQuest* will search for other *identical* items in your inventory and use those first. (Generally, that means pulling more arrows or whatever from a quiver or bandolier.) Note that there are many different types of arrows, and this works only if you have arrows that are exactly the same as the remaining arrow in your ammunition (ammo) slot.

Jewelry

There are two different kinds of jewelry in Norrath: enchanted and ordinary. Ordinary jewelry is a fashion statement. Enchanted jewelry is a method of strategically increasing your statistics to enhance your performance in the game. Enchanted Jewelry is the way to go ... once you can afford it.

Jewelry is created by combining a bar of precious metal (silver, electrum, gold or platinum) and a gemstone in a Jeweler's Kit, and then successfully using your Jeweler skill. You can buy both precious metals and gemstones from merchants, or you might find them or trade for them on your own.

A piece of jewelry will have the listed "Enchanted Effects" only if the metal bar has been enchanted (by an Enchanter) *before* it is made into jewelry. Only PC Enchanters will enchant a bar of metal for you, and the price they charge (if any) is totally up to them. (This is one of those "it pays to be nice and flatter the mage" situations.)

The listed values for all items are given in platinum pieces. As with all values in this book, these are approximate numbers. Merchants tend to pay you less, and charge more, than the value listed here for any item. Note also that merchants are unimpressed by enchanted items. No NPC merchants sell enchanted items, and they won't pay you any more for an enchanted bar of metal than for an unenchanted bar. They'll pay a little more for enchanted jewelry, but only about 5% — hardly worth the effort of creating it. (Of course, player characters are likely to value enchanted jewelry much higher than this. Capitalism can be your friend.)

Metal	Value (Platinum)
Silver Bar	.5
Electrum Bar	2.5
Gold Bar	10
Platinum Bar	100

Jewelry	Value (Plat.)		Enchanted Effects
	Unench.	Ench.	
Amber	**2.5**		**Strength Enhancer**
Silver Amber Ring	3.3	3.3	+2 STR
Electrum Amber Earring	5.5	5.8	+1 STR
Bloodstone	**0.5**		**Stamina Enhancer**
Silver Bloodstone Earring	1.1	1.1	+2 STA
Electrum Bloodstone Necklace	3.3	3.5	+3 STA
Gold Bloodstone Necklace	12	12	+5 STA
Black Pearl	**20**		**Agility & Dexterity Enhancer**
Blackened Pearl Silver Ring	23	24	+3 AGI & DEX
Black Pearl Electrum Choker	25	26	+4 AGI & DEX
Black Sapphire	**175**		**Health, Mana & Defense Enhancer**
Black Sapphire Silvered Necklace	193	202	+30 HP, +30 Mana & +3 AC
Black Sapphire Electrum Earring	195	204	+35 HP, +25 Mana & +2 AC
Carnelian	**0.85**		**Agility Enhancer**
Silver Carnelian Wedding Ring	1.5	1.5	+2 AGI
Electrum Carnelian Wedding Ring	3.7	3.9	+3 AGI
Gold Carnelian Wedding Ring	12	12	+5 AGI
Cat's Eye Agate	**0.2**		**Charisma Enhancer**
Silver Cat Eye Necklace	0.8	0.8	+3 CHA
Electrum Cat Eye Bracelet	3.0	3.1	+4 CHA
Golden Cat Eye Bracelet	11	12	+7 CHA
Diamond	**200**		**Enhanced Magical Resistance**
Silver Diamond Wedding Ring	221	231	+3 save vs. Magic, Fire, Cold, Disease & Poison
Diamond Electrum Mask	223	233	+3 save vs. Magic; +5 vs. Fire & Cold; +10 vs. Disease & Poison
Emerald	**13**		**Enhanced Defense & Fire Resistance**
Silver Emerald Ring	15	16	+2 AC & +5 save vs. Fire
Emerald Electrum Bracelet	17	18	+3 AC & +4 save vs. Fire
Fire Emerald	**85**		**Strength & Dexterity Enhancer**
Silvered Fire Emerald Ring	94	98	+3 STR & DEX
Fire Emerald Electrum Bracelet	96	101	+3 STR & +5 DEX
Fire Opal	**50**		**Enhanced Health & Defense**
Silver Fire Wedding Ring	56	58	+30 HP & +2 AC
Electrum Fire Wedding Ring	58	60	+35 HP & +3 AC

| Jewelry | Value (Plat.) | | Enchanted Effects |
	Unench.	Ench.	
Hematite	**0.15**		**Enhanced Fire Resistance**
Silver Hematite Ring	0.7	0.7	+2 save vs. Fire
Electrum Hematite Choker	2.9	3.0	+4 save vs. Fire
Golden Hematite Choker	11	12	+7 save vs. Fire
Platinum Hematite Ring	110	115	+7 save vs. Fire
Jacinth	**150**		**Modified Magic Resist. & Enhanced Defense**
Silver Jacinth Wedding Ring	166	137	-7 save vs. Magic & +10 AC
Jacinth Electrum Wedding Ring	168	175	-3 save vs. Magic & +7 AC
Jade	**3.5**		**Health, Mana & Defense Enhancer**
Jaded Silver Ring	4.4	4.6	+5 HP, +5 Mana & +1 AC
Jaded Electrum Bracelet	6.6	6.9	+10 HP, +10 Mana & +2 AC
Jasper	**0.75**		**Wisdom Enhancer**
Silver Jasper Ring	1.4	1.4	+2 WIS
Electrum Jasper Earring	3.6	3.7	+2 WIS
Jasper Gold Earring	12	12	+3 WIS
Lapis Lazuli	**0.09**		**Enhanced Disease Resistance**
Silver Lapis Lazuli Necklace	0.6	0.6	+2 save vs. Disease
Electrum Lapis Lazuli Earring	2.8	3.0	+3 save vs. Disease
Gold Lapis Lazuli Earring	11	12	+5 save vs. Disease
Malachite	**0.05**		**Enhanced Poison Resistance**
Silver Malachite Ring	0.6	0.6	+2 save vs. Poison
Electrum Malachite Bracelet	2.8	2.9	+3 save vs. Poison
Gold Malachite Bracelet	11	12	+5 save vs. Poison
Onyx	**0.65**		**Dexterity Enhancer**
Silver Onyx Bracelet	1.3	1.3	+2 DEX
Electrum Onyx Pendant	3.5	3.6	+3 DEX
Gold Onyx Pendant	12	12	+5 DEX
Opal	**17**		**Agility & Stamina Enhancer**
Silver Opal Engagement Ring	19	20	+2 AGI & +3 STA
Electrum Opal Amulet	21	22	+3 AGI & +4 STA
Pearl	**4.5**		**Enhanced Defense & Poison Resistance**
Silvered Pearl Ring	5.5	5.8	+2 AC & +4 save vs. Poison
Electrum Pearl Choker	7.7	8.1	+3 AC & +6 save vs. Poison
Peridot	**10**		**Enhanced Defense & Cold Resistance**
Silvered Peridot Ring	12	12	+2 AC & +5 save vs. Cold
Electrum Peridot Bracelet	14	14	+3 AC & +4 save vs. Cold

Jewelry	Value (Plat.)		Enchanted Effects
	Unench.	Ench.	
Ruby	**125**		**Enhanced Strength & Wisdom**
Silver Ruby Vail	138	144	+4 STR & WIS
Ruby Electrum Ring	140	147	+4 STR & +2 WIS
Sapphire	**100**		**Enhanced Strength & Intelligence**
Silvered Sapphire Necklace	111	116	+4 STR & INT
Sapphire Electrum Earring	113	116	+4 STR & +2 INT
Star Rose Quartz	**1**		**Enhanced Intelligence**
Silver Rose Engagement Ring	1.7	1.7	+2 INT
Electrum Star Amulet	3.9	4.0	+2 INT
Golden Star Amulet	12	13	+4 INT
Rose Platinum Engagement Ring	111	116	+4 INT
Star Ruby	**65**		**Enhanced Dexterity & Charisma**
Silvered Star Ruby Vail	72	75	+5 DEX & CHA
Electrum Star Ruby Ring	74	78	+7 DEX & +5 CHA
Topaz	**5**		**Enhanced Defense & Disease Resistance**
Topaz Silver Necklace	6.1	6.3	+3 AC & +5 save vs. Disease
Topaz Electrum Earring	8.3	8.6	+2 AC & +5 save vs. Disease
Turquoise	**0.11**		**Enhanced Cold Resistance**
Silver Turquoise Bracelet	0.7	0.7	+2 save vs. Cold
Electrum Turquoise Engagement Ring		2.9	3.0 +3 save vs. Cold
Gold Turquoise Engagement Ring	11	12	+5 save vs. Cold
Wolf's Eye Agate	**3**		**Enhanced Magic Resistance**
Silver Wolf's Eye Necklace	4.1	4.1	+4 save vs. Magic
Wolf's Eye Electrum Bracelet	6.3	6.6	+4 save vs. Magic

Containers

Pockets. Nobody but nobody's got pockets in *EverQuest*. Without some sort of container, your character is doomed to carry everything by hand ... and that's not very efficient. As a matter of fact, that's only six slots for goodies — two of which are usually devoted to food and drink.

The containers listed below range from the mundane to the exotic. (And we don't include everything — some things you just have to find on your own!) Each container's **Capacity** (**Cap.**, i.e., how many slots it has) is listed, along with the **Size Limit** (**Lim.**) for each slot. For example, a Small Bag can carry four items, each no larger than size 2 (Medium). Stackable items can also be stacked inside a container (at 20 per slot). Within each category below, containers are listed in order of their capacity, from the fewest slots to the most slots.

In a few cases, a container actually "reduces" the weight of the items it carries, either magically or by making it physically easier to haul its contents around. (For example, you can carry more weight in a pack on your shoulders, than you can in your arms.) In those cases, **W%** lists how much less weight the container's contents appear to weigh as you carry them around. **Value** gives an approximation of how much the item is worth to an NPC merchant. If a merchant won't buy or sell the container, it's listed as "**nfs**" (not for sale). If it can't be moved (to take it to a merchant), it is "**immobile**." In some cases, the container's value is far out of proportion to what it can carry. It may have other special properties — you'll have to put your hands on one and experiment to find what else it can do.

Trade Containers

You will need these containers to create items with your trade skills. For more information on creating items with trade skills, see **Trade Skills**, p. 104.

Container	Cap.	Lim.	W%	Value P G S C	Container	Cap.	Lim.	W%	Value P G S C
Brewing Barrel	6 or 10	3	–	immobile	**Pottery Wheels**				
Fletching Kit	8	3	–	1 0 0 0	Pottery Kit	6	3	–	2 0 0
Forges					Pottery Wheel	10	3	–	immobile
Sharpening Kit	2	3	–	1 0 0 0	**Ovens**				
Smithing Kit	6	3	–	immobile	Oven	6	3	–	immobile
Forge	10	3	–	immobile	Spit	6	4	–	2 0 0
Jeweller's Kit	4	3	–	1 0 0 0	**Sewing Kits**				
Key Maker	2	1	–	immobile	Small Sewing Kit	2	3	–	5 5 0
Kiln	10	3	–	immobile	Community Loom	6	4	–	immobile
Medicine Bag	6	3	–	1 0 0 0	Large Sewing Kit	8	4	–	1 0 0 0
Mixing Bowl	4	3	–	1 0 0 0	**Toolbox**	8	4	–	1 0 0 0
Mortar and Pestle	6	3	–	1 0 0 0					

Non-Trade Containers

These are everyday containers for simply holding, storing and carrying stuff.

Container	Cap.	Lim.	W%	Value P G S C
Backpacks				
Archeologist Pack	6	3	25	2 6 0 0
Featherweight Pouch	6	1	5	1 0 0 0
Backpack	8	3	–	5 5 0
Travelers Pack	8	3	20	1 0 0 0 0
Lionhide Backpack	8	3	35	6 8 0 0
Pierce's Pack	8	4	50	2 6 0 0 0
Shralok Pack	8	4	25	2 6 0 0
Rhinohide Backpack	8	3	–	5 5 0
Hand Made Backpack	10	3	–	9 0 0
Bank Box	10	3	–	3 0 0 0 0
Tracker's Terrapack	10	3	15	1 0 0 0 0 0
Bandoliers				
No standard bandoliers are currently available for sale, but look around and see what you can find ...				
Bags, Small				
Small Bag	4	2	–	1 8 0
Purse	4	1	–	1 5
Lady's Purse	4	1	–	1 5
Ration Bladder	4	1	–	2 0
Bags, Large				
Body Bag	2	3	–	7 5 0
Large Bag	6	3	–	3 0 0
Pierce's Pouch of Storing	8	3	20	1 1 5 0 0
Bag of the Tinkerers	10	4	100	5 0 0 0 0 0

Container	Cap.	Lim.	W%	Value P G S C
Pouches				
Zimbittle's Pouch	4	2	–	1 0
Cinched Stomach Pouch	4	2	–	1 2 5
Spider Silk Pouch	10	0	–	1 0 0 0
Pouches, Belt				
Belt Pouch	4	1	–	1 5 0
Pouches, Wrist				
Tattered Leather Pouch	2	0	–	5 0
Wrist Pouch	4	0	–	1 0 0
Travelers Pouch	4	1	25	7 5 0 0
Chests, Small				
Small Clay Jar	2	2	–	9 0
Small Metal Container	2	2	–	2 0 0
Momento Box	6	1	75	7 5 0 0
Small Box	8	2	–	2 0 0
Darkwood Trunk	10	4	100	7 5 0 0 0
Chests, Large				
Tower Coffin	2	3	–	1 0 0 0 0
Jade Inlaid Coffin	2	0	–	1 4 0 0 0 0
Medium Clay Jar	4	2	–	1 0 0
Medium Metal Container	4	2	–	3 5 0
Large Box	8	3	–	5 0 0
Treasure Chest	8	4	–	nfs
Large Clay Jar	8	2	–	1 1 0
Large Metal Container	8	2	–	5 0 0
Driftwood Treasure Chest	10	4	100	5 0 0 0 0

Shields & Blocking Items

Anything that acts like a shield — keeps other people's blows from landing — is listed below. Shields have the same stats as armor and clothing. All shields (and other blocking items, like a parrying dagger) add to your AC when you have them equipped (that is, in your hand). There are small, medium and large variations on several of the shields. In most cases, this only affects their weight (not their size or value), but note that small kite shields are Size 2, not 3 like the medium and large kite shields. Magical shields have the listed benefits, but might have other powers, as well.

Normal

Shield	Size	S	M	L	AC	Value	Shield	Size	S	M	L	AC	Value
Buckler	1	2.2	3	3.8	4	3 0 0	Round Shield	2	3.7	5	6.2	6	1 5 0 0
Combine Targ (Target) Shield	2		7.3		8	9 0 0 0	Shield of Prexus	2		6.5		8	25 0 0 0
Frogskin Shield	1		3		3	1 5 0	Targ (Target) Shield	2	5.6	7.5	9.3	7	3 0 0 0
Kite Shield	2/3/3	7.5	10	12.5	8	5 0 0 0	Tower Shield	3	11.2	15	18.7	10	100 0 0 0
Mithril Parrying Dagger	1		2.4		5	3 0 0 0	Wooden Kite Shield	2/3/3	9.3	12.5	15.6	7	3 0 0 0
Parrying Dagger	1		2.5		4	3 0 0	Wooden Shield	2	3.7	5	6.2	5	9 0 0
Qeynos Kite Shield	3		10		8	2 0 0 0							

Magical

Shield	Size	Sm	Md	Lg	AC	Value	Enhancements
Bark Shield	1		2.5		15	3 3 0 0	+5 AGI
Bone Shield	3	9.5	9.5	9.5	8	2 5 0 0	+1 save vs. Disease
Charred Guardian Shield	2		8		10	3 2 0 0	+9 WIS
Chitin Shell Shield	1		4		15	3 3 0 0	+10 save vs. Poison
Cracked Darkwood Shield	2		5		12	3 2 0 0	+9 STR
Crested Mistmoore Shield	2		6.5		10	4 5 0 0	+6 DEX; +10 save vs. Magic, Disease & Poison
Devlas Ilkvel	2		7		12	7 0 0 0	+ 5 DEX; + 7 save vs. Poison
Giant Laceless Sandal	3		5		15	2 2 0 0	+5 STA; -7 CHA
Runewood Shield	2		6		16	9 0 0 0	+8 WIS; +15 save vs. Fire
Scute Shield	2		8		15	4 5 0 0	+ 9 STA
Shimmering Orb	0		0.2		15	4 5 0 0	+20 HP
Shiny Brass Shield	2		8		10	3 2 0 0	+10 save vs. Magic
Silent Watch Shield	3		9.5		10	5 0 0 0	+10 WIS
Trueheart Shield	2		6.5		20	9 0 0 0	+5 STR, WIS & AGI

Creatures

Creatures of Norrath

Ah, wary traveler," Darna said as she pushed her blonde locks out of her eyes and wiped her ink-stained fingers on her tunic, "you come to me with queries about the creatures of this land. How very wise of you! My life's work is to compile useful information about the creatures of Norrath into this bestiary. Of course, I am not finished yet as our world is so vast. However, please feel free to peruse the descriptions of the creatures surrounding the larger cities . . .

Disclaimer. First, these stats only represent those creatures that venture closest to the cities. Second, they only represent an initial survey of even those creatures. This chronicler is sure that many more — and much more dangerous — creatures lie beyond the horizon.

When several creatures are listed under one heading (as with different varieties of bear to be found under "Bear"), the first stats are those shared by all of that type of creature. For example, all bears are "warriors." That stat is listed once and not repeated for each variety of bear. Then, each specific variety lists those stats that are different from other varieties of bear.

Class. All creatures of Norrath, intelligent or not, can be described by one of the adventuring classes. For example, most of the less intelligent creatures fit the Warrior pattern.

Typical Levels list the probable level of experience for each creature. **Typical Attributes** list the probable stats for the creature. In general, all of the "skills" (especially its ability to fight) are at about the same level, so one general **Typical Skill Level** is listed. The most common exception is **Swimming skill**; when it is different, the creature's Swimming skill is also listed.

Speed and **Attack Speed** are listed as *Slowest, Slower, Slow, Average, Fast, Faster, Fastest*. A typical human's Speed and Attack Speed are both Average.

Base Damage is how much damage the creature can inflict with a single strike. However, many creatures also have a **Combat Factor**, that can help increase this damage. The higher the Combat Factor, the better the creature fights, and the more damage it does. **Base AC** lists how well the creature's skin protects it from damage.

Awareness Range lists from how far away the creature is likely to spot you (*None, Shortest, Shorter, Short, Average, Long, Longer, Longest*). Average awareness range is about 600 feet. **Average Reaction Radius** lists from how far away the creature will Con you (*None, Smallest, Smaller, Small, Average, Large, Larger, Largest*). Average reaction radius is about 60 feet.

Frenzy. If a creature sees it can outnumber a potential target by at least 3-to-1, it might frenzy and attack. The chance that each creature might frenzy is listed next.

The final common stat listed is **Recuperation**, given as *Slowest, Slower, Slow, Average, Fast, Faster, Fastest*.

In addition, some creatures list special stats, like magical resistances or invulnerability to normal weapons. For example, the basilisk has a Stone breath that you would do well to avoid.

EverQuest: The Ruins of Kunark

Alligator

Warrior
Typical Levels 8-10
Typical Attributes
  STR 100
  STA 100
  DEX 80
  INT 20
  AGI 65
  WIS 20
Typical Skill Level 45
Typical Swimming skill 200
Speed Average
Attack Speed Average
Base Damage 10
Combat Factor 10
Base AC 4-6
Average Awareness Range
Average Reaction Radius
Likely to Frenzy
Average Recuperation

Aviak

An intelligent species, Aviak merchants will even deal with you.
Warrior
Typical Levels 8-30
Typical Attributes
  STR 85
  STA 85
  DEX 80
  INT 75
  AGI 80
  WIS 85
Typical Skill Level 145
Speed Average
Attack Speed Average
Base Damage 30
Combat Factor 16
Base AC 76
Average Awareness Range
Large Reaction Radius
Likely to Frenzy
Average Recuperation

Aviak Chick

Typical Levels 3-5
Typical Skill Level 20
Base Damage 5
Combat Factor 0
Base AC 0

Barracuda

Warrior
Typical Levels 4-10
Typical Attributes
  STR 80
  STA 75
  DEX 75
  INT 15
  AGI 95
  WIS 15
Typical Skill Level 45
Speed Average
Attack Speed Average
Base Damage 10
Shorter Awareness Range
Small Reaction Radius
Attacks all PCs in range
Least Likely to Frenzy
Average Recuperation

Bloodgills Faction

Typical Levels 35-44
Typical Attributes
  STR 95
Typical Skill Level 185
Attack Speed Fast
Base Damage 38
Combat Factor 34
Base AC 108
Unlikely to Frenzy

Basilisk

Warrior
Typical Levels 5-10
Typical Attributes
         STR 100
         STA 100
         DEX   80
         INT   22
         AGI   65
         WIS   20
Typical Skill Level 40
Typical Swimming skill 200
Speed Average
Attack Speed Average
Stone Breath
Base Damage 10
Average Awareness Range
Average Reaction Radius
Likely to Frenzy
Average Recuperation

Bat

Warrior
Typical Levels 1-2
Typical Attributes
         STR   20
         STA   60
         DEX   90
         INT   20
         AGI 100
         WIS   20
Typical Skill Level 5
Speed Fast
Attack Speed Average
Base Damage 2
Average Awareness Range
Average Reaction Radius
Least Likely to Frenzy
Faster Recuperation

Large Bat

Typical Levels 3-5
Typical Attributes
         STR   45
         AGI 120
Typical Skill Level 20
Speed Average
Base Damage 5
Large Reaction Radius
Less Likely to Frenzy
Average Recuperation

Giant Bat

Typical Levels 5-7
Typical Attributes
         STR   55
         STA   60
         DEX   90
         INT   30
         AGI 120
         WIS   15
Typical Skill Level 30
Speed Average
Base Damage 7
Average Awareness Range
Large Reaction Radius
Unlikely to Frenzy
Average Recuperation

Bear

Warrior
Typical Attributes
    STR   115
    STA   125
    DEX   80
    INT   20
    AGI   65
    WIS   60
Average Awareness Range

Black or Brown Bear

Typical Levels 3-5
Typical Skill Level 20
Speed Average
Attack Speed Average
Base Damage 5
Average Reaction Radius
Likely to Frenzy
Fast Recuperation

Grizzly or Kodiak Bear

Typical Levels 9-11
Typical Skill Level 50
Speed Average
Attack Speed Average
Base Damage 11
Average Reaction Radius
Likely to Frenzy
Average Recuperation

Polar Bear

Typical Levels 5-10
Typical Skill Level 35
Speed Average
Attack Speed Average
Base Damage 8
Small Reaction Radius
Less Likely to Frenzy
Average Recuperation

Iceberg Polar Bear

Wolves of the North Faction
Typical Levels 30-40
Typical Skill Level 175
Speed Faster
Attack Speed Fast
Base Damage 35
Combat Factor 30
Base AC 100
Small Reaction Radius
Less Likely to Frenzy
Average Recuperation
Cold Resistance 200

Glacier Bear

Typical Levels 25-30
Typical Skill Level 135
Speed Average
Attack Speed Average
Base Damage 30
Combat Factor 4
Base AC 70
Can only be hit with Magic
Small Reaction Radius
Less Likely to Frenzy
Average Recuperation
Cold Resistance 200

Beetle

Warrior
Typical Levels 1-14
Typical Attributes
    STR   90
    STA   100
    DEX   50
    INT   15
    AGI   80
    WIS   10
Typical Skill Level 10-65
Speed Slow
Attack Speed Average
Has Spit attack
Base Damage 3-14
Average Awareness Range
Average Reaction Radius
Less Likely to Frenzy
Faster Recuperation

Scarab Beetle

Typical Levels 7-9
Typical Attributes
    STR   60
Typical Skill Level 40
Base Damage 9
Slow Recuperation

Giant Scarab Beetle

Typical Levels 9-11
Typical Attributes
    STR   60
Typical Skill Level 50
Base Damage 11
Slow Recuperation

Beetle (cont.)

Lesser Scarab Beetle
Typical Levels 2
Typical Attributes
STR   50
Typical Skill Level 10
Base Damage 3

Minor Scarab Beetle
Typical Levels 4-6
Typical Attributes
STR   75
Typical Skill Level 25
Base Damage 6

Fire Beetle
Typical Levels 2-3
Typical Attributes
STR   50
Typical Skill Level 10
Base Damage 3

Ember Beetle
Typical Levels 1-2
Typical Attributes
STR   50
Typical Skill Level 5
Speed Fast
Base Damage 2
Likely to Frenzy

Giant Beetle
Typical Levels 6-8
Typical Attributes
STR   75
Typical Skill Level 35
Base Damage 8
Slow Recuperation

Pincer Beetle
Typical Levels 10-12
Typical Attributes
STR   75
Typical Skill Level 55
Base Damage 12
Base AC 4
Slow Recuperation

Borer Beetle
Typical Levels 14-16
Typical Attributes
STR   75
Typical Skill Level 75
Base Damage 16
Base AC 20
Slow Recuperation

She — at least he thought it was a female — was dying. The creature fascinated Marin, a bard by trade, a worshipper of Quellious, and follower of the Tranquil. She was as large as most Iksar and was completely covered in black and white fur. There was some sort of jewelry around her neck, perhaps signifying her place within a race of creatures such as herself. Or, the creature simply found the jewelry and thought it enticing for some reason. So far, she hadn't spoken any intelligible words and hadn't used her long, sharp claws in any offensive manner.

However, a well-concealed Marin crouched far outside her reach, just in case she changed her mind or any of her companions decided to retrieve her.

Bixie

Ranger
Many are in the Stone Hive
Bixies Faction
Typical Levels 1-2
Typical Attributes

STR 50
STA 70
DEX 100
INT 50
AGI 100
WIS 40

Typical Skill Level 5
Speed Average
Attack Speed Average
Has Poison
Base Damage 2
Average Awareness Range
Large Reaction Radius
Unlikely to Frenzy
Average Recuperation

Bixie Drone or Guard

Typical Levels 2-3
Typical Skill Level 10
No special abilities
Base Damage 3
Attacks all within range

Bixie Queen

Shaman
Stone Hive Bixies Faction
Typical Levels 3-5
Might have low-level spells
Typical Skill Level 25
Can cast Darkness
Base Damage 5
Attacks all within range
Poison Resistance 200

Brownie

Druid
Brownie Faction
Typical Levels 1-3
Might have low-level spells
Typical Attributes

STR 70
STA 70
DEX 100
INT 80
AGI 110
WIS 50

Typical Skill Level 10
Speed Average
Attack Speed Average
Base Damage 2-4
Average Awareness Range
Average Reaction Radius
Likely to Frenzy
Average Recuperation

Burynai

Warrior
Burynai Legion Faction
Typical Levels 10-18
Typical Attributes

STR 95
STA 95
DEX 75
INT 75
AGI 85
WIS 75

Typical Skill Level 75
Speed Average
Attack Speed Average
Base Damage 12-18
Base AC 4-28
Shorter Awareness Range
Small Reaction Radius
Unlikely to Frenzy
Average Recuperation

Centaur

Warrior
Typical Levels 15-35
Typical Attributes
STR 120
STA 120
DEX 100
INT 100
AGI 75
WIS 100
Equipment Hunting Bow, Arrow
Typical Skill Level 130
Speed Faster
Attack Speed Fast
Base Damage 15-35
Combat Factor 20
Base AC 30-80
No Awareness Range
No Reaction Radius
Won't Frenzy
Average Recuperation
Some have Resistances (at around 50)

Cyclops

Warrior
Typical Levels 28-32
Typical Attributes
STR 165
STA 165
DEX 65
INT 35
AGI 65
WIS 40
Typical Skill Level 150
Speed Fast
Attack Speed Fast
Base Damage 31
Combat Factor 20
Base AC 80
Average Awareness Range
Average Reaction Radius
Attacks all within range
Likely to Frenzy
Average Recuperation

Devourer

Warrior
Typical Levels 15-25
Typical Attributes
STR 80
STA 110
DEX 80
INT 75
AGI 85
WIS 75
Typical Skill Level 70-115
Speed Average
Attack Speed Average
Base Damage 15-25
Base AC 15-50
Can only be hit with Magic
Shorter Awareness Range
Small Reaction Radius
Attacks all PCs within range
Unlikely to Frenzy
Average Recuperation

Drake

Black and emerald drakes have been observed near some of the cities of Norrath; other, more exotic varieties are said to roost in more remote realms.

Warrior
Typical Levels 8-10
Typical Attributes

STR	85
STA	85
DEX	90
INT	50
AGI	100
WIS	50

Typical Skill Level 45
Speed Average
Attack Speed Average
Has Drake Breath
Base Damage 10
Average Awareness Range
Average Reaction Radius
Unlikely to Frenzy
Average Recuperation

Drixie

Warrior
Typical Levels 2-10
Typical Attributes

STR	75
STA	90
DEX	100
INT	50
AGI	100
WIS	40

Typical Skill Level 10-50
Speed Average
Attack Speed Average
Base Damage 3-10
Average Awareness Range
Large Reaction Radius
Average Chance to Frenzy
Average Recuperation
Some have Magic
Resistance 100

Elemental

There are a wide range of elementals. This listing gives a few of the more common stats.

Warrior
Elemental Faction
Typical Attributes

STR	150
STA	150
DEX	75
INT	50
AGI	50
WIS	50

Speed Average
Attack Speed Average
Some can only be hit with Magic
Average Awareness Range
Small Reaction Radius
Likely to Frenzy
Average Recuperation

Elephant

Warrior
Typical Levels 14-22
Typical Attributes
STR 125
STA 130
DEX 75
INT 30
AGI 50
WIS 50
Typical Skill Level 110
Speed Average
Attack Speed Average
Base Damage 21
Base AC 40
No Awareness Range
No Reaction Radius
Won't Frenzy
Average Recuperation

Elephant Calf

Typical Levels 10-14
Base Damage 13
Base AC 8

Faerie

Ranger
Fairie Faction
Typical Levels 6-23
Might have mid-level spells
Typical Attributes
STR 75
STA 75
DEX 100
INT 110
AGI 120
WIS 60
Typical Skill Level 35-110
Speed Average
Attack Speed Average
Base Damage 8-23
Base AC 10-48
Average Awareness Range
Average Reaction Radius
Unlikely to Frenzy
Average Recuperation

Fish

Warrior
Typical Levels 1-2
Typical Attributes
STR 15
STA 80
DEX 90
INT 15
AGI 115
WIS 15
Typical Skill Level 5
Typical Swimming skill 200
Speed Average
Attack Speed Average
Base Damage 2
Average Awareness Range
Small Reaction Radius
Least Likely to Frenzy
Faster Recuperation

Forest Giant

Warrior
The Kromdul Faction
Typical Levels 15-27
Typical Attributes

STR	125
STA	150
DEX	75
INT	65
AGI	75
WIS	60

Typical Skill Level 110
Speed Average
Attack Speed Average
Base Damage 18-26
Base AC 28-60
Shorter Awareness Range
Large Reaction Radius
Unlikely to Frenzy
Average Recuperation

Froglok

Frogloks can be Warrior, Shaman, Rogue, Necromancer, Wizard, Ranger
Guk and Kunark Froglok Factions
Typical Attributes

STR	85
STA	85
DEX	75
INT	75-125
AGI	85
WIS	65-120

Speed Average
Attack Speed Average
Base Damage 5-26
Base AC 8-60
Shorter Awareness Range
Small Reaction Radius
Unlikely to Frenzy
Average Recuperation

Froglok Tadpole

Warrior
Typical Levels 1
Typical Attributes

STR	75
STA	80
DEX	75
INT	75
AGI	90
WIS	65

Typical Skill Level 5
Typical Swimming skill 200
Base Damage 2
Average Awareness Range
Less Likely to Frenzy

Froglok Ghoul

All reported Froglok ghouls are warriors. Other than that, they have the same average stats as Frogloks.

Frost Giant

Warrior
Typical Levels 38-42
Typical Attributes

STR   175
STA   165
DEX   60
INT   50
AGI   65
WIS   30

Typical Skill Level 200
Speed Fast
Attack Speed Fast
Base Damage 41
Combat Factor 60
Base AC 120
Average Awareness Range
Average Reaction Radius
More Likely to Frenzy
Average Recuperation
Cold Resistance 200

Fungus Man

Ranger
Fungus Man Faction
Typical Levels 4-6
Might have low-level spells
Typical Attributes

STR   80
STA   90
DEX   90
INT   65
AGI   120
WIS   90

Typical Skill Level 25
Speed Average
Attack Speed Average
Base Damage 6
Average Awareness Range
Average Reaction Radius
More Likely to Frenzy
Faster Recuperation

Fungus Spore

Typical Levels 1
Typical Skill Level 5
Speed Slower
Base Damage 2
Poison Resistance 200

Fungus Spore Guardian

Typical Levels 9-11
Typical Skill Level 50
Has Snare attack
Base Damage 11
Poison Resistance 200

Ghoul

Warrior
Typical Levels 10-25
Typical Attributes

STR   120
STA   120
DEX   90
INT   45
AGI   75
WIS   15

Typical Skill Level 75
Speed Average
Attack Speed Average
Some see Invisible
(occasionally), have Ghoul
root
Base Damage 15-30
Base AC 20+
Can only be hit with Magic
Average Awareness Range
Average Reaction Radius
Likely to Frenzy
Average Recuperation

Gnoll

Warrior, Shaman,
Necromancer, Shadow
Knight
Factions: Split Paw Clan
and Sabertooths of
Blackburrow, plus a few
residents of Karana
Typical Attributes

STR	97
STA	105
DEX	75
INT	65
AGI	80
WIS	65

Typical Skill Level 80
Speed Average
Attack Speed Average
Base Damage 17
Base AC 24
Average Awareness Range
More Likely to Frenzy
Average Recuperation

Gnoll Pup

Warrior
Typical Levels 1-2
Typical Attributes

STR	70

Typical Skill Level 5
Base Damage 2

Goblin

Warrior, Wizard, Shaman,
Rogue
Factions include Clan
Runny Eye, Riptide Goblins
(aqua goblins), Vox (ice
goblins), Goblins of Cleaving
Tooth (Kunark goblins) and
Deeppockets, among others
Typical Attributes

STR	67
STA	82
DEX	75
INT	65
AGI	82
WIS	70

Speed Average
Attack Speed Average
Average Awareness Range
Smaller Reaction Radius
Average Recuperation

Goblin Whelp

Warrior
Typical Levels 1-4
Typical Skill Level 5
Base Damage 2-4
Average Reaction Radius

Golem

Warrior
Dreadguard Outer Faction
Typical Levels 13-22
Typical Attributes

STR	150
STA	150
DEX	75
INT	45
AGI	50
WIS	35

Typical Skill Level 90
Speed Slow
Attack Speed Average
Base Damage 16-21
Base AC 20-40
Some can only be hit with
Magic
Average Awareness Range
Larger Reaction Radius
Won't Frenzy
Average Recuperation

Griffin

Warrior
Typical Attributes

STR	135
STA	145
DEX	60
INT	45
AGI	60
WIS	45

Typical Skill Level 175
Speed Average
Average Awareness Range
Average Reaction Radius
Less Likely to Frenzy
Average Recuperation

Griffon (male)

Typical Levels 33-37
Attack Speed Fast
Base Damage 35
Combat Factor 40
Base AC 100
Can only be hit with Magic
Attacks all PCs within
range

Griffenne (female)

Typical Levels 23-27
Attack Speed Average
Base Damage 25
Base AC 60
Attacks all PCs within
range

Griffawn (young)

Typical Levels 13-17
Attack Speed Average
Base Damage 16
Base AC 20

Harpy

Warrior
Typical Levels 9-11
Might have low-level spells
Typical Attributes

STR	75
STA	90
DEX	90
INT	60
AGI	90
WIS	50

Typical Skill Level 50
Speed Average
Attack Speed Average
Has Breath attack
Base Damage 11
Average Awareness Range
Average Reaction Radius
Unlikely to Frenzy
Average Recuperation

Hill Giant

Warrior
Typical Levels 33-37
Typical Attributes

STR	170
STA	160
DEX	60
INT	50
AGI	65
WIS	30

Typical Skill Level 175
Speed Fast
Attack Speed Fast
Base Damage 36
Combat Factor 40
Base AC 100
Average Awareness Range
Average Reaction Radius
Attacks all PCs within
range
More Likely to Frenzy
Average Recuperation

Invisible Man

Warrior, Cleric,
Necromancer
Shadowed Men Faction
Typical Levels 24-26
Might have mid-level spells
Typical Attributes

STR	80
STA	80
DEX	80
INT	60-120
AGI	90
WIS	60-120

Typical Skill Level 125
Speed Fastest
Attack Speed Average
Base Damage 25
Base AC 60
Can only be hit with Magic
Average Awareness Range
Average Reaction Radius
Attacks all PCs within
range
Least Likely to Frenzy
Average Recuperation

Kobold

Warrior, Shaman
Kobold Faction
Typical Levels 6-8
Typical Attributes

STR	65
STA	80
DEX	75
INT	60
AGI	80
WIS	60

Speed Average
Attack Speed Average
Base Damage 8
Average Awareness Range
Smaller Reaction Radius
Average Chance to Frenzy
Average Recuperation
Some have Disease
Resistance 100
Some have Poison
Resistance 100

Kobold Runt

Warrior
Typical Levels 1-2
Typical Skill Level 5
Base Damage 2

Leech

*Leeches cover a wide range of
size and danger. The most
dangerous are said to infest
Kunark's Swamp of No
Hope.*
Warrior
Typical Levels 1-26
Typical Attributes

STR	80
STA	75
DEX	75
INT	10
AGI	75
WIS	10

Typical Skill Level 5-120
Speed Average
Attack Speed Average
Base Damage 2-25
Base AC 8-56
Shorter Awareness Range
Small Reaction Radius
Usually attacks all PCs
within range
Less Likely to Frenzy
Average Recuperation

Mammoth

Warrior
Typical Levels 22–26
Typical Attributes
STR 150
STA 150
DEX 85
INT 50
AGI 50
WIS 65
Typical Skill Level 120
Speed Average
Attack Speed Average
Base Damage 25
Base AC 55
No Awareness Range
No Reaction Radius
Won't Frenzy
Average Recuperation

Mammoth Calf

Typical Levels 10–14
Typical Attributes
STR 125
STA 130
DEX 75
INT 30
AGI 50
WIS 50
Typical Skill Level 60
Base Damage 13
Base AC 8

Lion

Warrior
Typical Attributes
STA 95
DEX 100
INT 20
AGI 110
WIS 20
Speed Fast
Attack Speed Average
Average Awareness Range
Average Reaction Radius
Average Recuperation

Lion (male)

Typical Levels 8–10
Typical Attributes
STR 95
Typical Skill Level 45
Base Damage 10
Unlikely to Frenzy

Lioness (female)

Typical Levels 6–8
Typical Attributes
STR 95
Typical Skill Level 35
Base Damage 8
Likely to Frenzy

Lion (young)

Typical Levels 3–6
Typical Attributes
STR 80
Typical Skill Level 20
Base Damage 5
Likely to Frenzy

Highland Lion

Typical Levels 13–15
Typical Attributes
STR 95
Typical Skill Level 70
Speed Faster
Base Damage 15
Base AC 16
Large Reaction Radius
Likely to Frenzy

Man Eating Plant

Includes Heartblood Fern, Weeping Mantrap, Bloodrose and Hangman
Warrior
Typical Levels 5-25
Typical Attributes

STR	95
STA	95
DEX	75
INT	10
AGI	75
WIS	10

Typical Skill Level 35-120
Speed Average
Attack Speed Average
Base Damage 5-25
Base AC 5-55
Shorter Awareness Range
Small Reaction Radius
Attacks all PCs within range
Unlikely to Frenzy
Average Recuperation

Minotaur

Warrior
Meldrath Faction
Typical Levels 9-36
Typical Attributes

STR	120
STA	120
DEX	85
INT	65
AGI	75
WIS	50

Some have Minotaur Battle Axe
Typical Skill Level 150
Speed Average
Attack Speed Fast
Base Damage 11-36
Combat Factor 13-40
Base AC 60-100
Average Awareness Range
Larger Reaction Radius
Stronger minotaurs attack all who come within range
Won't Frenzy
Average Recuperation

Mosquito

Warrior
Typical Levels 1-25
Typical Attributes

STR	55-80
STA	75
DEX	75
INT	10
AGI	85
WIS	10

Typical Skill Level 5-120
Speed Average
Attack Speed Average
Base Damage 2-25
Base AC 0-55
Shorter Awareness Range
Small Reaction Radius
Attacks all PCs within range
Least Likely to Frenzy
Average Recuperation

Orc

Warrior, Shaman, Shadow Knight

There are several orc factions, including the Death Fist Orcs, the Crushbone Orcs, and the Vox Faction

Typical Attributes

STR	90
STA	90
DEX	80
INT	67
AGI	82
WIS	67

Speed Average
Attack Speed Average
Average Awareness Range
Average Reaction Radius
More Likely to Frenzy
Average Recuperation
Some have Cold Resistance 25

Pegasus

Warrior
Typical Levels 10-20
Typical Attributes

STR	110
STA	120
DEX	75
INT	100
AGI	100
WIS	100

Typical Skill Level 120
Speed Faster
Attack Speed Average
Base Damage 16
Base AC 20
No Awareness Range
No Reaction Radius
Won't Frenzy
Average Recuperation

Piranha

Includes Pirahna, Pirhrana, Giant Piranha. The largest and strongest piranhas are rumored to lurk beneath the waters of Nektullos Forest.

Warrior
Typical Levels 2-14
Typical Attributes

STR	22-75
STA	85
DEX	90
INT	20
AGI	115
WIS	20

Typical Skill Level 10-60
Typical Swimming skill 200
Speed Fast
Attack Speed Average
Base Damage 3-13
Base AC 0-8
Average Awareness Range
Average Reaction Radius
Attacks all within range
Most Likely to Frenzy
Faster Recuperation

Pixie

Rogue, Ranger
Pixie Faction
Typical Attributes

STR	65
STA	70
DEX	100
INT	90
AGI	120
WIS	50

Speed Average
Attack Speed Average
Base Damage 3
Average Awareness Range
Average Reaction Radius
Unlikely to Frenzy
Average Recuperation

Puma

Warrior
Typical Levels 5-9
Typical Attributes

STR	90
STA	100
DEX	100
INT	20
AGI	110
WIS	20

Typical Skill Level 35
Speed Fast
Attack Speed Average
Base Damage 8
Average Awareness Range
Average Reaction Radius
Unlikely to Frenzy
Average Recuperation

Rat

Warrior
Typical Attributes

STR	65
STA	95
DEX	90
INT	30
AGI	105
WIS	20

Typical Swimming skill 50
Speed Average
Attack Speed Average
Average Chance to Frenzy
Fast Recuperation

Large Rat

Typical Levels 1-2
Typical Skill Level 5
Base Damage 2
Average Awareness Range
Average Reaction Radius
Unlikely to Frenzy

Giant Rat

Typical Levels 2-4
Typical Skill Level 15
Base Damage 4
Average Awareness Range
Average Reaction Radius
Least Likely to Frenzy

Plague Rat

Typical Levels 8-10
Typical Skill Level 45
Carries Plague Disease
Base Damage 10
Base AC 8
Average Awareness Range
Small Reaction Radius
Average Chance to Frenzy

Giant Plague Rat

Typical Levels 12-16
Typical Skill Level 70
Speed Average
Attack Speed Average
Carries Plague Disease
Base Damage 15
Base AC 16
Shortest Awareness Range
Small Reaction Radius
Average Chance to Frenzy

Sabertooth

Warrior

Typical Levels 2-24

Typical Attributes

STR	85
STA	75
DEX	75
INT	15
AGI	95
WIS	15

Typical Skill Level 10-115

Speed Fast

Attack Speed Average

Base Damage 3-24

Base AC 4-52

Shorter Awareness Range

Small Reaction Radius

Attacks all PCs within range

Least Likely to Frenzy

Average Recuperation

Sarnak

Warrior, Shaman

Sarnak Collective Faction

Typical Attributes

STR	90
STA	95
DEX	80
INT	75
AGI	80
WIS	75

Speed Average

Attack Speed Average

Base Damage 4-28

Base AC 4-68

Shorter Awareness Range

Small Reaction Radius

Unlikely to Frenzy

Average Recuperation

Scarecrow

Warrior

Typical Levels 13-17

Typical Attributes

STR	100
STA	125
DEX	75
INT	10
AGI	75
WIS	10

Typical Skill Level 75

Speed Average

Attack Speed Average

Sees Invisible (occasionally), has Fear attack

Base Damage 16

Base AC 20

Can only be hit with Magic

Average Awareness Range

Average Reaction Radius

Attacks all PCs within range

Less Likely to Frenzy

Average Recuperation

Lirahl, the Verishe Mal master of this arm of the Paw, shoved all the parchments from his desk. "You still have not solved the problem, Anozal!"

Anozal sighed and began to pick up the parchments upon which he had carefully outlined his plan for subjugating of the Splitpaw Gnolls, which included ignoring the hidden rebels. "The last rebel group is horribly fragmented and no real threat, Master."

The master stood and glared at his intelligent, but inexperienced, assistant. He stepped on the parchment Anozal was picking up and grabbed the younger gnoll by his ear. Drawing Anozal up, he snarled, "Are you willing to suffer my wrath every time a rebel surfaces?"

Anozal gulped, "And so my plan is to hunt down and kill every last rebel."

Scorpion

Warrior
Typical Levels 2-15
Typical Attributes

STR	75
STA	75
DEX	75
INT	10
AGI	90
WIS	10

Typical Skill Level 10-85
Speed Average
Attack Speed Average
Base Damage 3-15
Base AC 0-25
Shorter Awareness Range
Small Reaction Radius
Attacks all PCs within
range
Unlikely to Frenzy
Average Recuperation

Skeleton

Same class as when alive
Many are in Blood Sabers
Faction
Typical Levels 10-40
Might have low-level spells
Typical Attributes

STR	90
STA	80
DEX	80
INT	10-45
AGI	80
WIS	15

Often bear rusty weapons
Speed Average
Attack Speed Average
Some See Invisible
Base Damage 10-20
Base AC 5
Shorter Awareness Range
Small Reaction Radius
Unlikely to Frenzy
Average Recuperation
Disease Resistance 10
Poison Resistance 10

Skunk, Large

Warrior
Typical Levels 1-3
Typical Attributes

STR	75
STA	90
DEX	90
INT	20
AGI	90
WIS	20

Typical Skill Level 10
Speed Average
Attack Speed Average
Has Skunk spray
Base Damage 3
Average Awareness Range
Average Reaction Radius
Likely to Frenzy
Faster Recuperation

Snake

General Stats

Warrior
Typical Attributes
STA 100
DEX 90
INT 20
AGI 105
WIS 30
Typical Swimming skill 200
Speed Average
Attack Speed Average
Average Awareness Range
Average Reaction Radius

Snake, including Black, Green, Rattle, Water Moccasin

Typical Levels 1–2
Typical Attributes
STR 65
Typical Skill Level 5
Base Damage 2
Won't Frenzy
Faster Recuperation

Large Snake

Typical Levels 3–7
Typical Attributes
STR 75
Typical Skill Level 20
Has Weak Poison (most)
Base Damage 5–7
Likely to Frenzy
Average Recuperation

Giant Snake

Including Giant Green Snake & Rattlesnake
Typical Levels 7–11
Typical Attributes
STR 90
Typical Skill Level 40
Has Poison (most)
Base Damage 9–10
Likely to Frenzy
Average Recuperation

Snow Leopard

Warrior
Typical Levels 7–9
Typical Attributes
STR 90
STA 100
DEX 100
INT 20
AGI 110
WIS 20
Typical Skill Level 40
Speed Fast
Attack Speed Average
Base Damage 9
Average Awareness Range
Average Reaction Radius
Unlikely to Frenzy
Average Recuperation

Spectre

Warrior
Typical Levels 33–37
Typical Attributes
STR 100
STA 125
DEX 85
INT 85
AGI 85
WIS 20
Typical Skill Level 175
Speed Slow
Attack Speed Fast
Sees Invisible-to-Undead, has Lifetap, Stun attacks
Base Damage 36
Combat Factor 40
Base AC 100
Average Awareness Range
Small Reaction Radius
Attacks all within range
Likely to Frenzy
Average Recuperation

Spider

Warrior
Typical Levels 2-7
Typical Attributes
STR   75
STA   90
DEX   90
INT   20
AGI   125
WIS   20
Typical Skill Level 15-30
Speed Average
Attack Speed Average
Has Poison (feeble)
Base Damage 4-7
Average Awareness Range
Large Reaction Radius
Average Chance to Frenzy
Average Recuperation

Large Spider
Typical Levels 2-4
Typical Attributes
Typical Skill Level 15
Speed Average
Has Poison (feeble)
Base Damage 4

Giant Spider
Typical Levels 7-9
Typical Attributes
STR   85
STA   95
Typical Skill Level 40
Speed Average
Has Poison (weak)
Base Damage 9
Average Reaction Radius

Large Wooly Spider
Typical Levels 2-4
Typical Attributes
Typical Skill Level 15
Speed Average
Has Poison (feeble)
Base Damage 4

Giant Wooly Spider
Typical Levels 7-9
Typical Attributes
STR   85
STA   95
Typical Skill Level 40
Speed Average
Has Poison (weak)
Base Damage 9
Average Reaction Radius

Wooly Spiderling
Typical Levels 1-3
Typical Attributes
STR   70
AGI   100
Typical Skill Level 10
Speed Average
Base Damage 3

Rock Spiderling
Typical Levels 1-3
Typical Attributes
STR   70
STA   75
AGI   100
Typical Skill Level 10
Speed Average
Base Damage 3
Smaller Reaction Radius
Less Likely to Frenzy

Widow Hatchling Spider
Typical Levels 1-3
Typical Attributes
STR   85
STA   95
Typical Skill Level 10
Speed Average
Has Poison (feeble)
Base Damage 3
Base AC 4
Small Reaction Radius

Jungle Spider
Typical Levels 3-5
Typical Attributes
STR   70
AGI   100
Typical Skill Level 20
Speed Average
Base Damage 5
Less Likely to Frenzy

Jungle Spiderling
Typical Levels 1-3
Typical Attributes
STR   70
AGI   100
Typical Skill Level 10
Speed Average
Base Damage 3

Treant

Druid
Factions include Jagged Pine
Treefolk, Unkempt Druids
and Storm Reapers
Typical Levels 20-30
Might have mid-level spells
Typical Attributes

STR 150
STA 150
DEX 75
INT 80
AGI 50
WIS 125

Typical Skill Level 125
Speed Slow
Attack Speed Average
Base Damage 25-30
Base AC 60
Average Awareness Range
Average Reaction Radius
More Likely to Frenzy
Average Recuperation

Wasp

Warrior
Typical Levels 1
Might have low-level spells
Typical Attributes

STR 75
STA 75
DEX 75
INT 30
AGI 90
WIS 30

Typical Skill Level 5
Speed Average
Attack Speed Average
Base Damage 2
Average Awareness Range
Average Reaction Radius
More Likely to Frenzy
Average Recuperation

Giant Wasp

Warrior
Typical Levels 7-9
Might have low-level spells
Typical Attributes

STR 90

Typical Skill Level 40
Base Damage 9
Larger Reaction Radius

Werewolf

Warrior
Werewolf Faction
Typical Levels 18-32
Typical Attributes

STR 90
STA 110
DEX 90
INT 75
AGI 100
WIS 75

Typical Skill Level 110
Speed Faster
Attack Speed Average
Base Damage 20-30
Base AC 50-85
Average Awareness Range
Large Reaction Radius
Attacks all within range
Average Chance to Frenzy
Average Recuperation

Will-o-Wisp

Warrior
Typical Levels 9-11
Typical Attributes
> STR 30
> STA 75
> DEX 100
> INT 50
> AGI 100
> WIS 15

Typical Skill Level 50
Speed Average
Attack Speed Average
Base Damage 11
Can only be hit with Magic
Average Awareness Range
Average Reaction Radius
Won't Frenzy
Average Recuperation

Wolf

Warrior
Typical Attributes
> STR 75
> STA 90
> DEX 90
> INT 20
> AGI 90
> WIS 20

Typical Skill Level 20
Attack Speed Average
Average Awareness Range
Average Reaction Radius
Average Recuperation

Common Wolf

Typical Levels 1-4
Typical Skill Level 10
Speed Average
Base Damage 3
Least Likely to Frenzy

Gray Wolf

Typical Levels 3-10
Typical Skill Level 50
Speed Fast
Base Damage 11
Likely to Frenzy
Fast Recuperation

Black Wolf

Typical Levels 3-5
Typical Skill Level 20
Speed Fast
Base Damage 5
Likely to Frenzy

White Wolf

Typical Levels 2-4
Typical Skill Level 10
Speed Average
Base Damage 3
Least Likely to Frenzy

Scaled Wolf

Typical Levels 1-23
Typical Attributes
> STR 90

Typical Skill Level 110
Speed Average
Sees Invisible
Base Damage 23
Base AC 16-48
Shorter Awareness Range
Small Reaction Radius
Attacks all PCs within range
Less Likely to Frenzy

Yeti

Warrior
Typical Levels 7-25
Typical Attributes

STR 105
STA 105
DEX 80
INT 50
AGI 80
WIS 50

Typical Skill Level 40-115
Speed Average
Attack Speed Average
Base Damage 10-25
Base AC 10-50
Shorter Awareness Range
Small Reaction Radius
Attacks all PCs within range
Unlikely to Frenzy
Average Recuperation

Zombie

Warrior (also Necromancer, Cleric)
Typical Levels 6-10
Typical Attributes

STR 105
STA 125
DEX 75
INT 10
AGI 60
WIS 10

Typical Skill Level 40
Speed Slow
Attack Speed Average
Some see Invisible, some have rabies
Base Damage 10
Average Awareness Range
Average Reaction Radius
Attacks all within range
Likely to Frenzy
Average Recuperation

Two warriors pulled a third from the bloody water. They had had a fierce battle underwater and found this cave with an air pocket just as their water breathing spell had worn off. Merilan looked at her lifelong companion, Dereen, who was bleeding from several deep gashes across her chest. "Kasha, help Dereen."

Kasha cast a light spell and started to help Dereen. He touched her neck, took a deep breath and looked up at Merilan. "It's too late. She's gone." Merilan turned away. They were in a desperate situation. Without Dereen, it would be next to impossible to get out of here alive. The Veksar water creatures were too powerful.

A cold draft hit her wet body and Merilan shivered. A draft, she said to herself. She stood up and looked around. A small, dark opening led from the back of the cave. "Look," Merilan said as she pointed to the opening. "Dereen did not die in vain. The touch of her spirit as it was leaving her body alerted me to that passageway."

Spells

Spells

There are hundreds of spells in *EverQuest*. (Over a thousand, in fact.) We've detailed all spells up to level 24 — over 400 — and also listed those higher level spells that are more available in the game. The rest of the spells, like so much else in *EverQuest*, you're going to have to discover for yourself. Let's discussion the notation used, and then dive into the spells.

Casters is pretty obvious. This class of caster has access to the spell once he or she reaches the level in parentheses. For example, *Alacrity* is available at level 44 for Shamans and level 24 for Enchanters. **Mana Cost** and **Casting Skill** are also obvious.

Casting Time is how long it takes to cast the spell. **Casting Delay** is how long you must wait after casting this spell before you can cast another spell. It's nearly always about 2.5 seconds. The casting delay is listed only if it's shorter or longer than that. If a **Recasting Delay** is listed, you must wait that long until you can cast *this* spell again. *Alenia's Disenchanting Melody* has a recasting delay — it takes 3 seconds to cast, but then you may immediately cast any other spell. However, you must wait 12 seconds after casting it before you can cast it again.

Duration is how long the spell lasts. Sometimes this is based on the level of the caster. For example, if *Barbcoat* is cast by a level 20 Druid, it will last 60 minutes (3 x 20 = 60). All spell durations are listed in minutes and seconds.

Range is how far away the spell can be cast, in feet. **Radius of Effect** is how large an area the spell affects, also in feet. In some cases, such as *Alenia's Disenchanting Melody*, the spell affects creatures or even your own group, not a circle of land. In those cases, the spell affects all the people or creatures listed, who are in the radius of effect.

Target tells who you can cast the spell on. If it's "Anyone," you can also cast it on yourself.

Resistance Invoked lists the resistance a target uses to counter the spell. In some cases (especially with beneficial spells), there's no resistance listed, because the target usually *wants* the spell.

Effects are wide-ranged. We won't mention the obvious, but a few need further explanation.

Damage. A common measure of time in *EverQuest* is 6 seconds. For example, if a spell continues to inflict damage (DoT), the damage is usually inflicted every 6 seconds. Some spells inflict an immediate burst of damage, then continue inflicting more damage. For example, *Affliction* strikes with 36 HP of damage immediately, then deals another 6 HP every 6 seconds. If a spell lists only continuing damage (no immediate damage), it inflicts the listed amount immediately, and then again every 6 seconds.

> **Note:** To make everything fit nicely, a few spells are slightly out of alphabetical order. If you don't find a spell where you expect it, look just before and after that spell.

EverQuest: The Ruins of Kunark

Disease. Diseases come in a range of powers, as do their curatives. The lower the numerical rating for a disease, or a curative, the less power it has. Sending a 1 curative spell to heal a 7 disease isn't likely to produce a complete cure, but it might improve your patient's condition. If a spell lists multiple chances (like *Counteract Disease's* "2 chances, 4"), then the disease or curative has two chances to work its wonder. That means you can catch multiple diseases, and some spells might cure multiple diseases. If you only have one disease, a multiple curative has twice the opportunity to cure what ails you.

Poison spells (both inflictive and curative) work just like disease spells.

Magic dispelling spells, along with **Charm** and **Fear** spells, also work like disease spells, but the range of powers is expressed as *lowest* level, *low-level*, *mid-level*, *high-level* and *highest* level. Again, don't send a boy out to do a man's job — a low-level Dispel is unlikely to crack a high-level Charm.

Bonus HP are special HP that temporarily boost your total. If you're hit during the duration of a Bonus HP spell, you first reduce your Bonus HP before taking any actual damage.

Target's Reaction is what you see the spell's target do when hit with the spell. Anything given here in parentheses is what *you* feel or do. If you do the same thing as any other target, we don't list both reactions. And sometimes you can't tell if a spell has hit someone else, so the only reaction given here is in parentheses, to describe what you do.

Aanya's Animation

Casters	Enchanter (39)
Casting Skill	Conjuration

Aanya's Quickening

Casters	Enchanter (53)
Casting Skill	Alteration
Target's Reaction	Target experiences a quickening.

Abolish Disease

Casters	Shaman (49)
Casting Skill	Alteration

Abolish Poison

Casters	Cleric (49)
Casting Skill	Alteration

Abscond

Casters	Wizard (52)
Casting Skill	Alteration
Target's Reaction	Target fades away.

Abundant Drink

Casters	Cleric (29)
Casting Skill	Conjuration

Abundant Food

Casters	Cleric (34)
Casting Skill	Conjuration

Acumen

Casters	Shaman (56), Magician (10)
Mana Cost	75
Casting Skill	Divination
Casting Time (secs)	2
Casting Delay (secs)	2.25
Duration	3 + 3 x level minutes (max 63 m)
Range (feet)	100
Radius of Effect	60
Target	Anyone
Resistance Invoked	None
Effects	
See Invisible	
Ultravision	
Restores Fatigue points	10
Target's Reaction	(Your eyes tingle.)

Adorning Grace

Casters	Enchanter (49)
Casting Skill	Alteration
Target's Reaction	Target is adorned in an aura of radiant grace.

Aegis

Casters	Cleric (57)
Casting Skill	Abjuration
Target's Reaction	Target is shielded behind an aegis of pure faith. (An aegis of faith engulfs you.)

Aegis of Ro

Casters	Magician (60)
Casting Skill	Abjuration
Target's Reaction	Target is enveloped by the Aegis of Ro.

Affliction

Casters	Shaman (19)
Mana Cost	75
Casting Skill	Conjuration
Casting Time (secs)	2.75
Duration	2 minutes, 6 secs
Range (feet)	200
Target	Anyone
Resistance Invoked	Disease
Effects	
Disease	4
Initial Damage (HP)	36
Subsequent Damage (HP/6 seconds)	6

Alacrity

Casters	Shaman (44), Enchanter (24)
Mana Cost	115
Casting Skill	Alteration
Casting Time (secs)	4
Duration	1 minute + 12 seconds/level (max 11 m)
Range (feet)	100
Target	Anyone
Resistance Invoked	None
Effect	
Attack Speed boost	22% +1% / 2 levels (max 40% boost)
Target's Reaction	Target feels much faster.

Agility

Casters	Shaman (44)
Casting Skill	Alteration
Target's Reaction	Target looks agile.

Agilmente's Aria of Eagles

Casters	Bard (31)
Casting Skill	Wind Instruments
Target's Reaction	(The ayre lifts you from your feet.)

Alenia's Disenchanting Melody

Casters	Bard (22)
Mana Cost	0
Casting Skill	Stringed Instruments
Component	Lute
Casting Time (secs)	3
Casting Delay (secs)	none
Recasting Delay (secs)	12
Duration	Instantaneous
Range (feet)	0
Radius of Effect (feet)	25
Target	Your group
Resistance Invoked	None
Effect	
Cancel Magic	1 chance, low-level
Target's Reaction	(You feel a static pulse wash through you.)

Alliance

Casters	Enchanter (8)
Mana Cost	35
Casting Skill	Alteration
Casting Time (secs)	3.5
Recasting Delay (secs)	4.75
Duration	Instantaneous
Range (feet)	200
Target	Anyone
Resistance Invoked	Magic
Effect	
NPC Faction Standing Improved	+100
Target's Reaction	Target looks friendly. (You feel quite amicable.)

Alter Plane: Hate

Casters	Wizard (46)
Casting Skill	Alteration
Target's Reaction	Target creates a shimmering dimensional portal.

Alter Plane: Sky

Casters	Wizard (46)
Casting Skill	Alteration
Target's Reaction	Target creates a shimmering dimensional portal.

Allure

Casters	Enchanter (49)
Casting Skill	Alteration
Target's Reaction	(You have been charmed.)

Allure of Death

Casters	Necromancer (20)
Mana Cost	5
Casting Skill	Alteration
Casting Time (secs)	3
Recasting Delay (secs)	8.25
Duration	1 minute + 12 seconds/level
Range (feet)	0
Target	Yourself
Resistance Invoked	None
Effects	
Mana boost	4
Damage (HP)	8
Target's Reaction	Target looks sick. (You feel your health begin to drain.)

Allure of the Wild

Casters	Druid (44)
Casting Skill	Alteration
Target's Reaction	Target blinks.

Alluring Aura

Casters	Shaman (29)
Casting Skill	Alteration
Target's Reaction	Target is surrounded by an alluring aura. (You feel alluring.)

Anarchy

Casters	Enchanter (34)
Casting Skill	Evocation
Target's Reaction	Target's world dissolves into Anarchy.

Angstlich's Appalling Screech

Casters	Bard (26)
Casting Skill	Brass Instruments
Target's Reaction	Target flees in terror. (Your mind snaps in terror.)

Angstlich's Assonance

Casters	Bard (60)
Casting Skill	Brass Instruments
Target's Reaction	Target has been deafened.

Animate Dead

Casters	Shadow Knight (39), Necromancer (20)
Mana Cost	200
Casting Skill	Conjuration
Components	2 Bone Chips
Casting Time (secs)	10
Duration	Instantaneous
Range (feet)	0
Target	Yourself
Resistance Invoked	None
Effect	
Create Undead	Skeleton (Circle 6)
Target's Reaction	Skeleton rises from the dead.

Annul Magic

Casters	Cleric (53), Druid (55), Shaman (55), Necromancer (53), Wizard (53), Magician (53)
Casting Skill	Abjuration
Target's Reaction	Target feels annulled.

Anthem de Arms

Casters	Bard (10)
Mana Cost	0
Casting Skill	Singing
Casting Time (secs)	3
Casting Delay (secs)	none
Recasting Delay (secs)	12
Duration	12 seconds
Range (feet)	0
Radius of Effect (feet)	50
Target	Your group
Resistance Invoked	None
Effects	
Attack Speed boost	10
STR boost	5 + 1 / 2 levels
Target's Reaction	(A burst of strength surges through your body.)

Antidote

Casters	Cleric (58)
Casting Skill	Alteration

Arch Shielding

Casters	Necromancer (44), Wizard (44), Magician (44), Enchanter (44)
Casting Skill	Abjuration
Target's Reaction	(You feel armored.)

Armor of Faith

Casters	Cleric (39), Paladin (53)
Casting Skill	Abjuration
Target's Reaction	Target feels the favor of the gods upon them.

Asphyxiate

Casters	Enchanter (59)
Casting Skill	Alteration
Target's Reaction	Target begins to choke. (You feel a shortness of breath.)

Assiduous Vision

Casters	Shaman (39)
Casting Skill	Divination
Target's Reaction	Target eyes shimmer. (Your spirit drifts from your body.)

Asystole

Casters	Shadow Knight (60), Necromancer (44)
Casting Skill	Alteration
Target's Reaction	Target clutches their chest. (Your heart stops.)

Atol's Spectral Shackles

Casters	Wizard (51)
Casting Skill	Alteration
Target's Reaction	Target's feet are shackled to the ground. (Spectral shackles bind your feet to the ground.)

Atone

Casters	Cleric (34)
Casting Skill	Alteration
Target's Reaction	Target calms down. (You feel forgiveness in your mind.)

Augment

Casters	Enchanter (56)
Casting Skill	Alteration
Target's Reaction	Target's body pulses with energy.

Augment Death

Casters	Necromancer (39)
Casting Skill	Alteration
Target's Reaction	Target's eyes gleam with madness.

Augmentation

Casters	Enchanter (29)
Casting Skill	Alteration

Avalanche

Casters	Druid (39)
Casting Skill	Evocation
Target's Reaction	Target is entombed in ice.

Avatar

Casters	Shaman (60)
Casting Skill	Alteration
Target's Reaction	Target has been infused with the power of an Avatar. (Your body screams with the power of an Avatar.)

Bandoleer of Luclin

Casters	Magician (54)
Casting Skill	Conjuration

Bane of Nife

Casters	Shaman (56)
Casting Skill	Conjuration
Target's Reaction	Target's veins have been filled with deadly poison.

Banish Summoned

Casters	Cleric (56), Druid (44), Magician (49)
Casting Skill	Evocation
Target's Reaction	Target staggers.

Banish Undead

Casters	Cleric (44), Necromancer (49)
Casting Skill	Evocation
Target's Reaction	Target staggers.

Banishment

Casters	Druid (60), Magician (60)
Casting Skill	Evocation

Banishment of Shadows

Casters	Cleric (60), Necromancer (60)
Casting Skill	Evocation

Banshee Aura

Casters	Shadow Knight (54), Necromancer (16)
Mana Cost	60
Casting Skill	Abjuration
Component	Pearl (not consumed)
Casting Time (secs)	5
Recasting Delay (secs)	11.75
Duration	6 seconds/level (max 3 m)
Range (feet)	0
Target	Yourself
Resistance Invoked	Cold
Effect	
Reflect Damage (HP)	8
Target's Reaction	Target is surrounded by a shrieking aura. (A shrieking aura surrounds you.)

Barbcoat

Casters	Ranger (30), Druid (19)
Mana Cost	50
Casting Skill	Abjuration
Casting Time (secs)	2
Duration	3 x level minutes
Range (feet)	0
Target	Yourself
Resistance Invoked	Magic
Effects	
AC boost	18 +1/level (max 42)
Reflect Damage (HP)	2
Target's Reaction	Target's skin sprouts barbs. (Barbs spring from your skin.)

Barrier of Combustion

Casters	Magician (39)
Casting Skill	Abjuration
Target's Reaction	Target is enveloped in flame.

Bedlam

Casters	Enchanter (58)
Casting Skill	Alteration
Target's Reaction	Target's eyes gleam with bedlam.

Befriend Animal

Casters	Druid (14), Shaman (29)
Mana Cost	70
Casting Skill	Alteration
Casting Time (secs)	4
Recasting Delay (secs)	10.25
Duration	1 minute + 18 seconds/level
Range (feet)	200
Target	Animal
Resistance Invoked	Magic
Effect	
Charm	Lowest-level
Target's Reaction	Target blinks.

Beguile

Casters	Enchanter (24)
Mana Cost	120
Casting Skill	Alteration
Casting Time (secs)	3.5
Duration	1 minute + 18 seconds/level
Range (feet)	200
Target	Anyone
Resistance Invoked	Magic
Effect	
Charm	Mid-level
Target's Reaction	(You have been charmed.)

Beguile Animals

Casters	Druid (34)
Casting Skill	Alteration
Target's Reaction	Target blinks.

Beguile Plants

Casters	Druid (29)
Casting Skill	Alteration
Target's Reaction	Target blinks.

Beguile Undead

Casters	Necromancer (34)
Casting Skill	Alteration
Target's Reaction	Target moans.

Benevolence

Casters	Enchanter (20)
Mana Cost	50
Casting Skill	Alteration
Casting Time (secs)	4
Recasting Delay (secs)	5.75
Duration	Instantaneous
Range (feet)	200
Target	Anyone
Resistance Invoked	Magic
Effect	
NPC Faction Standing Improved	+200
Target's Reaction	Target looks friendly. (You feel quite amicable.)

Berserker Spirit

Casters	Enchanter (49)
Casting Skill	Alteration
Target's Reaction	Target lets lose a berserk yell. (Your spirit screams with berserker strength.)

Berserker Strength

Casters	Enchanter (20)
Mana Cost	45
Casting Skill	Alteration
Casting Time (secs)	3
Recasting Delay (secs)	10.25
Duration	6 seconds/level (max 3 m)
Range (feet)	100
Target	Anyone
Resistance Invoked	None
Effects	
STR boost	10 + 1 / 2 levels (max 25)
Bonus HP	20 + 1 / 2 levels
AGI loss	1 + 1 / 2 levels (max 15)

Bladecoat

Casters	Druid (56)
Casting Skill	Abjuration
Target's Reaction	Target's skin sprouts blades. (Blades spring from your skin.)

Blanket of Forgetfulness

Casters	Enchanter (49)
Casting Skill	Alteration
Target's Reaction	Target blinks a few times. (You feel your mind fog.)

Bind Affinity

Casters	Cleric (14), Druid (14), Shaman (14), Necromancer (12), Wizard (12), Magician (12), Enchanter (12)
Mana Cost	100
Casting Skill	Alteration
Casting Time (secs)	6
Recasting Delay (secs)	14.25
Duration	Instantaneous
Range (feet)	100
Target	Anyone
Resistance Invoked	None
Effect	
Bind Affinity	Caster classes can be bound anywhere; others only in cities.
Target's Reaction	Target is bound to the area.

Bind Sight

Casters	Ranger (22), Wizard (16), Enchanter (8)
Mana Cost	15
Casting Skill	Divination
Casting Time (secs)	4
Recasting Delay (secs)	12.25
Duration	1 minute + 12 seconds/level
Range (feet)	10000
Target	Anyone
Resistance Invoked	None
Effects	
Caster sees Target's View	
Fatigues Caster	2 points
Target's Reaction	Target eyes gleam and then go dark. (You bind your sight.)

Blaze

Casters	Magician (34)
Casting Skill	Evocation
Target's Reaction	Target's skin ignites.

Blinding Luminance

Casters	Cleric (34), Shaman (39)
Casting Skill	Divination
Target's Reaction	Target is blinded by a flash of light.

Blizzard

Casters	Druid (54)
Casting Skill	Evocation
Target's Reaction	Target is caught within a raging blizzard.

Blizzard Blast

Casters	Shaman (44)
Casting Skill	Evocation
Target's Reaction	Target staggers as spirits of frost slam against them.

Boil Blood

Casters	Shadow Knight (53), Necromancer (29)
Casting Skill	Alteration
Target's Reaction	Target's blood boils.

Bolt of Flame

Casters	Magician (20)
Mana Cost	105
Casting Skill	Evocation
Casting Time (secs)	3.25
Duration	Instantaneous
Range (feet)	300
Target	Anyone
Resistance Invoked	Fire
Effect	
Damage (HP)	106 +2/level (max 156)
Target's Reaction	Target is bathed in fire. (A stream of fire washes over you.)

Boltran's Agacerie

Casters	Enchanter (53)
Casting Skill	Alteration
Target's Reaction	(You have been charmed.)

Boltran's Animation

Casters	Enchanter (34)
Casting Skill	Conjuration

Bond of Death

Casters	Necromancer (49)
Casting Skill	Alteration
Target's Reaction	Target staggers. (You feel you lifeforce drain away.)

Bonds of Force

Casters	Wizard (29)
Casting Skill	Alteration
Target's Reaction	Target's feet are bound by strands of force. (Bonds of force stick your feet to the ground.)

Bonds of Tunare

Casters	Druid (57)
Casting Skill	Alteration
Target's Reaction	Target's feet are wrapped in dark vines. (Dark vines drag your feet into the ground.)

Bone Walk

Casters	Shadow Knight (15), Necromancer (8)
Mana Cost	80
Casting Skill	Conjuration
Components	2 Bone Chips
Casting Time (secs)	7
Recasting Delay (secs)	11.75
Duration	Instantaneous
Range (feet)	0
Target	Yourself
Resistance Invoked	None
Effect	
Create Undead	Skeleton (Circle 3)
Target's Reaction	Skeleton rises from the dead.

Boon of Immolation

Casters	Magician (53)
Casting Skill	Abjuration
Target's Reaction	Target is enveloped in flame. (You are enveloped in lava.)

Boon of the Clear Mind

Casters	Enchanter (52)
Casting Skill	Alteration
Target's Reaction	Target looks tranquil. (A cool breeze slips through your mind.)

Bravery

Casters	Cleric (24)
Mana Cost	70
Casting Skill	Abjuration
Casting Time (secs)	2.75
Duration	45 minutes
Range (feet)	100
Target	Anyone
Resistance Invoked	None
Effects	
AC boost	20 + 1 / 2 levels (max 35)
Bonus HP	90 +1/level
Target's Reaction	Target looks brave. (You feel very brave.)

Bramblecoat

Casters	Ranger (49), Druid (29)
Casting Skill	Abjuration
Target's Reaction	Target's skin sprouts brambles. (Brambles spring from your skin.)

Breath of Karana

Casters	Druid (56)
Casting Skill	Conjuration
Target's Reaction	Target is slammed by an intense gust of wind.

Breath of Ro

Casters	Druid (52)
Casting Skill	Evocation
Target's Reaction	Target is immolated in blazing flames.

Breath of the Dead

Casters	Shadow Knight (49), Necromancer (24)
Mana Cost	45
Casting Skill	Alteration
Component	Fish Scales
Casting Time (secs)	2.5
Duration	27 minutes
Range (feet)	0
Target	Yourself
Resistance Invoked	None
Effect	
Magic Breathing	
Target's Reaction	Target stops breathing. (You feel your heart stop beating.)

Breeze

Casters	Enchanter (16)
Mana Cost	35
Casting Skill	Alteration
Casting Time (secs)	2.5
Duration	27 minutes
Range (feet)	200
Target	Anyone
Resistance Invoked	None
Effect	
Mana boost/6 secs	2
Target's Reaction	Target looks slightly tranquil. (A light breeze slips through your mind.)

Brilliance

Casters	Enchanter (44)
Casting Skill	Alteration
Target's Reaction	Target gains a flash of insight. (Your mind clears.)

Bristlebane's Bundle

Casters	Magician (52)
Casting Skill	Conjuration

Brusco's Boastful Bellow

Casters	Bard (12)
Mana Cost	0
Casting Skill	Singing
Casting Time (secs)	3
Casting Delay (secs)	30
Recasting Delay (secs)	60
Duration	Instantaneous
Range (feet)	100
Target	Anyone
Resistance Invoked	Magic
Effects	
Damage (HP)	1 + 1 / 2 levels
Knockback	1 foot
Target's Reaction	Target reels in pain. (You reel in pain as every bone in your body goes numb.)

Bulwark of Faith

Casters	Cleric (57)
Casting Skill	Abjuration
Target's Reaction	Target is engulfed within a bulwark of pure faith. (A bulwark of faith engulfs you.)

Burn

Casters	Magician (4)
Mana Cost	15
Casting Skill	Evocation
Casting Time (secs)	1.75
Duration	Instantaneous
Range (feet)	200
Target	Anyone
Resistance Invoked	Fire
Effect	
Damage (HP)	9 + 1 / 2 levels (max 14)
Target's Reaction	Target's skin blisters and burns.

Burnout

Casters	Magician (12)
Mana Cost	35
Casting Skill	Alteration
Casting Time (secs)	5
Recasting Delay (secs)	12.5
Duration	15 minutes
Range (feet)	100
Target	Your pet
Resistance Invoked	None
Effects	
AC boost	25
STR boost	15
Attack Speed boost	9% +1% / 3 levels (max 15%)
Target's Reaction	Target goes berserk.

Burnout II

Casters	Magician (29)
Casting Skill	Alteration
Target's Reaction	Target goes berserk.

Burnout III

Casters	Magician (49)
Casting Skill	Alteration
Target's Reaction	Target goes berserk.
Effect	
Damage (HP)	3 + 1 / 2 levels (max 5)
Target's Reaction	Target singes as the Burst of Flame hits them.

Burst of Strength

Casters	Shaman (14)
Mana Cost	15
Casting Skill	Abjuration
Casting Time (secs)	0.5
Recasting Delay (secs)	14.25
Duration	18 seconds
Range (feet)	100
Target	Anyone
Resistance Invoked	None
Effects	
Restores Fatigue	
Point	1
STR boost	20
AC boost	25
DEX boost	20
Target's Reaction	Target looks stronger. (Your muscles scream with strength.)

Burst of Fire

Casters	Ranger (15), Druid (5)
Mana Cost	15
Casting Skill	Evocation
Casting Time (secs)	1.75
Duration	Instantaneous
Range (feet)	200
Target	Anyone
Resistance Invoked	Fire
Effect	
Damage (HP)	10 + 1 / 2 levels (max 15)
Target's Reaction	Target singes as the Burst of Fire hits them.

Burst of Flame

Casters	Druid (1), Shaman (1), Magician (1)
Mana Cost	7
Casting Skill	Evocation
Casting Time (secs)	1.5
Duration	Instantaneous
Range (feet)	200
Target	Anyone
Resistance Invoked	Fire

Cackling Bones

Casters	Shadow Knight (58), Necromancer (44)
Casting Skill	Conjuration

Cadeau of Flame

Casters	Magician (56)
Casting Skill	Abjuration
Target's Reaction	Target is enveloped in a cadeau of flame.

Cajole Undead

Casters	Necromancer (49)
Casting Skill	Alteration
Target's Reaction	Target moans.

Cajoling Whispers

Casters	Enchanter (39)
Casting Skill	Alteration
Target's Reaction	(You have been charmed.)

Call of Bones

Casters	Necromancer (34)
Casting Skill	Alteration
Target's Reaction	Target's skin peels away. (You feel the skin peel away from your bones.)

Call of Karana

Casters	Druid (52)
Casting Skill	Alteration
Target's Reaction	Target blinks.

Call of the Hero

Casters	Magician (55)
Casting Skill	Conjuration
Target's Reaction	Target steps into a mystic portal.

Calm

Casters	Cleric (19), Paladin (49), Enchanter (20)
Mana Cost	50
Casting Skill	Alteration
Casting Time (secs)	2.5
Recasting Delay (secs)	7.25
Duration	3 minutes
Range (feet)	200
Target	Anyone
Resistance Invoked	Magic
Effects	
Target's Reaction Range	5 feet
Target's Help Radius	5 feet
Target much less likely to attack	
Target's Reaction	Target looks less aggressive. (You feel your aggression subside.)

Calm Animal

Casters	Ranger (39), Druid (19)
Mana Cost	45
Casting Skill	Alteration
Casting Time (secs)	2.5
Recasting Delay (secs)	7.25
Duration	3 minutes
Range (feet)	200
Target	Animal
Resistance Invoked	Magic
Effects	
Target's Reaction Range	5 feet
Target's Help Radius	10 feet
Target much less likely to attack	
Target's Reaction	Target looks less aggressive. (You feel your aggression subside.)

Camouflage

Casters	Ranger (15), Druid (5)
Mana Cost	15
Casting Skill	Divination
Outdoors only	
Casting Time (secs)	5
Duration	3 x level minutes (max 20 m)
Range (feet)	100
Target	Anyone
Resistance Invoked	None
Effect	
Invisibility	
Target's Reaction	Target fades away.

Cancel Magic

Casters	Cleric (14), Paladin (39), Ranger (30), Druid (19), Shaman (19), Shadow Knight (39), Necromancer (16), Wizard (12), Magician (12), Enchanter (8)
Mana Cost	30
Casting Skill	Abjuration
Casting Time (secs)	3.5
Recasting Delay (secs)	7.25
Duration	Instantaneous
Range (feet)	200
Target	Anyone
Resistance Invoked	None
Effect	
Cancel Magic	1 chance, low-level
Target's Reaction	Target feels a bit dispelled.

Cannibalize

Casters	Shaman (24)
Mana Cost	0
Casting Skill	Alteration
Casting Time (secs)	1.25
Duration	Instantaneous
Range (feet)	0
Target	Yourself
Resistance Invoked	None
Effects	
Damage (HP)	50
Mana boost	16 + 1 / 6 levels
Target's Reaction	Target winces. (Your body aches as your mind clears.)

Cannibalize II

Casters	Shaman (39)
Casting Skill	Alteration
Target's Reaction	Target winces. (Your body aches as your mind clears.)

Cannibalize III

Casters	Shaman (54)
Casting Skill	Alteration
Target's Reaction	Target winces. (Your body aches as your mind clears.)

Cantana of Replenishment

Casters	Bard (55)
Casting Skill	Stringed Instruments
Target's Reaction	(You feel replenished.)

Careless Lightning

Casters	Ranger (39), Druid (19)
Mana Cost	70
Casting Skill	Evocation
Casting Time (secs)	2.75
Duration	Instantaneous
Range (feet)	200
Target	Anyone
Resistance Invoked	Magic
Effect	
Damage (HP)	75 +1/level (max 99)
Target's Reaction	Target has been struck by lightning. (Lightning surges through your body.)

Cascade of Hail

Casters	Druid (14)
Mana Cost	62
Casting Skill	Evocation
Casting Time (secs)	2.75
Recasting Delay (secs)	14.5
Duration	Instantaneous
Impact Duration (secs)	7.5
Range (feet)	150
Radius of Effect (feet)	20
Target	Area
Resistance Invoked	Cold
Effect	
Damage (HP)	27
Target's Reaction	Target is pelted by hailstones.

Cascading Darkness

Casters	Shadow Knight (59), Necromancer (49)
Casting Skill	Conjuration
Target's Reaction	Target is engulfed in darkness.

Cassindra's Chorus of Clarity

Casters	Bard (32)
Casting Skill	Singing
Target's Reaction	(Your mind clears.)

Cassindra's Elegy

Casters	Bard (44)
Casting Skill	Singing
Target's Reaction	(Your mind sharpens.)

Cassindra's Insipid Ditty

Casters	Bard (57)
Casting Skill	Stringed Instruments
Target's Reaction	Target winces in an asinine way. (You feel asinine.)

Cast Force

Casters	Wizard (24)
Mana Cost	123
Casting Skill	Evocation
Casting Time (secs)	3.15
Recasting Delay (secs)	8.5
Duration	Instantaneous
Range (feet)	0
Radius of Effect (feet)	20
Target	Area (but not your group)
Resistance Invoked	Magic
Effect	
Damage (HP)	42 +2/level (max 101)
Target's Reaction	Target is covered in raging energy. (Energy race across your body.)

Cast Sight

Casters	Enchanter (34)
Casting Skill	Divination
Target's Reaction	Target eyes gleam and then go dark. (You cast your sight.)

Cavorting Bones

Casters	Necromancer (1)
Mana Cost	15
Casting Skill	Conjuration
Component	Bone Chips
Casting Time (secs)	5
Recasting Delay (secs)	6.25
Duration	Instantaneous
Range (feet)	0
Target	Yourself
Resistance Invoked	None
Effect	
Create Undead	Skeleton (Circle 1)
Target's Reaction	Skeleton rises from the dead.

Cazic Gate

Casters	Wizard (24)
Mana Cost	150
Casting Skill	Alteration
Casting Time (secs)	7
Recasting Delay (secs)	12.25
Duration	Instantaneous
Range (feet)	0
Target	Yourself
Resistance Invoked	None
Effect	
Teleports you to	Cazic Thule
Target's Reaction	Target fades away.

Cazic Portal

Casters	Wizard (34)
Casting Skill	Alteration
Target's Reaction	Target creates a shimmering portal.

Celerity

Casters	Shaman (56), Enchanter (39)
Casting Skill	Alteration
Target's Reaction	Target feels much faster.

Celestial Elixir

Casters	Cleric (59)
Casting Skill	Alteration
Target's Reaction	Target's body is covered with a soft glow. (Celestial Elixir pumps through your body.)

Center

Casters	Cleric (9), Paladin (22)
Mana Cost	40
Casting Skill	Abjuration
Casting Time (secs)	4
Recasting Delay (secs)	10.5
Duration	27 minutes
Range (feet)	100
Target	Anyone
Resistance Invoked	None
Effects	
AC boost	13 + 1 / 2 levels (max 20)
Bonus HP	35 +1/level
Target's Reaction	Target is surrounded by a divine aura. (You feel magnanimous of spirit.)

Cessation of Cor

Casters	Necromancer (56)
Casting Skill	Alteration
Target's Reaction	Target blood stills within their veins. (The blood within your veins stops.)

Chant of Battle

Casters	Bard (1)
Mana Cost	0
Casting Skill	Percussion Instruments
Casting Time (secs)	3
Casting Delay (secs)	none
Recasting Delay (sccs)	12
Duration	12 seconds
Range (feet)	0
Radius of Effect (feet)	50
Target	Your group
Resistance Invoked	None
Effects	
AC boost	5 + 1 / 4 levels
STR boost	5 + 1 / 4 levels
DEX boost	5 + 1 / 4 levels
Target's Reaction	(You feel your pulse quicken.)

Char

Casters	Magician (52)
Casting Skill	Evocation
Target's Reaction	Target's skin ignites and chars. (You feel your skin ignite and char.)

Chaos Flux

Casters	Enchanter (24)
Mana Cost	100
Casting Skill	Evocation
Casting Time (secs)	3.5
Recasting Delay (secs)	10.5
Duration	Instantaneous
Range (feet)	200
Target	Anyone
Resistance Invoked	Magic
Effects	
Damage (HP)	95 +2/level (max 150)
Stun	Can disrupt spellcasting
Knockback	1 foot
Target's Reaction	Target is surrounded by fluxing strands of chaos. (Your world goes mad as chaos fluxes through you.)

Chaotic Feedback

Casters	Enchanter (8)
Mana Cost	45
Casting Skill	Evocation
Casting Time (secs)	2.1
Recasting Delay (secs)	10.5
Duration	Instantaneous
Range (feet)	200
Target	Anyone
Resistance Invoked	Magic
Effects	
Damage (HP)	35 +1/level (max 48)
Stun	Can disrupt spellcasting
Knockback	1/2 foot
Target's Reaction	Target's brain begins to smolder.

Charm

Casters	Enchanter (12)
Mana Cost	60
Casting Skill	Alteration
Casting Time (secs)	2.4
Duration	1 minute + 18 seconds/level
Range (feet)	200
Target	Anyone
Resistance Invoked	Magic
Effect	
Charm	Lowest-level
Target's Reaction	(You have been charmed.)

Charm Animals

Casters	Druid (24)
Mana Cost	120
Casting Skill	Alteration
Casting Time (secs)	5
Recasting Delay (secs)	12.25
Duration	1 minute + 18 seconds/level
Range (feet)	200
Target	Animal
Resistance Invoked	Magic
Effect	
Charm	Mid-level
Target's Reaction	Target blinks.

Charisma

Casters	Shaman (49)
Casting Skill	Alteration
Target's Reaction	Target look charismatic.

Chase the Moon

Casters	Enchanter (16)
Mana Cost	70
Casting Skill	Alteration
Casting Time (secs)	3.5
Duration	36 secs
Range (feet)	200
Target	Anyone
Resistance Invoked	Magic
Effect	
Fear	Low-level
Target's Reaction	Target begins to run.

Chill Bones

Casters	Necromancer (55)
Casting Skill	Evocation
Target's Reaction	Target's skin frosts away. (You feel your skin frost from your body.)

Chill Sight

Casters	Ranger (56), Wizard (39)
Casting Skill	Divination
Target's Reaction	Target's eyes glow violet. (You eyes tingle.)

Chloroplast

Casters	Druid (44), Shaman (39)
Casting Skill	Alteration
Target's Reaction	Target begins to regenerate.

Choke

Casters	Enchanter (12)
Mana Cost	50
Casting Skill	Alteration
Casting Time (secs)	2.25
Duration	30 secs
Range (feet)	200
Target	Anyone
Resistance Invoked	Magic
Effects	
Immediate Damage (HP)	24 + 1 / 2 levels (max 32)
Subsequent Damage (HP/6 secs)	12
STR loss	1 + 1 / 2 levels (max 10)
AGI loss	1 + 1 / 2 levels (max 10)
Target's Reaction	Target begins to choke. (You feel a shortness of breath.)

Chords of Dissonance

Casters	Bard (2)
Mana Cost	0
Casting Skill	Stringed Instruments
Casting Time (secs)	3
Casting Delay (secs)	none
Recasting Delay (secs)	12
Duration	12 seconds
Range (feet)	0
Radius of Effect (feet)	30
Target	Area (but not your group)
Resistance Invoked	Magic
Effect	
Damage (HP/6 secs)	2 + 1 / 4 levels
Target's Reaction	Target winces. (Jagged notes tear through your body.)

Circle of Butcher

Casters	Druid (29)
Casting Skill	Alteration
Target's Reaction	Target creates a mystic portal.

Circle of Commons

Casters	Druid (29)
Casting Skill	Alteration
Target's Reaction	Target creates a mystic portal.

Circle of Feerrott

Casters	Druid (34)
Casting Skill	Alteration
Target's Reaction	Target creates a mystic portal.

Circle of Force

Casters	Wizard (34)
Casting Skill	Evocation
Target's Reaction	Target is immolated in raging energy.

Circle of Karana

Casters	Druid (29)
Casting Skill	Alteration
Target's Reaction	Target creates a mystic portal.

Circle of Lavastorm

Casters	Druid (34)
Casting Skill	Alteration
Target's Reaction	Target creates a mystic portal.

Circle of Misty

Casters	Druid (39)
Casting Skill	Alteration
Target's Reaction	Target creates a mystic portal.

Circle of Ro

Casters	Druid (34)
Casting Skill	Alteration
Target's Reaction	Target creates a mystic portal.

Circle of Steamfont

Casters	Druid (34)
Casting Skill	Alteration
Target's Reaction	Target creates a mystic portal.

Circle of Summer

Casters	Druid (52)
Casting Skill	Abjuration
Target's Reaction	Target is surrounded by a summer haze.

Circle of the Combines

Casters	Druid (34)
Casting Skill	Alteration
Target's Reaction	Target creates a mystic portal.

Circle of Toxxulia

Casters	Druid (29)
Casting Skill	Alteration
Target's Reaction	Target creates a mystic portal.

Circle of Winter

Casters	Druid (51)
Casting Skill	Abjuration
Target's Reaction	Target is surrounded by a winter haze.

Cinda's Charismatic Carillon

Casters	Bard (11)
Mana Cost	0
Casting Skill	Wind Instruments
Casting Time (secs)	3
Casting Delay (secs)	none
Recasting Delay (secs)	12
Duration	12 seconds
Range (feet)	100
Target	Anyone
Resistance Invoked	Magic
Effect	
NPC Faction Standing Improvement	10 +10/level
Target's Reaction	(You feel the enchantment fade.)

Cinder Bolt

Casters	Magician (34)
Casting Skill	Evocation
Target's Reaction	Target is bathed in fire. (A stream of fire washes over you.)

Clarify Mana

Casters	Enchanter (29)
Casting Skill	Alteration

Clinging Darkness

Casters	Shadow Knight (15), Necromancer (4)
Mana Cost	20
Casting Skill	Alteration
Casting Time (secs)	1.75
Recasting Delay (secs)	6.5
Duration	36 secs
Range (feet)	200
Target	Anyone
Resistance Invoked	Magic
Effects	
Damage (HP/6 secs)	5
Movement rate loss	20% +1% / level (max 30%)
Target's Reaction	Target is surrounded by darkness. (You are in the grip of darkness.)

Clarity

Casters	Enchanter (29)
Casting Skill	Alteration
Target's Reaction	Target looks tranquil. (A cool breeze slips through your mind.)

Clarity II

Casters	Enchanter (54)
Casting Skill	Alteration
Target's Reaction	Target looks very tranquil. (A soft breeze slips through your mind.)

Cloud

Casters	Enchanter (20)
Mana Cost	40
Casting Skill	Abjuration
Casting Time (secs)	4
Duration	36 minutes
Range (feet)	100
Target	Anyone
Resistance Invoked	None
Effect	
AC boost	10 +1/level (max 35)
Target's Reaction	Target's image clouds.

Coldlight

Casters	Necromancer (1)
Mana Cost	15
Casting Skill	Conjuration
Casting Time (secs)	2
Recasting Delay (secs)	8.25
Duration	Instantaneous
Range (feet)	0
Target	Yourself
Resistance Invoked	None
Effect	
Create Item	Coldlight
Target's Reaction	Target's hands pulse blue. (A globe of Cold Light forms in your hand.)

Collaboration

Casters	Enchanter (51)
Casting Skill	Alteration
Target's Reaction	Target looks friendly. (You feel quite amicable.)

Color Flux

Casters	Enchanter (4)
Mana Cost	20
Casting Skill	Divination
Casting Time (secs)	1
Recasting Delay (secs)	14.25
Duration	Instantaneous
Range (feet)	0
Radius of Effect (feet)	20
Target	Area (but not your group)
Resistance Invoked	Magic
Effects	
Stun	4 seconds
Knockback	1/2 foot
Target's Reaction	Target is stunned by scintillating colors. (Scintillating colors pound through your brain.)

Color Shift

Casters	Enchanter (20)
Mana Cost	40
Casting Skill	Divination
Casting Time (secs)	1.5
Recasting Delay (secs)	14.25
Duration	Instantaneous
Range (feet)	0
Radius of Effect (feet)	25
Target	Area (but not your group)
Resistance Invoked	Magic
Effects	
Stun	6 seconds
Knockback	1/2 foot
Target's Reaction	Target is stunned by scintillating colors. (Scintillating colors pound through your brain.)

Color Skew

Casters	Enchanter (44)
Casting Skill	Divination
Target's Reaction	Target is stunned by scintillating colors. (Scintillating colors pound through your brain.)

Color Slant

Casters	Enchanter (52)
Casting Skill	Divination
Target's Reaction	Target is throttled by scintillating colors. (Scintillating colors throttle your brain.)

Column of Fire

Casters	Magician (12)
Mana Cost	65
Casting Skill	Evocation
Casting Time (secs)	3.25
Recasting Delay (secs)	8.5
Duration	Instantaneous
Range (feet)	200
Radius of Effect (feet)	10
Target	Area
Resistance Invoked	Fire
Effect	
Damage (HP)	37 +1/level (max 51)
Target's Reaction	Target is immolated in flame.

Column of Frost

Casters	Wizard (8)
Mana Cost	39
Casting Skill	Evocation
Casting Time (secs)	2.7
Recasting Delay (secs)	8.5
Duration	Instantaneous
Range (feet)	200
Radius of Effect (feet)	15
Target	Area
Resistance Invoked	Cold
Effect	
Damage (HP)	19 +1/level (max 31)
Target's Reaction	Target is encased in frost.

Column of Lightning

Casters	Wizard (24)
Mana Cost	130
Casting Skill	Evocation
Casting Time (secs)	3.6
Recasting Delay (secs)	8.5
Duration	Instantaneous
Range (feet)	200
Radius of Effect (feet)	15
Target	Area
Resistance Invoked	Fire
Effect	
Damage (HP)	80 +2/level (max 136)
Target's Reaction	Target is engulfed in lightning.

Combine Portal

Casters	Wizard (34)
Casting Skill	Alteration
Target's Reaction	Target creates a shimmering portal.

Combust

Casters	Ranger (52), Druid (29)
Casting Skill	Evocation
Target's Reaction	Target's skin combusts.

Common Gate

Casters	Wizard (24)
Mana Cost	150
Casting Skill	Alteration
Casting Time (secs)	7
Recasting Delay (secs)	12.25
Duration	Instantaneous
Range (feet)	0
Target	Yourself
Resistance Invoked	None
Effect	
Teleports you to	West Commonlands
Target's Reaction	Target fades away.

Common Portal

Casters	Wizard (39)
Casting Skill	Alteration
Target's Reaction	Target creates a shimmering portal.

Companion Spirit

Casters	Shaman (34)
Casting Skill	Conjuration
Target's Reaction	Target summons a companion spirit.

Complete Healing

Casters	Cleric (39)
Casting Skill	Alteration

Concussion

Casters	Wizard (39)
Casting Skill	Alteration
Target's Reaction	Target staggers from a blow to the head.

Conflagration

Casters	Wizard (44)
Casting Skill	Evocation
Target's Reaction	Target combusts. (You feel your skin combust.)

Conjuration: Air

Casters	Magician (44)
Casting Skill	Conjuration

Conjuration: Earth

Casters	Magician (44)
Casting Skill	Conjuration

Conjuration: Fire

Casters	Magician (44)
Casting Skill	Conjuration

Conjuration: Water

Casters	Magician (44)
Casting Skill	Conjuration

Conjure Corpse

Casters	Necromancer (57)
Casting Skill	Conjuration

Convergence

Casters	Necromancer (53)
Casting Skill	Alteration

Convoke Shadow

Casters	Shadow Knight (22), Necromancer (12)
Mana Cost	120
Casting Skill	Conjuration
Components	2 Bone Chips
Casting Time (secs)	8
Recasting Delay (secs)	13.25
Duration	Instantaneous
Range (feet)	0
Target	Yourself
Resistance Invoked	None
Effect	
Create Undead	Skeleton (Circle 4)

Cornucopia

Casters	Magician (24)
Mana Cost	25
Casting Skill	Conjuration
Casting Time (secs)	4
Duration	Instantaneous
Range (feet)	0
Target	Yourself
Resistance Invoked	None
Effect	
Create Item	1 black bread + 1 more loaf / 6 levels

Counteract Disease

Casters	Cleric (29), Paladin (56), Druid (29), Shaman (24), Necromancer (39)
Mana Cost	50
Casting Skill	Alteration
Casting Time (secs)	4
Duration	Instantaneous
Range (feet)	100
Target	Anyone
Resistance Invoked	None
Effect	
Disease Reduction	2 chances, 4

Counteract Poison

Casters	Cleric (24), Paladin (39), Druid (29), Shaman (29)
Mana Cost	50
Casting Skill	Alteration
Casting Time (secs)	4
Duration	Instantaneous
Range (feet)	100
Target	Anyone
Resistance Invoked	None
Effect	
Poison Reduction	2 chances, 4

Courage

Casters	Cleric (1), Paladin (9)
Mana Cost	12
Casting Skill	Abjuration
Casting Time (secs)	2
Recasting Delay (secs)	5.5
Duration	3 + 3 x level minutes (max 27 m)
Range (feet)	100
Target	Anyone
Resistance Invoked	None
Effects	
AC boost	10 + 1 / 2 levels (max 15)
Bonus HP	10 +1/level (max 20)
Target's Reaction	Target looks courageous. (You feel a rush of courage.)

Covetous Subversion

Casters	Necromancer (44)
Casting Skill	Alteration
Target's Reaction	Target twitches. (A foreign surge of mana refreshes your mind.)

Creeping Crud

Casters	Druid (24)
Mana Cost	100
Casting Skill	Conjuration
Casting Time (secs)	2.45
Duration	1 minute
Range (feet)	250
Target	Anyone
Resistance Invoked	Magic
Effect	
Damage (HP/6 secs)	21
Target's Reaction	Target is engulfed in a swarm. (You feel the pain of a thousand stings.)

Creeping Vision

Casters	Shaman (24)
Mana Cost	20
Casting Skill	Divination
Casting Time (secs)	2.5
Recasting Delay (secs)	32.25
Duration	1 minute
Range (feet)	0
Target	Yourself
Resistance Invoked	None
Effect	
Telescope	See farther and farther until the spell expires.
Target's Reaction	Target eyes shimmer and gleam. (Your eyes begin to focus.)

Cripple

Casters	Shaman (53), Enchanter (53)
Casting Skill	Alteration
Target's Reaction	Target has been crippled.

Crission's Pixie Strike

Casters	Bard (28)
Casting Skill	Wind Instruments
Target's Reaction	Target's eyes glaze over. (You send forth music.)

Crystallize Mana

Casters	Enchanter (20)
Mana Cost	400
Casting Skill	Alteration
Components	Peridot, Emerald, Poison Vial
Casting Time (secs)	6
Duration	Instantaneous
Range (feet)	0
Target	Yourself
Resistance Invoked	None
Effect	
Create Item	1 vial of Cloudy Mana + 1 more / level

Cure Blindness

Casters	Cleric (5), Shaman (9)
Mana Cost	20
Casting Skill	Alteration
Casting Time (secs)	2
Recasting Delay (secs)	5.25
Duration	Instantaneous
Range (feet)	100
Target	Anyone
Resistance Invoked	None
Effect	
Blindness healed	
Target's Reaction	Target's eyes sparkle.

Cure Disease

Casters	Cleric (5), Paladin (15), Druid (5), Shaman (1), Necromancer (16)
Mana Cost	20
Casting Skill	Alteration
Casting Time (secs)	2
Recasting Delay (secs)	5.25
Duration	Instantaneous
Range (feet)	100
Target	Anyone
Resistance Invoked	None
Effect	
Disease Reduction	1

Curse of the Simple Mind

Casters	Enchanter (29)
Casting Skill	Alteration
Target's Reaction	Target looks stupid.

Cure Poison

Casters	Cleric (1), Paladin (9), Ranger (15), Druid (5), Shaman (5)
Mana Cost	20
Casting Skill	Alteration
Casting Time (secs)	2
Recasting Delay (secs)	5.25
Duration	Instantaneous
Range (feet)	100
Target	Anyone
Resistance Invoked	None
Effect	
Poison Reduction	1

Dagger of Symbols

Casters	Magician (39)
Casting Skill	Conjuration

Dance of the Fireflies

Casters	Ranger (15), Druid (1)
Mana Cost	10
Casting Skill	Conjuration
Outdoors only	
Casting Time (secs)	3
Recasting Delay (secs)	8.25
Duration	Instantaneous
Range (feet)	0
Target	Yourself
Resistance Invoked	None
Effect	
Create Item	Firefly Globe
Target's Reaction	Target's hands flicker. (A swarm of fireflies shimmer around your hand.)

Daring

Casters	Cleric (19), Paladin (39)
Mana Cost	60
Casting Skill	Abjuration
Casting Time (secs)	2.5
Duration	36 minutes
Range (feet)	100
Target	Anyone
Resistance Invoked	None
Effects	
AC boost	17 + 1 / 2 levels (max 30)
Bonus HP	65 + 1 / level
Target's Reaction	Target looks daring.

Dark Empathy

Casters	Shadow Knight (22), Necromancer (8)
Mana Cost	20
Casting Skill	Alteration
Casting Time (secs)	4
Recasting Delay (secs)	10
Duration	Instantaneous
Range (feet)	100
Target	Anyone (flows from you)
Resistance Invoked	None
Effect	
Healing (HP)	30
Target's Reaction	Target's wounds disappear.

Dark Pact

Casters	Necromancer (8)
Mana Cost	5
Casting Skill	Alteration
Casting Time (secs)	3
Recasting Delay (secs)	8.25
Duration	1 minute + 6 seconds/level
Range (feet)	0
Target	Yourself
Resistance Invoked	None
Effects	
Mana boost/6 secs	2
Damage (HP/6 secs)	4
Target's Reaction	Target looks sick. (You feel your health begin to drain.)

Dazzle

Casters	Enchanter (49)
Casting Skill	Conjuration
Target's Reaction	Target has been mesmerized.

Dead Man Floating

Casters	Necromancer (44)
Casting Skill	Abjuration
Target's Reaction	Target looks dead. (You become like the dead.)

Death Pact

Casters	Cleric (51)
Casting Skill	Abjuration
Target's Reaction	Target is covered in a foreboding aura. (You are surrounded by a foreboding aura.)

Deadeye

Casters	Shadow Knight (22), Necromancer (8)
Mana Cost	35
Casting Skill	Divination
Casting Time (secs)	3
Duration	3 x level minutes (max 27 m)
Range (feet)	0
Target	Yourself
Resistance Invoked	None
Effects	
Infravision	
See Invisible	
Target's Reaction	Target's eyes glow red. (Your vision shifts.)

Deflux

Casters	Necromancer (54)
Casting Skill	Alteration
Target's Reaction	Target staggers. (You feel you lifeforce drain away.)

Defoliate

Casters	Necromancer (29)
Casting Skill	Evocation
Target's Reaction	Target wilts.

Defoliation

Casters	Necromancer (52)
Casting Skill	Evocation
Target's Reaction	Target wilts.

Deftness

Casters	Shaman (39)
Casting Skill	Alteration
Target's Reaction	Target looks dexterous.

Deliriously Nimble

Casters	Shaman (53)
Casting Skill	Alteration
Target's Reaction	Target twitches, deliriously nimble. (You feel deliriously nimble.)

Dementia

Casters	Enchanter (54)
Casting Skill	Evocation
Target's Reaction	Target's mind warps. (Twisted logic warps your mind.)

Demi Lich

Casters	Necromancer (60)
Casting Skill	Alteration
Target's Reaction	Target's skin peels away. (You feel the skin peel from your bones.)

Denon's Bereavement

Casters	Bard (59)
Casting Skill	Stringed Instruments
Target's Reaction	Target convulses. (Venomous notes seep through your body.)

Denon's Desperate Dirge

Casters	Bard (43)
Casting Skill	Singing
Target's Reaction	Target staggers back a step. (You stagger in pain as every bone in your body pulses.)

Denon's Disruptive Discord

Casters	Bard (18)
Mana Cost	0
Casting Skill	Brass Instruments
Casting Time (secs)	3
Casting Delay (secs)	none
Recasting Delay (secs)	12
Duration	12 seconds
Range (feet)	0
Radius of Effect (feet)	35
Target	Area (but not your group)
Resistance Invoked	Magic
Effects	
Damage (HP/6 secs)	4 + 1 / 4 levels
AC loss	1 +1/level
Target's Reaction	Target winces. (Jagged notes tear through your body.)

Denon's Dissension

Casters	Bard (35)
Casting Skill	Brass Instruments
Target's Reaction	Target winces. (Jagged notes tear through your mind.)

Devouring Darkness

Casters	Necromancer (59)
Casting Skill	Conjuration
Target's Reaction	Target is engulfed in devouring darkness.

Dexterity

Casters	Shaman (49)
Casting Skill	Alteration
Target's Reaction	Target looks dexterous.

Dexterous Aura

Casters	Shaman (1)
Mana Cost	10
Casting Skill	Alteration
Casting Time (secs)	3
Duration	3 + 3 x level minutes (max 27 m)
Range (feet)	100
Target	Anyone
Resistance Invoked	None
Effect	
DEX boost	4 +1/level (max 10)
Target's Reaction	Target looks more dexterous.

Diamondskin

Casters	Necromancer (44), Wizard (44)
Casting Skill	Abjuration
Target's Reaction	Target's skin looks like diamond.

Dictate

Casters	Enchanter (60)
Casting Skill	Alteration
Target's Reaction	(You have been charmed.)

Dimensional Hole

Casters	Magician (34)
Casting Skill	Conjuration

Dimensional Pocket

Casters	Magician (8)
Mana Cost	40
Casting Skill	Conjuration
Casting Time (secs)	6
Recasting Delay (secs)	8.25
Duration	Instantaneous
Range (feet)	0
Target	Yourself
Resistance Invoked	None
Effect	
Create Item	1 Dimensional Pocket + 1 more / level

Discordant Mind

Casters	Enchanter (44)
Casting Skill	Evocation
Target's Reaction	Target's brain begins to melt. (You feel part of your mind melt away.)

Disease Cloud

Casters	Shadow Knight (9), Necromancer (1)
Mana Cost	10
Casting Skill	Conjuration
Casting Time (secs)	1.5
Recasting Delay (secs)	8.5
Duration	3 x level minutes (max 6 m)
Range (feet)	200
Target	Anyone
Resistance Invoked	Disease
Effects	
Disease	1
Immediate Damage (HP)	6
Subsequent Damage (HP/6 secs)	1
Target's Reaction	Target doubles over in pain. (Your stomach begins to cramp.)

Disempower

Casters	Shaman (14), Enchanter (16)
Mana Cost	45
Casting Skill	Alteration
Casting Time (secs)	2.25
Duration	6 seconds/level (max 2 m)
Range (feet)	200
Target	Anyone
Resistance Invoked	Magic
Effects	
STA loss	3 + 1 / 2 levels (max 20)
STR loss	7 + 1 / 2 levels (max 15)
AC loss	16 + 1 / 2 levels (max 30)
Target's Reaction	Target looks frail.

Disintegrate

Casters	Wizard (60)
Casting Skill	Evocation

Distill Mana

Casters	Enchanter (39)
Casting Skill	Alteration

Dismiss Summoned

Casters	Cleric (39), Ranger (39), Druid (24), Magician (29)
Mana Cost	90
Casting Skill	Evocation
Casting Time (secs)	3.3
Duration	Instantaneous
Range (feet)	200
Target	Summoned creature
Resistance Invoked	Magic
Effect	
Damage (HP)	92 +2/level (max 162)
Target's Reaction	Target staggers.

Dismiss Undead

Casters	Cleric (24), Paladin (49), Shadow Knight (49), Necromancer (29)
Mana Cost	90
Casting Skill	Evocation
Casting Time (secs)	3.3
Duration	Instantaneous
Range (feet)	200
Target	Undead
Resistance Invoked	Magic
Effect	
Damage (HP)	92 +2/level (max 162)
Target's Reaction	Target staggers.

Divine Aura

Casters	Cleric (1), Paladin (58)
Mana Cost	10
Casting Skill	Abjuration
Casting Time (secs)	1
Recasting Delay	15 minutes
Duration	18 secs
Range (feet)	0
Target	Yourself
Resistance Invoked	None
Effect	
Invulnerability	
Target's Reaction	(The gods have rendered you invulnerable.)

Divine Barrier

Casters	Cleric (29)
Casting Skill	Abjuration
Target's Reaction	Target is surrounded by a divine barrier.

Divine Intervention

Casters	Cleric (60)
Casting Skill	Abjuration
Target's Reaction	Target feels the watchful eyes of the gods upon him.

Divine Light

Casters	Cleric (53)
Casting Skill	Alteration
Target's Reaction	Target is bathed in a divine light.

Dizzying Wind

Casters	Druid (19)
Mana Cost	80
Casting Skill	Conjuration
Outdoors only	
Casting Time (secs)	2.75
Recasting Delay (secs)	14.5
Duration	Instantaneous
Range (feet)	200
Target	Anyone
Resistance Invoked	Magic
Effects	
Damage (HP)	72 +2/level (max 122)
Stun	Can disrupt spellcasting
Lift and Knockback	2 feet each
Target's Reaction	Target is slammed by an intense gust of wind.

Dominate Undead

Casters	Necromancer (20)
Mana Cost	100
Casting Skill	Alteration
Casting Time (secs)	5
Recasting Delay (secs)	12.25
Duration	1 minute + 18 seconds/level
Range (feet)	200
Target	Undead
Resistance Invoked	Magic
Effect	
Charm	Lowest-level
Target's Reaction	Target moans.

Dooming Darkness

Casters	Shadow Knight (49), Necromancer (29)
Casting Skill	Conjuration
Target's Reaction	Target is engulfed in darkness.

Drain Soul

Casters	Necromancer (49)
Casting Skill	Alteration
Target's Reaction	Target staggers. (You feel you lifeforce drain away.)

Drain Spirit

Casters	Shadow Knight (60), Necromancer (39)
Casting Skill	Alteration
Target's Reaction	Target staggers. (You feel you lifeforce drain away.)

Draught of Fire

Casters	Wizard (51)
Casting Skill	Evocation
Target's Reaction	Target is caught in a torrent of fire.

Draught of Ice

Casters	Wizard (57)
Casting Skill	Evocation
Target's Reaction	Target is caught in a torrent of jagged ice.

Draught of Jiva

Casters	Wizard (55)
Casting Skill	Evocation
Target's Reaction	Target is caught in a torrent of reckless magic.

Dread of Night

Casters	Cleric (51), Necromancer (51)
Casting Skill	Alteration
Target's Reaction	Target has been instilled with the dread of night. (Your bones tingle.)

Drifting Death

Casters	Druid (44)
Casting Skill	Conjuration
Target's Reaction	Target is engulfed in a swarm. (You feel the pain of a thousand stings.)

Drones of Doom

Casters	Ranger (54), Druid (34)
Casting Skill	Conjuration
Target's Reaction	Target is engulfed in a swarm. (You feel the pain of a thousand stings.)

Drowsy

Casters	Shaman (5)
Mana Cost	20
Casting Skill	Alteration
Casting Time (secs)	2.5
Recasting Delay (secs)	7.25
Duration	12 seconds + 6 seconds / 2 levels
Range (feet)	200
Target	Anyone
Resistance Invoked	Magic
Effect	
Attack Speed loss	10% +1% / 4 levels
Target's Reaction	Target yawns. (You feel drowsy.)

Dyn's Dizzying Draught

Casters	Enchanter (29)
Casting Skill	Alteration
Target's Reaction	Target begins to spin.

Dyzil's Deafening Decoy

Casters	Magician (56)
Casting Skill	Conjuration

Earthquake

Casters	Cleric (44), Druid (34)
Casting Skill	Evocation
Target's Reaction	Target is smashed by the moving ground. (You feel the ground shake.)

Ebbing Strength

Casters	Enchanter (12)
Mana Cost	35
Casting Skill	Alteration
Casting Time (secs)	2
Recasting Delay (secs)	5.75
Duration	1 minute + 6 seconds/level
Range (feet)	200
Target	Anyone
Resistance Invoked	Magic
Effect	
STR loss	15 + 1 / 2 levels (max 25)
Target's Reaction	Target weakens. (You feel weaker.)

Egress

Casters	Druid (52)
Casting Skill	Alteration
Target's Reaction	Target sinks into the ground.

Elemental Armor

Casters	Wizard (44), Magician (44)
Casting Skill	Abjuration
Target's Reaction	Target feels protected from fire and ice.

Elemental: Air

Casters	Magician (12)
Mana Cost	120
Casting Skill	Conjuration
Components	Broom of Trilon (not consumed), Lapis Lazuli
Casting Time (secs)	8
Duration	Instantaneous
Range (feet)	0
Target	Yourself
Resistance Invoked	None
Effect	
Summon Elemental	Air Elemental (Circle 4)

Elemental: Earth

Casters	Magician (12)
Mana Cost	120
Casting Skill	Conjuration
Components	Shovel of Ponz (not consumed), Lapis Lazuli
Casting Time (secs)	8
Duration	Instantaneous
Range (feet)	0
Target	Yourself
Resistance Invoked	None
Effect	
Summon Elemental	Earth Elemental (Circle 4)

Elemental: Fire

Casters	Magician (12)
Mana Cost	120
Casting Skill	Conjuration
Components	Torch of Alna (not consumed), Lapis Lazuli
Casting Time (secs)	8
Duration	Instantaneous
Range (feet)	0
Target	Yourself
Resistance Invoked	None
Effect	
Summon Elemental	Fire Elemental (Circle 4)

Elemental: Water

Casters	Magician (12)
Mana Cost	120
Casting Skill	Conjuration
Components	Stein of Ulissa (not consumed), Lapis Lazuli
Casting Time (secs)	8
Duration	Instantaneous
Range (feet)	0
Target	Yourself
Resistance Invoked	None
Effect	
Summon Elemental	Water Elemental (Circle 4)

Elemental Rhythms

Casters	Bard (9)
Mana Cost	0
Casting Skill	Percussion Instruments
Casting Time (secs)	3
Casting Delay (secs)	none
Recasting Delay (secs)	12
Duration	12 seconds
Range (feet)	0
Radius of Effect (feet)	50
Target	Your group
Resistance Invoked	None
Effects	
Resist Magic boost	5 + 1 / 2 levels
Resist Cold boost	5 + 1 / 2 levels
Resist Fire boost	5 + 1 / 2 levels
AC boost	5 + 1 / 4 levels
Target's Reaction	(You feel an aura of elemental protection surround you.)

Elemental Shield

Casters	Wizard (20), Magician (20)
Mana Cost	50
Casting Skill	Abjuration
Casting Time (secs)	3
Duration	27 minutes
Range (feet)	0
Target	Yourself
Resistance Invoked	None
Effects	
Resist Fire boost	15
Resist Cold boost	15
Target's Reaction	Target feels protected from fire and ice.

Elementaling: Air

Casters	Magician (8)
Mana Cost	80
Casting Skill	Conjuration
Components	Broom of Trilon (not consumed), Malachite
Casting Time (secs)	7
Duration	Instantaneous
Range (feet)	0
Target	Yourself
Resistance Invoked	None
Effect	
Summon Elemental	Air Elemental (Circle 3)

Elementaling: Earth

Casters	Magician (8)
Mana Cost	80
Casting Skill	Conjuration
Components	Shovel of Ponz (not consumed), Malachite
Casting Time (secs)	7
Duration	Instantaneous
Range (feet)	0
Target	Yourself
Resistance Invoked	None
Effect	
Summon Elemental	Earth Elemental (Circle 3)

Elementaling: Fire

Casters	Magician (8)
Mana Cost	80
Casting Skill	Conjuration
Components	Torch of Alna (not consumed), Malachite
Casting Time (secs)	7
Duration	Instantaneous
Range (feet)	0
Target	Yourself
Resistance Invoked	None
Effect	
Summon Elemental	Fire Elemental (Circle 3)

Elementaling: Water

Casters	Magician (8)
Mana Cost	80
Casting Skill	Conjuration
Components	Stein of Ulissa (not consumed), Malachite
Casting Time (secs)	7
Duration	Instantaneous
Range (feet)	0
Target	Yourself
Resistance Invoked	None
Effect	
Summon Elemental	Water Elemental (Circle 3)

Elementalkin: Air

Casters	Magician (4)
Mana Cost	40
Casting Skill	Conjuration
Components	Broom of Trilon (not consumed), Malachite
Casting Time (secs)	6
Duration	Instantaneous
Range (feet)	0
Target	Yourself
Resistance Invoked	None
Effect	
Summon Elemental	Air Elemental (Circle 2)

Elementalkin: Earth

Casters	Magician (4)
Mana Cost	40
Casting Skill	Conjuration
Components	Shovel of Ponz (not consumed), Malachite
Casting Time (secs)	6
Duration	Instantaneous
Range (feet)	0
Target	Yourself
Resistance Invoked	None
Effect	
Summon Elemental	Earth Elemental (Circle 2)

Elementalkin: Fire

Casters	Magician (4)
Mana Cost	40
Casting Skill	Conjuration
Components	Torch of Alna (not consumed), Malachite
Casting Time (secs)	6
Duration	Instantaneous
Range (feet)	0
Target	Yourself
Resistance Invoked	None
Effect	
Summon Elemental	Fire Elemental (Circle 2)

Elementalkin: Water

Casters	Magician (4)
Mana Cost	40
Casting Skill	Conjuration
Components	Stein of Ulissa (not consumed), Malachite
Casting Time (secs)	6
Duration	Instantaneous
Range (feet)	0
Target	Yourself
Resistance Invoked	None
Effect	
Summon Elemental	Water Elemental (Circle 2)

Emissary of Thule

Casters	Necromancer (59)
Casting Skill	Conjuration

Enchant Electrum

Casters	Enchanter (16)
Mana Cost	75
Casting Skill	Alteration
Component	Electrum Bar
Casting Time (secs)	6
Duration	Instantaneous
Range (feet)	0
Target	Yourself
Resistance Invoked	None
Effect	
Create Item	1 enchanted electrum bar + 1 more / level

Enchant Platinum

Casters	Enchanter (34)
Casting Skill	Alteration

Enchant Gold

Casters	Enchanter (24)
Mana Cost	150
Casting Skill	Alteration
Component	Gold Bar
Casting Time (secs)	6
Duration	Instantaneous
Range (feet)	0
Target	Yourself
Resistance Invoked	None

Effect
  Create Item — 1 enchanted gold bar + 1 more / level

Enchant Silver

Casters	Enchanter (8)
Mana Cost	80
Casting Skill	Alteration
Component	Silver Bar
Casting Time (secs)	6
Duration	Instantaneous
Range (feet)	0
Turget	Yourself
Resistance Invoked	None

Effect
  Create Item — 1 enchanted silver bar + 1 more / level

Endure Cold

Casters	Cleric (14), Druid (9), Shaman (1), Shadow Knight (15), Necromancer (4)
Mana Cost	20
Casting Skill	Abjuration
Casting Time (secs)	2.5
Duration	3 x level minutes (max 27 m)
Range (feet)	100
Target	Anyone
Resistance Invoked	None

Effect
  Resist Cold boost — 10 +1/level (max 20)
  Target's Reaction — Target is protected from cold.

Endure Disease

Casters	Cleric (14), Paladin (39), Druid (19), Shaman (9), Shadow Knight (30), Necromancer (12)
Mana Cost	20
Casting Skill	Abjuration
Casting Time (secs)	2.5
Duration	27 minutes
Range (feet)	100
Target	Anyone
Resistance Invoked	None

Effect
  Resist Disease boost — 10 +1/level (max 20)
  Target's Reaction — Target is protected from disease.

Endure Fire

Casters	Cleric (9), Ranger (9), Druid (1), Shaman (5)
Mana Cost	20
Casting Skill	Abjuration
Casting Time (secs)	2.5
Duration	3 x level minutes (max 27 m)
Range (feet)	100
Target	Anyone
Resistance Invoked	None

Effect
  Resist Fire boost — 10 +1/level (max 20)
  Target's Reaction — Target is protected from fire.

Endure Magic

Casters	Cleric (19), Druid (34), Shaman (19), Enchanter (20)
Mana Cost	40
Casting Skill	Abjuration
Casting Time (secs)	2.5
Duration	27 minutes
Range (feet)	100
Target	Anyone
Resistance Invoked	None

Effect
  Resist Magic boost — 20
  Turget's Reaction — Target is protected from magic.

Endure Poison

Casters	Cleric (9), Paladin (22), Druid (19), Shaman (14)
Mana Cost	20
Casting Skill	Abjuration
Casting Time (secs)	2.5
Duration	27 minutes
Range (feet)	100
Target	Anyone
Resistance Invoked	None
Effect	
Resist Poison boost	10 +1/level (max 20)
Target's Reaction	Target is protected from poison.

Enduring Breath

Casters	Ranger (22), Druid (9), Shaman (14), Enchanter (12)
Mana Cost	35
Casting Skill	Alteration
Component	Fish Scales
Casting Time (secs)	4
Duration	27 minutes
Range (feet)	100
Target	Anyone
Resistance Invoked	None
Effect	
Magic Breathing	
Target's Reaction	Target doesn't seem to be breathing anymore. (You feel no need to breathe.)

Energy Storm

Casters	Wizard (29)
Casting Skill	Evocation
Target's Reaction	Target's skin blisters as energy rains down from above.

Enfeeblement

Casters	Enchanter (4)
Mana Cost	20
Casting Skill	Alteration
Casting Time (secs)	1.75
Duration	1 minute + 6 seconds/level (max 6 m)
Range (feet)	200
Target	Anyone
Resistance Invoked	Magic
Effects	
STR loss	16 + 1 / 2 levels (max 20)
AC loss	10
Target's Reaction	Target is enfeebled.

Enforced Reverence

Casters	Cleric (58)
Casting Skill	Evocation
Target's Reaction	Target staggers in reverent awe. (You are stunned with reverent awe.)

Engorging Roots

Casters	Druid (56)
Casting Skill	Alteration
Target's Reaction	Target's feet become entwined.

Engulfing Darkness

Casters	Shadow Knight (22), Necromancer (12)
Mana Cost	60
Casting Skill	Conjuration
Casting Time (secs)	2.45
Recasting Delay (secs)	6.5
Duration	1 minute
Range (feet)	200
Target	Anyone
Resistance Invoked	Magic
Effects	
Damage (HP/6 secs)	11
Movement Rate loss	40%
Target's Reaction	Target is engulfed in darkness.

Engulfing Roots

Casters	Druid (49)
Casting Skill	Alteration
Target's Reaction	Target's feet become entwined.

Enlightenment

Casters	Enchanter (57)
Casting Skill	Alteration
Target's Reaction	Target has been enlightened.

Enslave Death

Casters	Necromancer (60)
Casting Skill	Alteration
Target's Reaction	Target moans.

Ensnare

Casters	Ranger (51), Druid (29)
Casting Skill	Alteration
Target's Reaction	Target has been ensnared.

Ensnaring Roots

Casters	Ranger (49), Druid (24)
Mana Cost	60
Casting Skill	Alteration
Casting Time (secs)	2.5
Duration	1 min, 36 secs
Range (feet)	200
Target	Anyone
Resistance Invoked	Magic
Effects	
Immobilizes	
One-Time Damage (HP)	10 +1/level (max 60)
Target's Reaction	Target's feet become entwined.

Enstill

Casters	Cleric (29), Paladin (54), Shaman (34), Necromancer (53), Wizard (20), Enchanter (29)
Mana Cost	60
Casting Skill	Alteration
Casting Time (secs)	2.5
Duration	1 min, 36 secs
Range (feet)	200
Target	Anyone
Resistance Invoked	Magic
Effect	
Immobilizes	
Target's Reaction	Target's feet adhere to the ground.

Enthrall

Casters	Enchanter (16)
Mana Cost	50
Casting Skill	Conjuration
Casting Time (secs)	2.5
Recasting Delay (secs)	4.75
Duration	48 secs
Range (feet)	200
Target	Anyone
Resistance Invoked	Magic
Effect	
Mesmerization	
Target's Reaction	Target has been enthralled.

Entrance

Casters	Enchanter (34)
Casting Skill	Conjuration
Target's Reaction	Target has been entranced.

Entrapping Roots

Casters	Druid (60)
Casting Skill	Alteration
Target's Reaction	Target's feet become entwined.

Enveloping Roots

Casters	Ranger (60), Druid (39)
Casting Skill	Alteration
Target's Reaction	Target's feet become entwined.

Envenomed Bolt

Casters	Shaman (49), Necromancer (51)
Casting Skill	Conjuration
Target's Reaction	Target has been poisoned.

Envenomed Breath

Casters	Shaman (24)
Mana Cost	100
Casting Skill	Conjuration
Casting Time (secs)	3.1
Duration	42 secs
Range (feet)	200
Target	Anyone
Resistance Invoked	Poison
Effects	
Poison	0
Immediate Damage (HP)	57
Subsequent Damage (HP/6 secs)	27
Knockback	1/2 foot
Target's Reaction	Target has been poisoned.

Evacuate

Casters	Wizard (57)
Casting Skill	Alteration
Target's Reaction	Target creates a mystic portal.

Evacuate: Fay

Casters	Wizard (34)
Casting Skill	Alteration
Target's Reaction	Target creates a shimmering portal.

Evacuate: Nek

Casters	Wizard (44)
Casting Skill	Alteration
Target's Reaction	Target creates a shimmering portal.

Evacuate: North

Casters	Wizard (29)
Casting Skill	Alteration
Target's Reaction	Target creates a shimmering portal.

Evacuate: Ro

Casters	Wizard (39)
Casting Skill	Alteration
Target's Reaction	Target creates a shimmering portal.

Evacuate: West

Casters	Wizard (49)
Casting Skill	Alteration
Target's Reaction	Target creates a shimmering portal.

Everfount

Casters	Magician (24)
Mana Cost	25
Casting Skill	Conjuration
Casting Time (secs)	4
Duration	Instantaneous
Range (feet)	0
Target	Yourself
Resistance Invoked	None
Effect	
Create Item	1 globe of water + 1 more globe / 6 levels

Exile Summoned

Casters	Druid (55), Magician (56)
Casting Skill	Evocation
Target's Reaction	Target staggers.

Exile Undead

Casters	Cleric (55), Necromancer (57)
Casting Skill	Evocation
Target's Reaction	Target staggers.

Expel Summoned

Casters	Cleric (49), Druid (34), Magician (39)
Casting Skill	Evocation

Expel Undead

Casters	Cleric (34), Paladin (54), Shadow Knight (55), Necromancer (39)
Casting Skill	Evocation
Target's Reaction	Target staggers.

Expulse Summoned

Casters	Cleric (29), Druid (14), Magician (20)
Mana Cost	60
Casting Skill	Evocation
Casting Time (secs)	2.75
Duration	Instantaneous
Range (feet)	200
Target	Summoned creature
Resistance Invoked	Magic
Effect	
Damage (HP)	74 +1/level (max 94)

Expulse Undead

Casters	Cleric (14), Paladin (30), Shadow Knight (39), Necromancer (20)
Mana Cost	60
Casting Skill	Evocation
Casting Time (secs)	2.75
Duration	Instantaneous
Range (feet)	200
Target	Undead
Resistance Invoked	Magic
Effect	
Damage (HP)	74 +1/level (max 94)

Extinguish Fatigue

Casters	Cleric (19), Ranger (52), Druid (29), Shaman (39), Enchanter (44)
Mana Cost	35
Casting Skill	Alteration
Casting Time (secs)	3.5
Recasting Delay (secs)	5.75
Duration	Instantaneous
Range (feet)	100
Target	Anyone
Resistance Invoked	None
Effect	
Restores Fatigue Points	90
Target's Reaction	Target looks energized (Your body zings with energy.)

Eye of Confusion

Casters	Enchanter (8)
Mana Cost	25
Casting Skill	Alteration
Casting Time (secs)	3
Recasting Delay (secs)	7.25
Duration	18 secs
Range (feet)	200
Target	Anyone
Resistance Invoked	Magic
Effect	
Blindness	
Target's Reaction	Target looks confused.

Eye of Tallon

Casters	Wizard (57), Magician (57)
Casting Skill	Conjuration

Eye of Zomm

Casters	Wizard (8), Magician (8)
Mana Cost	30
Casting Skill	Conjuration
Casting Time (secs)	6
Recasting Delay (secs)	12.25
Duration	30 secs
Range (feet)	5
Target	Yourself
Resistance Invoked	None
Effect	
You see from NPC point of view	

Eyes of the Cat

Casters	Ranger (30)
Casting Skill	Divination
Target's Reaction	Target's eyes glow green. (Your vision shifts.)

Fade

Casters	Wizard (4)
Mana Cost	10
Casting Skill	Alteration
Casting Time (secs)	1
Recasting Delay (secs)	7.25
Duration	Instantaneous
Range (feet)	350
Target	Yourself
Resistance Invoked	None
Effect	
Random Teleport	
Target's Reaction	Target fades. (You fade out.)

Fascination

Casters	Enchanter (52)
Casting Skill	Conjuration
Target's Reaction	Target has been fascinated. (You are fascinated by the pretty colors.)

Fay Gate

Casters	Wizard (20)
Mana Cost	150
Casting Skill	Alteration
Casting Time (secs)	7
Recasting Delay (secs)	12.25
Duration	Instantaneous
Range (feet)	0
Target	Yourself
Resistance Invoked	None
Effect	
Teleports you to	Greater Faydark
Target's Reaction	Target fades away.

Fay Portal

Casters	Wizard (29)
Casting Skill	Alteration
Target's Reaction	Target creates a shimmering portal.

Fear

Casters	Cleric (9), Shadow Knight (15), Necromancer (4), Enchanter (4)
Mana Cost	40
Casting Skill	Alteration
Casting Time (secs)	3.5
Recasting Delay (secs)	9.25
Duration	18 secs
Range (feet)	200
Target	Anyone
Resistance Invoked	Magic
Effect	
Fear	Low-level
Target's Reaction	Target looks very afraid. (Your mind fills with fear.)

Feckless Might

Casters	Enchanter (20)
Mana Cost	45
Casting Skill	Alteration
Casting Time (secs)	2.5
Duration	6 seconds/level
Range (feet)	200
Target	Anyone
Resistance Invoked	Magic
Effect	
STR loss	16 + 1 / 2 levels (max 30)
Target's Reaction	Target is weakened. (You feel weak.)

Feedback

Casters	Enchanter (29)
Casting Skill	Abjuration
Target's Reaction	Target is enveloped in blazing energy.

Feet like Cat

Casters	Ranger (15), Shaman (5)
Mana Cost	40
Casting Skill	Alteration
Casting Time (secs)	5
Duration	3 + 3 x level minutes (max 36 m)
Range (feet)	100
Target	Anyone
Resistance Invoked	None
Effect	
AGI boost	9 +1/level (max 18)
Target's Reaction	Target looks more agile.

Feign Death

Casters	Shadow Knight (30), Necromancer (16)
Mana Cost	60
Casting Skill	Abjuration
Casting Time (secs)	1.5
Recasting Delay (secs)	17.25
Duration	Instantaneous
Range (feet)	0
Target	Yourself
Resistance Invoked	None
Effect	
Feign Death	
Target's Reaction	Target dies.

Feral Spirit

Casters	Druid (19)
Mana Cost	50
Casting Skill	Alteration
Casting Time (secs)	6
Recasting Delay (secs)	14.25
Duration	1 minute + 6 seconds/level
Range (feet)	100
Target	Your pet
Resistance Invoked	None
Effects	
Attack Speed boost	12% +1% / 4 levels (max 20% boost)
STR boost	12 + 1 / 4 levels (max 20)
AC boost	15 + 1 / 2 levels
Target's Reaction	Target foams at the mouth.

Fetter

Casters	Wizard (58), Enchanter (58)
Casting Skill	Alteration
Target's Reaction	Target's feet adhere to ground.

Fingers of Fire

Casters	Wizard (8)
Mana Cost	47
Casting Skill	Evocation
Casting Time (secs)	1.85
Recasting Delay (secs)	8.5
Duration	Instantaneous
Range (feet)	0
Radius of Effect (feet)	25
Target	Area (but not your group)
Resistance Invoked	Fire
Effect	
Damage (HP)	14 +1/level (max 28)
Target's Reaction	Target is covered in flames. (Flames dance across your body.)

Fire

Casters	Druid (49)
Casting Skill	Evocation
Target's Reaction	Target is immolated in flame.

Fire Bolt

Casters	Wizard (8)
Mana Cost	40
Casting Skill	Evocation
Casting Time (secs)	2.25
Duration	Instantaneous
Range (feet)	300
Target	Anyone
Resistance Invoked	Fire
Effect	
Damage (HP)	37 +1/level (max 51)
Target's Reaction	Target is bathed in fire. (A stream of fire washes over you.)

Fire Flux

Casters	Magician (4)
Mana Cost	23
Casting Skill	Evocation
Casting Time (secs)	1.75
Recasting Delay (secs)	8.5
Duration	Instantaneous
Range (feet)	0
Radius of Effect (feet)	20
Target	Area (but not your group)
Resistance Invoked	Fire
Effect	
Damage (HP)	8 + 1 / 2 levels (max 12)
Target's Reaction	Target is covered in flames. (Flames race across your body.)

Fire Spiral of Al'Kabor

Casters	Wizard (20)
Mana Cost	150
Casting Skill	Evocation
Casting Time (secs)	3.6
Recasting Delay (secs)	11.5
Duration	Instantaneous
Range (feet)	200
Radius of Effect (feet)	35
Target	Area
Resistance Invoked	Fire
Effect	
Damage (HP)	51 +1/level (max 76)
Target's Reaction	Target is blasted by blazing winds.

Firefist

Casters	Druid (9)
Mana Cost	30
Casting Skill	Evocation
Casting Time (secs)	3.5
Recasting Delay (secs)	9.25
Duration	12 minutes
Range (feet)	0
Target	Yourself
Resistance Invoked	None
Effect	
Attack Skill boost	1 + 1 / 2 levels (max 10)
Target's Reaction	Target's fist bursts into flame.

Firestorm

Casters	Wizard (12)
Mana Cost	62
Casting Skill	Evocation
Casting Time (secs)	2.5
Recasting Delay (secs)	14.5
Duration	Instantaneous
Impact Duration (secs)	7.5
Range (feet)	150
Radius of Effect (feet)	25
Target	Area
Resistance Invoked	Fire
Effect	
Damage (HP)	28
Target's Reaction	Target's skin blisters as fire rains down from above.

Firestrike
Casters	Ranger (59), Druid (39)
Casting Skill	Evocation
Target's Reaction	Target's skin ignites.

Fist of Karana
Casters	Druid (58)
Casting Skill	Evocation
Target's Reaction	Target has been struck by the shocking Fist of Karana.

Flame Arc
Casters	Magician (39)
Casting Skill	Evocation
Target's Reaction	Target is covered in flames.

Flame Bolt
Casters	Magician (8)
Mana Cost	40
Casting Skill	Evocation
Casting Time (secs)	2.5
Duration	Instantaneous
Range (feet)	300
Target	Anyone
Resistance Invoked	Fire
Effect	
Damage (HP)	33 +1/level (max 47)
Target's Reaction	Target is bathed in fire. (A stream of fire washes over you.)

Flame Flux
Casters	Magician (24)
Mana Cost	123
Casting Skill	Evocation
Casting Time (secs)	3.5
Recasting Delay (secs)	8.5
Duration	Instantaneous
Range (feet)	0
Radius of Effect (feet)	20
Target	Area (but not your group)
Resistance Invoked	Fire
Effect	
Damage (HP)	67 +1/level (max 96)
Target's Reaction	Target is covered in flames. (Flames race across your body.)

Flame Lick
Casters	Ranger (9), Druid (1)
Mana Cost	10
Casting Skill	Evocation
Component	Fire Beetle Eye (not consumed)
Casting Time (secs)	1.5
Duration	48 secs
Range (feet)	200
Target	Anyone
Resistance Invoked	Fire
Effects	
AC loss	12
Damage (HP/6 secs)	1 + 1 / 2 levels (max 3)
Target's Reaction	Target is surrounded by flickering flames.

Flame Shock
Casters	Wizard (16)
Mana Cost	75
Casting Skill	Evocation
Casting Time (secs)	2.5
Duration	Instantaneous
Range (feet)	200
Target	Anyone
Resistance Invoked	Fire
Effect	
Damage (HP)	70 +2/level (max 110)
Target's Reaction	Target combusts. (You feel your skin combust.)

Flaming Sword of Xuzl
Casters	Wizard (59)
Casting Skill	Conjuration

Flare
Casters	Magician (1)
Mana Cost	3
Casting Skill	Evocation
Casting Time (secs)	2.5
Recasting Delay (secs)	20.25
Duration	Instantaneous
Range (feet)	400
Target	Anyone
Resistance Invoked	None
Effect	
Restores Fatigue Point	1

Flash of Light

Casters	Cleric (1), Paladin (9), Shaman (1)
Mana Cost	12
Casting Skill	Divination
Casting Time (secs)	1.5
Recasting Delay (secs)	5.25
Duration	12 seconds
Range (feet)	200
Target	Anyone
Resistance Invoked	Magic
Effects	
Blindness	
Attack Skill loss	5
Target's Reaction	Target is blinded by a flash of light.

Fleeting Fury

Casters	Shaman (5)
Mana Cost	10
Casting Skill	Abjuration
Casting Time (secs)	0.5
Recasting Delay (secs)	6.25
Duration	18 secs
Range (feet)	100
Target	Anyone
Resistance Invoked	None
Effects	
Restores Fatigue Point	1
STR boost	15
AC boost	20
DEX boost	20
Target's Reaction	Target simmers with fury.

Force Shock

Casters	Wizard (20)
Mana Cost	120
Casting Skill	Evocation
Casting Time (secs)	2.8
Recasting Delay (secs)	14.5
Duration	Instantaneous
Range (feet)	200
Target	Anyone
Resistance Invoked	Magic
Effects	
Damage (HP)	131 +2/level (max 179)
Stun	Can disrupt spellcasting
Knockback	1 foot

Force

Casters	Cleric (34), Paladin (52)
Casting Skill	Evocation
Target's Reaction	Target is stunned.

Force Spiral of Al'Kabor

Casters	Wizard (39)
Casting Skill	Evocation
Target's Reaction	Target is blasted by energy laden winds.

Force Strike

Casters	Wizard (44)
Casting Skill	Evocation

Forlorn Deeds

Casters	Enchanter (57)
Casting Skill	Alteration
Target's Reaction	Target slows down.

Form of the Great Wolf

Casters	Druid (44)
Casting Skill	Alteration
Target's Reaction	Target turns into a wolf.

Form of the Howler

Casters	Druid (54)
Casting Skill	Alteration
Target's Reaction	Target turns into a wolf.

Form of the Hunter

Casters	Druid (60)
Casting Skill	Alteration
Target's Reaction	Target turns into a wolf.

Fortitude

Casters	Cleric (55)
Casting Skill	Abjuration
Target's Reaction	Target's body pulses with mystic fortitude. (An aura of fortitude fills you.)

Frenzied Spirit

Casters	Shaman (49)
Casting Skill	Conjuration
Target's Reaction	Target summons a frenzied spirit.

Frenzied Strength

Casters	Cleric (34), Paladin (52)
Casting Skill	Alteration
Target's Reaction	Target's muscles bulge with frenzied strength. (Your muscles erupt with frenzied strength.)

Frenzy

Casters	Shaman (19)
Mana Cost	25
Casting Skill	Abjuration
Casting Time (secs)	2
Casting Delay (secs)	30
Duration	1 minute + 18 seconds/level
Range (feet)	0
Target	Yourself
Resistance Invoked	None
Effects	
Mana loss	10 + 1 / 2 levels
STR boost	15 + 1 / 4 levels
AC boost	15 + 1 / 2 levels (max 35)
Healing (HP)	2 + 1 / 6 levels
Target's Reaction	Target goes berserk.

Frost

Casters	Druid (57)
Casting Skill	Evocation
Target's Reaction	Target is iced by an intense cone of frost. (Your blood freezes as you are iced by an intense cone of frost.)

Frost Bolt

Casters	Wizard (1)
Mana Cost	10
Casting Skill	Evocation
Casting Time (secs)	1.8
Duration	Instantaneous
Range (feet)	300
Target	Anyone
Resistance Invoked	Cold
Effects	
Damage (HP)	4 + 1 / 2 levels (max 7)
Knockback	1/3 foot
Target's Reaction	Target is chilled by a bolt of frost.

Frost Rift

Casters	Shaman (5)
Mana Cost	15
Casting Skill	Evocation
Casting Time (secs)	1.75
Duration	Instantaneous
Range (feet)	200
Target	Anyone
Resistance Invoked	Cold
Effect	
Damage (HP)	10 + 1 / 2 levels (max 15)
Target's Reaction	Target is struck by the frost rift. (You feel your skin numb as the frost rift strikes you.)

Frost Shock

Casters	Wizard (24)
Mana Cost	110
Casting Skill	Evocation
Casting Time (secs)	3.15
Duration	Instantaneous
Range (feet)	200
Target	Anyone
Resistance Invoked	Cold
Effect	
Damage (HP)	97 +3/level (max 187)
Target's Reaction	Target's skin freezes over.

Frost Spiral of Al'Kabor

Casters	Wizard (12)
Mana Cost	100
Casting Skill	Evocation
Casting Time (secs)	3.15
Recasting Delay (secs)	11.5
Duration	Instantaneous
Range (feet)	200
Radius of Effect (feet)	35
Target	Area
Resistance Invoked	Cold
Effect	
Damage (HP)	36 + 1 / 2 levels (max 44)
Target's Reaction	Target is blasted by freezing winds.

Frost Storm

Casters	Wizard (44)
Casting Skill	Evocation
Target's Reaction	Target's skin freezes as frost rains down from above.

Frost Strike

Casters	Shaman (24)
Mana Cost	100
Casting Skill	Evocation
Casting Time (secs)	3.1
Duration	Instantaneous
Range (feet)	200
Target	Anyone
Resistance Invoked	Cold
Effect	
Damage (HP)	89 +2/level (max 149)
Target's Reaction	Target staggers as spirits of frost slam against them.

Fufil's Curtailing Chant

Casters	Bard (30)
Casting Skill	Percussion Instruments
Target's Reaction	Target's hair stands on end. (You feel a static pulse engulf you.)

Furious Strength

Casters	Shaman (39)
Casting Skill	Alteration
Target's Reaction	Target looks stronger.

Furor

Casters	Cleric (5)
Mana Cost	20
Casting Skill	Evocation
Casting Time (secs)	1.75
Duration	Instantaneous
Range (feet)	200
Target	Anyone
Resistance Invoked	Magic
Effects	
Damage (HP)	14 + 1 / 2 levels (max 19)
Knockback	1/2 foot
Target's Reaction	Target is struck by a sudden burst of force.

Fury

Casters	Shaman (34)
Casting Skill	Abjuration
Target's Reaction	Target goes berserk.

Gale of Poison

Casters	Shaman (39)
Casting Skill	Evocation
Target's Reaction	Target's skin blisters. (Your skin blisters as poison rains down on you.)

Gasping Embrace

Casters	Enchanter (49)
Casting Skill	Alteration
Target's Reaction	Target begins to choke. (You feel a shortness of breath.)

Gate

Casters	Cleric (5), Druid (5), Shaman (5), Necromancer (4), Wizard (4), Magician (4), Enchanter (4)
Mana Cost	70
Casting Skill	Alteration
Casting Time (secs)	5
Recasting Delay (secs)	10.25
Duration	Instantaneous
Range (feet)	0
Target	Yourself
Resistance Invoked	None
Effect	
Teleport to	Wherever you're bound (see Bind Affinity)
Target's Reaction	Target fades away.

Gather Shadows

Casters	Shadow Knight (30), Necromancer (8)
Mana Cost	35
Casting Skill	Divination
Casting Time (secs)	5
Duration	20 minutes
Range (feet)	0
Target	Yourself
Resistance Invoked	None
Effect	
Invisibility	
Target's Reaction	Target steps into the shadows and disappears. (You gather shadows about you.)

Gaze

Casters	Wizard (12)
Mana Cost	15
Casting Skill	Divination
Casting Time (secs)	2.5
Recasting Delay (secs)	5.25
Duration	Level minutes
Range (feet)	0
Target	Yourself
Resistance Invoked	None
Effect	
Telescope	See twice as far
Target's Reaction	Target eyes gleam. (Your eyes feel stronger.)

Gift of Pure Thought

Casters	Enchanter (59)
Casting Skill	Alteration
Target's Reaction	Target looks very tranquil. (A soft breeze slips through your mind.)

Gift of Xev

Casters	Magician (51)
Casting Skill	Conjuration

Girdle of Karana

Casters	Druid (55)
Casting Skill	Alteration
Target's Reaction	Target looks stronger. (You feel the strength of Karana infuse you.)

Glamour

Casters	Shaman (39)
Casting Skill	Alteration
Target's Reaction	Target looks charismatic.

Glamour of Kintaz

Casters	Enchanter (54)
Casting Skill	Conjuration
Target's Reaction	Target has been mesmerized by the Glamour of Kintaz.

Glamour of Tunare

Casters	Druid (53)
Casting Skill	Abjuration
Target's Reaction	Target is surrounded by a Tunarian glamour.

Glimpse

Casters	Ranger (9), Wizard (4)
Mana Cost	5
Casting Skill	Divination
Casting Time (secs)	1.5
Recasting Delay (secs)	14.25
Duration	12 seconds
Range (feet)	0
Target	Yourself
Resistance Invoked	None
Effect	
Telescope	See almost twice as far
Target's Reaction	Target eyes gleam. (Your eyes feel stronger.)

Grasping Roots

Casters	Ranger (15), Druid (5)
Mana Cost	35
Casting Skill	Alteration
Casting Time (secs)	2
Duration	48 secs
Range (feet)	200
Target	Anyone
Resistance Invoked	Magic
Effects	
Immobilizes	
One-Time Damage (HP)	10
Target's Reaction	Target's feet become entwined.

Gravity Flux

Casters	Wizard (44), Enchanter (39)
Casting Skill	Alteration
Target's Reaction	Target rises chaotically into the air. (You experience chaotic weightless.)

Greater Conjuration: Air

Casters	Magician (49)
Casting Skill	Conjuration

Greater Conjuration: Earth

Casters	Magician (49)
Casting Skill	Conjuration

Greater Conjuration: Fire

Casters	Magician (49)
Casting Skill	Conjuration

Greater Conjuration: Water

Casters	Magician (49)
Casting Skill	Conjuration

Greater Healing

Casters	Cleric (24), Paladin (39), Ranger (57), Druid (29), Shaman (29)
Mana Cost	150
Casting Skill	Alteration
Casting Time (secs)	3.75
Duration	Instantaneous
Range (feet)	100
Target	Anyone
Resistance Invoked	None
Effect	
Healing (HP)	240 +2/level (max 300)

Greater Shielding

Casters	Necromancer (34), Wizard (34), Magician (34), Enchanter (34)
Casting Skill	Abjuration
Target's Reaction	(You feel armored.)

Greater Summoning: Air

Casters	Magician (29)
Casting Skill	Conjuration

Greater Summoning: Earth

Casters	Magician (29)
Casting Skill	Conjuration

Greater Summoning: Fire

Casters	Magician (29)
Casting Skill	Conjuration

Greater Summoning: Water

Casters	Magician (29)
Casting Skill	Conjuration

Greater Vocaration: Air

Casters	Magician (59)
Casting Skill	Conjuration

Greater Vocaration: Earth

Casters	Magician (57)
Casting Skill	Conjuration

Greater Vocaration: Fire

Casters	Magician (58)
Casting Skill	Conjuration

Greater Vocaration: Water

Casters	Magician (60)
Casting Skill	Conjuration

Greater Wolf Form

Casters	Ranger (56), Druid (34)
Casting Skill	Alteration
Target's Reaction	Target turns into a wolf.

Grim Aura

Casters	Necromancer (4)
Mana Cost	25
Casting Skill	Alteration
Casting Time (secs)	3
Duration	3 x level minutes (max 27 m)
Range (feet)	0
Target	Yourself
Resistance Invoked	None
Effect	
Attack Skill boost	5
Target's Reaction	Target's hand is covered with a dull aura. (A dull aura covers your hand.)

Group Resist Magic

Casters	Enchanter (49)
Casting Skill	Abjuration
Target's Reaction	Target is resistant to magic. (You feel protected from magic.)

Guard

Casters	Cleric (29), Paladin (49)
Casting Skill	Abjuration

Guardian

Casters	Shaman (44)
Casting Skill	Abjuration
Target's Reaction	Target is surrounded by a spirit aura. (The protective presence of a guardian spirit surrounds you.)

Guardian Spirit

Casters	Shaman (44)
Casting Skill	Conjuration
Target's Reaction	Target summons a guardian spirit.

Guardian Rhythms

Casters	Bard (17)
Mana Cost	0
Casting Skill	Percussion Instruments
Casting Time (secs)	3
Casting Delay (secs)	none
Recasting Delay (secs)	12
Duration	12 seconds
Range (feet)	0
Radius of Effect (feet)	50
Target	Your group
Resistance Invoked	None
Effects	
AC boost	5 + 1 / 2 levels
Resist Magic boost	5 + 1 / 2 levels
Target's Reaction	(You feel an aura of mystic protection surround you.)

Halo of Light

Casters	Cleric (14), Paladin (22), Druid (14), Wizard (12)
Mana Cost	40
Casting Skill	Conjuration
Casting Time (secs)	5
Recasting Delay (secs)	12.25
Duration	Instantaneous
Range (feet)	0
Target	Yourself
Resistance Invoked	None
Effect	
Create Item	Halo of Light
Target's Reaction	Target's hands are bathed in light. (A Halo of Light solidifies in your hand.)

Hammer of Striking

Casters	Cleric (24), Paladin (30)
Mana Cost	100
Casting Skill	Conjuration
Casting Time (secs)	6
Recasting Delay (secs)	14.25
Duration	Instantaneous
Range (feet)	0
Target	Yourself
Resistance Invoked	None
Effect	
Create Item	1 Hammer of Striking + 1 more / level
Target's Reaction	(A magical hammer appears in your hand.)

Hammer of Requital

Casters	Cleric (44), Paladin (54)
Casting Skill	Conjuration
Target's Reaction	(A magical hammer appears in your hand.)

Hammer of Wrath

Casters	Cleric (9), Paladin (15)
Mana Cost	50
Casting Skill	Conjuration
Casting Time (secs)	4
Recasting Delay (secs)	14.25
Duration	Instantaneous
Range (feet)	0
Target	Yourself
Resistance Invoked	None
Effect	
Create Item	1 Hammer of Wrath + 1 more / level
Target's Reaction	(A magical hammer appears in your hand.)

Harm Touch

Casters	Shadow Knight (1)
Mana Cost	0
Casting Skill	None
Casting Time (secs)	0
Recasting Delay	72 minutes
Duration	Instantaneous
Range (feet)	50
Target	Anyone
Resistance Invoked	Magic
Effects	
Damage (HP)	1 +10/level
Knockback	1/3 foot
Target's Reaction	Target writhes in the grip of agony.

Harmshield

Casters	Necromancer (20)
Mana Cost	85
Casting Skill	Abjuration
Casting Time (secs)	1
Recasting Delay (secs)	602.5
Duration	18 secs
Range (feet)	0
Target	Yourself
Resistance Invoked	None
Effects	
One-Time Damage (HP)	20
Invulnerability	
Target's Reaction	(You no longer feel pain.)

Harmony

Casters	Ranger (22), Druid (5)
Mana Cost	25
Casting Skill	Abjuration
Outdoors only	
Casting Time (secs)	3
Recasting Delay (secs)	14.25
Duration	2 minutes
Range (feet)	200
Radius of Effect (feet)	40
Target	Area
Resistance Invoked	None
Effects	
Target's Reaction Range (feet)	15 feet
Target's Help Radius	15 feet

Haunting Corpse

Casters	Necromancer (24)
Mana Cost	240
Casting Skill	Conjuration
Components	2 Bone Chips
Casting Time (secs)	11
Duration	Instantaneous
Range (feet)	0
Target	Yourself
Resistance Invoked	None
Effect	
Create Undead	Skeleton (Circle 7)
Target's Reaction	Skeleton rises from the dead.

Haze

Casters	Enchanter (4)
Mana Cost	25
Casting Skill	Abjuration
Casting Time (secs)	2
Recasting Delay (secs)	6.25
Duration	3 x level minutes (max 27 m)
Range (feet)	100
Target	Anyone
Resistance Invoked	None
Effect	
AC boost	11 + 1 / 2 levels (max 15)
Target's Reaction	Target's image blurs.

Healing

Casters	Cleric (14), Paladin (30), Ranger (39), Druid (19), Shaman (19)
Mana Cost	60
Casting Skill	Alteration
Casting Time (secs)	3
Duration	Instantaneous
Range (feet)	100
Target	Anyone
Resistance Invoked	None
Effect	
Healing (HP)	70 +1/level (max 100)

Health

Casters	Shaman (34)
Casting Skill	Alteration
Target's Reaction	Target looks healthy.

Heart Flutter

Casters	Shadow Knight (39), Necromancer (16)
Mana Cost	80
Casting Skill	Alteration
Casting Time (secs)	2.75
Recasting Delay (secs)	9.5
Duration	1 min, 12 secs
Range (feet)	200
Target	Anyone
Resistance Invoked	Disease
Effects	
STR loss	7 + 1 / 2 levels (max 20)
AC loss	18 + 1 / 2 levels (max 30)
Damage (HP/6 secs)	12
Target's Reaction	Target clutches their chest. (Your heartbeat becomes irregular.)

Heat Blood

Casters	Shadow Knight (30), Necromancer (12)
Mana Cost	72
Casting Skill	Alteration
Casting Time (secs)	2.45
Recasting Delay (secs)	6.5
Duration	1 minute
Range (feet)	200
Target	Anyone
Resistance Invoked	Fire
Effect	
Damage (HP/6 secs)	17
Target's Reaction	Target's blood simmers.

Heat Sight

Casters	Wizard (16)
Mana Cost	30
Casting Skill	Divination
Casting Time (secs)	5
Recasting Delay (secs)	9.75
Duration	27 minutes
Range (feet)	0
Target	Yourself
Resistance Invoked	None
Effect	
Infravision	
Target's Reaction	Target eyes glow red. (Your eyes tingle.)

Heroic Bond

Casters	Cleric (52)
Casting Skill	Abjuration
Target's Reaction	Target eyes gleam with heroic resolution. (You feel heroic.)

Heroism

Casters	Cleric (52)
Casting Skill	Abjuration
Target's Reaction	Target eyes gleam with heroic resolution. (You feel heroic.)

Holy Armor

Casters	Cleric (5), Paladin (15)
Mana Cost	20
Casting Skill	Abjuration
Casting Time (secs)	2
Duration	3 x level minutes (max 27 m)
Range (feet)	100
Target	Anyone
Resistance Invoked	None
Effect	
AC boost	20

Holy Might

Casters	Cleric (19), Paladin (49)
Mana Cost	60
Casting Skill	Evocation
Casting Time (secs)	2
Recasting Delay (secs)	20.5
Duration	Instantaneous
Range (feet)	200
Target	Anyone
Resistance Invoked	Magic
Effects	
Stun	6 seconds
Damage (HP)	10 +1/level
Target's Reaction	Target is stunned.

Hungry Earth

Casters	Necromancer (16)
Mana Cost	30
Casting Skill	Alteration
Casting Time (secs)	2
Recasting Delay (secs)	10
Duration	48 secs
Range (feet)	200
Target	Undead
Resistance Invoked	Magic
Effects	
Immobilizes	
One-Time Damage (HP)	10 +1/level
Target's Reaction	Target's feet sink into ground.

Hymn of Restoration

Casters	Bard (6)
Mana Cost	0
Casting Skill	Stringed Instruments
Casting Time (secs)	3
Casting Delay (secs)	none
Recasting Delay (secs)	12
Duration	12 seconds
Range (feet)	0
Radius of Effect (feet)	30
Target	Your group
Resistance Invoked	None
Effect	
Healing (HP)	1 + 1 / 6 levels

Ice

Casters	Druid (49)
Casting Skill	Evocation
Target's Reaction	Target is encased in frost.

Ice Comet

Casters	Wizard (49)
Casting Skill	Evocation
Target's Reaction	Target's skin freezes.

Ice Shock

Casters	Wizard (34)
Casting Skill	Evocation
Target's Reaction	Target's skin freezes over.

Ice Strike

Casters	Shaman (54)
Casting Skill	Evocation
Target's Reaction	Target staggers as ice of frost slam against them. (You stagger as spirits of ice slam against you.)

Icestrike

Casters	Wizard (4)
Mana Cost	30
Casting Skill	Evocation
Casting Time (secs)	1.8
Recasting Delay (secs)	14.5
Duration	Instantaneous
Duration of impact (secs)	7.5
Range (feet)	150
Radius of Effect (feet)	25
Target	Area
Resistance Invoked	Cold
Effect	
Damage (HP)	10
Target's Reaction	Target is pelted by sleet.

Identify

Casters	Necromancer (20), Wizard (16), Magician (16), Enchanter (16)
Mana Cost	50
Casting Skill	Divination
Casting Time (secs)	5
Duration	Instantaneous
Range (feet)	100
Target	Anyone
Resistance Invoked	None
Effect	
Identify 1 Item	

Ignite

Casters	Ranger (22), Druid (9)
Mana Cost	30
Casting Skill	Evocation
Casting Time (secs)	2.1
Duration	Instantaneous
Range (feet)	200
Target	Anyone
Resistance Invoked	Fire
Effect	
Damage (HP)	23 +1/level (max 37)
Target's Reaction	Target's skin ignites.

Ignite Blood

Casters	Necromancer (49)
Casting Skill	Alteration
Target's Reaction	Target's blood ignites.

Ignite Bones

Casters	Necromancer (44)
Casting Skill	Evocation
Target's Reaction	Target's skin burns away. (You feel your skin burn from your body.)

Illusion: Air Elemental

Casters	Enchanter (29)
Casting Skill	Divination
Target's Reaction	Target's image shimmers. (You feel different.)

Illusion: Barbarian

Casters	Enchanter (16)
Mana Cost	30
Casting Skill	Divination
Casting Time (secs)	3
Recasting Delay (secs)	8.25
Duration	36 minutes
Range (feet)	0
Target	Yourself
Resistance Invoked	None
Effect	
Change Form	Barbarian
Target's Reaction	Target's image shimmers. (You feel different.)

Illusion: Dark Elf

Casters	Enchanter (12)
Mana Cost	30
Casting Skill	Divination
Casting Time (secs)	3
Recasting Delay (secs)	8.25
Duration	36 minutes
Range (feet)	0
Target	Yourself
Resistance Invoked	None
Effect	
Change Form	Dark Elf
Target's Reaction	Target's image shimmers. (You feel different.)

Illusion: Drybone

Casters	Enchanter (39)
Casting Skill	Divination
Target's Reaction	Target's image shimmers. (You feel different.)

Illusion: Dwarf

Casters	Enchanter (16)
Mana Cost	30
Casting Skill	Divination
Casting Time (secs)	3
Recasting Delay (secs)	8.25
Duration	36 minutes
Range (feet)	0
Target	Yourself
Resistance Invoked	None
Effect	
Change Form	Dwarf
Target's Reaction	Target's image shimmers. (You feel different.)

Illusion: Earth Elemental

Casters	Enchanter (24)
Mana Cost	50
Casting Skill	Divination
Casting Time (secs)	3
Recasting Delay (secs)	8.25
Duration	36 minutes
Range (feet)	0
Target	Yourself
Resistance Invoked	None
Effects	
Change Form	Earth Elemental
STR boost	10
Target's Reaction	Target's image shimmers. (You feel different.)

Illusion: Erudite

Casters	Enchanter (12)
Mana Cost	30
Casting Skill	Divination
Casting Time (secs)	3
Recasting Delay (secs)	8.25
Duration	36 minutes
Range (feet)	0
Target	Yourself
Resistance Invoked	None
Effect	
Change Form	Erudite
Target's Reaction	Target's image shimmers. (You feel different.)

Illusion: Fire Elemental

Casters	Enchanter (34)
Casting Skill	Divination
Target's Reaction	Target's image shimmers. (You feel different.)

Illusion: Gnome

Casters	Enchanter (8)
Mana Cost	10
Casting Skill	Divination
Casting Time (secs)	3
Recasting Delay (secs)	8.25
Duration	3 x level minutes (max 36 m)
Range (feet)	0
Target	Yourself
Resistance Invoked	None
Effect	
Change Form	Gnome
Target's Reaction	Target's image shimmers. (You feel different.)

Illusion: Half-Elf

Casters	Enchanter (4)
Mana Cost	10
Casting Skill	Divination
Casting Time (secs)	3
Recasting Delay (secs)	8.25
Duration	3 x level minutes (max 36 m)
Range (feet)	0
Target	Yourself
Resistance Invoked	None
Effect	
Change Form	Half-Elf
Target's Reaction	Target's image shimmers. (You feel different.)

Illusion: Halfling

Casters	Enchanter (12)
Mana Cost	30
Casting Skill	Divination
Casting Time (secs)	3
Recasting Delay (secs)	8.25
Duration	36 minutes
Range (feet)	0
Target	Yourself
Resistance Invoked	None
Effect	
Change Form	Halfling
Target's Reaction	Target's image shimmers. (You feel different.)

Illusion: High Elf

Casters	Enchanter (12)
Mana Cost	30
Casting Skill	Divination
Casting Time (secs)	3
Recasting Delay (secs)	8.25
Duration	36 minutes
Range (feet)	0
Target	Yourself
Resistance Invoked	None
Effect	
Change Form	High Elf
Target's Reaction	Target's image shimmers. (You feel different.)

Illusion: Human

Casters	Enchanter (4)
Mana Cost	10
Casting Skill	Divination
Casting Time (secs)	3
Recasting Delay (secs)	8.25
Duration	3 x level minutes (max 36 m)
Range (feet)	0
Target	Yourself
Resistance Invoked	None
Effect	
Change Form	Human
Target's Reaction	Target's image shimmers. (You feel different.)

Illusion: Iksar

Casters	Enchanter (20)
Mana Cost	50
Casting Skill	Divination
Casting Time (secs)	3
Recasting Delay (secs)	8.5
Duration	36 minutes
Range (feet)	0
Target	Yourself
Resistance Invoked	None
Effect	
Change Form	Iksar
Target's Reaction	Target's image shimmers. (You feel different.)

Illusion: Ogre

Casters	Enchanter (20)
Mana Cost	50
Casting Skill	Divination
Casting Time (secs)	3
Recasting Delay (secs)	8.25
Duration	36 minutes
Range (feet)	0
Target	Yourself
Resistance Invoked	None
Effect	
Change Form	Ogre
Target's Reaction	Target's image shimmers. (You feel different.)

Illusion: Spirit Wolf

Casters	Enchanter (39)
Casting Skill	Divination
Target's Reaction	Target's image shimmers. (You feel different.)

Illusion: Skeleton

Casters	Enchanter (24)
Mana Cost	50
Casting Skill	Divination
Casting Time (secs)	3
Recasting Delay (secs)	8.25
Duration	36 minutes
Range (feet)	0
Target	Yourself
Resistance Invoked	None
Effect	
Change Form	Skeleton
Target's Reaction	Target's image shimmers. (You feel different.)

Illusion: Tree

Casters	Enchanter (16)
Mana Cost	30
Casting Skill	Divination
Outdoors only	
Casting Time (secs)	3
Recasting Delay (secs)	8.25
Duration	36 minutes
Range (feet)	0
Target	Yourself
Resistance Invoked	None
Effects	
Change Form	Tree
Immobilizes	
Target's Reaction	Target's image shimmers. (You feel different.)

Illusion: Troll

Casters	Enchanter (20)
Mana Cost	100
Casting Skill	Divination
Casting Time (secs)	3
Recasting Delay (secs)	8.25
Duration	36 minutes
Range (feet)	0
Target	Yourself
Resistance Invoked	None
Effects	
Change Form	Troll
Healing	1
(HP/6 secs)	
Target's Reaction	Target's image shimmers. (You feel different.)

Illusion: Water Elemental

Casters	Enchanter (29)
Casting Skill	Divination
Target's Reaction	Target's image shimmers. (You feel different.)

Illusion: Werewolf

Casters	Enchanter (44)
Casting Skill	Divination
Target's Reaction	Target's image shimmers. (You feel different.)

Illusion: Wood Elf

Casters	Enchanter (8)
Mana Cost	10
Casting Skill	Divination
Casting Time (secs)	3
Recasting Delay (secs)	8.25
Duration	3 x level minutes (max 36 m)
Range (feet)	0
Target	Yourself
Resistance Invoked	None
Effect	
Change Form	Wood Elf
Target's Reaction	Target's image shimmers. (You feel different.)

Immobilize

Casters	Cleric (49), Shaman (51), Necromancer (58), Wizard (39), Enchanter (39)
Casting Skill	Alteration
Target's Reaction	Target's feet adhere to the ground.

Immolate

Casters	Ranger (49), Druid (29)
Casting Skill	Evocation
Target's Reaction	Target is surrounded by blazing flames.

Impart Strength

Casters	Necromancer (8)
Mana Cost	15
Casting Skill	Alteration
Casting Time (secs)	4
Recasting Delay (secs)	7.25
Duration	6 minutes
Range (feet)	100
Target	Anyone (STR flows from you)
Resistance Invoked	None
Effect	
STR boost	10
Target's Reaction	Target looks stronger.

Incapacitate

Casters	Shaman (44), Enchanter (44)
Casting Skill	Alteration
Target's Reaction	Target looks frail.

Infectious Cloud

Casters	Shaman (19), Necromancer (16)
Mana Cost	78
Casting Skill	Conjuration
Casting Time (secs)	2.75
Duration	2 minutes, 6 seconds
Range (feet)	200
Radius of Effect (feet)	15
Target	Area
Resistance Invoked	Disease
Effects	
Disease	1
Immediate Damage (HP)	25
Subsequent Damage (HP/6 secs)	5
Target's Reaction	Target starts to wretch. (The bile wells up in your throat.)

Inferno of Al'Kabor

Casters	Wizard (53)
Casting Skill	Evocation
Target's Reaction	Target burns within the inferno of Al'Kabor.

Inferno Shield

Casters	Magician (29)
Casting Skill	Abjuration
Target's Reaction	Target is enveloped in flame.

Inferno Shock

Casters	Wizard (29)
Casting Skill	Evocation
Target's Reaction	Target's skin ignites.

Infusion

Casters	Necromancer (55)
Casting Skill	Alteration
Target's Reaction	Target radiates with essence. (Your mind clears as a rush of essence fills you.)

Insidious Decay

Casters	Shaman (52)
Casting Skill	Conjuration
Target's Reaction	Target sweats and shivers, looking feverish. (You feel a fever settle upon you.)

Inner Fire

Casters	Shaman (1)
Mana Cost	10
Casting Skill	Abjuration
Casting Time (secs)	3
Duration	3 + 3 x level minutes (max 27)
Range (feet)	100
Target	Anyone
Resistance Invoked	None
Effects	
AC boost	5 + 1 / 2 levels (max 10)
Bonus HP	10 +1/level (max 20)
Target's Reaction	Target's body pulses with energy.

Insidious Fever

Casters	Shaman (19)
Mana Cost	30
Casting Skill	Conjuration
Casting Time (secs)	1
Recasting Delay (secs)	7.5
Duration	1 minute + 12 seconds/level
Range (feet)	200
Target	Anyone
Resistance Invoked	Disease
Effects	
Disease	4
Disease Resistance lowered	10 + 1 / 2 levels
Target's Reaction	Target sweats and shivers, looking feverish. (You feel a fever settle upon you.)

Insidious Malady

Casters	Shaman (39)
Casting Skill	Conjuration
Target's Reaction	Target sweats and shivers, looking feverish. (You feel a fever settle upon you.)

Insight

Casters	Enchanter (39)
Casting Skill	Alteration
Target's Reaction	Target looks wise. (Your mind fills with wisdom.)

Insipid Weakness

Casters	Enchanter (34)
Casting Skill	Alteration
Target's Reaction	Target is weakened. (You feel weak.)

Inspire Fear

Casters	Cleric (24)
Mana Cost	80
Casting Skill	Alteration
Casting Time (secs)	4
Recasting Delay (secs)	10.25
Duration	30 secs
Range (feet)	200
Target	Anyone
Resistance Invoked	Magic
Effect	
Fear	Low-level
Target's Reaction	Target looks very afraid. (Your mind fills with fear.)

Intensify Death

Casters	Necromancer (24)
Mana Cost	50
Casting Skill	Alteration
Casting Time (secs)	6
Recasting Delay (secs)	32.25
Duration	1 minute + 6 seconds/level
Range (feet)	100
Target	Your pet
Resistance Invoked	None
Effects	
Attack Speed boost	10% +1% / 2 levels (max 30% boost)
STR boost	20 + 1 / 4 levels
AC boost	15 + 1 / 4 levels
Target's Reaction	Target's eyes gleam with madness.

Invert Gravity

Casters	Wizard (59)
Casting Skill	Alteration
Target's Reaction	Target rises chaotically into the air. (You feel gravity reverse.)

Invigor

Casters	Cleric (9), Paladin (22), Ranger (30), Druid (14), Shaman (24), Enchanter (24)
Mana Cost	20
Casting Skill	Alteration
Casting Time (secs)	3.5
Recasting Delay (secs)	5.75
Duration	12 seconds
Range (feet)	100
Target	Anyone
Resistance Invoked	None
Effect	
Restores Fatigue Points	35
Target's Reaction	Target looks energized. (Your body zings with energy.)

Invisibility

Casters	Shaman (29), Wizard (16), Magician (8), Enchanter (4)
Mana Cost	30
Casting Skill	Divination
Casting Time (secs)	5
Duration	3 x level minutes (max 20 m)
Range (feet)	100
Target	Anyone
Resistance Invoked	None
Effect	
Invisibility	
Target's Reaction	Target fades away. (You vanish.)

Invisibility versus Animals

Casters	Druid (9), Shaman (14)
Mana Cost	30
Casting Skill	Divination
Casting Time (secs)	3
Recasting Delay (secs)	8.25
Duration	3 x level minutes max 36 m)
Range (feet)	100
Target	Anyone
Resistance Invoked	None
Effect	
Invisible to Animals	
Target's Reaction	Target is surrounded by an aura which shimmers, and then fades away. (Part of your image fades away.)

Invisibility versus Undead

Casters	Cleric (14), Necromancer (1), Shadow Knight (9), Paladin (22), Enchanter (16)
Mana Cost	40
Casting Skill	Divination
Casting Time (secs)	4
Recasting Delay (secs)	6.25
Duration	3 x level minutes (max 27 m)
Range (feet)	100
Target	Anyone
Resistance Invoked	None
Effect	
Invisible to Undead	
Target's Reaction	Target fades a little. (You feel your skin tingle.)

Invoke Death

Casters	Necromancer (49)
Casting Skill	Conjuration

Invoke Fear

Casters	Cleric (39), Shadow Knight (49), Necromancer (34), Enchanter (39)
Casting Skill	Alteration
Target's Reaction	Target looks very afraid. (Your mind fills with fear.)

Invoke Lightning

Casters	Ranger (15), Druid (5)
Mana Cost	32
Casting Skill	Evocation
Outdoors only	
Casting Time (secs)	2.5
Recasting Delay (secs)	8.5
Duration	Instantaneous
Range (feet)	200
Radius of Effect (feet)	10
Target	Area
Resistance Invoked	Magic
Effect	
Damage (HP)	16 +1/level (max 25)
Target's Reaction	Target has been struck by lightning. (Lightning surges through your body.)

Invoke Shadow

Casters	Necromancer (34)
Casting Skill	Conjuration

Jaxan's Jig o' Vigor

Casters	Bard (3)
Mana Cost	0
Casting Skill	Percussion Instruments
Casting Time (secs)	3
Casting Delay (secs)	none
Recasting Delay (secs)	12
Duration	12 seconds
Range (feet)	0
Radius of Effect (feet)	35
Target	Your group
Resistance Invoked	None
Effect	
Restores Fatigue Points	10 + 1 / 4 levels
Target's Reaction	(The jig sends energy zinging through your body.)

Jonthan's Inspiration

Casters	Bard (58)
Casting Skill	Brass Instruments
Target's Reaction	(You feel inspired.)

Jonthan's Provocation

Casters	Bard (45)
Casting Skill	Brass Instruments
Target's Reaction	(You feel provoked.)

Jonthan's Whistling Warsong

Casters	Bard (7)
Mana Cost	0
Casting Skill	Singing
Casting Time (secs)	3
Casting Delay (secs)	none
Recasting Delay (secs)	12
Duration	12 seconds
Range (feet)	0
Target	Yourself
Resistance Invoked	None
Effects	
Attack Speed boost	15% +1% / 4 levels (max 25% boost)
AC boost	5 + 1 / 2 levels
STR boost	5 + 1 / 2 levels
Target's Reaction	(You whistle an ancient warsong.)

Juli's Animation

Casters	Enchanter (4)
Mana Cost	24
Casting Skill	Conjuration
Components	2 Tiny Daggers
Casting Time (secs)	2
Recasting Delay (secs)	6.25
Duration	Instantaneous
Range (feet)	0
Target	Yourself
Resistance Invoked	None
Effect	
Summon Animation	Animated Sword and Shield (Circle 2)

Jyll's Static Pulse

Casters	Wizard (53)
Casting Skill	Evocation
Target's Reaction	Target is slammed by a static pulse. (A static pulse slams through you.)

Jyll's Wave of Heat

Casters	Wizard (59)
Casting Skill	Evocation
Target's Reaction	Target is ashed by an intense wave of heat. (A wave of heat screams through you.)

Jyll's Zephyr of Ice

Casters	Wizard (56)
Casting Skill	Evocation
Target's Reaction	Target is torn by a zephyr of ice. (A zephyr of ice tears through you.)

Kazumi's Note of Preservation

Casters	Bard (60)
Casting Skill	Wind Instruments
Target's Reaction	(You feel protected.)

Kelin's Lucid Lullaby

Casters	Bard (15)
Mana Cost	0
Casting Skill	Stringed Instruments
Component	Lute
Casting Time (secs)	3
Casting Delay (secs)	none
Recasting Delay (secs)	12
Duration	6 seconds
Range (feet)	0
Radius of Effect (feet)	30
Target	Area (but not your group)
Resistance Invoked	Magic
Effect	
Mesmerization	
Target's Reaction	Target's head nods. (You feel quite drowsy.)

Kelin's Lugubrious Lament

Casters	Bard (8)
Mana Cost	0
Casting Skill	Stringed Instruments
Component	Lute
Casting Time (secs)	3
Casting Delay (secs)	none
Recasting Delay (secs)	12
Duration	12 seconds
Range (feet)	200
Target	Anyone
Resistance Invoked	Magic
Effects	
Target's Reaction Range (feet)	5 feet
Target's Help Radius	10 feet
Target much less likely to attack	
Target's Reaction	Target looks sad. (You feel a strong sense of loss.)

Kilan's Animation

Casters	Enchanter (12)
Mana Cost	65
Casting Skill	Conjuration
Component	Tiny Dagger
Casting Time (secs)	4
Recasting Delay (secs)	10.25
Duration	Instantaneous
Range (feet)	0
Target	Yourself
Resistance Invoked	None
Effect	
Summon Animation	Animated Sword and Shield (Circle 4)

Kintaz's Animation

Casters	Enchanter (49)
Casting Skill	Conjuration

Languid Pace

Casters	Enchanter (12)
Mana Cost	50
Casting Skill	Alteration
Casting Time (secs)	2.25
Duration	12 seconds + 6 seconds / 2 levels
Range (feet)	250
Target	Anyone
Resistance Invoked	Magic
Effect	
Attack Speed loss	15% +1% / 4 levels (max 30% loss)
Target's Reaction	Target slows down.

Largarn's Lamentation

Casters	Enchanter (55)
Casting Skill	Evocation
Target's Reaction	Target begins to weep. (You are very sad.)

Largo's Absonant Binding

Casters	Bard (51)
Casting Skill	Singing
Target's Reaction	Target is bound in strands of solid music. (Strands of solid music bind your body.)

Largo's Melodic Binding

Casters	Bard (20)
Mana Cost	0
Casting Skill	Singing
Casting Time (secs)	3
Casting Delay (secs)	none
Recasting Delay (secs)	12
Duration	12 seconds
Range (feet)	0
Radius of Effect (feet)	30
Target	Area (but not your group)
Resistance Invoked	Magic
Effects	
AC loss	5 + 1 / 2 levels
Attack Speed loss	95 + 1 / 2 levels
Target's Reaction	Target is bound in strands of solid music. (Strands of solid music bind your body.)

Lava Bolt

Casters	Magician (49)
Casting Skill	Evocation
Target's Reaction	Target is bathed in fire. (Stream of fire washes over you.)

Lava Storm

Casters	Wizard (34)
Casting Skill	Evocation
Target's Reaction	Target's skin blisters as fire rains down from above.

Lay on Hands

Casters	Paladin (1)
Mana Cost	0
Casting Skill	None
Casting Time (secs)	0
Recasting Delay (secs)	Once a day
Duration	Instantaneous
Range (feet)	50
Target	Anyone
Resistance Invoked	None
Effect	
Healing (HP)	1 +32/level
Target's Reaction	Target feels a healing touch.

Leach

Casters	Necromancer (12)
Mana Cost	72
Casting Skill	Alteration
Casting Time (secs)	2.4
Recasting Delay (secs)	12.5
Duration	54 secs
Range (feet)	200
Target	Anyone (HP flow to you)
Resistance Invoked	Magic
Effect	
Damage (HP/6 secs)	8
Target's Reaction	Target pales. (You feel your blood begin to leach away.)

Leatherskin

Casters	Necromancer (24), Wizard (24)
Mana Cost	83
Casting Skill	Abjuration
Component	Bloodstone
Casting Time (secs)	4
Duration	54 minutes
Range (feet)	0
Target	Yourself
Resistance Invoked	None
Effect	
Bonus HP	118
Target's Reaction	Target's skin looks like leather.

Leering Corpse

Casters	Shadow Knight (9), Necromancer (4)
Mana Cost	40
Casting Skill	Conjuration
Components	2 Bone Chips
Casting Time (secs)	6
Recasting Delay (secs)	11.75
Duration	Instantaneous
Range (feet)	0
Target	Yourself
Resistance Invoked	None
Effect	
Create Undead	Skeleton (Circle 2)
Target's Reaction	Skeleton rises from the dead.

Legacy of Spike

Casters	Druid (51)
Casting Skill	Abjuration
Target's Reaction	Target is surrounded by a thorny barrier.

Legacy of Thorn

Casters	Druid (59)
Casting Skill	Abjuration
Target's Reaction	Target is surrounded by a thorny barrier.

Lesser Conjuration: Air

Casters	Magician (39)
Casting Skill	Conjuration

Lesser Conjuration: Earth

Casters	Magician (39)
Casting Skill	Conjuration

Lesser Conjuration: Fire

Casters	Magician (39)
Casting Skill	Conjuration

Lesser Conjuration: Water

Casters	Magician (39)
Casting Skill	Conjuration

Lesser Shielding

Casters	Necromancer (8), Wizard (8), Magician (8), Enchanter (8)
Mana Cost	25
Casting Skill	Abjuration
Casting Time (secs)	4
Duration	3 x level minutes (max 27 m)
Range (feet)	0
Target	Yourself
Resistance Invoked	None
Effects	
Bonus HP	12 +1/level (max 30)
AC boost	12 +1/level (max 30)
Resist Magic boost	5 + 1 / 4 levels (max 10)
Target's Reaction	(You feel armored.)

Lesser Summoning: Air

Casters	Magician (20)
Mana Cost	200
Casting Skill	Conjuration
Components	Broom of Trilon (not consumed), Malachite
Casting Time (secs)	10
Duration	Instantaneous
Range (feet)	0
Target	Yourself
Resistance Invoked	None
Effect	
Summon Elemental	Air Elemental (Circle 6)

Lesser Summoning: Earth

Casters	Magician (20)
Mana Cost	200
Casting Skill	Conjuration
Components	Shovel of Ponz (not consumed), Malachite
Casting Time (secs)	10
Duration	Instantaneous
Range (feet)	0
Target	Yourself
Resistance Invoked	None
Effect	
Summon Elemental	Earth Elemental (Circle 6)

Lesser Summoning: Fire

Casters	Magician (20)
Mana Cost	200
Casting Skill	Conjuration
Components	Torch of Alna (not consumed), Malachite
Casting Time (secs)	10
Duration	Instantaneous
Range (feet)	0
Target	Yourself
Resistance Invoked	None
Effect	
Summon Elemental	Fire Elemental (Circle 6)

Lesser Summoning: Water

Casters	Magician (20)
Mana Cost	200
Casting Skill	Conjuration
Components	Stein of Ulissa (not consumed), Malachite
Casting Time (secs)	10
Duration	Instantaneous
Range (feet)	0
Target	Yourself
Resistance Invoked	None
Effect	
Summon Elemental	Water Elemental (Circle 6)

Levant

Casters	Necromancer (55)
Casting Skill	Alteration
Target's Reaction	Target steps into the shadows.

Levitate

Casters	Ranger (39), Druid (14), Shaman (14), Wizard (24), Enchanter (16)
Mana Cost	30
Casting Skill	Alteration
Component	Bat Wing
Casting Time (secs)	3
Recasting Delay (secs)	7.25
Duration	1 minute + 18 seconds/level
Range (feet)	100
Target	Anyone
Resistance Invoked	None
Effect	
Levitation	
Target's Reaction	Target's feet leave the ground.

Lich

Casters	Necromancer (49)
Casting Skill	Alteration
Target's Reaction	Target's skin peels off. (You feel the skin peel from your bones.)

Lifedraw

Casters	Shadow Knight (30), Necromancer (12)
Mana Cost	63
Casting Skill	Alteration
Casting Time (secs)	2.45
Duration	Instantaneous
Range (feet)	200
Target	Anyone (HP flow to you)
Resistance Invoked	Magic
Effect	
Damage (HP)	27 +1/level (max 45)
Target's Reaction	Target staggers. (You feel your lifeforce drain away.)

Lifespike

Casters	Shadow Knight (15), Necromancer (4)
Mana Cost	18
Casting Skill	Alteration
Casting Time (secs)	1.75
Duration	Instantaneous
Range (feet)	200
Target	Anyone(flows to you)
Resistance Invoked	Magic
Effect	
Damage (HP)	7 + 1 / 2 levels (max 11)
Target's Reaction	Target staggers. (You feel you lifeforce drain away.)

Lifetap

Casters	Shadow Knight (9), Necromancer (1)
Mana Cost	9
Casting Skill	Alteration
Casting Time (secs)	1.5
Duration	Instantaneous
Range (feet)	200
Target	Anyone (HP flow to you)
Resistance Invoked	Magic
Effect	
Damage (HP)	3 + 1 / 2 levels (max 5)
Target's Reaction	Target staggers. (You feel you lifeforce drain away.)

Light Healing

Casters	Cleric (5), Paladin (15), Ranger (22), Druid (9), Shaman (9)
Mana Cost	25
Casting Skill	Alteration
Casting Time (secs)	2
Duration	Instantaneous
Range (feet)	100
Target	Anyone
Resistance Invoked	None
Effect	
Healing (HP)	24 + 1 / 2 levels (max 33)

Lightning Blast

Casters	Druid (49)
Casting Skill	Evocation
Target's Reaction	Target has been struck by lightning. (Lightning surges through your body.)

Lightning Bolt

Casters	Wizard (16)
Mana Cost	85
Casting Skill	Evocation
Casting Time (secs)	2.7
Duration	Instantaneous
Range (feet)	300
Target	Anyone
Resistance Invoked	Magic
Effects	
Damage (HP)	85 +2/level (max 125)
Knockback	1/3 foot
Target's Reaction	Target's body spasms as a bolt of lightning arcs through them.

Lightning Shock

Casters	Wizard (39)
Casting Skill	Evocation
Target's Reaction	Target's skin ignites.

Lightning Storm

Casters	Wizard (24)
Mana Cost	137
Casting Skill	Evocation
Casting Time (secs)	3.6
Recasting Delay (secs)	14.5
Duration	Instantaneous
Impact Duration (secs)	7.5
Range (feet)	150
Radius of Effect (feet)	25
Target	Area
Resistance Invoked	Magic
Effect	
Damage (HP)	75
Target's Reaction	Target's skin blisters as lightning rains down from above.

Lightning Strike

Casters	Druid (34)
Casting Skill	Evocation
Target's Reaction	Target has been struck by lightning. (Lightning surges through your body.)

Listless Power

Casters	Shaman (29), Enchanter (29)
Casting Skill	Alteration
Target's Reaction	Target looks frail.

Locate Corpse

Casters	Shadow Knight (9), Necromancer (1)
Mana Cost	5
Casting Skill	Divination
Casting Time (secs)	1.5
Recasting Delay (secs)	5.25
Duration	Instantaneous
Range (feet)	10,000
Radius of Effect (feet)	1000
Target	Yourself
Resistance Invoked	None
Effect	
Locate Corpse	

Lull

Casters	Cleric (1), Paladin (15), Enchanter (1)
Mana Cost	10
Casting Skill	Alteration
Casting Time (secs)	1.5
Recasting Delay (secs)	5.25
Duration	1 minute + 12 seconds/level (max 2 m)
Range (feet)	200
Target	Anyone
Resistance Invoked	Magic
Effects	
Target's Reaction Range (feet)	15 feet
Target's Help Radius	15 feet
Target's Reaction	Target looks less aggressive.

Lull Animal

Casters	Ranger (9), Druid (1)
Mana Cost	10
Casting Skill	Alteration
Casting Time (secs)	1.5
Recasting Delay (secs)	5.25
Duration	1 minute + 12 seconds/level (max 2 m)
Range (feet)	200
Target	Animal
Resistance Invoked	Magic
Effects	
Target's Reaction Range (feet)	15 feet
Target's Help Radius	25 feet
Target much less likely to attack	

Lure of Flame

Casters	Wizard (55)
Casting Skill	Evocation
Target's Reaction	Target succumbs to the lure of flame. (You succumb to the lure of flame.)

Lure of Frost

Casters	Wizard (52)
Casting Skill	Evocation
Target's Reaction	Target succumbs to the lure of frost.

Lure of Ice

Casters	Wizard (60)
Casting Skill	Evocation
Target's Reaction	Target succumbs to the lure of ice.

Lure of Lightning

Casters	Wizard (58)
Casting Skill	Evocation
Target's Reaction	Target succumbs to lure of lightning. (You succumb to the lure of lightning.)

Lyssa's Cataloging Librello

Casters	Bard (14)
Mana Cost	0
Casting Skill	Singing
Casting Time (secs)	3
Casting Delay (secs)	none
Recasting Delay (secs)	12
Duration	Instantaneous
Range (feet)	100
Target	Anyone
Resistance Invoked	None
Effect	
Identify 1 Item	
Target's Reaction	(Long forgotten knowledge sifts through your mind.)

Lyssa's Locating Lyric

Casters	Bard (4)
Mana Cost	0
Casting Skill	Singing
Casting Time (secs)	3
Casting Delay (secs)	none
Recasting Delay (secs)	12
Duration	Instantaneous
Range (feet)	0
Radius of Effect (feet)	900
Target	Yourself
Resistance Invoked	None
Effect	
Locate Corpse	
Target's Reaction	(A tune pervades your mind and beckons you.)

Lyssa's Solidarity of Vision

Casters	Bard (34)
Casting Skill	Wind Instruments
Target's Reaction	Target's eyes are covered by notes of solid music. (Strands of music cover your eyes.)

Lyssa's Veracious Concord

Casters	Bard (24)
Mana Cost	0
Casting Skill	Wind Instruments
Component	Wooden Flute
Casting Time (secs)	3
Casting Delay (secs)	none
Recasting Delay (secs)	12
Duration	12 seconds
Range (feet)	0
Radius of Effect (feet)	80
Target	Your group
Resistance Invoked	None
Effects	
See Invisible, Ultravision	
Target's Reaction	(Music floods your mind and sharpens your sight.)

Magnify

Casters	Wizard (29)
Casting Skill	Divination
Target's Reaction	Target eyes gleam. (Your eyes feel stronger.)

Major Shielding

Casters	Necromancer (24), Wizard (24), Magician (24), Enchanter (24)
Mana Cost	80
Casting Skill	Abjuration
Casting Time (secs)	5
Duration	45 minutes
Range (feet)	0
Target	Yourself
Resistance Invoked	None
Effects	
Bonus HP	45 +1/level (max 75)
AC boost	32 +1/level (max 60)
Resist Magic boost	14
Target's Reaction	(You feel armored.)

Mala

Casters	Magician (60)
Casting Skill	Alteration
Target's Reaction	Target looks very uncomfortable. (You feel very vulnerable.)

Malignant Dead

Casters	Shadow Knight (52), Necromancer (39)
Casting Skill	Conjuration

Malise

Casters	Shaman (19), Magician (24)
Mana Cost	60
Casting Skill	Alteration
Casting Time (secs)	3
Recasting Delay (secs)	8.25
Duration	1 minute + 12 seconds/level
Range (feet)	200
Target	Anyone
Resistance Invoked	Magic
Effects	
Fire Resistance lowered	6 + 1 / 2 levels (max 20)
Cold Resistance lowered	6 + 1 / 2 levels (max 20)
Magic Resistance lowered	6 + 1 / 2 levels (max 20)
Poison Resistance lowered	6 + 1 / 2 levels (max 20)
Target's Reaction	Target looks uncomfortable.

Malisement

Casters	Shaman (34), Magician (44)
Casting Skill	Alteration
Target's Reaction	Target looks uncomfortable.

Malo

Casters	Shaman (60)
Casting Skill	Alteration
Target's Reaction	Target looks very uncomfortable. (You feel very vulnerable.)

Malosi

Casters	Shaman (49), Magician (51)
Casting Skill	Alteration
Target's Reaction	Target looks very uncomfortable.

Malosini

Casters	Shaman (57), Magician (58)
Casting Skill	Alteration
Target's Reaction	Target looks very uncomfortable. (You feel very vulnerable.)

Mana Sieve

Casters	Enchanter (34)
Casting Skill	Alteration
Target's Reaction	Target staggers in pain. (You feel your mental energies slip away.)

Manasink

Casters	Wizard (58)
Casting Skill	Abjuration
Target's Reaction	Target's skin is slicked in a silver glow. (A silver force slicks your skin.)

Manaskin

Casters	Necromancer (52), Wizard (52)
Casting Skill	Abjuration
Target's Reaction	Target's skin gleams with an incandescent glow.

Manastorm

Casters	Magician (59)
Casting Skill	Evocation
Target's Reaction	Target's skin numbs as deadly mana rains down from above.

Manicial Strength

Casters	Shaman (57)
Casting Skill	Alteration
Target's Reaction	Target's muscles fill with manicial strength. (You are filled with manicial strength.)

Mark of Karn

Casters	Cleric (56)
Casting Skill	Abjuration
Target's Reaction	Target's skin gleams with a pure aura.

Markar's Clash

Casters	Wizard (49)
Casting Skill	Evocation
Target's Reaction	Target is stunned.

Markar's Discord

Casters	Wizard (56)
Casting Skill	Evocation
Target's Reaction	Target is stunned.

Mask of the Hunter

Casters	Druid (60)
Casting Skill	Alteration
Target's Reaction	Target's features sharpen.

McVaxius' Berserker Crescendo

Casters	Bard (42)
Casting Skill	Brass Instruments
Target's Reaction	(You go berserk.)

McVaxius' Rousing Rondo

Casters	Bard (57)
Casting Skill	Brass Instruments
Target's Reaction	(You are roused.)

Melanie's Mellifluous Motion

Casters	Bard (21)
Mana Cost	0
Casting Skill	Wind Instruments
Casting Time (secs)	3
Casting Delay (secs)	none
Recasting Delay (secs)	12
Duration	Instantaneous
Range (feet)	600
Radius of Effect (feet)	200
Target	Your group
Resistance Invoked	None
Effect	
Random Teleport	
Target's Reaction	Target is swept away by a mellifluous melody. (A mellifluous melody sweeps you away.)

Memory Blur

Casters	Enchanter (12)
Mana Cost	40
Casting Skill	Alteration
Casting Time (secs)	2.5
Recasting Delay (secs)	14.25
Duration	Instantaneous
Range (feet)	200
Target	Anyone
Resistance Invoked	Magic
Effect	
NPC Hate List erased	
Target's Reaction	Target blinks a few times. (You feel your mind fog.)

Memory Flux

Casters	Enchanter (55)
Casting Skill	Alteration
Target's Reaction	Target blinks a few times. (You feel your mind fog.)

Mend Bones

Casters	Necromancer (8)
Mana Cost	25
Casting Skill	Alteration
Casting Time (secs)	3.5
Recasting Delay (secs)	9
Duration	Instantaneous
Range (feet)	100
Target	Undead
Resistance Invoked	None
Effect	
Healing (HP)	25 +1/level (max 50)
Target's Reaction	Target begins to mend.

Mesmerization

Casters	Enchanter (16)
Mana Cost	70
Casting Skill	Conjuration
Casting Time (secs)	3
Duration	24 secs
Range (feet)	200
Radius of Effect (feet)	30
Target	Area
Resistance Invoked	Magic
Effect	
Mesmerization	
Target's Reaction	Target has been mesmerized.

Mesmerize

Casters	Enchanter (4)
Mana Cost	20
Casting Skill	Conjuration
Casting Time (secs)	2.5
Duration	24 secs
Range (feet)	200
Target	Anyone
Resistance Invoked	Magic
Effect	
Mesmerization	
Target's Reaction	Target has been mesmerized.

Mind Wipe

Casters	Enchanter (39)
Casting Skill	Alteration
Target's Reaction	Target blinks a few times. (You feel your mind fog.)

Minion of Shadows

Casters	Necromancer (53)
Casting Skill	Conjuration

Minor Conjuration: Air
Casters	Magician (34)
Casting Skill	Conjuration

Minor Conjuration: Earth
Casters	Magician (34)
Casting Skill	Conjuration

Minor Conjuration: Fire
Casters	Magician (34)
Casting Skill	Conjuration

Minor Conjuration: Water
Casters	Magician (34)
Casting Skill	Conjuration

Minor Healing
Casters	Cleric (1), Paladin (9), Ranger (9), Druid (1), Shaman (1)
Mana Cost	10
Custing Skill	Alteration
Casting Time (secs)	1
Duration	Instantaneous
Range (feet)	100
Target	Anyone
Resistance Invoked	None
Effect	
Healing (HP)	10
Target's Reaction	Target feels a little better.

Minor Illusion
Casters	Enchanter (1)
Mana Cost	10
Casting Skill	Divination
Casting Time (secs)	3
Recasting Delay (secs)	8.25
Duration	3 x level minutes (max 36 m)
Range (feet)	0
Target	Yourself
Resistance Invoked	None
Effects	
Change Form	to that of nearest object
Movement Rate loss	Immobile
Target's Reaction	(You feel different.)

Minor Shielding
Casters	Necromancer (1), Wizard (1), Magician (1), Enchanter (1)
Mana Cost	10
Casting Skill	Abjuration
Casting Time (secs)	2.5
Duration	3 + 3 x level minutes (max 27 m)
Range (feet)	0
Target	Yourself
Resistance Invoked	None
Effects	
Bonus HP	5 +1/level (max 10)
AC boost	10 +1/level (max 15)
Target's Reaction	Target is surrounded by a translucent shield. (You feel armored.)

Minor Summoning: Air
Casters	Magician (16)
Mana Cost	160
Casting Skill	Conjuration
Components	Broom of Trilon (not consumed), Lapis Lazuli
Casting Time (secs)	9
Duration	Instantaneous
Range (feet)	0
Target	Yourself
Resistance Invoked	None
Effect	
Summon Elemental	Air Elemental (Circle 5)

Minor Summoning: Earth
Casters	Magician (16)
Mana Cost	160
Casting Skill	Conjuration
Components	Shovel of Ponz (not consumed), Lapis Lazuli
Casting Time (secs)	9
Duration	Instantaneous
Range (feet)	0
Target	Yourself
Resistance Invoked	None
Effect	
Summon Elemental	Earth Elemental (Circle 5)

Minor Summoning: Fire

Casters	Magician (16)
Mana Cost	160
Casting Skill	Conjuration
Components	Torch of Alna (not consumed), Lapis Lazuli
Casting Time (secs)	9
Duration	Instantaneous
Range (feet)	0
Target	Yourself
Resistance Invoked	None
Effect	
Summon Elemental	Fire Elemental (Circle 5)

Minor Summoning: Water

Casters	Magician (16)
Mana Cost	160
Casting Skill	Conjuration
Components	Stein of Ulissa (not consumed), Lapis Lazuli
Casting Time (secs)	9
Duration	Instantaneous
Range (feet)	0
Target	Yourself
Resistance Invoked	None
Effect	
Summon Elemental	Water Elemental (Circle 5)

Mircyl's Animation

Casters	Enchanter (8)
Mana Cost	45
Casting Skill	Conjuration
Components	3 Tiny Daggers
Casting Time (secs)	3
Recasting Delay (secs)	8.25
Duration	Instantaneous
Range (feet)	0
Target	Yourself
Resistance Invoked	None
Effect	
Summon Animation	Animated Sword and Shield (Circle 3)

Mist

Casters	Enchanter (12)
Mana Cost	30
Casting Skill	Abjuration
Casting Time (secs)	3
Duration	27 minutes
Range (feet)	100
Target	Anyone
Resistance Invoked	None
Effect	
AC boost	9 +1/level (max 25)
Target's Reaction	Target's image blurs.

Modulating Rod

Casters	Magician (44)
Casting Skill	Conjuration

Mortal Deftness

Casters	Shaman (58)
Casting Skill	Alteration
Target's Reaction	Target begins to move with mortal deftness. (Your muscles move with mortal deftness.)

Muzzle of Mardu

Casters	Magician (56)
Casting Skill	Conjuration

Natureskin

Casters	Druid (57)
Casting Skill	Abjuration
Target's Reaction	Target's skin shimmers.

Nek Gate

Casters	Wizard (24)
Mana Cost	150
Casting Skill	Alteration
Casting Time (secs)	7
Recasting Delay (secs)	12.25
Duration	Instantaneous
Range (feet)	0
Target	Yourself
Resistance Invoked	None
Effect	
Teleports you to	Nektulos Forest
Target's Reaction	Target fades away.

Nek Portal

Casters	Wizard (34)
Casting Skill	Alteration
Target's Reaction	Target creates a shimmering portal.

Nillipus' March of the Wee

Casters	Bard (52)
Casting Skill	Percussion Instruments
Target's Reaction	(You feel small.)

Nimble

Casters	Shaman (34)
Casting Skill	Alteration
Target's Reaction	Target looks nimble.

Niv's Harmonic

Casters	Bard (58)
Casting Skill	Singing
Target's Reaction	(The harmony surrounds you.)

Niv's Melody of Preservation

Casters	Bard (47)
Casting Skill	Stringed Instruments
Target's Reaction	(You feel an aura of protection engulf you.)

North Gate

Casters	Wizard (20)
Mana Cost	150
Casting Skill	Alteration
Casting Time (secs)	7
Recasting Delay (secs)	12.25
Duration	Instantaneous
Range (feet)	0
Target	Yourself
Resistance Invoked	None
Effect	
Teleports you to	North Karana
Target's Reaction	Target fades away.

North Portal

Casters	Wizard (29)
Casting Skill	Alteration
Target's Reaction	Target creates a shimmering portal.

Nullify Magic

Casters	Cleric (39), Paladin (58), Ranger (58), Druid (44), Shaman (44), Shadow Knight (58), Necromancer (39), Wizard (34), Magician (34), Enchanter (29)
Casting Skill	Abjuration
Target's Reaction	Target feels dispelled.

Numb the Dead

Casters	Shadow Knight (15), Necromancer (4)
Mana Cost	20
Casting Skill	Abjuration
Component	Bone Chips
Casting Time (secs)	2
Recasting Delay (secs)	5.25
Duration	1 minute + 6 seconds/level (max 2 m)
Range (feet)	200
Target	Undead
Resistance Invoked	Magic
Effects	
Target's Reaction Range (feet)	15 feet
Target's Help Radius	25 feet
Target much less likely to attack	
Target's Reaction	Target looks ambivalent.

Numbing Cold

Casters	Wizard (1)
Mana Cost	13
Casting Skill	Evocation
Casting Time (secs)	1.35
Recasting Delay (secs)	8.5
Duration	Instantaneous
Range (feet)	0
Radius of Effect (feet)	25
Target	Area (but not your group)
Resistance Invoked	Cold
Effects	
Damage (HP)	5 +1/level (max 7)
Knockback	1 foot
Target's Reaction	Target looks stone cold.

Obscure

Casters	Enchanter (29)
Casting Skill	Abjuration
Target's Reaction	Target's image shifts out of focus. (You image has been obscured.)

Overwhelming Splendor

Casters	Enchanter (56)
Casting Skill	Alteration
Target's Reaction	Target is adorned in an aura of radiant grace.

O'Keils Radiation

Casters	Wizard (4)
Mana Cost	15
Casting Skill	Abjuration
Casting Time (secs)	3
Recasting Delay (secs)	8.25
Duration	Level minutes + 10
Range (feet)	100
Target	Anyone
Resistance Invoked	Fire
Effects	
Reflect Damage (HP)	2
Resist Fire boost	5 + 1 / 2 levels (max 10)
Target's Reaction	Target begins to radiate.

Pacify

Casters	Cleric (39), Paladin (51), Enchanter (39)
Casting Skill	Alteration
Target's Reaction	Target looks less aggressive. (You feel your aggression subside.)

Pack Chloroplast

Casters	Druid (49)
Casting Skill	Alteration
Target's Reaction	Target begins to regenerate.

Pack Regeneration

Casters	Druid (39)
Casting Skill	Alteration
Target's Reaction	Target begins to regenerate.

Pack Spirit

Casters	Druid (39)
Casting Skill	Alteration
Target's Reaction	Target is surrounded by a brief lupine aura.

Pact of Shadow

Casters	Necromancer (44)
Casting Skill	Alteration
Target's Reaction	Target pulses with a blue-green aura. (Your wounds begin to heal.)

Panic Animal

Casters	Druid (1)
Mana Cost	10
Casting Skill	Alteration
Casting Time (secs)	2
Recasting Delay (secs)	6.25
Duration	18 secs
Range (feet)	200
Target	Animal
Resistance Invoked	Magic
Effect	
Fear	Low-level

Panic the Dead

Casters	Cleric (29), Shadow Knight (54), Necromancer (29)
Casting Skill	Alteration
Target's Reaction	Target has the fear of life put in them. (Your bones tingle.)

Paralyzing Earth

Casters	Cleric (56), Shaman (56), Necromancer (49), Wizard (49), Enchanter (49)
Casting Skill	Alteration
Target's Reaction	Target's feet adhere to the ground.

Pendril's Animation

Casters	Enchanter (1)
Mana Cost	12
Casting Skill	Conjuration
Component	Tiny Dagger
Casting Time (secs)	1.5
Recasting Delay (secs)	4.25
Duration	Instantaneous
Range (feet)	0
Target	Yourself
Resistance Invoked	None
Effect	
Summon Animation	Animated Sword and Shield (Circle 1)

Phantom Armor

Casters	Magician (52)
Casting Skill	Abjuration
Target's Reaction	Target dons gleaming armor. (You are covered in illusionary armor.)

Phantom Chain

Casters	Magician (29)
Casting Skill	Abjuration
Target's Reaction	Target dons chainmail armor. (You are covered in illusionary chainmail armor.)

Phantom Leather

Casters	Magician (16)
Mana Cost	60
Casting Skill	Abjuration
Component	Cat's Eye Agate
Casting Time (secs)	4
Duration	45 minutes
Range (feet)	0
Target	Yourself
Resistance Invoked	None
Effects	
Healing (HP)	1
AC boost	20 + 1 / 2 levels (max 30)
Target's Reaction	Target dons leather armor. (You are covered in illusionary leather armor.)

Phantom Plate

Casters	Magician (44)
Casting Skill	Abjuration
Target's Reaction	Target dons platemail armor. (You are covered in illusionary platemail armor.)

Pillage Enchantment

Casters	Enchanter (44)
Casting Skill	Abjuration

Pillar of Fire

Casters	Wizard (16)
Mana Cost	84
Casting Skill	Evocation
Casting Time (secs)	3.15
Recasting Delay (secs)	8.5
Duration	Instantaneous
Range (feet)	200
Radius of Effect (feet)	15
Target	Area
Resistance Invoked	Fire
Effect	
Damage (HP)	36 +2/level (max 76)
Target's Reaction	Target is immolated in flame.

Pillar of Flame

Casters	Wizard (57)
Casting Skill	Evocation
Target's Reaction	Target is immolated in a pillar of flame.

Pillar of Frost

Casters	Wizard (51)
Casting Skill	Evocation
Target's Reaction	Target is encased within a pillar of frost.

Pillar of Lightning

Casters	Wizard (54)
Casting Skill	Evocation
Target's Reaction	Target is immolated in a pillar of raging lightning.

Plague

Casters	Shaman (49), Necromancer (52)
Casting Skill	Conjuration
Target's Reaction	Target sweats and shivers, looking feverish. (You feel feverish.)

Plainsight

Casters	Wizard (55)
Casting Skill	Divination
Target's Reaction	Target's eyes glow violet. (You eyes tingle.)

Pogonip

Casters	Druid (24)
Mana Cost	125
Casting Skill	Evocation
Casting Time (secs)	3.5
Recasting Delay (secs)	14.5
Duration	Instantaneous
Impact Duration (secs)	7.5
Range (feet)	150
Radius of Effect (feet)	20
Target	Area
Resistance Invoked	Cold
Effect	
Damage (HP)	62
Target's Reaction	Target is sheathed in ice crystals.

Poison Bolt

Casters	Necromancer (4)
Mana Cost	30
Casting Skill	Conjuration
Casting Time (secs)	1.75
Duration	42 secs
Range (feet)	200
Target	Anyone
Resistance Invoked	Poison
Effects	
Poison	1
Immediate Damage (HP)	11
Subsequent Damage (HP/6 secs)	5
Knockback	1/2 foot
Target's Reaction	Target has been poisoned.

Poison Storm

Casters	Shaman (24)
Mana Cost	125
Casting Skill	Evocation
Casting Time (secs)	3.5
Recasting Delay (secs)	14.5
Duration	Instantaneous
Impact Duration (secs)	7.5
Range (feet)	150
Radius of Effect (feet)	20
Target	Area
Resistance Invoked	Poison
Effect	
Damage (HP)	60
Target's Reaction	Target's skin blisters. (Your skin blisters as poison rains down on you.)

Pouch of Quellious

Casters	Magician (55)
Casting Skill	Conjuration

Pox of Bertoxxulous

Casters	Shaman (59)
Casting Skill	Conjuration
Target's Reaction	Target's skin erupts in purulent pock marks.

Project Lightning

Casters	Wizard (16)
Mana Cost	85
Casting Skill	Evocation
Casting Time (secs)	2.5
Recasting Delay (secs)	8.5
Duration	Instantaneous
Range (feet)	0
Radius of Effect (feet)	25
Target	Area (but not your group)
Resistance Invoked	Magic
Effects	
Damage (HP)	41 +1/level (max 62)
Knockback	3 feet
Target's Reaction	Target is consumed by lightning. (Lightning bursts through your body.)

Protect

Casters	Shaman (24)
Mana Cost	75
Casting Skill	Abjuration
Casting Time (secs)	6
Recasting Delay (secs)	14.25
Duration	36 minutes
Range (feet)	100
Target	Anyone
Resistance Invoked	None
Effect	
AC boost	17 +1/level (max 45)
Target's Reaction	Target is covered in a aura. (A protective aura settles over you.)

Psalm of Cooling

Casters	Bard (33)
Casting Skill	Singing
Target's Reaction	(You feel protected from fire.)

Psalm of Mystic Shielding

Casters	Bard (41)
Casting Skill	Singing
Target's Reaction	(You feel protected from magic.)

Psalm of Purity

Casters	Bard (37)
Casting Skill	Singing
Target's Reaction	(You feel protected from poison.)

Psalm of Vitality

Casters	Bard (29)
Casting Skill	Singing
Target's Reaction	(You feel protected from disease.)

Psalm of Warmth

Casters	Bard (25)
Casting Skill	Singing
Target's Reaction	(You feel protected from cold.)

Purify Mana

Casters	Enchanter (49)
Casting Skill	Alteration

Purifying Rhythms

Casters	Bard (13)
Mana Cost	0
Casting Skill	Percussion Instruments
Casting Time (secs)	3
Casting Delay (secs)	none
Recasting Delay (secs)	12
Duration	12 seconds
Range (feet)	0
Radius of Effect (feet)	50
Target	Your group
Resistance Invoked	None
Effects	
Resist Magic boost	5 + 1 / 2 levels
Resist Poison boost	5 + 1 / 2 levels
Resist Disease boost	5 + 1 / 2 levels
AC boost	5 + 1 / 4 levels
Target's Reaction	(You feel an aura of vigorous protection surround you.)

Pyrocruor

Casters	Necromancer (58)
Casting Skill	Alteration
Target's Reaction	Target's blood ignites.

Quickness

Casters	Shaman (29), Enchanter (16)
Mana Cost	80
Casting Skill	Alteration
Casting Time (secs)	3.1
Duration	1 minute + 12 seconds/level (max 11 m)
Range (feet)	100
Target	Anyone
Resistance Invoked	None
Effect	
Attack Speed boost	20% +1% / 2 levels (max 30% boost)
Target's Reaction	Target feels much faster.

Quiver of Marr

Casters	Magician (53)
Casting Skill	Conjuration

Quivering Veil of Xarn

Casters	Necromancer (58)
Casting Skill	Abjuration
Target's Reaction	Target has been surrounded by the Quivering Veil of Xarn.

Radiant Visage

Casters	Enchanter (34)
Casting Skill	Alteration
Target's Reaction	Target's face takes on a radiant visage. (You feel radiant.)

Radius of Fear 2

Casters	Cleric (24)
Mana Cost	120
Casting Skill	Alteration
Casting Time (secs)	4.5
Recasting Delay (secs)	11.25
Duration	Instantaneous
Range (feet)	200
Radius of Effect (feet)	10
Target	Anyone
Resistance Invoked	Magic
Effect	
Stun	6 seconds
Target's Reaction	Target looks very afraid. (Your mind fills with fear.)

Rage

Casters	Shaman (49)
Casting Skill	Abjuration
Target's Reaction	Target goes berserk. (You lose yourself in your rage and go berserk.)

Rage of Zomm

Casters	Magician (55)
Casting Skill	Conjuration

Raging Strength

Casters	Shaman (29)
Casting Skill	Alteration
Target's Reaction	Target looks stronger.

Rain of Blades

Casters	Magician (12)
Mana Cost	62
Casting Skill	Evocation
Casting Time (secs)	2.75
Recasting Delay (secs)	14.5
Duration	Instantaneous
Impact Duration (secs)	7.5
Range (feet)	150
Radius of Effect (feet)	20
Target	Area
Resistance Invoked	Magic
Effect	
Damage (HP)	26
Target's Reaction	Target's skin shreads as blades rain down from above.

Rain of Fire

Casters	Magician (20)
Mana Cost	125
Casting Skill	Evocation
Casting Time (secs)	3.5
Recasting Delay (secs)	14.5
Duration	Instantaneous
Impact Duration (secs)	7.5
Range (feet)	150
Radius of Effect (feet)	20
Target	Area
Resistance Invoked	Fire
Effect	
Damage (HP)	56
Target's Reaction	Target's skin blisters as fire rains down from above.

Rain of Lava

Casters	Magician (39)
Casting Skill	Evocation
Target's Reaction	Target's skin blisters as lava rains down from above.

Rain of Spikes

Casters	Magician (29)
Casting Skill	Evocation
Target's Reaction	Target's skin shreads as spikes rain down from above.

Rain of Swords

Casters	Magician (49)
Casting Skill	Evocation
Target's Reaction	Target's skin shreads as swords rain down from above.

Rampage

Casters	Enchanter (39)
Casting Skill	Alteration
Target's Reaction	Target begins to rampage. (You feel the urge to rampage.)

Rapacious Subversion

Casters	Necromancer (24)
Mana Cost	200
Casting Skill	Alteration
Casting Time (secs)	3
Recasting Delay (secs)	10.25
Duration	Instantaneous
Range (feet)	200
Target	Anyone
Resistance Invoked	None
Effect	
Mana boost	60
Target's Reaction	Target twitches. (A foreign surge of mana refreshes your mind.)

Rapture

Casters	Enchanter (59)
Casting Skill	Conjuration
Target's Reaction	Target swoons in raptured bliss.

Recant Magic

Casters	Enchanter (53)
Casting Skill	Abjuration
Target's Reaction	Target's enchantments begin to fade. (You feel your enchantments being stripped away.)

Reckoning

Casters	Cleric (54)
Casting Skill	Evocation
Target's Reaction	Target has been struck by the judgement of the gods.

Reckless Strength

Casters	Cleric (5), Paladin (22)
Mana Cost	30
Casting Skill	Alteration
Casting Time (secs)	3
Recasting Delay (secs)	8.25
Duration	3 minutes
Range (feet)	100
Target	Anyone
Resistance Invoked	None
Effect	
STR boost	20 - 1 / 6 seconds (ending at -10 STR)
Target's Reaction	Target's muscles bulge with reckless strength. (Your muscles erupt with r. s.)

Reclaim Energy

Casters	Necromancer (1), Magician (1), Enchanter (1)
Mana Cost	5
Casting Skill	Conjuration
Casting Time (secs)	2.5
Duration	Instantaneous
Range (feet)	100
Target	Your pet
Resistance Invoked	None
Effect	
Reclaim Energy	Restores a bit of mana
Target's Reaction	Target disperses.

Regeneration

Casters	Ranger (55), Druid (34), Shaman (24)
Mana Cost	100
Casting Skill	Alteration
Casting Time (secs)	6
Duration	1 minute + 18 seconds/level
Range (feet)	100
Target	Anyone
Resistance Invoked	None
Effect	
Healing (HP/6 secs)	5
Target's Reaction	Target begins to regenerate.

Regrowth

Casters	Druid (54), Shaman (52)
Casting Skill	Alteration
Target's Reaction	Target begins to regenerate

Regrowth of the Grove

Casters	Druid (58)
Casting Skill	Alteration
Target's Reaction	Target begins to regenerate.

Remedy

Casters	Cleric (51)
Casting Skill	Alteration
Target's Reaction	Target's wounds fade away.

Rend

Casters	Wizard (49)
Casting Skill	Evocation
Target's Reaction	Target screams as a magic force rends away their flesh.

Renew Bones

Casters	Necromancer (29)
Casting Skill	Alteration

Renew Elements

Casters	Magician (8)
Mana Cost	25
Casting Skill	Alteration
Casting Time (secs)	3
Recasting Delay (secs)	9
Duration	Instantaneous
Range (feet)	100
Target	Your pet
Resistance Invoked	None
Effect	
Healing (HP)	25 +1/level (max 50)
Target's Reaction	Target form pulses blue.

Renew Summoning

Casters	Magician (20)
Mana Cost	100
Casting Skill	Alteration
Casting Time (secs)	3.5
Recasting Delay (secs)	10
Duration	Instantaneous
Range (feet)	100
Target	Your pet
Resistance Invoked	None
Effect	
Healing (HP)	100 +2/level
Target's Reaction	Target form shimmers blue.

Reoccurring Amnesia

Casters	Enchanter (49)
Casting Skill	Alteration
Target's Reaction	Target blinks a few times. (You feel your mind fog.)

Repulse Animal

Casters	Druid (51)
Casting Skill	Alteration

Resist Cold

Casters	Cleric (39), Druid (34), Shaman (24), Shadow Knight (39), Necromancer (24)
Mana Cost	50
Casting Skill	Abjuration
Casting Time (secs)	4.5
Duration	36 minutes
Range (feet)	100
Target	Anyone
Resistance Invoked	None
Effect	
Resist Cold boost	15 +1/level (max 40)
Target's Reaction	Target is resistant to cold.

Resist Disease

Casters	Cleric (39), Druid (44), Shaman (34), Necromancer (34)
Casting Skill	Abjuration
Target's Reaction	Target is resistant to disease.

Resist Fire

Casters	Cleric (34), Ranger (49), Druid (24), Shaman (29)
Mana Cost	50
Casting Skill	Abjuration
Casting Time (secs)	4.5
Duration	36 minutes
Range (feet)	100
Target	Anyone
Resistance Invoked	None
Effect	
Resist Fire boost	10 +1/level (max 40)
Target's Reaction	Target is resistant to fire.

Resist Magic

Casters	Cleric (44), Druid (49), Shaman (44), Enchanter (39)
Casting Skill	Abjuration
Target's Reaction	Target is resistant to magic.

Resist Poison

Casters	Cleric (34), Druid (44), Shaman (39)
Casting Skill	Abjuration
Target's Reaction	Target is resistant to poison.

Resistant Skin

Casters	Wizard (12)
Mana Cost	35
Casting Skill	Abjuration
Casting Time (secs)	4.5
Duration	27 minutes
Range (feet)	100
Target	Yourself
Resistance Invoked	None
Effects	
Resist Poison boost	5 + 1 / 2 levels (max 15)
Resist Disease boost	5 + 1 / 2 levels (max 15)
Target's Reaction	Target's skin shines.

Resolution

Casters	Cleric (44), Paladin (60)
Casting Skill	Abjuration
Target's Reaction	Target looks resolute.

Rest the Dead

Casters	Shadow Knight (52), Necromancer (24)
Mana Cost	75
Casting Skill	Abjuration
Casting Time (secs)	3
Duration	3 minutes
Range (feet)	200
Target	Undead
Resistance Invoked	Magic
Effects	
Target's Reaction Range (feet)	1 foot
Target's Help Radius	1 foot
Target much less likely to attack	
Target's Reaction	Target looks ambivalent.

Restless Bones

Casters	Shadow Knight (30), Necromancer (16)
Mana Cost	160
Casting Skill	Conjuration
Components	2 Bone Chips
Casting Time (secs)	9
Duration	Instantaneous
Range (feet)	0
Target	Yourself
Resistance Invoked	None
Effect	
Create Undead	Skeleton (Circle 5)
Target's Reaction	Skeleton rises from the dead.

Resurrection

Casters	Cleric (49), Paladin (59)
Casting Skill	Alteration

Resuscitate

Casters	Cleric (39), Paladin (59)
Casting Skill	Alteration

Retribution

Casters	Cleric (44)
Casting Skill	Evocation
Target's Reaction	Target has been struck by the wrath of the gods.

Retribution of Al'Kabor

Casters	Wizard (56)
Casting Skill	Evocation
Target's Reaction	Target is frozen by the retribution of Al'Kabor.

Revive

Casters	Cleric (29), Paladin (49)
Casting Skill	Alteration

Reviviscence

Casters	Cleric (56)
Casting Skill	Alteration

Ring of Butcher

Casters	Druid (19)
Mana Cost	150
Casting Skill	Alteration
Casting Time (secs)	7
Recasting Delay (secs)	12.25
Duration	Instantaneous
Range (feet)	0
Target	Yourself
Resistance Invoked	None
Effect	
Teleports you to	Butcherblock Mountains
Target's Reaction	Target fades away.

Ring of Commons

Casters	Druid (19)
Mana Cost	150
Casting Skill	Alteration
Casting Time (secs)	7
Recasting Delay (secs)	12.25
Duration	Instantaneous
Range (feet)	0
Target	Yourself
Resistance Invoked	None
Effect	
Teleports you to	West Commonlands
Target's Reaction	Target fades away.

Ring of Feerrott

Casters	Druid (24)
Mana Cost	150
Casting Skill	Alteration
Casting Time (secs)	7
Recasting Delay (secs)	12.25
Duration	Instantaneous
Range (feet)	0
Target	Yourself
Resistance Invoked	None
Effect	
Teleports you to	The Feerrott
Target's Reaction	Target fades away.

Ring of Karana

Casters	Druid (19)
Mana Cost	150
Casting Skill	Alteration
Casting Time (secs)	7
Recasting Delay (secs)	12.25
Duration	Instantaneous
Range (feet)	0
Target	Yourself
Resistance Invoked	None
Effect	
Teleports you to	North Karana
Target's Reaction	Target fades away.

Ring of Lavastorm

Casters	Druid (24)
Mana Cost	150
Casting Skill	Alteration
Casting Time (secs)	7
Recasting Delay (secs)	12.25
Duration	Instantaneous
Range (feet)	0
Target	Yourself
Resistance Invoked	None
Effect	
Teleports you to	Lavastorm
Target's Reaction	Target fades away.

Ring of Misty

Casters	Druid (29)
Casting Skill	Alteration
Target's Reaction	Target fades away.

Ring of Ro

Casters	Druid (24)
Mana Cost	150
Casting Skill	Alteration
Casting Time (secs)	7
Recasting Delay (secs)	12.25
Duration	Instantaneous
Range (feet)	0
Target	Yourself
Resistance Invoked	None
Effect	
Teleports you to	South Ro
Target's Reaction	Target fades away.

Ring of Steamfont

Casters	Druid (24)
Mana Cost	150
Casting Skill	Alteration
Casting Time (secs)	7
Recasting Delay (secs)	12.25
Duration	Instantaneous
Range (feet)	0
Target	Yourself
Resistance Invoked	None
Effect	
Teleports you to	Steamfont Mountains
Target's Reaction	Target fades away.

Ring of Toxxulia

Casters	Druid (19)
Mana Cost	150
Casting Skill	Alteration
Casting Time (secs)	7
Recasting Delay (secs)	12.25
Duration	Instantaneous
Range (feet)	0
Target	Yourself
Resistance Invoked	None
Effect	
Teleports you to	Toxxulia Forest
Target's Reaction	Target fades away.

Riotous Health

Casters	Shaman (54)
Casting Skill	Alteration
Target's Reaction	Target's body shines with riotous health.

Rising Dexterity

Casters	Shaman (29)
Casting Skill	Alteration
Target's Reaction	Target looks dexterous.

Ro Gate

Casters	Wizard (24)
Mana Cost	150
Casting Skill	Alteration
Casting Time (secs)	7
Recasting Delay (secs)	12.25
Duration	Instantaneous
Range (feet)	0
Target	Yourself
Resistance Invoked	None
Effect	
Teleports you to	North Ro
Target's Reaction	Target fades away.

Ro Portal

Casters	Wizard (39)
Casting Skill	Alteration
Target's Reaction	Target creates a shimmering portal.

Root

Casters	Cleric (9), Paladin (22), Shaman (14), Wizard (4), Necromancer (34), Enchanter (8)
Mana Cost	30
Casting Skill	Alteration
Casting Time (secs)	2
Duration	48 secs
Range (feet)	200
Target	Anyone
Resistance Invoked	Magic
Effect	
Immobilizes	
Target's Reaction	Target's feet adhere to the ground.

Rune I

Casters	Enchanter (16)
Mana Cost	41
Casting Skill	Abjuration
Component	Cat's Eye Agate
Casting Time (secs)	3.5
Duration	36 minutes
Range (feet)	100
Target	Anyone
Resistance Invoked	None
Effect	
Bonus HP	55
Target's Reaction	Target is surrounded by a shimmer of runes. (A light shimmer of runes surround you.)

Rune II

Casters	Enchanter (24)
Mana Cost	83
Casting Skill	Abjuration
Component	Bloodstone
Casting Time (secs)	4
Duration	54 minutes
Range (feet)	100
Target	Anyone
Resistance Invoked	None
Effect	
Bonus HP	118
Target's Reaction	Target is surrounded by a shimmer of runes. (A shimmer of runes surround you.)

Rune III

Casters	Enchanter (34)
Casting Skill	Abjuration
Target's Reaction	Target is surrounded by a shimmer of runes. (A dark shimmer of runes surround you.)

Rune IV

Casters	Enchanter (44)
Casting Skill	Abjuration
Target's Reaction	Target is surrounded by a shimmer of runes. (A coat of shimmer of runes surround you.)

Rune V

Casters	Enchanter (52)
Casting Skill	Abjuration
Target's Reaction	Target is surrounded by a shimmer of runes. (A coat of shimmer of runes surround you.)

Sacrifice

Casters	Necromancer (51)
Casting Skill	Alteration

Sagar's Animation

Casters	Enchanter (24)
Mana Cost	130
Casting Skill	Conjuration
Component	Tiny Dagger
Casting Time (secs)	7
Recasting Delay (secs)	16.25
Duration	Instantaneous
Range (feet)	0
Target	Yourself
Resistance Invoked	None
Effect	
Summon Animation	Animated Sword and Shield (Circle 7)

Sanity Warp

Casters	Enchanter (16)
Mana Cost	75
Casting Skill	Evocation
Casting Time (secs)	2.75
Recasting Delay (secs)	10.5
Duration	Instantaneous
Range (feet)	200
Target	Anyone
Resistance Invoked	Magic
Effects	
Damage (HP)	72 +1/level (max 95)
Stun	Can disrupt spellcasting
Knockback	1/2 foot
Target's Reaction	Target looks delirious. (Reality goes amok.)

Savage Spirit

Casters	Druid (44)
Casting Skill	Alteration
Target's Reaction	Target's eyes gleam with madness.

Scale Skin

Casters	Shaman (5)
Mana Cost	25
Casting Skill	Abjuration
Component	Snake Scales
Casting Time (secs)	2.5
Recasting Delay (secs)	6.75
Duration	3 x level minutes (max 27 m)
Range (feet)	100
Target	Anyone
Resistance Invoked	None
Effect	
AC boost	11 +1/level (max 20)
Target's Reaction	Target grows scales.

Scale of Wolf

Casters	Druid (29), Shaman (24)
Mana Cost	60
Casting Skill	Alteration
Casting Time (secs)	4.5
Recasting Delay (secs)	6
Duration	45 minutes (If target attacks or casts a spell, this spell is cancelled.)
Range (feet)	100
Target	Anyone
Resistance Invoked	None
Effect	
Movement Rate boost	40% + 1% / 2 levels (max 65%)
Target's Reaction	Target is surrounded by a dark lupine aura. (You feel the spirit-scale of wolf enter you.)

Scars of Sigil

Casters	Magician (54)
Casting Skill	Evocation
Target's Reaction	Target is burned by the Scars of Sigil. (The Scars of Sigil burn you.)

Scent of Darkness

Casters	Necromancer (39)
Casting Skill	Alteration
Target's Reaction	Target is surrounded by a dark haze. (You smell the faint scent of darkness.)

Scent of Dusk

Casters	Necromancer (12)
Mana Cost	50
Casting Skill	Alteration
Casting Time (secs)	3
Recasting Delay (secs)	8.25
Duration	1 minute + 12 seconds/level
Range (feet)	200
Target	Anyone
Resistance Invoked	Poison
Effects	
Poison	1
Fire Resistance loss	1 + 1 / 2 levels (max 9)
Poison Resist. loss	1 + 1 / 2 levels (max 9)
Disease Resist. loss	1 + 1 / 2 levels (max 9)
Target's Reaction	Target is surrounded by a dull haze. (You smell the faint scent of dusk.)

Scent of Shadow

Casters	Necromancer (24)
Mana Cost	100
Casting Skill	Alteration
Casting Time (secs)	3
Recasting Delay (secs)	8.25
Duration	1 minute + 12 seconds/level
Range (feet)	200
Target	Anyone
Resistance Invoked	Poison
Effects	
Poison	4
Fire Resistance lowered	2 + 1 / 2 levels (max 18)
Poison Resistance lowered	2 + 1 / 2 levels (max 18)
Disease Resistance lowered	2 + 1 / 2 levels (max 18)
Target's Reaction	Target is surrounded by a dim haze. (You smell the faint scent of shadow.)

Scent of Terris

Casters	Necromancer (52)
Casting Skill	Alteration
Target's Reaction	Target is surrounded by a dark haze. (You smell the faint scent of Terris.)

Scintillation

Casters	Magician (51)
Casting Skill	Evocation
Target's Reaction	Target is covered in scintillating flames. (Scintillating flames race across your body.)

Scourge

Casters	Shaman (34), Necromancer (39)
Casting Skill	Conjuration
Target's Reaction	Target sweats and shivers, looking feverish. (You feel feverish.)

Scoriae

Casters	Druid (54)
Casting Skill	Evocation
Target's Reaction	Target's skin melts.

Screaming Terror

Casters	Necromancer (24)
Mana Cost	60
Casting Skill	Alteration
Casting Time (secs)	2.6
Recasting Delay (secs)	8.75
Duration	18 secs
Range (feet)	200
Target	Anyone
Resistance Invoked	Magic
Effect	
Mesmerization	
Target's Reaction	Target begins to scream.

Sedulous Subversion

Casters	Necromancer (56)
Casting Skill	Alteration
Target's Reaction	Target twitches. (A foreign surge of mana refreshes your mind.)

See Invisible

Casters	Druid (14), Wizard (4), Magician (16), Enchanter (8)
Mana Cost	25
Casting Skill	Divination
Casting Time (secs)	2
Duration	3 + 3 x level minutes (max 27 m)
Range (feet)	100
Radius of Effect (feet)	60
Target	Anyone
Resistance Invoked	None
Effect	
See Invisible	
Target's Reaction	(Your eyes tingle.)

Seeking Flame of Seukor

Casters	Magician (59)
Casting Skill	Evocation
Target's Reaction	Target is burnt by the Seeking Flame of Seukor.

Selo's Accelerando

Casters	Bard (5)
Mana Cost	0
Casting Skill	Percussion Instruments
Outdoors only	
Casting Time (secs)	3
Casting Delay (secs)	none
Recasting Delay (secs)	12
Duration	12 seconds
Range (feet)	0
Radius of Effect (feet)	150
Target	Your group
Resistance Invoked	None
Effect	
Movement Rate boost	15% +1% / level
Target's Reaction	(Your feet move faster.)

Selo's Assonait Strane

Casters	Bard (54)
Casting Skill	Stringed Instruments
Target's Reaction	Target is bound in silver strands of music. (Silver strands of music bind you.)

Selo's Chords of Cessation

Casters	Bard (48)
Casting Skill	Stringed Instruments
Target's Reaction	Target is bound in chords of music. (Chords of music bind your hands.)

Selo's Consonant Chain

Casters	Bard (23)
Mana Cost	0
Casting Skill	Singing
Casting Time (secs)	3
Casting Delay (secs)	none
Recasting Delay (secs)	12
Duration	12 seconds
Range (feet)	150
Target	Anyone
Resistance Invoked	Magic
Effect	
Movement Rate loss	30% +1% / level
Attack Speed loss	5% +1% / 2 levels
Target's Reaction	Target is surrounded by chains of music. (Your voice binds chords into chains.)

Selo's Song of Travel

Casters	Bard (51)
Casting Skill	Percussion Instruments
Target's Reaction	(Your feet blur as they leave the ground.)

Sense Animals

Casters	Druid (1), Shaman (9)
Mana Cost	5
Casting Skill	Divination
Casting Time (secs)	2
Recasting Delay (secs)	6.25
Duration	Instantaneous
Range (feet)	0
Radius of Effect (feet)	240
Target	Yourself
Resistance Invoked	None
Effect	
Detect Animals	

Sense Summoned

Casters	Cleric (14), Wizard (8), Magician (4)
Mana Cost	5
Casting Skill	Divination
Casting Time (secs)	2
Duration	Instantaneous
Range (feet)	0
Radius of Effect (feet)	240
Target	Yourself
Resistance Invoked	None
Effect	
Detect Summoned	

Sense the Dead

Casters	Cleric (9), Paladin (15), Shadow Knight (9), Necromancer (1)
Mana Cost	5
Casting Skill	Divination
Casting Time (secs)	2
Duration	Instantaneous
Range (feet)	0
Radius of Effect (feet)	240
Target	Yourself
Resistance Invoked	None
Effect	
Detect Undead	

Sentinel

Casters	Enchanter (8)
Mana Cost	25
Casting Skill	Divination
Casting Time (secs)	2.5
Recasting Delay (secs)	7.25
Duration	Instantaneous
Impact Duration (secs)	360
Range (feet)	0
Radius of Effect (feet)	40
Target	Area
Resistance Invoked	None
Effect	
You are notified of anything entering the area	
Target's Reaction	(You sense that you are being watched.)

Serpent Sight

Casters	Shaman (9), Enchanter (12)
Mana Cost	30
Casting Skill	Divination
Casting Time (secs)	5
Duration	27 minutes
Range (feet)	100
Target	Anyone
Resistance Invoked	None
Effect	
Infravision	
Target's Reaction	Target eyes glow red. (Your eyes tingle.)

Servent of Bones

Casters	Necromancer (56)
Casting Skill	Conjuration
Target's Reaction	Skeleton rises from the dead.

Shade

Casters	Enchanter (39)
Casting Skill	Abjuration
Target's Reaction	Target's image fades around the edges. (Your image fades.)

Shadow

Casters	Enchanter (49)
Casting Skill	Abjuration
Target's Reaction	Target's image fades into the shadows.

Shadow Compact

Casters	Necromancer (20)
Mana Cost	10
Casting Skill	Alteration
Casting Time (secs)	2
Recasting Delay (secs)	14.5
Duration	24 secs
Range (feet)	100
Target	Anyone
Resistance Invoked	None
Effect	
Healing (HP/6 secs)	20
Target's Reaction	Target pulses with a blue-green aura. (Your wounds begin to heal.)

Shadow Sight

Casters	Shadow Knight (49), Necromancer (24)
Mana Cost	50
Casting Skill	Divination
Casting Time (secs)	3
Duration	27 minutes
Range (feet)	100
Target	Yourself
Resistance Invoked	None
Effect	
Ultravision	
Target's Reaction	Target eyes glow violet. (The shadows fade.)

Shadow Step

Casters	Shadow Knight (15), Necromancer (8), Wizard (8)
Mana Cost	10
Casting Skill	Alteration
Casting Time (secs)	1
Recasting Delay (secs)	7.25
Duration	Instantaneous
Range (feet)	900
Target	Yourself
Resistance Invoked	None
Effect	
Random Teleport	
Target's Reaction	Target fades away.

Shadow Vortex

Casters	Shadow Knight (39), Necromancer (20)
Mana Cost	40
Casting Skill	Alteration
Casting Time (secs)	1.5
Recasting Delay (secs)	8.25
Duration	1 minute + 6 seconds/level
Range (feet)	200
Target	Anyone(flows to you)
Resistance Invoked	Magic
Effect	
AC loss	10 +1/level (max 40)
Target's Reaction	Target is surrounded by a vortex of shadows. (You feel a shadow pass over you.)

Shadowbond

Casters	Necromancer (54)
Casting Skill	Alteration
Target's Reaction	Target pulses with a blue-green aura. (Your wounds begin to heal.)

Shalee's Animation

Casters	Enchanter (16)
Mana Cost	85
Casting Skill	Conjuration
Components	2 Tiny Daggers
Casting Time (secs)	5
Recasting Delay (secs)	12.25
Duration	Instantaneous
Range (feet)	0
Target	Yourself
Resistance Invoked	None
Effect	
Summon Animation	Animated Sword and Shield (Circle 5)

Share Wolf Form

Casters	Druid (39)
Casting Skill	Alteration
Target's Reaction	Target turns into a wolf. (You are now a wolf.)

Shallow Breath

Casters	Enchanter (1)
Mana Cost	7
Casting Skill	Alteration
Casting Time (secs)	1.5
Duration	12 seconds
Range (feet)	200
Target	Anyone
Resistance Invoked	Magic
Effects	
One-Time Damage (HP)	3 + 1 / 2 levels (max 5)
STR loss	5
AGI loss	5
Target's Reaction	Target begins to choke. (You feel a shortness of breath.)

Shauri's Sonorous Clouding

Casters	Bard (19)
Mana Cost	0
Casting Skill	Wind Instruments
Components	2 Wooden Flutes (1 not consumed)
Casting Time (secs)	3
Casting Delay (secs)	none
Recasting Delay (secs)	12
Duration	18 secs
Range (feet)	0
Radius of Effect (feet)	45
Target	Your group
Resistance Invoked	None
Effects	
Invisibility	
See Invisible	
Target's Reaction	(A soft mist surrounds you.)

Shield of Barbs

Casters	Druid (19)
Mana Cost	60
Casting Skill	Abjuration
Casting Time (secs)	2.5
Duration	6 seconds/level
Range (feet)	100
Target	Anyone
Resistance Invoked	Magic
Effect	
Reflect Damage (HP)	3 + 1 / 4 levels (max 9)
Target's Reaction	Target is surrounded by a thorny barrier.

Shield of Blades

Casters	Druid (58)
Casting Skill	Abjuration
Target's Reaction	Target is surrounded by a thorny barrier of blades.

Shield of Brambles

Casters	Ranger (49), Druid (29)
Casting Skill	Abjuration
Target's Reaction	Target is surrounded by a thorny barrier.

Shield of Fire

Casters	Magician (8)
Mana Cost	40
Casting Skill	Abjuration
Casting Time (secs)	2
Duration	6 seconds/level
Range (feet)	100
Target	Anyone
Resistance Invoked	Fire
Effects	
Reflect Damage (HP)	3 + 1 / 4 levels (max 6)
Resist Fire boost	10
Target's Reaction	Target is enveloped in flame.

Shield of Flame

Casters	Magician (20)
Mana Cost	60`
Casting Skill	Abjuration
Casting Time (secs)	4
Duration	6 seconds/level
Range (feet)	100
Target	Anyone
Resistance Invoked	Fire
Effects	
Reflect Damage (HP)	3 + 1 / 4 levels (max 9)
Resist Fire boost	15
Target's Reaction	Target is enveloped in flame.

Shield of Lava

Casters	Magician (49)
Casting Skill	Abjuration
Target's Reaction	Target is enveloped in flame. (You are enveloped in lava.)

Shield of Spikes

Casters	Ranger (58), Druid (39)
Casting Skill	Abjuration
Target's Reaction	Target is surrounded by a thorny barrier.

Shield of the Magi

Casters	Necromancer (54), Wizard (54), Magician (54), Enchanter (54)
Casting Skill	Abjuration
Target's Reaction	(You feel armored.)

Shield of Thistles

Casters	Ranger (30), Druid (9)
Mana Cost	40
Casting Skill	Abjuration
Casting Time (secs)	2.5
Duration	6 seconds/level
Range (feet)	100
Target	Anyone
Resistance Invoked	Magic
Effect	
Reflect Damage (HP)	3 + 1 / 4 levels (max 6)
Target's Reaction	Target is surrounded by a thorny barrier.

Shield of Thorns

Casters	Druid (49)
Casting Skill	Abjuration
Target's Reaction	Target is surrounded by a thorny barrier.

Shield of Words

Casters	Cleric (49), Paladin (60)
Casting Skill	Abjuration
Target's Reaction	Target feels the favor of the gods upon them.

Shielding

Casters	Necromancer (16), Wizard (16), Magician (16), Enchanter (16)
Mana Cost	50
Casting Skill	Abjuration
Casting Time (secs)	5
Duration	36 minutes
Range (feet)	0
Target	Yourself
Resistance Invoked	None
Effects	
Bonus HP	30 +1/level (max 50)
AC boost	24 +1/level (max 45)
Resist Magic boost	12
Target's Reaction	(You feel armored.)

Shieldskin

Casters	Shadow Knight (39), Necromancer (16), Wizard (16)
Mana Cost	41
Casting Skill	Abjuration
Component	Cat's Eye Agate
Casting Time (secs)	3.5
Duration	36 minutes
Range (feet)	0
Target	Yourself
Resistance Invoked	None
Effect	
Bonus HP	55
Target's Reaction	Target's skin is covered in a mystic glow. (A mystic force shields your skin.)

Shiftless Deeds

Casters	Enchanter (44)
Casting Skill	Alteration
Target's Reaction	Target slows down.

Shifting Shield

Casters	Shaman (34)
Casting Skill	Abjuration
Target's Reaction	Target is surrounded by a shifting spirit shield. (A shifting spirit shield surrounds you.)

Shifting Sight

Casters	Wizard (39), Enchanter (20)
Mana Cost	30
Casting Skill	Divination
Casting Time (secs)	4
Duration	1 minute + 18 seconds/level
Duration of impact (secs)	7.5
Range (feet)	10,000
Target	Anyone
Resistance Invoked	None
Effect	
You see from Target's View	
Fatigue	2 points
Infravision	
Target's Reaction	Target eyes gleam and then go dark. (You shift your sight.)

Shock of Blades

Casters	Magician (8)
Mana Cost	30
Casting Skill	Conjuration
Casting Time (secs)	2.1
Duration	Instantaneous
Range (feet)	200
Target	Anyone
Resistance Invoked	Magic
Effects	
Damage (HP)	23 +1/level (max 35)
Knockback	1/2 foot
Target's Reaction	Target is lacerated by steel. (You have been lacerated.)

Shock of Fire

Casters	Wizard (4)
Mana Cost	15
Casting Skill	Evocation
Casting Time (secs)	1.35
Duration	Instantaneous
Range (feet)	200
Target	Anyone
Resistance Invoked	Fire
Effect	
Damage (HP)	11 + 1 / 2 levels (max 16)
Target's Reaction	Target combusts. (You feel your skin combust.)

Shock of Flame

Casters	Magician (16)
Mana Cost	70
Casting Skill	Evocation
Casting Time (secs)	2.75
Duration	Instantaneous
Range (feet)	200
Target	Anyone
Resistance Invoked	Fire
Effect	
Damage (HP)	75 +1/level (max 96)
Target's Reaction	Target's skin ignites.

Shock of Frost

Casters	Wizard (1)
Mana Cost	8
Casting Skill	Evocation
Casting Time (secs)	1.1
Duration	Instantaneous
Range (feet)	200
Target	Anyone
Resistance Invoked	Cold
Effect	
Damage (HP)	4 + 1 / 2 levels (max 6)
Target's Reaction	Target's skin freezes.

Shock of Ice

Casters	Wizard (8)
Mana Cost	30
Casting Skill	Evocation
Casting Time (secs)	1.85
Duration	Instantaneous
Range (feet)	200
Target	Anyone
Resistance Invoked	Cold
Effect	
Damage (HP)	26 +1/level (max 38)
Target's Reaction	Target's skin freezes over.

Shock of Steel

Casters	Magician (57)
Casting Skill	Conjuration
Target's Reaction	Target is lacerated by deadly steel.

Shock of Lightning

Casters	Wizard (12)
Mana Cost	60
Casting Skill	Evocation
Casting Time (secs)	2.2
Duration	Instantaneous
Range (feet)	200
Target	Anyone
Resistance Invoked	Magic
Effects	
Damage (HP)	66 +1/level (max 83)
Knockback	2 feet
Target's Reaction	Target convulses as lightning arcs through them.

Shock of Poison

Casters	Necromancer (24)
Mana Cost	100
Casting Skill	Conjuration
Casting Time (secs)	3.5
Duration	Instantaneous
Range (feet)	200
Target	Anyone
Resistance Invoked	Poison
Effect	
Damage (HP)	74 +3/level (max 160)
Target's Reaction	Target screams in agony. (You feel your skin burn as poison seeps through your skin.)

Shock of Spikes

Casters	Magician (24)
Mana Cost	110
Casting Skill	Conjuration
Casting Time (secs)	3.5
Duration	Instantaneous
Range (feet)	200
Target	Anyone
Resistance Invoked	Magic
Effects	
Damage (HP)	86 +3/level (max 176)
Knockback	1/2 foot
Target's Reaction	Target is lacerated by steel. (You have been lacerated.)

Shock of Swords

Casters	Magician (11)
Casting Skill	Conjuration
Target's Reaction	Target is lacerated by steel. (You have been lacerated.)

Shock Spiral of Al'Kabor

Casters	Wizard (29)
Casting Skill	Evocation
Target's Reaction	Target is blasted by static wind.

Shrink

Casters	Shaman (19)
Mana Cost	50
Casting Skill	Alteration
Indoors only	
Casting Time (secs)	4
Duration	Instantaneous
Range (feet)	200
Target	Anyone
Resistance Invoked	None
Effect	
Get Smaller	
Target's Reaction	Target shrinks. (You feel smaller.)

Shroud of the Spirits

Casters	Shaman (54)
Casting Skill	Abjuration
Target's Reaction	Target is surrounded by a spirit shroud. (A protective spirit shroud cloaks you.)

Sicken

Casters	Shaman (5)
Mana Cost	30
Casting Skill	Conjuration
Casting Time (secs)	1.75
Duration	1 minute + 6 secs/level (max 2 m, 6 s)
Range (feet)	200
Target	Anyone
Resistance Invoked	Disease
Effects	
Disease	1
Immediate Damage (HP)	10
Subsequent Damage (HP/6 secs)	2
Target's Reaction	Target sweats and shivers, looking feverish. (You feel feverish.)

Sight

Casters	Wizard (20)
Mana Cost	20
Casting Skill	Divination
Casting Time (secs)	2.5
Recasting Delay (secs)	14.25
Duration	Level minutes
Range (feet)	0
Target	Yourself
Resistance Invoked	None
Effects	
Telescope	See more than twice as far
Infravision	
Target's Reaction	Target eyes gleam. (Your eyes feel stronger.)

Sight Graft

Casters	Necromancer (12)
Mana Cost	10
Casting Skill	Divination
Casting Time (secs)	5
Recasting Delay (secs)	12.25
Duration	27 minutes
Range (feet)	100
Target	Your pet
Resistance Invoked	None
Effect	
You see from your pet's view	
Target's Reaction	Target eyes shimmer.

Siphon Life

Casters	Shadow Knight (51), Necromancer (20)
Mana Cost	72
Casting Skill	Alteration
Casting Time (secs)	3.1
Duration	Instantaneous
Range (feet)	200
Target	Anyone (flows to you)
Resistance Invoked	Magic
Effect	
Damage (HP)	25 +2 / level (max 75)
Target's Reaction	Target staggers. (You feel you lifeforce drain away.)

Siphon Strength

Casters	Shadow Knight (9), Necromancer (1)
Mana Cost	5
Casting Skill	Alteration
Casting Time (secs)	1.5
Recasting Delay (secs)	8.25
Duration	3 x level minutes (max 6 m)
Range (feet)	200
Target	Anyone (flows to you)
Resistance Invoked	Magic
Effect	
STR loss	5 + 1 / 2 levels (max 10)
Target's Reaction	Target weakens. (You feel your strength dwindle.)

Sirocco

Casters	Magician (55)
Casting Skill	Evocation
Target's Reaction	Target's skin blisters as lava rains down from above.

Sisna's Animation

Casters	Enchanter (20)
Mana Cost	105
Casting Skill	Conjuration
Components	3 Tiny Daggers
Casting Time (secs)	6
Recasting Delay (secs)	14.25
Duration	Instantaneous
Range (feet)	0
Target	Yourself
Resistance Invoked	None
Effect	
Summon Animation	Animated Sword and Shield (Circle 6)

Skin like Diamond

Casters	Ranger (54), Druid (39)
Casting Skill	Abjuration
Target's Reaction	Target's skin turns hard as diamond.

Skin like Nature

Casters	Druid (49)
Casting Skill	Abjuration
Target's Reaction	Target's skin shimmers with divine power.

Skin like Rock

Casters	Ranger (22), Druid (14)
Mana Cost	60
Casting Skill	Abjuration
Casting Time (secs)	5
Recasting Delay (secs)	10.5
Duration	27 minutes
Range (feet)	100
Target	Anyone
Resistance Invoked	None
Effects	
AC boost	16 + 1 / 2 levels (max 25)
Bonus HP	40 +1/level
Target's Reaction	T's skin turns hard as stone.

Skin like Steel

Casters	Ranger (39), Druid (24)
Mana Cost	100
Casting Skill	Abjuration
Casting Time (secs)	6
Recasting Delay (secs)	11.5
Duration	36 minutes
Range (feet)	100
Target	Anyone
Resistance Invoked	None
Effects	
AC boost	20 + 1 / 2 levels (max 35)
Bonus HP	50 +1/level
Target's Reaction	T's skin turns hard as steel.

Skin like Wood

Casters	Ranger (9), Druid (1)
Mana Cost	10
Casting Skill	Abjuration
Casting Time (secs)	3
Recasting Delay (secs)	8.25
Duration	3 + 3 x level minutes (max 27 m)
Range (feet)	100
Target	Anyone
Resistance Invoked	None
Effects	
AC boost	10 + 1 / 2 levels (max 15)
Bonus HP	10 +1/level (max 20)

Skin of the Shadow

Casters	Necromancer (55)
Casting Skill	Alteration
Target's Reaction	Target's skin turns to shadow. (Your skin becomes shadow.)

Smite

Casters	Cleric (14)
Mana Cost	70
Casting Skill	Evocation
Casting Time (secs)	2.45
Recasting Delay (secs)	8.5
Duration	Instantaneous
Range (feet)	200
Target	Anyone
Resistance Invoked	Magic
Effects	
Damage (HP)	60 +1/level (max 83)
Knockback	1 foot

Snare

Casters	Ranger (9), Druid (1)
Mana Cost	15
Casting Skill	Alteration
Casting Time (secs)	2
Recasting Delay (secs)	6.25
Duration	Level minutes + 10
Range (feet)	200
Target	Anyone
Resistance Invoked	Magic
Effect	
Movement Rate loss	40% +1% / level (max 55%)
Target's Reaction	Target has been ensnared.

Solon's Bewitching Bravura

Casters	Bard (39)
Casting Skill	Wind Instruments
Target's Reaction	Target's eyes glaze over. (You are captivated by the bewitching tune.)

Solon's Charismatic Concord

Casters	Bard (59)
Casting Skill	Singing
Target's Reaction	(You feel charismatic.)

Solon's Song of the Sirens

Casters	Bard (27)
Casting Skill	Wind Instruments
Target's Reaction	Target's eyes glaze over. (You are captivated by the haunting tune.)

Song of Dawn

Casters	Bard (53)
Casting Skill	Wind Instruments
Target's Reaction	Target winks.

Song of Highsun

Casters	Bard (56)
Casting Skill	Wind Instruments
Target's Reaction	(You feel a static pulse wash through you.)

Song of Midnight

Casters	Bard (56)
Casting Skill	Brass Instruments
Target's Reaction	Target flees in nocturn terror. (Your mind snaps in terror.)

Song of Twilight

Casters	Bard (53)
Casting Skill	Wind Instruments
Target's Reaction	Target stumbles towards you. (You hear the music of twilight.)

Soothe

Casters	Cleric (9), Paladin (30), Enchanter (8)
Mana Cost	30
Casting Skill	Alteration
Casting Time (secs)	2
Recasting Delay (secs)	6.25
Duration	1 minute + 6 seconds/level (max 2 m, 30 s)
Range (feet)	200
Target	Anyone
Resistance Invoked	Magic
Effects	
Target's Reaction Range (feet)	10 feet
Target's Help Radius	10 feet
Target much less likely to attack	
Target's Reaction	Target looks less aggressive. (You feel your aggression subside.)

Sound of Force

Casters	Cleric (49)
Casting Skill	Evocation
Target's Reaction	Target is stunned.

Spikecoat

Casters	Druid (39)
Casting Skill	Abjuration
Target's Reaction	Target's skin sprouts spikes. (Spikes spring from your skin.)

Spear of Warding

Casters	Magician (20)
Mana Cost	60
Casting Skill	Conjuration
Casting Time (secs)	6
Recasting Delay (secs)	8.25
Duration	Instantaneous
Range (feet)	0
Target	Yourself
Resistance Invoked	None
Effect	
Create Item	1 Spear of Warding, + 1 more / level

Sphere of Light

Casters	Wizard (1)
Mana Cost	10
Casting Skill	Divination
Casting Time (secs)	4
Recasting Delay (secs)	10.25
Duration	Instantaneous
Range (feet)	0
Target	Yourself
Resistance Invoked	None
Effect	
Create Item	1 light globe + 1 more / level

Spirit Armor

Casters	Cleric (19), Paladin (30), Necromancer (16)
Mana Cost	75
Casting Skill	Abjuration
Casting Time (secs)	6
Duration	36 minutes
Range (feet)	100
Target	Anyone
Resistance Invoked	None
Effect	
AC boost	21 +1/level (max 45)
Target's Reaction	Target is coated in translucent armor. (Translucent armor gathers around you.)

Spirit of Bear

Casters	Shaman (9)
Mana Cost	40
Casting Skill	Abjuration
Casting Time (secs)	5
Duration	3 x level minutes (max 36 m)
Range (feet)	100
Target	Anyone
Resistance Invoked	None
Effect	
STA boost	8 + 1 / 2 levels (max 15)
Target's Reaction	Target is surrounded by a brief ursine aura. (You feel the spirit of bear enter you.)

Spirit of Cat

Casters	Shaman (19)
Mana Cost	60
Casting Skill	Alteration
Casting Time (secs)	5
Duration	45 minutes
Range (feet)	100
Target	Anyone
Resistance Invoked	None
Effect	
AGI boost	4 +1/level (max 27)
Target's Reaction	Target is surrounded by a brief feline aura. (You feel the spirit of cat enter you.)

Spirit of Cheetah

Casters	Druid (24), Shaman (24)
Mana Cost	20
Casting Skill	Alteration
Outdoors only	
Casting Time (secs)	0.5
Recasting Delay (secs)	602.25
Duration	48 secs
Range (feet)	0
Target	Yourself
Resistance Invoked	None
Effect	
Movement Rate boost	75% +1%/level (max 115% boost)
Target's Reaction	Target is surrounded by a brief feline aura. (You feel the spirit of cheetah enter you.)

Spirit of the Howler

Casters	Shaman (55)
Casting Skill	Conjuration
Target's Reaction	Target summons a howling spirit.

Spirit of Monkey

Casters	Shaman (24)
Mana Cost	40
Casting Skill	Alteration
Casting Time (secs)	5
Duration	36 minutes
Range (feet)	100
Target	Anyone
Resistance Invoked	None
Effect	
DEX boost	20
Target's Reaction	Target is surrounded by a brief aura. (You feel the spirit of monkey enter you.)

Spirit of Oak

Casters	Druid (59)
Casting Skill	Alteration
Target's Reaction	Target turns into a tree. (You have taken root.)

Spirit of Ox

Casters	Shaman (24)
Mana Cost	60
Casting Skill	Alteration
Casting Time (secs)	5
Duration	45 minutes
Range (feet)	100
Target	Anyone
Resistance Invoked	None
Effect	
STA boost	9 + 1 / 2 levels (max 23)
Target's Reaction	Target is surrounded by a brief bovine aura. (You feel the spirit of ox enter you.)

Spirit of Scale

Casters	Druid (53), Shaman (52)
Casting Skill	Alteration
Target's Reaction	Target is surrounded by a brief lupine aura. (You feel the spirit of the scaled wolf enter you.)

Spirit of Snake

Casters	Shaman (14)
Mana Cost	40
Casting Skill	Alteration
Casting Time (secs)	5
Duration	36 minutes
Range (feet)	100
Target	Anyone
Resistance Invoked	None
Effect	
CHA boost	6 + 1 / 2 levels (max 15)
Target's Reaction	Target is surrounded by a brief serpentine aura. (You feel the spirit of snake enter you.)

Spirit of Wolf

Casters	Ranger (39), Druid (14), Shaman (9)
Mana Cost	40
Casting Skill	Alteration
Outdoors only	
Casting Time (secs)	4.5
Recasting Delay (secs)	5.75
Duration	3 x level minutes (max 36 m)
Range (feet)	100
Target	Anyone
Resistance Invoked	None
Effect	
Movement Rate boost	30% + 1% / 2 levels
Target's Reaction	Target is surrounded by a brief lupine aura. (You feel the spirit of wolf enter you.)

Spirit Pouch

Casters	Shaman (5)
Mana Cost	40
Casting Skill	Conjuration
Casting Time (secs)	5
Recasting Delay (secs)	12.25
Duration	Instantaneous
Range (feet)	0
Target	Yourself
Resistance Invoked	None
Effect	
Create Item	1 Spirit Pouch + 1 more / level

Spirit Sight

Casters	Shaman (9)
Mana Cost	20
Casting Skill	Divination
Casting Time (secs)	2
Duration	27 minutes
Range (feet)	100
Radius of Effect (feet)	60
Target	Anyone
Resistance Invoked	None
Effect	
See Invisible	
Target's Reaction	(Your eyes tingle.)

Spirit Strength

Casters	Shaman (19)
Mana Cost	40
Casting Skill	Alteration
Casting Time (secs)	5
Duration	36 minutes
Range (feet)	100
Target	Anyone
Resistance Invoked	None
Effect	
STR boost	7 + 1 / 2 levels (max 18)
Target's Reaction	Target looks stronger.

Spirit Strike

Casters	Shaman (14)
Mana Cost	75
Casting Skill	Evocation
Casting Time (secs)	2.45
Duration	Instantaneous
Range (feet)	200
Target	Anyone
Resistance Invoked	Cold
Effect	
Damage (HP)	60 +1/level (max 81)
Target's Reaction	Target staggers as spirits of frost slam against them.

Spirit Tap

Casters	Shadow Knight (56), Necromancer (29)
Casting Skill	Alteration
Target's Reaction	Target staggers. (You feel you lifeforce drain away.)

Splurt

Casters	Necromancer (51)
Casting Skill	Alteration
Target's Reaction	Target's body begins to splurt.

Spook the Dead

Casters	Cleric (1), Paladin (9), Shadow Knight (22), Necromancer (12)
Mana Cost	10
Casting Skill	Alteration
Casting Time (secs)	2
Recasting Delay (secs)	6.25
Duration	18 secs
Range (feet)	200
Target	Undead
Resistance Invoked	Magic
Effect	
Fear	Low-level
Target's Reaction	Target has the fear of life put in them. (Your bones tingle.)

Staff of Runes

Casters	Magician (24)
Mana Cost	60
Casting Skill	Conjuration
Casting Time (secs)	6
Recasting Delay (secs)	8.25
Duration	Instantaneous
Range (feet)	0
Target	Yourself
Resistance Invoked	None
Effect	
Create Item	1 Staff of Runes + 1 more / level

Staff of Symbols

Casters	Magician (34)
Casting Skill	Conjuration

Staff of Tracing

Casters	Magician (8)
Mana Cost	20
Casting Skill	Conjuration
Casting Time (secs)	6
Recasting Delay (secs)	8.25
Duration	Instantaneous
Range (feet)	0
Target	Yourself
Resistance Invoked	None
Effect	
Create Item	1 Staff of Tracing + 1 more / level

Staff of Warding

Casters	Magician (16)
Mana Cost	40
Casting Skill	Conjuration
Casting Time (secs)	6
Recasting Delay (secs)	8.25
Duration	Instantaneous
Range (feet)	0
Target	Yourself
Resistance Invoked	None
Effect	
Create Item	1 Staff of Warding + 1 more / level

Stamina

Casters	Shaman (44)
Casting Skill	Alteration
Target's Reaction	Target looks robust.

Starfire

Casters	Druid (49)
Casting Skill	Evocation
Target's Reaction	Target is bathed in starfire. (You feel the glare of the heavens.)

Starshine

Casters	Druid (9)
Mana Cost	50
Casting Skill	Conjuration
Outdoors only	
Casting Time (secs)	5
Recasting Delay (secs)	12.25
Duration	Instantaneous
Range (feet)	0
Target	Yourself
Resistance Invoked	None
Effect	
Create Item	Globe of Stars
Target's Reaction	Target's hands pulse softly. (A globe of stars form within your hands.)

Steelskin

Casters	Shadow Knight (56), Necromancer (34), Wizard (34)
Casting Skill	Abjuration
Target's Reaction	Target's skin looks like steel.

Stinging Swarm

Casters	Ranger (30), Druid (14)
Mana Cost	65
Casting Skill	Conjuration
Casting Time (secs)	2.45
Duration	54 secs
Range (feet)	250
Target	Anyone
Resistance Invoked	Magic
Effect	
Damage (HP/6 secs)	13
Target's Reaction	Target is engulfed in a swarm. (You feel the pain of a thousand stings.)

Storm Strength

Casters	Ranger (53), Druid (44)
Casting Skill	Alteration
Target's Reaction	Target looks stronger.

Strength

Casters	Shaman (49)
Casting Skill	Alteration
Target's Reaction	Target looks strong.

Strength of Earth

Casters	Ranger (30), Druid (9)
Mana Cost	40
Casting Skill	Alteration
Casting Time (secs)	5
Recasting Delay (secs)	4.75
Duration	27 minutes
Range (feet)	100
Target	Anyone
Resistance Invoked	None
Effect	
STR boost	5 + 1 / 2 levels (max 15)
Target's Reaction	Target looks stronger.

Strength of Stone

Casters	Ranger (53), Druid (34)
Casting Skill	Alteration
Target's Reaction	Target looks stronger.

Strengthen

Casters	Shaman (1), Enchanter (1)
Mana Cost	10
Casting Skill	Alteration
Casting Time (secs)	2
Duration	3 + 3 x level minutes (max 27 m)
Range (feet)	100
Target	Anyone
Resistance Invoked	None
Effect	
STR boost	1 +1/level (max 10)
Target's Reaction	Target looks stronger.

Strike

Casters	Cleric (1)
Mana Cost	12
Casting Skill	Evocation
Casting Time (secs)	1.5
Duration	Instantaneous
Range (feet)	200
Target	Anyone
Resistance Invoked	Magic
Effects	
Damage (HP)	6 + 1 / 2 levels (max 8)
Knockback	1/2 foot

Strip Enchantment

Casters	Enchanter (24)
Mana Cost	70
Casting Skill	Abjuration
Casting Time (secs)	3.5
Recasting Delay (secs)	7.25
Duration	Instantaneous
Range (feet)	200
Target	Anyone
Resistance Invoked	Magic
Effect	
Cancel Magic	4 chances, all low-level

Stun

Casters	Cleric (5), Paladin (30)
Mana Cost	35
Casting Skill	Evocation
Casting Time (secs)	1.5
Recasting Delay (secs)	14.25
Duration	Instantaneous
Range (feet)	200
Target	Anyone
Resistance Invoked	Magic
Effect	
Stun	4 seconds
Target's Reaction	Target is stunned.

Succor

Casters	Druid (57)
Casting Skill	Alteration
Target's Reaction	Target creates a mystic portal.

Succor: Butcher

Casters	Druid (34)
Casting Skill	Alteration
Target's Reaction	Target creates a mystic portal.

Succor: East

Casters	Druid (29)
Casting Skill	Alteration
Target's Reaction	Target creates a mystic portal.

Succor: Lavastorm

Casters	Druid (44)
Casting Skill	Alteration
Target's Reaction	Target creates a mystic portal.

Succor: North

Casters	Druid (49)
Casting Skill	Alteration
Target's Reaction	Target creates a mystic portal.

Succor: Ro

Casters	Druid (39)
Casting Skill	Alteration
Target's Reaction	Target creates a mystic portal.

Suffocate

Casters	Enchanter (29)
Casting Skill	Alteration
Target's Reaction	Target begins to choke. (You feel a shortness of breath.)

Suffocating Sphere

Casters	Enchanter (4)
Mana Cost	20
Casting Skill	Alteration
Casting Time (secs)	1.75
Duration	12 seconds
Range (feet)	200
Target	Anyone
Resistance Invoked	Magic
Effects	
Immediate Damage (HP)	18
Subsequent Damage (HP/6 secs)	8
STR loss	5
AGI loss	5
Target's Reaction	Target gasps for breath.

Summon Arrows

Casters	Magician (20)
Mana Cost	30
Casting Skill	Conjuration
Casting Time (secs)	4
Duration	Instantaneous
Range (feet)	0
Target	Yourself
Resistance Invoked	None
Effect	
Create Item	1 arrow, + 1 more / 4 levels

Summon Bandages

Casters	Magician (4)
Mana Cost	15
Casting Skill	Conjuration
Casting Time (secs)	5
Recasting Delay (secs)	8.25
Duration	Instantaneous
Range (feet)	0
Target	Yourself
Resistance Invoked	None
Effect	
Create Item	1 bandage + 1 more / 2 levels (max 5)

Summon Coldstone

Casters	Magician (29)
Casting Skill	Conjuration

Summon Corpse

Casters	Necromancer (39)
Casting Skill	Conjuration

Summon Dagger

Casters	Magician (1)
Mana Cost	10
Casting Skill	Conjuration
Casting Time (secs)	5
Recasting Delay (secs)	8.25
Duration	Instantaneous
Range (feet)	0
Target	Yourself
Resistance Invoked	None
Effect	
Create Item	1 dagger + 1 more / level

Summon Dead

Casters	Shadow Knight (49), Necromancer (29)
Casting Skill	Conjuration

Summon Drink

Casters	Cleric (5), Druid (14), Shaman (5), Magician (1)
Mana Cost	10
Casting Skill	Conjuration
Casting Time (secs)	4
Duration	Instantaneous
Range (feet)	0
Target	Yourself
Resistance Invoked	None
Effect	
Create Item	1 globe of water + 1 more / level

Summon Fang

Casters	Magician (12)
Mana Cost	40
Casting Skill	Conjuration
Casting Time (secs)	6
Recasting Delay (secs)	8.25
Duration	Instantaneous
Range (feet)	0
Target	Yourself
Resistance Invoked	None
Effect	
Create Item	1 snake fang + 1 more / level

Summon Food

Casters	Cleric (9), Druid (14), Shaman (9), Magician (1)
Mana Cost	10
Casting Skill	Conjuration
Casting Time (secs)	4
Duration	Instantaneous
Range (feet)	0
Target	Yourself
Resistance Invoked	None
Effect	
Create Item	1 black bread + 1 more / level

Summon Heatstone

Casters	Magician (16)
Mana Cost	40
Casting Skill	Conjuration
Casting Time (secs)	7
Recasting Delay (secs)	8.25
Duration	Instantaneous
Range (feet)	0
Target	Yourself
Resistance Invoked	None
Effect	
Create Item	1 Heatstone + 1 more / level

Summon Ring of Flight

Casters	Magician (39)
Casting Skill	Conjuration

Summon Throwing Dagger

Casters	Magician (16)
Mana Cost	20
Casting Skill	Conjuration
Casting Time (secs)	4
Duration	Instantaneous
Range (feet)	0
Target	Yourself
Resistance Invoked	None
Effect	
Create Item	1 throwing dagger + 1 more / 4 levels

Summon Waterstone

Casters	Magician (20)
Mana Cost	40
Casting Skill	Conjuration
Casting Time (secs)	4
Duration	Instantaneous
Range (feet)	0
Target	Yourself
Resistance Invoked	None
Effect	
Create Item	1 Waterstone + 1 more / 4 levels

Summon Wisp

Casters	Magician (4)
Mana Cost	30
Casting Skill	Conjuration
Casting Time (secs)	5
Recasting Delay (secs)	8.25
Duration	Instantaneous
Range (feet)	0
Target	Yourself
Resistance Invoked	None
Effect	
Create Item	Wisp Stone
Target's Reaction	Target's hands pulse soft light. (A wisp settles into your hand.)

Summoning: Air

Casters	Magician (24)
Mana Cost	240
Casting Skill	Conjuration
Components	Broom of Trilon (not consumed), Malachite
Casting Time (secs)	12
Duration	Instantaneous
Range (feet)	0
Target	Yourself
Resistance Invoked	None
Effect	
Summon Elemental	Air Elemental (Circle 7)

Summoning: Earth

Casters	Magician (24)
Mana Cost	240
Casting Skill	Conjuration
Components	Shovel of Ponz (not consumed), Malachite
Casting Time (secs)	12
Duration	Instantaneous
Range (feet)	0
Target	Yourself
Resistance Invoked	None
Effect	
Summon Elemental	Earth Elemental (Circle 7)

Summoning: Fire

Casters	Magician (24)
Mana Cost	240
Casting Skill	Conjuration
Components	Torch of Alna (not consumed), Malachite
Casting Time (secs)	12
Duration	Instantaneous
Range (feet)	0
Target	Yourself
Resistance Invoked	None
Effect	
Summon Elemental	Fire Elemental (Circle 7)

Summoning: Water

Casters	Magician (24)
Mana Cost	240
Casting Skill	Conjuration
Components	Stein of Ulissa (not consumed), Malachite
Casting Time (secs)	12
Duration	Instantaneous
Range (feet)	0
Target	Yourself
Resistance Invoked	None
Effect	
Summon Elemental	Water Elemental (Circle 7)

Sunbeam

Casters	Druid (24)
Mana Cost	40
Casting Skill	Divination
Outdoors only	
Casting Time (secs)	3
Recasting Delay (secs)	14.25
Duration	12 seconds
Range (feet)	200
Radius of Effect (feet)	20
Target	Area
Resistance Invoked	Magic
Effect	
Blindness	
Target's Reaction	Target is blinded by a sunbeam.

Sunskin

Casters	Cleric (51)
Casting Skill	Divination
Target's Reaction	Target fades a little. (You feel your skin tingle.)

Sunstrike

Casters	Wizard (60)
Casting Skill	Evocation
Target's Reaction	Target is consumed by the flames of the sun.

Superior Camouflage

Casters	Ranger (49), Druid (19)
Mana Cost	40
Casting Skill	Divination
Casting Time (secs)	5
Duration	24 minutes
Range (feet)	100
Target	Anyone
Resistance Invoked	None
Effect	
Invisibility	
Target's Reaction	Target fades away. (You vanish.)

Superior Healing

Casters	Cleric (34), Paladin (57), Druid (53), Shaman (53)
Casting Skill	Alteration
Target's Reaction	Target feels much better.

Supernova

Casters	Wizard (49)
Casting Skill	Evocation
Target's Reaction	Target is immolated in flame.

Surge of Enfeeblement

Casters	Necromancer (34)
Casting Skill	Alteration
Target's Reaction	Target weakens. (You feel your strength dwindle.)

Swift like the Wind

Casters	Enchanter (49)
Casting Skill	Alteration
Target's Reaction	Target feels much faster.

Sword of Runes

Casters	Magician (29)
Casting Skill	Conjuration

Symbol of Marzin

Casters	Cleric (54)
Casting Skill	Abjuration
Target's Reaction	Target is cloaked in a shimmer of glowing symbols. (A mystic symbol flashes before your eyes.)

Symbol of Naltron

Casters	Cleric (44), Paladin (58)
Casting Skill	Abjuration
Target's Reaction	Target is cloaked in a shimmer of glowing symbols. (A mystic symbol flashes before your eyes.)

Symbol of Pinzarn

Casters	Cleric (34), Paladin (49)
Casting Skill	Abjuration
Target's Reaction	Target is cloaked in a shimmer of glowing symbols. (A mystic symbol flashes before your eyes.)

Symbol of Ryltan

Casters	Cleric (24), Paladin (39)
Mana Cost	111
Casting Skill	Abjuration
Component	Bloodstone
Casting Time (secs)	4
Duration	36 minutes
Range (feet)	100
Target	Anyone
Resistance Invoked	None
Effect	
Bonus HP	118 + 10/level (max 158)
Target's Reaction	Target is cloaked in a shimmer of glowing symbols. (A mystic symbol flashes before your eyes.)

Symbol of Transal

Casters	Cleric (14), Paladin (30)
Mana Cost	55
Casting Skill	Abjuration
Component	Cat's Eye Agate
Casting Time (secs)	3.5
Duration	27 minutes
Range (feet)	100
Target	Anyone
Resistance Invoked	None
Effect	
Bonus HP	73
Target's Reaction	Target is cloaked in a shimmer of glowing symbols. (A mystic symbol flashes before your eyes.)

Syvelian's Anti-Magic Aria

Casters	Bard (40)
Casting Skill	Singing
Target's Reaction	(You feel a static pulse wash through you.)

Sympathetic Aura

Casters	Enchanter (20)
Mana Cost	40
Casting Skill	Alteration
Casting Time (secs)	5
Duration	36 minutes
Range (feet)	100
Target	Anyone
Resistance Invoked	None
Effect	
CHA boost	6 + 1 / 2 levels (max 18)
Target's Reaction	Target is surrounded by a warm aura. (You feel a warm aura surround you.)

Tagar's Insects

Casters	Shaman (29)
Casting Skill	Alteration
Target's Reaction	Target yawns. (You feel drowsy.)

Tainted Breath

Casters	Shaman (9)
Mana Cost	40
Casting Skill	Conjuration
Casting Time (secs)	2.1
Duration	42 seconds
Range (feet)	200
Target	Anyone
Resistance Invoked	Poison
Effects	
Poison	5
Immediate Damage (HP)	18
Subsequent Damage (HP/6 secs)	8
Target's Reaction	Target has been poisoned.

Talisman of Altuna

Casters	Shaman (44)
Casting Skill	Alteration
Target's Reaction	Target looks tougher. (You feel tough.)

Talisman of Jasinth

Casters	Shaman (51)
Casting Skill	Abjuration
Target's Reaction	Target has been protected by the Talisman of Jasinth.

Talisman of Kragg

Casters	Shaman (55)
Casting Skill	Alteration
Target's Reaction	Target looks tougher.

Talisman of Shadoo

Casters	Shaman (53)
Casting Skill	Abjuration
Target's Reaction	Target has been protected by the Talisman of Shadoo.

Talisman of the Brute

Casters	Shaman (57)
Casting Skill	Alteration
Target's Reaction	Target looks robust. (You feel the spirit of the brute channel through you.)

Talisman of the Cat

Casters	Shaman (57)
Casting Skill	Alteration
Target's Reaction	Target looks agile. You feel the spirit of the cat channel through you.)

Talisman of the Raptor

Casters	Shaman (59)
Casting Skill	Alteration
Target's Reaction	Target looks dexterous. (You feel the spirit of the raptor channel through you.)

Talisman of the Rhino

Casters	Shaman (58)
Casting Skill	Alteration
Target's Reaction	Target looks strong. (You feel the spirit of the rhino channel through you.)

Talisman of the Serpent

Casters	Shaman (58)
Casting Skill	Alteration
Target's Reaction	Target look charismatic. (You feel the spirit of the serpent channel through you.)

Talisman of Tnarg

Casters	Shaman (34)
Casting Skill	Alteration
Target's Reaction	Target looks tougher. (You feel tough.)

Taper Enchantment

Casters	Enchanter (1)
Mana Cost	5
Casting Skill	Abjuration
Casting Time (secs)	3
Duration	Instantaneous
Range (feet)	200
Target	Anyone
Resistance Invoked	None
Effect	
Cancel Magic	1 chance, lowest level
Target's Reaction	Target is surrounded by a pulse of static air. (The air crackles around you.)

Tarew's Aquatic Ayre

Casters	Bard (16)
Mana Cost	0
Casting Skill	Wind Instruments
Component	Wooden Flute
Casting Time (secs)	3
Casting Delay (secs)	none
Recasting Delay (secs)	12
Duration	24 seconds
Range (feet)	0
Radius of Effect (feet)	125
Target	Your group
Resistance Invoked	None
Effect	
Magic Breathing	
Target's Reaction	(Tiny bubbles of music surround your head.)

Tashan

Casters	Enchanter (4)
Mana Cost	10
Casting Skill	Abjuration
Casting Time (secs)	1
Duration	1 minute + 12 seconds/level
Range (feet)	200
Target	Anyone
Resistance Invoked	None
Effects	
Poison	1
Magic Resistance lowered	5 +1/level (max 13)
Target's Reaction	Target glances nervously about. (You hear the barking of Tashan.)

Tashani

Casters	Enchanter (20)
Mana Cost	20
Casting Skill	Abjuration
Casting Time (secs)	1
Duration	1 minute + 12 seconds/level
Range (feet)	200
Target	Anyone
Resistance Invoked	None
Effects	
Poison	1
Magic Resistance lowered	10 + 1 / 2 levels (max 23)
Target's Reaction	Target glances nervously about. (You hear the barking of the Tashani.)

Tashania

Casters	Enchanter (44)
Casting Skill	Abjuration
Target's Reaction	Target glances nervously about. (You hear the barking of Tashania.)

Tashanian

Casters	Enchanter (57)
Casting Skill	Abjuration
Target's Reaction	Target glances nervously about. (You hear the barking of Tashania.)

Tears of Druzzil

Casters	Wizard (52)
Casting Skill	Evocation
Target's Reaction	Target's skin blisters as the tears of Druzzil rain upon them.

Tears of Prexus

Casters	Wizard (58)
Casting Skill	Evocation
Target's Reaction	Target's skin freezes as the tears of Prexus rain upon them.

Tears of Solusek

Casters	Wizard (55)
Casting Skill	Evocation
Target's Reaction	Target's skin blisters as the tears of Solusek rain upon them.

Tepid Deeds

Casters	Enchanter (24)
Mana Cost	100
Casting Skill	Alteration
Casting Time (secs)	3.5
Duration	12 seconds + 3 seconds/level
Range (feet)	250
Target	Anyone
Resistance Invoked	Magic
Effect	
Attack Speed loss	20% +1% / 2 levels
Target's Reaction	Target slows down.

Terrorize Animal

Casters	Druid (19)
Mana Cost	30
Casting Skill	Alteration
Casting Time (secs)	1.75
Duration	54 secs
Range (feet)	200
Target	Animal
Resistance Invoked	Magic
Effect	
Fear	Low-level

The Unspoken Word

Casters	Cleric (59)
Casting Skill	Evocation
Target's Reaction	Target writhes and staggers. (Your mind bleeds with wonder.)

Theft of Thought

Casters	Enchanter (51)
Casting Skill	Alteration
Target's Reaction	Target staggers. (You feel your mental energies drain away.)

Thicken Mana

Casters	Enchanter (12)
Mana Cost	200
Casting Skill	Alteration
Components	Pearl, Poison Vial
Casting Time (secs)	6
Duration	Instantaneous
Range (feet)	0
Target	Yourself
Resistance Invoked	None
Effect	
Create Item	1 vial of Viscous Mana + 1 more / level

Thistlecoat

Casters	Ranger (15), Druid (9)
Mana Cost	25
Casting Skill	Abjuration
Casting Time (secs)	2
Duration	3 x level minutes
Range (feet)	0
Target	Yourself
Resistance Invoked	Magic
Effects	
AC boost	7 +1/level (max 21)
Reflect Damage (HP)	1
Target's Reaction	Target's skin sprouts thistles. (Thistles spring from your skin.)

Thorncoat

Casters	Ranger (60), Druid (49)
Casting Skill	Abjuration
Target's Reaction	Target's skin sprouts thorns. (Thorns spring from your skin.)

Thrall of Bones

Casters	Necromancer (54)
Casting Skill	Alteration
Target's Reaction	Target moans.

Thunder Strike

Casters	Wizard (29)
Casting Skill	Evocation
Target's Reaction	Target has been struck by a Thunder Bolt. (You have been thunder struck.)

Thunderbold

Casters	Wizard (54)
Casting Skill	Evocation
Target's Reaction	Target has been thunder stunned.

Thunderclap

Casters	Wizard (34)
Casting Skill	Evocation
Target's Reaction	Target has been thunder struck.

Tigir's Insects

Casters	Shaman (58)
Casting Skill	Alteration
Target's Reaction	Target yawns. (You feel drowsy.)

Tishan's Clash

Casters	Wizard (20)
Mana Cost	65
Casting Skill	Evocation
Casting Time (secs)	2.5
Recasting Delay (secs)	20.5
Duration	Instantaneous
Range (feet)	200
Target	Anyone
Resistance Invoked	Magic
Effects	
Damage (HP)	10 +1/level (max 50)
Stun	5 seconds
Target's Reaction	Target is stunned.

Tishan's Discord

Casters	Wizard (51)
Casting Skill	Evocation
Target's Reaction	Target is stunned.

Togor's Insects

Casters	Shaman (39)
Casting Skill	Alteration
Target's Reaction	Target yawns. (You feel drowsy.)

Torment of Argli

Casters	Enchanter (56)
Casting Skill	Evocation
Target's Reaction	Target screams from the Torment of Argli. (Your thoughts muddle from the Torment of Argli.)

Torpor

Casters	Shaman (60)
Casting Skill	Alteration
Target's Reaction	Target falls into a state of torpor.

Torrent of Poison

Casters	Shaman (55)
Casting Skill	Evocation
Target's Reaction	Target's skin steams and melts. (Your skin steams and melts as poison rains down on you.)

Touch of Night

Casters	Necromancer (59)
Casting Skill	Alteration
Target's Reaction	Target staggers. (Your lifeforce drains at the Touch of Night.)

Tox Gate

Casters	Wizard (20)
Mana Cost	150
Casting Skill	Alteration
Casting Time (secs)	7
Recasting Delay (secs)	12.25
Duration	Instantaneous
Range (feet)	0
Target	Yourself
Resistance Invoked	None
Effect	
Teleports you to	Toxxulia Forest
Target's Reaction	Target fades away.

Tox Portal

Casters	Wizard (29)
Casting Skill	Alteration
Target's Reaction	Target creates a shimmering portal.

Track Corpse

Casters	Wizard (20)
Mana Cost	15
Casting Skill	Divination
Casting Time (secs)	1.5
Recasting Delay (secs)	5.5
Duration	12 minutes
Range (feet)	10,000
Radius of Effect (feet)	1000
Target	Yourself
Resistance Invoked	None
Effect	
Locate Corpse	

Treeform

Casters	Druid (9)
Mana Cost	30
Casting Skill	Alteration
Outdoors only	
Casting Time (secs)	4
Duration	3 x level minutes (max 36 m)
Range (feet)	0
Target	Yourself
Resistance Invoked	None
Effects	
Change Form	Tree
Immobilizes	
Healing (HP)	1 + 1 / 6 levels (max 5)
Fire Resistance lowered	10
Target's Reaction	Target turns into a tree. (You have taken root.)

Tremor

Casters	Cleric (34), Druid (24)
Mana Cost	200
Casting Skill	Evocation
Casting Time (secs)	4
Recasting Delay (secs)	12.5
Duration	Instantaneous
Range (feet)	0
Radius of Effect (feet)	30
Target	Area (but not your group)
Resistance Invoked	Magic
Effects	
Damage (HP)	64 +2/level (max 122)
Knockback	1 foot
Target's Reaction	(You feel the ground rumble.)

Trepidation

Casters	Cleric (57), Necromancer (56), Enchanter (56)
Casting Skill	Alteration
Target's Reaction	Target is filled with trepidation. (Your mind fills with trepidation.)

Trucidation

Casters	Necromancer (60)
Casting Skill	Alteration
Target's Reaction	Target drains away. (Your essence drains away.)

EverQuest: The Ruins of Kunark

True North

Casters	Cleric (1), Paladin (9), Shaman (1), Necromancer (4), Wizard (1), Magician (1), Enchanter (1)
Mana Cost	5
Casting Skill	Divination
Casting Time (secs)	2
Recasting Delay (secs)	6.25
Duration	Instantaneous
Range (feet)	0
Target	Yourself
Resistance Invoked	None
Effect	
True North Shown	
Target's Reaction	(You spin to face north.)

Tunare's Request

Casters	Druid (55)
Casting Skill	Alteration
Target's Reaction	Target blinks.

Turgur's Insects

Casters	Shaman (51)
Casting Skill	Alteration
Target's Reaction	Target yawns. (You feel drowsy.)

Turtle Skin

Casters	Shaman (14)
Mana Cost	50
Casting Skill	Abjuration
Casting Time (secs)	5
Recasting Delay (secs)	9.75
Duration	36 minutes
Range (feet)	100
Target	Anyone
Resistance Invoked	None
Effect	
AC boost	17 +1/level (max 35)
Target's Reaction	Target's skin looks greener. (Your skin turns hard as turtle shell.)

Tuyen's Chant of Flame

Casters	Bard (38)
Casting Skill	Percussion Instruments
Target's Reaction	Target begins to chant.

Tuyen's Chant of Frost

Casters	Bard (46)
Casting Skill	Percussion Instruments
Target's Reaction	Target begins to chant.

Uleen's Animation

Casters	Enchanter (29)
Casting Skill	Conjuration

Ultravision

Casters	Shaman (29), Enchanter (29)
Casting Skill	Divination
Target's Reaction	Target's eyes glow violet. (Your eyes tingle.)

Umbra

Casters	Enchanter (57)
Casting Skill	Abjuration
Target's Reaction	Target's image fades into the umbra.

Unfailing Reverence

Casters	Shaman (59)
Casting Skill	Alteration
Target's Reaction	Target exudes an aura of massive charisma. (People look at you with unfailing reverence.)

United Resolve

Casters	Cleric (54)
Casting Skill	Abjuration
Target's Reaction	Target looks resolute.

Unswerving Hammer of Faith

Casters	Cleric (54)
Casting Skill	Conjuration

Upheaval

Casters	Cleric (52), Druid (51)
Casting Skill	Evocation
Target's Reaction	Target is mauled by the moving ground. (You feel the ground scream and heave.)

Valor

Casters	Cleric (34), Paladin (49)
Casting Skill	Abjuration
Target's Reaction	Target looks valorous.

Velocity

Casters	Magician (58)
Casting Skill	Alteration
Target's Reaction	Target's shimmers and blurs.

Vampiric Curse

Casters	Shadow Knight (57), Necromancer (29)
Casting Skill	Alteration
Target's Reaction	Target pales. (You feel your blood being drained away.)

Vampiric Embrace

Casters	Shadow Knight (22), Necromancer (8)
Mana Cost	30
Casting Skill	Alteration
Casting Time (secs)	3
Recasting Delay (secs)	8.25
Duration	1 minute + 6 seconds/level
Range (feet)	0
Target	Yourself
Resistance Invoked	None
Effect	
Contact Ability	Might cast *Cripple* on next successful melee strike
Target's Reaction	Target's hands begin to glow.

Vengeance of Al'Kabor

Casters	Wizard (59)
Casting Skill	Evocation
Target's Reaction	Target is blasted by the Vengeance of Al'Kabor.

Venom of the Snake

Casters	Shaman (39), Necromancer (34)
Casting Skill	Conjuration
Target's Reaction	Target has been poisoned.

Verses of Victory

Casters	Bard (50)
Casting Skill	Singing
Target's Reaction	(You feel your pulse quicken.)

Vexing Mordinia

Casters	Necromancer (57)
Casting Skill	Alteration
Target's Reaction	Target staggers under the curse of Vexing Mordinia. (Vexing Mordinia begins to drain your life away.)

Vigilant Spirit

Casters	Shaman (39)
Casting Skill	Conjuration
Target's Reaction	Target summons a companion spirit. (You summon a vigilant spirit.)

Vilia's Chorus of Celerity

Casters	Bard (54)
Casting Skill	Singing
Target's Reaction	(The beat of your heart increases to match the music.)

Vilia's Verses of Celerity

Casters	Bard (36)
Casting Skill	Singing
Target's Reaction	(A burst of speed surges through your body.)

Vision

Casters	Shaman (19)
Mana Cost	10
Casting Skill	Divination
Casting Time (secs)	4
Recasting Delay (secs)	12.25
Duration	1 minute + 12 seconds/level
Range (feet)	10,000
Target	Anyone
Resistance Invoked	None
Effect	
You see from Target's View	
Ultravision	
Target's Reaction	Target eyes shimmer. (Your spirit drifts from your body.)

Visions of Grandeur

Casters	Enchanter (60)
Casting Skill	Alteration
Target's Reaction	Target experiences visions of grandeur. (You experience visions of grandeur.)

Vocarate: Earth

Casters	Magician (51)
Casting Skill	Conjuration

Vocerate: Air

Casters	Magician (53)
Casting Skill	Conjuration

Vocerate: Fire

Casters	Magician (52)
Casting Skill	Conjuration

Vocerate: Water

Casters	Magician (54)
Casting Skill	Conjuration

Voice Graft

Casters	Necromancer (16)
Mana Cost	10
Casting Skill	Divination
Casting Time (secs)	6
Recasting Delay (secs)	14.25
Duration	27 minutes
Range (feet)	100
Target	Your pet
Resistance Invoked	None
Effect	
Ventriloquism	
Target's Reaction	Target's head shimmers.

Voice of the Berserker

Casters	Shaman (59)
Casting Skill	Abjuration
Target's Reaction	Target goes berserk. (You lose yourself in your rage and go berserk.)

Voltaic Draugh

Casters	Wizard (54)
Casting Skill	Evocation
Target's Reaction	Target is caught in a torrent of lightning.

Wake of Karana

Casters	Druid (56)
Casting Skill	Alteration
Target's Reaction	(You call out to Karana.)

Wake of Tranquility

Casters	Cleric (55), Enchanter (51)
Casting Skill	Alteration
Target's Reaction	Target looks less aggressive. (You feel your aggression subside.)

Walking Sleep

Casters	Shaman (14)
Mana Cost	60
Casting Skill	Alteration
Casting Time (secs)	3.25
Recasting Delay (secs)	7.25
Duration	12 seconds + 6 seconds / 2 levels
Range (feet)	200
Target	Anyone
Resistance Invoked	Magic
Effect	
Attack Speed loss	80 + 1 / 4 levels
Target's Reaction	Target yawns. (You feel drowsy.)

Ward Summoned

Casters	Cleric (19), Ranger (22), Druid (5), Magician (12)
Mana Cost	30
Casting Skill	Evocation
Casting Time (secs)	2.1
Duration	Instantaneous
Range (feet)	200
Target	Summoned creature
Resistance Invoked	Magic
Effect	
Damage (HP)	41
Target's Reaction	Target staggers.

Ward Undead

Casters	Cleric (5), Paladin (15), Shadow Knight (22), Necromancer (8)
Mana Cost	30
Casting Skill	Evocation
Casting Time (secs)	2.1
Duration	Instantaneous
Range (feet)	200
Target	Undead
Resistance Invoked	Magic
Effect	
Damage (HP)	30 +1/level (max 41)

Wave of Enfeeblement

Casters	Shadow Knight (30), Necromancer (12)
Mana Cost	40
Casting Skill	Alteration
Casting Time (secs)	2.5
Recasting Delay (secs)	7.75
Duration	1 minute + 6 seconds/level (max 4 m)
Range (feet)	0
Radius of Effect (feet)	30
Target	Area (but not your group)
Resistance Invoked	Magic
Effect	
STR loss	5 + 1 / 2 levels (max 15)
Target's Reaction	Target weakens. (You feel your strength dwindle.)

Wave of Fear

Casters	Cleric (24)
Mana Cost	90
Casting Skill	Alteration
Casting Time (secs)	4.5
Recasting Delay (secs)	11.25
Duration	18 secs
Range (feet)	0
Radius of Effect (feet)	15
Target	Area (but not your group)
Resistance Invoked	Magic
Effect	
Fear	Low-level
Target's Reaction	Target looks very afraid. (Your mind fills with fear.)

Weaken

Casters	Enchanter (1)
Mana Cost	8
Casting Skill	Alteration
Casting Time (secs)	1.5
Duration	1 minute + 6 seconds/level (max 6 m)
Range (feet)	200
Target	Anyone
Resistance Invoked	Magic
Effect	
STR loss	10 + 1 / 2 levels (max 15)
Target's Reaction	Target weakens. (You feel weaker.)

Weakness

Casters	Enchanter (44)
Casting Skill	Alteration
Target's Reaction	Target is weakened. (You feel weak.)

West Gate

Casters	Wizard (24)
Mana Cost	150
Casting Skill	Alteration
Casting Time (secs)	7
Recasting Delay (secs)	12.25
Duration	Instantaneous
Range (feet)	0
Target	Yourself
Resistance Invoked	None
Effect	
Teleports you to	West Karana
Target's Reaction	Target fades away.

West Portal

Casters	Wizard (39)
Casting Skill	Alteration
Target's Reaction	Target creates a shimmering portal.

Whirl Till You Hurl

Casters	Enchanter (12)
Mana Cost	55
Casting Skill	Alteration
Casting Time (secs)	2.5
Recasting Delay (secs)	8.75
Duration	12 secs
Range (feet)	200
Target	Anyone
Resistance Invoked	Magic
Effect	
Spin Target	
Target's Reaction	Target begins to spin.

Whirling Wind

Casters	Druid (5)
Mana Cost	24
Casting Skill	Conjuration
Outdoors only	
Casting Time (secs)	1.75
Recasting Delay (secs)	14.5
Duration	Instantaneous
Range (feet)	200
Target	Anyone
Resistance Invoked	Magic
Effects	
Damage (HP)	20 + 1 / 2 levels (max 25)
Stun	Can disrupt spellcasting
Lift and Knockback	2 feet
Target's Reaction	Target is slammed by an intense gust of wind.

Wildfire

Casters	Druid (59)
Casting Skill	Evocation
Target's Reaction	Target's skin ignites as wildfire courses over them.

Wind of Tishani

Casters	Enchanter (55)
Casting Skill	Abjuration
Target's Reaction	Target glances nervously about. (You hear the barking of the Tashani.)

Wind of Tishanian

Casters	Enchanter (60)
Casting Skill	Abjuration
Target's Reaction	Target glances nervously about. (You hear the barking of Tashania.)

Winds of Gelid

Casters	Wizard (60)
Casting Skill	Evocation
Target's Reaction	Target's body is rended by freezing winds. (Freezing winds rend your body.)

Winged Death

Casters	Druid (53)
Casting Skill	Conjuration
Target's Reaction	Target is engulfed in a swarm of deadly insects. (You feel the pain of a million stings.)

Winter's Roar

Casters	Shaman (34)
Casting Skill	Evocation
Target's Reaction	Target staggers as spirits of frost slam against them.

Wolf Form

Casters	Ranger (49), Druid (24)
Mana Cost	60
Casting Skill	Alteration
Outdoors only	
Casting Time (secs)	4
Recasting Delay (secs)	10.25
Duration	72 minutes
Range (feet)	0
Target	Yourself
Resistance Invoked	None
Effects	
Change Form	Wolf Elemental
Movement Rate boost	30% + 1% / 2 levels
Attack Skill boost	1 +1/level (max 30)
Target's Reaction	Target turns into a wolf. (You are now a wolf.)

Wonderous Rapidity

Casters	Enchanter (58)
Casting Skill	Alteration
Target's Reaction	Target begins to move with wonderous rapidity.

Word Divine

Casters	Cleric (49)
Casting Skill	Evocation
Target's Reaction	Target writhes in pain. (You are wracked with pain.)

Word of Healing

Casters	Cleric (49)
Casting Skill	Alteration
Target's Reaction	Target feels much better.

Word of Health

Casters	Cleric (34)
Casting Skill	Alteration
Target's Reaction	Target feels much better.

Word of Pain

Casters	Cleric (9)
Mana Cost	47
Casting Skill	Evocation
Casting Time (secs)	2.1
Recasting Delay (secs)	11.5
Duration	Instantaneous
Range (feet)	0
Radius of Effect (feet)	20
Target	Area (but not your group)
Resistance Invoked	Magic
Effects	
Damage (HP)	15 +1/level (max 29)
Knockback	1 foot
Target's Reaction	Target writhes in pain. (You are wracked with pain.)

Word of Redemption

Casters	Cleric (60)
Casting Skill	Alteration
Target's Reaction	Target feels the touch of Redemption.

Word of Restoration

Casters	Cleric (57)
Casting Skill	Alteration
Target's Reaction	Target feels restored.

Word of Shadow

Casters	Cleric (19), Necromancer (20)
Mana Cost	85
Casting Skill	Evocation
Casting Time (secs)	2.75
Recasting Delay (secs)	11.5
Duration	Instantaneous
Range (feet)	0
Radius of Effect (feet)	20
Target	Area (but not your group)
Resistance Invoked	Magic
Effects	
Damage (HP)	33 +1/level (max 58)
Knockback	1 foot
Target's Reaction	Target writhes in pain. (You are wracked with pain.)

Word of Souls

Casters	Cleric (39), Necromancer (39)
Casting Skill	Evocation
Target's Reaction	Target writhes in pain. (You are wracked with pain.)

Word of Spirit

Casters	Cleric (29), Shadow Knight (49), Necromancer (29)
Casting Skill	Evocation
Target's Reaction	Target writhes in pain. (You are wracked with pain.)

Word of Vigor

Casters	Cleric (52)
Casting Skill	Alteration
Target's Reaction	Target looks vigorous.

Wrath

Casters	Cleric (29)
Casting Skill	Evocation
Target's Reaction	Target has been struck down by wrath.

Wrath of Al'Kabor

Casters	Wizard (49)
Casting Skill	Evocation
Target's Reaction	Target is blasted by freezing winds.

Yaulp

Casters	Cleric (1), Paladin (9)
Mana Cost	5
Casting Skill	Abjuration
Casting Time (secs)	0.5
Recasting Delay (secs)	20.25
Duration	18 secs
Range (feet)	0
Target	Yourself
Resistance Invoked	None
Effects	
AC boost	20
STR boost	10
Restores Fatigue Point	1
Target's Reaction	Target lets loose a mighty yaulp. (You feel a surge of strength as you let forth a mighty yaulp.)

Yaulp II

Casters	Cleric (19), Paladin (39)
Mana Cost	15
Casting Skill	Abjuration
Casting Time (secs)	0.5
Recasting Delay (secs)	20.25
Duration	18 secs
Range (feet)	0
Target	Yourself
Resistance Invoked	None
Effects	
AC boost	30
STR boost	20
Restores Fatigue Point	1
Target's Reaction	Target lets loose a mighty yaulp. (You feel a surge of strength as you let forth a mighty yaulp.)

Yaulp III

Casters	Cleric (44), Paladin (56)
Casting Skill	Abjuration
Target's Reaction	Target lets loose a mighty yaulp. You feel a surge of strength as you let forth a mighty yaulp.)

Yaulp IV

Casters	Cleric (53)
Casting Skill	Abjuration
Target's Reaction	Target lets loose a mighty yaulp. (You feel a surge of strength as you let forth a mighty yaulp.)

Yegoreff's Animation

Casters	Enchanter (44)
Casting Skill	Conjuration

Yonder

Casters	Wizard (29)
Casting Skill	Alteration
Target's Reaction	Target fades away.

Zumaik's Animation

Casters	Enchanter (55)
Casting Skill	Conjuration

"Are you sure these things will allow us to breathe underwater?" Briddle asked. "It seems like a long way down there." They were both only scholars and this journey scared him.

"That's why we need these artifacts," Sord replied. "They work all the time as long as we keep them around our necks. They give off light as well as let us breathe water."

Briddle shrugged his shoulders and tentatively dropped into the ocean at the outskirts of the Cauldron. Eventually, they found the structure they had heard about in Freeport, the abandoned settlement of the mysterious Kedge.

They didn't find anything of obvious value, but picked up a number of things that they wanted to study later. They were about to leave when Sord pointed to a room at the end of a long hallway. In the room they found large green orbs, a roomful of them.

Sadly, that's where this tale ends. Briddle returned incoherently babbling about his journey. When asked about his friend, Sord, Briddle only breaks out into fearful screams.

Kack dug next to a goblin that he'd sort of made friends with. His name was Forg. Just as they were getting ready to regroup, eat and go to sleep, Kack saw Forg grab a sparkling gem from the dirt and stuff it into his dirty tunic.

"Are you crazy?" Kack whispered.

"No," Forg said with a gleam in his eye. "This means my freedom. The guard said he'd look away while I escaped … if I got him a good stone."

Kack tried to stop the one he now hesitated to call friend, but Forg just grinned and walked up to the guard. Kack watched as the guard listened to Forg and took the stone. Then, the guard grabbed the collar of Forg's tunic and drug him away.

Kack just shook his head and trudged off to eat.